W9-BWD-415

The Norton Scores

Seventh Edition

VOLUME II

Donated
To
St. Francis College

The Norton Scores

A Study Anthology

Seventh Edition
in Two Volumes

EDITED BY

KRISTINE FORNEY

Professor of Music
California State University, Long Beach

VOLUME II:
Schubert to the Present

W. W. NORTON & COMPANY
New York • London

The Library
WITHDRAWN
Saint Francis College
Fort Wayne, Indiana 46808

Acknowledgments

The text translation for item 12 is from *The Ring of Words: An Anthology of Song Texts*, edited by Philip Miller (New York: W. W. Norton, 1973).
The text translation for item 28 is reprinted through the courtesy of London Records, a Division of Polygram Classics, Inc.
The text translation for item 41 is from Federico García Lorca, *Selected Poems,* translated by W. S. Merwin (New York: New Directions, 1955).

Copyright © 1995, 1990, 1984, 1977, 1970, 1968 by W. W. Norton & Company, Inc.

All rights reserved
Printed in the United States of America
First Edition

The text of this book is composed in Garamond Book
with the display set in Zapf Chancery
Composition by University Graphics, Inc.
Manufacturing by R. R. Donnelley

ISBN 0-393-96687-9

W. W. Norton & Company, Inc., 500 Fifth Avenue, New York, N.Y. 10110
W. W. Norton & Company, Ltd., 10 Coptic Street, London WC1A 1PU

1 2 3 4 5 6 7 8 9 0

Contents

Preface ix

How to Follow the Highlighted Scores xiii

A Note on the Recordings xiv

1. FRANZ SCHUBERT, *Erlkönig (Erlking)* 1
2. HECTOR BERLIOZ, *Symphonie fantastique,* Fifth Movement 8
3. FELIX MENDELSSOHN, *A Midsummer Night's Dream,* Overture 62
4. FRÉDÉRIC FRANÇOIS CHOPIN, Prelude in E minor, Op. 28, No. 4 116
5. CHOPIN, Polonaise in A-flat major, Op. 53 117
6. ROBERT SCHUMANN, Piano Concerto in A minor, Op. 54, First Movement 127
7. FRANZ LISZT, *Wilde Jagd (Wild Hunt),* Transcendental Etude No. 8 168
8. RICHARD WAGNER, *Die Walküre,* Act III, Finale 179
9. GIUSEPPE VERDI, *La traviata,* Act II, Finale 189
10. CLARA SCHUMANN, Scherzo, Op. 10 226
11. JOHANNES BRAHMS, *A German Requiem,* Fourth Movement 236
12. BRAHMS, *Vergebliches Ständchen (Futile Serenade)* 247
13. BRAHMS, Symphony No. 4 in E minor, Fourth Movement 252
14. GEORGES BIZET, *Carmen,* Act I, excerpt 283
15. MODEST PETROVICH MUSORGSKY, *Pictures at an Exhibition,* Three Movements
    - *Promenade* 317
    - 9. *The Hut on Fowl's Legs (Baba-Yaga)* 322
    - 10. *The Great Gate of Kiev* 352
16. PETER ILYICH TCHAIKOVSKY, *The Nutcracker,* Three Dances from Act II
    - *March* 377
    - *Dance of the Sugar Plum Fairy* 401
    - *Trepak* (Russian Dance) 410

17. ANTONÍN DVOŘÁK, Symphony No. 9 in E minor, *From the New World,* Second Movement 424

18. RUGGERO LEONCAVALLO, *Pagliacci,* Act I, Canio's Aria 442

19. GUSTAV MAHLER, *Das Lied von der Erde (The Song of the Earth),* Third Movement 447

20. CLAUDE DEBUSSY, *Prélude à "L'après-midi d'un faune" (Prelude to "The Afternoon of a Faun")* 458

21. RICHARD STRAUSS, *Der Rosenkavalier* (The Cavalier of the Rose), Act III, Trio 489

22. ARNOLD SCHOENBERG, *Pierrot lunaire,* Op. 21
No. 18. "Der Mondfleck" 499
No. 21. "O alter Duft" 505

23. CHARLES IVES, *The Fourth of July,* from *A Symphony: New England Holidays* 509

24. MAURICE RAVEL, *Chansons madécasses (Songs of Madagascar),* Second Movement 570

25. BÉLA BARTÓK, *Music for Strings, Percussion, and Celesta,* Fourth Movement 578

26. IGOR STRAVINSKY, *Petrushka,* First Tableau 628

27. ANTON WEBERN, Symphony, Op. 21, Second Movement 684

28. ALBAN BERG, *Wozzeck,* Act III, Scenes 4 and 5 692

29. SERGEI PROKOFIEV, *Alexander Nevsky,* Seventh Movement 717

30. RICHARD RODGERS, *My Funny Valentine*
Original Version, from *Babes in Arms* (1937) 730
Gerry Mulligan Quartet Version (1953) 734

31. LOUIS ARMSTRONG AND THE SAVOY BALLROOM FIVE, *West End Blues,* excerpt 737

32. DUKE ELLINGTON, *Ko-Ko* 739

33. AARON COPLAND, *Billy the Kid,* Scene 1, *Street in a Frontier Town* 758

34. RUTH CRAWFORD, *Rat Riddles,* from Three Songs (1933) 799

35. WITOLD LUTOSŁAWSKI, *Jeux vénitiens (Venetian Games),* First Movement 817

36. ELLIOTT CARTER, Sonata for Flute, Oboe, Cello, and Harpsichord, First Movement 822

37. MILTON BABBITT, *Phonemena,* excerpt 833

38. LEONARD BERNSTEIN, Symphonic Dances from *West Side Story,* excerpts 840

39. GYÖRGY LIGETI, *Désordre (Disorder),* from Etudes for Piano, Book I 875

40. PIERRE BOULEZ, *Le marteau sans maître (The Hammer Without a Master)*
1. *Avant "L'artisanat furieux" (Before "Furious Artisans")* 880
3. *L'artisanat furieux (Furious Artisans)* 886
7. *Après "L'artisanat furieux" (After "Furious Artisans")* 889

41. GEORGE CRUMB, *Ancient Voices of Children,* First Movement: *El niño busca su voz* 893

42. JOAN TOWER, *Petroushskates* 896

43. JOHN ADAMS, *Nixon in China,* Act I, Scene 3, Finale 928

44. TOD MACHOVER, *Bug-Mudra,* excerpt 961

Appendix A. Reading a Musical Score 1011

Appendix B. Instrumental Names and Abbreviations 1013

Appendix C. Glossary of Musical Terms Used in the Scores 1018

Appendix D. Concordance Table for Recordings and *The Enjoyment of Music* Listening Guides 1025

Index of Forms and Genres 1029

Preface

This score anthology is designed for use in courses that focus on the great masterworks of Western music literature. The selections, which range from Gregorian chant through contemporary computer music, span a wide variety of forms and genres. Many works are presented in their entirety; others are represented by one or more movements or an excerpt. (In the case of some twentieth-century works, issues of copyright and practicality prevented the inclusion of a complete score.) Operatic excerpts and some choral works are given in piano/vocal scores, while other pieces are in full scores. Translations are provided for all foreign-texted vocal works; in operatic excerpts, these appear in the score as nonliteral singing translations. The anthology is arranged chronologically by the birthdate of the composer and, within a composer's output, by order of composition.

This collection of scores can serve a variety of teaching needs:

1. as a core anthology or ancillary for a masterworks-oriented music appreciation class, to aid students in improving their listening and music-reading abilities;
2. as a study anthology for a music history course, in which students focus on repertory, genres, and musical styles;
3. as an anthology for an analysis course, providing students with a variety of forms and styles for in-depth study;
4. as a central text for a capstone course in musical styles, in which students learn or review standard repertory through listening and score study;
5. as an ancillary to a beginning conducting course, where the highlighting aids students in following full orchestral scores.

In addition, *The Norton Scores* can function as an independent study tool for students wishing to expand their knowledge of repertory and styles, or as a resource for the instructor teaching any of the courses listed above.

The Norton Scores can be used either independently or with an introductory text. The repertory coordinates with that of *The Enjoyment of Music*, Seventh Edition, by Joseph Machlis and Kristine Forney. A package of recordings (eight CDs or cassettes) accompanies this seventh edition of *The Norton Scores*. (A sixth edition of this score anthology was bypassed in order to synchronize the edition numbers of *The Enjoyment of Music, The*

Norton Scores, and the recording package.) Also available is a new CD-ROM disk (*The Norton CD-ROM Masterworks*, vol. 1), which includes interactive analyses of twelve works chosen from *The Norton Scores*, spanning Gregorian chant through the twentieth century.

A unique system of highlighting is employed in the full scores of this anthology. The highlighting directs those who are just beginning to develop music-reading skills to preselected elements in the score, thus enhancing their listening experience. Students with good music-reading skills will, of course, perceive many additional details. Each system (or group of staves) is covered with a light gray screen, within which the most prominent musical lines are highlighted by white bands. Where two or more simultaneous lines are equally prominent, they are each highlighted. Multiple musical systems on a single page are separated by thin white bands running the full width of the page. (For more information, see "How to Follow the Highlighted Scores" on p. xiii.) This highlighting technique has been employed largely for instrumental music; in vocal works, the text serves to guide the less-experienced score reader through the work.

The highlighting is not intended as an analysis of the melodic structure, contrapuntal texture, or any other aspect of the work. In order to follow the most prominent musical line, the highlighting may shift mid-phrase from one instrument or vocal line to another. Since performances differ in interpretation, the highlighting may not always correspond exactly to what is heard in a specific recording. In some twentieth-century works, it is impossible to isolate a single musical line that shows the continuity of the piece. In these works, the listener's attention is directed to the most audible musical events, and the highlighting is kept as simple as possible.

The repertory chosen for *The Norton Scores* includes numerous mainstream works that reflect important cross-cultural influences from traditional, popular, and non-Western styles. Such mergers of musical styles occur in the following compositions: traditional and popular song or dance styles in John Gay's *Beggar's Opera;* Haydn's String Quartet, Op. 76, No. 2 *(Quinten);* Chopin's Polonaise in A flat, Op. 53; Brahms's *Vergebliches Ständchen (Futile Serenade);* Bizet's *Carmen;* Ives's *Fourth of July;* Bartók's *Music for Strings, Percussion, and Celesta;* Stravinsky's *Petrushka;* Copland's *Billy the Kid;* and Bernstein's *West Side Story;* and non-Western styles, instruments, and settings in Haydn's Symphony No. 100 *(Military);* Dvořák's Symphony No. 9 *(From the New World);* Tchaikovsky's *Nutcracker;* Mahler's *Das Lied von der Erde (The Song of the Earth);* Debussy's *Prélude à "L'après-midi d'un faune" (Prelude to "The Afternoon of a Faun");* Ravel's *Chansons madécasses (Songs of Madagascar);* and Crumb's *Ancient Voices of Children.* Specific information about the multicultural elements of each of these compositions can be found in *The Enjoyment of Music,* Seventh Edition, particularly in the text's new Cultural Perspectives.

The role of women in music is prominently reflected in the repertory

chosen for this edition of *The Norton Scores*. Five pieces by women composers, covering the full chronological gamut, are included: a scene from Hildegard von Bingen's *Ordo virtutum (The Play of the Virtues);* a work from Elisabeth-Claude Jacquet de la Guerre's *Pièces de clavecin;* Clara Schumann's Scherzo, Op. 10, for solo piano; Ruth Crawford's song *Rat Riddles;* and Joan Tower's chamber work *Petroushskates*. In addition, several works written expressly for female performers emphasize the important historic role women have played as interpreters of music. These include Marenzio's madrigal *Cantate Ninfe,* written for the famous *Concerto delle donne* (referring to the Singing Ladies of Ferrara); Mozart's Piano Concerto in G major, K. 453, written for his student Barbara Ployer; and Babbitt's *Phonemena*, written for virtuoso singer Bethany Beardslee.

I should like to thank a number of people for assistance in preparing this, my first edition of *The Norton Scores:* Paula Sabin, Roger Hickman, and my husband, William Prizer, who have all made invaluable musical contributions to these volumes; David Hamilton, who has expertly guided the coordination of the recordings with the scores; Suzanne La Plante and Gabrielle Karp of W. W. Norton, who have ably edited this anthology; Claire Brook, who has generously counseled me throughout this endeavor; and Susan Gaustad, who has served as project coordinator at W. W. Norton. To all of them I express my heartfelt gratitude.

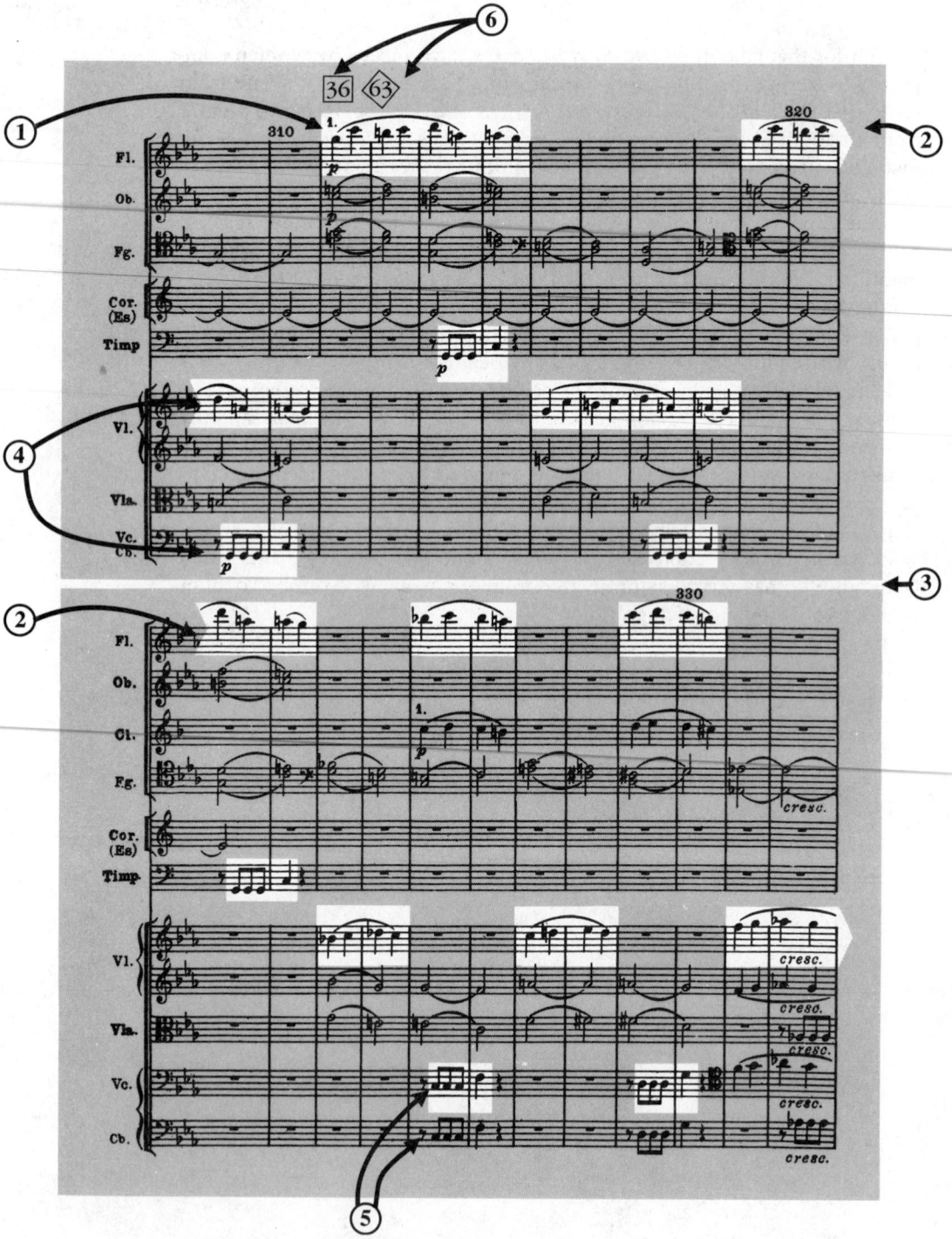

Editor's note: The track numbers in this illustration actually occur in measure 307 (see page 490 of *The Norton Scores,* volume one).

How to Follow the Highlighted Scores

By following the highlighted bands throughout a work, the listener will be able to read the score and recognize the most important or most audible musical lines.

1. The musical line that is most prominent at any time is highlighted by a white band shown against light gray screening.
2. When a highlighted line continues from one system (group of staves) or page to the next, the white band ends with an arrow head (>) that indicates the continuation of the highlighted line, which begins with an indented arrow shape.
3. Multiple score systems (more than one on a page) are separated by narrow white bands across the full width of the page. Watch carefully for these bands so that you do not overlook a portion of the score.
4. At times, two musical lines are highlighted simultaneously, indicating that they are equally audible. On first listening, it may be best to follow only one of these.
5. When more than one instrument plays the same musical line, in unison or octaves (called doubling), the instrument whose line is most audible is highlighted.
6. CD track numbers are given throughout the scores at the beginning of each movement and at important structural points within movements. They appear in a □ for the 8-CD set and in a ◇ for the 3-CD set, where appropriate.

A Note on the Recordings

Sets of recordings of the works in *The Norton Scores* are available from the publisher. There are five sets in all: an eight-cassette or eight-CD set that includes all the works in the two volumes of the anthology; a three-cassette or three-CD set that includes selected works from both volumes; and a CD-ROM disk that includes twelve of the works selected from the two volumes, with interactive analyses. The location of each work in the various recording packages is noted in the score to the right of the title.

Symbols employed:

cassettes compact discs

(MW) *Norton CD-ROM Masterworks,* vol. 1

Example (for Schubert's *Erlkönig*)

8:5A/1 8:5/ [1] - [7]

3:2A/4 3:2/ ⟨20⟩ - ⟨26⟩ (MW)

Following the cassette symbol: a numeral indicates whether the reference is to the eight- or three-cassette package; after the colon, a number designates the individual cassette within the set and a letter indicates side A or B of the cassette; after a diagonal slash, a numeral gives the selection number(s) on that cassette side.

Following the CD symbol: a numeral indicates whether the reference is to the eight- or three-CD package; after the colon, a number designates the individual CD within the set; after a diagonal slash, a boxed number gives the track or tracks on that CD devoted to the work. (The three-CD package tracks are enclosed in a diamond-shaped box.)

For an overview of which works appear on the various recording sets, see Appendix D.

The Norton Scores

Seventh Edition

VOLUME II

1. Franz Schubert (1797–1828)

8:5A/1 8:5/1 - 7

MW

Erlkönig (Erlking), D. 328 (1815)

3:2A/4 3:2/20 - 26

Editor's note: In performance, this Lied is often transposed to F minor, and occasionally to E minor.

Kind; er hat den Kna - ben wohl in dem Arm, er fasst ihn
sicher, er hält ihn warm. Mein
Sohn, was birgst du so bang dein Ge_sicht? Siehst, Va - - ter,
du den Erl - kö - nig nicht? den Er - - len -
kö - nig mit Kron' und Schweif? Mein Sohn, es ist ein

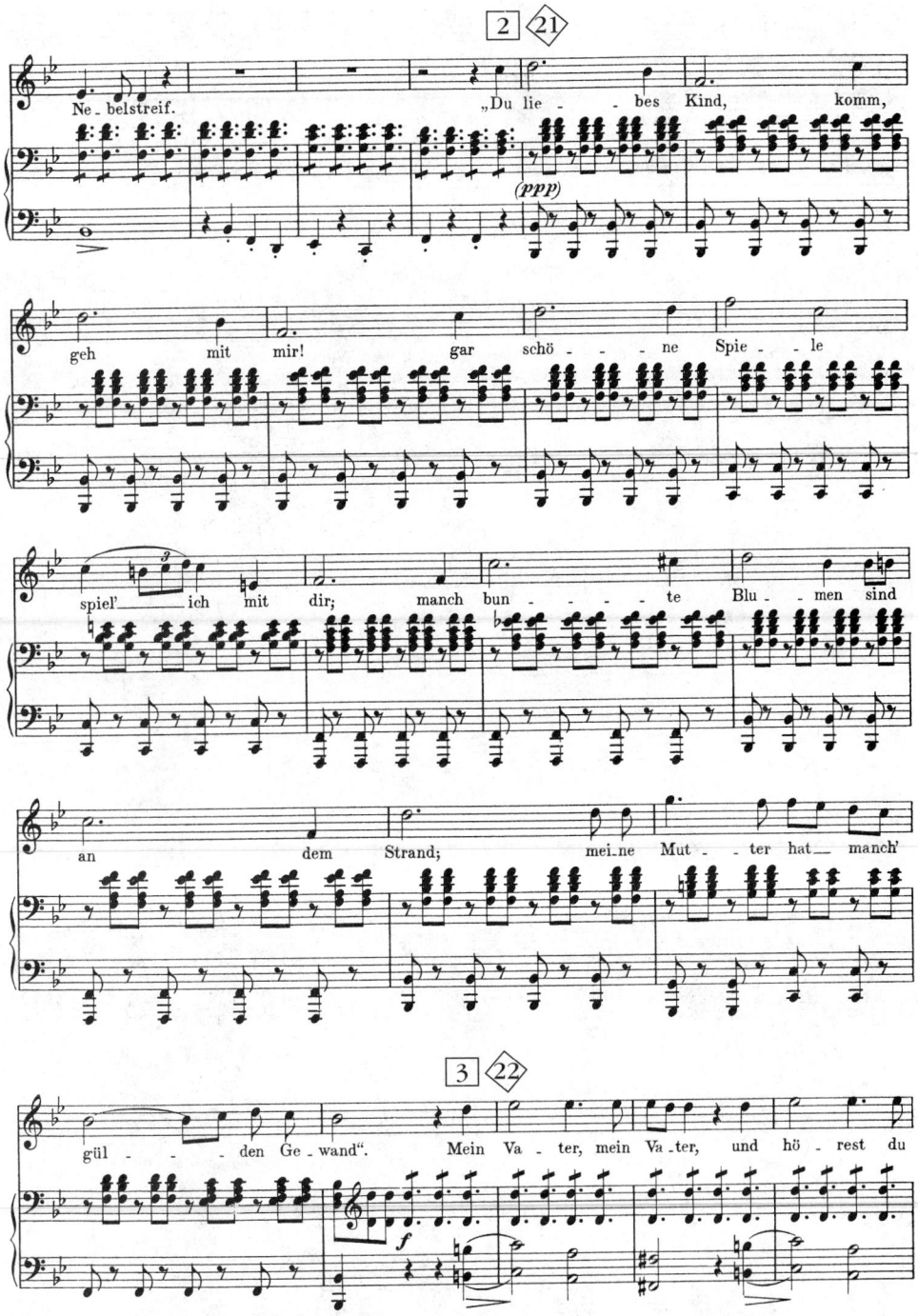
2 21
Ne_belstreif. „Du lie_ _bes Kind, komm,
(ppp)
geh mit mir! gar schö_ _ne Spie_le
spiel'_ ich mit dir; manch bun_ _te Blu_men sind
an dem Strand; mei_ne Mut_ter hat_ manch'
3 22
gül_ _den Ge_wand". Mein Va_ter, mein Va_ter, und hö_rest du
f

nicht, was Er-len-könig mir lei - se verspricht? Sei ru-hig, bleibe
p
decresc.
4
23
ru-hig, mein Kind; in dür-ren Blättern säu-selt der Wind. „Willst,
fei - ner Kna - be, du mit mir gehn? mei-ne Töch - ter sol - len dich
ppp
war - ten schön; mei-ne Töch - ter füh - ren den nächt - li-chen Reihn, und
wie - gen und tan - zen und sin - gen dich ein, sie wie - gen und tan - zen und sin - gen dich ein".
f

5
24
Mein Va - ter, mein Va - ter, und siehst du nicht dort Erl -
kö-nigs Töchter am dü - stern Ort? Mein Sohn, mein Sohn, ich
decresc.
seh' es ge - nau; es scheinen die al - ten Wei - den so grau.
cresc.
ff
6
25
„Ich lie - be dich, mich
p
pp
reizt dei-ne schö-ne Ge - stalt; und bist du nicht wil - lig, so brauch' ich Ge-

7
26
walt'. Mein Va - ter, mein Va - ter, jetzt fasst er mich an! Erl - kö - nig
fff
hat mir ein Leids ge - than! Dem Va - - ter
fz
f
accelerando
grau - set's, er rei - tet geschwind, er hält in Ar - men das
cresc.
äch - zen - de Kind, er - reicht den
ff
Hof mit Müh und Noth; in seinen Armen das Kind war todt.
Recit.
Andante.
fp
pp
p

TEXT AND TRANSLATION

Wer reitet so spät durch Nacht und Wind?
Es ist der Vater mit seinem Kind;
er hat den Knaben wohl in dem Arm,
er fasst ihn sicher, er hält ihn warm.

"Mein Sohn, was birgst du so bang dein Gesicht?"
"Siehst, Vater, du den Erlkönig nicht?
den Erlenkönig mit Kron' und Schweif?"
"Mein Sohn, es ist ein Nebelstreif."

"Du liebes Kind, komm, geh mit mir!
gar schöne Spiele spiel' ich mit dir;
manch' bunte Blumen sind an dem Strand;
meine Mutter hat manch' gülden Gewand."

"Mein Vater, mein Vater, und hörest du nicht,
was Erlenkönig mir leise verspricht?"
"Sei ruhig, bleibe ruhig, mein Kind;
in dürren Blättern säuselt der Wind."

"Willst, feiner Knabe, du mit mir geh'n?
meine Töchter sollen dich warten schön;
meine Töchter führen den nächtlichen Reih'n
und wiegen und tanzen und singen dich ein."

"Mein Vater, mein Vater, und siehst du nicht dort,
Erlkönigs Töchter am düstern Ort?"

"Mein Sohn, mein Sohn, ich seh' es genau,
es scheinen die alten Weiden so grau."

"Ich liebe dich, mich reizt deine schöne Gestalt,
und bist du nicht willig, so brauch' ich Gewalt."
"Mein Vater, mein Vater, jetzt fasst er mich an!
Erlkönig hat mir ein Leids gethan!"

Dem Vater grauset's, er reitet geschwind,
er hält in Armen das ächzende Kind,
erreicht den Hof mit Müh und Noth:

in seinem Armen das Kind war todt.

JOHANN WOLFGANG VON GOETHE

Who rides so late through night and wind?
It is a father with his child:
he has the boy close in his arm,
he holds him tight, he keeps him warm.

"My son, why do you hide your face in fear?"
"Father, don't you see the Erlking?
The Erlking with his crown and train?"
"My son, it is a streak of mist."

"You dear child, come with me!
I'll play very lovely games with you.
There are lots of colorful flowers by the shore;
my mother has some golden robes."

"My father, my father, and don't you hear
the Erlking whispering promises to me?"
"Be still, stay calm, my child;
it's the wind rustling in the dry leaves."

"My fine lad, do you want to come with me?
My daughters will take care of you;
my daughters lead off the nightly dance,
and they'll rock and dance and sing you to sleep."

"My father, my father, and don't you see

the Erlking's daughters over there in the shadows?"
"My son, my son, I see it clearly,
it's the gray sheen of the old willows."

"I love you, your beautiful form delights me!
And if you are not willing, then I'll use force."
"My father, my father, now he's grasping me!
The Erlking has hurt me!"

The father shudders, he rides swiftly,
he holds the moaning child in his arms;
with effort and urgency he reaches the courtyard:
in his arms the child was dead.

2. *Hector Berlioz (1803–1869)*

Symphonie fantastique,
Fifth Movement (1830)

8:5A/2 8:5/ 8 - 12

3:2B/2 3:2/ 37 - 41

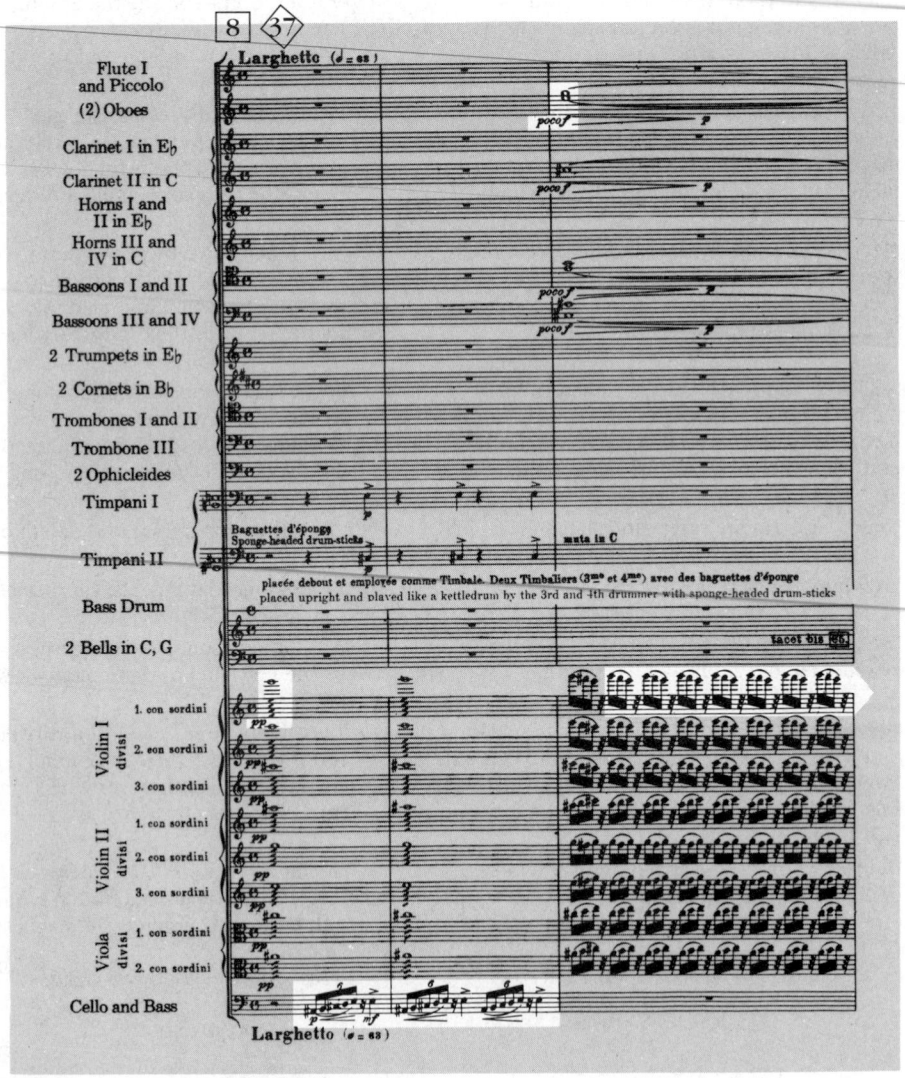

4
60
pizz.
Vcllo.
C.B.
div.
60

7
Fl. Solo
Fl.picc. Solo
a 2.
Soli
dim.
61
I. Solo
Solo III. bouché avec les cylindres
ppp stopped, with valves
II.
Deux timbaliers. roulement avec des baguettes à tête d'éponge sur la Grande Caisse placée debout
Two timpanists, rolling with sponge-headed sticks on the upright Bass Drum.
arco
unis.
pp

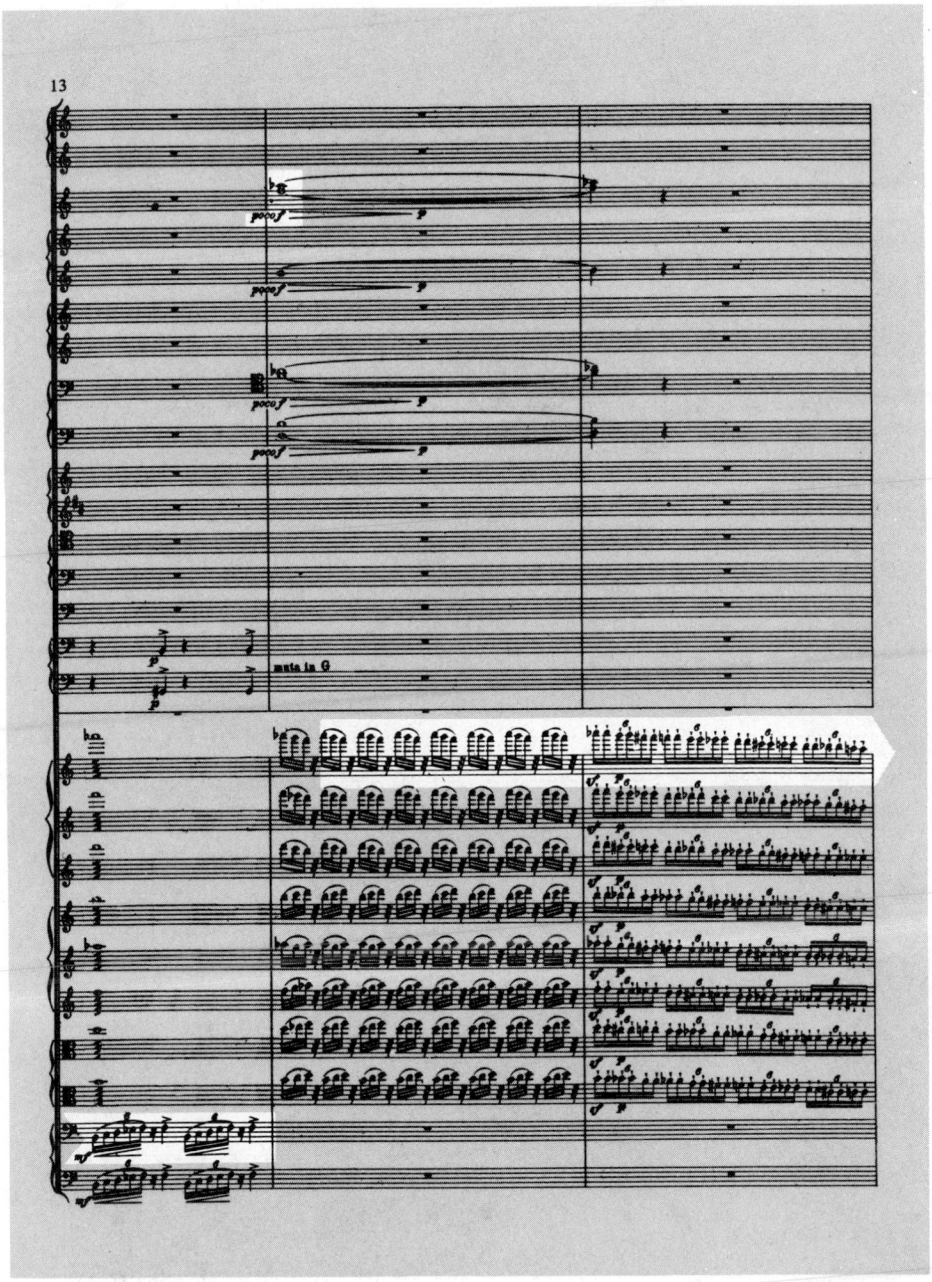
13
poco f
p
poco f
p
poco f
p
poco f
p
mute in G

16
62
Solo I
dim.
Solo III. bouché avec les cylindres
éponges
ôtez les sourdines
div.
62

9
38
21
Allegro (♩.= 112)
Allegro assai (o = 76)
Solo lointain distant
ppp
cresc.
ouvert avec les cylindres
open, with valves
a2
p cresc. poco a poco
Sur les deux timbales
cresc. poco a poco
sans sourdine
sans sourdine
Allegro (♩.= 112)
Allegro assai (o = 76)

32
a2.
a2.

63
40
Allegro (♩.= 104)
Fl. picc.
Ob.
poco f
Clar. I in E♭
Solo
poco f
cresc.
Clar. II in C
poco f
Fag.
unis.
Viol. I unis.
Viol. II unis.
Viola unis.
Vcllo.
C.B.
Allegro (♩.= 104)
63

49
Fl. picc.
Ob.
Clar.
Fag.
Viol.

55
Fl.
Fl.picc.
Ob.
a2
Clar.
Cor.
Fag.
Viol.

61
64
Fl.
Fl.pic.
Ob.
Clar.
Cor.
Fag.
(cresc.)
Viol.
cresc.
64

67
Fl.
Fl. picc.
Ob.
Clar.
Cor.
a 2.
Fag.
unis.
Tr.
Ctti
Tromb.
Oph.
Timp.
Viol.

74
a 2.
unis.

83
Fag.
unis.
(dim.)
ppp
Viol.
(dim.)
ppp
(dim.)
ppp

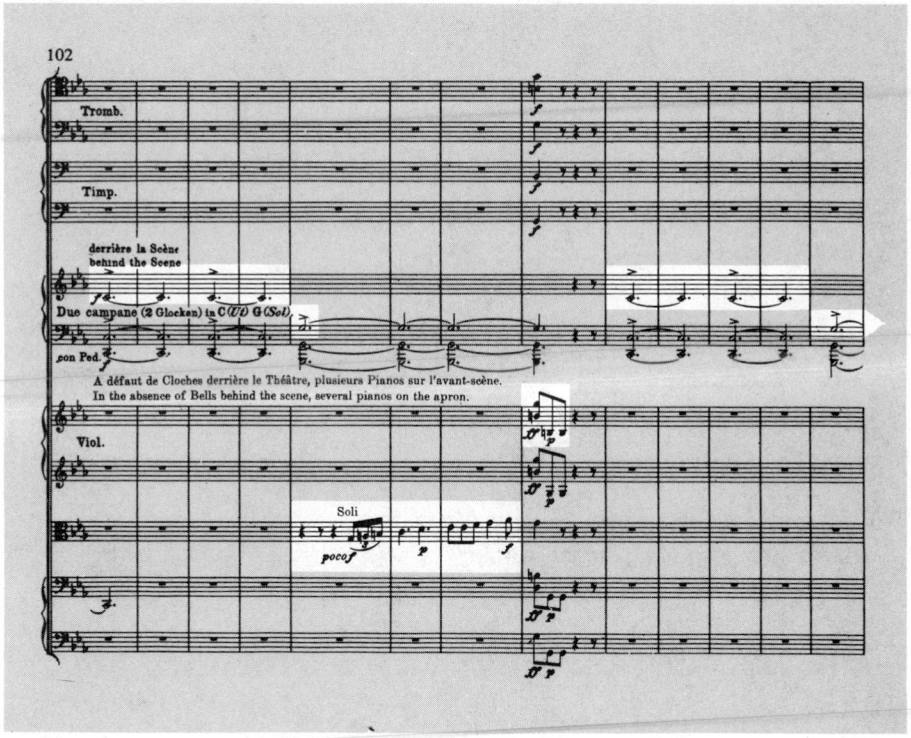
102
Tromb.
Timp.
derrière la Scène
behind the Scene
Due campane (2 Glocken) in C(D) G(Sol)
con Ped.
A défaut de Cloches derrière le Théâtre, plusieurs Pianos sur l'avant-scène.
In the absence of Bells behind the scene, several pianos on the apron.
Viol.
Soli
poco f

115
Ob. I.
Solo
a 2.
Cor.
Tr.
Tromb.
Timp.
Camp.
Viol.
66
10
39
Dies iræ
127
sans presser
Fag.
unis.
Oph.
a 2.
Soli
Camp.
Viol.
sans presser

146
Fl.
Fl. picc.
Ob.
Clar.
Cor.
Fag.
Tr.
Ctti
Tromb
Oph.
Gr. Tamb.
Camp.
Viol.
pizz.
pizz.
pizz.

159
67
f
ff
f
ff
arco
f
arco
f
arco
f
pizz.
f
pizz.
f
67

171
pizz.
pizz.
pizz.

184
68
arco
arco
arco
arco
tenu
arco
tenu
68

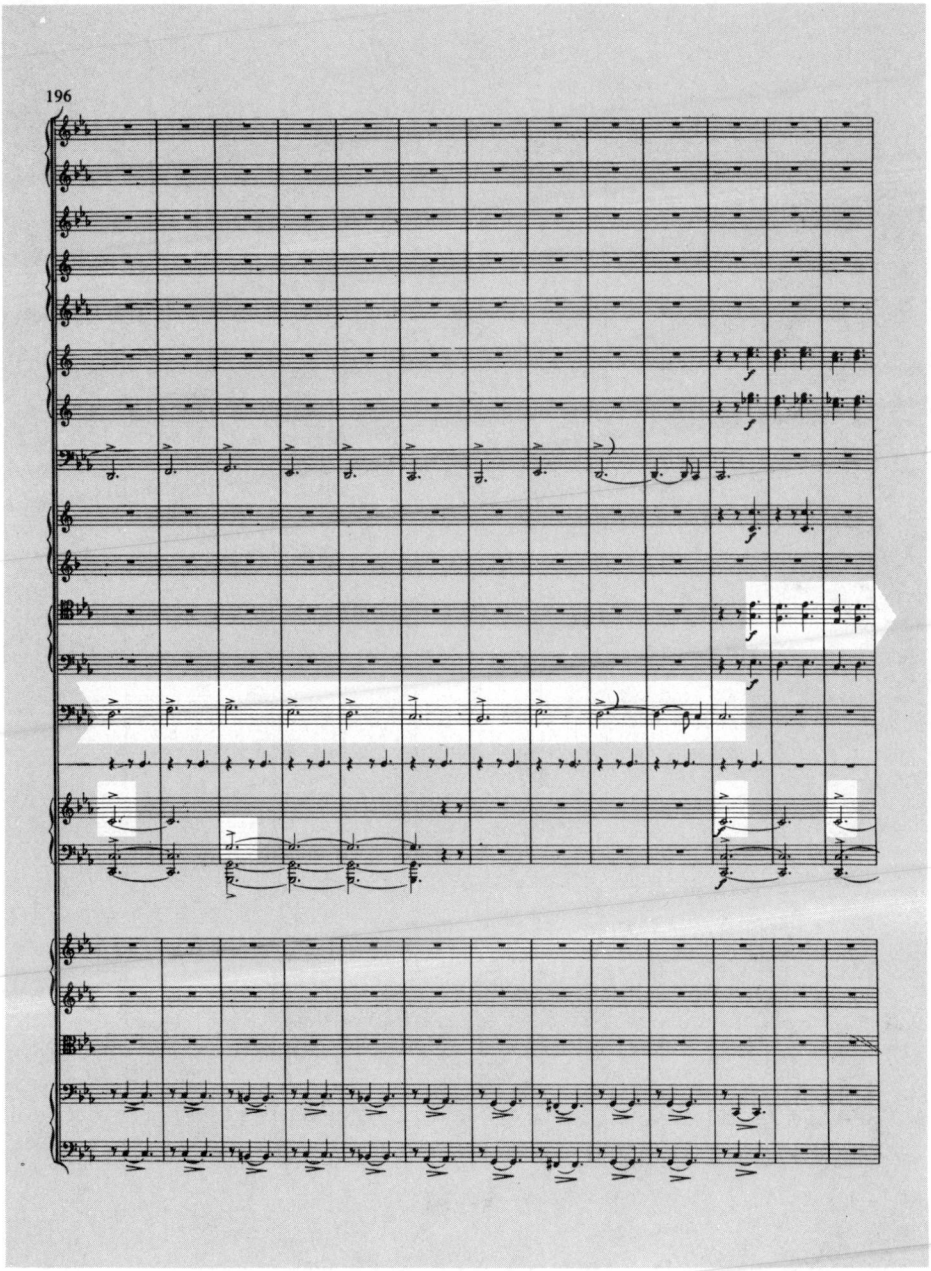
196

209
pizz.
pizz.
pizz.

221
69
a 2.
a 2.
G-Caisse roulante, deux Timbaliers
Bass-Drum roll, two timpanists
arco
arco
arco
69

231
70
Fl.
Fl. picc.
Ob.
Clar.
Cor.
Fag.
Tr.
Ctti
Tromb.
Oph.
Baguettes d'éponge
Sponge-headed sticks
Timp.
Baguettes d'éponge
Sponge-headed sticks
Viol.
70

11
40
Ronde du Sabbat
Witches' round dance
241
Un peu retenu
Un peu retenu

250
71
I.
71

257
I.
a 2.
a 2.
unis.

265
72
unis.
a 2.
a 2.
cresc.
72

272
a 2.
cresc.
cresc.
cresc.
cresc.
cresc.

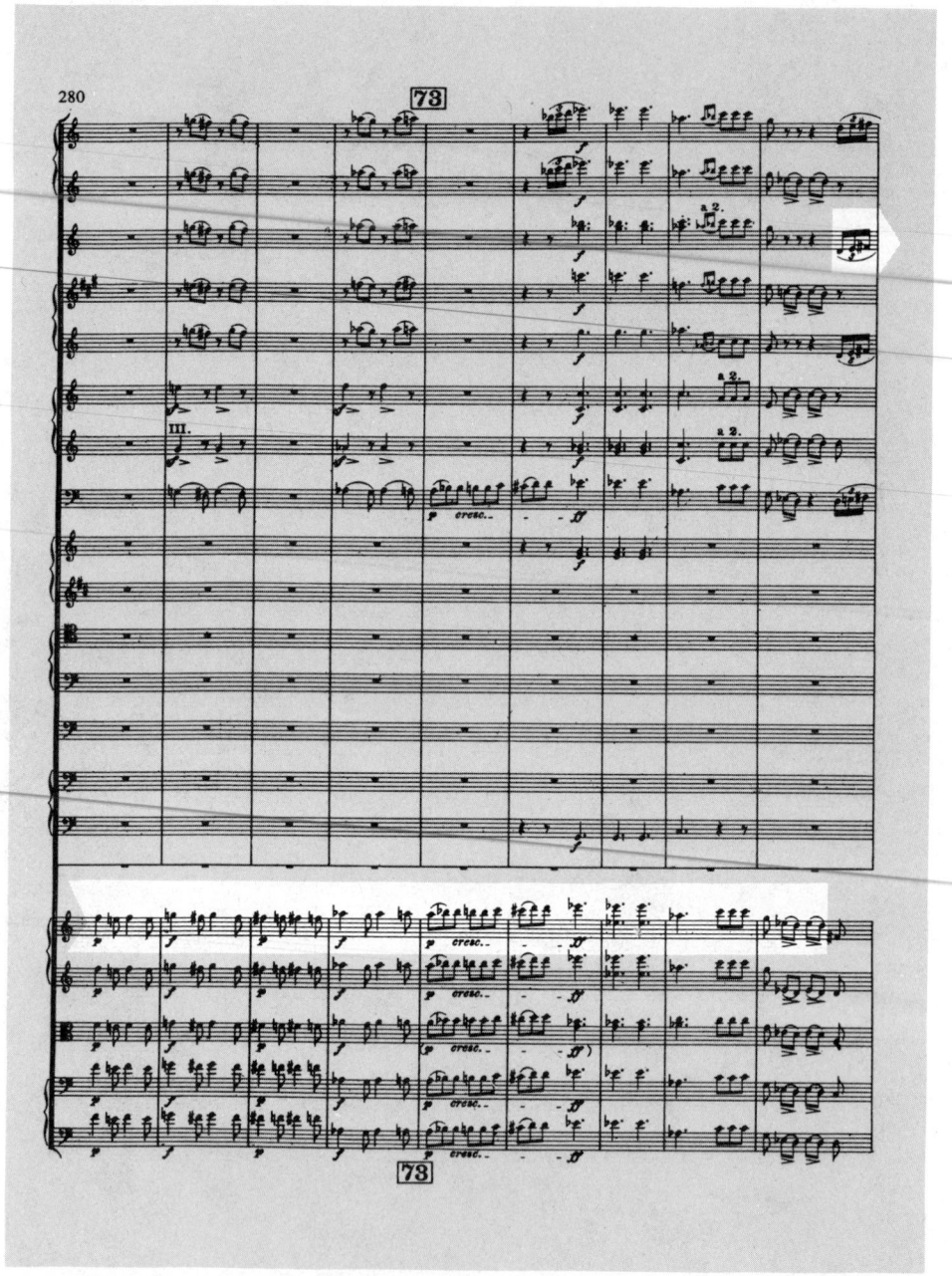
280
73
III.
a 2.
cresc.
73

289
(cresc.)
(cresc.)

297
74
a 2.
III.
unis.
a 2.
74

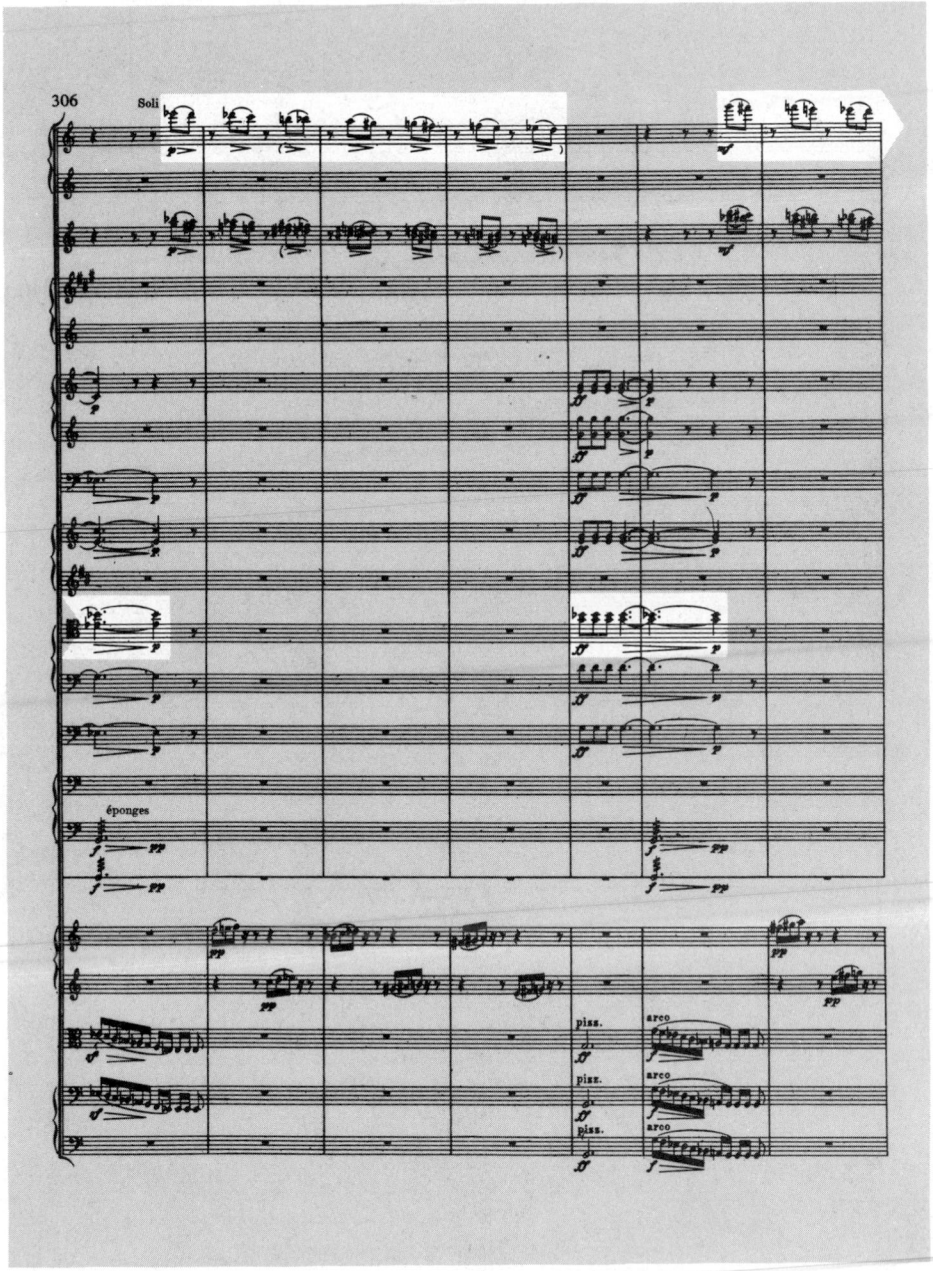
306
Soli
éponges
piss.
arco
piss.
arco
piss.
arco

313
f dimin.
a 2.
pizz.
arco

320
75
a 2.
unis.
a 2.
a 2.
a 2.
pizz.
pizz.
75

327
76
I.
III.
Soli
dim.
pp
Soli
unis. Soli
arco
arco
en dim. toujours
en dim. toujours
(en dim. toujours)
piss.
poco f
piss.
poco f
76

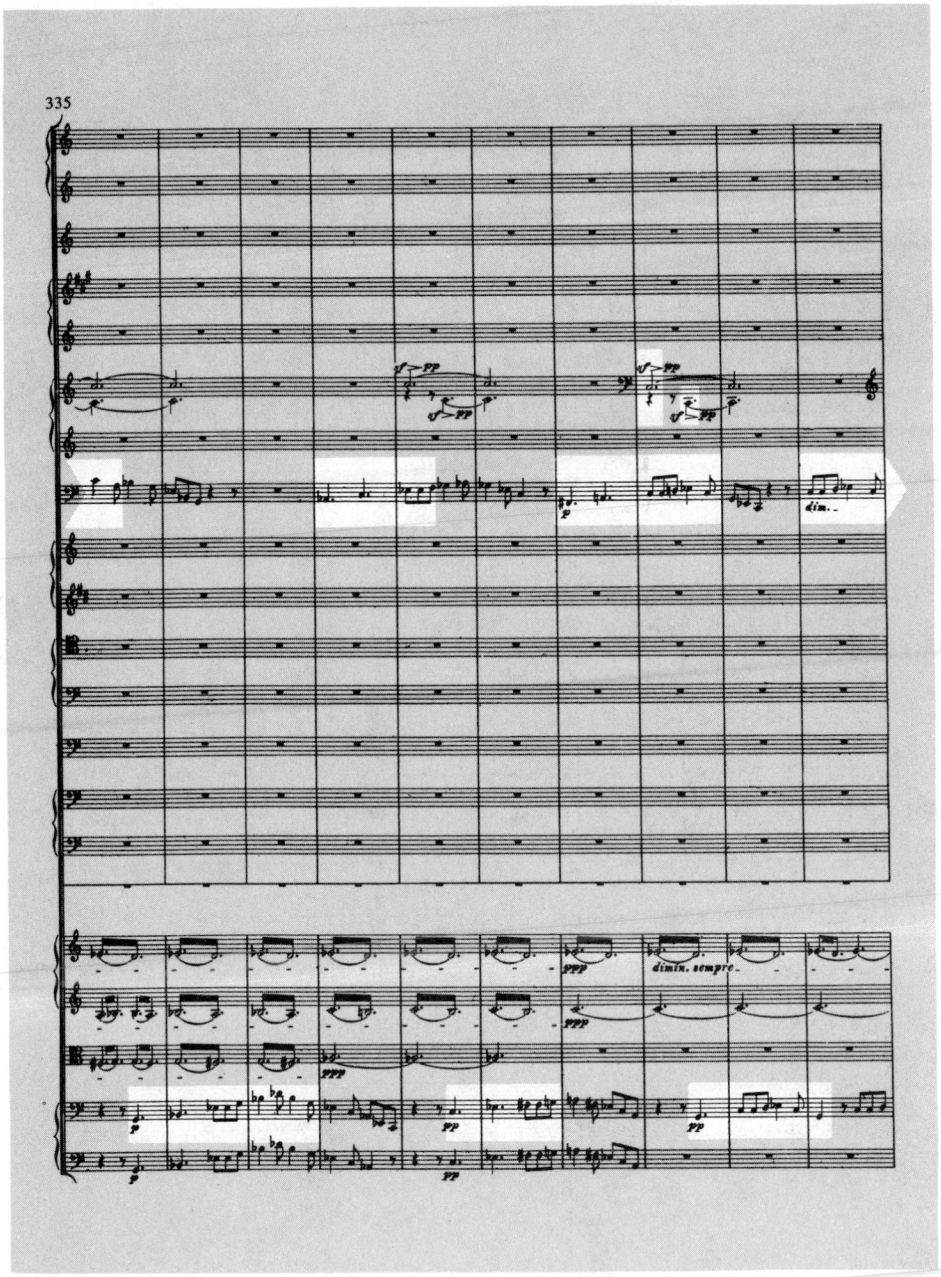
335
dim.
ppp
diminu. sempre
ppp
ppp
p
pp
pp
p
pp

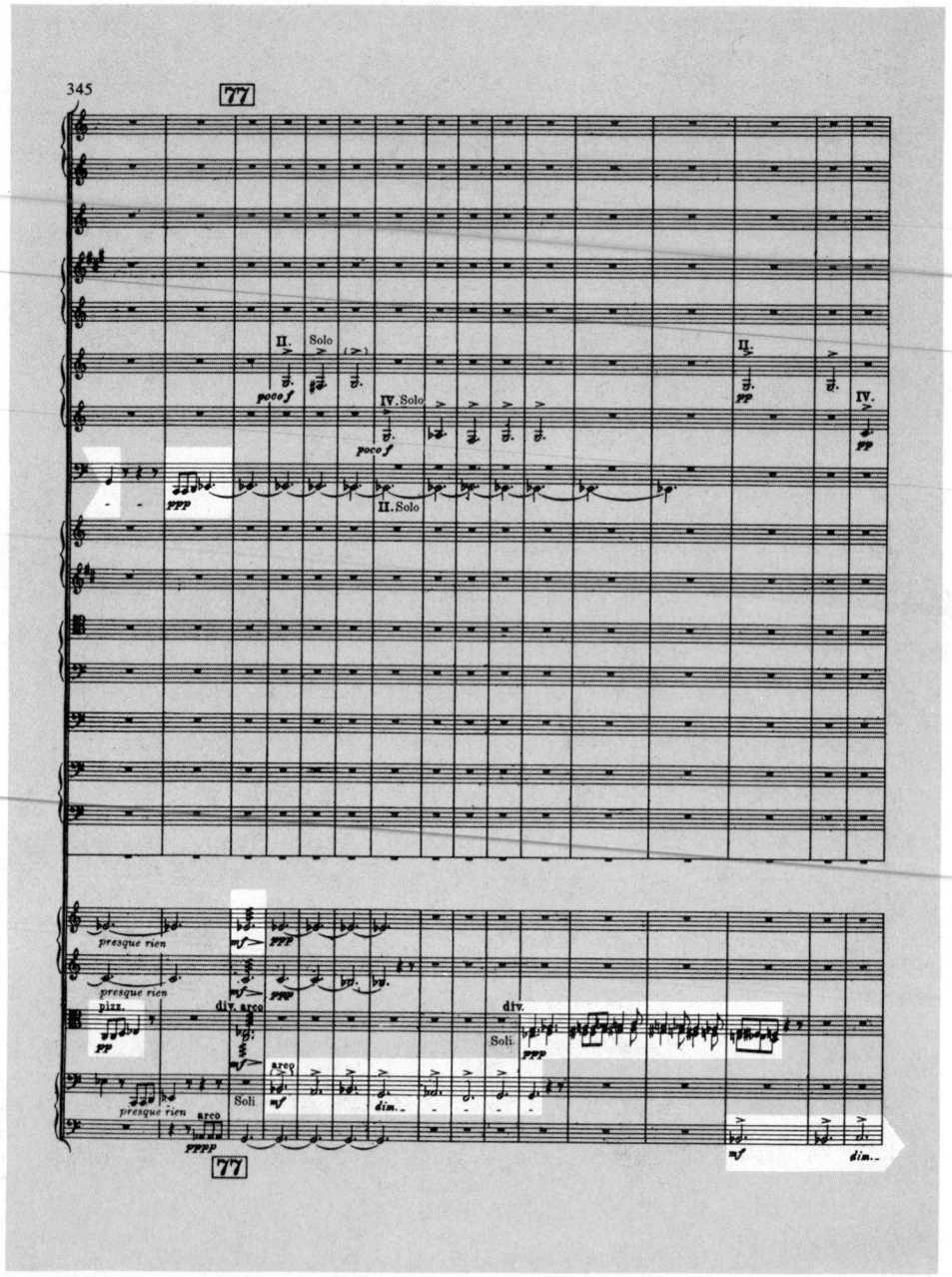
345
77
II.
Solo
poco f
IV. Solo
poco f
II. Solo
II.
pp
IV.
pp
ppp
presque rien
ppp
presque rien
ppp
pizz.
pp
div. arco
arco
Soli
mf
dim..
div.
Soli
ppp
presque rien
arco
pppp
77
mf
dim..

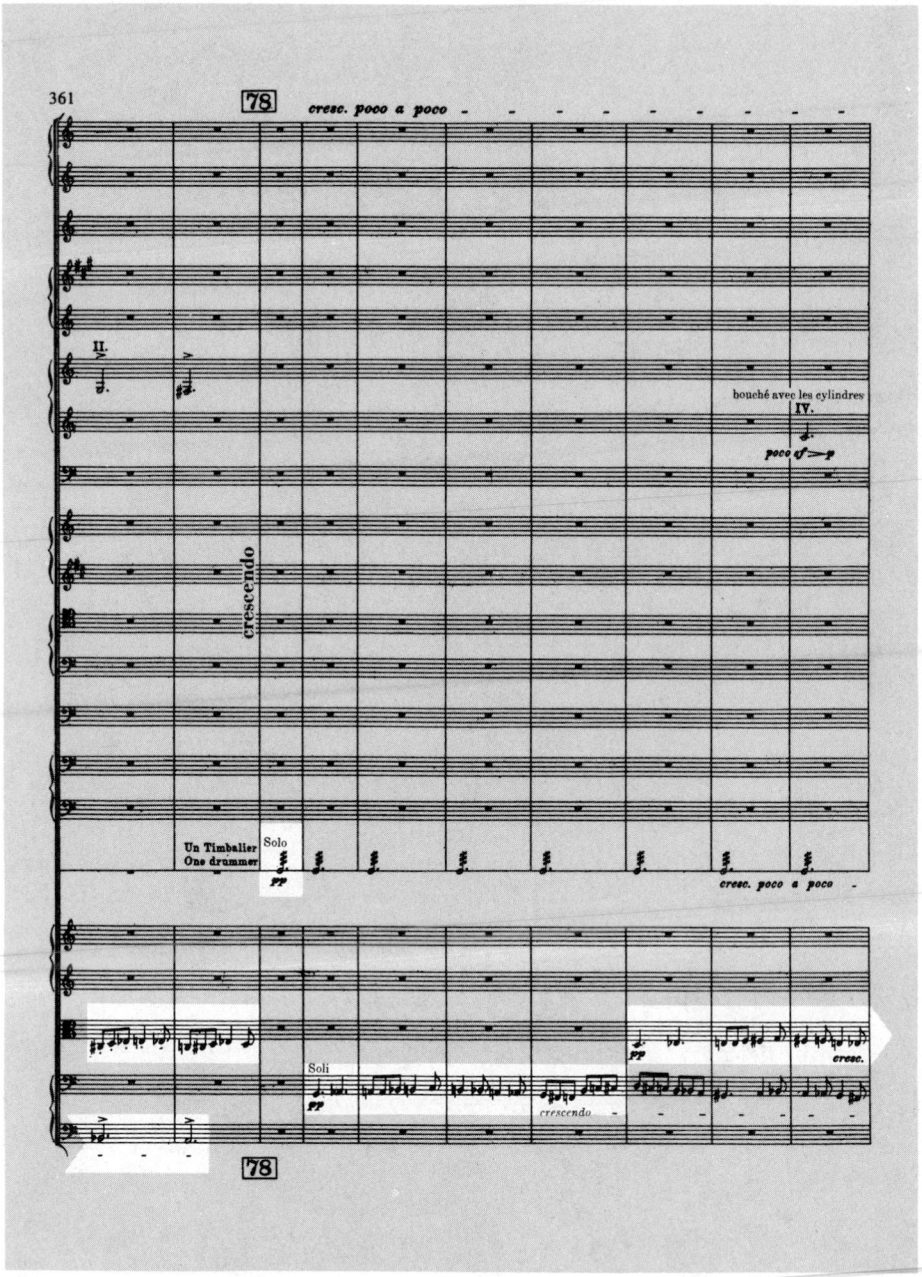
361
78
cresc. poco a poco
II.
bouché avec les cylindres
IV.
poco sf
p
crescendo
Un Timballier
One drummer
Solo
pp
cresc. poco a poco
Soli
pp
crescendo
pp
cresc.
78

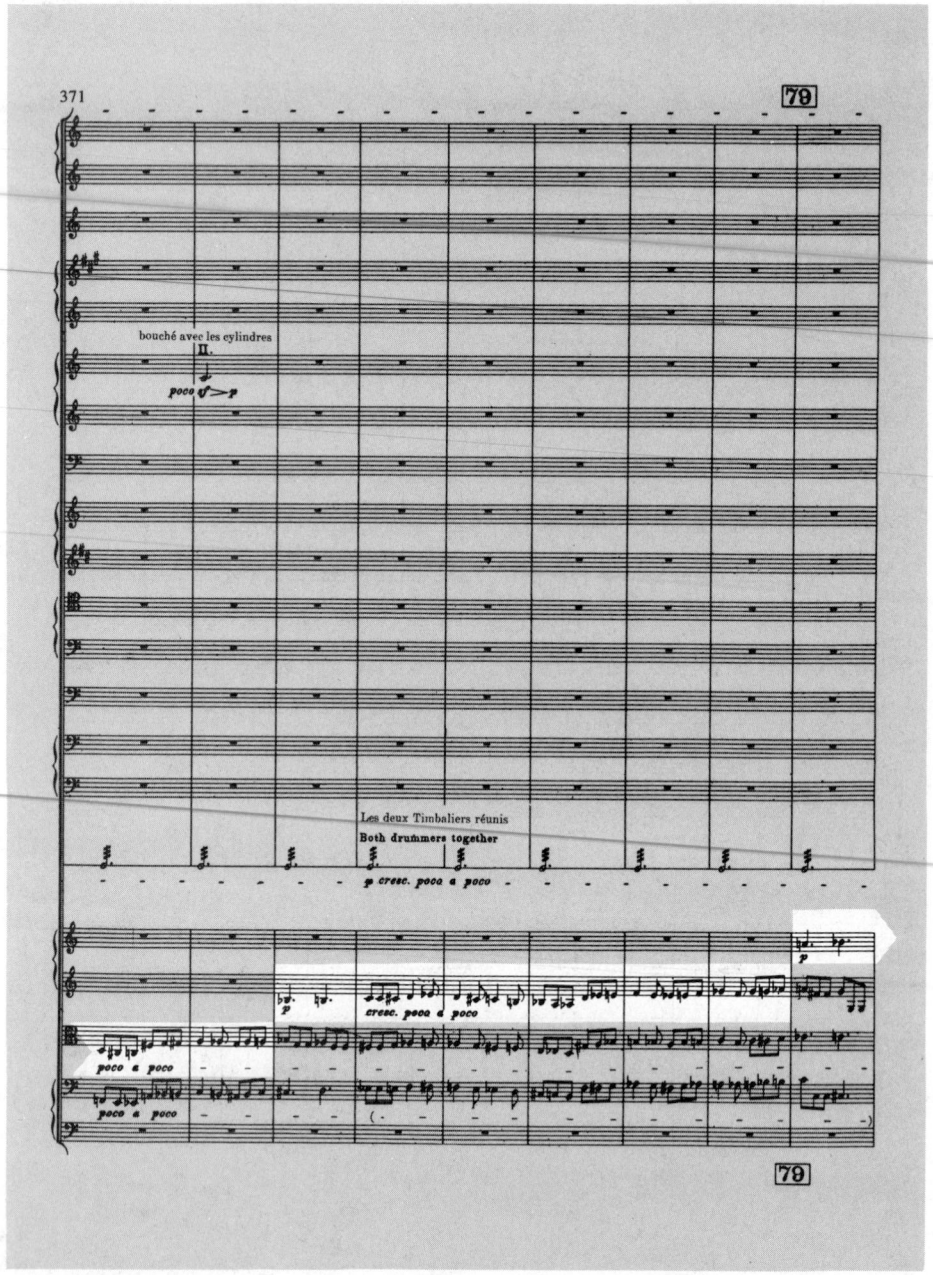
371
79
bouché avec les cylindres
II.
poco sf
p
Les deux Timbaliers réunis
Both drummers together
p cresc. poco a poco
p
cresc. poco a poco
poco a poco
poco a poco
79

380
mf
cresc.
I.
cresc. sempre
cresc. poco a poco
cresc. sempre
f cresc. sempre

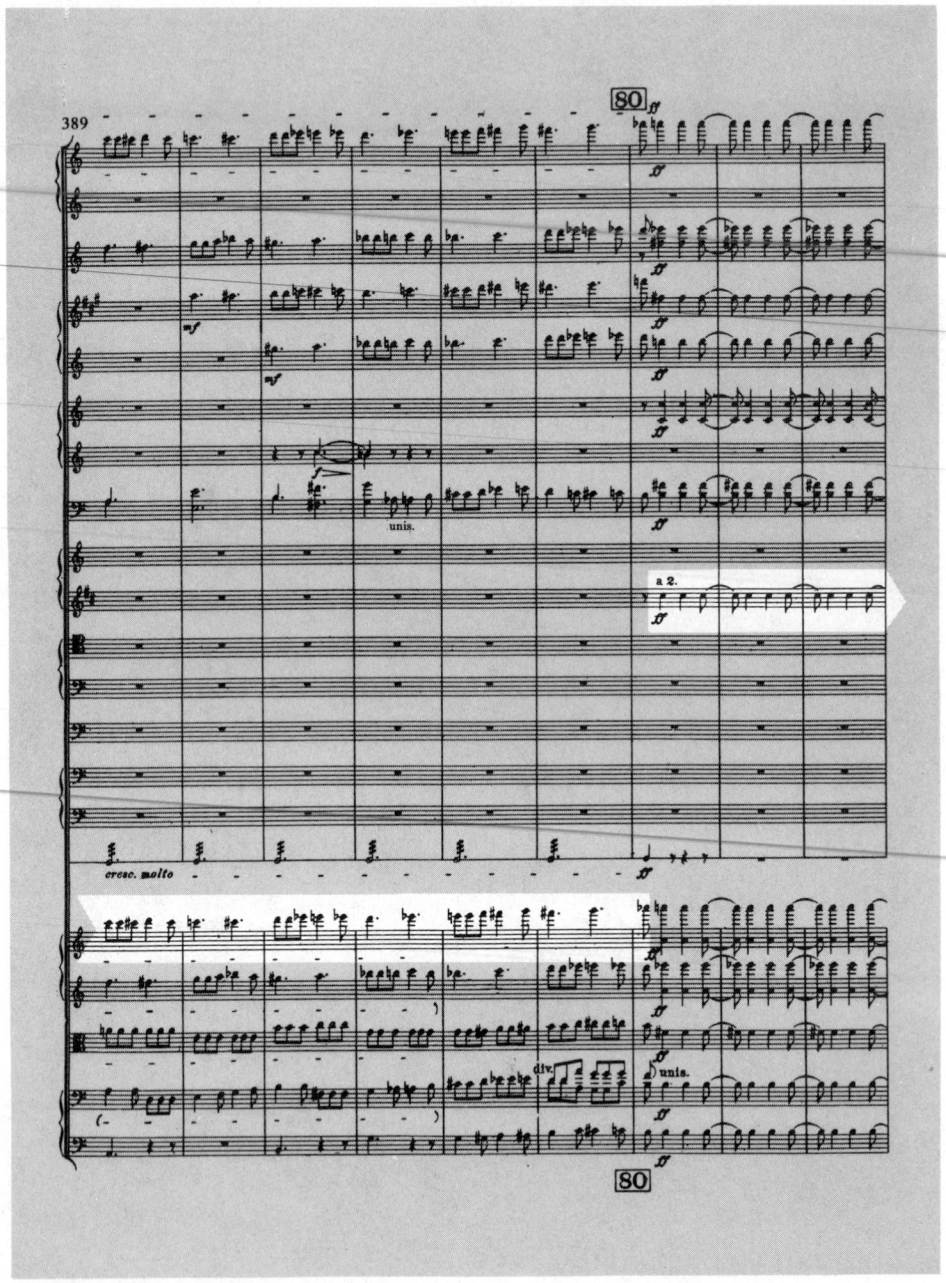
389
80
unis.
a 2.
cresc. molto
div.
unis.
80

398

407
81
81

12
41
Dies irae et Ronde du Sabbat ensemble
414 Dies irae and witches' round dance together
a 2.
unis.
a 2.
a 2.
a 2.

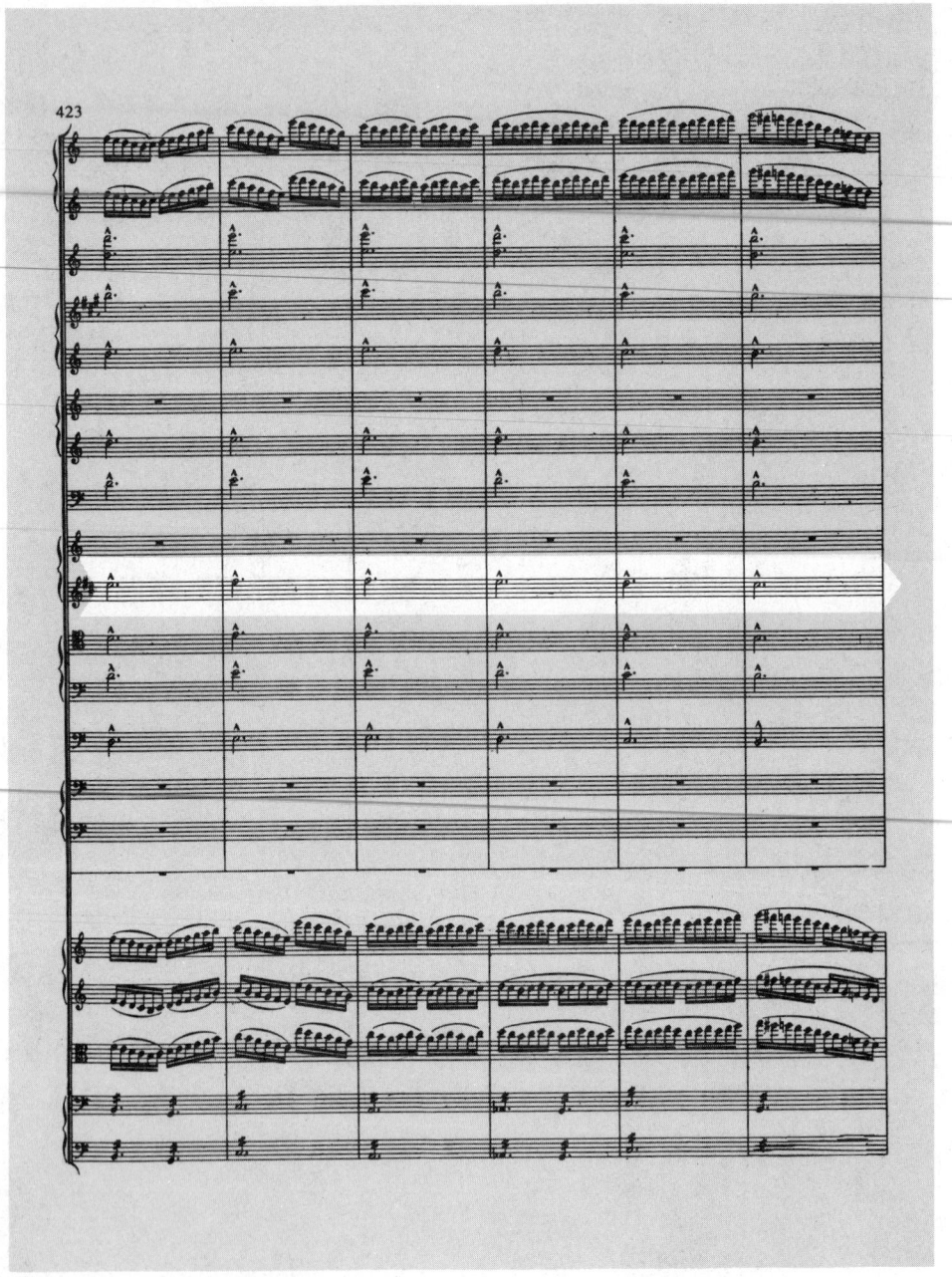
423

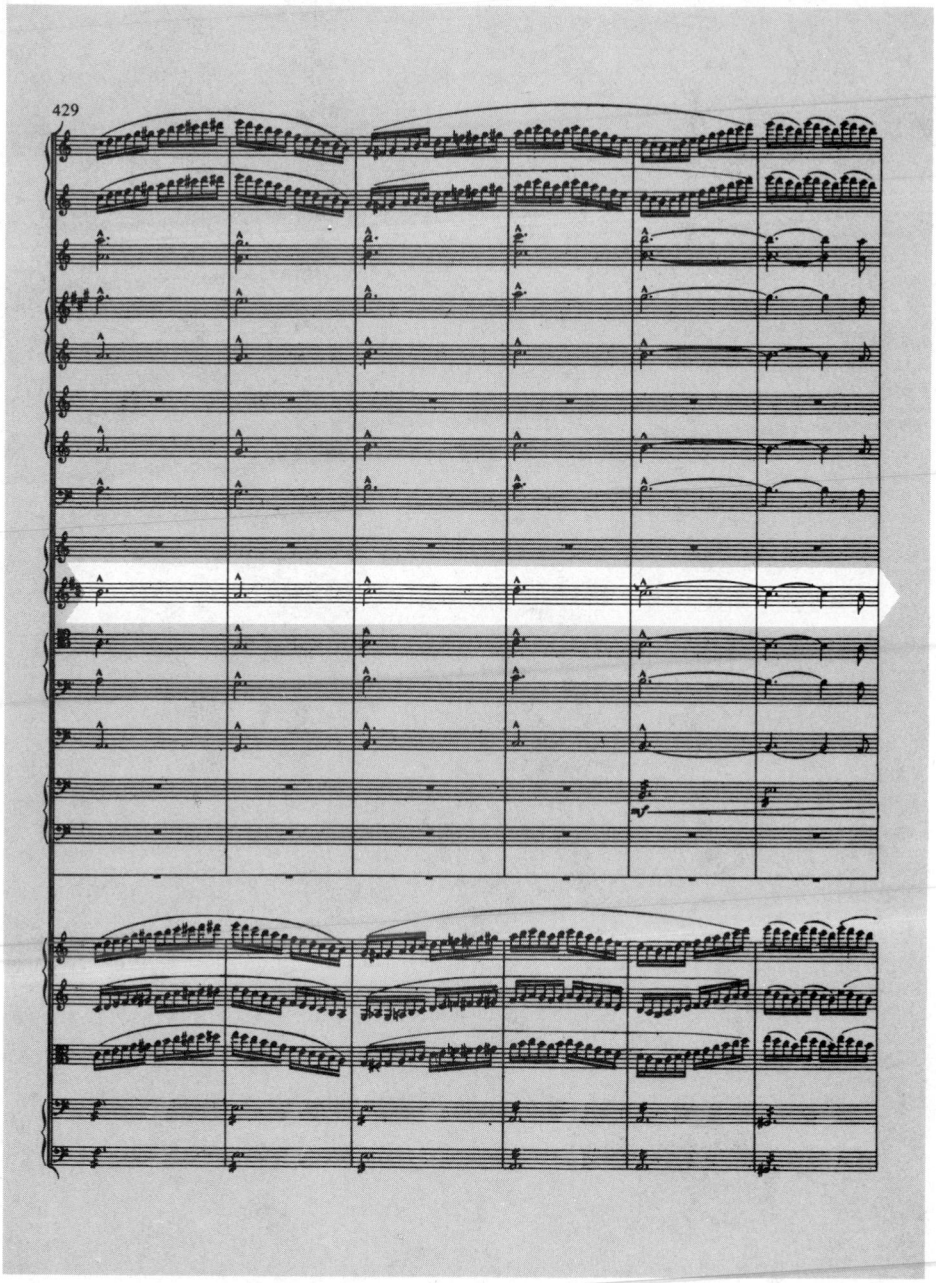

The Library
Saint Francis College
Fort Wayne, Indiana 46808

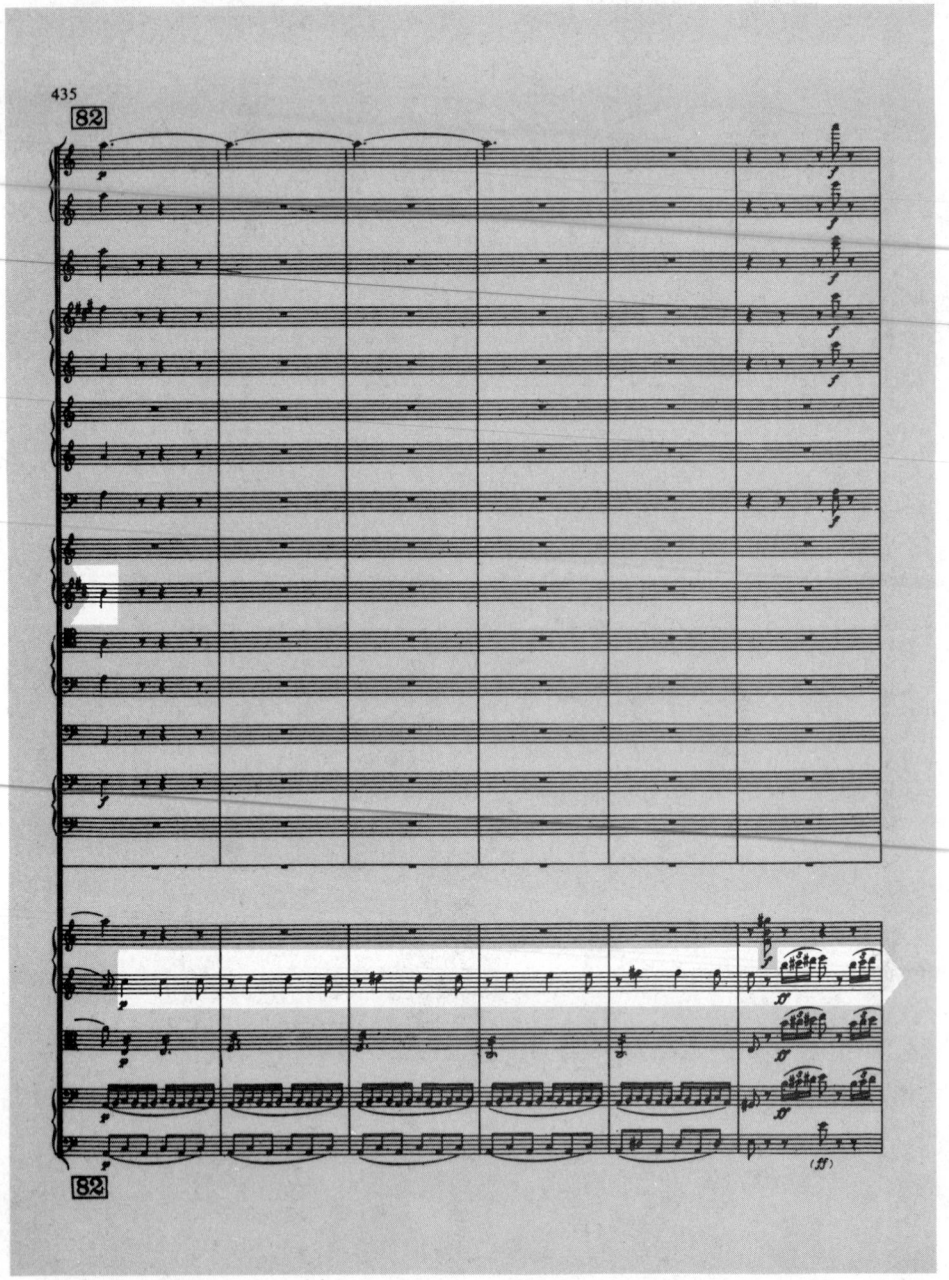
435
82
82

441
83
a 2.
unis.
frappez avec les bois de l'archet
frappez avec les bois de l'archet
frappez avec les bois de l'archet
(col legno battuta)
div.
83

448
pizz.
pp
pizz.
pp

456
Soli
p légèrement
I.
p légèrement
p légèrement
I.
p légèrement
arco

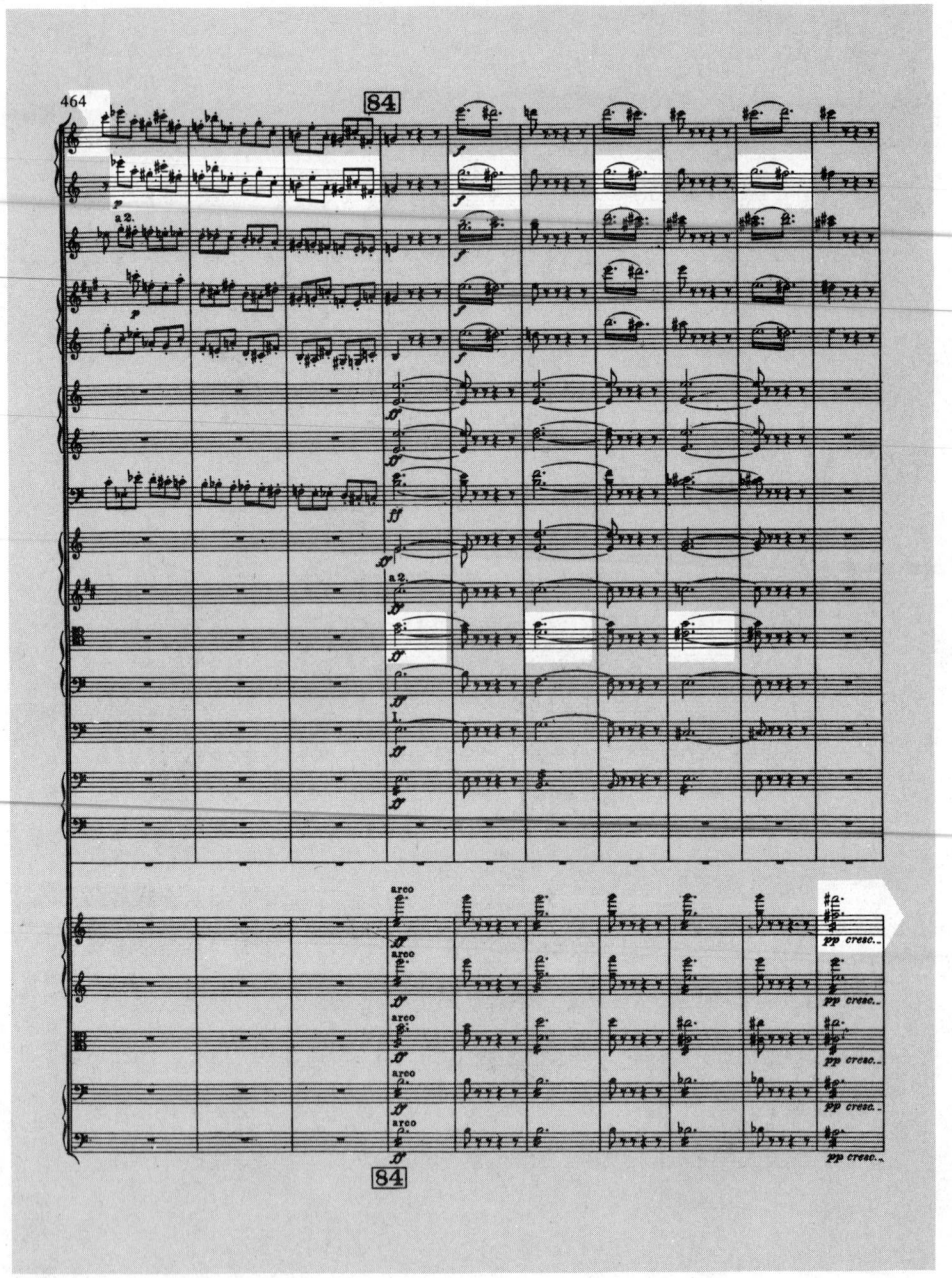
464
84
a 2.
arco
pp cresc.
84

474
Soli
mf
cresc.
a 2.
unis.

483
85
Solo II.
a 2.
unis.
a 2.
cresc. molto
a 2
a 2.
85

493
animez un peu
a 2.
animez un peu

504
86
unis.
a 2.
a 2.
I.
div.
unis.
86

515
tenu
unis.
Coup frappé sur une Cymbale avec une baguette couverte d'éponge ou un tampon
Struck on a cymbal with a sponge-headed drum-stick or a padded stick
Cinelli.

3. *Felix Mendelssohn (1809–1847)*

A Midsummer Night's Dream,
Overture (1826)

8:5A/3 8:5/13 - 21

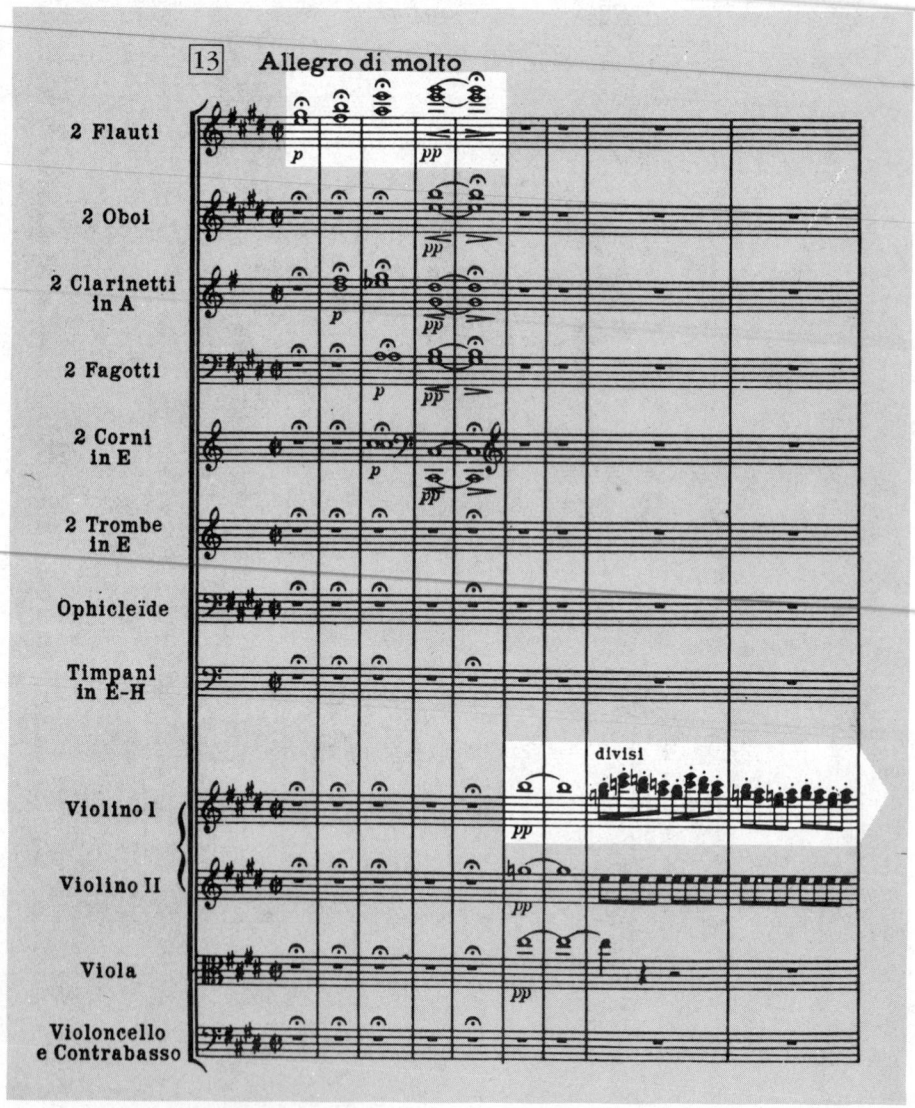

10
Vl.
sempre stacc.
div.
sempre stacc.
20
Vl.
unis.
div.
pizz.
Vla.
p
Vl.
pp stacc.
stacc.
pp pizz.
pizz.
Vla.
pp
30
Vl.
unis.
arco
Vla.
Vl.
div.

40
Fl.
pp
Cl. (A)
pp
Fg.
pp
Cor. (E)
pp
Vl.
div.
arco
pizz.
pizz.
Vla.

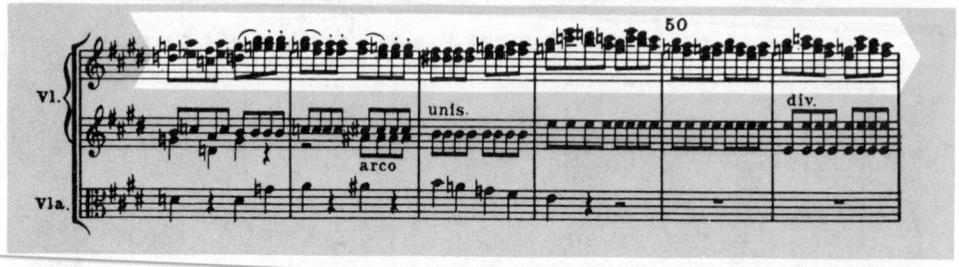
50
Vl.
unis.
arco
div.
Vla.

Fl.
pp
Cl. (A)
Fg.
Cor. (E)
pp
Vl.
pp
pp

14
60
Fl.
Ob.
Cl. (A)
Fg.
Cor. (E)
Tr. (E)
Oph.
Timp.
Vl.
Vla.
Vc. e Cb.
ff
unis.
arco

70
Fl.
Ob.
Cl. (A)
Fg.
Cor. (E)
Tr. (E)
Oph.
Timp.
Vl.
Vla.
Vc. e Cb.
ff
sf

80
Fl.
Ob.
Cl. (A)
Fg.
Cor. (E)
Tr. (E)
Oph.
Timp.
Vl.
Vla.
Vc. e Cb.
a 2
a 2
a 2

Fl.
a 2
sf
ff
Ob.
a 2
sf
ff
Cl. (A)
ff
Fg.
ff
Cor. (E)
ff
Tr. (E)
ff
Oph.
ff
ff
Timp.
ff
Vl.
ff
ff
Vla.
ff
Vc. e Cb.
ff

90
a 2
Fl.
Ob.
Cl. (A)
Fg.
Cor. (E)
Tr. (E)
Oph.
Timp.
Vl.
Vla.
Vc. e Cb.
sf
f

Ob.
Cl. (A)
Fg.
Cor. (E)
Vl.
Vla.
Vc.
Cb.
cresc.
ff
a 2
f
1.
100
Fl.
Oph.
Vc.

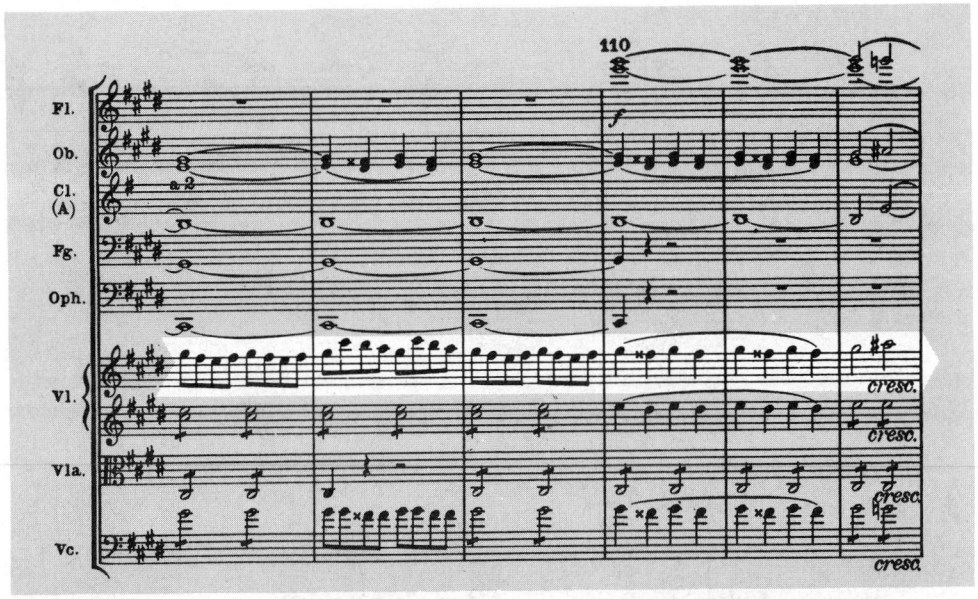
110
Fl.
Ob.
Cl. (A)
a 2
Fg.
Oph.
Vl.
Vla.
Vc.
f
cresc.

Ob.
Cl. (A)
Fg.
Cor. (E)
Tr. (E)
Oph.
Timp.
Vl.
Vla.
Vc.
Cb.
cresc.
ff
f
tr.

120
Fl.
Ob.
Cl. (A)
Fg.
Cor. (E)
Tr. (E)
Oph.
Timp.
Vl.
Vla.
Vc. e Cb.
Bassi
pizz.

130
Fl.
Cl. (A)
Fg.
Cor. (E)
Oph.
Vla.
Vc.
arco

15
140
Fl.
Cl. (A)
Fg.
Cor. (E)
Vl.
Vla.
Vc.
pp
p
div.
Bassi
150
Vc. e Cb.
160

170
Fl.
Ob.
Cl. (A)
a 2
Fg.
Cor. (E)
Tr. (E)
Oph.
Timp.
Vl.
Vla.
Vc.
Cb.
cresc.
dolce
pizz.

180
Fl.
Ob.
Cl. (A)
Fg.
Cor. (E)
Tr. (E)
Timp.
Vl.
Vla.
Vc.
Cb.
f
mf
pp
p
cresc.
arco

Cl. (A)
Fg.
Cor. (E)
Vl.
Vla.
Vc. e Cb.
Bassi
mf
cresc.
f
più f
190
Ob.
Tr. (E)
Oph.
Timp.
a 2
ff

16
200
Fl.
Ob.
Cl. (A)
Fg.
Cor. (E)
Oph.
Timp.
Vl.
Vla.
Vc. e Cb.
ff
f

210
Fl.
Ob.
Cl. (A)
Fg.
Cor. (E)
Oph.
Timp.
Vl.
Vla.
Vc. e Cb.
f
ff

220
Fl.
Ob.
Cl. (A)
Fg.
Cor. (E)
Tr. (E)
Oph.
Timp.
Vl.
Vla.
Vc. e Cb.
ff
f

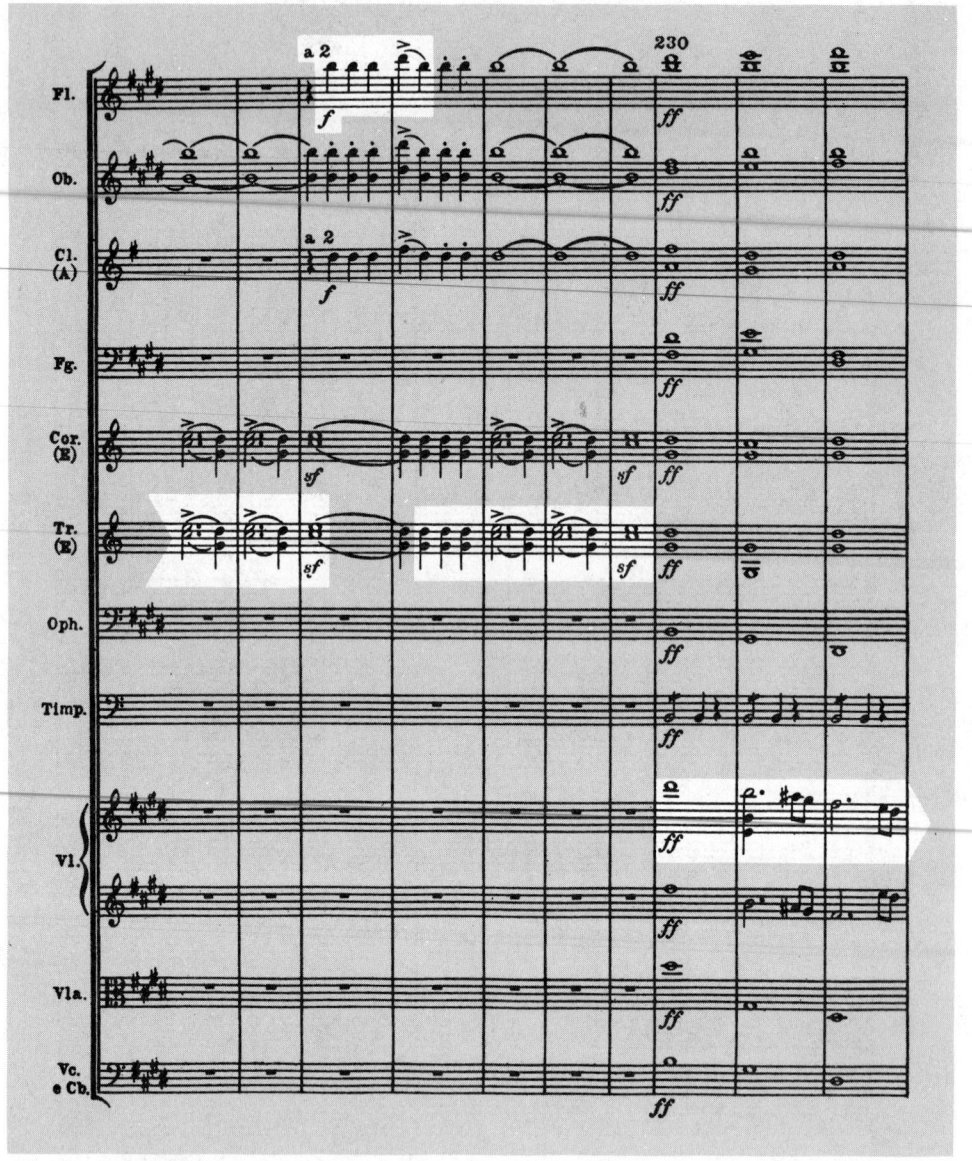
230
a 2
Fl.
Ob.
Cl. (A)
Fg.
Cor. (E)
Tr. (E)
Oph.
Timp.
Vl.
Vla.
Vc. e Cb.
f
ff
sf

240
Fl.
Ob.
Cl. (A)
Fg.
Cor. (E)
Tr. (E)
a 2
Oph.
Timp.
Vl.
Vla.
Vc. e Cb.
sf
f

17
250
Fl.
Ob.
Cl. (A)
Fg.
Cor. (E)
Tr. (E)
Oph.
Timp.
Vl.
Vla.
Vc. e Cb.
a 2
div.
pp stacc.
Ob.
Vl.
div.

260
Fl.
Ob.
Cl. (A)
Fg.
Cor. (E)
Timp.
Vl.
Vla.
pp
unis.

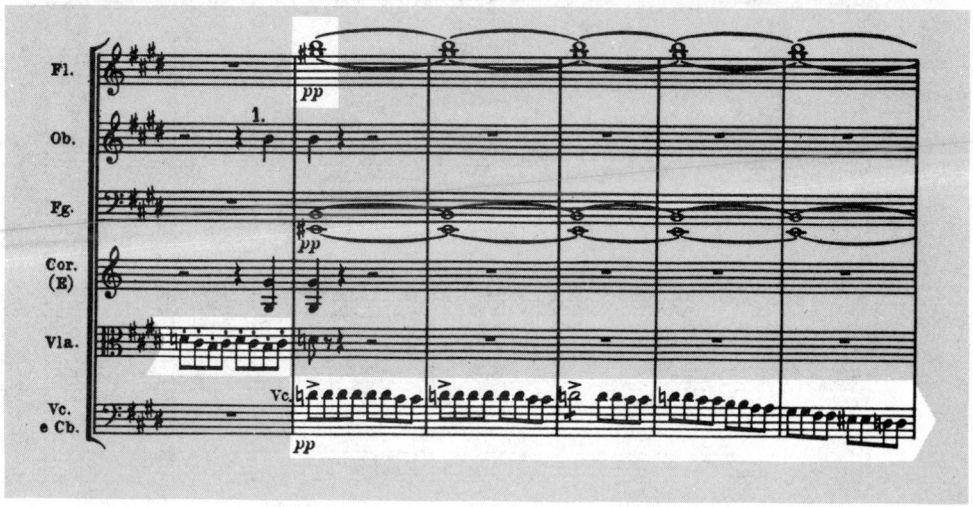
Fl.
Ob.
Fg.
Cor. (E)
Vla.
Vc. e Cb.
1.
Vc.
pp

270
Fl.
Ob.
Cl. (A)
Fg.
Vl.
Vc.
1.
pp
div.
280
Cor. (E)
unis.
Vc. e Cb.
Bassi

Fl.
Ob.
Cl. (A)
Fg.
Cor. (E)
Tr. (E)
Timp.
Vl.
Vla.
Vc.
Cb.
8
pp
p
a 2
Tutti
Tutti

290
Fl.
Ob.
Cl. (A)
Fg.
Cor. (E)
Tr. (E)
Timp.
Vl.
Vc.
Cb.
pp
con tutta la forza
a 2
ff
dim. poco a poco
div.
Vla.
sempre pp

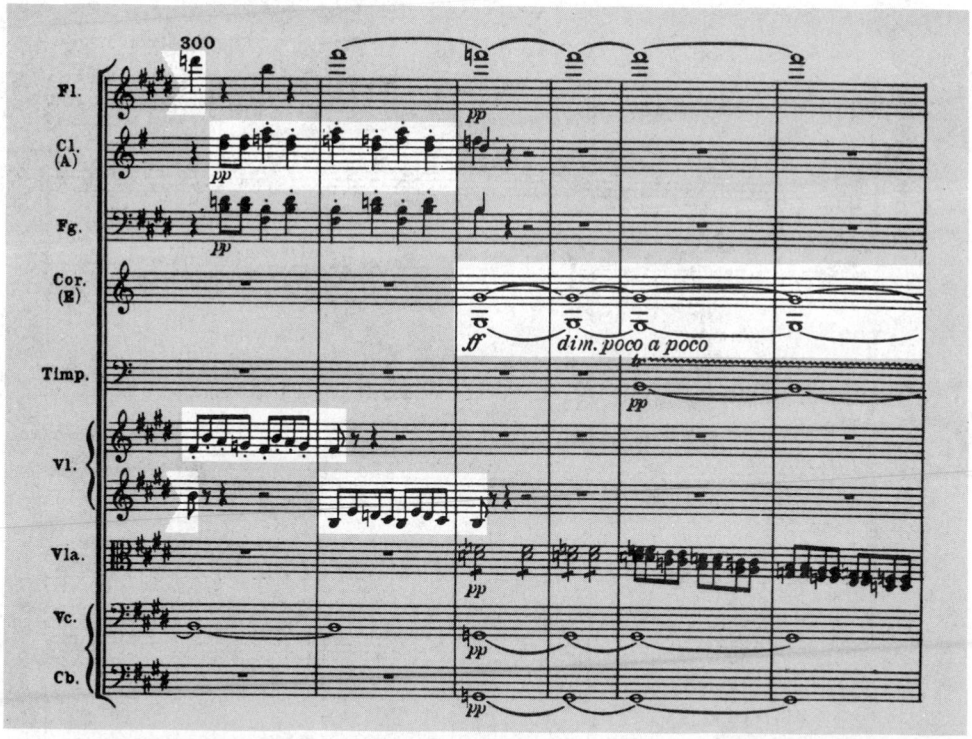
300
Fl.
Cl. (A)
Fg.
Cor. (E)
Timp.
Vl.
Vla.
Vc.
Cb.
pp
ff
dim. poco a poco
tr

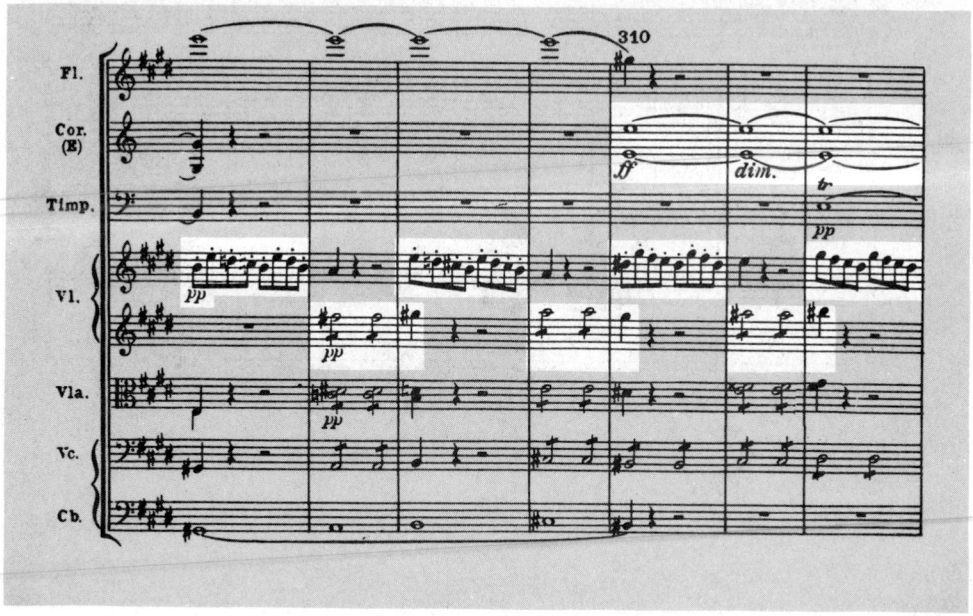
310
Fl.
Cor. (E)
Timp.
Vl.
Vla.
Vc.
Cb.
pp
ff
dim.
tr

Fl.
Ob.
Cl. (A)
Fg.
Cor. (E)
Tr. (E)
Timp.
Vl.
Vla.
Vc.
Cb.
pp
1.
a 2
p

320
Fl.
Ob.
Cl. (A)
Fg
Cor. (E)
Tr. (E)
Vl.
Vla.
Vc. e Cb.
p
Vc.

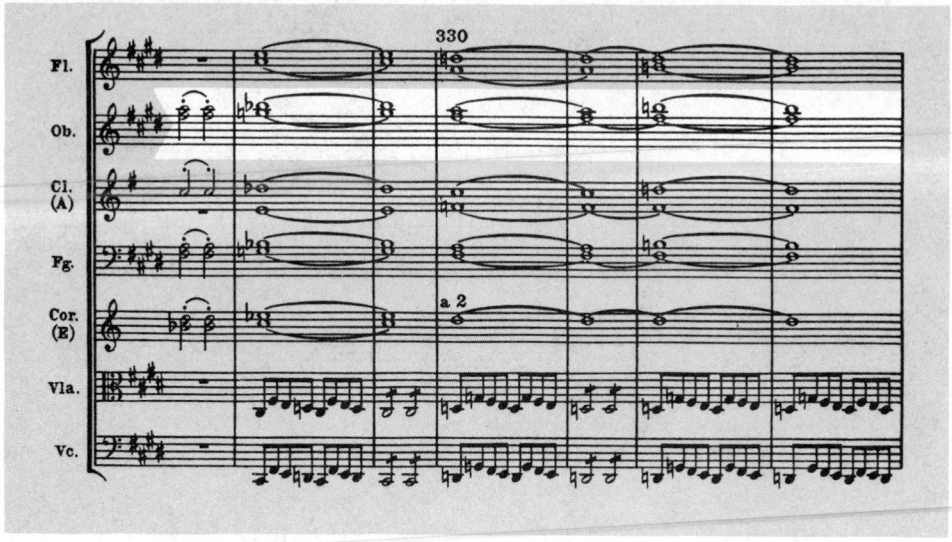
330
Fl.
Ob.
Cl. (A)
Fg.
Cor. (E)
a 2
Vla.
Vc.

340
a 2
Fl.
Ob.
Cl. (A)
Fg.
Cor. (E)
1.
Timp.
pp
div.
pizz.
arco
Vl.
Vla.
Vc.
Bassi pizz.

350
Fl.
Ob.
Cl. (A)
Fg.
Cor. (E)
Timp.
Vl.
Vla.
Vc.
pp
1.
pizz.
arco
Bassi
(pizz.)

360
Fl.
Fg.
Vl.
Vla.
Vc.
Cb.
unis.
pp
arco

370
Fl.
Cl. (A)
Fg.
Cor. (E)
Vl.
Vla.
Vc.
Cb.
1.
pp

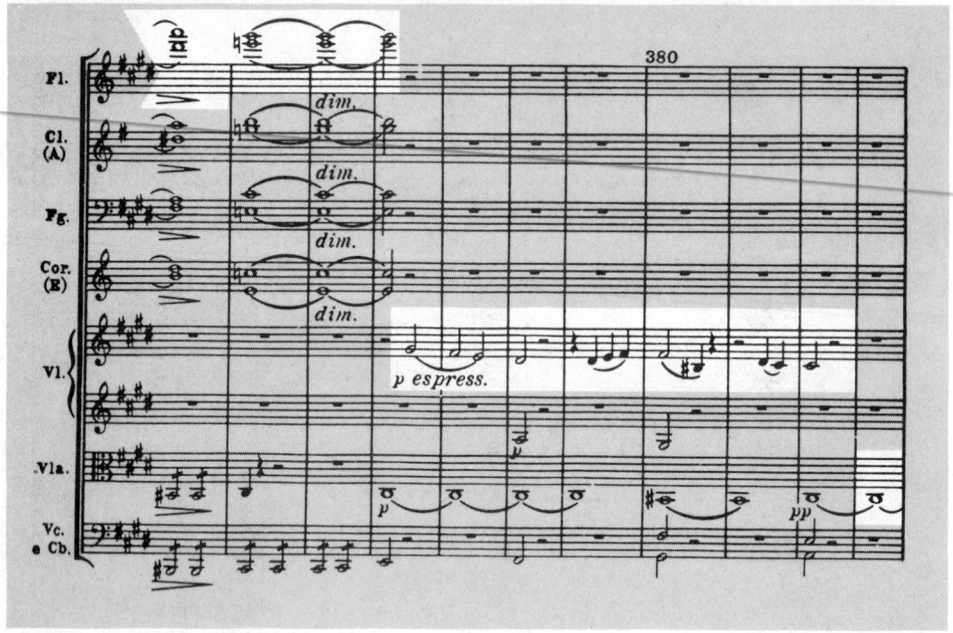
380
Fl.
Cl. (A)
Fg.
Cor. (E)
Vl.
Vla.
Vc. e Cb.
dim.
p espress.
p
pp

ritard.
390
Vl.
Vla.
Vc.
e Cb.
18
400
Fl.
Ob.
Cl.
(A)
Fg.
Cor.
(E)
div.
Vl.
Vla.
Vc.
e Cb.
pizz.

410
Fl.
Ob.
Cl. (A)
Vl.
div.
Fg.
Cor. (E)
Oph.
unis.
div.
420
Timp.
arco
pizz.

430
Fl.
Ob.
Cor. (E)
Oph.
Timp.
Vl.
Vc. e Cb.
pp
unis.
arco
pizz.

440
Fl.
Ob.
Cl. (A)
Cor. (E)
Oph.
Timp.
Vl.
Vc. e Cb.
1.
pp
div.

Fl.
Ob.
Cl. (A)
Cor. (E)
Vl.
Vla.
Vc. e Cb.
p
unis.
pp
arco
pp

450
Fl.
Ob.
Cl. (A)
Fg.
Cor. (E)
Vl. I
Vla.
Vc.
arco
p

19
460
Fl.
Ob.
Cl. (A)
Fg.
Cor. (E)
Vl.
Vla.
Vc. e Cb.
p
div.
Bassi
p arco

470
1.
Fl.
Cl. (A)
Cor. (E)
Vl.
Vla.
Vc. e Cb.
p
unis.

480
1.
a 2
Fl.
cresc.
f
Ob.
f
Cl. (A)
a 2
p
f
Fg.
p
Cor. (E)
p
mf
Tr. (E)
mf
Oph.
mf
Timp.
mf
Vl.
cresc.
cresc.
Vla.
sf cresc.
Vc. e Cb.
cresc.

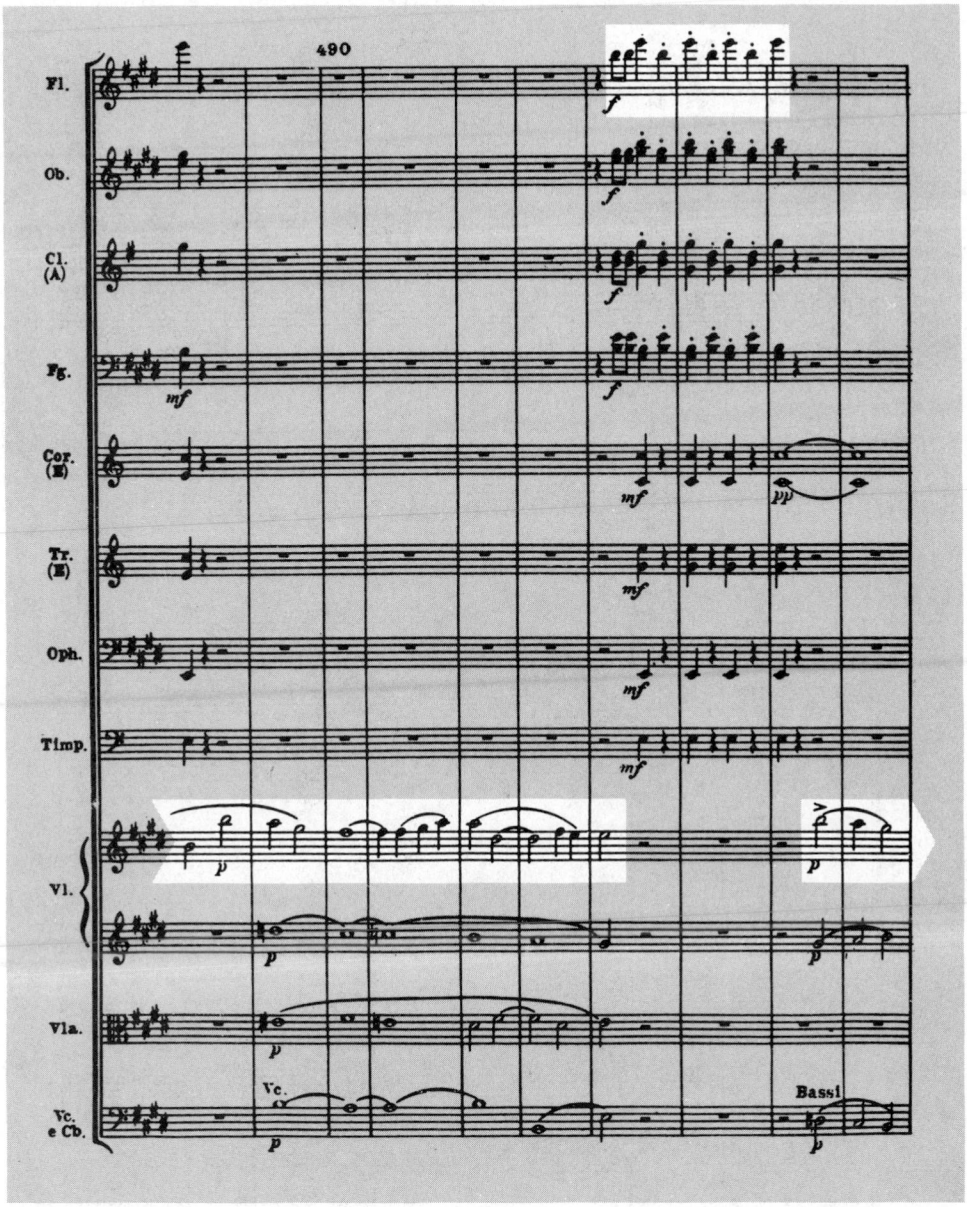
490
Fl.
Ob.
Cl. (A)
Fg.
Cor. (E)
Tr. (E)
Oph.
Timp.
Vl.
Vla.
Vc. e Cb.
Vc.
Bassi

500
Cl. (A)
Fg.
Cor. (E)
Vl.
Vla.
Vc. e Cb.
cresc.
mf
f
più f
510
Cl. (A)
Fg.
Cor. (E)
Oph.
Timp.
Vl.
Vla.
Vc. e Cb.
cresc.
f
ff

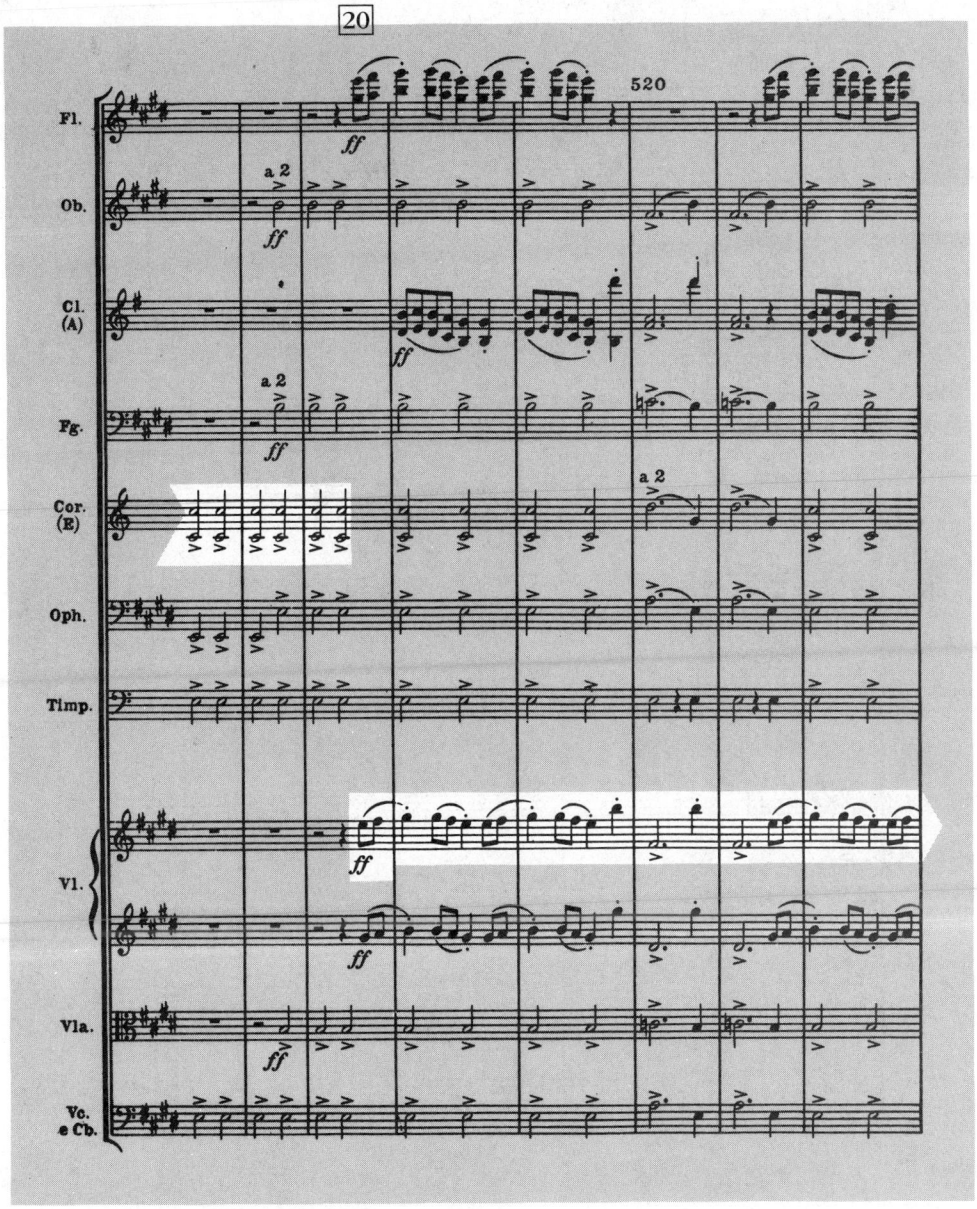
20
520
Fl.
Ob.
Cl. (A)
Fg.
Cor. (E)
Oph.
Timp.
Vl.
Vla.
Vc. e Cb.
ff
a 2

530
Fl.
Ob.
Cl. (A)
Fg.
Cor. (E)
a 2
Oph.
Timp.
Vl.
Vla.
Vc. e Cb.
f

540
Fl.
Ob.
Cl. (A)
Fg.
Cor. (E)
Oph.
Timp.
Vl.
Vla.
Vc. e Cb.
ff
a 2

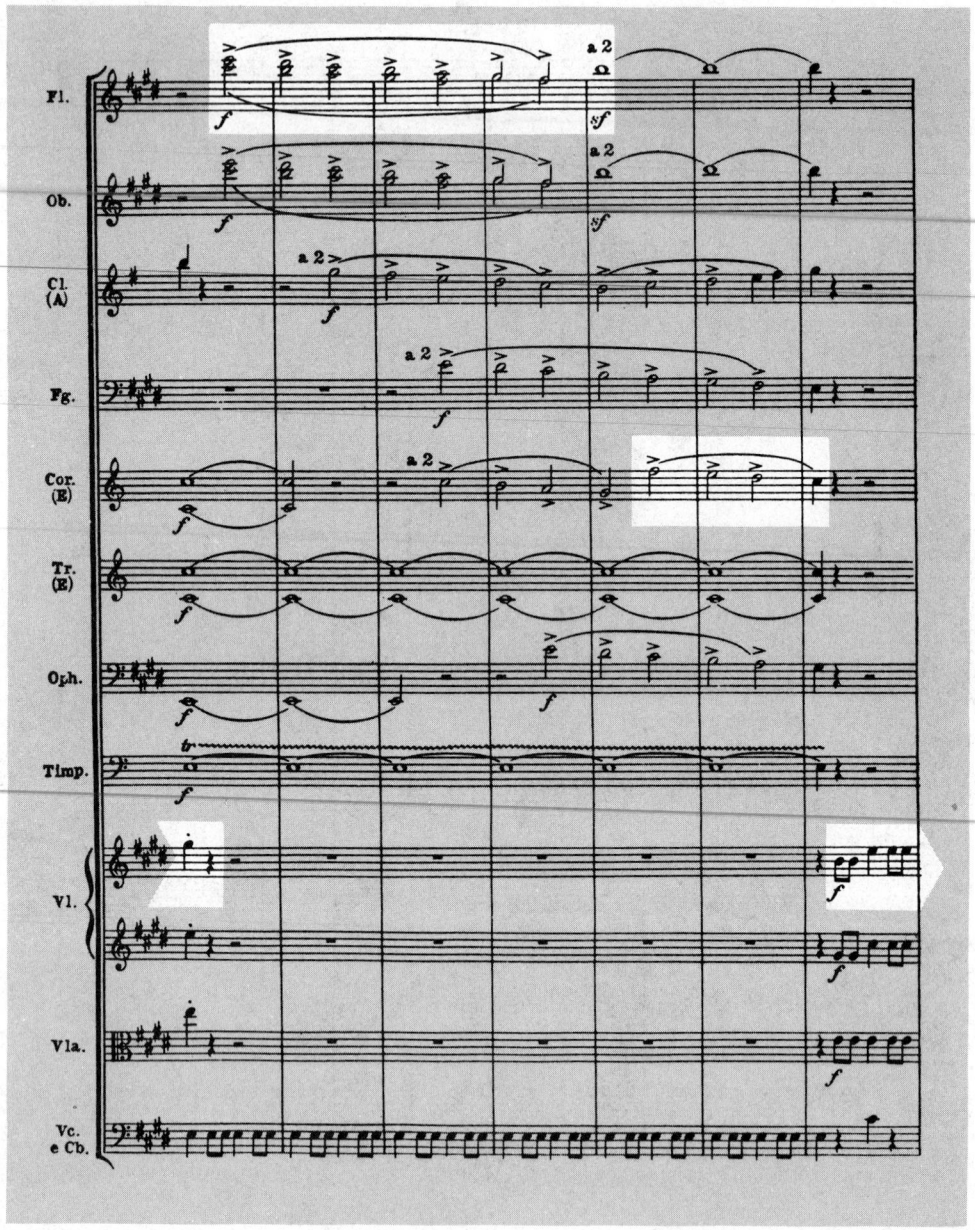
Fl.
Ob.
Cl. (A)
Fg.
Cor. (E)
Tr. (E)
Oph.
Timp.
Vl.
Vla.
Vc. e Cb.
a 2
a 2
a 2
a 2
a 2
f
sf
sf
f
f
f
f
f
f
f
f
f
f
f

550
a 2
a 2
a 2
Fl.
Ob.
Cl. (A)
Fg.
Cor. (E)
Tr. (E)
Oph.
Timp.
Vl.
Vla.
Vc. e Cb.

560
Fl.
Ob.
a 2
f sempre
Cl. (A)
f
f sempre
Fg.
f sempre
Cor. (E)
a 2
f
f sempre
Oph.
f sempre
Timp.
Vl.
f
Via.
Vc. e Cb.

Fl.
Ob.
Cl. (A)
Fg.
Cor. (E)
Tr. (E)
Oph.
Timp.
Vl.
Vla.
Vc. e Cb.
a 2
f
f sempre

570
580
Fl.
Ob.
Cl. (A)
Fg.
Cor. (E)
a 2
Tr. (E)
Oph.
Timp.
Vl.
Vla.
Vc. e Cb.

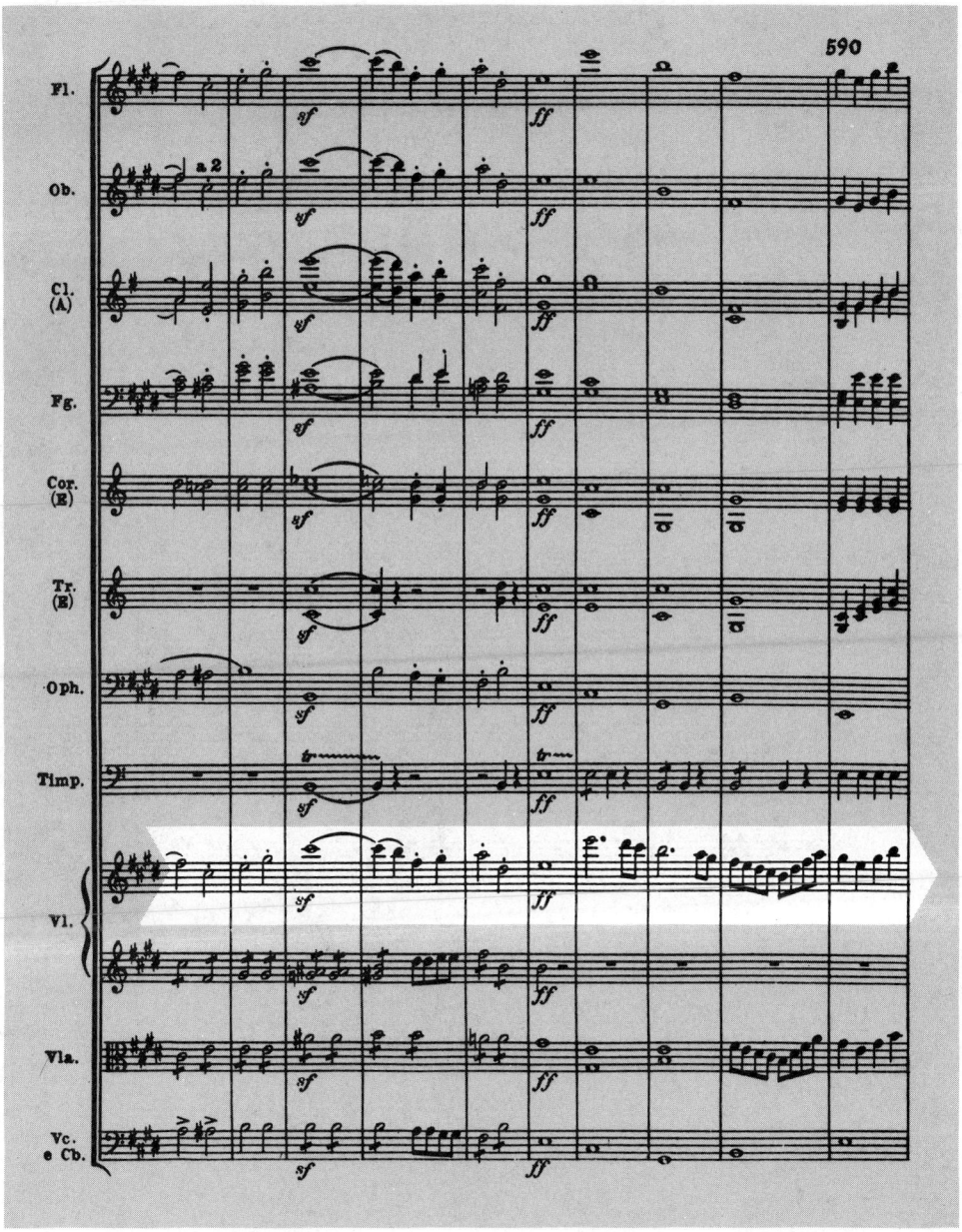
590
Fl.
Ob.
a 2
Cl. (A)
Fg.
Cor. (E)
Tr. (E)
Oph.
Timp.
Vl.
Vla.
Vc. e Cb.
sf
ff

Fl.
Ob.
Cl. (A)
Fg.
Cor. (E)
Tr. (E)
a 2
Oph.
Timp.
Vl.
Vla.
Vc. e Cb.

600
610
Fl.
Ob.
Cl. (A)
Fg.
Cor. (E)
Tr. (E)
a 2
Oph.
Timp.
Vl.
Vla.
Vc. e Cb.
ff
f

21
620
Fl.
Ob.
Cl. (A)
Fg.
Cor. (E)
Tr. (E)
Oph.
Timp.
Vl.
Vla.
Vc.
Cb.
a 2
ff
sf
con tutta la forza ff
div.
pp

Vl.
unis.
Ob.
Cl. (A)
Vl.
div.
630
Fl.
Cl. (A)
Vl.
Fl.
Ob.
Cl. (A)
Vl.
640
div.

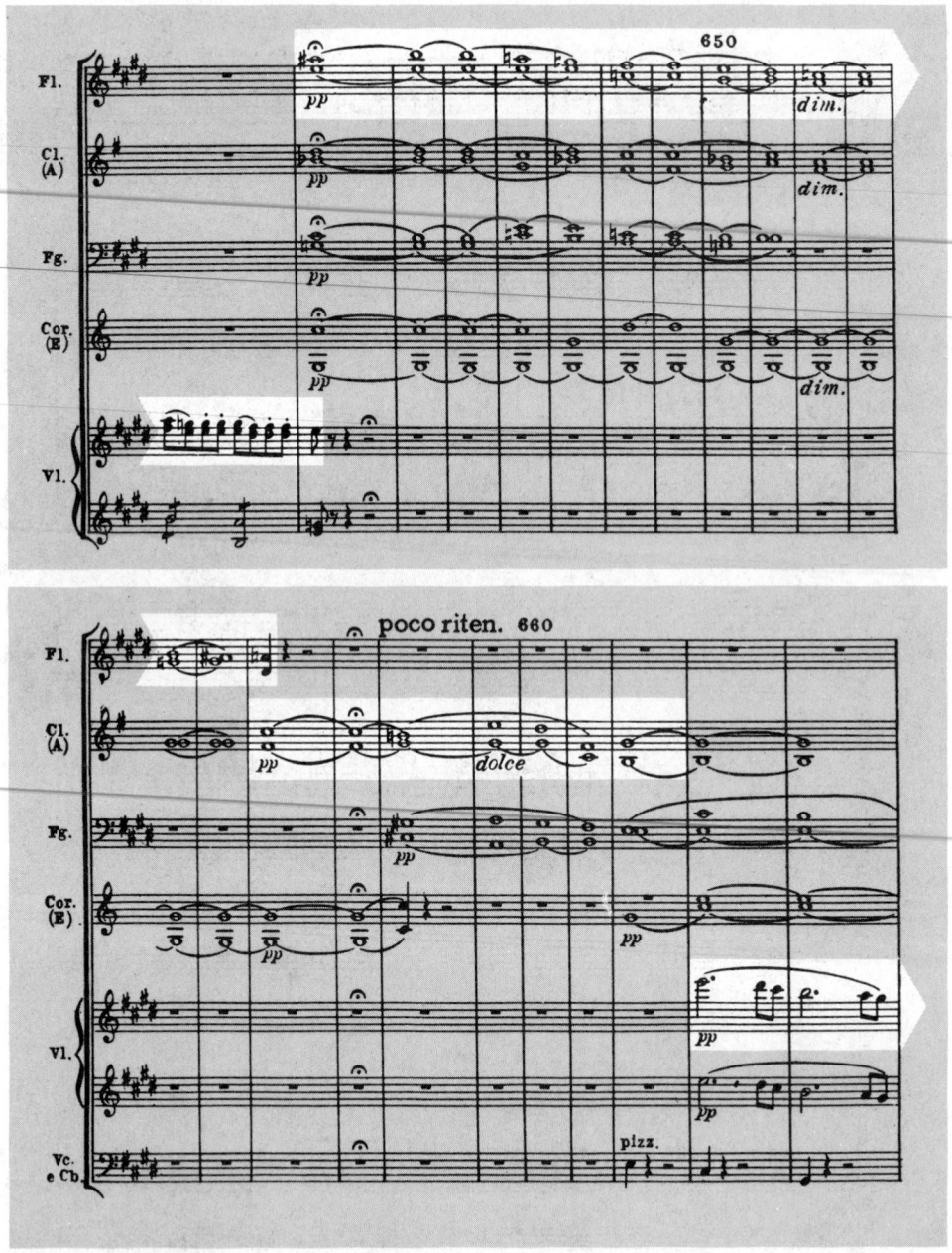
650
Fl.
Cl. (A)
Fg.
Cor. (E)
Vl.
pp
dim.
poco riten. 660
dolce
Vc. e Cb.
pizz.

670
Fg.
pp dolce
Cor. (E)
pp dolce
Vl.
Vc. e Cb.

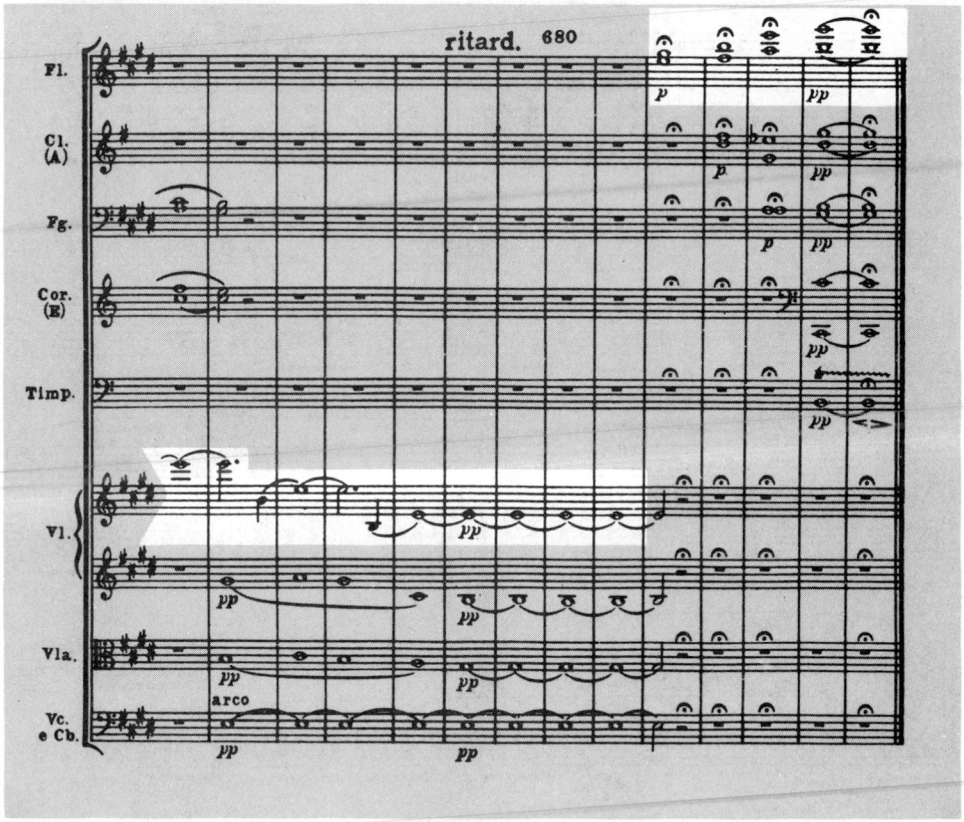
ritard.
680
Fl.
p
pp
Cl. (A)
p
pp
Fg.
p
pp
Cor. (E)
pp
Timp.
pp
Vl.
pp
pp
Vla.
pp
pp
arco
Vc. e Cb.
pp
pp

4. *Frédéric François Chopin (1810–1849)*

Prelude in E minor, Op. 28,
No. 4 (published 1839)

8:5A/4 8:5/22 - 23

5. *Chopin*

Polonaise in A-flat major,
Op. 53 (1842)

8:5A/5 8:5/24 - 27

3:2A/5 3:2/27 - 30

MW

tr
cresc.
ff
3
8

tr
tr
Ped.
8
f
8
sostenuto
f
tr
tr
tr

cresc.
ff

26
29
ff
pp
sf
sotto voce
staccato
poco
poco
cresc.
f
cresc.
ff

sf pp
staccato
poco a poco
cresc.
f
cresc.
ff
Ped.
Ped.
Ped.

p

tr
tr
tr
Ped.
Ped.
Ped.
Ped.
Ped.
Ped.
Ped.
Ped.
Ped.
Ped.
Ped.
Ped.
Ped.
Ped.
Ped.
Ped.
Ped.
Ped.
Ped.
Ped.
smorz.
Ped.
Ped.
Ped.
Ped.
Ped.
Ped.

cresc.
27
30
f
tr

sempre f
ff
sff

6. Robert Schumann (1810–1856)

Piano Concerto in A minor, Op. 54,
First Movement (1841)

8:5B/1 8:5/28 - 34

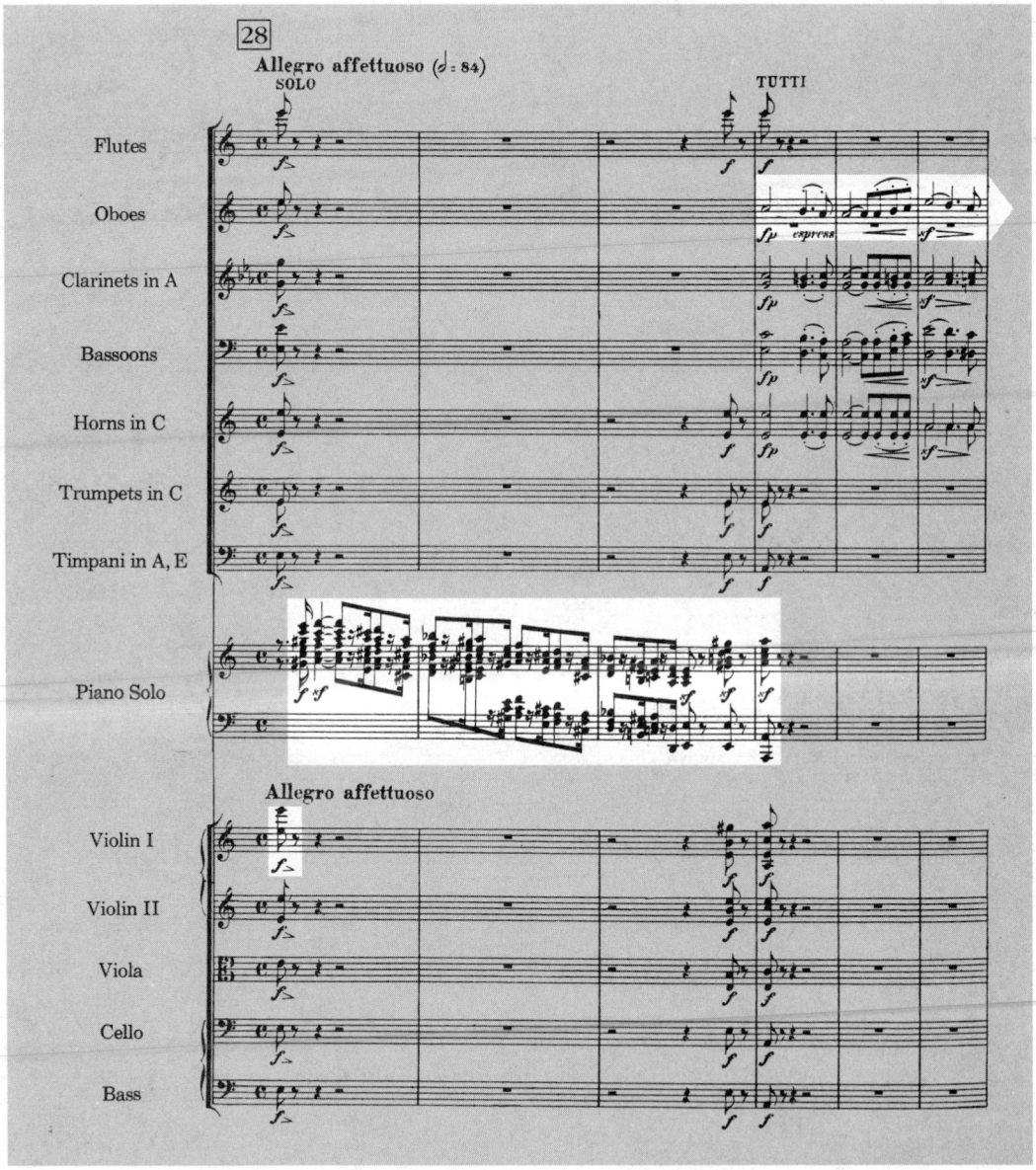

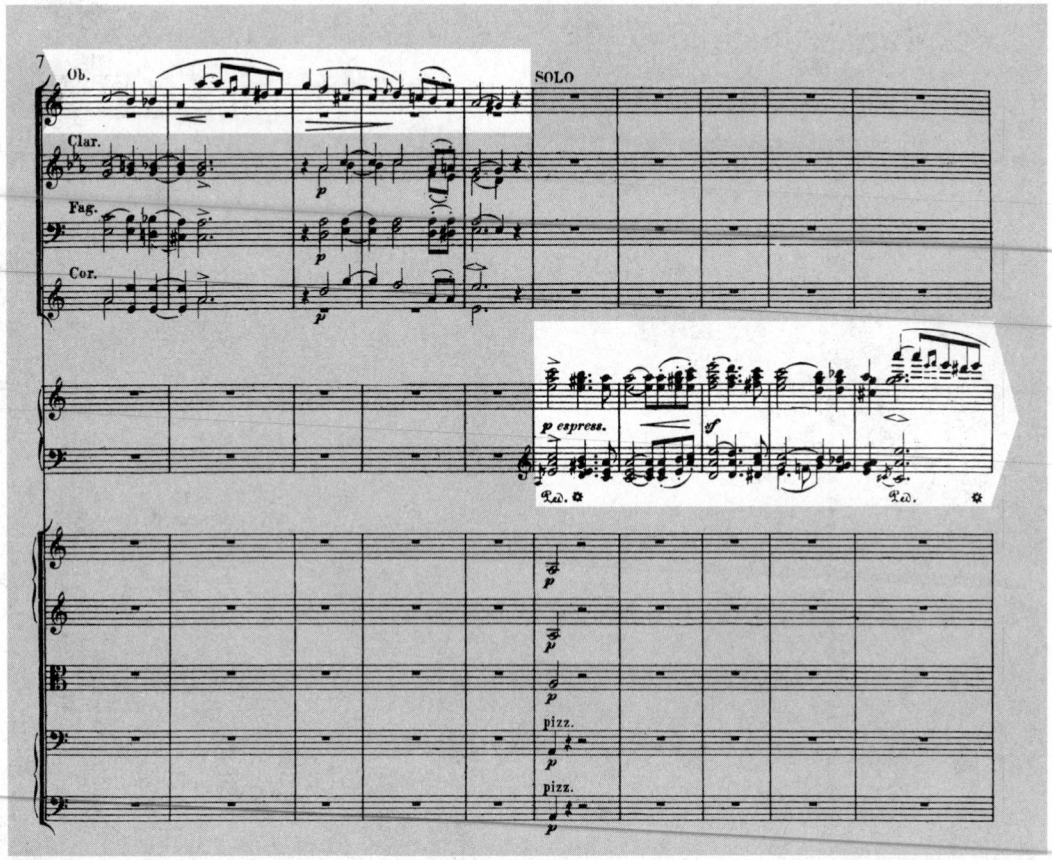
7
Ob.
SOLO
Clar.
Fag.
Cor.
p espress.
pizz.
pizz.

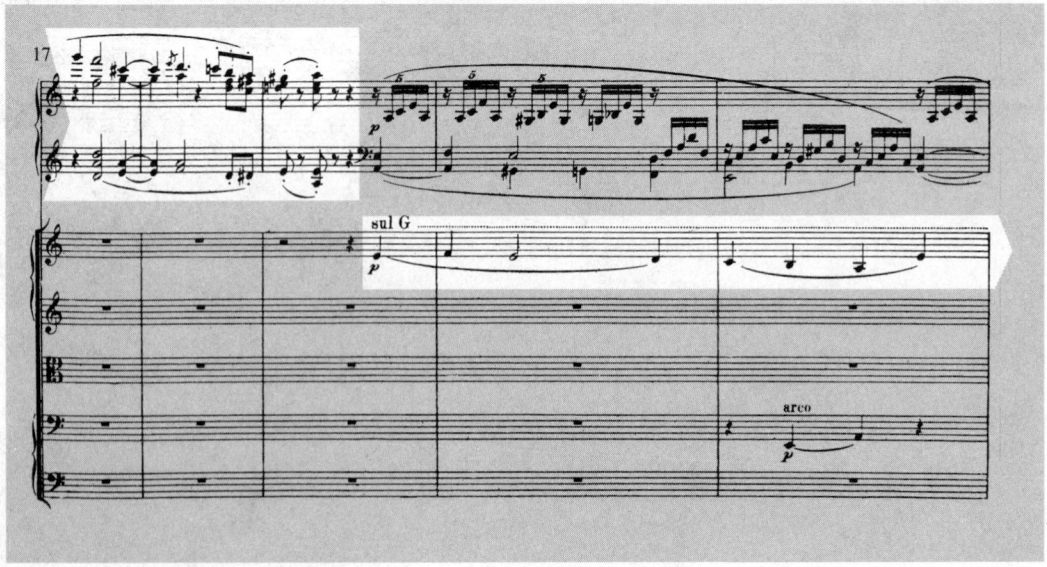
17
sul G
arco

22
p
p
26
Fl.
Clar.
Fag.
p
p
p
cresc.
p
cresc.
p
cresc.
p
cresc.
p
arco
cresc.

30
cresc.
p
35
Cor.
TUTTI
marc.
div.

42
A
SOLO.
p
espress.
A
49
un poco

56
Cor.
ri - tar - dan - do
a tempo
a tempo
ri - tar - dan - do
ri -
pizz.
pizz.
pizz.
pizz.

29
65
Clar.
Animato
- tar - dan - do
pp espress.
dim.
arco
arco
arco
arco

71

76
p
p
p
p
p
82
Clar.
Fag.
Cor.
p
p
p

87
Ob.
Clar.
Fag.
Cor.
92
Ob.
Clar.
Cor.

97
Clar.
sf
p
p
p
p
p

102
Ob
Clar.
sf
sf
p
p
p
pizz.
p
pizz.
p

107
Ob.
Clar.
Fag.
Cor.
B
ritard.
arco
112
a tempo, animato
Violoncello
117
Cor.
sempre cresc.

122
p
div.
p
127
f

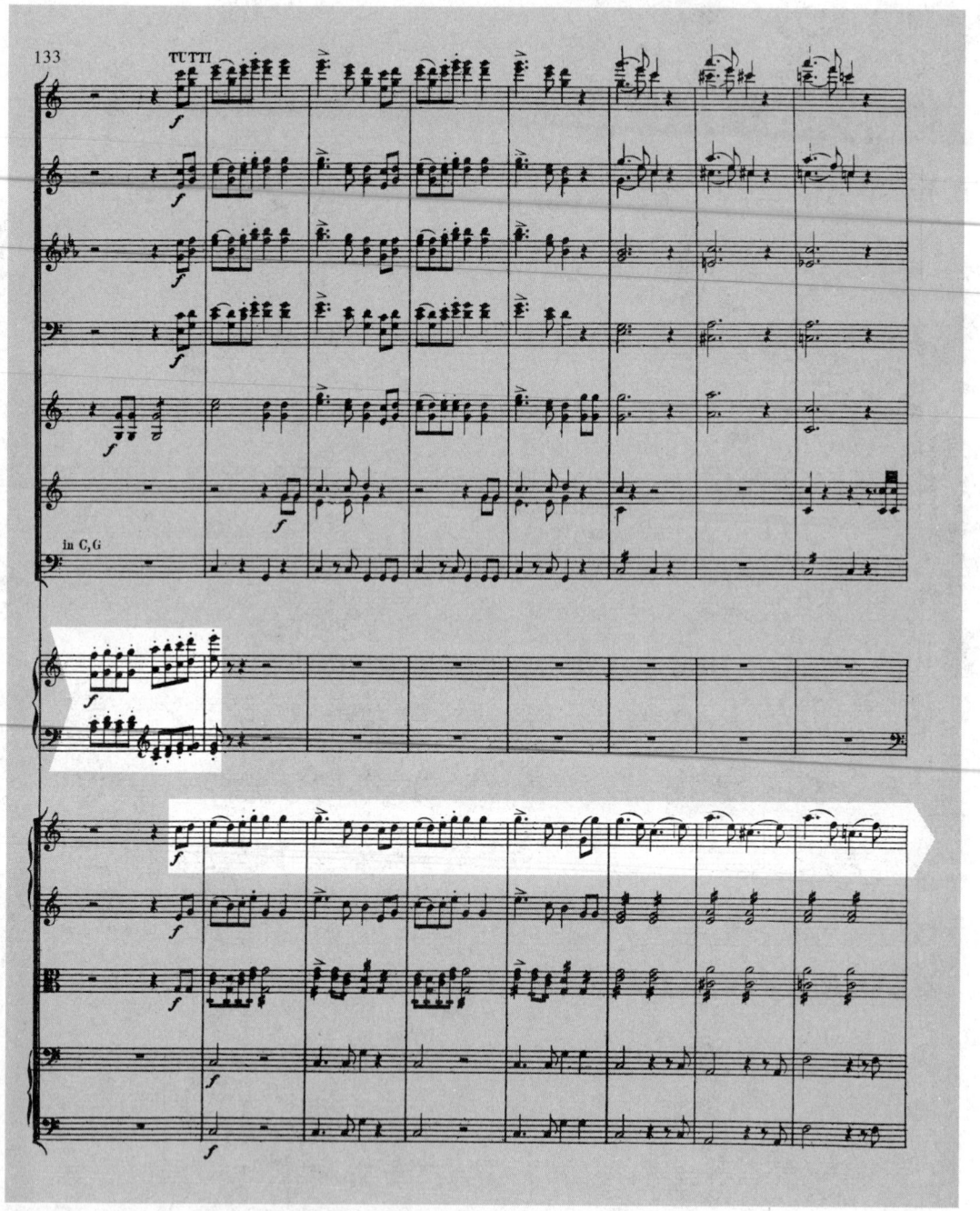
133
TUTTI
in C, G

141

149
ri - tar - dan - do
dim.
p
in B
ri tar - dan - do
dim. ri tar - dan - do

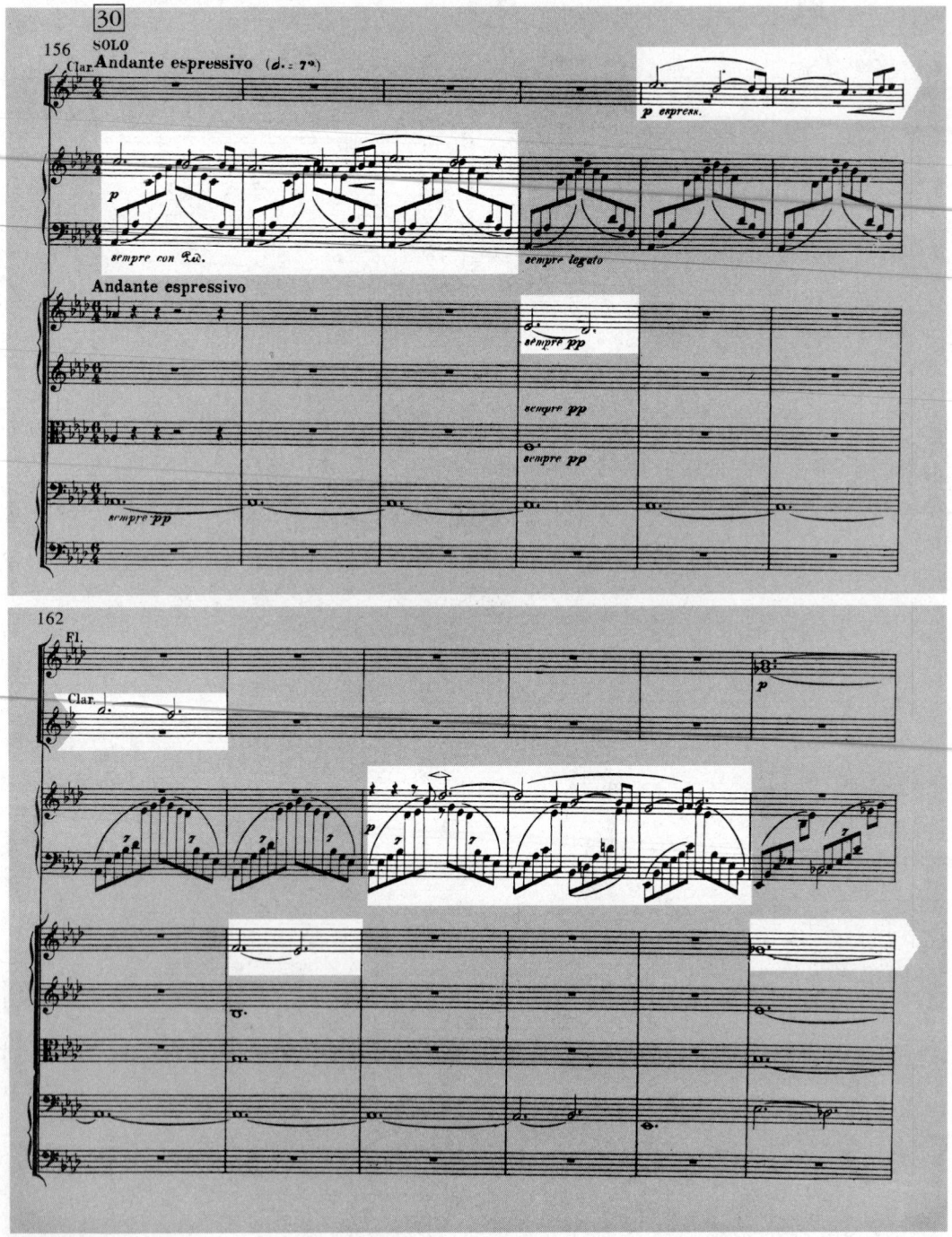
30
156
SOLO
Clar.
Andante espressivo
p espress.
p
sempre con Ped.
sempre legato
Andante espressivo
sempre pp
sempre pp
sempre pp
sempre pp
162
Fl.
Clar.
p
p

168

174
Fl.
Clar.
Fag.
f
p
f

180
ri - tar - dan - - do
p
ri - tar - dan - - do
ri - tar - dan - - do
185
C Allegro (Tempo I)
Fl.
Ob.
Clar.
Fag.
Cor.
Ped.
Ped.
C Allegro (Tempo I)
div.

190
div.
div.
195

201
Fl.
Ob.
Clar.
Fag.
Cor.
Tr.
ritardando
Più animato
poco a poco
cresc.
ritardando
Passionato
poco a poco
ore
scen -
Più animato
ritardando
207
Fl.
do
pizz.
pizz.

212
217
222

227
Fl.
p
cresc.
poco a poco
poco a poco
poco a poco
poco a poco
poc a poco
232 Fl.
Fag.
p
cresc.
cresc.
cresc.
cresc.
cresc.

237
242
ff
arco
arco

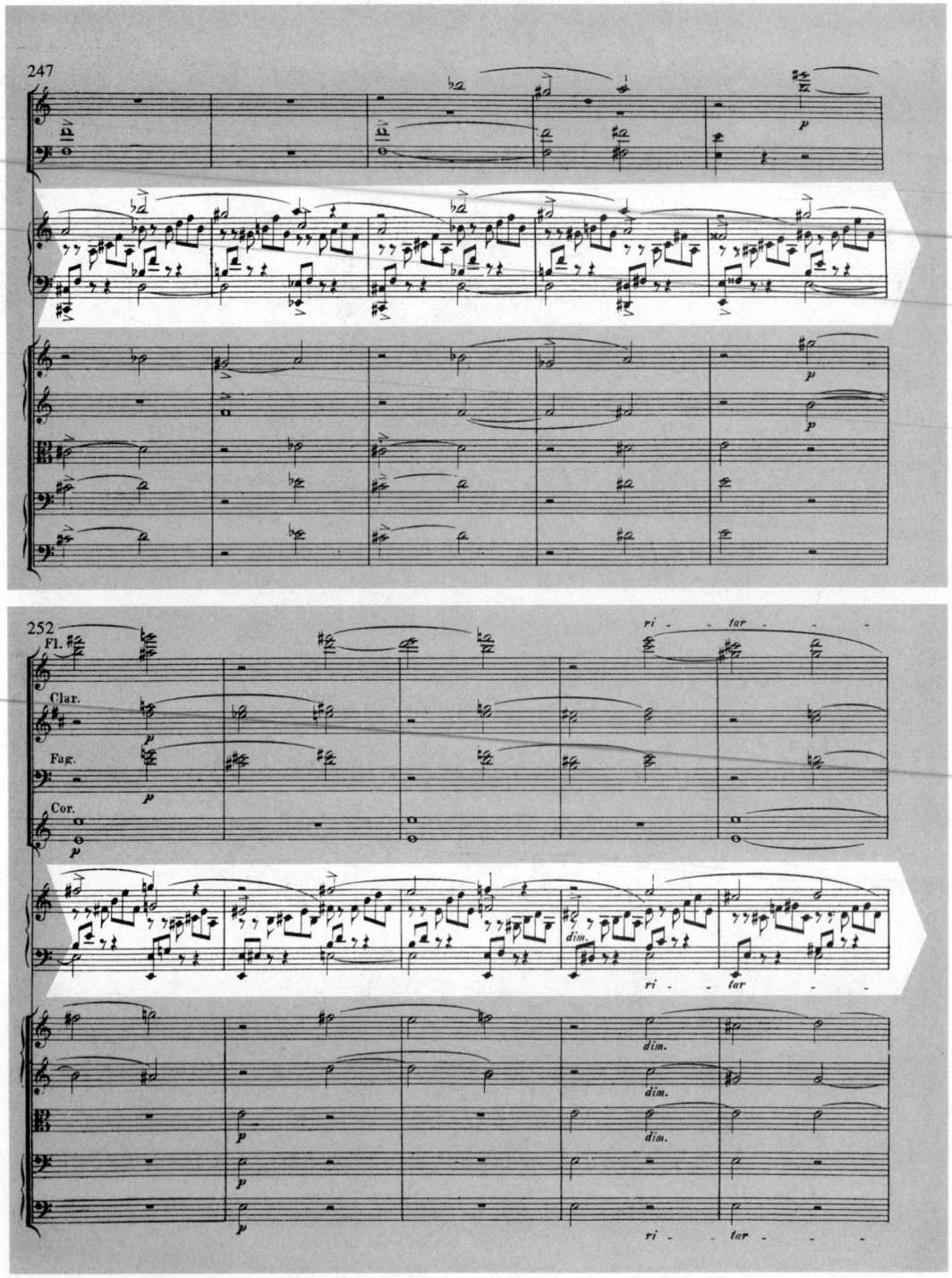
247
p
p
p
252
Fl.
Clar.
Fag.
Cor.
p
p
p
ri - - tar - - -
dim.
ri - - tar
dim.
dim.
dim.
p
p
p
ri - - tar - - -

31
257 Fl.
dan - - - - - do
D Tempo I
TUTTI
Ob.
Clar.
Fag.
Cor.
Timp. in A, E
dan - - - - - do
D Tempo I
dan - - - - - do
267 SOLO
sul G
pizz.
pizz.

275
279
Fl.
Clar.
Fag.
in A
cresc.
arco

283
Clar in A
cresc.
cresc.
cresc.
cresc.
p
cresc.
cresc.
p
cresc.
p
cresc.
cresc.
287
dim.
p
p
p
p
p
p
p
p

293
Fl.
Ob.
Clar.
Fag.
TUTTI
marc.
div.
300
SOLO

307
Cor. in A.
ri - tar - tan - - do
a tempo
pizz.

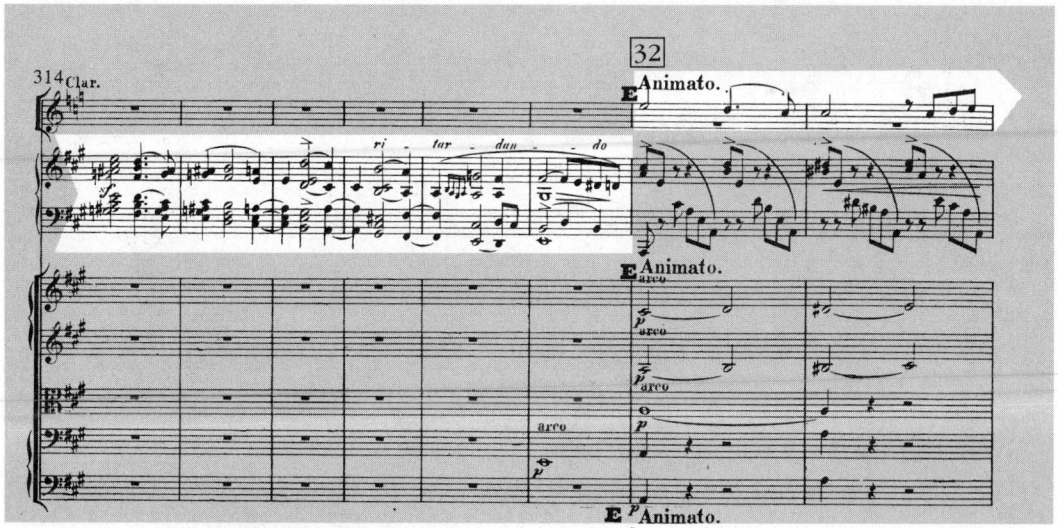
314
Clar.
ri - tar - dan - - do
32
E Animato.
arco

322

327
332
337 Ob.
Clar.
Fag.

342
Ob.

347
Ob.
Clar.
fp
fp
fp
fp
fp
div.

352
Ob.
Clar.
pizz.
pizz.
357
Ob.

362
Ob.
Clar.
Fag.
Cor.
ritard.
F a tempo, animato
p
p
p
p
sf
ritard.
F a tempo, animato
arco
arco
ritard.
367
p
sf

372
Cor.
f
p
p
p
p

378
Ob.
Fag.
Cor.
cresc.
cresc.
f
cresc.
cresc.
div.
cresc.
cresc.
cresc.

384
TUTTI
G
Accelerando
poco a poco
G
Accelerando
poco a poco
Accelerando
poco a poco
div.

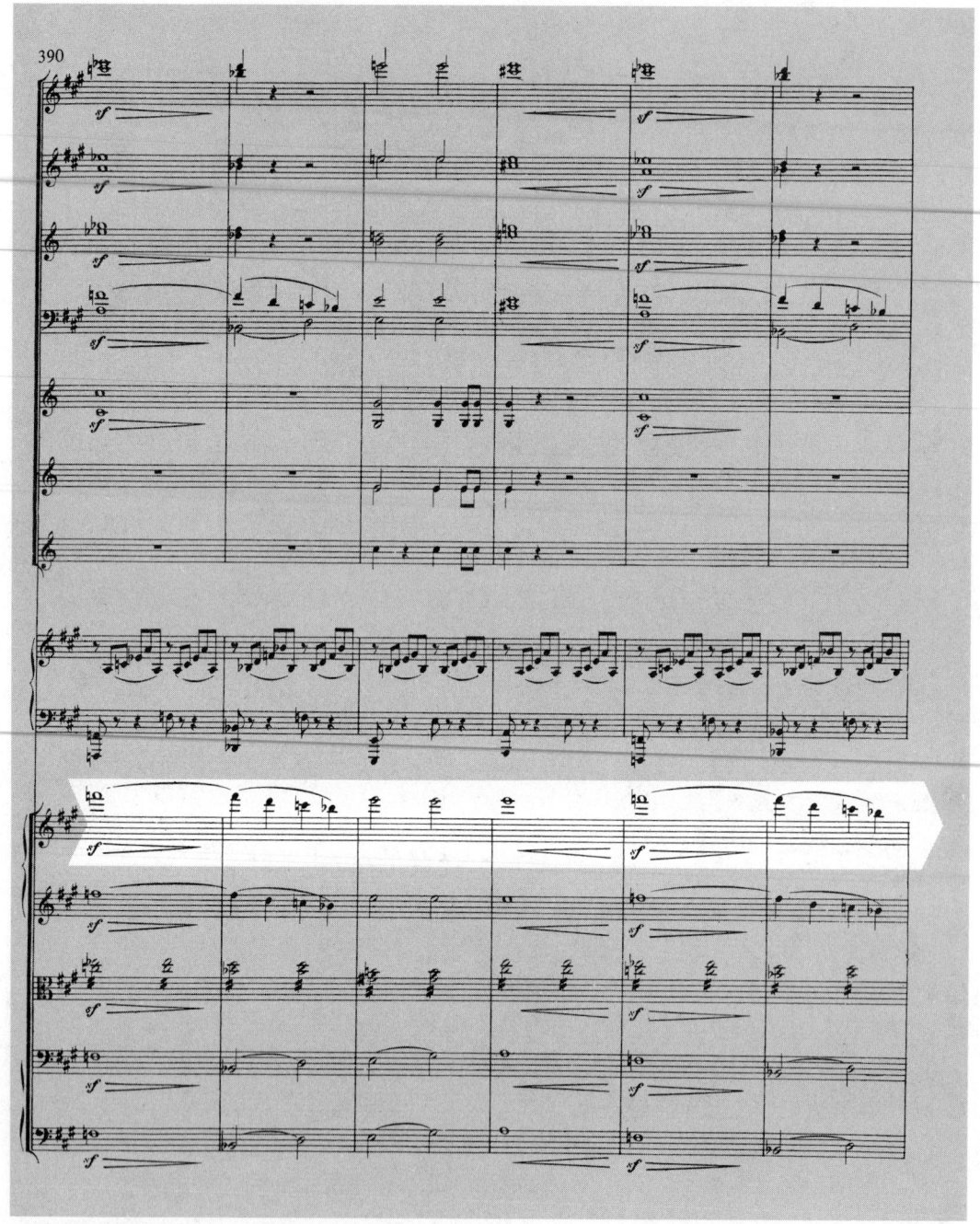
390

396
SOLO
ritard.
33
Cadenza
(Die ♩ wie vorher die ♩)
espressivo
poco a poco più strin - gendo e cre -

cen - do
ri - tar - dan - do
Un poco Andante
dim.

34
402
Allegro molto
Ob.
Clar.
Fag.
Allegro molto
411
Fl.
Ob.
Clar.
Fag.

419
426
Cor.
p
f
f
f

433
443
dim.

452
Ob.
Clar.
Fag.
pp
p
461
dim.

470
cresc.
pp
478
cresc.

7. *Franz Liszt (1811–1886)*

8:5A/6 8:5/35 - 37

Wilde Jagd (Wild Hunt),
Transcendental Etude No. 8 (1851)

Ped.
p
ff
ff

rinf.
rinf.
rinf.

36
in tempo
mp ma sempre marcato e staccato
mf
cresc.
ff
ten.
poco rallent.

un poco rit. a capriccio
espressivo
pp
rallent.
leggieramente e staccato
dimin.

languendo
cresc.
8
molto rinf.
Ped.
Ped.

fff molto appassionato
simile
poco a poco dimin.
riten. molto
e rallent.
smorz.
37
Tempo I.
pp

sempre pp
cresc.
più cresc.

fff con brio
ff
Ped.

leggieramente
p e sempre più animato
Ossia.
cresc.
molto
ben marcato il canto
p agitato ed appassionato assai
cresc.

fff
marcatissimo
Ped.
rfz
sempre fff

8. Richard Wagner (1813–1883)

Die Walküre, Act III, Finale (1856)

8:5B/2 8:5/38 - 41

3:2B/5 3:2/54 - 55

38

Langsam. **WOTAN.**

Der Au - gen leuch - tendes Paar, das oft ich lä - chelndge-
Thy bright - ly glit - tering eyes, that, smil - ing, oft I ca-

sempre legatissimo e tenuto

pp

kos't, wenn Kam - pfeslusteinKuss dir lohn - te, wenn kin - disch lallend der
ressed, when val - ourwon a kiss as guer - don, when child-ish lispings of

p

P. + P. + P. +

Editor's note: Shorter Norton recording begins on page 183.

English translation by Frederick Jameson and Andrew Porter. Copyright © 1936 (renewed) G. Schirmer, Inc. (ASCAP). International copyright secured. All rights reserved. Reprinted by permission.

WOTAN.
Hel - den Lob von hol - den Lippen dir floss: dieser Au - gen strahlendes Paar das
he - roes' praise from sweetest lips has flowed forth: those gleaming ra - di - ant eyes that
p
poco cresc.
mf
dim.
p
oft im Sturm mir ge - glänzt wenn Hoff - nungsseh - nen das Herz mir
oft in storms on me shone, when hope - less yearning my heart had
p
seng - te, nach Wel - ten - won - ne mein Wunsch ver - langte, aus wild we - bendem
wast - ed, when world's de - lights all my wish - es wakened, thro' wild wil - dering
fp
mf
Ban - gen: zum letz - ten Mal letz' es mich heut' mit des
sad - ness: once more to - day, lured by their light, my
poco rall.
dim.
p
dolce
più p

WOTAN.
Le - be - woh - les letz - tem Kuss! Dem glück - licher'n Man - ne glän - ze sein
lips shall give them love's fare - well! On mor - tal more blessed once may they
pp
dolce
cresc.
Stern: dem un - se - li - gen Ew' - - gen muss es schei - dend sich
beam: on me, hap - less im - mor - - tal, must they close now for
dim.
f
(Er fasst ihr Haupt in beide Hände.)
(He clasps her head in his hands.)
schlies - sen. Denn so kehrt der Gott sich dir
e - - ver. For so turns the god now from
p
più p
pp espress.
39
(Er küsst sie lange auf die Augen.)
(He kisses her long on the eyes.)
ab, so küsst er die Gott - heit von dir!
thee, so kis - ses thy god - hood a - way!
pp
ppp
dolcissimo
P. (u.c.)

(Sie sinkt mit geschlossenen Augen, sanft ermattend, in seine Arme zurück. Er geleitet sie zart auf einen niedrigen Mooshügel
(She sinks back with closed eyes, unconscions, in his arms. He gently bears her to a low mossy mound, which is overshadowed
sempre pp
pp
(Er betrachtet sie und schliesst
(He looks upon her and closes
zu liegen, über den sich eine breitästige Tanne ausstreckt.)
by a wide-spreading fir tree, and lays her upon it.)
la melodia molto cantabile
l'accompagnamento sempre legatissimo e dolcissimo
più p
pp
poco cresc.
P.
ihr den Helm; sein Auge weilt dann auf der Gestalt der Schlafenden, die er nun mit dem grossen Stahlschilde der Walküren ganz
her helmet; his eyes then rest on the form of the sleeper, which he now completely covers with the great steel shield of the
dim.
ppp
zudeckt. — Langsam kehrt er sich ab, mit einem schmerzlichen Blicke wendet er sich noch einmal um.)
Valkyrie. — He turns slowly away, then again turns round with a sorrowful look.)
più pp
mf
dim.

pp
più pp
P.
pp
p
p
cresc.
f
tre corde
40
54
WOTAN (Er schreitet mit feierlichem Entschlusse in die Mitte der Bühne, und kehrt die Spitze seines Speeres gegen einen mächtigen Felsstein.)
(He strides with solemn decision to the middle of the stage and directs the point of his spear towards a large rock.)
Lo - ge hör'!
Lo - ge hear!
Mässig bewegt.
f
fp
più p
P.
lau - sche hie-her!
List to my word!
Wie zuerst ich dich fand, als feu - ri - ge
As I found thee of old, a glim - mering
p
più p
Gluth, wie dann einst du mir schwandest, als schweifen-de Lo-he; wie ich dich band,
flame, as from me thou didst va-nish, in wan - dering fire; as once I stayed thee,
cresc
f
P.

WOTAN.
bann' ich dich heut'!
stir I thee now!
Her - auf,
Ap - pear!
wa - bern - de
come, wav - ing
p
fp
P.
Lo - he,
fire
um - lod' - re mir
and wind thee in
feu - rig den
flames round the
mf
poco cresc.
dim.
tr
(Er stösst mit dem Folgenden dreimal mit dem Speer auf den Stein.)
(During the following he strikes the rock thrice with his spear.)
(Erster Stoss.)
(First stroke.)
Fels!
fell!
Lo - ge!
Lo - ge!
cresc.
più cresc.
(Zweiter.)
(Second.)
(Dritter.)
(Third.)
(Dem Stein entfährt ein Feuerstrahl.)
(A flash of flame issues from
Lo - ge!
Lo - ge!
hie - her!
ap - pear!
f

der zur allmälich immer helleren Flammenglut anschwillt.)
the rock, which swells to an ever-brightening fiery glow.)
f
più f
41
55
(Hier bricht die lichte Flackerlohe aus.)
(Here flickering flames break forth.)
p
sempre stacc
cresc. poco a poco
sempre cresc.
f
Lichte Brunst umgiebt Wotan mit wildem Flackern. Er weis't mit dem Speere gebie-
Bright shooting flames surround Wotan. With his spear he directs the sea of fire
ff

terisch dem Feuermeere den Umkreis des Felsenrandes zur Strömung an; alsbald zieht es sich nach dem Hintergrunde, wo es nun
to encircle the rocks; it presently spreads toward the background where it encloses the mountain in flames.)
sempre stacc.
dim.
fortwährend den Bergsaum umlodert.)
sempre legato
dolce
sempre stacc.
WOTAN.
Wer mei - nes Spee - - - - res
He who my spear - - - - point's
cresc. - poco -
Spit - - - ze fürch - - - - tet durch-
sharp - - - ness fear - - - - eth shall
a poco
schrei - - te das Feu - - - er nie!
cross not the flam - - - ing fire!

(Er streckt den Speer wie zum Banne aus.)
(He stretches out the spear as a spell.)
f
più cresc.
pesante
marcato
ff
(Er blickt schmerzlich auf Brünnhilde zurück)
(He gazes sorrowfully back on Brünnhilde.)
dim.
p
sehr ausdrucksvoll
dim.
più p

(Er wendet sich langsam zum Gehen.)
(Slowly he turns to depart.)
p dolce
più p
sempre più p
(Er wendet sich nochmals mit dem Haupt und blickt zurück.)
(He turns his head again and locks back.)
mp
pp
(Er verschwindet durch das Feuer.)
He disappears through the fire.
mp
pp
pp
(Vorhang fällt.)
Curtain falls.
più pp
ppp

9. *Giuseppe Verdi (1813–1901)*

La traviata, Act II, Finale (1853)

8:6A/1 8:6/1 - 5

3:3A/1 3:3/1 - 2

Editor's note: Shorter Norton recording begins on page 200.

English translation by Ruth and Thomas Martin. Copyright © 1946, 1961 (renewed) G. Schirmer, Inc. (ASCAP). All rights reserved. Reprinted by permission.

Alfred. (enters)
Mi chia-ma-ste? che bra-ma-te?
You have called me? Well, what is it?
Violetta.
Que-sti
You must
Str.
p
luo-ghi abban-do-na-te; un pe-riglio vi so-vra-sta.
waste no time in leav-ing. If you stay here, you're in dan-ger!
Alfred.
Ah com-
Oh, I
pren-do! Ba-sta, basta. E sì vi-le mi cre-de-te?
see it! What an in-sult! And you think me such a cow-ard?
Violetta.
Ah no, no,
No, no, be-
Alfred.
ma-i! Ma che te-me-te?
lieve me! Then why be fright ened?
Violetta.
Tremo sem-pre del ba-ro-ne.
I'm a-fraid Dou phol might harm you.
Alfred
E fra
Do not
noi mor-tal qui-stione. S'ei ca-drà per ma-no mi-a, un sol
let the thought a-larm you. But, of course, if I should kill him, With one

col - po vi tor - ri - a, un sol col - po vi tor - ri - a col - l'a -
blow I would de - prive you, With one blow I would de - prive you Of your
Violetta.
man - te il pro - tet - to - re _ Vat - ter - ri - sce tal scia - gura? Ma s'ei
lov - er and pro - tect - or! Does that pros - pect make you trem - ble? But if
Wind sustain
fos - se l'uc - ci - so - re! ec - co l'u - ni - ca sven - tu - ra ch'io pa -
he in - stead should kill you That would be the one mis - for - tune I would
Alfred.
ven - to a me fa - ta - le. La mia mor - te! _ che ven
dread a - bove all oth - ers. If he killed me? Why should
Violetta.
Alfred.
ca - le? Deh, par - ti - te _ e sul - l'i - stante. Par - ti -
you care? Do not stay here! De - part this in stant! I shall

rò, ma giu-ra in-nan-te che do-vun-que se-gui-ra-i, se-gui-
go; but not un-til You prom-ise on your word of hon-or To re-
Violetta.
Ah no, giam-ma-i. Va, sciagu-
Ah no, I can-not! You must be-
rai i pas-si mie-i. No, giam-ma-i?
turn to the coun-try. So you can not?
ra-to! scorda un no-me ch'è in-fa-ma-to, va, mi la-scia sul mo-
lieve me and for-get me. Go and leave me at this mo-ment. I im-
men-to di fug-gir-ti un giu-ra-men-to sa-cro jo
plore you, for I gave my sol-emn word That I will

Alfred.
fe - ci. A chi? dil - lo — chi po - te - a? A chi
leave you. To whom? Tell me? Who could ask it? One who
Violetta.
drit - to pien n'a - ve - a. Fu Dou - phol?
had the right to ask it. It's the Bar-on?
Alfred.
Violetta. (with utmost will power)
Sì. Dun - que l'a - - mi? Eb -
Yes. Then you love him?
Violetta.
ben — l'a - mo. Or tut - ti a
Yes . . . I love him . . . Come here at
Alfred. (runs furiously to the door and calls)
me!
once!
(Everybody enters in confusion.)
ff Tutti.

Flora.
Ne ap - pel - laste? che vo - le - te?
What has hap-pened? Well, what is it?
Alfred (indicating Violetta)
Questa don - - na co - no-
Do you all here know this
Gaston.
Ne ap - pel - laste? che vo - le - te?
What has hap-pened? Well, what is it?
Chorus.
Ne ap - pel - la-ste? che vo - le - te?
What has hap-pened? Well, what is it?
Ne ap - pel - la-ste? che vo - le - te?
What has hap-pened? Well, what is it?
Baron, Doctor and Marquis with BASS.
Str.
p
Vl.
dim.
Cello
Fag Ophicleide & D-b.
Chi! Vio-let-ta?
Who? Vio-let-ta?
(softly to Alfred)
Violetta.
(Ah! ta-ci.)
Don't say it!
Flora.
No.
No!
sce-te?
Che fa - ces - - se non sa - pe-te?
wom-an?
What she did, you do not know yet?
Chi! Vio-let-ta?
Who? Vio-let-ta?
No.
No!
Chi! Vio-let-ta?
Who? Vio-let-ta?
No.
No!
Chi! Vio-let-ta?
Who? Vio-let-ta?
No.
No!
ff
Tutti.

2
Allegro sostenuto.
Alfred.
O - gni suo aver tal fem-mi-na per a-mor mio sper-de-a, io
All she pos-sessed, this wom-an here Squan-dered on me, un-spar-ing. And
p
Str.
cie-co, vi-le, mi - sero, tut-to accettar po-te - a.
blind-ly, vile-ly, reck - less-ly, I took it all, un-car - ing.
Wind.
animato
Ma è tempo anco - ra! ter - ger-mi da tan-ta mac - chia bra - mo,
But there is time to clear my-self, Time to re-pay such kind - ness.
Ob. & Cl.
animato
qui te - sti-mon vi chiamo, or te-stimon vi chia - mo,
I call you all to wit-ness, I call you all to wit - ness,
or te-sti-mon vi chia - mo che qui, che qui pa-ga-ta io
I call you all to tes ti-fy That I have paid her back in
ff
Tutti.

3
(With furious contempt he throws a purse at Violetta's feet. She faints into the arms of Flora.)
(At this moment Germont enters.)
Velocissimo.
I'ho!
full!
Gaston.
Oh, in-famia or-ri-bi-le tu commet-te-sti! un cor sen-si-bi-le co-si uc-ci-de-sti! Di donne i-gno-bi-le in-sul-ta-to-re, di qua al-lon-scend-ed! You have in-sult-ed and deep-ly of-fend-ed A per-son
Oh, what an in-fam-ous act you com-mit-ted! To shameless slander and lies you de-scend-ed! You have in-sult-ed and deep-ly of-fend-ed A per-son
Baron, Doctor and Marquis.
Chorus.
Velocissimo.
Tutti.

ta - na - ti, ne de-stior - ror! Va, va, va, va, va, va, ne
whom we re - spect and es - teem! Go go go go go. Leave this
Marquis 2nd Bass.
ta - na - ti, ne de-stior - ror! Va, va, va, va, va, va, ne
whom we re - spect and es - teem! Go go go go go. Leave this
ta - na - ti, ne de-stior - ror! Va, va, va, va, va, va, ne
whom we re - spect and es - teem! Go go go go go. Leave this
ta - na - ti, ne de-stior - ror! Va, va, va, va, va, va, ne
whom we re - spect and es - teem! Go go go go go. Leave this
de-stior - ror! Di don-nej - gno - bi - le. in - sul - ta - to - re, di qua al-lon-
house at once! Such shame-less con-duct we nev - er have wit-nessed, Such low bru-
de-stior - ror! Di don-nej - gno - bi - le in - sul - ta - to - re, di qua al-lon-
house at once! Such shame-less con-duct we nev - er have wit-nessed, Such low bru-
de-stior - ror! Di don-nej - gno - bi - le in - sul - ta - to - re, di qua al-lon-
house at once! Such shame-less con-duct we nev - er have wit-nessed, Such low bru-
de-stior - ror! Di don-nej - gno - bi - le in - sul - ta - to - re, di qua al-lon-
house at once! Such shame-less con-duct we nev - er have wit-nessed, Such low bru-

ta - na - ti, ne de-stior-ror, ne de-stior-ror, ne de-stior - ror, ne
tal - i - ty we nev - er saw. You are no long - er one of us; De-
ta - na - ti, ne de-stior-ror, ne de-stior-ror, ne de-stior - ror, ne
tal - i - ty we nev - er saw. You are no long - er one of us; De-
ta - na - ti, ne de-stior-ror, ne de-stior-ror, ne de-stior - ror, ne
tal - i - ty we nev - er saw. You are no long - er one of us; De-
ta - na - ti, ne de-stior-ror, ne de-stior-ror, ne de-stior - ror, ne
tal - i - ty we nev - er saw. You are no long - er one of us; De-
de-stior-ror, ne de-stior-ror, ne de - stior - ror, ne de-stior-
part at once and leave this house! Go, Leave this house You are no
de-stior-ror, ne de-stior-ror, ne de - stior - ror, ne de-stior-
part at once and leave this house! Go, Leave this house You are no
de-stior-ror, ne de-stior-ror, ne de - stior - ror, ne de-stior-
part at once and leave this house! Go, Leave this house. You are no
de-stior-ror, ne de-stior-ror, ne de - stior - ror, ne de-stior-
part at once and leave this house! Go, Leave this house. You are no

ror, ne de-stior - ror, ne de-stior - ror, ne de-stior - ror,
long-er one of us; De - part at once and leave this house!
ror, ne de-stior - ror, ne de-stior - ror, ne de-stior - ror,
long-er one of us; De - part at once and leave this house!
ror, ne de-stior - ror, ne de-stior - ror, ne de-stior - ror,
long-er one of us; De - part at once and leave this house!
ror, ne de-stior - ror, ne de-stior - ror, ne de-stior - ror,
long-er one of us; De - part at once and leave this house!
ff
ne de - stior - ror!
Go, Leave this house!
ff
ne de - stior ror!
Go, Leave this house!
ff
ne de - stior - ror!
Go, Leave this house!
ff
ne de - stior - ror!
Go, Leave this house!
ff
ff

No. 15. "Di sprezzo degno se stesso rende"
Continuation of Finale

Alfred (to himself)
sotto voce
(Ah sì! che fe - ci! ne sento or - ro - re! Ge - lo - sa sma - nia, de - lu - so a -
Germont. What-ev-er caused me to act so blind-ly? My life was shat-tered; I was un-
so.
know.
Str.
mo - re mi strazian l'al - ma, più non ra - gio - no — da lei per - do - no più non a -
hap-py... My heart was brok-en... I lost my rea-son, No hope of par-don is left to
vrò. Vo - lea fug - gir - la, non ho po - tu - to, dal - l'i - ra spin - to son qui ve -
me. My pride was wound ed.. I could not bear it... In rag - ing ha-tred I want-ed
nu - to! Or che lo sdegno ho di - sfo - ga - to, me scia - gu - ra - to! ri - mor - so
venge-ance. Now that my an-ger has lost its fu-ry, I am in mis-'ry, full of re -

Violetta.
Flora. (to Violetta)
ppp
O quan-to pe-ni! ma pur fa
Oh, how you suf-fer, you must take
Alfred.
n'ho!
morse.
Che
How
Caston.
ppp
O quan-to pe-ni! ma pu-re fa
Oh, how you suf-fer, you must take
Germont. (to himself)
ppp
(Io sol fra tan-ti so-qual vir-
I on-ly know the truth she is
Baron. (softly to Alfred)
ppp
A que-sta, a que-sta don-na, a que-sta don-na la-tro-ce in-
The in-sult to this la-dy Is so out-ra-geous That it de-
Doctor.
ppp
O quan-to pe-ni! ma pur fa
Oh, how you suf-fer, you must take
Marquis.
ppp
O quan-to pe-ni! ma pur fa
Oh, how you suf-fer, you must take
Chorus.
ppp
O quan-to pe-ni! ma pur fa
Oh, how you suf-fer, you must take
ppp
O quan-to pe-ni! ma pur fa
Oh, how you suf-fer, you must take
ppp
O quan-to pe-ni! ma pur fa
Oh, how you suf-fer, you must take
p Tutti
Wind

cor, qui sof-fre o-gnu - no del tuo do -
heart, For we who know you will take your
fe - ci!
dread - ful!
ohi-
Oh
cor, qui sof-fre o-gnu - no del tu - o do -
heart, For we who know you will take your
tu - de di quel-la mi - se - ra il sen rac -
hid - ing, All of the an - guish she is not con -
sul - to qui tut - ti of-fe - se, ma non i - nul - to fia tan-to ol-
mands in - stant sat - is - fac - tion. And to this pur - pose I shall take
Tutti.
Wind.

lor; fra ca - ria - mi - ci qui sei sol -
part. We love you dear - ly, we stand be -
mè! chi - mè, che fe - ci! ne sen - to or -
Lord! What ev - er caused me to act so
lor; fra ca - ria - mi - ci qui sei sol -
part. We love you dear - ly, we stand be -
chiu - de, io so che l'a - ma, che gli è fe -
fid - ing. I know she loves him, that she is
trag - gio, pro - var vi vo - glio, pro - var vi
ac - tion. Here is my chal - lenge; I am de -
lor; fra ca - ria - mi - ci qui sei sol -
part. We love you dear - ly, we stand be -
lor, fra ca - ria - mi - ci qui sei sol -
part. We love you dear - ly, we stand be -
lor; fra ca - ria - mi - ci qui sei sol -
part. We love you dear - ly, we stand be -
lor; fra ca - ria - mi - ci qui sei sol -
part. We love you dear - ly, we stand be -
lor; fra ca - ria - mi - ci qui sei sol -
part. We love you dear - ly, we stand be -
p

5
2
(reviving; in a very weak but passionate tone)
Al-fre-do, Al-
Oh Al-fred,
tan-to, ra-sciu-ga il pian-to che t'i-non-dò.
side you, He is un-wor-thy of your de-spair.
ro-re, da lei per-do-no più non a-vrò.)
blind-ly? No hope of par-don is left to me.
tan-to, ra-sciu-ga il pian-to che t'i-non-dò.
side you, He is un-wor-thy of your de-spair.
de-le; ep-pur cru-de-le ta-cer do-vrò!)
faith-ful, But I must cruel-ly con-ceal the truth.
vo-glio che il vo-stro or-go-glio fiac-car sa-prò!
ter-mined There shall be jus-tice in this af-fair.
tan-to, ra-sciu-ga il pian-to che t'i-non-dò.
side you, He is un-wor-thy of your de-spair.
tan-to, ra-sciu-ga il pian-to che t'i-non-dò.
side you, He is un-wor-thy of your de-spair.
tan-to, ra-sciu-ga il pian-to che t'i-non-dò.
side you, He is un-wor-thy of your de-spair.
tan-to, ra-sciu-ga il pian-to che t'i-non-dò.
side you, He is un-wor-thy of your de-spair.
ff Tutti
pp Cl. Cor. & Fag.
Str.
fre-do, di que-sto co-re non puoi compren-de-re tut-to la-
Al-fred, you can't im-ag-ine What you have been to me, And how I
Wind.

mo - re, tu non co - no - sci che fi - no a prez - zo del tuo di -
love you. You do not know yet how much you mean to me, How much I
ancora pianissimo
sprez - zo pro-va-to io l'ho. Ma ver - rà
suf - fer beneath your disdain. The day will
Quan-to pe - ni! fa cor!
Dry your tears and take heart.
Ohimè! che fe - ci! ne sento orror!
I am in mis-'ry, full of re-morse!
Quan-to pe - ni! fa cor!
Dry your tears and take heart.
Pro-var vi vog-lio
Here is my chal-lenge:
Quan-to pe - ni! fa cor!
Dry your tears and take heart.
Quan-to pe - ni! fa cor!
Dry your tears and take heart.
Quan-to pe - ni! fa cor!
Dry your tears and take heart.
Quan-to pe - ni! fa cor!
Dry your tears and take heart.
Quan-to pe - ni! fa cor!
Dry your tears and take heart.
Wind.
Oh.

tem - po, in che il sa - pra - i co-me t'a -
come, though, when you will re - a - lize; How much I
quan-to pe - ni! fa cor!
Do not weep an - y more,
Oh me! che fe - ci! ne sen-to or-ror!
I am in mis'ry, full of re-morse!
quan-to pe - ni! fa cor!
Do not weep an - y more,
(Io so che l'a - ma,
I know she loves him,
che il vo - - stro orgoglio
There shall be jus tice
quan-to pe - ni! fa cor!
Do not weep an - y more,
quan-to pe - ni! fa cor!
Do not weep an - y more,
quan-to pe - ni! fa cor!
Do not weep an - y more,
quan-to pe - ni! fa cor!
Do not weep an - y more,
quan-to pe - ni! fa cor!
Do not weep an - y more,

mas - si con-fes-se-ra - i, Dio dai ri -
loved you, and always will love you. May God pre -
quan-to pe - ni! fa cor!
Do not weep an - y more,
oh me! che fe - ci! ne sen-to or-ror!
I am in mis 'ry, full of re - morse!
quan-to pe - ni! fa cor!
Do not weep an - y more,
che gli è fe - de - - le;
that she is faith - - ful,
fiac-car sa-prò!
in this af-fair.
quan-to pe - ni! fa cor!
Do not weep an - y more,
quan-to pe - ni! fa cor!
Do not weep an - y more,
quan-to pe - ni! fa cor!
Do not weep an - y more,
quan-to pe - ni! fa cor!
Do not weep an - y more,
quan-to pe - ni! fa cor!
Do not weep an - y more,
quan-to pe - ni! fa cor!
Do not weep an - y more,

mor-si ti sal - vi al-lo-ra, dai ri-mor-si, dai ri-mor-si Dio ti salvi, salvial-
serve you from sad re-pentance; May He save you from re-morse,-may-God pre-serve you-from re-
Fra ca-ri-a-mi-ci sei!
You are a-mong dear friends.
Ge-lo-sa sma-nia, de-lu-so a-mor!
My jeal-ous ha-tred has made me blind.
Fra ca-ri-a-mi-ci!
You are a-mong dear friends.
Ep pur cru-de-le!
Yet I may not re-veal,
Che il vo-stro or-go-glio,
And I shall a-venge her.
Fra ca-ri-a-mi-ci sei!
You are a-mong dear friends.
Fra ca-ri-a-mi-ci sei!
You are a-mong dear friends.
mn staccato

dim.
lor, ah io spen - ta an-
morse. Ah, I'll nev - er
ra - sciu - ga il
He is not
ohimè! che fe - ci! ne sento or-ro - re! ge-lo - sa sma-nia, de - lu-so a-
What-ev-er caused me to act so blind-ly? My life was shat-tered; I was un-
ra - sciu - ga il
He is not
ep - pur cru -
But yet I
che il vo - stro or -
There shall be
ra - sciu - ga il
He is not
ra - sciu - ga il
He is not
ra - sciu - ga il
He is not
ra - sciu - ga il
He is not
ra - sciu - ga il
He is not
Vl. Ob. & Cl.

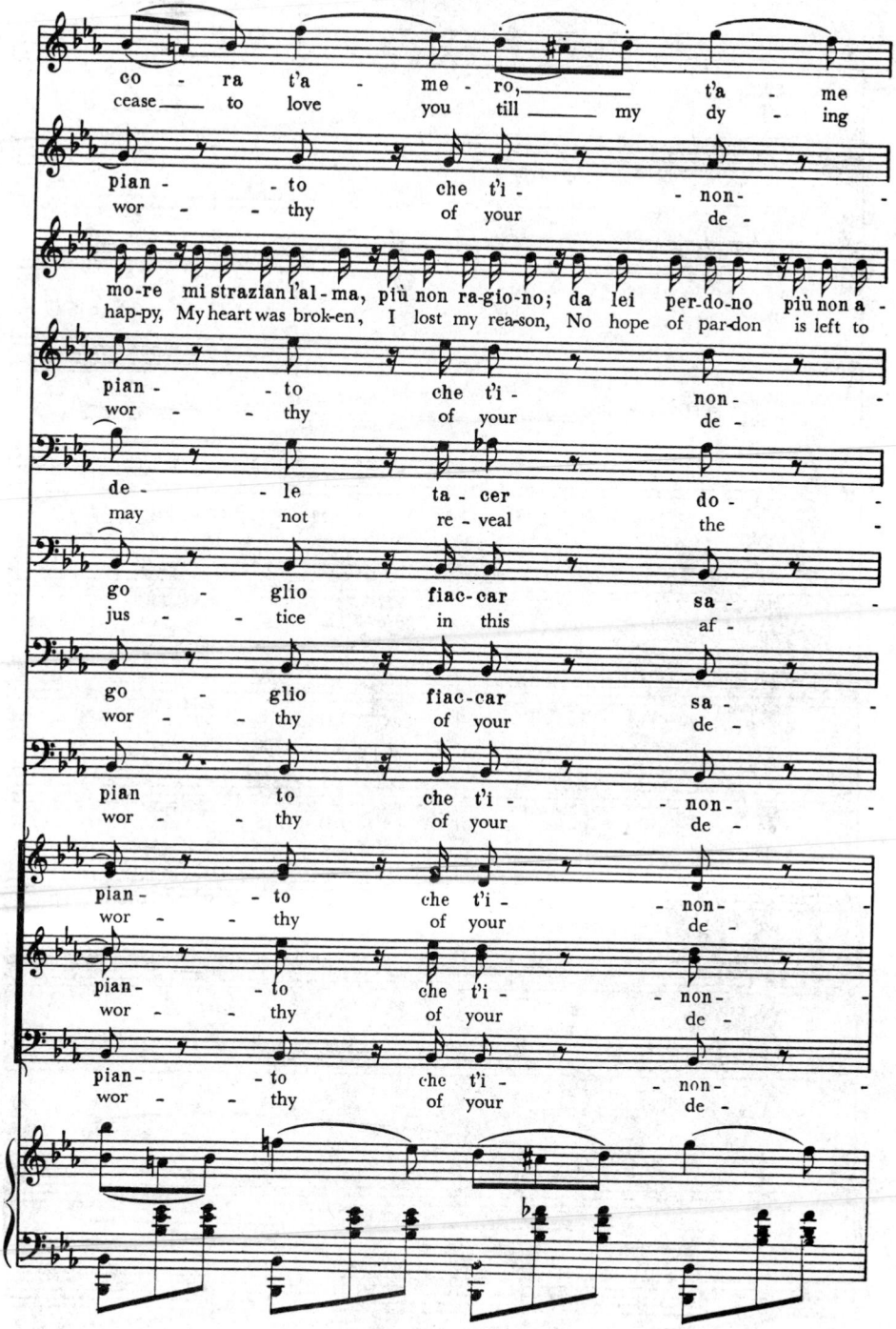
co - ra t'a - me - ro, t'a - me
cease to love you till my dy - ing
pian - to che t'i - non -
wor - thy of your de -
mo-re mi strazian l'al-ma, più non ra-gio-no; da lei per-do-no più non a -
hap-py, My heart was brok-en, I lost my rea-son, No hope of par-don is left to
pian - to che t'i - non -
wor - thy of your de -
de - le ta - cer do -
may not re - veal the -
go - glio fiac-car sa -
jus - tice in this af -
go - glio fiac-car sa -
wor - thy of your de -
pian to che t'i - non -
wor - thy of your de -
pian - to che t'i - non -
wor - thy of your de -
pian - to che t'i - non -
wor - thy of your de -
pian - to che t'i - non -
wor - thy of your de -

rò. Dai ri-
day. May
dò, ra-
spair, We
vrò. Vo - lea fug - gir - la, non ho po-
me. My pride was wound - - ed . . . I could not -
dò, ra-
spair, We
vrò, io so che l'a - ma, che gli è fe-
truth. I know she loves him, her heart is
prò, a que - sta don - ha l'a - tro - ce in-
fair. The in - - sult to this la - dy is
prò, ahi quan - to pe - ni! ma pur fa
spair, We are your friends and hold you
dò, ahi quan - to pe - ni! ma pur fa
spair, We are your friends and hold you
dò, ah! sì, fra
spair. You see your
dò, ah! sì, fra
spair. You see your
dò, ah! sì, fra
spair. You see your
Tutti.

mor - si Dio ti sal - vi al - lor
God pre - serve you from sad re - morse!
sciu - - - - ga il pian - to
love you dear - ly,
tu - to, dal - li-ra spin - to son qui ve - nu - to! or che lo
bear it, rag - ing with hate I want-ed venge-ance. Now that my
sciu - - - - ga il pian - to
love you dear - ly,
del, è fe - del, ep - pur cru -
faith - - - - ful to him but I may
sul - to qui tut - ti of - fe - se, ma non i - nul-to fia tan-to ol -
so out - ra - geous That it de - mands an in - stant sat - is -
co - re, qui sof-fre o - gnu-no del tu - o do - lo - re, fra ca-ri a -
dear, He is un - wor-thy of your de - spair, Your friends are
co - re, qui sof-fre o - gnu-no del tu - o do - lo - re, fra ca-ri a -
dear. He is un - wor-thy of your de - spair, Your friends are
ca - ria - mi - ci sei, ah!
friends are all with you, take
ca - ria - mi - ci sei, ah!
friends are all with you, take
ca - ria - mi - ci sei, ah!
friends are all with you, take

spen - ta an - co - ra pur t'a - me -
I will al - ways love you till my dy - ing
che t'i - non -
Now dry your
sde - gno ho di - sfo - ga - to, me scia-gu-ra - to! ri - morso
an - ger has lost its fu - ry, I am in mis - 'ry, full of re -
che t'i - non -
Now dry your
de - le ta - cer do - vrò,
not re - veal the truth.
trag-gio, pre - var vi voglio che tan - to or - go-glio fiac - car sa -
fac - tion. And to this pur-pose I shall take ac-tion. Of that be
mi - ci tu se - i sol - tan - to, ra - sciuga il pian-to che t'i - non -
all with you. You see your friends are all with you, take
mi - ci tu se - i sol - tan - to, ra - sciuga il pian-to che t'i - non -
all with you. You see your friends are all with you, take
sì, fra ca - ria - mi - ci
heart, Your friends are all with
sì, fra ca - ria - mi - ci
heart, Your friends are all with
sì, fra ca - ria - mi - ci
heart, Your friends are all with

rò, ah spen - ta an -
day. I'll nev - er cease to
dò, ra - - -
tears, He
n'ho, ri - mor-so n'ho, ri - mor - so n'ho! or che lo sde - -
morse, Bit - ter re - morse, Bit - ter re - morse, Now that my an - -
dò, ra - - -
tears He
ep-pur cru - del, ep-pur cru - del, ta - - -
Though it is hard, though it is hard. Though
prò, pro - var vi vo-glio che tan - to or - go-glio fiac - car sa -
cer - tain. Here is my chal lenge; I am de - ter mined There shall be
dò, fra ca - ri a - mi - ci tu sei sol - tan - to, ra - sciu-ga il
heart, Your friends are all with you. He is un - wor - thy
dò, fra ca - ri a - mi - ci tu sei sol - tan - to, ra - sciu-ga il
heart, Your friends are all with you. He is un - wor - thy
sei, ra - sciu - ga il pian - to che
you. He is un - wor - thy of
sei, ra - sciu - ga il pian - to che
you. He is un - wor - thy of
sei, ra - sciu - ga il pian - to che
you. He is un - wor - thy of

co - ra, spen - ta an - co - ra, t'a - me - rò, t'a - me -
love you, dear - est Al - fred, I shall al - ways hold you
sciu - ga il pian - to che t'i - non - dò, che t'i - non -
is un - wor - thy, We are your friends and hold you
gno ho di - sfoga - - to, ri - mor - so n'ho, ri - mor - so
ger has lost its fu - - ry, Bit - ter re - morse tor - ments my
sciu - ga il pian - to che t'i - non - dò, che t'i - non -
is un - - wor - thy, We are your friends and hold you
cer, ep - pur cru - de - le, ep - pur cru - del ta - cer do -
it is hard and cru - el, I may not yet re - veal the
prò, pro - var vi vo - glio che tan - to or - go - glio fiac - car sa -
jus - tice in this af - fair There shall be jus - tice in this af -
pianto che t'i - non - dò, ra - sciuga il pianto che t'i - non -
of all your de - spair. We are your friends and hold you
pianto che t'i - non - dò, ra - sciuga il pianto che t'i - non -
of all your de - spair. We are your friends and hold you
t'i - non - dò, che t'i - non - dò, che t'i - non -
your de - spair. We are your friends and hold you
t'i - non - dò, ra - sciu - ga il pian -
your de - spair. We are your friends and hold you
t'i - non - dò, ra - sciuga il pianto che t'i - non -
your de - spair. We are your friends and hold you

rò; dai ri - mor - si
dear. May God pre-serve
dò, ra - sciu - -
dear. We love
pp
n'ho! Vo - lea fug - gir - la, non ho po - tu - to, dal - li - ra
heart! My pride was wound - ed . . . I could not bear it rag - ing with
dò, ra - sciu - -
dear. We love
pp
vrò; io so che l'a - ma, che gli è fe - del,
truth. I know she loves him, that she is faith - - -
prò; a que - sta do - na l'a - tro - ce in - sul - to qui tut - ti of -
fair. The in - sult to this la - dy is so out - ra - geous
dò; ahi quan - to pe - ni! ma pur fa co - re, qui sof - fre o -
dear. We are your friends and hold you dear. He is un -
dò; ahi quan - to pe - ni! ma pur fa co - re, qui sof - fre o -
dear. We are your friends and hold you dear. He is un -
pp
dò, ah sì, fra ca - ria -
dear. You see your friends are
pp
to, ah sì, fra ca - ria -
dear. You see your friends are
pp
dò, ah sì, fra ca - ria -
dear. You see your friends are
p

Dio ti sal - vi al - lor, spen - ta an -
you from sad re - morse. I will
- gail pian - to che
you dear - ly, now
spin - to son qui ve - nu - to! or che lo sde - gno ho di - sfo -
hate, I want - ed venge-ance. Now that my an - ger has lost its
- gail pian - to che
you dear - ly, now
è fe - del, ep-pur cru - de - le ta - cer do -
ful to him. But I may not re - veal the
fe - se, ma non i - nul-to fia tan-to ol-trag-gio, pro - var vi
That it de - mands an in - stant sat - is - fac - tion. And to this
gnuno del tu - o do - lo - re, fra ca - ri a - mi - ci tu se - i sol -
wor - thy of your de - spair. Your friends are all with you. You
gnuno del tu - o do - lo - re, fra ca - ri a - mi - ci tu se - i sol -
wor - thy of your de - spair. Your friends are all with you. You
mi - ci sei, ah! sì, fra
all with you, take heart. Your
mi - ci sei, ah! sì, fra
all with you, take heart. Your
mi - ci sei, ah! sì, fra
all with you, take heart. Your

co - ra pur t'a - me - rò;
al - ways love you to my dy - ing day.
t'i - - - non - dò,
dry your tears.
ga - to, me scia-gu-ra - to! ri - mor-so n'ho, ri-mor-so
fu - ry, I am in mis - 'ry, full of re-morse, Bit-ter re-
t'i - - - - non - dò,
dry your tears.
vrò, ep-pur cru-del,
truth. Though it is hard,
vo-glio, che tan-to or - go-glio fiac-car sa - prò, pro-var vi
pur pose I shall take ac-tion. Of that be cer - tain, Here is my
tan-to, ra - sciu-ga il pian-to che t'i - non - dò, fra ca - ria-
see your friends are all with you, take heart. Your friends are
tan-to, ra - sciu-ga il pian-to che t'i - non - dò, fra ca - ria-
see your friends are all with you, take heart. Your friends are
ca - ria - - mi - ci sei, ra -
friends are all with you. He
ca - ria - - mi - ci sei, ra -
friends are all with you. He
ca - ria - - mi - ci sei, ra -
friends are all with you. He

ah spen - - ta an - co - ra, spen - ta an-
I'll nev - er cease to love you, dear - est
ra - - - sciu - ga il
He is un - -
n'ho, ri-mor-so n'ho! or che lo sde - gno ho di-sfo-ga - -
morse, Bit-ter re-morse, Now that my an - ger has lost its fu - -
ra - - sciù - ga il
He is un - -
ep-pur cru-del ta - - cer, ep - per cru-
though it is hard. Though it is hard and
vo-glio, che tan - to or - go - glio fiac - car sa - prò, pro - var vi
chal lenge; I am de - ter mined There shall be jus-tice in this af -
mi-ci tu sei sol - tan-to, ra - sciu-ga il pian-to che t'i - non-
all with you. He is un - wor - thy of all your de -
mi-ci tu sei sol - tan-to, ra - sciu-ga il pian-to che t'i - non-
all with you. He is un - wor - thy of all your de -
sciu - ga il pian - - to che t'i - - non - -
is un - wor - - thy of your de - -
sciu - ga il pian - - to che t'i - - non - -
is un - wor - - thy of your de - -
sciu - ga il pian - - to che t'i - - non - -
is un - wor - - thy of your de - -
cresc.

co - ra t'a - me - rò, t'a - me - rò, ah!
Al - fred I shall al - ways hold you dear. Ah
pian - to che t'i - non - dò, che t'i - non - dò, ah!
wor - thy, We are your friends and hold you dear. Ah
to, ri - mor - so n'ho, ri - mor - so n'ho! me scia - gu -
ry, Bit - ter re - morse tor - ments my heart! Ah Bit - ter re -
pian - to che t'i - non - dò, che t'i - non - dò, sì, ra - sciu - ga il
wor - thy, We are your friends and hold you dear. Do not weep an - y
de - le, ep - pur cru - del ta - cer do - vrò; so che l'a - ma, che
cru - el, I may not yet re - veal the truth. I a - lone know she
vo - glio, che tan - to or - go - glio fiac - car sa - prò, e che tan - to or -
fair. There shall be jus - tice in this af - fair. I'll de - mand sat - is -
dò, ra - sciu - ga il pian - to che t'i - non - dò, sì, ra - sciu - ga il
spair. We are your friends and hold you dear. Do not weep an - y
dò, ra - sciu - ga il pian - to che t'i - non - dò, sì, ra - sciu - ga il
spair We are your friends and hold you dear. Do not weep an - y
dò, che t'i - non - dò, che t'i - non - dò, ah!
spair. We are your friends and hold you dear. Ah
dò, ra - sciu - ga il pian - tò, sì, ra - sciu - ga il
spair. We are your friends and hold you dear. Do not weep an - y
dò, ra - sciu - ga il pian - to che t'i - non - dò, sì, ra - sciu - ga il
spair. We are your friends and hold you dear. Do not weep an - y

ppp
pp
t'a - me - rò, io spenta an-cor, pur t'a-me-rò, pur t'a-me-
You will see the day will come, when you will know my faith-ful
fa cor, qui sof-fre o-gnun, qui soffre o-gnun del tuo do-
take heart! We are your friends and hold you dear. We hold you
ra-to! ri-mor-so io n'ho, ri-mor-so n'ho, ri-mor-so n'ho, ri-mor-so
morse is tor-ment-ing my heart! Bit-ter re-morse, Bit-ter re-morse now fills my
pianto che t'i-non - dò, qui sof-fre o-gnun, qui soffre o-gnun del tuo do-
more Dry your tears and take heart. We are your friends and hold you dear. We hold you
l'a-ma, che gli è fe - del, che gli è fe-del, ep-pur crudel, ta-cer do-
loves him and that she is true. Though it is hard, I may not speak. I may not
go-glio fiac-car sa - prò, fiac-car sa-prò, fiac-car sa-prò, fiac-car sa-
fac-tion. For what you have done I shall de-mand jus-tice from you, jus-tice from
pian-to che t'i-non - dò, fa cor, fa cor, qui sof-fre o-gnun del tuo do-
more Dry your tears and take heart. We are your friends and hold you dear. We hold you
pian-to che t'i-non - dò, fa cor, fa cor, qui sof-fre o-gnun del tuo do-
more Dry your tears and take heart. We are your friends and hold you dear. We hold you
fa cor,
take heart.
pian-to che t'i-non - dò,
more Dry your tears and take heart.
pian-to che t'i-non - dò,
more Dry your tears and take heart.
pp Wind
pp

ff
ppp
rò, ah t'a - me - rò, io spen-ta an-
heart. Ah You will know, The day will
lor, ah fa cor, qui sof - fre o-
dear. Ah take heart. We are your
n'ho, me scia - gu - ra - to, ri - mor - so io n'ho, ri - mor - so
heart! Ah Bit - ter re-morse is tor-ment-ing my heart! Bit - ter re -
lor, sì, ra - sciu - ga il pian - to che t'i - non - dò, qui sof - fre o-
dear. Do not weep an - y more, Dry your tears and take heart. We are your
vrò, so che l'a - ma, che l'a - ma, che gli è fe - del, che gli è fe -
speak. I a - lone know she loves him and that she is true. Though it is
prò, e che tan - to or - go - glio fiac - ca - re sa - prò, fiac - car sa-
you, I'll de - mand sat - is - fac - tion for what you have done, I shall de -
lor, sì, ra - sciu - ga il pian - to che t'i - non - dò, fa cor, fa
dear. Do not weep an - y more, Dry your tears and take heart. We are your
lor, sì, ra - sciu - ga il pian - to che t'i - non - dò, fa cor, fa
dear. Do not weep an - y more, Dry your tears and take heart. We are your
ah fa cor,
Ah take heart.
sì, ra - sciu - ga il pian - to che t'i - non - dò,
Do not weep an - y more, Dry your tears and take heart.
sì, ra - sciu - ga il pian - to che t'i - non - dò,
Do not weep an - y more, Dry your tears and take heart.
Tutti
pp Wind

pp
cor pur t'a - me - rò, pur t'a - me - rò, pur
come, when you will know my faith-ful heart, my
gnun, qui sof-fre o-gnun del tuo do - lor, fa
friends and hold you dear. We are your friends and
n'ho, ri - mor - so n'ho, ri - mor - so n'ho, ah sì, che fe - ci! ne sento or-
morse, Bit - ter re - morse now fills my heart! What-ev-er caused me to act so
gnun, qui sof-fre o-gnun del tuo do - lor, fa
friends and hold you dear. We are your friends and
del, ep - pur cru - del, ta - cer do - vrò, ta - - -
hard, I may not speak, I may not speak. Though
prò, fiac-car sa - prò, fiac-car sa - prò, che tan - to or -
mand jus - tice from you, jus-tice from you. There shall be
cor, qui sof-fre o-gnun del tuo do - lor, ra - sciu - ga il
friends and hold you dear. We are your friends and hold you
cor, qui sof-fre o-gnun del tuo do - lor, ra - sciu - ga il
friends and hold you dear. We are your friends and hold you
fa
Take
fa
Take
fa
Take
Str. & Cor.
Fag.
Cello & C.B.

(Germont draws Alfred with him. The Baron follows him. Violetta is led by Flora into another room. The others disperse.)

End of the Second Act.

10. Clara Schumann (1819–1896)

Scherzo, Op. 10 (c. 1838)

8:6A/2 8:6/ 6 - 11

3:2B/1 3:2/ 31 - 36

From Clara Wieck-Schumann: Ausgewählte Klavierwerke. *Copyright © 1987 by G. Henle Verlag, Munich. Reprinted by permission of G. Henle Verlag, Munich.*

26
31
36
42
48
54
sf
p
mf
(f)
f
dim.

60
sf
sf
66
(sf)
sf
p
72
mf
78
f
p
84
sf
f
sf
sf
sf
90
sf
dim.
p

96
p
102
p
p
108
mf
cresc.
114
fp
p
120
dim.
126
cresc.
f

8
33
132
un poco calando
assai dim.
ben legato
doloroso
138
mf
ben marcato la melodia
146
8
un poco ritenuto
stringendo
p dolce
152
159
cresc.
Tempo I
f
165
ff
sf
sf

171
poco a poco crescendo
177
legato
tranquillo
183
9
34
ff
sf
189
195
mf
p
201

10
35
la melodia ben marcato
207
p
l'accompagnemento pp
mf
215
dim.
223
mf
231
rubato
un poco ritenuto
cresc.
pp
*
239
a tempo
leggierissimo
244

250
doloroso
pp
stringendo
258
poco a poco stringendo
265
cresc.
271
p
277
f
poco a poco dim.
283
sf
f

11
36
289
295
301
307
313
p leggieramente
pesante

319
sf
sf
p
325
p
ff
sf
sf
331
sf
sf
fpp
misterioso
poco a poco
stringendo e
337
crescendo
ff
precipitato
342
6
sf
ff
*

11. Johannes Brahms (1833–1897)

***A German Requiem*,**
Fourth Movement (1868)

8:5B/3 8:5/42 - 46
3:2B/4 3:2/49 - 53

From Edition Peters No. 3672. Used by permission of C. F. Peters Corporation.

Ze - - ba - oth, dei - ne Woh - nun -
Ze - - ba - oth, dei - ne Woh - nun -
Ze - - ba - oth, dei - ne Woh - nun -
Ze - - ba - oth, dei - ne Woh - nun -
Fl.
Hob.
Hr.
Kl.
gen, Herr Ze - - - - - - - - - - - - ba -
gen, Herr Ze - - - - - - - - - - - - ba -
gen, Herr Ze - - - - - - - - - - - - ba - - -
gen, Herr Ze - - ba - oth, Herr Ze - - - ba - - -
Viol.
A
oth!
oth!
oth! Wie lieb - - - - - lich sind dei - ne Woh - nun -
oth!
A
espress.
p
espress.
con Ped.

p espress.
Wie lieb - - - -
p espress.
Wie lieb - - - lich
gen, Herr Ze - - - - ba oth! Wie
p espress.
Wie lieb - - - - - - - lich
- lich sind dei - - ne Woh - - nun - gen, Herr Ze - - -
sind dei - - ne Woh - - nun - gen, Herr Ze - - -
lieb - - - lich sind dei - - ne Woh - - nun - gen, Herr
sind dei - - ne Woh - nun - gen, Herr Ze - - -
43
50
- - - ba - oth! Mei - ne See - - -
- - - ba - oth! Mei - ne See - - -
Ze - - ba - oth! Mei - ne See - - -
ba - - - oth! Mei - ne See - - -
Holzbl.
p

cresc.
le ver -
le ver - lan - get und
le ver - lan - get und seh - net, ver - lan - - -
le ver - lan - get und seh - net, ver - lan - get und seh - net, ver - lan - - -
lan - get und seh - net, und seh - net sich nach den
seh - net, ver - lan - get und seh - - - net sich nach den
get und seh - - - - - - net sich nach den
get und seh - net, seh - net sich nach den
Fl. u. Kl.
Vor - - hö - fen des Herrn; mein
Vor - - hö - fen des Herrn; mein
Vor - - hö - fen des Herrn; mein
Vor - - hö - fen des Herrn; mein
Hob.

B
Leib und See - le freu - en sich in dem le - ben - - -
Leib und See - le freu - en sich in dem le - ben - di - gen
Leib und See - le freu - en sich in dem le - ben - di - gen
Leib und See - le freu - en sich in dem le - ben - di - gen
B Str.
- - di - gen Gott, freu - en sich
Gott, mein Leib und See - le freu - en sich
Gott, mein Leib und See - le freu - en sich
Gott, mein Leib und See - le freu - en sich
cresc.
in dem le - ben - - - - - - di - gen
in dem le - ben - di - gen, in dem le - ben - - - - - di - gen
in dem le - ben - - - di - gen, in dem le - ben - - di - gen
in dem le - ben - - - di - gen, in dem le - ben - di - gen

44 51
Gott.
Wie
Viol.
Fl.
Kl.
Hr.
lieb - lich sind dei - ne Woh - nun - gen, Herr Ze - - - - ba -
lieb - lich sind dei - ne Woh - nun - gen, Herr Ze - - - - ba -
lieb - lich sind dei - ne Woh - nun - gen, Herr Ze - - - - ba -
lieb - - - lich sind dei - ne Woh - nun - gen, Herr Ze - ba -
oth, Herr Ze - ba - oth, dei - ne
oth, Herr Ze - ba - oth, dei - ne
oth, Herr Ze - ba - oth, dei - ne
oth, Herr Ze - ba - oth, dei - ne
Hob.

Woh - nun - gen, Herr Ze - - - - - - - - - ba -
Woh - nun - gen, Herr Ze - - - - - - - - - ba -
Woh - nun - gen, Herr Ze - - - - - - - - ba - - -
Woh - nun - gen, Herr Ze - ba - oth, Herr Ze - - - - ba -
Kl.
Viol.
oth! Wohl de - - -
oth! Wohl de - - -
oth! Wohl de - - -
oth! Wohl de - - -
p legato espress.
con Ped.
C
nen, wohl de - - nen, die
nen, wohl de - - nen, die
nen, wohl de - - nen, die
nen, wohl de - - nen, die
C

45
52
cresc.
in dei - nem Hau - se woh - nen, die
in dei - nem Hau - se woh - nen,
in dei - nem Hau - se woh - nen,
in dei - nem Hau - se woh - nen,
lo - ben - dich im - mer - dar,
die lo - ben dich im - mer - dar, im - mer - dar, im - mer,
die lo - ben dich im - mer - dar, lo - ben dich, lo - ben
die lo - ben dich im - mer - dar, die lo - ben, die lo - ben, die
die lo - ben dich, die lo - ben dich im - mer -
im - mer-dar, im - mer-dar, die lo - ben dich im - mer - dar,
dich im - mer - dar, die lo - ben dich im - mer - dar,
lo - ben, die lo - ben dich, die lo - ben dich im - mer -

dar, im - mer - dar, die
die lo - - ben dich im - mer -
die lo - - ben dich im - mer - dar, die lo - ben dich im - mer -
dar, im - mer - dar, die lo - ben dich im - mer - dar,
lo - ben, die lo - - ben, die lo - - ben, die
dar, die lo - - ben, die lo - - - ben, die lo - - ben,
dar, die lo - ben, die lo - ben, die lo - ben, die lo - ben,
die lo - ben, die lo - ben, die lo -
46 53
p dimin.
lo - - - - ben dich im - - - - - - mer - - - - -
lo - - - ben dich im - - - - - - mer - - - - -
die lo - ben dich im - - - - - - mer - - - - -
ben, die lo - ben dich im - - - - - - mer - - - - -
Fl.
Hob.
pp Str. pizz.
p es-

D
p dolce
dar! Wie lieb - - - lich, wie lieb - - lich,
dar! Wie
dar! Wie lieb - - lich, wie lieb - - lich,
dar! Wie
D
press.
Viol.
espress.
p
lieb - - - lich, wie lieb - - - lich, wie lieb - - - lich, wie
lieb - - - lich, wie lieb - - - lich, wie lieb - - - lich, wie
Fl.
Hob.
cresc.
Holzbl.
lieb - - - lich sind dei - - ne
lieb - - - lich, wie lieb - - lich sind dei - - ne
lieb - - - lich sind dei - - ne
lieb - - - lich, wie lieb - - lich sind dei - - ne
legato
Str.
f

TEXT AND TRANSLATION

Wie lieblich sind deine
Wohnungen, Herr Zebaoth!
Meine Seele verlanget und sehnet
sich nach den Vorhöfen des Herrn:
mein Leib und Seele freuen sich
in dem lebendigen Gott.
Wie lieblich . . .
Wohl denen, die in deinem
Hause wohnen, die loben
dich immerdar!
Wie lieblich . . .

How lovely is Thy dwelling
place, O Lord of hosts!
My soul longs and even
faints for the courts of the Lord;
my flesh and soul rejoice
in the living God.
How lovely . . .
Blessed are they that live in
Thy house, that praise
Thee evermore!
How lovely . . .

12. Brahms

8:5B/4 8:5/47 - 50

Vergebliches Ständchen
(Futile Serenade), Op. 84, No. 4 (1881)

(Sie.)
Mein' Tür ist ver - schlos - sen, ich lass' dich nicht
ein, ich lass' dich nicht ein;
p
Mut - ter, die rät mir klug, wärst du her - ein mit Fug, wär's mit mir vor -
pp
49
bei, wär's mit mir, wär's mit mir, wär's mit mir vor - bei!
poco f

(Er.)
So_ kalt ist die Nacht, so ei - sig der
Wind, so ei - sig der Wind,
p
dass mir das Herz er - friert, mein' Lieb' er - lö-schen wird, öff-ne mir, mein Kind,
50
Lebhafter.
öff-ne mir, öff-ne mir, öff-ne mir, mein Kind!
Lebhafter.
p
f

(Sie.)
Löschet dein' Lieb', lass sie lö- -schen nur, lass sie
f
lö- -schen nur! Lö-schet sie im-mer-zu, geh' heim zu
p legg.
Bett, zur Ruh', gu-te Nacht, mein Knab', gu-te Nacht, gu-te Nacht,
gu-te Nacht, mein Knab'!
f
sf

TEXT AND TRANSLATION

ER (HE)

Guten Abend, mein Schatz,
Guten Abend, mein Kind!
Ich komm' aus Lieb' zu dir,
Ach, mach' mir auf die Tür!
Mach' mir auf die Tür!

Good evening, my love,
Good evening, my child!
I come out of love for you,
Ah, open the door for me!
Open the door for me!

SIE (SHE)

Mein Tür ist verschlossen,
Ich lass' dich nicht ein;
Mutter, die rät mir klug,
Wär'st du herein mit Fug,
Wär's mit mir vorbei!

My door is locked,
I will not let you in.
Mother warned me
That if I let you in willingly,
All would be over with me!

ER (HE)

So kalt ist die Nacht,
So eisig der Wind,
Dass mir das Herz erfriert,
Mein' Lieb' erlöschen wird;
Öffne mir, mein Kind!

The night is so cold,
The wind is so icy,
That my heart is freezing.
My love will be extinguished;
Open up for me, child!

SIE (SHE)

Löschet dein Lieb',
Lass sie löschen nur!
Löschet sie immer zu,
Geh' heim zu Bett, zur Ruh',
Gute Nacht, mein Knab'!

If your love is extinguished,
Just let it go out!
Just keep on extinguishing it;
Go home to bed, to rest!
Good night, my boy!

TRADITIONAL

Translated by Philip Miller

13. *Brahms*

8:6A/3 8:6/12 - 14

Symphony No. 4 in E minor, Fourth Movement (1885)

A
15
Fl.
Ob.
Klar. (A)
Fag.
K.-Fag.
(E)
Hr.
(C)
Trpt. (E)
Pos.
Pk.
1.Viol.
2.Viol.
Br.
Vcl.
K.-B.
mp
cresc.
f ben marc.
f ben marc.
f ben marc.
f ben marc.
f ben marc.
f ben marc.
p
a 2
p
ben marc.
a 2
p
f
f
f
f
f
mp ma marc.
div.
mp ma marc.
arco
f
cresc.
arco
mp ma marc.
cresc.
f
A

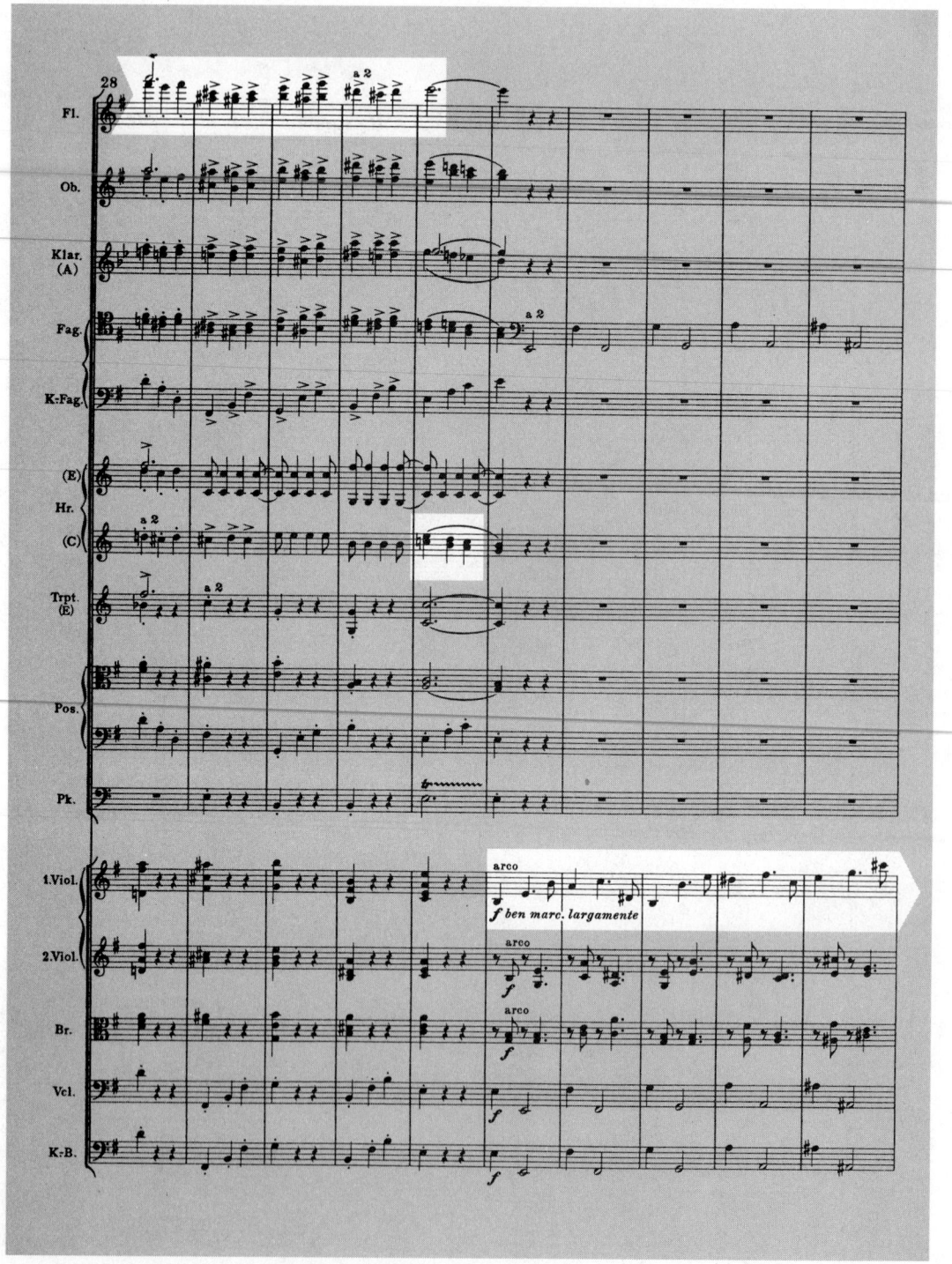
28
Fl.
Ob.
Klar. (A)
Fag.
K.-Fag.
(E)
Hr.
(C)
Trpt. (E)
Pos.
Pk.
1.Viol.
2.Viol.
Br.
Vcl.
K.-B.
a 2
arco
f ben marc. largamente
f

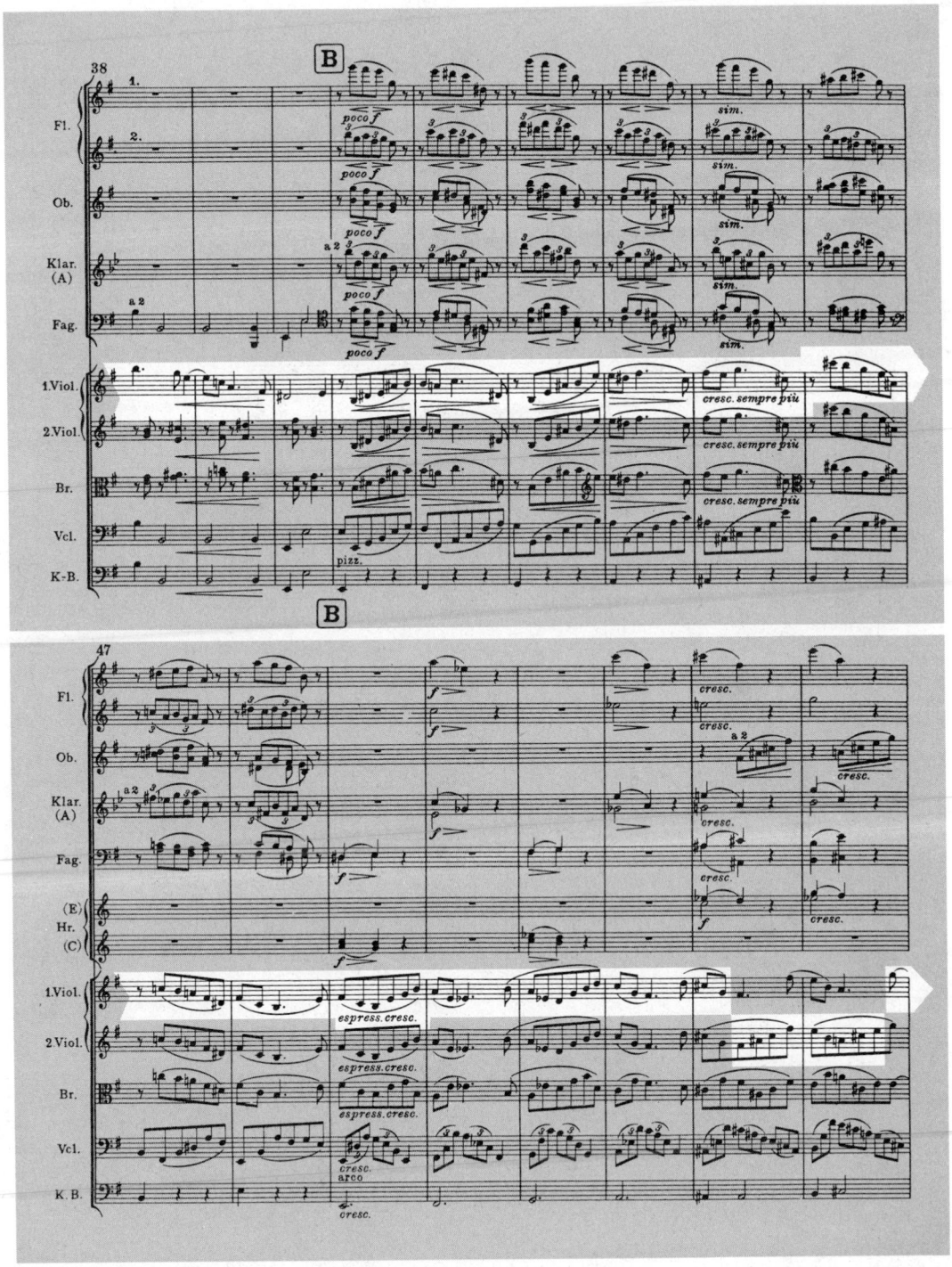
38
B
Fl.
Ob.
Klar. (A)
Fag.
1.Viol.
2.Viol.
Br.
Vcl.
K-B.
poco f
sim.
a 2
cresc. sempre più
pizz.
47
(E)
Hr.
(C)
cresc.
espress. cresc.
arco

55
C
Fl.
Ob.
Klar. (A)
Fag.
K.-Fag.
(E) Hr. (C)
1.Viol.
2.Viol.
Br.
Vcl.
K.-B.
più f
cresc.
f ben marc.
62
a 2

68
Fl.
Ob.
Klar. (A)
Fag.
(E) Hr. (C)
Trpt. (E)
Pk.
1.Viol.
2.Viol.
Br.
Vcl.
K.-B.
1.
fp
dim.
p
sf

73
Fl.
Ob.
Klar. (A)
Fag.
(E) Hr. (C)
Trpt. (E)
Pk.
1.Viol.
2.Viol.
Br.
Vcl.
K.-B.
1.
2.
f
fp dim.
p dim.
sf

78
D
Fl.
Ob.
Klar. (A)
Fag.
(E) Hr. (C)
Trpt. (E)
Pk.
1.Viol.
2.Viol.
Br.
Vcl.
K.-B.
p dim.
poco cresc.
pp
89
p dolce
dolce
a 2
p molto dolce
dim.
pizz.

13
espressivo
97
Fl.
Ob.
Klar. (A)
Fag.
(E) Hr. (C)
a 2
p dolce
poco cresc.
1.Viol.
2.Viol.
Br.
Vcl.
K.-B.

102
Fl.
Ob.
Klar. (A)
Fag.
(E) Hr. (C)
a2
dim.
espress.
dolce
1.Viol.
2.Viol.
Br.
Vcl.
K.-B.
arco
pp dolce

108
Fl.
Ob.
Klar. (A)
Fag.
(E) Hr. (C)
1.Viol.
2.Viol.
Br.
Vcl.
K.-B.
poco cresc.
dim.
a 2
113
E
pp
espress.
p
ppp
dolce
div.

120
Fl.
Ob.
Klar. (A)
Fag.
K.-Fag.
(E)
Hr.
(C)
Trpt. (E)
Pos.
Pk.
1.Viol.
2.Viol.
Br.
Vcl.
K.-B.
pp
p
ppp
a 2

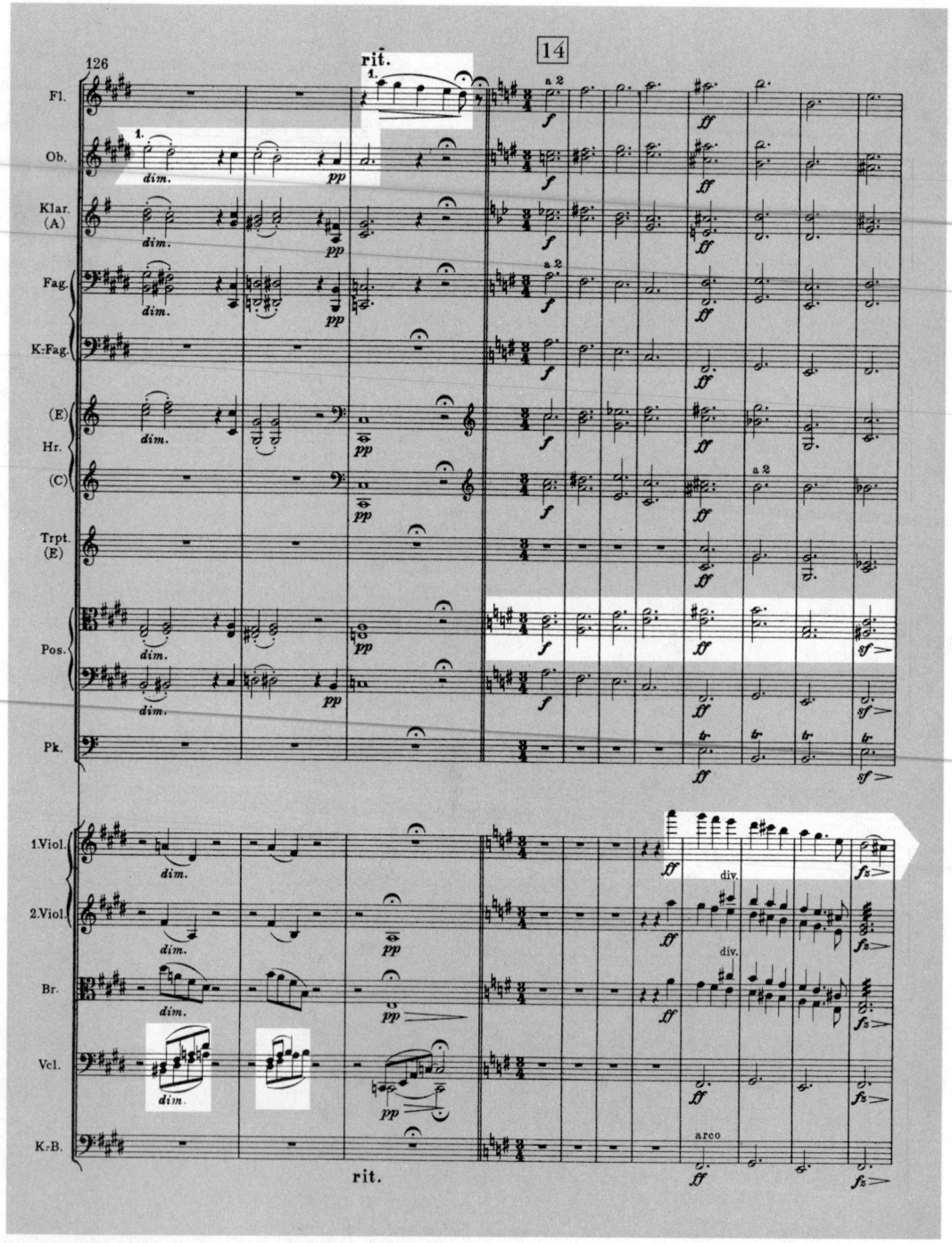
126
rit.
14
Fl.
Ob.
Klar. (A)
Fag.
K.-Fag.
(E)
Hr.
(C)
Trpt. (E)
Pos.
Pk.
1.Viol.
2.Viol.
Br.
Vcl.
K.-B.
a 2
dim.
pp
f
ff
div.
arco
rit.

F
137
Fl.
Ob.
Klar. (A)
Fag.
K-Fag.
(E)
Hr.
(C)
Trpt. (E)
Pos.
Pk.
1.Viol.
2.Viol.
Br.
Vcl.
K-B.
a 2
div.
F

149
Fl.
Ob.
Klar. (A)
Fag.
K.Fag.
(E)
Hr.
(C)
Trpt. (E)
Pos.
Pk.
1.Viol.
2.Viol.
Br.
Vcl.
K.B.
a 2
cresc.
f
p

157
Fl.
Ob.
Klar. (A)
Fag.
K.-Fag.
(E)
Hr.
(C)
Trpt. (E)
Pos.
Pk.
1.Viol.
2.Viol.
Br.
Vcl.
K.-B.
sf
a 2
f marc.

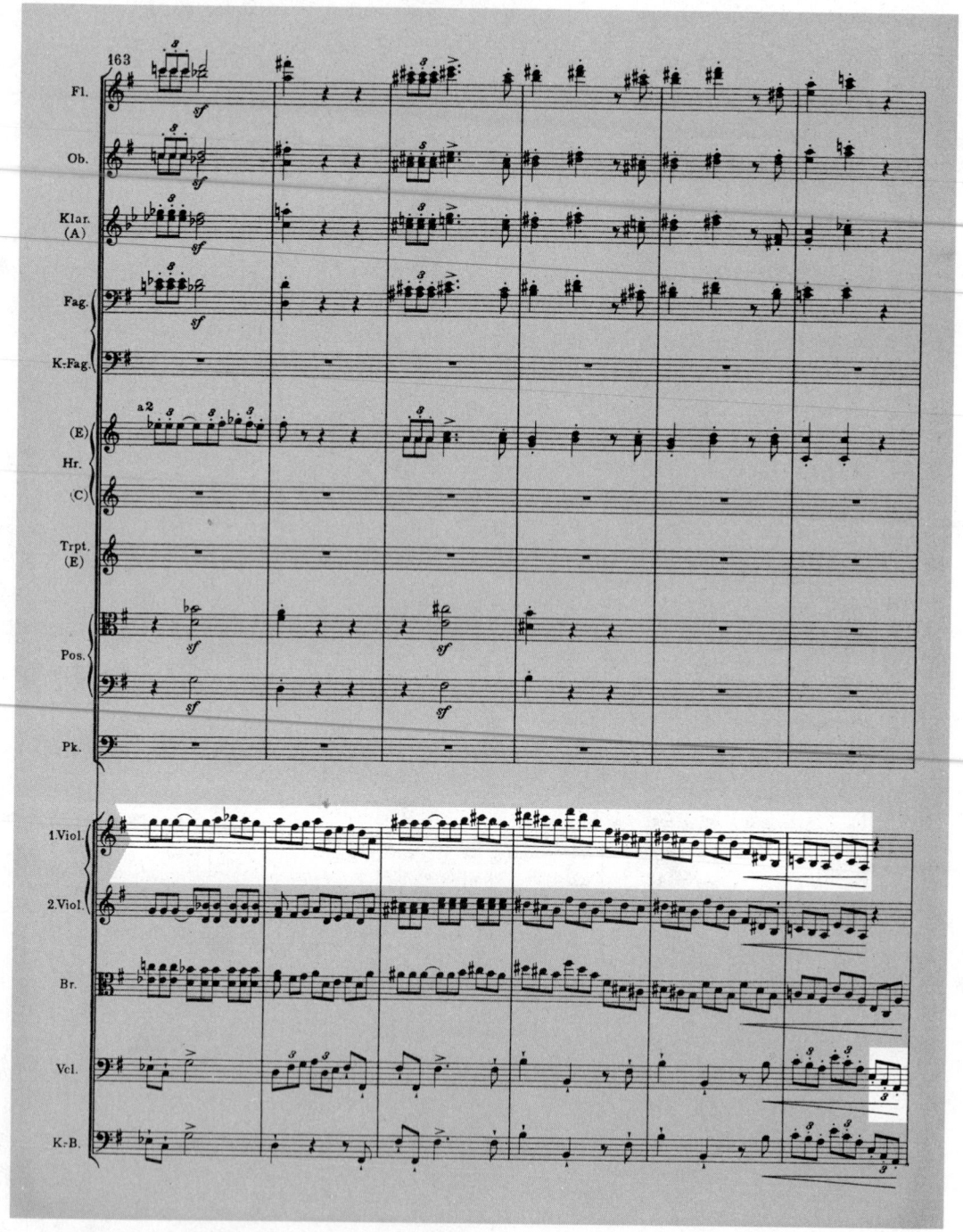
163
Fl.
Ob.
Klar. (A)
Fag.
K.-Fag.
(E)
Hr.
(C)
Trpt. (E)
Pos.
Pk.
1.Viol.
2.Viol.
Br.
Vcl.
K.-B.
a2
sf

G
169
a 2
Fl.
Ob.
Klar. (A)
Fag.
K.-Fag.
(E)
Hr.
(C)
Trpt (E)
a 2
Pos.
Pk.
1.Viol.
2.Viol.
Br.
Vcl.
K.-B.
G

175
Fl.
Ob.
Klar. (A)
Fag.
K.-Fag.
(E)
Hr.
(C)
Trpt. (E)
Pos.
Pk.
1.Viol.
2.Viol.
Br.
Vcl.
K.-B.

180
H
Fl.
Ob.
Klar. (A)
Fag.
(E)
Hr.
(C)
1.Viol.
2.Viol.
Br.
Vcl.
K.-B.
pp
f
a 2
dim.
sf
H
187
Fl.
Ob.
Klar. (A)
Fag.
(E)
Hr.
(C)
Trpt. (E)
Pk.
1.Viol.
2.Viol.
Br.
Vcl.
K.-B.
div.

193
Fl.
Ob.
a 2
Klar. (A)
Fag.
K:Fag.
(E)
Hr.
(C)
Trpt. (E)
Pos.
Pk.
1.Viol.
2.Viol.
Br.
div.
Vcl.
K.-B.
ff
f
ff marc.

201
Fl.
sf sempre
Ob.
a2
Klar. (A)
sf sempre
Fag.
K.-Fag.
sf sempre
(E)
Hr.
sf sempre
(C)
sf sempre
Trpt. (E)
sf sempre
Pos.
sf sempre
sf sempre
Pk.
sf sempre
1.Viol.
div.
2.Viol.
div.
Br.
Vcl.
sf sempre
K.-B.
sf sempre

209
I
Fl.
Ob.
Klar. (A)
Fag.
K.-Fag.
(E)
Hr.
(C)
Trpt. (E)
Pos.
Pk.
1.Viol.
2.Viol.
Br.
Vcl.
K.-B.
p
3.
fp
I

215
Fl.
Ob.
Klar. (A)
Fag.
(E)
Hr.
(C)
1.Viol.
2.Viol.
Br.
Vcl.
K.-B.
p dolce
p dim.
dim.
div.
pizz.
K
223
poco f
p legg.
legg.

230
Fl.
Ob.
Klar. (A)
Fag.
(E) Hr. (C)
1.Viol.
2.Viol.
Br.
Vcl.
K.-B.
dim.
p
p dolce
a 2
pizz.
237
L
K.-Fag.
Trpt. (E)
arco
div.
f
marc.

245
poco ritard.
Fl.
Ob.
cresc.
Klar. (A)
cresc.
Fag.
cresc.
K.-Fag.
cresc.
(E)
Hr.
(C)
cresc.
f cresc.
Trpt. (E)
Pos.
Pk.
mf
cresc.
1.Viol.
sempre più f
2.Viol.
sempre più f
Br.
cresc.
Vcl.
sempre più f
K.-B.
sempre più f
poco ritard.

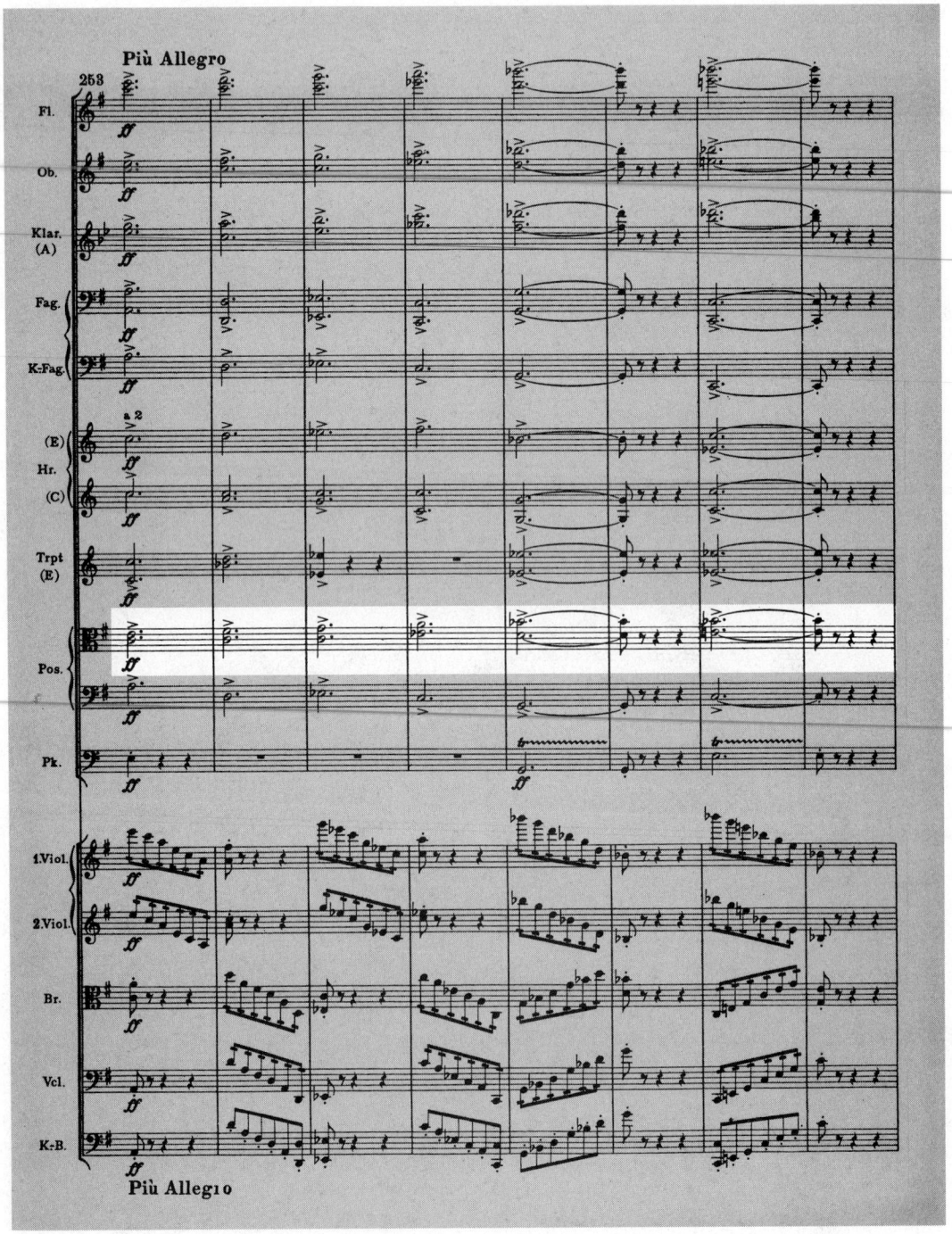
Più Allegro
253
Fl.
Ob.
Klar. (A)
Fag.
K.-Fag.
a 2
(E)
Hr.
(C)
Trpt (E)
Pos.
Pk.
1.Viol.
2.Viol.
Br.
Vcl.
K.-B.
Più Allegro

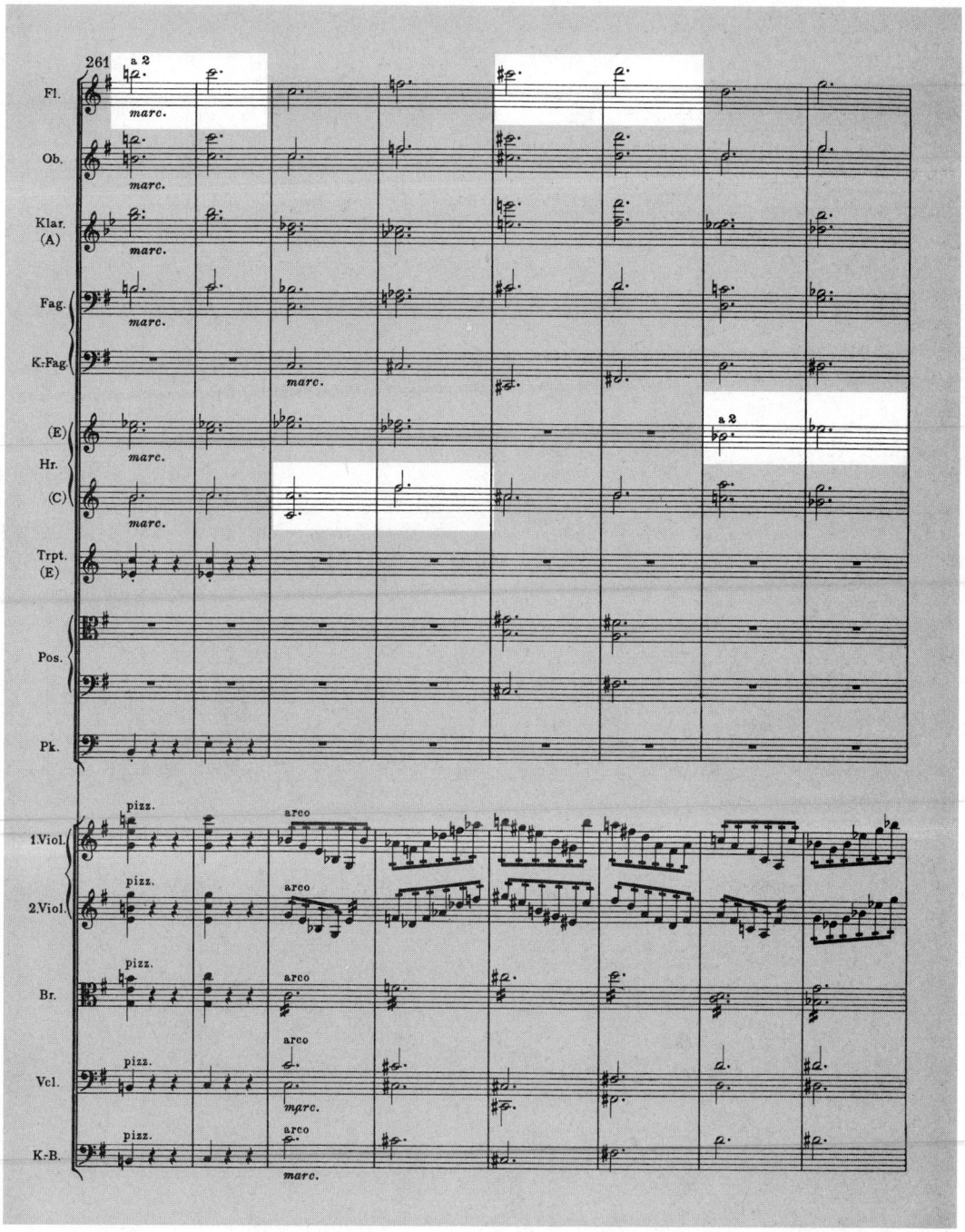
261
a 2
Fl.
marc.
Ob.
marc.
Klar.
(A)
marc.
Fag.
marc.
K.-Fag.
marc.
(E)
Hr.
marc.
a 2
(C)
marc.
Trpt.
(E)
Pos.
Pk.
pizz.
arco
1.Viol.
pizz.
arco
2.Viol.
pizz.
arco
Br.
arco
pizz.
Vcl.
marc.
arco
pizz.
K.-B.
marc.

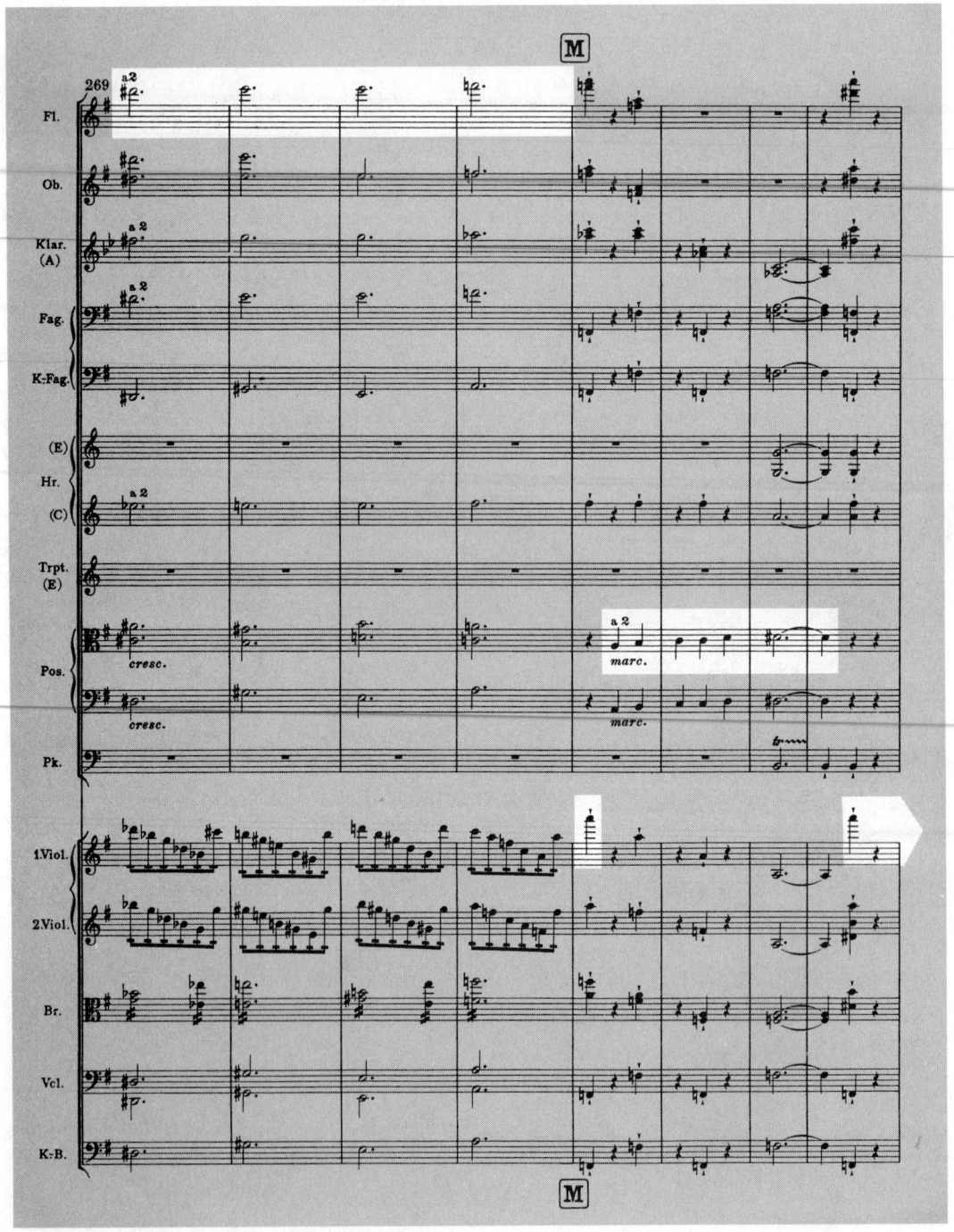
M
269
Fl.
Ob.
Klar. (A)
Fag.
K.-Fag.
(E)
Hr.
(C)
Trpt. (E)
Pos.
Pk.
1.Viol.
2.Viol.
Br.
Vcl.
K.-B.
a2
a 2
cresc.
marc.
M

277
Fl.
Ob.
Klar. (A)
Fag.
K-Fag.
(E)
Hr.
(C)
Trpt. (E)
Pos.
Pk.
1.Viol.
2.Viol.
Br.
Vcl.
K-B.
p cresc.
cresc.
div.

285
Fl.
Ob.
Klar. (A)
Fag.
K.-Fag.
(E)
Hr.
(C)
Trpt. (E)
Pos.
Pk.
div.
1.Viol.
div.
2.Viol.
Br.
Vcl.
K.-B.

292
Fl.
Ob.
Klar. (A)
Fag.
K.-Fag.
(E)
Hr.
(C)
Trpt. (E)
Pos.
Pk.
1.Viol.
2.Viol.
Br.
Vcl.
K.-B.
a 2
sf
ff

302
a 2
Fl.
Ob.
Klar. (A)
Fag.
K.-Fag.
(E)
Hr.
(C)
Trpt. (E)
Pos.
Pk.
1.Viol.
2.Viol.
Br.
Vcl.
K.-B.
sf

14. Georges Bizet (1838–1875)

8:6A/4 8:6/15 - 22

Carmen, Act I, excerpt (1875)

Scene No. 3

English translation by Ruth and Thomas Martin. Copyright © 1958 (renewed) G. Schirmer, Inc. (ASCAP). All rights reserved. Reprinted by permission.

ten.
ten.
a -
(The relief appears:
poco a poco cresc.
first a bugler and fifer, then a crowd of street-boys. — Following the latter, Lieutenant Zuniga and
ten.
ten.
Corporal Don José, then the dragoons. — During Street-boys' Chorus, the relief forms in front of the
mf
guard going off duty.)
f

pp
a
poco
a
poco
cresc. molto
ff
f ben ritmato, quasi staccato.
A - vec la gar - de mon-tan-te, Nous ar - ri-vons, nous voi-là! Son - ne, trom-
We are sol-diers marching proudly, Here we come to change the guard. Boys, blow your
p
petite e-cla-tan- te! Ta ra ta ta ta ra ta ta. Nous mar-chons la tê - te hau - te
bu-gles loud-ly! See us march in per-fect man-ner,
ff
f
cresc.
f
p
Com - me de pe - tits sol - dats, Mar - quant sans fai - re de fau - te,
We are nev - er out of step. Fol - low the wav - ing ban - ner,

(spoken.)
mf
Une, deux, mar - quant le pas. Les é - pau - les en ar - riè - re
One two, one two, hep, hep! Straight in line be - side our neigh-bors.
cresc.
f
pp
Et la poi - trine en de - hors, Les bras de cet - te ma - niè - re,
Shoul-ders back and heads up high. We raise our trust-y sa - bers,
Tom - bant tout le long du corps. A - vec la gar -
And sa - lute you go - ing by. We are sol - diers
cresc. molto.
de mon - tan - te, Nous ar - ri - vons, nous voi - là! Son - ne, trom -
march-ing proud-ly, Here we come to change the guard. Boys, blow your
cresc. molto.
ff
f
pette é - cla - tan - te, Ta ra ta ta ta ra ta ta, ta ra ta ta ra ta
bu - gles loud - ly,
f
p

ta, ta ra ta ta ra ta ta ta, ta ra ta ta ra ta ta ra ta ta ra ta ta ra
ff
ta ta ra ta ta ta; Ta ra ta ta ra ta ta, ta ra ta ta ra ta ta ta, ta ra
sf
mf
ta ta ra ta ta ra ta ta ra ta ta ra ta ta ra ta ta ta ta.
mf unis.
Nous mar-chons la
See us march in
p
tê-te haute Com-me de pe-tits sol-dats, Mar-quant sans tai-
per-fect man-ner, We are nev-er out of step, Fol-low-ing the
f
mf
re de faute, (spoken.) Une, deux, mar-quant le pas. Les é-pau-les
wav-ing ban-ner, One two, one two, hep, hep. Straight in line be-
p

cresc. molto.
en ar-rière Et la poi-tri-ne en de-hors,
side our neigh-bors, Shoul-ders back, heads up high.
ff
Les bras de cet-
We pre-sent our
te ma-niè-re, Tom-bant tout le long du corps.
trust-y sa-bers, And sa-lute you go-ing by.
Nous ar-ri-vons!
Com-pa-ny halt!
Nous voi-là!
Stand at ease!
Ta ra ta ta ra ta ta ra ta ta ta ta, ta ra ta ta.
fff
16
Recit.
Morales.
U-ne jeu-ne fil-le char-man-te Vient de nous de-man-
I have a mes-sage for you from a young and charm-ing
der si tu n'é-tais pas là!
girl who asked to speak to you.
Ju-pe bleue et nat-te tom-
Light blue skirt and ver-y long

Don José.
ban - te.
braids.
Ce doit ê - tre Mi - ca - ë - la!
I am sure that was Mi - ca - e - la.
17
(Exeunt guard going off duty. — Street-boys march off behind bugler and fifer of the retiring guard, in the same manner as they followed those of the relief.)
f
ff
Et la gar - de des - cendan - te Ren - tre chez elle
We are sol - diers march - ing proud - ly, Leav - ing with the
ten.
et s'en va. — Son - ne, trom - pette é - cla - tan - te!
chang - ing guard. Boys, blow your bu - gles — loud - ly!
Ta ra ta ta ta
tr
ra ta ta.
Nous mar - chons la tê - te bau - te Com - me de pe -
See us march in per - fect man - ner, We are nev - er
meno f

(spoken.)
tits sol - dats, Mar - quant sans fai - re de fau - te, Une, deux, mar -
out of step. Fol - low the wav - ing — ban - ner, One two, one
ten.
quant le pas.
two, hep, hep! Ta ra ta ta ra ta ta, — ta ra ta ta ra ta ta
mf
ta, ta ra ta ta ra ta ta ra ta ta ra ta ta ra ta ta ra ta ta
unis.
ta, — ta ra ta ta ra ta ta — ta ra ta ta ra ta ta ta, ta ra
dim.
ta ta ra ta ta ra ta ta ra ta ta ra ta ta ra ta ta ta.
p

sempre dim.
pp
pp possibile.

Recitative

18
Moderato.
Recit.
Zuniga.
C'est bien là, n'est - ce
Don Jo - sé, is it
Piano.
f
pas, dans ce grand bâ - ti - ment Que tra - vail - lent les ci - ga -
true that in that fac-to-ry there man - y pret - ty wom - en are
Don José.
riè - res? C'est - là, mon of - fi - cier, et bien cer - tai - ne -
work - ing? In - deed, sir, that is so, and ev - 'ry - bod - y
mf
ment On ne vit nul - le part, fil - les aus - si lé -
knows that these cig - a - rette girls are of ver - y eas - y
p
Zuniga.
gè - res. Mais au moins sont - el - les jo -
vir - tue. Are they al - so eas - y to
alla misura e legg.

Don José.
li - es?
look at?
Mon of - fi - cier, je n'en sais
Sir, I don't know much a - bout
rien, Et m'oc - cupe as - sez peu de ces ga - lan - te - ri -
that, for I am not con - cerned with wom - en of that na -
Zuniga.
es.
ture.
Ce qui t'oc - cupe, a -
What con - cerns you, my
poco più allegro.
mi, je le sais bien,
friend, I think I know.
U - ne jeu - ne fil - le char-
You're in love with one charm-ing
p
man - te
girl.
Qu'on ap - pel - le Mi - ca - ë - la,
Mi - ca - e - la is her name.

Ju - pe bleue et nat - te tom - ban - te.
"Light blue skirt and ver - y long braids!"
Don José.
Tu ne ré - ponds rien à ce - la? Je ré - ponds que c'est
Well, am I right a - bout that? I ad - mit you are
vrai, je ré - ponds que je l'ai - me!
right. I con - fess, she's the girl I love.
Recit.
Quant aux ou-vri - è - res d'i - ci, Quant à leur beau-
And as for the fac - to - ry girls, When you hear the
té, les voi - ci! Et vous pou - vez ju - ger vous - mê - me.
bell, they'll be here. Then you can judge their looks quite well.
attacca subito.

Scene No. 4

19
Allegro.
Carmen.
Sopranos I & II.
(Cigarette-girls).
Tenors.
(Young men).
Basses.
(Townspeople)
Chorus.
(The factory-bell is ringing.)
(Don José sits down and pays no attention to the shifting scenes. He repairs the
Allegro. (♩.= 104.)
Piano.
pp
chain of his saber.)
(the bell stops.)
cresc. molto.
ff
Allegretto moderato. (♩= 104.)
pp

TENORS.
p leggieramente.
La cloche a son - né; nous, des ouv - ri - è - res, Nous ven-ons i -
Ev - 'ry day at noon, you will find us here, 'Wait-ing for the
ci guet - ter le re - tour; Et nous vous sui - vrons,
time when the girls ap - pear. Charm-ing to the eye,
poco sf
bru - nes ci - ga - riè - res, En vous mur - mu - rant des pro - pos d'a -
how we love to court them, Hop - ing that our fond wish-es may come
mour! En vous mur - mu - rant des pro - pos d'a - mour!
true, Hop-ing that our fond wish - es may come true,
dim.
Più lento.
sempre più lento.
lunga.
des pro - pos d'a - mour! des pro - pos d'a - mour!
As all lov - ers do, As all lov - ers do.

20
Andantino. (♩.= 60.)
BASSES. (Enter Cigarette-girls, smoking cigarettes, and slowly descending to the stage.)
p
Voy - ez
Here they
pp
les! re - gards im - pu - dents, Mi - ne co -
are, the bright - eyed co - quettes, Keen and au -
quet - te! Fu - mant tou - tes, du bout des dents
da - cious, I - dly smok - ing their cig - a - rettes,
La ci - ga - ret - - - - te.
And so flir - ta - - - - tious!
sf
p
dim.
pp

(Beat 3/4).
SOPRANOS I.
SOPRANOS II.
Dans l'air nous sui - vons des yeux La fu -
Smoke rings make their la - zy way, Soft - ly
Dans l'air nous sui - vons des yeux
Smoke rings make their la - zy way,
mé - e, La fu - mé - e Qui vers les cieux Mon - te,
curl - ing, soft - ly curl - ing. Sky - ward they stray In a
poco cresc.
La fu - mé - e, La fu - mé - e Qui vers les cieux Mon - te,
Soft - ly curl - ing, soft - ly curl - ing. Skyward they stray In a
poco cresc.
mon - te par - fu - mé - e; Ce - la mon - te
fra - grant cloud un - furl - ing. Their per - fume per -
dim.
mon - te par - fu - mé - e; Ce - la mon -
fra - grant cloud un - furl - ing. Their per - fume
dim.

gen - ti - ment A la tê - te, à la tê - te, Tout dou - ce -
vades the air, Gent-ly steal-ing, gent-ly steal-ing, Sooth-ing our
te gen - ti - ment A la tê - te, à la tê - te,
per - vades the air, Gent-ly steal - ing, gent-ly steal - ing,
poco cresc. dim.
ment, Ce - la vous met l'â - me en fê - te!
mind To a mel - low pleas - ant feel - ing.
poco cresc. dim.
Tout dou - ce - ment, Ce - la vous met l'â - me en fê - te!
Sooth-ing our mind To a mel - low pleas - ant feel - ing.
poco cresc. dim.
pp e molto stacc.
Le doux par - ler, le doux par - ler des a - mants,
Those ten - der words you lov - ers say ev - ry day
mf
C'est fu - mé - e!
Fade a - way!
pp
pp
Leurs trans - ports, leurs transports et leurs serments,
Your prom-is - es, too, like the smoke in the blue
mf
C'est fu - mé - e!
Fade a - way!

pp
Le doux parler des amants,
Those ten-der words lov-ers say
mf
C'est fu-mé-e!
Fade a-way.
pp
Leurs transports et leurs serments, Oui
Your prom-is-es ev-'ry day They
C'est fu-mé-e!
Fade a-way.
c'est fu-mé-e, c'est fu-mé
fade a-way, they fade a-way.
sf
pp
Oui c'est fu-mé-e, c'est fu-mé-e!
They fade a-way, fade a-way.
sf
dim.
Ped.
p
e!
Dans l'air nous sui-
Smoke rings rise and
Dans l'air nous sui-vons des yeux, Dans l'air
Smoke rings rise and float a-way, Smoke rings
pp
vons des yeux, des yeux, La fu-mé-e!
float a-way, a-way in the blue,
cresc.
nous sui-vons des yeux, La fu-
rise and float a-way, of the
marcato.
cresc.
Ped.

cresc.
La fu - mé - e! Dans l'air
in the blue. See there
cresc.
me - e! La fu - mé - e! Ah!
sky, of the sky. Ah!
f
f
mosso.
Ped.
Ped.
dim.
nous sui - vons la fu - mé - e Qui monte en tour -
See them curl - ing and ris - ing and van - ish at
nous sui - vons la fu - mé - e Qui monte en tour -
See them curl - ing and ris - ing and van - ish at
dim.
p
nant, en tour - nant vers les cieux!
last in the blue of the sky.
p
nant, en tour - nant vers les cieux!
last in the blue of the sky.
p
La fu - mé - - - - e!
See them rise
La fu - mé - - - - e!
See them rise
dim.
pp
dim.

pp
smorzando.
La fu - mé - - - - - -
To the skies.
pp
smorzando.
La fu - mé - - - - - -
To the skies.
ppp
smorzando.
e!
e!
pppp
21
Allegretto molto. (♩.= 108.)
BASSES.
mf
Mais nous ne voyons pas
But where's Carmen to-day?
f
p

Allegro moderato. (♩= 92.)
(Entrance of Carmen.)
la Carmen - ci - ta!
Why is she mis-sing?
ff
TENORS.
f
La voi-là!
There she is!
BASSES.
f
La voi-là!
Look at her!
p
cresc.
SOPRANOS.
ff
La voi-là!
Where she is
voi - là la Carmen-
there is al-ways ex-
TENORS.
ff
La voi-là!
Where she is
voi - là la Carmen-
there is al-ways ex-
BASSES.
ff
f
ff

ci - ta!
cite - ment!
(to Carmen.)
mf
ci - ta!
cite - ment!
Car - men! sur tes pas nous nous pres - sons
At last! We've been anx - ious - ly wait - ing for
(♩.= 100.)
p
tous!
you!
Car - men! sois gen - til - le au moins réponds-
We men want, at least, an an-swer from
nous,
you.
Et dis-nous quel jour tu nous ai - me - ras!
O Car-men, why must you tease us this way?
sf
dim.
p
Car - men, dis - nous quel jour tu nous ai - me - ras!
When will you give your love? Won't you name the day?
p
pp

Carmen.
quasi Recit.
mf guily.
(after a swift glance at Don José.)
Quand je vous ai - me - rai? ma foi, je ne sais
When I'll give you my love? Who knows, it's hard to
a tempo Andantino.
colla voce.
p
colla voce.
a tempo.
f
p
pas, Peut - ê - tre ja - mais! peut - ê - tre de -
tell! Per - haps not at all. Per - haps ver - y
a tempo.
p
pp
(resolutely.)
main.
soon!
Mais pas au - jour -
But one thing I'll
pp
d'hui
say:
c'est cer - tain.
Not to - day.
pp
mf
attacca.

Scene No. 5

22
Allegretto, quasi Andantino.
Carmen.
p
L'amour
Love is
Sopranos I & II.
(Cigarette-girls).
Tenors.
(Young men).
Basses.
(Workingmen).
Chorus.
Allegretto, quasi Andantino. (♩= 72.)
Piano.
pp
est un oi-seau re - bel-le Que nul ne peut ap-pri-voi - ser, Et c'est
free as the way-ward breeze, It can be shy, it can be bold. Love can
portamento.
bien en vain qu'on l'ap - pel-le, S'il lui con - vient de re - fu - ser. Rien n'y
fas-ci-nate, love can tease, Its whims and moods are thou-sand-fold. All at
portamento.
fait, menace ou pri - è-re, L'un par-le bien, l'au-tre se tait; Et c'est
once it ar-rives and lin-gers For just how long can't be fore-told. Then it
*) Imitated from a Spanish song.

l'au-tre que je pré - fè - re Il n'a rien dit; mais il me
deft-ly slips through your fin-gers, For love's a thing no force can
espress.
plait. L'a - mour! l'a -
hold. That's love for
Sopr.
pp legg.
L'a-mour est un oi-seau re - bel-le Que nul ne peut ap-pri-voi-
Love is free as the way-ward breeze, It can be shy, it can be
Ten.
pp legg.
L'a-mour est un oi-seau re - bel-le Que nul ne peut ap-pri-voi-
Love is free as the way-ward breeze, It can be shy, it can be
mour! l'a - mour!
you, That's love
ser, Et c'est bien en vain qu'on l'ap - pel-le S'il lui con-
bold. Love can fas-ci-nate, love can tease, Its whims and
ser, Et c'est bien en vain qu'on l'ap - pel-le S'il lui con-
bold. Love can fas-ci-nate, love can tease, Its whims and

p
l'a - mour! L'amour est en - fant de Bo - hême, Il n'a ja -
for you! A heart in love is quick-ly burned, It knows no
vient de re - fu - ser!
moods are thou - sand - fold.
vient de re - fu - ser!
moods are thou - sand - fold.
mais, jamais connu de loi, Si tu ne m'ai - mes pas, je t'ai - me; Si
law ex - cept its own de - sire. If I should love you and you spurn me, I'm
je t'aime, prends garde à toi! Si tu ne m'ai - mes pas, si
warning you, you play with fire! If I'm in love with you, don't
f
Prends garde à toi!
You play with fire!
f
Prends garde à toi!
You play with fire!
f
f
pp

cresc.
tu ne m'aimes pas, je t'ai - me! Mais si je t'ai-me, si je
ev-er, ev-er try to spurn me. My friend, re-mem-ber, if I
Prends garde à toi!
You play with fire.
Prends garde à toi!
You play with fire.
f
pp
cresc.
t'aime, prends gar - de à toi!
love you, you play with fire.
mf
L'amour est en - fant de Bo - hême, Il n'a ja -
A heart in love is quick-ly burned, It knows no
p
L'a - - - mour
A heart
mf
mf
mais, jamais con-nu de loi, Si tu ne m'ai-mes pas, je t'ai - me; Si
law ex-cept its own de - sire. If I should love you and you spurn me, I'm
est en - fant de Bo - - -
in love is quick - -

Carmen.
Si tu ne m'ai-mes pas, si
If I'm in love with you, don't
je t'ai-me, prends garde à toi! Prends garde à toi!
warning you, you play with fire, you play with fire!
hê - - - - me! Prends garde à toi!
ly burned, you play with fire!
tu ne m'aimes pas, je t'ai - me! Mais si je t'ai-me, si je
ev-er, ev-er try to spurn me. My friend, re-mem-ber, if I
Prends garde à toi!
You play with fire!
Prends garde à toi!
You play with fire!
cresc.
cresc.

t'ai - me, prends garde à toi!
love you, you play with fire.
cresc.
à toi!
with fire.
L'oiseau que tu croy - ais sur - prendre Battit de l'aile et s'en - vo -
Wait for love and you wait for - ev - er, Don't wait at all, it comes to
la; L'amour est loin, tu peux l'at - ten - dre; Tu ne l'at - tends plus, il est
you. Try to grasp it, It's far too clev - er, It flies a - way in - to the

portamento.
la! Tout au - tour de toi vi - te, vi - te, Il vient, s'en va, puis il re -
blue. Love has so man-y forms and shapes, Each day it wears a new dis -
portamento.
vient; Tu crois le te - nir, il t'é - vi - te; Tu crois l'é - vi - ter, il te
guise. Think you've caught it and it es - capes To catch you lat - er by sur -
tient! L'a - mour! l'a -
prise. That's love for
Sopr. pp legg.
Tout au - tour de toi vi - te, vite Il vient, s'en va, puis il re -
Ten. pp legg.
Love has so man-y forms and shapes, Each day it wears a new dis -
mour! l'a - mour! l'a -
you, That's love for
vient; Tu crois le te - nir, il t'é - vi - te; Tu crois l'é - vi - ter, il te
guise. Think you've caught it and it es - capes To catch you lat - er by sur -

p
mour! L'amour est en - fant de Bo - hême, Il n'a ja - mais, jamais connu de
you! A heart in love is quick-ly burned, It knows no law ex - cept its own de -
tient!
prise.
loi, Si tu ne m'ai - mes pas, je t'ai - me: Si je t'ai - me prends garde à
sire, If I should love you and you spurn — me, I'm warning you, you play with
toi! Si tu ne m'ai - mes pas, Si tu ne m'aimes pas, je
fire! If I'm in love with you, don't ev - er, ev - er try to
f
Prends garde à toi!
You play with fire!
f
Prends garde à toi!
You play with fire!
f
f
pp

cresc.
t'ai - me; Mais si je t'ai-me, si je t'ai-me prends gar - de à
spurn me, My friend, re-mem-ber, if I love you, you play — with
Prends garde à toi!
You play with fire!
Prends garde à toi!
You play with fire!
f
pp
cresc.
mf
toi!
fire!
L'amour est en - fant de Bo - hême, Il n'a ja - mais, jamais con-nu de
A heart in love is quick-ly burned, It knows no law ex - cept its own de -
L'a - - - mour est en -
A heart in
p

loi, Si tu ne m'ai - mes pas, je t'ai - me; Si je t'ai-me prends garde à
sire. If I should love you and you spurn me, I'm warning you, you play with
fant de Bo - - - hê - - - -
love is quick - - - ly
Carmen.
p
Si tu ne m'ai - mes pas. Si
If I'm in love with you, don't
f
toi! Prends garde à toi!
fire! You play with fire!
f
me! Prends garde à toi!
burned. You play with fire!
f
f
p

p cresc.
tu ne m'aimes pas, je t'ai - me;
ev - er, ev - er try to spurn me.
Mais si je
My friend, re -
f
Prends garde à toi!
You play with fire,
f
Prends garde à toi!
You play with fire,
f
f
p
f
t'ai - me, si je t'ai - me, prends garde à toi!
mem-ber, if I love you, you play with fire!
p cresc.
à toi!
with fire!
p cresc.
à toi!
with fire!
p cresc.
f
f
f
f ff
cresc.
attacca subito.

15. Modest Petrovich Musorgsky (1839–1881)

Pictures at an Exhibition, Three Movements (1874; orchestrated by Ravel, 1922)

8:6B/1-2 8:6/23 - 33

3:2B/3 3:2/42 - 48

Promenade

Editor's note: The pianoforte part at the bottom of each score system shows the original piano version; it is not part of the orchestral score.

© *Copyright 1929 by Boosey & Hawkes, Inc.; copyright renewed. Reprinted by permission of Boosey & Hawkes, Inc.*

Cor. I.II
Tr. I.II
Trb.III Tuba
Pfte.
Ob. I.II.
Cl. I.II
Fg. I.II
Cfg.
Cor. I.II.
Vl.I
Vl.II
Vla.
Vc.
Cb.
Pfte.
mf
div.
unis.
pizz.
arco

Fl.
Fl. picc.
I.II
Ob.
III
Cl. I.II
Cl.b.
Fg. I.II
Cfg.
I.II
Cor.
III. IV
Tr. I.II
VI.I
VI.II
Vla.
Vc.
Cb.
Pfte.
Muta in Flauto grande
div.
unis.
pizz.
arco
pizz.
arco
pizz.
pizz.

I.II
Fl.
III
Ob.
I.II.III
Cl.
I.II
Cl.b.
Fg.
Cfg.
I.II
Cor
III.IV
Tr.
I.II.III
Trb.I
VI.I
VI.II
Vla.
Vc.
Cb.
Pfte.
a 2
div.
unis.
arco

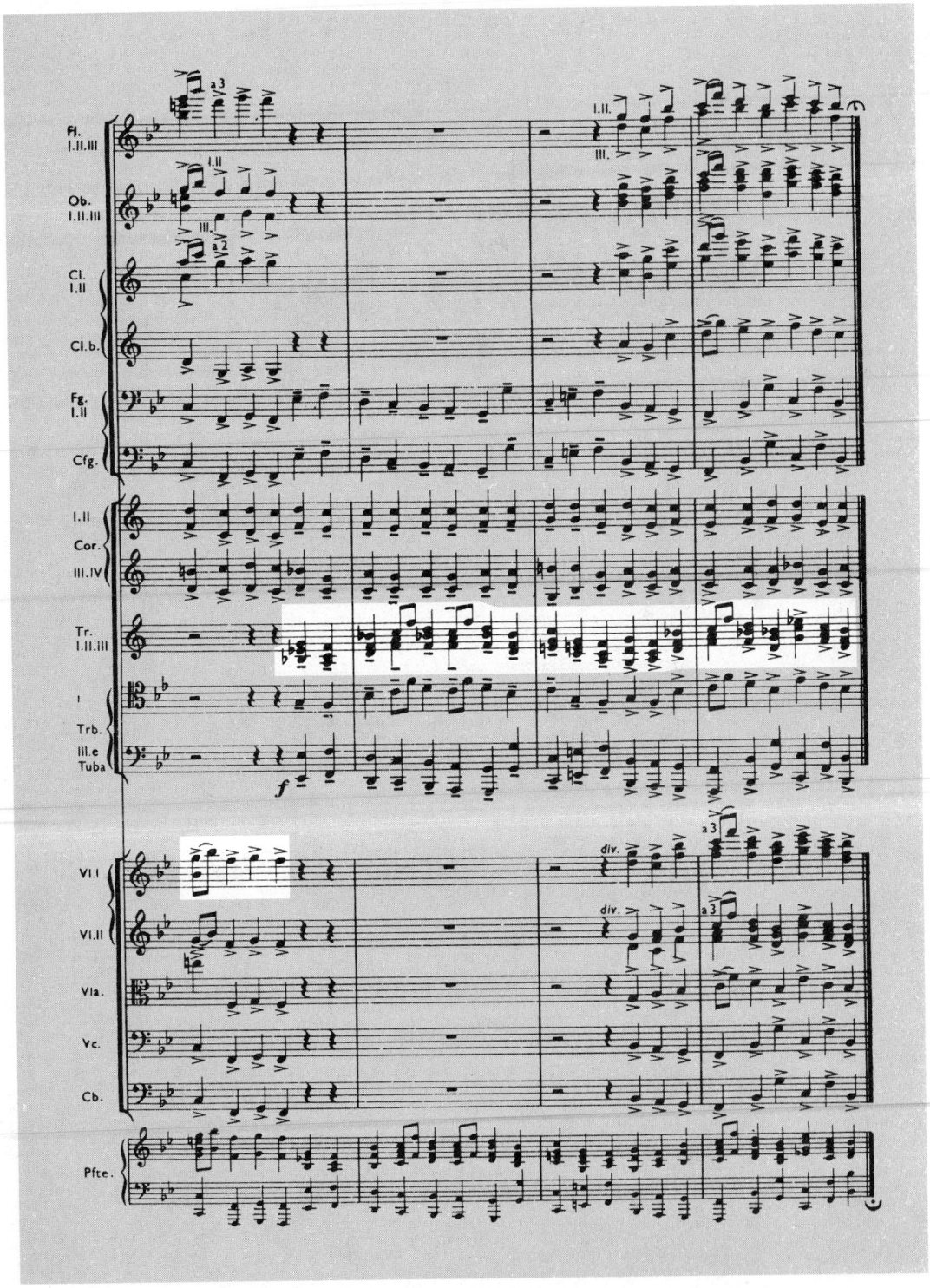
Fl.
I.II.III
Ob.
I.II.III
Cl.
I.II
Cl.b.
Fg.
I.II
Cfg.
I.II
Cor.
III.IV
Tr.
I.II.III
I
Trb.
III.e
Tuba
Vl.I
Vl.II
Vla.
Vc.
Cb.
Pfte.
a 3
a 2
I.II.
III.
div.
f

9. *The Hut on Fowl's Legs (Baba-Yaga)*

C.I
Cl. I. II
a 2
Cl.b
Fg. I. II
a2
Cfg.
mf
I. II
Cor.
III. IV
ff
Timp.
Muta Fa♯(F♯) in Mi (E)
Gr.C.
Arpa
mf
Vl. I.
Vl. II
Vla
Vc
Cb.
mf
Pfte.
mf
sf

Fl. I, II
Ob. I, II
Cl.b
Fg. I, II
Cfg.
I, II
Cor.
III, IV
Trb I, II
Trb. III. Tuba
Tuba
Gr.C.
Arpa
Solo(G)
Vl. I
Vl. II
Vla
Vc
Cb.
pizz.
arco
cresc.
Pfte.

Fl. I. II
Ob. I. II
C.I
Cl. I. II
Cl.b
Fg. I. II
Cfg.
I. II
Cor.
III. IV
Trb. II.
Trb. III
Tuba
Gr.C.
Vl. I
Vl. II
Vla
Vc
Cb.
Pfte.
a2
div.
pizz.
unis.
arco

Cl.b
Fg. I. II
Cfg.
I. II
Cor.
III. IV
Tr.
Trb. I. II.
Trb. III. Tuba
Ptti.
Gr.C.
Vl. I.
Vl. II
Vla
Vc.
Cb.
Pfte.
pizz.
arco
pizz.

Fl. I. II
Fl. picc.
Ob. I. II
C.I
Cl I. II
Cl.b
Fg. I. II
Cfg.
Cor.
Tr.
Trb. I. II
Trb III
Tuba
Timp.
Tamb.
Ptti.
Gr.C.
Arpa
Vl. I.
Vl. II
Vla
Vc
Cb.
Pfte.
pizz.
arco
div.
unis.
simile
Tamb.
Ptti.

Fl. I. II
Fl. picc.
Ob. I. II
C.I
Cl I. II
Cl.b
Fg. I. II
Cfg.
Cor.
Tr.
Trb. I. II
Timp.
Trg.
Tamb.
Pcci.
Arpa
Vl. I
Vl. II
Vla
Vc
Cb.
Pfte.
a2
a4
I. II.
f
ff
pizz.
unis. arco
arco
div.
unis.
sf

Fl. I. II
Fl. picc.
Ob. I. II
C.I
Cl. I. II
Cl.b
Fg. I. II
Cfg.
Cor.
Trb. I. II
Trb. III
Tuba
Timp.
Ptti.
Gr.C.
Vl. I
Vl. II
Vla
Vc
Cb.
Pfte.
a 2
ff
pizz.
arco

Fl. I.II
Ob. I.II
C.I.
Cl. I.II
Cl.b
Fg. I.II
Cfg.
Cor.
Trb.III Tuba
Timp.
Vl.I
Vl.II
Vla.
Vc
Cb.
Pfte.
pizz.
arco

Fl. I.II
Fl. picc.
Ob. I.II
C.I.
Cl. I.II
Cl.b.
Fg. I.II
Cfg.
Cor.
Tr.
Trb. I.II
Trb.III Tuba
Pcti.
Gr. C.
Vl.I
Vl.II
Vla
Vc.
Cb.
Pfte.
a2
p
ff
mf
tr
glss.
pizz.

Fl. I.II
Fl. picc.
Ob. I.II
C.I.
Cl. I.II
Cl.b.
Fg. I.II
Cfg.
Cor.
Tr.
Trb. I.II
Trb.III Tuba
Timp.
Trg.
Tamb.
Ptcl.
Gr.C.
Vl.I
Vl.II
Vla.
Vc.
Cb.
Pfte.
a 2
arco
I.III.
II.IV.
II.III.
ff
f

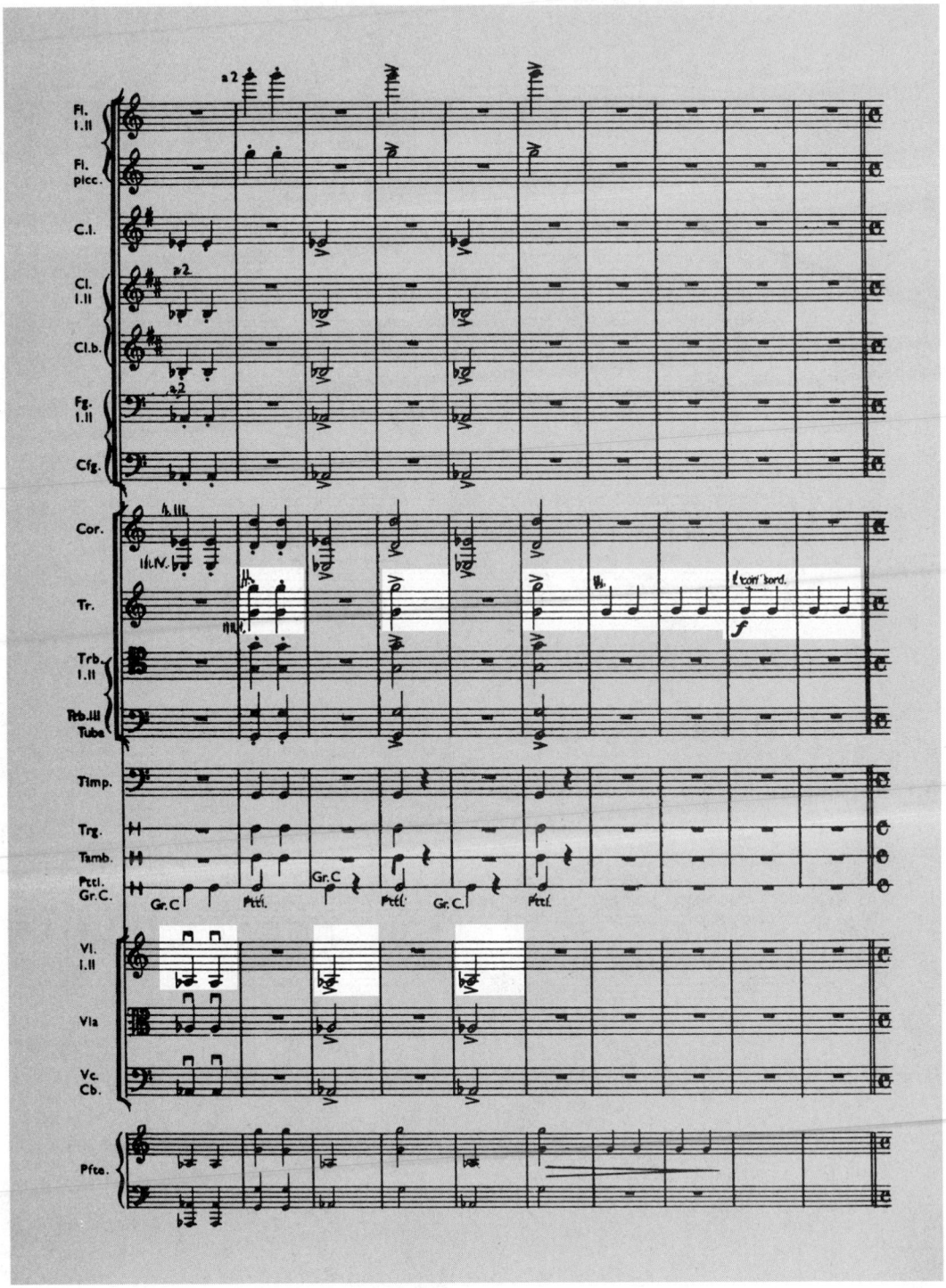
Fl. I.II
Fl. picc.
C.I.
Cl. I.II
Cl.b.
Fg. I.II
Cfg.
Cor.
Tr.
Trb. I.II
Trb.III Tuba
Timp.
Trg.
Tamb.
Ptcl. Gr.C.
Vl. I.II
Vla
Vc. Cb.
Pfte.
a2
Gr.C
Ptcl.
l'corn' bord.
f

25
Andante mosso. ♩= 72
Fl. I.II
Fg. I.II
Cb.
Pfte.
I.
p
L'Solo
mf
pizz.
non legato

Fl. I.II
Cl. I.II
Fg. I.II
Vl.I
Vl.II
Vc.
Cb.
Pfte.
Fl. II. muta in Fl. picc.
(Sul D)
(Sul A)
pizz.
arco

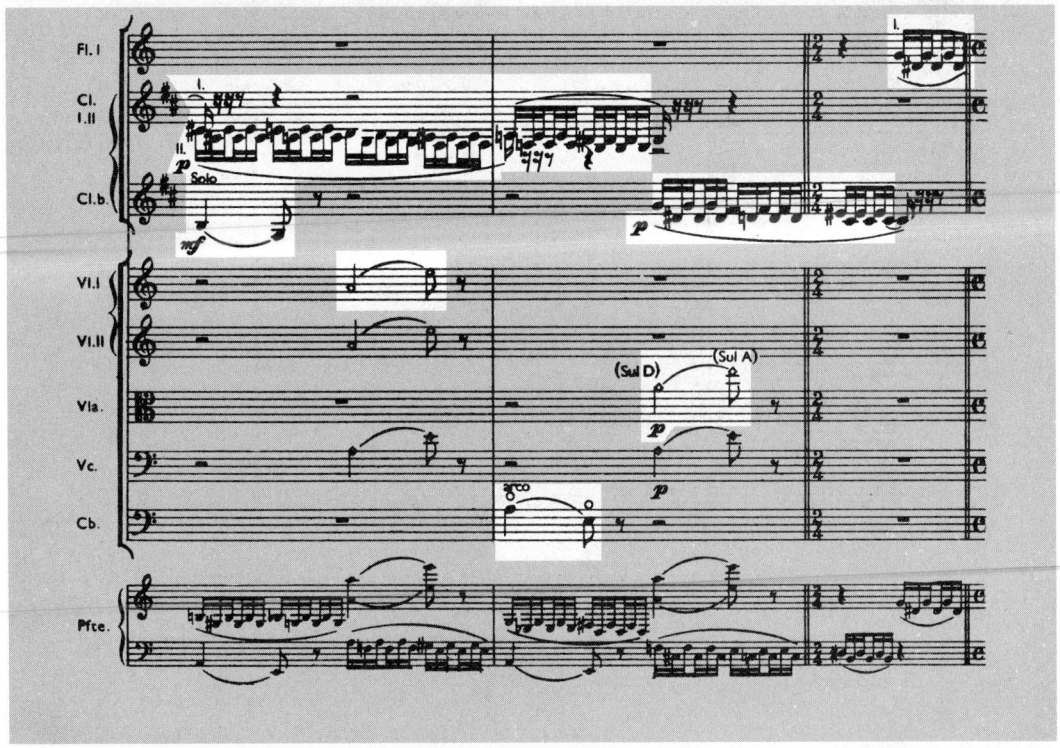
Fl. I
Cl. I.II
Cl.b.
Vl.I
Vl.II
Vla.
Vc.
Cb.
Pfte.
Solo
(Sul D)
(Sul A)

Fl. I
Fl. picc.
Tuba
Ptti.
(baguette d'éponge)
Xylo.
Cel.
Arpa
Si♭(B♮)
Ut♭(C♭)
Vl. I
div.
pizz.
unis.
Vl. II
con sord.
Vla.
Vc.
Cb.
m.d.
Pfte.
ten.
non legato

Fl. I
Fl. picc. II
Fl. picc. II. muta in Fl.
Tuba
Ptcl.
Xylo.
Cel.
Arpa
unis.
div.
Vl. I
Vl. II
Vla.
con sord.
Vc.
Cb.
m.d.
Pfce.
ten.
marcato

Fl. I.II
Fl. picc.
Ob. I.II
Cl. I.II
Cfg.
Xylo.
Vl.I
Vl.II
Vla.
Vc.
Cb.
Pfte.
f
unis.
senza sord.
mp
pizz.
mf
con sord.
arco
p

26
Allegro molto
Fl. I.II
Fl. picc.
Ob. I.II
Cl. I.II
Cl.b.
Fg. I.II
Cfg.
Cor.
Tuba
Gr.C.
Tam.T.
Xylo.
Vl.I
Vl.II
Vla.
Vc.
Cb.
Pfte.
a2
I.III.
II.IV.
senza sord.
pizz.
arco
con sord.
dimin.

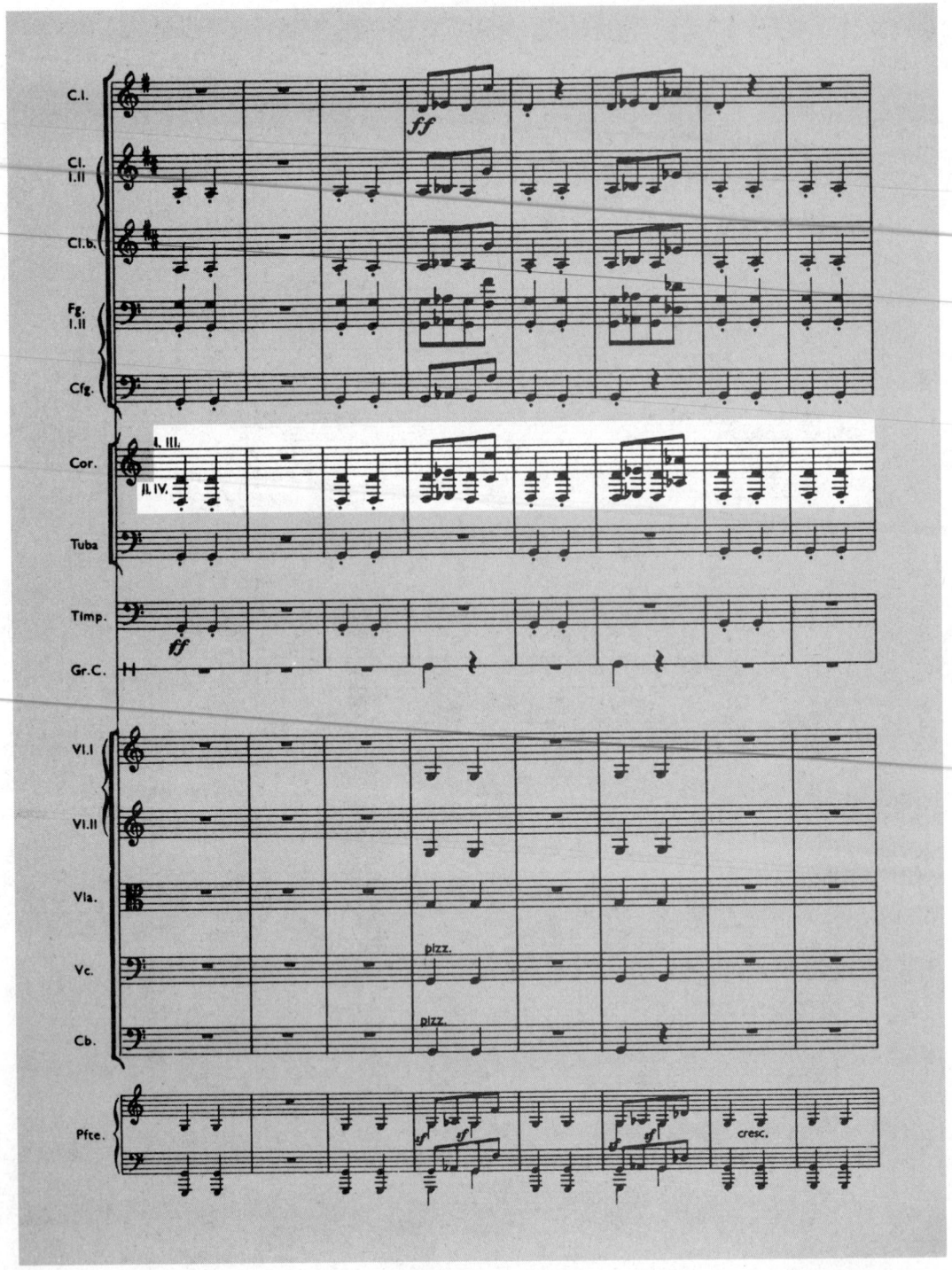
C.I.
ff
Cl. I.II
Cl.b.
Fg. I.II
Cfg.
Cor.
I. III.
II. IV.
Tuba
Timp.
ff
Gr.C.
VI.I
VI.II
Vla.
Vc.
pizz.
Cb.
pizz.
Pfte.
sf
sf
sf
sf
cresc.

Fl. I.II
Ob. I.II
C.I.
Cl. I.II
Cl.b
Fg. I.II
Cfg.
a 2
Cor.
I.III.
II.IV.
Trb. I.II
Trb.III Tuba
Gr.C.
Arpa
Solo (G)
Vl.I
Vl.II
div.
pizz.
arco
Via.
Vc. Cb.
Vc.
Pfte.

Ob I.II
C.I.
Cl. I.II
Cl.b.
Fg. I.II
Cfg.
I.II
Cor.
III.IV
Tr.
Trb. I.II
Trb.III
Tuba
Ptti.
Gr.C.
Vl.I
Vl.II
Vla.
Vc.
Cb.
Pfte.
a 2
unis.
arco
div.
pizz.

Fl. I.II
Ob. I.II
C.I.
Cl. I.II
Cl.b.
Fg. I.II
Cfg.
Cor.
Tr.
Trb. I.II
Trb.III Tuba
Ptti. Tamb.
Gr.C.
Arpa
VI.I
VI.II
Vla.
Vc.
Cb.
Pfte.
a 2
I.III. a 2
a 4
Tamb.
pizz.
arco

Fl. I.II
Fl. picc.
Ob. I.II
C.I.
Cl. I.II
Cl.b.
Fg. I.II
Cfg.
Cor.
Tr.
Trb. I.II
Timp.
Tamb. Ptcl.
Arpa
Vl.I
Vl.II
Vla.
Vc.
Cb.
Pfte.
(simile)
a2
a4
I.
I.II.
Ptcl.
Tamb.
Silk(B♭)
arco
pizz.
div.

Fl. I.II
Fl. picc.
Ob. I.II
C.I.
Cl. I.II
Cl.b.
Fg. I.II
Cfg.
Cor.
Tr.
Trb. I.II
Trb.III Tuba
Timp.
Trg. Tamb.
Pctl.
Arpa
Vl.I
Vl.II
Vla.
Vc. Cb.
Pfte.
a2
a4
I.II.
I.
ff
f
Trg.
Tamb.
Gr.C.
unis.
arco
div.
pizz.

Fl. I.II
Fl. picc.
Ob. I.II
C.I.
Cl. I.II
Cl.b.
Fg. I.II
Cfg.
Cor.
I.III.
II.IV.
Vl.I
Vl.II
Vla.
Vc.
Cb.
Pfte.
a2
pizz.
arco

Fl. I.II
a2
Ob. I.II
a2
C.I.
Cl. I.II
Cl.b.
a2
a2
a2
a2
Fg. I.II
Cfg.
(hauteur réelle)
I.III
II.IV
Cor.
Trb.III Tuba
VI.I
VI.II
Vla.
Vc.
Cb.
div.
Pfte.

Fl. I.II
Fl. picc.
Ob. I.II
C.I.
Cl. I.II
Cl.b.
Fg. I.II
Cfg.
Cor.
Tr.
Trb. I.II
Trb.III Tuba
Pcci. Gr.C.
Vl.I
Vl.II
Vla.
Vc.
Cb.
Pfte.
a2
gliss.
pizz.
Pcci.
Gr.C.

Ob. I.II
a2
CODA
C.I.
Cl. I.II
a2
Cl.b.
Fg. I.II
a2
Cfg.
ff
Pctl.
Vl.I
CODA
Vl.II
Vla.
Vc.
Cb.
Pfte.

Fl. I.II
Fl. picc.
Ob. I.II
C.I.
Cl. I.II
Cl.b.
Fg. I.II
Cfg.
Pctl.
Vl.I
Vl.II
Vla.
Vc.
Cb.
Pfte.
a2

Fl. I.II
Fl. picc.
Ob. I.II
C.I.
Cl. I.II
Cl.b.
Fg. I.II
Crec.
Tamb.
Ptti.
Vl.I
Vl.II
Vla.
Vc.
Cb.
Pfte.
a2
poco ritard.
attacca

10. *The Great Gate of Kiev*

Fl.
Ob.
Cl. I.II
Cl.b.
Fg. I.II
Cfg
I.II Cor. III.IV
Tr.
Trb. I.II
Trb.III Tuba
Timp.
Gr.C.
Vl.I
Vl.II
Vla.
Vc. Cb
Pfte.

Fl.
Ob.
Cl.I.II
Cl.b.
Fg.
I.II
Cfg.
I.II
Cor.
III.IV
Tr.
Trb.
I.II
Trb.III
Tuba
Timp.
Ptci.
Gr.C.
Vl.I
Vl.II
Vla.
Vc.
Cb.
Pfte.
a3
I.III.
II.
III.
a2
div.
unis.
cresc.

28
43
Fl.
Flauto III. Muta in Flauto piccolo
Ob.
Oboe III. Muta in Corno Inglese
Cl. I.II
Cl.b.
Fg. I.II
Cfg.
(senza espressione)
(senza espressione)
I.II Cor. III.IV
Tr.
Trb. I.II
Trb.III Tuba
Timp.
Ptcl. Gr.C.
Ptcl.
Gr. C.
Vl.I
Vl.II
Vla.
Vc.
Cb.
div.
Pfte.
(senza espressione)

29
44
Fl. I.II
Fl. picc.
Ob. I.II
Cl. I.II
Fg. I.II
Cfg.
I.II Cor. III.IV
Trb.III Tuba
Timp.
Arpa I
Arpa II
VI.I
VI.II
Vla.
Vc.
Cb.
Pfte.
a 2
unis.
dimin.
energico.

Fl. I.II
muta in Fl. grande
Fl. picc.
Ob. I.II
C.I.
Cl. I.II
a2
Cl.b.
Fg. I.II
Cfg.
I.II
Cor. III.IV
Trb.III Tuba
Timp.
Gr.C.
Arpa I
Arpa II
Vl.I
Vl.II
Vla.
Vc.
div.
unis.
Cb.
Pfte.

Fl.
Ob. I.II
C.I.
Cl. I.II
Cl.b.
Fg. I.II
Cfg.
I.II Cor.
III.IV
Tr.
Trb. I.II
Trb.III Tuba
Timp.
Pttl. Gr.C.
Arpa I.II
Vl.I
Vl.II
Vla.
Vc.
Cb.
Pfte.
a2
Gr.C.
Pttl.
8va bassa
Sul G (Sol)
unis.
div.

Fl.
Ob. I.II
Cl. I.II
Cl.b.
Fg. I.II
Cfg.
I.II Cor.
III.IV
Tr.
Trb. I.II
Trb.III Tuba
Timp.
Ptti. Gr.C.
Arpa I.II
8va bassa
Vl.I
Vl.II
Vla.
Vc.
Cb.
Pfte.
a3
a2
I.III
II.
Tuba
Gr.C.
Ptti.
Sul G (Sol)
div.
unis
unis.

30
45
Fl.
Ob. I.II
C.I.
Cl. I.II
Cl.b.
Fg. I.II
Cfg.
Cor.
Tr.
Trb. I.II
Trb.III Tuba
Timp.
Arpa I.II
Vl.I
Vl.II
Vla.
Vc.
Cb.
Pfte.
a3
a2
muta in Oboe
p senza espress
a4
unis
ff
senza espr.

31
46
Fl.
III, muta in Fl. piccolo
Cl. I.II
Cl.b.
Fg. I.II
I.II
Cor.
III.IV
Tuba
Ptcl.
Tam.T.
Ptcl.
T.Tam.
vibr.
vibr.
Camp.
Arpa
Vl.I
Vl.II
Vla.
pizz.
pizz.
Vc.
Cb.
pizz
Pfte.
dimin.

Cl.b.
I.II
Cor.
III.IV
Tuba
Pcl.
Tam.T.
Camp.
Arpa I
VI.I
VI.II
div.
p
arco
Vla.
div.
p
arco
Vc.
div.
p
Cb.
Pfte.

Fl. I.II
Fl. picc.
Ob.
Cl. I.II
Cl.b
Fg. I.II
cresc.
a2
I.II
Cor.
III.IV
Trb. I.II
Trb.III Tuba
Tuba
3° Trb.
Timp.
Ptti. Tam.T.
Ptti.
Tam.T.
Camp.
Arpa I
div
Vl.I
Vl.II
Vla.
arco
pizz.
Vc.
Cb.
Pfte.

32
47
Fl. I.II
Fl. picc.
Muta in Flauto Grande
Ob.
Cl. I.II
Cl.b.
Fg. I.II
Cfg.
I.II Cor.
III.IV
Tr.
Trb. I.II
Trb.III Tuba
Timp.
Pcti. Tam.T.
Tam.T.
Pcti.
Camp.
Arpa I
Arpa II
gliss.
div. in 3
pizz.
Vl.I
Vl.II
Vla.
div.
Vc.
unis.
Cb.
Pfte.

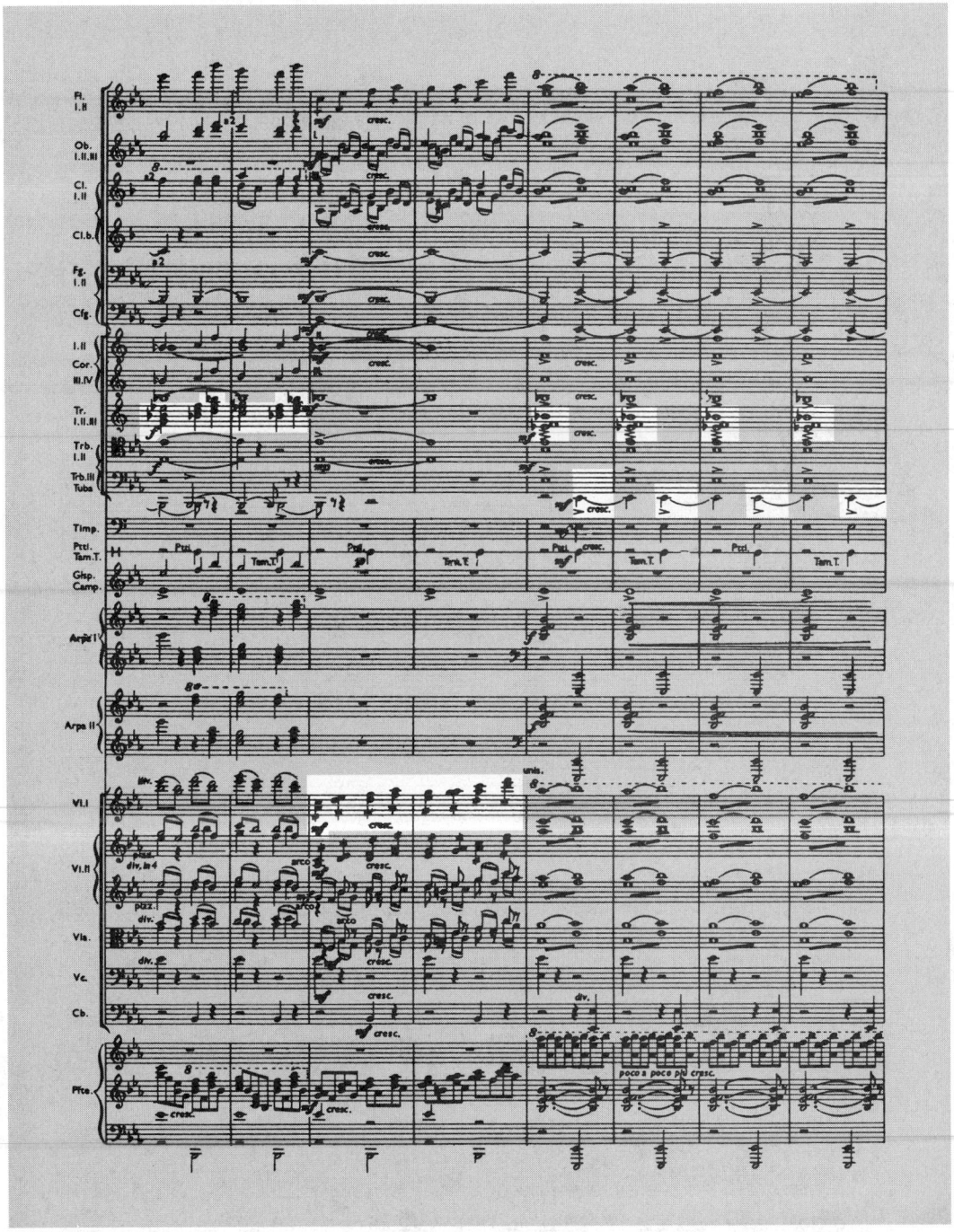
Fl. I.II
Ob. I.II.III
Cl. I.II
Cl.b.
Fg. I.II
Cfg.
Cor. I.II
Cor. III.IV
Tr. I.II.III
Trb. I.II
Trb. III Tuba
Timp.
Perc. Tam.T.
Glsp. Camp.
Arpa I
Arpa II
Vl.I
Vl.II
Vla.
Vc.
Cb.
Pfte.
cresc.
poco a poco più cresc.

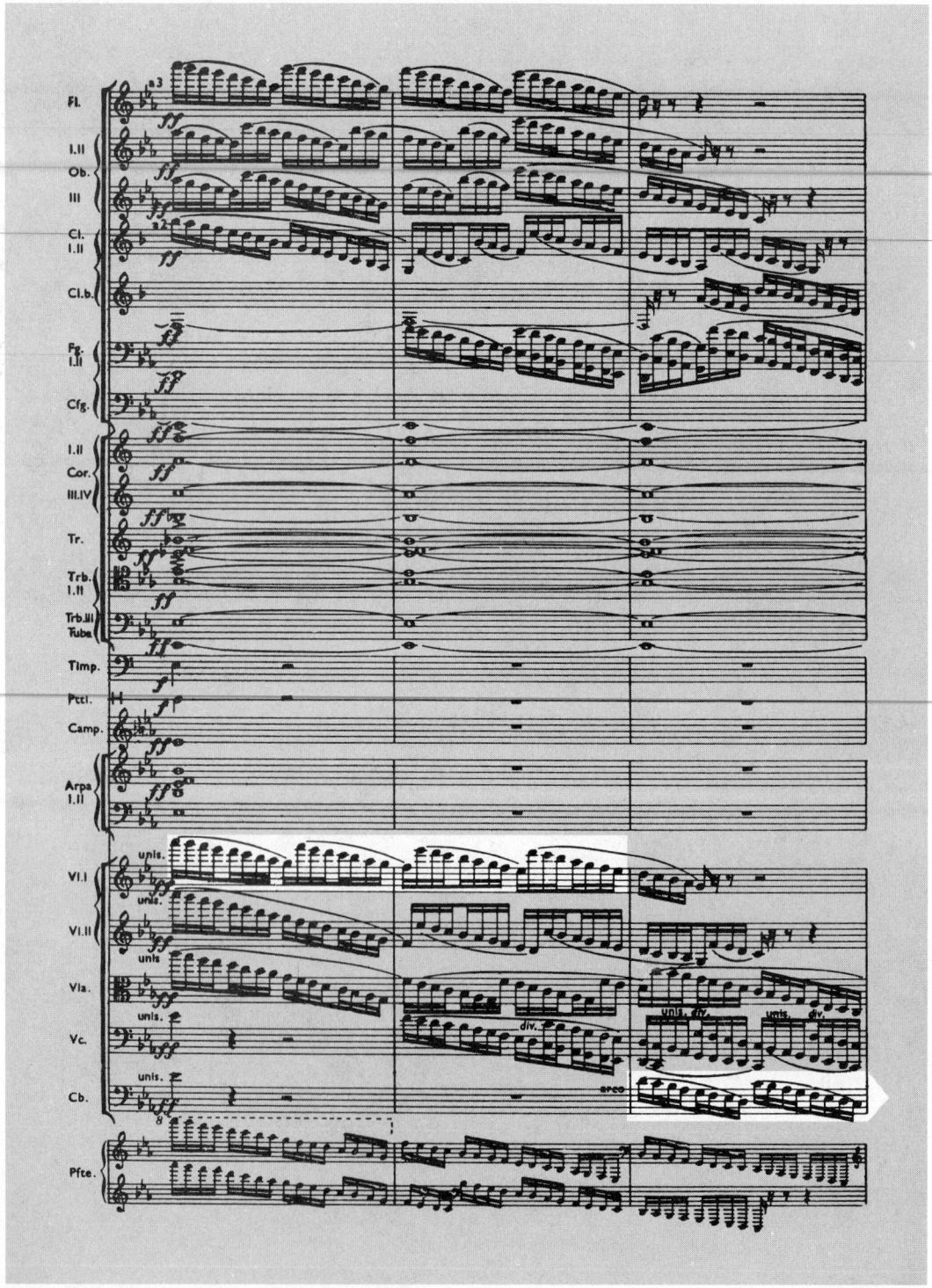
Fl.
I.II
Ob.
III
Cl.
I.II
Cl.b.
Fg.
I.II
Cfg.
I.II
Cor.
III.IV
Tr.
Trb.
I.II
Trb.III
Tuba
Timp.
Pctl.
Camp.
Arpa
I.II
Vl.I
Vl.II
Vla.
Vc.
Cb.
Pfte.
unis.
div.
arco

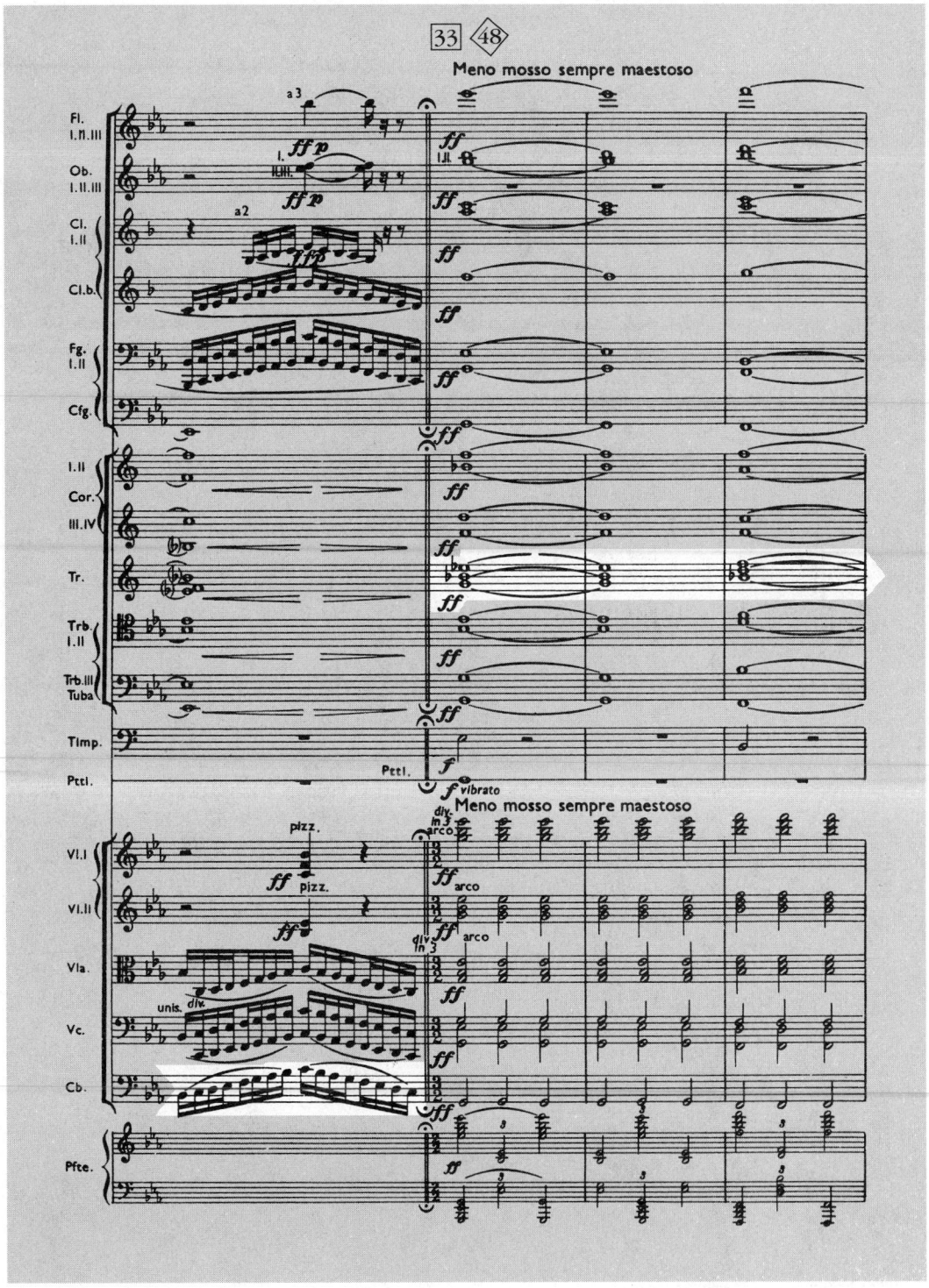
33
48
Meno mosso sempre maestoso
Fl.
I.II.III
Ob.
I.II.III
Cl.
I.II
Cl.b.
Fg.
I.II
Cfg.
I.II
Cor.
III.IV
Tr.
Trb.
I.II
Trb.III
Tuba
Timp.
Pttl.
Pttl.
vibrato
Meno mosso sempre maestoso
Vl.I
Vl.II
Vla.
Vc.
Cb.
Pfte.
a 3
a 2
pizz.
arco
div.
unis.

Fl. I.II.III
Ob. I.II.III
Cl. I.II
Cl.b.
Fg. I.II
Cfg.
I.II Cor.
III.IV
Tr.
Trb. I.II
Trb.III Tuba
Timp.
Pctl. Gr.C
Vl.I
Vl.II
Vla.
Vc.
Cb.
Pfte.
a2
a3
ff
Gr.C.
Pctl
unis.
div.

Fl. I.II.III
Ob. I.II.III
Cl. I.II
Cl.b.
Fg. I.II
Cfg.
I.II Cor. III.IV
Tr.
Trb. I.II
Trb.III Tuba
Timp.
Pcci. Gr.C.
Gr.C.
Pcci.
Vl.I
Vl.II
Vla.
Vc.
Cb.
Pfte.
a3
a2
unis.
div.

Fl. I.II.III
Ob. I.II.III
Cl. I.II
Cl.b.
Fg. I.II
Cfg.
I.II Cor. III.IV
Tr.
Trb. I.II.
Trb.III Tuba
Timp.
Perc.
Vl.I
Vl.II
Vla.
Vc.
Cb.
Pfte.
mf
div.
unis.

I.II
Fl.
III
Ob.
I.II
Cl.
I.II
Cl.b.
Fg.
I.II
I.II
Cor.
III.IV
VI.I
VI.II
Vla.
Vc.
Cb.
Pfte.
cresc.
mf
II.
III.
unis.

Fl.
I.II
Ob.
I.II
Cl.
I.II
Cl.b.
Fg.
I.II
Cfg.
I.II
Cor.
III.IV
VI.I
VI.II
Vla.
Vc.
Cb.
Pfte.
cresc.

I.II
Fl.
III
Ob.
I.II.III
Cl.
I.II
Cl.b.
Fg.
Cfg.
I.II
Cor.
III.IV
Tr.
Trb.
I.II
Trb.III
Tuba
Timp.
Vl.I
Vl.II
Vla.
Vc.
Cb.
Pfte.
cresc.
cresc. sempre
a2
div.
in 3

Poco a poco rallentando
a2
I.II
Fl.
III
I.II
Ob.
III
Cl.
I.II
Cl.b.
Fg.
I.II
Cfg.
I.II
Cor.
III.IV
Tr.
Trb.
I.II
Trb.III
Tuba
Timp.
Pctl.
Gr.C.
Pctl.
Gr.C.
Pctl.
Gr.C.
Poco a poco rallentando
in 2
unis.
div.
VI.I
VI.II
Vla.
Vc.
Cb.
Poco a poco rall.
Pfte.

Fl. I.II.III
Ob. I.II.III
Cl. I.II
Cl.b.
Fg. I.II
Cfg.
I.II Cor. III.IV
Tr.
Trb. I.II
Trb.III Tuba
Timp.
Trg.
Ptti.
Gr.C.
Tam.T.
Camp.
Arpa I.II
Vl.I
Vl.II
Vla.
Vc.
Cb.
Pfte.
vibrato
div.
unis.

Fl. I.II.III.
Ob. I.II.III
Cl. I.II
Cl.b.
Fg. I.II
Cfg.
I.II
Cor. III.IV
Tr.
Trb. I.II
Trb.III Tuba
Timp.
Trg.
Pcti.
Gr.C. Tam.T.
Camp.
Arpa I.II
Vl.I
Vl.II
Vla.
Vc.
Cb.
Pfte.
avec baguette
Tam.T.
Gr.C.

16. Peter Ilyich Tchaikovsky (1840–1893)

The Nutcracker, Three Dances from Act II (1892)

8:6B/3-5 8:6/34 - 42

March

Fl.
Gr. Fl.
Ob.
Cl.
Fg.
Cor. (F)
Trbe. (A)
Tbni. Tuba
Piat.
Mit Paukenschlägel.
Vl.
Vle.
Celli
C.-B.
pizz.
pizz.

10
Fl.
Ob.
Cl.
Fg.
Cor. (F)
Trbe. (A)
Tbni. Tuba
Piat.
Vl.
Vle.
Celli
C.-B.
pizz.
pizz.

Fl.
Ob.
Cl.
Fg.
Cor. (F)
Trbe. (A)
Tbni. Tuba
Piat.
Vl.
Vle.
Celli
C.-B.
cre - - - scen - - - do
Mit Paukenschlägel.

20
Fl.
Ob.
Cl.
Fg.
Cor. (F)
Trbe. (A)
Tbni. Tuba
Piat.
Vl.
Vle.
Celli
C.-B.
pizz.
pizz.
arco
arco
arco

Fl.
Ob.
Cl.
Fg.
Cor. (F)
Trbe. (A)
Tbni. Tuba
Piat.
Vl.
Vle.
Celli
C.-B.

30
Fl.
Ob.
Cl.
Fg.
Cor. (F)
Trbe. (A)
Tbni. Tuba
Piat.
Vl.
Vle.
Celli
C.-B.
pizz.
pizz.

Fl.
Ob.
Cl.
Fg.
Cor. (F)
Trbe. (A)
Tbni.
Tuba
Mit Paukenschlägel.
Piat.
Vl.
Vle.
Celli
C.-B.

40
Fl.
Ob.
Cl.
pp
cre - - scen - - do
f
Fg.
Cor. (F)
Trbe. (A)
Tbni. Tuba
Piat.
Mit Paukenschlägel.
Vl.
Vle.
pizz.
Celli
C.-B.
p

35
Fl.
Ob.
Cl.
Fg.
Cor. (F)
Trbe. (A)
Tbni. Tuba
Piat.
Vl.
Vle.
Celli
C.-B.
mf
marcato
arco

Fl.
Ob.
Cl.
Fg.
Cor. (F)
Trbe. (A)
Tbni. Tuba
Piat.
Vl.
Vle.
Celli
C.-B.

36
Fl.
Ob.
Cl.
Fg.
marcato
marcato
Cor. (F)
Trbe. (A)
Tbni. Tuba
Piat.
Vl.
Vle.
Celli
C.-B.

50
Fl.
Ob.
Cl.
Fg.
Cor. (F)
Trbe. (A)
Tbni. Tuba
Piat.
Vl.
Vle.
Celli
C.-B.

Fl.
Ob.
Cl.
Fg.
Cor. (F)
Trbe. (A)
Tbni. Tuba
Piat.
Vl.
Vle.
Celli
C.-B.
mf
cresc.
pizz.

Fl.
Ob.
Cl.
Fg.
Cor. (F)
Trbe. (A)
Tbni. Tuba
Mit Paukenschlägel.
Piat.
Vl.
Vle.
arco
Celli
arco
C.-B.

60
Fl.
Ob.
Cl.
Fg.
Cor. (F)
Trbe. (A)
Tbni. Tuba
Piat.
Vl.
Vle.
Celli
C.-B.
pizz.
pizz.

Fl.
Ob.
Cl.
Fg.
Cor. (F)
Trbe. (A)
Tbni. Tuba
Piat.
Vl.
Vle.
Celli
C.-B.
mf cresc.
cresc.
Mit Paukenschlägel.

Fl.
Ob.
Cl.
Fg.
Cor. (F)
Trbe. (A)
Tbni. Tuba
Piat.
Vl.
Vle.
Celli
C.-B.
mf
f
pizz.

70
Fl.
Ob.
Cl.
Fg.
Cor. (F)
Trbe. (A)
Tbni. Tuba
Piat.
Vl.
Vle.
Celli
C.-B.
arco
arco
arco

Fl.
Ob.
Cl.
Fg.
Cor. (F)
Trbe. (A)
Tbni. Tuba
Piat.
Vl.
Vle.
Celli
C.-B.

Fl.
Ob.
Cl.
Fg.
Cor. (F)
Trbe. (A)
Tbni. Tuba
Piat.
Vl.
Vle.
Celli
C.-B.
mf
cresc.
pizz.

80
Fl.
Ob.
Cl.
Fg.
Cor. (F)
Trbe. (A)
Tbni.
Tuba
Mit Paukenschlägel.
Piat.
Vl.
Vle.
Celli
C.-B.
arco
arco

Fl.
Ob.
Cl.
Fg.
Cor. (F)
Trbe. (A)
Tbni. Tuba
Piat.
Vl.
Vle.
Celli
C.-B.
pizz.
pizz.

Fl.
Ob.
Cl.
Fg.
Cor. (F)
Trbe. (A)
Tbni. Tuba
Piat.
Vl.
Vle.
Celli
C.-B.
mf cresc.
cresc.
f
ff
Mit Paukenschlägel.
arco

Dance of the Sugar Plum Fairy

Cl.b.
10
mf
fp
Cel.
f
Vl.
Vle.
Celli
C.-B.
Cl.
Cl.b.
I.
p
pp
Cel.
mf
Vl.
Vle.
Celli
C.-B.

20
Fl.
Ob.
C.Ingl.
Cl.
Cl.b.
Fg.
Cor. (F)
Cel.
div.
Vl.
Vle.
Celli
C.-B.
arco
arco
arco
arco

38
Fl.
Ob.
C.Ingl.
Cl.
Cl. b.
Fg.
Cor. (F)
Cel.
Vl.
Vle.
Celli
C.-B.
arco

Fl.
Ob.
C.Ingl.
Cl.
Cl.b.
Fg.
Cor. (F)
Cel.
Vl.
Vle.
Celli
C.-B.

30
Fl.
Ob.
Clngl.
Cl.
Cl.b.
Fg.
Cor. (F)
Cel.
Vl.
Vle.
Celli
C.-B.

Cel.
Cel.
39
Fl.
Fg.
Cel.
Vl.
Vle.
Celli
C.-B.
pp a punto d'arco
pp a punto d'arco
pp a punto d'arco
pp a punto d'arco

40
I.
Cl.
Cel.
Vl.
Vle.
Celli
C.-B.
p
mf
pp
cresc.
ff
f

50.
Fl.
Ob.
C.Ingl.
Cl.
Cl. b.
Fg.
Cor. (F)
Cel.
Vl.
div.
Vle.
Celli
C.-B.
pizz.

Trepak (Russian Dance)

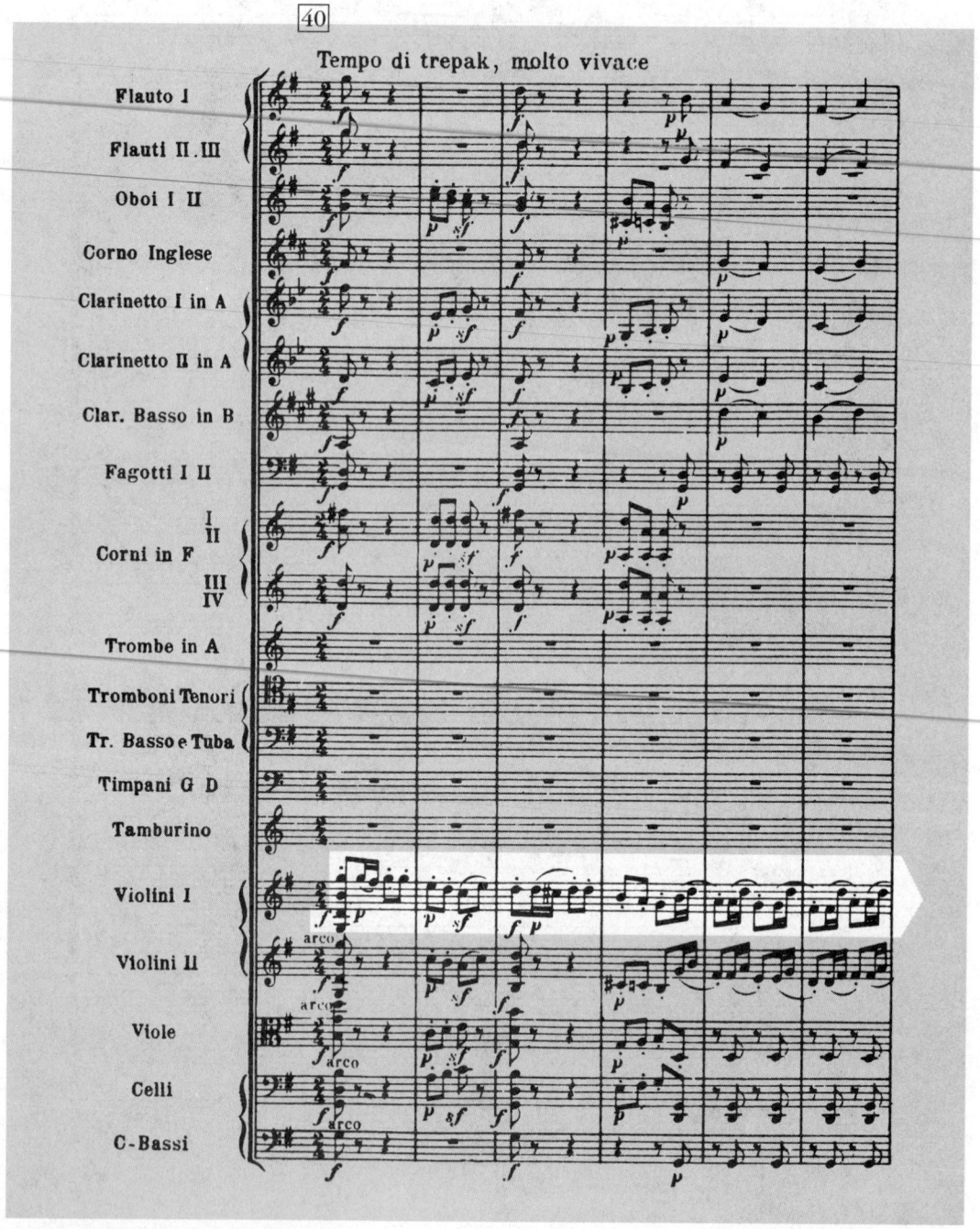

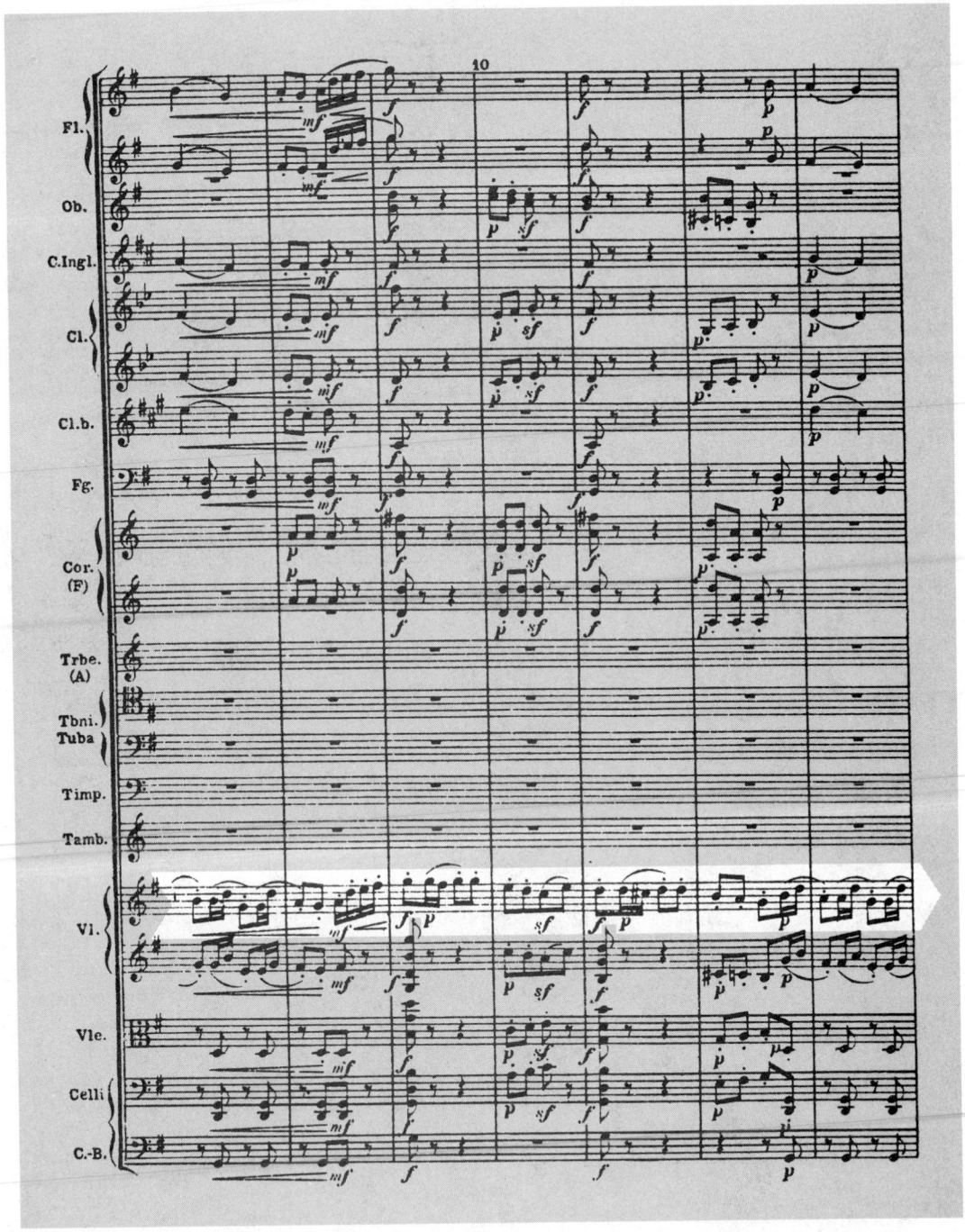
10
Fl.
Ob.
C.Ingl.
Cl.
Cl.b.
Fg.
Cor. (F)
Trbe. (A)
Tbni.
Tuba
Timp.
Tamb.
Vl.
Vle.
Celli
C.-B.

20
Fl.
Ob.
C.Ingl.
Cl.
Cl.b.
Fg.
Còr. (F)
Trbe. (A)
Tbni.
Tuba
Timp.
Tamb.
Vl.
Vle.
Celli
C.-B.

Fl.
Ob.
C.Ingl.
Cl.
Cl.b.
Fg.
Cor. (F)
Trbe. (A)
Tbni. Tuba
Timp.
Tamb.
Vl.
Vle.
Celli
C.-B.

41
30
Fl.
Cb.
C.Ingl.
Cl.
Cl.b.
Fg.
Cor. (F)
Trbe. (A)
Tbni.
Tuba
Timp.
Tamb.
Vl.
Vle.
Celli
C.-B.

Fl.
sempre staccato
sempre staccato
Ob.
C.Ingl.
Cl.
Cl.b.
Fg.
Cor. (F)
mf
mf
mf
Trbe. (A)
Tbni. Tuba
mf
Timp.
Tamb.
Vl.
Vle.
cresc.
Celli
cresc.
C.-B.
cresc.

40
Fl.
a 2.
Ob.
C.Ingl.
Cl.
Cl. b.
Fg.
Cor. (F)
Trbe. (A)
Tbni. Tuba
Timp.
Tamb.
Vl.
sempre ff
Vle.
Celli
C.-B.

50
a 2.
Fl.
Ob.
C.Ingl.
Cl.
Cl.b.
Fg.
Cor. (F)
Trbe. (A)
Tbni.
Tuba
Timp.
Tamb.
Vl.
Vle.
Celli
C.-B.

Fl.
Ob.
Ingl.
Cl.
Cl.b.
Fg.
Cor. (F)
Trbe. (A)
Tbni. Tuba
Timp.
Tamb.
Vl.
Vle.
Celli
C.-B.

42
60
Fl.
Ob.
C.Ingl.
Cl.
Cl.b.
Fg.
a 2.
Cor. (F)
Trbe. (A)
Tbni.
Tuba
Timp.
Tamb.
Vl.
Vle.
Celli
C.-B.

Fl.
Ob.
C.Ingl.
Cl.
Cl.b.
Fg.
Cor. (F)
Trbe. (A)
Tbni.
Tuba
Timp.
Tamb.
Vl.
Vle.
Celli
C.-B.

70
stringendo
Fl.
Ob.
C.Ingl.
Cl.
Cl.b.
Fg.
Cor. (F)
Trbe. (A)
Tbni.
Tuba
Timp.
Tamb.
Vl.
Vle.
Celli
C.-B.
sempre fff

Fl.
Ob.
C.Ingl.
Cl.
Cl.b.
Fg.
Cor. (F)
Trbe. (A)
Tbni. Tuba
Timp.
Tamb.
Vl.
Vle.
Celli
C.-B.

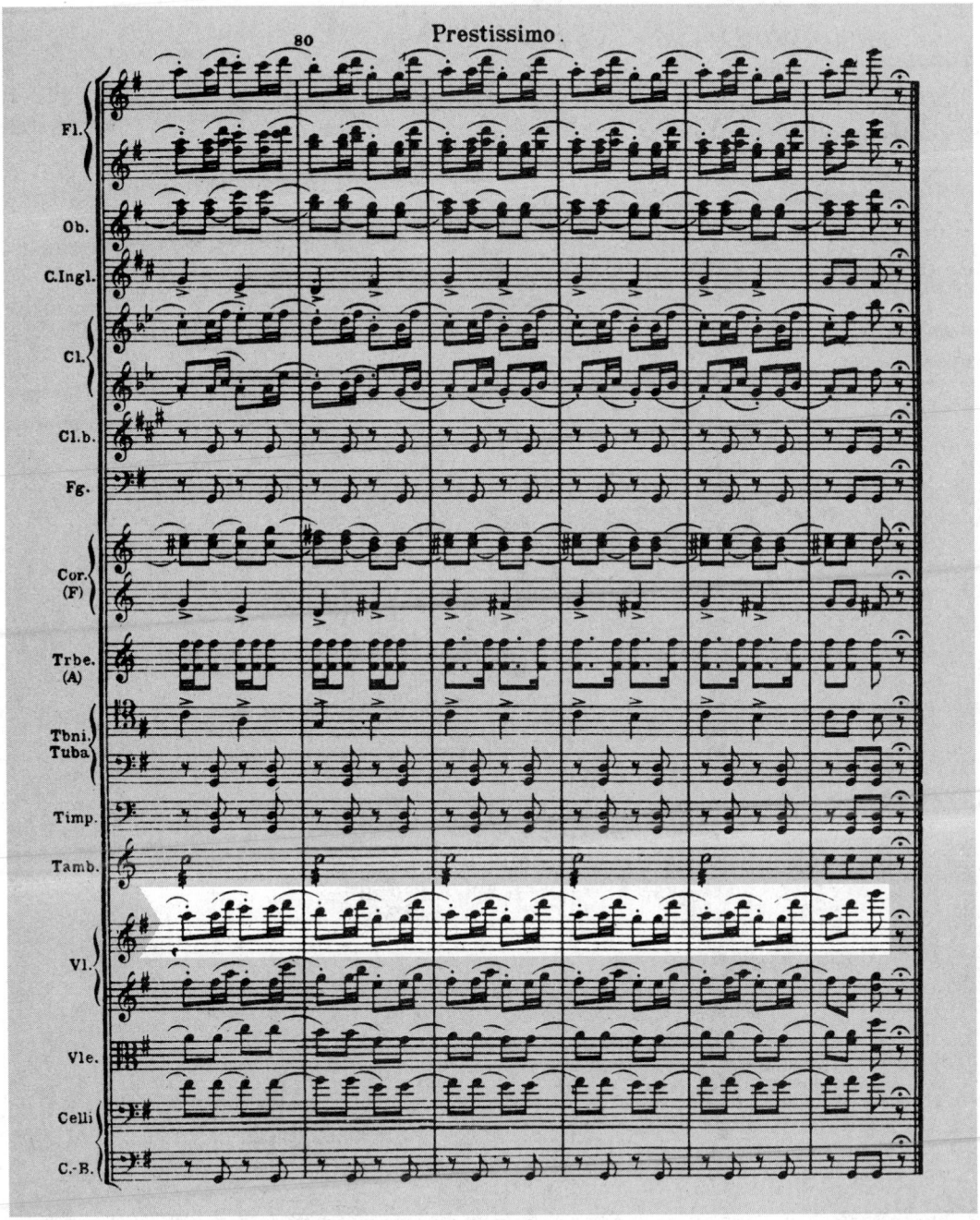
80
Prestissimo.
Fl.
Ob.
C.Ingl.
Cl.
Cl.b.
Fg.
Cor. (F)
Trbe. (A)
Tbni. Tuba
Timp.
Tamb.
Vl.
Vle.
Celli
C.-B.

17. Antonín Dvořák (1841–1904)

Symphony No. 9 in E minor,
From the New World,
Second Movement (1893)

8:6B/6 8:6/43 - 45

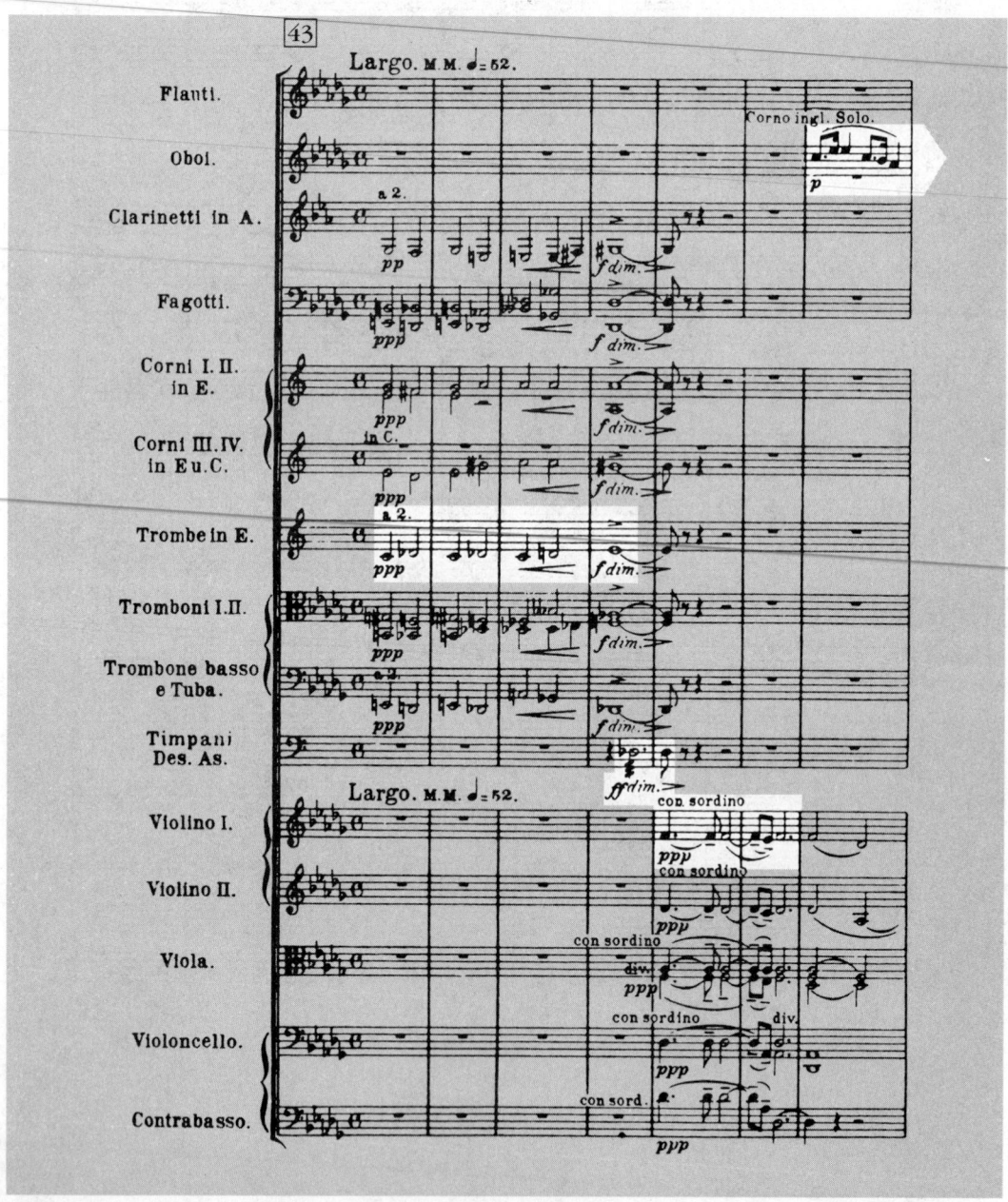

Cor. ingl.
Cl. in B
Vl. I
Vl. II
Vla.
Vc.
Cb.
in B
a 2
Fl.
Cor. ingl.
Cl. in B
Fg.
Cor. III in E
in E.
molto cresc.
Vl. I
Vl. II
Vla.
Vc.
Cb.

Fl.
Ob.
Ob. II.
I.
Cl. in B
Fg.
I. II.
Cor. in E
III. IV.
Trbe. in E
Trbni. I. II
Tromb.
Trbne. basso
Timp. Des. As
Vl. I
Vl. II
Vla.
Vc.
Cb.
cresc.
pp
fz
ff
p
ppp

Vl.I
Vl.II
Vla.
Vc.
Cb.
cresc.
dim.
p
pp
Cor. ingl.
Cl. in B
Fg.
f
ppp
fz
div.

44
Un poco più mosso.
Fl.
Ob.
Cor. I, II in E
con sordini
senza sord.
Vl. I
Vl. II
Vla.
Vc.
Cb.
pp
p
dim.
ppp
cresc.
f
mf

poco ritard.
Poco meno mosso.
Fl.
Ob.
Cl. in A
in A
Fg.
a 2.
Vl. I.
Vl. II.
molto cresc.
div.
Vla.
dim.
Vc.
Cb.
pizz.
a 2.

Fl.
Ob.
Cl. in A
Vl. I
Vl. II
Vla.
Vc.
Cb.
p
fz
pp
pizz.
cresc.
mf
dim.

3
Poco più mosso.
Fl.
Ob.
a 2.
Cl. in A
pp
cresc
f
Poco più mosso.
Vl. I
Vl. II
arco
pp
cresc.
f
dim.
Vla.
Vc.
Cb.
3

Fl.
Ob.
Cl. in A
dim.
p
f
cresc.
Vl. I
Vl. II
Vla.
Vc.
Cb.
pp
cresc.

Fl.
Ob.
Cl. in A
Vl. I
Vl. II
Vla.
Vc.
Cb.
fz
cresc.
f
ff
mf
dim.
fp

Cl. in A
Meno.
pp
Vl. I
Vl. II
Vla.
Vc.
Cb.
dim.
Meno.
sul G
pizz.
ppp
arco
tremolo

Cl. in A
Vl. I
Vl. II
Vla.
Vc.
Cb.
cresc.
cresc.
cresc.
cresc.

Cl. in A
mf
dim.
p
Vl. I
mf
dim.
pp
pp
Vl. II
arco
mf
dim.
pp
pp
Vla.
dim.
pp
pp
Vc.
dim.
pp
pp
Cb.
pp

Ob.
Vl.I
Vl.II
Vla.
Vc.
Cb.
p
dim.
Fl.
a 2.
Cl.in A
p leggiero
cresc.
pp cresc.

Fl.
Ob.
Cl. in A
Fg.
I.II.
Cor. in E
III.IV.
Trbe. in E
Trbni. I.II
Trbne. basso
Timp. Des. As
Vl. I
Vl. II
Vla.
Vc.
Cb.
a 2.
cresc.
mf
p
f

Fl.
Ob.
Cl. in A
Fg.
I. II. in E
Corni
III. IV. in C
in C
Trbe. in C
in C
cresc.
a 2.
Trbni. I. II
Trbne. basso
Timp.. Des. As (Cis)
Vl. I
Vl. II
Vla.
Vc.
Cb.
cresc.

Fl.
Ob.
Cl. in A
Fg.
I. II. in E
Corni
III. IV. in C
Trbe. in C
Trbni. I. II
Trbne.
basso
Timp.
Des. As
(Cis)
Vl. I
Vl. II
Vla.
Vc.
Cb.
a 2.
ff
dim.
mf
f
p
mp

45
rit.
5
Meno mosso, Tempo I. ♩= 52.
Fl.
Solo Corno inglese.
p
dimin. pp
Cb.
Cl. in A
in B.
Fg.
I. II. in E
Corni
III. IV. in C
Trbe. in C
pp
pp
Trbni. I. II
Trbne. basso
Timp.
Des. As
(Cis)
ppp
rit.
Meno mosso, Tempo I. ♩= 52.
Vl. I
p
4 Violini.
pp
Vl. II
p
4 Violini.
pp
Vla.
p
4 Viole.
pp
div.
Vc.
p
4 Celli.
pp
Cb.
p
pp
5

Cor. ingl.
sempre più diminuendo
Vl. I
2 Violini con sordini.
Solo.
pp
Vl. II
2 Violini con sordini.
Vla.
2 Viole con sordini.
Solo.
pp
Vc.
2 Celli.
pp
Solo.
pp
Cb.
2 Bassi.
pp. sempre più diminuendo

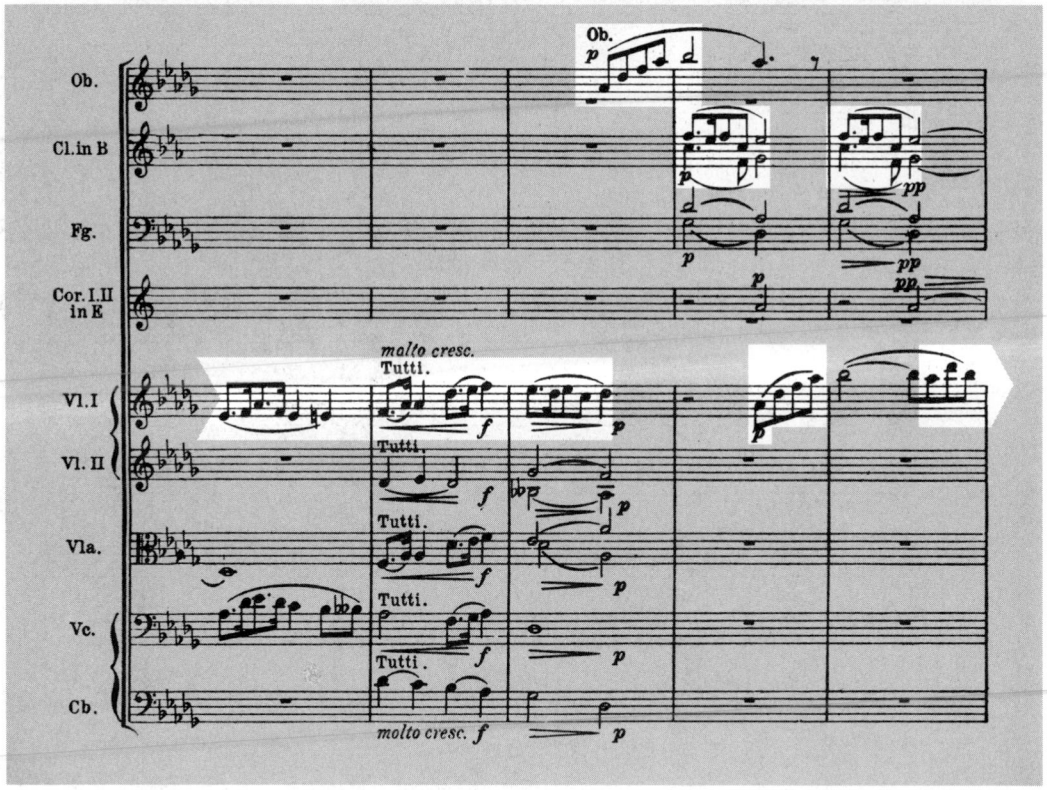
Ob.
p
Cl. in B
p
pp
Fg.
p
pp
Cor. I. II in E
p
pp
Vl. I
malto cresc.
Tutti.
f
p
p
Vl. II
Tutti.
f
p
Vla.
Tutti.
f
p
Vc.
Tutti.
f
p
Cb.
Tutti.
molto cresc. f
p

ritard.
in tempo
Fl.
Ob.
Cl. in B
Fg.
pp
I. II.
Cor. in E
III. IV.
in E.
a 2.
pp
Trbe. in C
Trbni. I. II
pp
Trbne. basso e Tuba
a 2.
pp
Timp. Des. As
ritard.
in tempo
Vl. I
dimin.
pp
dim.
ppp
Vl. II
Vla.
Vc.
Cb.

ritard. Molto Adagio.
Fl.
Ob.
Cl. in B
Fg.
I. II.
Cor. in E
III. IV.
Trbe. in C
Trbni. I. II
Trbne. basso e Tuba
Timp. Des. As
Vl. I
Vl. II
Vla.
Vc.
Cb.
pp
p dim.
f
p
tr
fz
dim.
ppp
mf
div.

18. Ruggero Leoncavallo (1857–1919)

Pagliacci, Act I, Canio's Aria (1892)

8:6B/7 | 8:6/46 - 47 | MW
3:2B/6 | 3:2/56 - 57

English translation by Ruth and Thomas Martin. Copyright © 1960 (renewed) G. Schirmer, Inc. (ASCAP). All rights reserved. Reprinted by permission.

string. un poco
(angrily)
C.
d'uo - po... sfor - za - ti! Bah! sei tu for-se un uom?
have to force my - self! Bah, can't you be a man?
col canto
precipitato
(laughing bitterly)
Ah!Ah!Ah!Ah! Ah!
rit.
(taking his head in his hands in despair)
C.
Tu se' Pa - gliaccio!
You're a Co - me - dian!
pp
K. dr.
47
57
Arioso
Adagio (♩= 46)
declamando con dolore
C.
Ve - sti la giub - ba e la fac - cia in - fa - ri - na. La gen - te
On with your cos - tume, and your face bright - ly pain - ted. Your pub - lic

portando
C.
pa - ga e ri - der vuo - le qua. E se Ar-lec - chin t'in -
pays you, and they must be a - mused. Though Co - lum - bine and
violento
Opp.
vo - la Co - lom - bi - na, ri - di, Pa - gliac-cio... e o - gnun ap-plau-di -
Har - le - quin be - tray you, Laugh, clown, be mer - ry and they will all ap -
poco rit.
a tempo
rà! Tra - mu - ta in laz - zi lo spa - smo ed il pian - to;
plaud! You must trans - form your des - pair in - to laugh - ter;
col canto
a tempo

affrett.
cresc.
rit.
C.
in u - na smor-fia il sin - ghiozzo e'l do - lor... Ah!
And make a jest of your sob-bing, of your pain... Ah!
col canto
cresc.
poco rit.
a piena voce, straziante
Ri - di, Pa - gliac - cio, sul tuo a - mo - re in -
Laugh and a - muse them, though your love has be -
f molto rit.
con grande espressione
(sobbing)
fran - to! Ri - di del duol che t'av - ve - le - na il
trayed you! Laugh, through the tor - ment that em - bit - ters your
cedendo
(moves slowly towards the theatre, weeping; reaching the curtain which opens on the
cor!
heart!
Lo stesso movimento
cantabile con molta espressione
mf sonoro
r.h.

stage, he pushes it roughly, as if not wishing to enter; then, seized by a new
cresc. sempre
fit of sobbing, he again buries his face in his
f
poco rit. con dolore
p
(The curtain begins to fall slowly)
hands; takes three or four steps towards the curtain, from which he had
rianimando
recoiled in fury, and [on these chords] enters and disappears)
rit. ed accentato molto
marcato il canto
r.h.
End of Act I

19. Gustav Mahler (1860–1911)

8:6B/8 8:6/48 - 50

Das Lied von der Erde (The Song of the Earth), Third Movement (1908-9)

3. "Von der Jugend" ("Of Youth")

Copyright 1912 by Universal Edition A.G., Vienna. Copyright renewed, assigned 1952 to Universal Edition (London) Ltd., London. © This edition, revised by the Internationale Gustav-Mahler-Gesellschaft, copyright 1962 by Universal Edition (London) Ltd., London. © renewed. All rights reserved. Used by permission of European American Music Distributors Corporation, sole U.S. and Canadian agent for Universal Edition A.G., Vienna, and Universal Edition (London) Ltd., London.

kl. Fl.
1.2. Fl.
1. Ob.
2. Ob.
1. Kl. in B
2. Kl.
1.2. Fag.
1. Vl.
2. Vl.
Br.
Ten.-St.
Vlc.
cresc.
zu 2
stacc.
lon aus grü-nem und aus wei-ßem Porzel-lan.
Wie der Rücken ei-nes Ti-gers wölbt die
p subito
dim.
Brücke sich aus Ja-de zu dem Pa-vil-lon hin-ü-ber.
pizz.

49
kl. Fl.
1.2. Fl.
1. Ob.
2. Ob.
1.2. Kl. in B
.2. Fag.
1.3. Hr. in F
2.4. Hr.
1. Trp. in B
Trgl.
gr. Tr. Beck.
1. Vl.
2. Vl.
Br.
Ten-St.
Vlc. get.
Kb.
sempre f
zu 2
dim.
in B
mit Dämpfer
pp
sempre pp
Griffbrett
pp Zart, aber
In dem
arco
pizz.

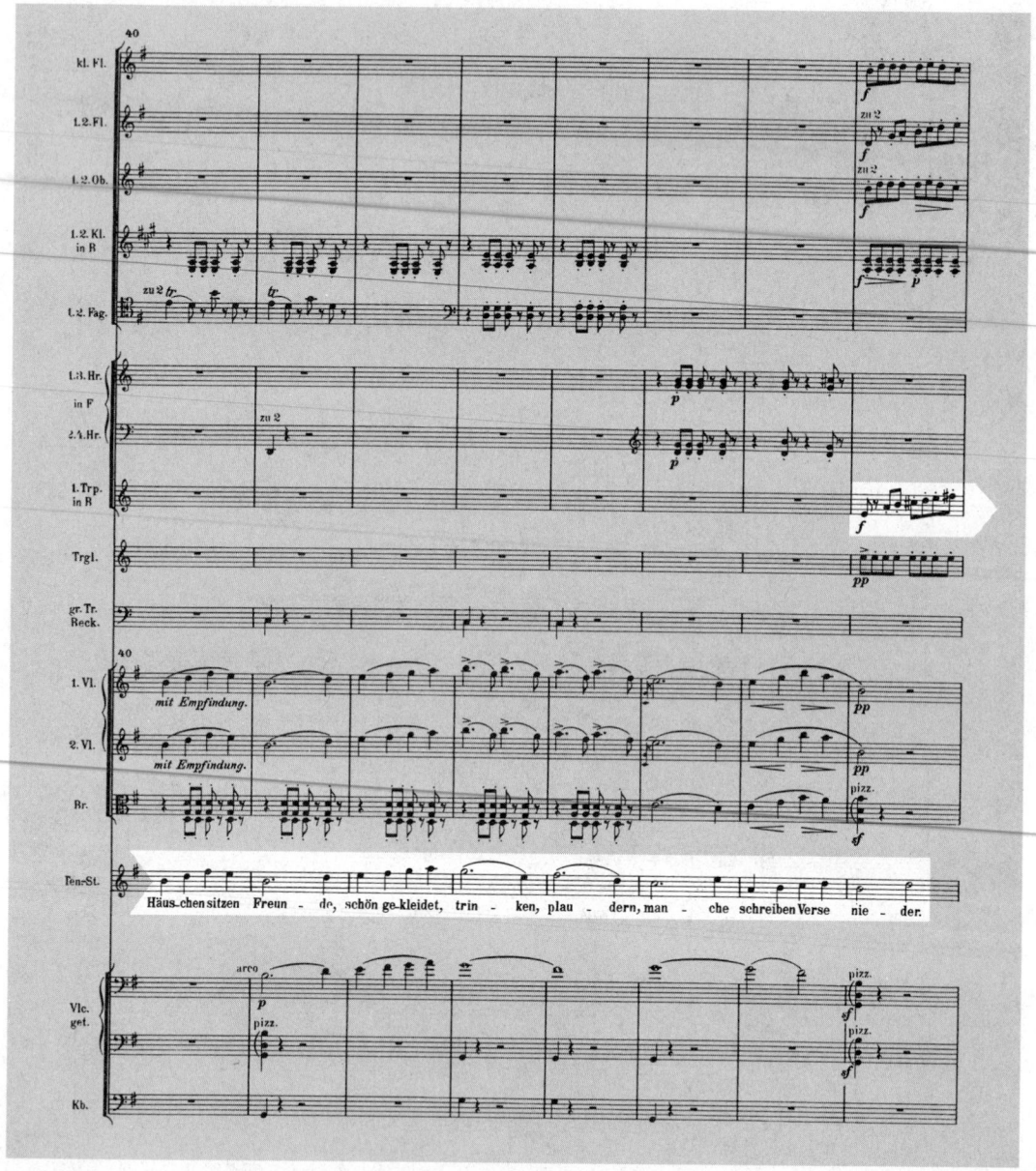
40
kl. Fl.
1.2. Fl.
1.2. Ob.
1.2. Kl. in B
1.2. Fag.
zu 2
1.3. Hr. in F
2.4. Hr.
1. Trp. in B
Trgl.
gr. Tr. Beck.
1. Vl.
2. Vl.
mit Empfindung.
Br.
pizz.
Ten.-St.
Häus-chen sitzen Freun - de, schön ge-kleidet, trin - ken, plau - dern, man - che schreiben Verse nie - der.
Vlc. gef.
arco
Kb.

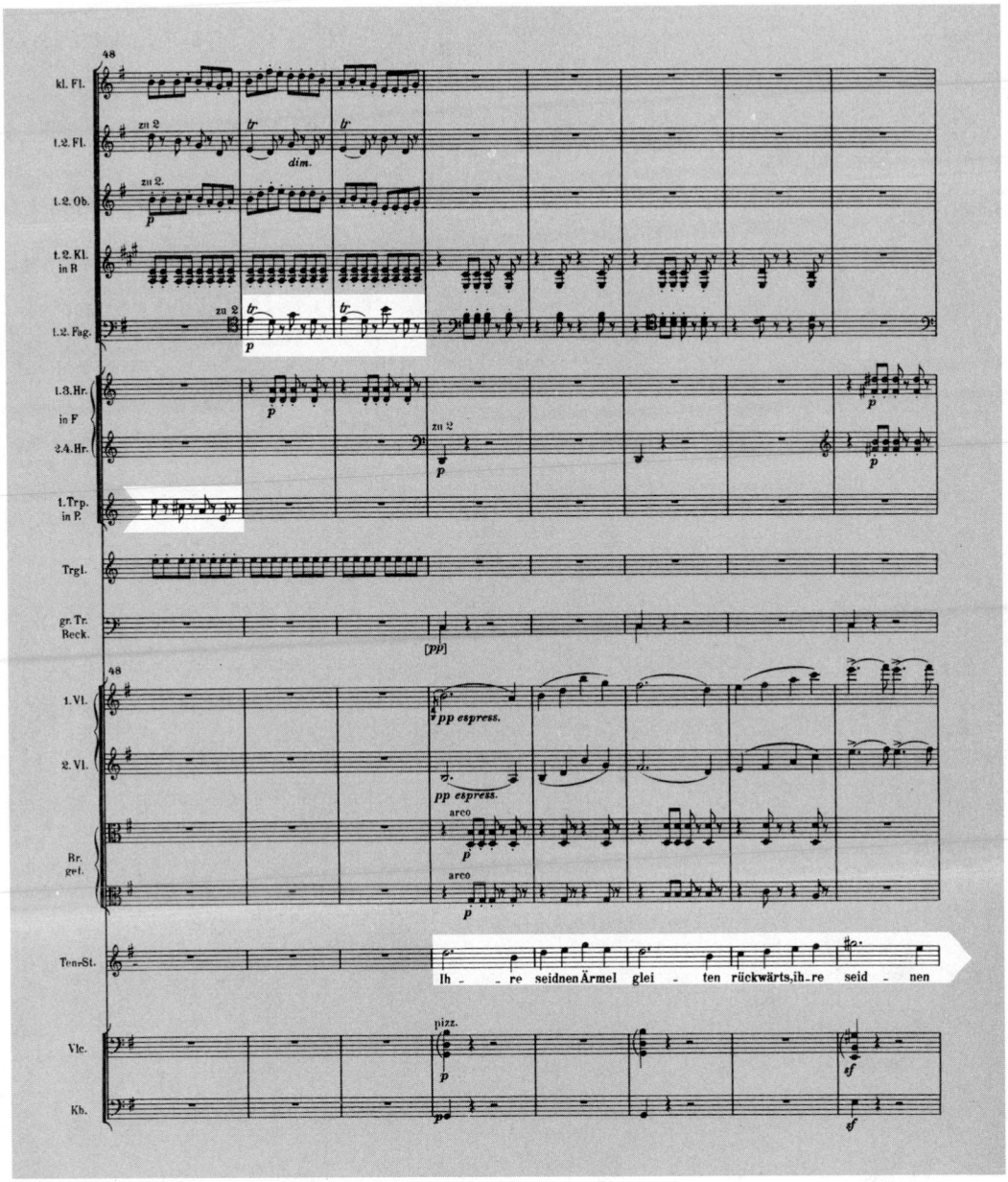
48
kl. Fl.
1.2. Fl.
zu 2
tr
dim.
1.2. Ob.
zu 2.
p
1.2. Kl. in B
1.2. Fag.
zu 2
1.3. Hr. in F
2.4. Hr.
zu 2
1. Trp. in P.
Trgl.
gr. Tr. Reck.
[pp]
48
1. Vl.
pp espress.
2. Vl.
pp espress.
Br. get.
arco
arco
Ten-St.
Ih - re seidnen Ärmel glei - ten rückwärts, ih - re seid - nen
Vlc.
pizz.
Kb.

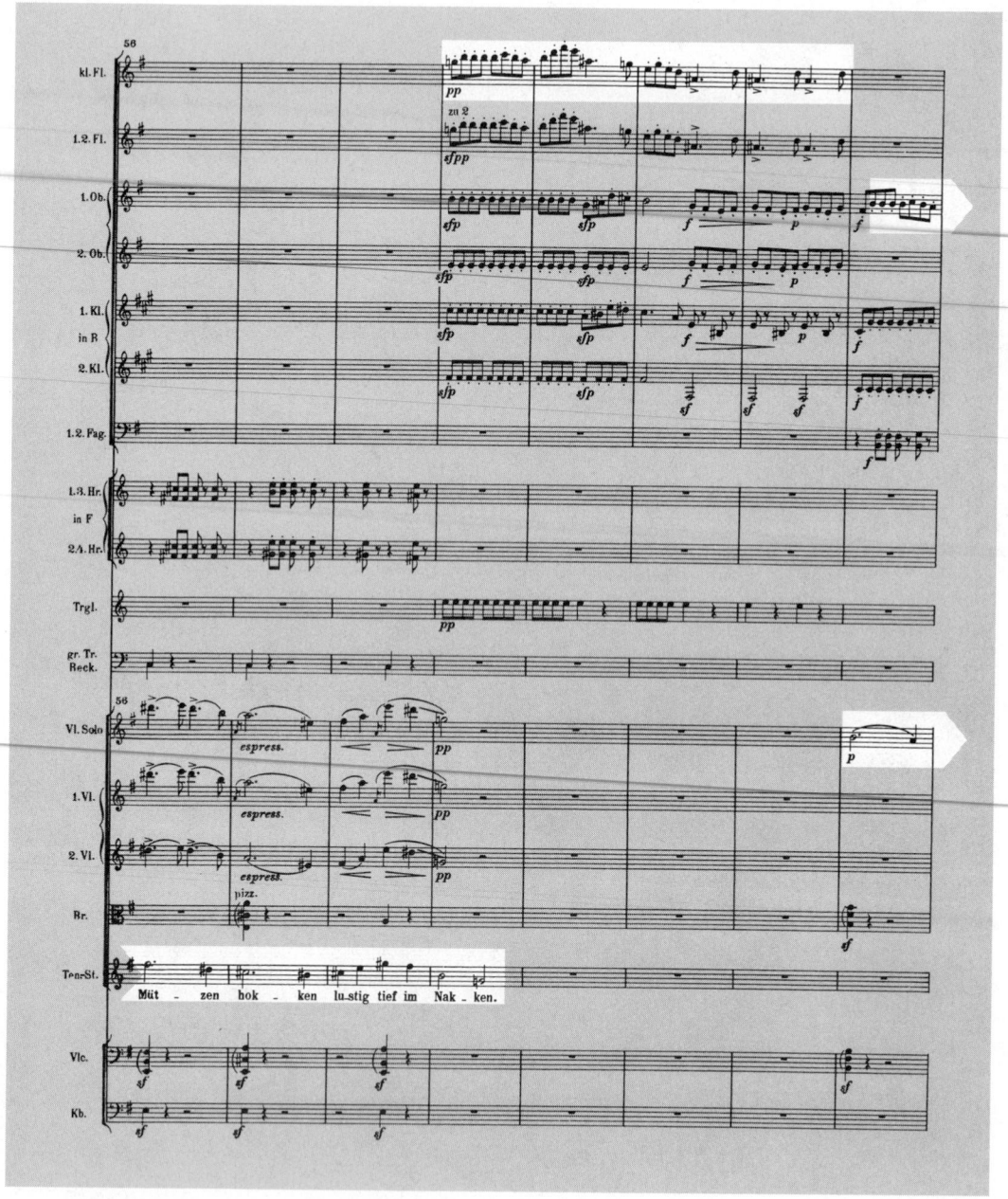
56
kl. Fl.
1. 2. Fl.
zu 2
1. Ob.
2. Ob.
1. Kl.
in B
2. Kl.
1. 2. Fag.
1. 3. Hr.
in F
2/4. Hr.
Trgl.
gr. Tr.
Beck.
56
Vl. Solo
espress.
1. Vl.
2. Vl.
Br.
pizz.
Ten-St.
Müt - zen hok - ken lu-stig tief im Nak - ken.
Vlc.
Kb.

64
Ruhiger
kl. Fl.
1. 2. Fl.
1. Ob.
2. Ob.
1. Kl.
in B
2. Kl.
1. 2. Fag.
1. 3. Hr.
in F
2. 4. Hr.
zu 2
gr. Tr.
Beck.
Solo-Vl.
1. Vl.
2. Vl.
Br.
Ten.-St.
Vlc.
Kb.
arco
pizz.
Auf des klei - nen,

Langsam
kl. Fl.
1. 2. Fl.
1. 2. Ob.
1. 2. Kl. in B
1. 2. Fag.
1. 2. Hr. in F
gr. Tr. Beck.
1. Vl.
2. Vl.
Br.
Ten-St.
klei - nen Tei - ches stil - ler, stil - ler Was - ser - flä - che zeigt sich al - les wun - der-
Vlc.
Kb.
Poco rit.
Rit. molto
Tempo (etwas mäßig)
lich im Spie - gel - bil - - de.
mit Dämpfer
[mit Dämpfer]

50
Rit.
A tempo (mäßig)
Rit.
Molto rit.
Tempo I subito
1.2. Fl.
1.2. Ob.
1.2. Kl. in B
1.2. Fag.
1.2. Hr. in F
4. Hr.
Trgl.
gr. Tr. Beck.
(ohne Dämpfer)
1. Vl.
2. Vl.
Br.
Vlc.
Kb.
espress. molto
Tutti
p molto espress.
arco
pizz.
Dämpfer ab!
1. Hr. in F
Ten.-St.
stacc.
Al - les auf dem Kop - fe ste - hend in dem Pa - vil - lon aus grü - nem und aus wei - ßem

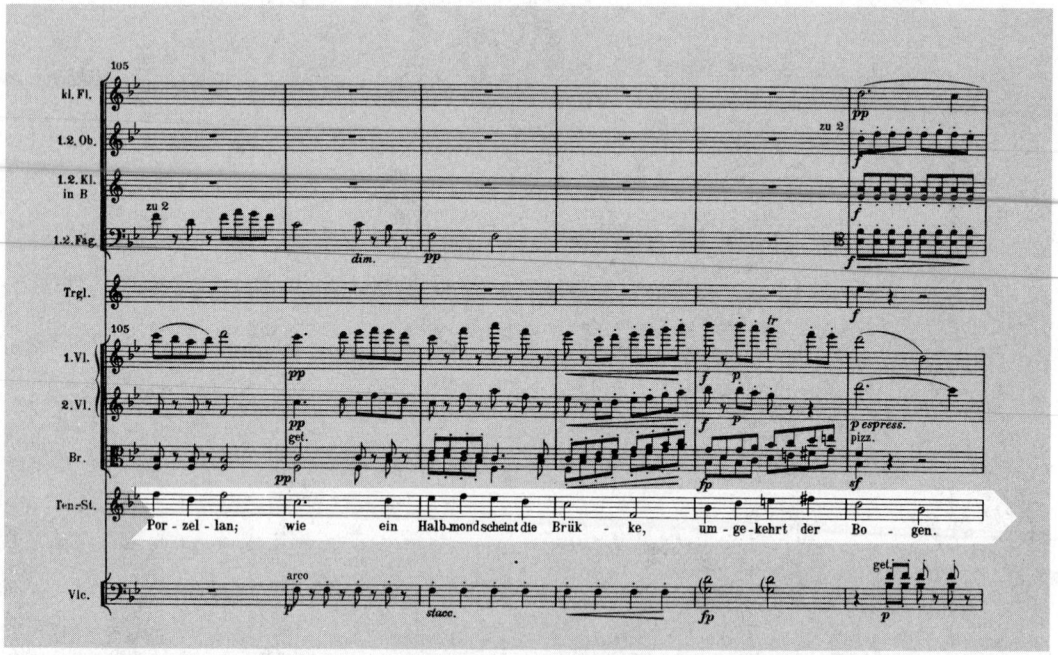
105
kl. Fl.
1.2. Ob.
1.2. Kl. in B
1.2. Fag.
Trgl.
1.Vl.
2.Vl.
Br.
Ten.-St.
Vlc.
zu 2
dim.
pp
f
tr
p espress.
pizz.
fp
sf
get.
arco
stacc.
Por - zel - lan; wie ein Halb-mond scheint die Brük - ke, um - ge - kehrt der Bo - gen.

111
(118)
kl. Fl.
1.2. Fl.
1.2. Ob.
1.2. Kl. in B
1.2. Fag.
1.Vl.
2.Vl.
Br.
Ten.-St.
Vlc.
zu 2
stacc.
dim.
p
pp
ppp
morendo
arco
Freun - de, schön ge - klei - det, trin - ken, plau - dern.

TEXT AND TRANSLATION

Mitten in dem kleinen Teiche
steht ein Pavillon aus grünem
und aus weissem Porzellan.

Wie der Rücken eines Tigers
wölbt die Brücke sich aus
Jade zu dem Pavillon hinüber.

In dem Häuschen sitzen Freunde,
schön gekleidet, trinken, plaudern,
manche schreiben Verse nieder.

Ihre seidnen Ärmel gleiten
rückwärts, ihre seidnen Mützen
hokken lustig tief im Nakken.

Auf des kleinen Teiches stiller
Wasserfläche zeigt sich alles
wunderlich im Spiegelbilde.

Alles auf dem Kopfe stehend
in dem Pavillon aus grünem
und aus weissem Porzellan;

wie ein Halbmond scheint die Brükke
umgekehrt der Bogen.
Freunde, schön gekleidet,
trinken, plaudern.

In the middle of the little pool
stands a pavilion of green
and of white porcelain.

Like the back of a tiger
arches the bridge of
jade over to the pavilion.

In the little house, friends are sitting
beautifully dressed, drinking, chatting;
several are writing verses.

Their silken sleeves slip
backwards, their silken caps
perch gaily on the back of their necks.

On the little pool's still
surface everything appears
fantastically in a mirror image.

Everything is standing on its head
in the pavilion of green
and of white porcelain;

like a half-moon stands the bridge,
upside-down its arch.
Friends, beautifully dressed, are
drinking, chatting.

20. Claude Debussy (1862–1918)

8:7A/1 8:7/1 - 4

Prélude à "L'après-midi d'un faune" (Prelude to "The Afternoon of a Faun") (1894)

3:3A/2 3:3/3 - 6

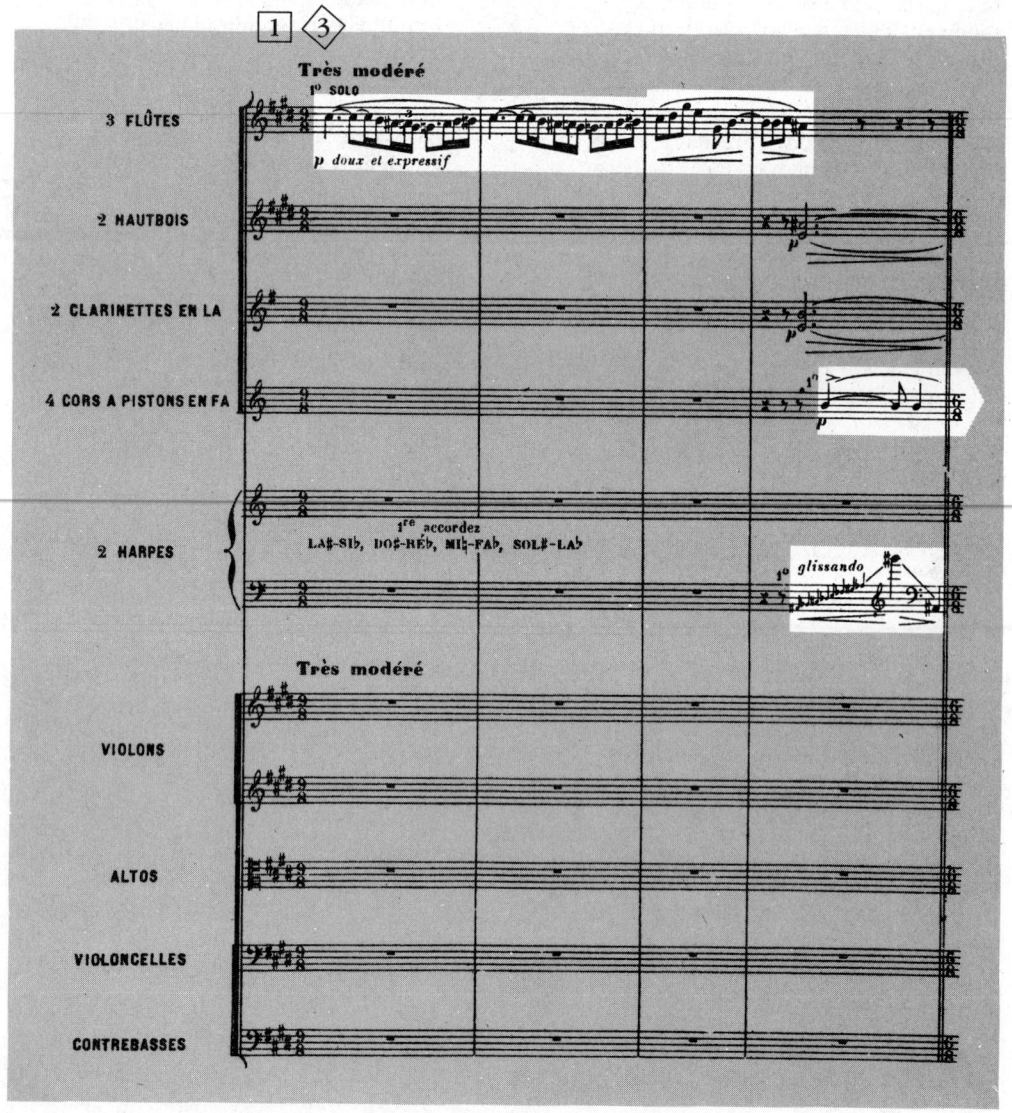

HAUTB.
CL.
1°
CORS
3°
1re HARPE
glissando
2e HARPE
(sourdine)
Div.
(sourdine)
Div.
(sourdine)
Div.
(sourdine)

1
1re Fl.
SOLO
p
HAUTB.
p
expressif
Cl.
pp
pp
Bons
1°
p
1°
p
CORS
3°
p
1
Div.
(sur la touche)
pp
(sur la touche)
pp
(sur la touche)
pp
à 2
pp

FL.
1° et 2°
p cre - scen - do f
HAUTB.
à 2
p cre - scen - do f
COR ANGL.
p cre - scen - do f
CL.
à 2
p cre scen - do f
dim. et retenu
BONS
à 2
p cre - scen - do f
1. 2.
(1)
p cre - scen - do f
dim.
CORS
3. 4.
(3)
p cre - scen - do f
dim.
Div.
cresc. - - - f
position nat.
cre - scen - do f
position nat.
cre - scen - do f
position nat.
cre - scen - do f
Unies.
cresc - - - f

1re FL.
SOLO
légèrement et expressif
CORS
1re HARPE
2e HARPE
Div.
pizz.

1re FL.
CL.
8pds
1er COR
1re HARPE
2e HARPE
Unis
pizz.
pizz.
Unis.
pizz.

FL.
2°
CL.
BONS
CORS
2° et 4°
pp
1re HARPE
2e HARPE p
Div.
arco
Div.
arco
arco

EL.
BOIS
Div.
Unis
arco
Unis
tim.
dim.
Div.
Div.
dim.
1er FL.
CL
CORS
1er HARPE
sourdines
sourdines
ôtez vite les sourdines
ôtez vite les sourdines
ôtez vite les sourdines
pizz.

1re FL.
CL.
BONS
CORS
1re HARPE
pizz.
arco
Div.

2
4
4
En animant
1re FL.
HAUTB.
1° SOLO
doux et expressif
CL.
BOUN.
1°
CORG
1re HARPE
4
En animant
pizz.
Div.
arco
pizz.
pizz.
arco
pizz.
Unis

HAUTB.
(à 2)
cre - - scen - - do
mf
COR ANGL.
cre - - scen - - do
mf
CL.
1°
cresc.
(2)
BONS
cresc.
mf
1. 2.
cresc.
CORS
3. 4.
p
3°
mf
arco
cresc.
mf
cre - - scen - - do
mf
cre - - scen - - do
mf
arco
cre - - scen - - do
mf
Div.
p
arco
mf

5
Toujours en animant
cresc.
FL.
HAUTB.
COR ANGL.
CL.
Changez en Sib
à 2
BOUS
CORS
Div.
Fin

FL.
HAUTB.
COR ANGL.
CL.
Bons
CORS
mf
f
f très en dehors
f très en dehors
1°
dim.
f (en dehors)
3° (en dehors)
più f
Div.

retenu
1er mouv!
FL.
HAUTB.
COR ANGL.
CL.
Solo
p doux et expressif
BONS
CORS
1er HARPE
2e HARPE
retenu
Div.
1er mouv!
pizz.

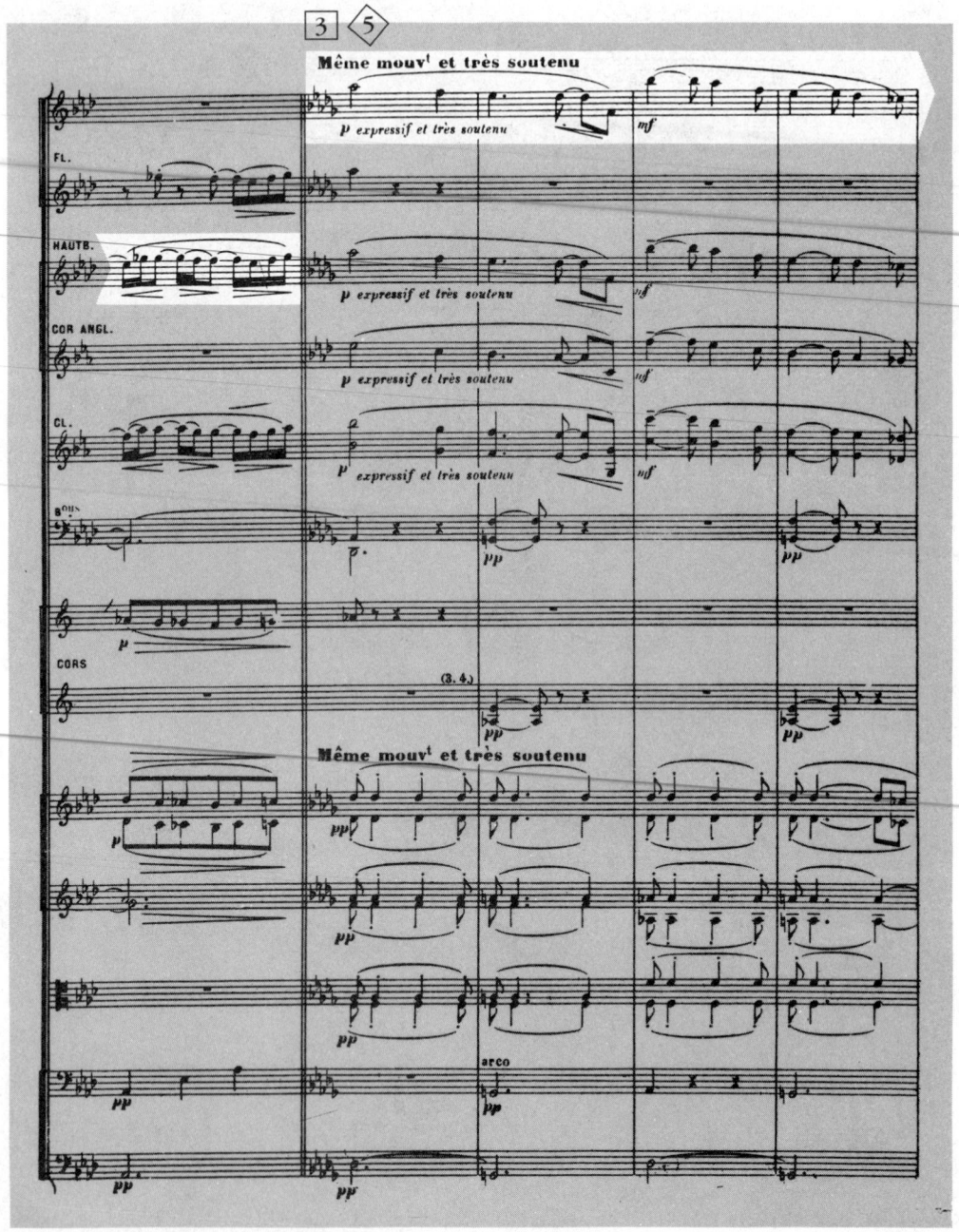
3
5
Même mouv^t et très soutenu
p expressif et très soutenu
mf
FL.
HAUTB.
COR ANGL.
CL.
BSON.
CORS
(3. 4.)
Même mouv^t et très soutenu
arco

7
p cre - - scen - - do
f
FL.
2° et 3°
HAUTB.
à 2
COR ANGL.
CL.
BOHS
1°
cresc
mf
1.2.
CORS
3.4.
4°
cresc
Unis
pp
Div.

FL.
HAUTB.
COR ANGL.
CL.
BONS
CORS
1re HARPE
2e HARPE
Unis
très expressif et très soutenu
Div.
pp subito
cre
pp
à 2

FL.
HAUTB.
COR ANGL.
CL.
BOUS
CORS
1er HARPE
2e HARPE
scen - - - do
mp cre - - scen - - do molto

FL.
HAUTB.
COR ANGL.
CL.
BONS
à 2
CORS
1re HARPE
2e HARPE

FL.
CL.
1°
p très doux
8ons
p espressif et doux
CORS
3°
1re HARPE
1er VON SOLO
p doux et expressif
sourdines
sourdines
sourdines
sourdines
Div.

HAUTB.
CL.
CORS
Vcelle SOLO
pp très doux
ppp
pp
p
4
6
1er FL.
8 Mouvt du Début
doux et expressif
HAUTB.
CL.
CORS
1er HARPE
Vcelle SOLO
8 Mouvt du Début
(1rs Vlns)
Div.

1re FL.
Un peu plus animé
HAUTB.
CL.
Bons
1. 2.
sourdines
CORS
3. 4.
sourdines
3e
1re HARPE
préparez le ton de Mib
Un peu plus animé
pizz.
pizz.
pizz.
pizz.

1
FL.
2, 3.
HAUTB.
sfz
COR ANGL.
CL.
Bons
CORS
sur la touche
arco
sur la touche
arco
sur la touche
arco
pizz
arco
sur la touche
Div.
arco
pizz
arco

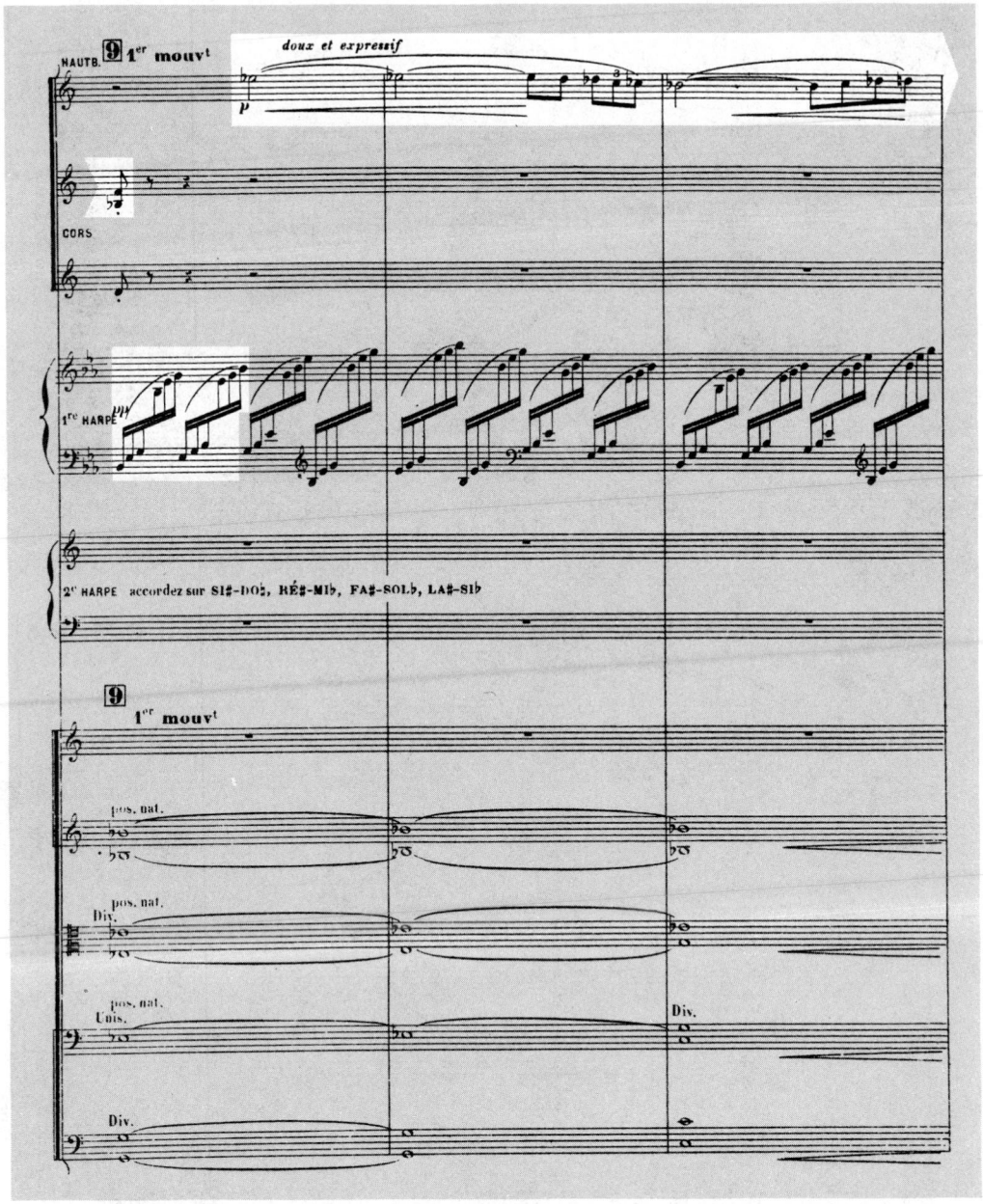
HAUTB.
9 1er mouvt
doux et expressif
p
CORS
1re HARPE
pp
2e HARPE accordez sur SI♯-DO♯, RÉ♯-MI♭, FA♯-SOL♭, LA♯-SI♭
9
1er mouvt
pos. nat.
pos. nat.
Div.
pos. nat.
Unis.
Div.
Div.

dans le mouvt plus animé
1.
FL.
2. 3.
HAUTB.
COR ANGL.
CL.
Changez en La♭
BONS
CORS
1re HARPE
2e HARPE
glissando
dans le mouvt plus animé
pizz.
pizz.
pizz.
pizz.

1.
FL.
2. 3.
HAUTB.
COR ANGL.
CL.
BASS.
CORS
1o cuivré
glissando
2e HARPE
arco
arco Div.
pizz.
arco Unis.
arco
pizz.
arco Unis.

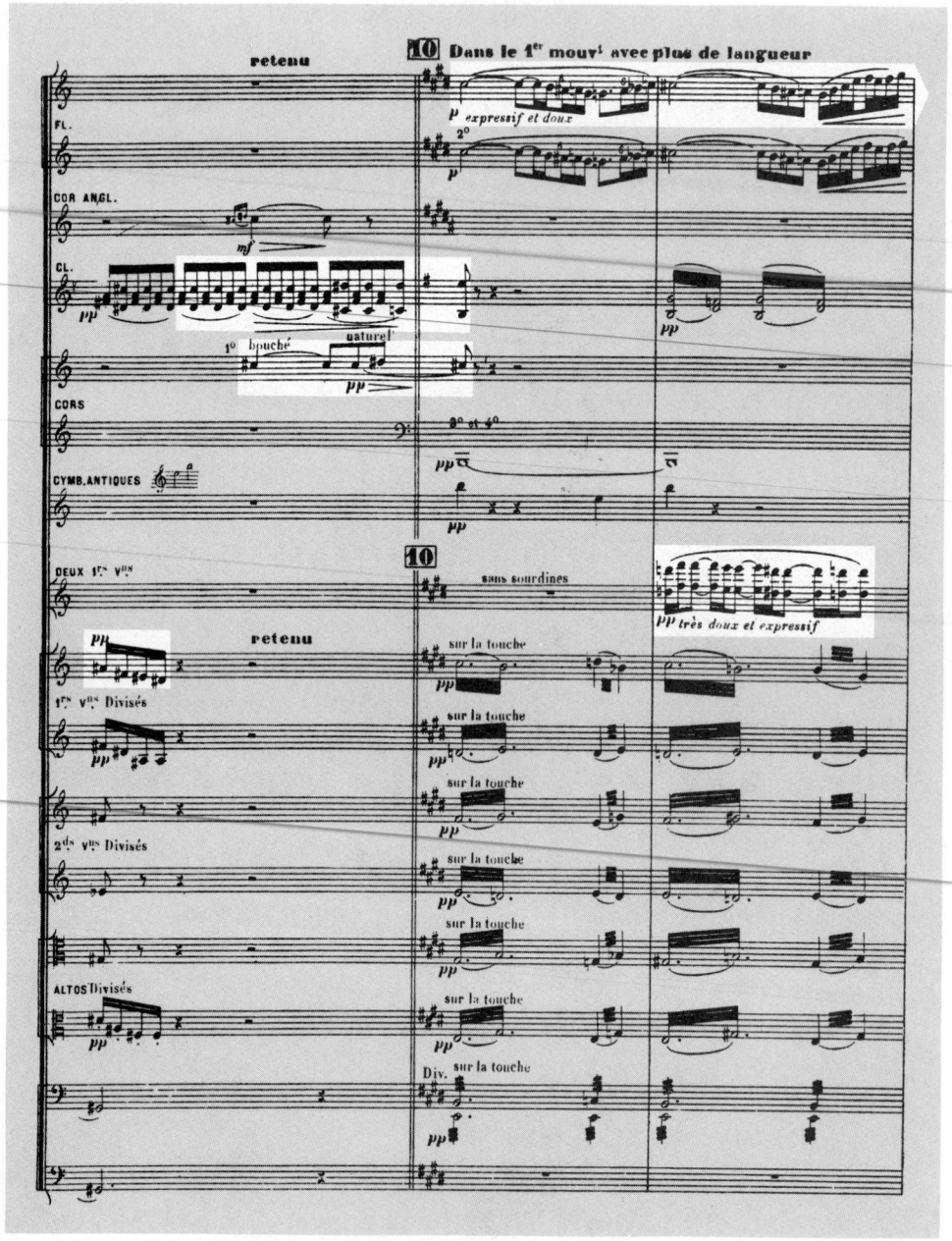
retenu
10 Dans le 1er mouv.t avec plus de langueur
FL.
p expressif et doux
2°
COR ANGL.
mf
CL.
pp
1° bouché
naturel
CORS
3° et 4°
CYMB. ANTIQUES
10
DEUX 1ers Vns
sans sourdines
pp très doux et expressif
pp
retenu
sur la touche
1ers Vns Divisés
2ds Vns Divisés
ALTOS Divisés
Div.

FL.
HAUTB.
CL.
à 2
BONS
CORS
3° et 4°
1° sourdine
CYMB. ANT.
1 VLLE SOLO

FL.
MAUTB.
CL.
CORS
sourdine
CYMB. ANT.
1re HARPE
pos. nat.
pos. nat.
pos. nat.
pos. nat.
pos. nat.
pos. nat.
1 Vlle SOLO

11
Retenu
(a tempo)
Très retenu
1er Fl.
HAUTB.
SOLO
COR ANGL.
CL.
BONS
CORS
2e
11
Très retenu
Retenu
(a tempo)

12
Très lent et très retenu jusqu'à la fin
FL.
NAUTR.
(sourdines)
1. 2.
CORS
(sourdines)
3. 4.
CYMB. ANT.
1er et 2e HARPES
1ère
2. 3.
12
Très lent et très retenu jusqu'à la fin
Unis
Div.
pizz.
pizz.

21. Richard Strauss (1864–1949)

8:7A/2 8:7/5 - 6

Der Rosenkavalier (The Cavalier of the Rose), Act III, Trio (1909–10)

English translation by Alfred Kalisch. © Copyright 1911 by Adolph Furstner. Copyright renewed 1940 by Furstner, Ltd., London. © Copyright assigned 1943 to Boosey & Hawkes, Ltd., London, for all countries except Germany, Danzig, Italy, and Portugal. All rights reserved. Reprinted in the U.S. by permission of Boosey & Hawkes, Inc. Used in the world excluding the U.S. by permission of European American Music Distributors Corporation, agent for Furstner, Ltd., London.

Marsch.
lieb zu ha - ben in der rich - ti - gen Weis', dass ich
love him right - ly, As a good wo - man should, E'en to
Sophie
Sophie (vor sich) (To herself)
Mir ist wie in der
I feel as one at
Marsch.
selbst sein Lieb' zu ei - ner an - dern noch
love the love he bore a - no - ther I
Oct.
Octavian (vor sich) (To himself)
Es ist was
What thing so
Sophie
Kirch' - n, hei - lig ist mir
wor - ship, ho - li - est thoughts
Marsch.
lieb hab'! Hab' mir frei - lich nicht ge - dacht,
pro - mised. But in truth, I did not think
Oct.
(ausdrucksvoll) (With much expression)
kom - men und ist was g'scheh'n. Ich möcht' sie
won - d'rous has come to pass? I fain would
espr.
dim.

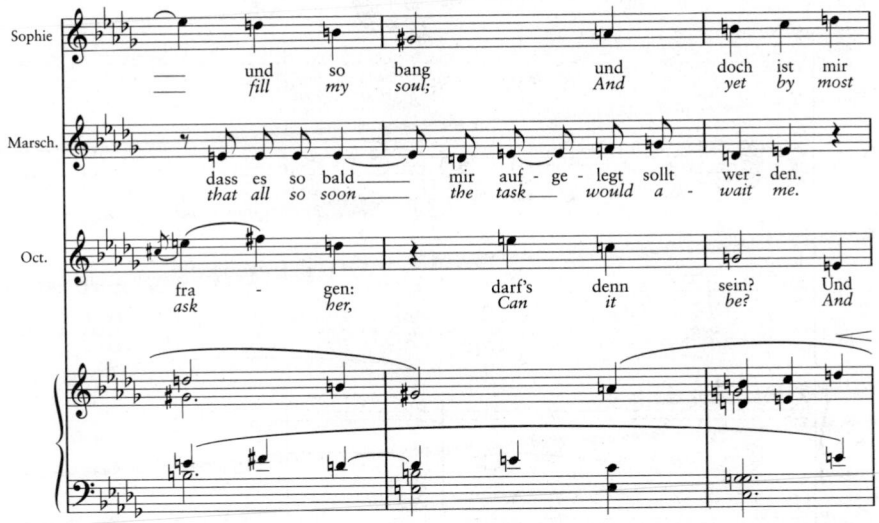
Sophie
und so bang und doch ist mir
fill my soul; And yet by most
Marsch.
dass es so bald mir auf - ge - legt sollt wer - den.
that all so soon the task would a - wait me.
Oct.
fra - gen: darf's denn sein? Und
ask her, Can it be? And

Sophie
un - hei - lig auch! Ich
un - ho - ly thought, and
(suefzend) (Sighing)
Marsch.
3
Es sind die meh- re- ren Din - ge auf der Welt,
Full many a thing is or - dai - ned in this world,
Oct.
g'rad' die Frag' die spür' ich, dass sie mir ver-
just that ques - tion that I know I can - not

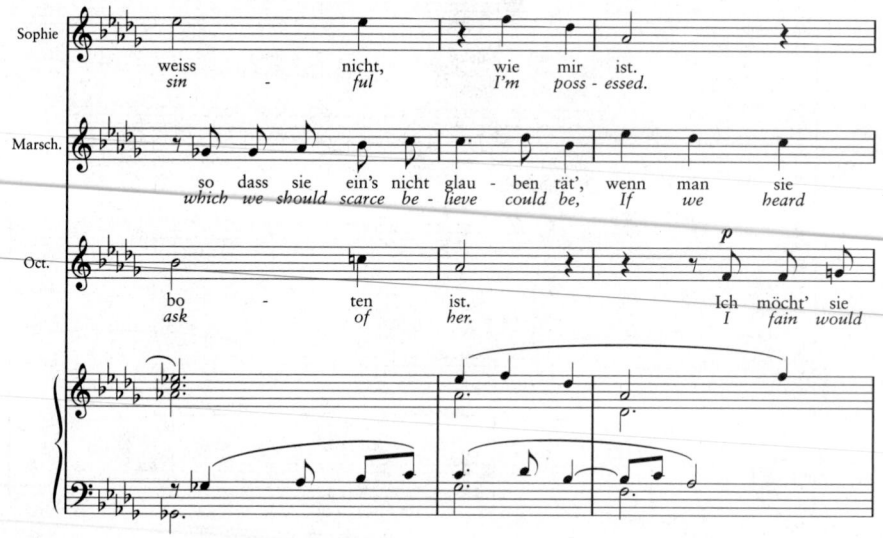
Sophie
weiss nicht, wie mir ist.
sin - ful I'm poss - essed.
Marsch.
so dass sie ein's nicht glau - ben tät', wenn man sie
which we should scarce be - lieve could be, If we heard
Oct.
p
bo - ten ist. Ich möcht' sie
ask of her. I fain would

Sophie
p
Wie in der Kirch'n so hei - lig so bang.
With ho - liest thoughts my soul is filled.
Marsch.
möcht' er - zäh - len hör'n.
o - thers tell of them;
Oct.
fra - gen, ich möcht' sie
ask her, I fain would
cresc.

(ausdrucksvoll)
(With much expression)
Sophie
Ich möcht' mich nie - der knien
At yon - der la - dy's feet
Marsch.
Al - lei - nig, wer's er - lebt,
But some day whom they wound
Oct.
fra - gen: wa - rum, wa - rum zit - tert was in
ask her: oh why, oh why trem - bles all my
8
Sophie
dort vor der Frau und möcht' ihr was
I fain would kneel, yet fain would I
Marsch.
der glaubt da - ran und weiss nicht
be - lieves in them, and knows not
Oct.
mir? Ist denn ein gro - sses Un - recht ge -
soul? Has a great wrong, a foul deed been
8
f
8

Sophie
an - tun; denn ich spür', sie gibt mir
harm her; For I feel, she gives him to
Marsch.
wie
how
Oct.
scheh'n? Und g'rad' an die,
done? And just of her,
♩ = 80
fp
espr.
Sophie
ihn und nimmt mir was von ihm zu -
me and yet robs me of part of
Oct.
und g'rad' an die, und g'rad' an die, an die darf
and just of her, and just of her, of her, I
cresc.
Sophie
gleich. Weiss gar - nicht, wie mir ist.
him. So strange - ly I'm dis - traught.
Oct.
ich die Frag', die Frag' nicht tun.
may not ask, the ques - tion I may not ask.
poco accelerando
f

6
Sophie
Möcht' al - les ver - steh'n und möcht' auch
All things I would know, yet fear to
Princess Marschallin
f
Marsch.
Da steht der Bub und da steh'
There stands the boy, And here stand
Oct.
Und dann seh' ich dich an, So-
And then on your dear face I
tempo primo
p
3
p subito
espr.
Sophie
nichts ver steh'n. Möcht' fra gen
know the truth Now long - ing
Marsch.
ich, und mit dem frem - den
I; and with his love, new -
Oct.
phie und seh' nur dich, spür' nur
gaze, and see but you, Know but
mf
3
cresc.
mf
cresc.

Sophie
und nicht fra - gen, wird mir heiss und kalt.
to ask, now fea - ring; hot am I and cold.
Marsch.
Mä - del dort
found this day
cresc.
Oct.
dich, spür' nur dich, So -
you You, So - phi - a, but
(Aug' in Aug' mit Octavian)
(Gazing into Octavian's eyes)
Sophie
Und spür' nur dich und weiss nur eins:
And know but you, know but this one
Marsch.
wird er so glück - - - -
He will have hap - - - -
Oct.
phie, und seh' nur dich und weiss von
you, and see but you, and no - thing
♩ = 88

Sophie
cresc.
ff
thing, that I love dich hab'
you, you
Marsch.
cresc.
ff
- lich sein, als wie halt Män -
- pi - ness Such as a man
Oct.
cresc.
ff
nichts als nur: dich,
know but this: you,
8
♩ = 84
cresc.
ff
Sophie
ich lieb, dich hab' ich
I love you, you I
Marsch.
- ner das Glück - lich - sein ver -
thinks the best the world can
Oct.
ff
dich hab' ich
you you I
8
♩ = 80
ff

Sophie
lieb.
love.
Marsch.
steh'n.
give.
In Got - tes
'Tis done so
Oct.
lieb.
love.
mf espr.
Breit ♩ = 72
ff
ff
(Die Marschallin geht leise links hinein,
die Beiden bemerken es gar nicht.)
(The Princess goes quietly into the room on the left;
the two others do not notice her.)
Marsch.
Na - men.
be it.
f
espr.
dim.
p
dim.

22. Arnold Schoenberg (1874–1951)

Pierrot lunaire, Op. 21, Nos. 18 and 21 (1912)

8:7A/3-4 | 8:7/7 - 10 | 3:3A/4-5 | 3:3/16 - 19 | MW

No. 18. "Der Mondfleck"

7 16

Sehr rasche ♪ (ca 144)

Piccolo.

Klarinette in B.

Geige.

Violoncell.

Rezitation.

Klavier.

Einen wei - ßen Fleck des hel - len Mon - des auf dem Rük - ken

Pic.

Kl. (B)

G.

Vcl.

mf quasi kadenzierend

quasi kadenzierend

sei - nes schwar - zen Rok - kes, so spaziert Pier -

Copyright © 1914 by Universal Edition. Copyright renewed. All rights reserved. Used in the world excluding the U.S. by permission of European American Music Distributors Corporation, agent for Universal Edition. Used in the U.S. by permission of Belmont Music Publishers, Pacific Palisades, CA 90272.

Pic.
Kl. (B)
G.
Vcl.
rot im lauen A_bend,
auf_ zu_ suchen Glück und A _ ben_teu_er.
cresc.
Plötzlich stört ihn was an sei_nem An _ zug, er be_

8
17
Pic.
Kl. (B)
G.
Vcl.
cresc.
ff
dim.
pp
mf
f
p
mfp
sieht sich rings und fin_det rich_tig- ei_nen wei_ßen Fleck
10
ppp
des hel_len Mon_ _des auf dem Rük_ken sei_nes schwarzen Rockes. War_te!

Pic.
Kl. (B)
G.
Vcl.
denkt er: das ist so ein Gips - fleck!
Wischt und wischt, doch
(ärgerlich)
bringt ihn nicht her - un - ter!
(erregt)
Und so geht er
15
cresc.

ohne größere Pause, bloß 𝄐 aushalten, folgt:

Serenade.

Klavier, Violoncell

Übergang zu Heimfahrt kommen dazu Flöte, Klarinette in A, Geige.

TEXT AND TRANSLATION

Einen weissen Fleck des hellen Mondes
Auf dem Rücken seines schwarzen Rockes,
So spaziert Pierrot im lauen Abend,
Aufzusuchen Glück und Abenteuer.

Plötzlich stört ihn was an seinem Anzug,
Er besieht sich rings und findet richtig—
Einen weissen Fleck des hellen Mondes
Auf dem Rücken seines schwarzen Rockes.

Warte! denkt er: das ist so ein Gipsfleck!
Wischt und wischt, doch—bringt ihn nicht herunter!
Und so geht er, giftgeschwollen, weiter,
Reibt und reibt bis an den frühen Morgen—
Einen weissen Fleck des hellen Mondes.

With a fleck of white—from the bright moon—
On the back of his black jacket,
Pierrot strolls about in the mild evening
Seeking his fortune and adventure.

Suddenly something strikes him as wrong,
He checks his clothes and sure enough finds
A fleck of white—from the bright moon—
On the back of his black jacket.

Damn! he thinks: that's a spot of plaster!
Wipes and wipes, but—he can't get it off.

And so goes on his way, his pleasure poisoned,
Rubs and rubs till the early morning—
A fleck of white—from the bright moon.

No. 21. "O alter Duft"

10 19
poco rit. - - - - - - Tempo
rit. - - Tempo
Fl.
Kl. (A)
nimmt Baß Klarinette in B
G.
nimmt Bratsche
Vcl.
poco rit. - - - - - - Tempo
rit. - - Tempo
sehr innig
Wünschen macht mich froh nach Freu - den, die ich lang ver - ach - - tet.
O
poco rit. - - - - - - Tempo
rit. - - Tempo
p espress.
poco rit. - - - - - - Tempo
Fl.
Baß-Klarinette (B)
Bratsche.
Vcl.
p espress.
15
poco rit. - - - - - - Tempo
15 al - ter Duft aus Mär - chen - zeit, be - rau - schest wie - der mich.
All meinen
poco rit. - - - ppp - - Tempo
Ped.

nimmt Piccolo
Fl.
B-Kl (B)
Br.
Vcl.
20
Un_mut geb ich preis; aus meinem sonnumrahm_ten Fenster beschau ich frei die lie_be Welt und
Piccolo.
rit.
Tempo
molto rit.
Dämpfer aufsetzen
mit Dämpfer
25
29
träum hin_aus in sel_ge Weiten... O al_ter Duft aus Mär_chen_zeit!

TEXT AND TRANSLATION

O alter Duft aus Märchenzeit,
Berauschest wieder meine Sinne!
Ein närrisch Heer von Schelmerein
Durchschwirrt die leichte Luft.

Ein glückhaft Wünschen macht mich froh
Nach Freuden, die ich lang verachtet:
O alter Duft aus Märchenzeit,
Berauschest wieder mich!

All meinen Unmut geb ich preis:
Aus meinem sonnumrahmten Fenster
Beschau ich frei die liebe Welt
Und träum hinaus in selge Weiten . . .
O alter Duft aus Märchenzeit!

O scent of fabled yesteryear,
Intoxicating my senses once again!
A foolish swarm of idle fancies
Pervades the gentle air.

A happy desire makes me yearn for
Joys that I have long scorned:
O scent of fabled yesteryear,
Intoxicating me again.

All my ill humor is dispelled:
From my sun-drenched window
I look out freely on the lovely world
And dream of beyond the horizon . . .
O scent of fabled yesteryear!

23. Charles Ives (1874–1954)

8:7A/5 8:7/11 - 18

The Fourth of July, from *A Symphony: New England Holidays* (1911-13)

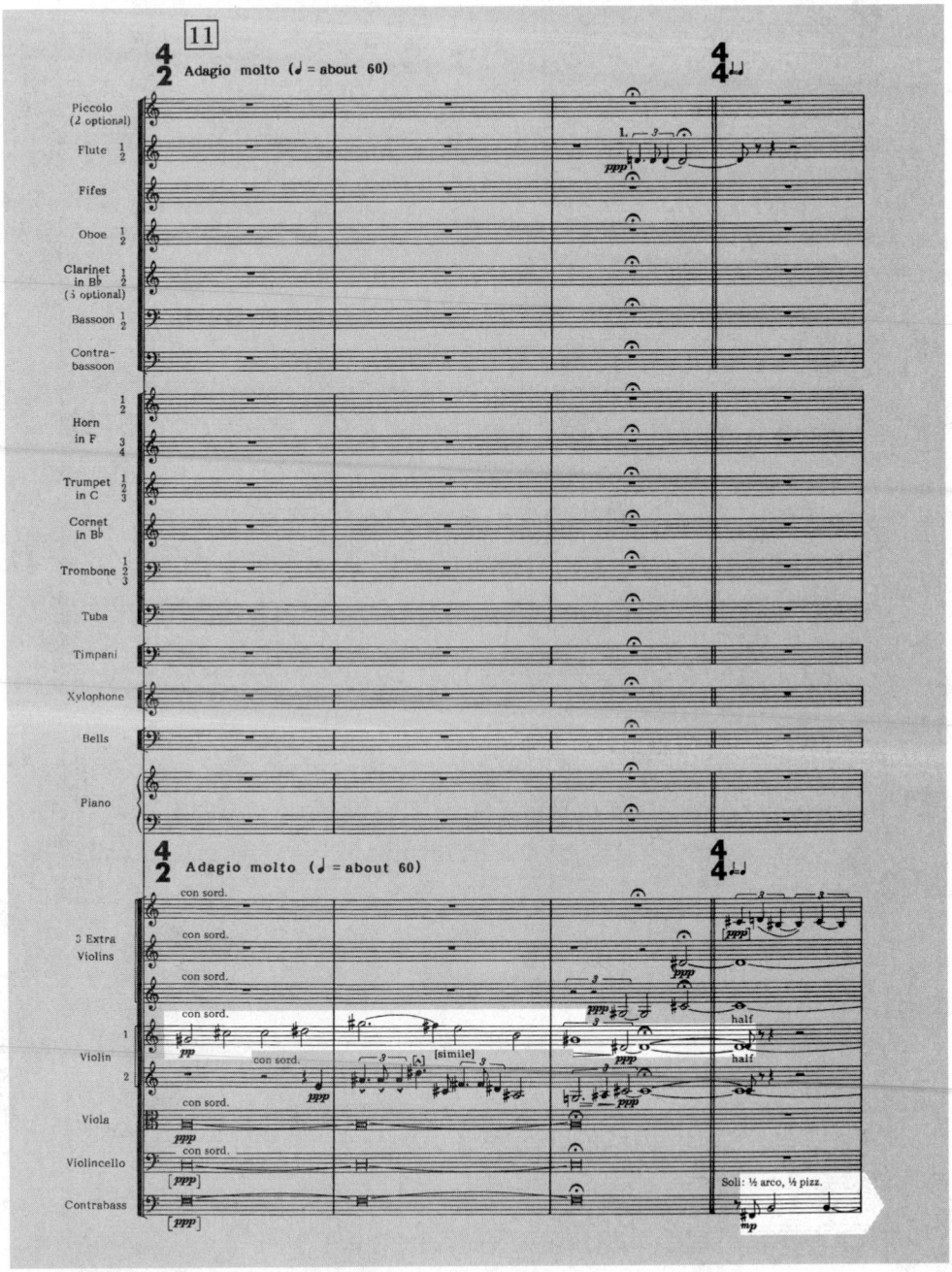

Copyright © 1932 (renewed) by Associated Music Publishers, Inc. (BMI). New edition (1992) edited by Wayne D. Shirley. International copyright secured. All rights reserved. Reprinted by permission.

5
Pic.
Fl. 1 2
Ob. 1
Cl. (B♭) 1
Bn. 1
1 2
Hn. (F)
3 4
Tpt. (C)
Tbn.
Tba.
pp
Timp.
Perc.
Pno.
3 extra Vlns.
Vln. 1 div.
ppp
Vln. 2 div.
[ppp]
pp
Vla. div.
Vlc.
Cb.
mf
Tutti arco
(octaves ad lib.)
p

10
Andante (con moto), a little faster
(♩ = about 72-76)
Pic.
Fl. 1 2
Ob. 1
Cl. (B♭) 1
Bn. 1
Hn. (F) 1 2 3 4
Tpt. (C)
Tbn.
Tba.
Timp.
Perc.
Pno.
Andante (con moto), a little faster
(♩ = about 72-76)
3 extra Vlns.
Vln. 1 div.
Vln. 2 div.
Vla. div.
Vlc.
Cb. div.

14
Pic.
Fl.
Ob.
Cl. (B♭)
Bn.
Hn. (F)
Tpt. (C)
Tbn.
Tba.
Timp.
Perc.
Pno.
3 extra Vlns.
Vln. 1 div.
Vln. 2 div.
Vla. div.
Vlc.
Cb. div.
a 2
div.
unis.

18
Pic.
Fl.
Ob.
Cl. (B♭)
Bn.
Hn. (F)
Tpt. (C)
Tbn.
Tba.
Timp.
Perc.
Pno.
3 extra Vlns.
Vln. 1 div.
Vln. 2 div.
Vla. div.
Vlc. div.
Cb. div.
a 2
[1.]
1.
senza sord.

22
Pic.
Fl.
Ob.
Cl. (B♭)
Bn.
Hn. (F)
Tpt. (C)
Tbn.
Tba.
Timp.
Perc.
Pno.
3 extra Vlns.
Vln. 1 div.
Vln. 2 div.
Vla. div.
Vlc. div.
Cb. div.
[div.]
[unis.]

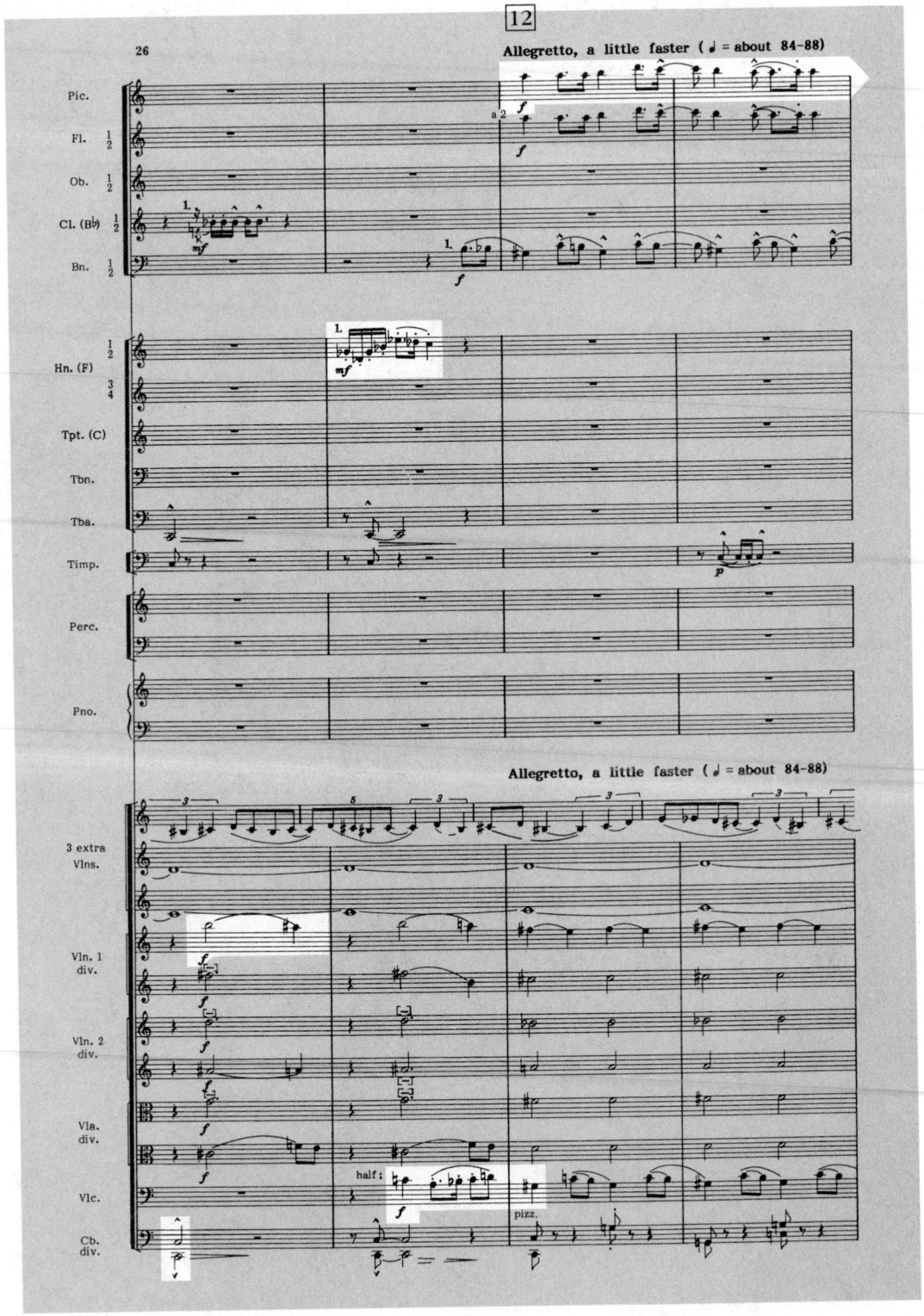
12
26
Allegretto, a little faster (♩ = about 84-88)
Pic.
Fl.
Ob.
Cl. (B♭)
Bn.
a 2
Hn. (F)
Tpt. (C)
Tbn.
Tba.
Timp.
Perc.
Pno.
Allegretto, a little faster (♩ = about 84-88)
3 extra Vlns.
Vln. 1 div.
Vln. 2 div.
Vla. div.
Vlc.
Cb. div.
half:
pizz.

30
Pic.
Fl. 1 2
Ob. 1 2
Cl. (B♭) 1 2
Bn. 1 2
Hn. (F) 1 2 3 4
Tpt. (C)
Tbn.
Tba.
Timp.
Perc.
Pno.
3 extra Vlns.
Vln. 1 div.
Vln. 2 div.
Vla. div.
Vlc.
Cb. div.
[divisi]
arco, div.
first half, divisi
second half

34
Pic.
Fl. 1/2
Ob. 1/2
Cl. (B♭) 1/2
Bn. 1/2
Hn. (F) 1/2 3/4
Tpt. (C) 1
mp
Tbn.
Tba.
Timp.
p
pp
Perc.
Pno.
3 extra Vlns.
Vln. 1 div.
Vln. 2 div.
Vla. div.
Vlc. div.
half, divisi in 2
Cb.

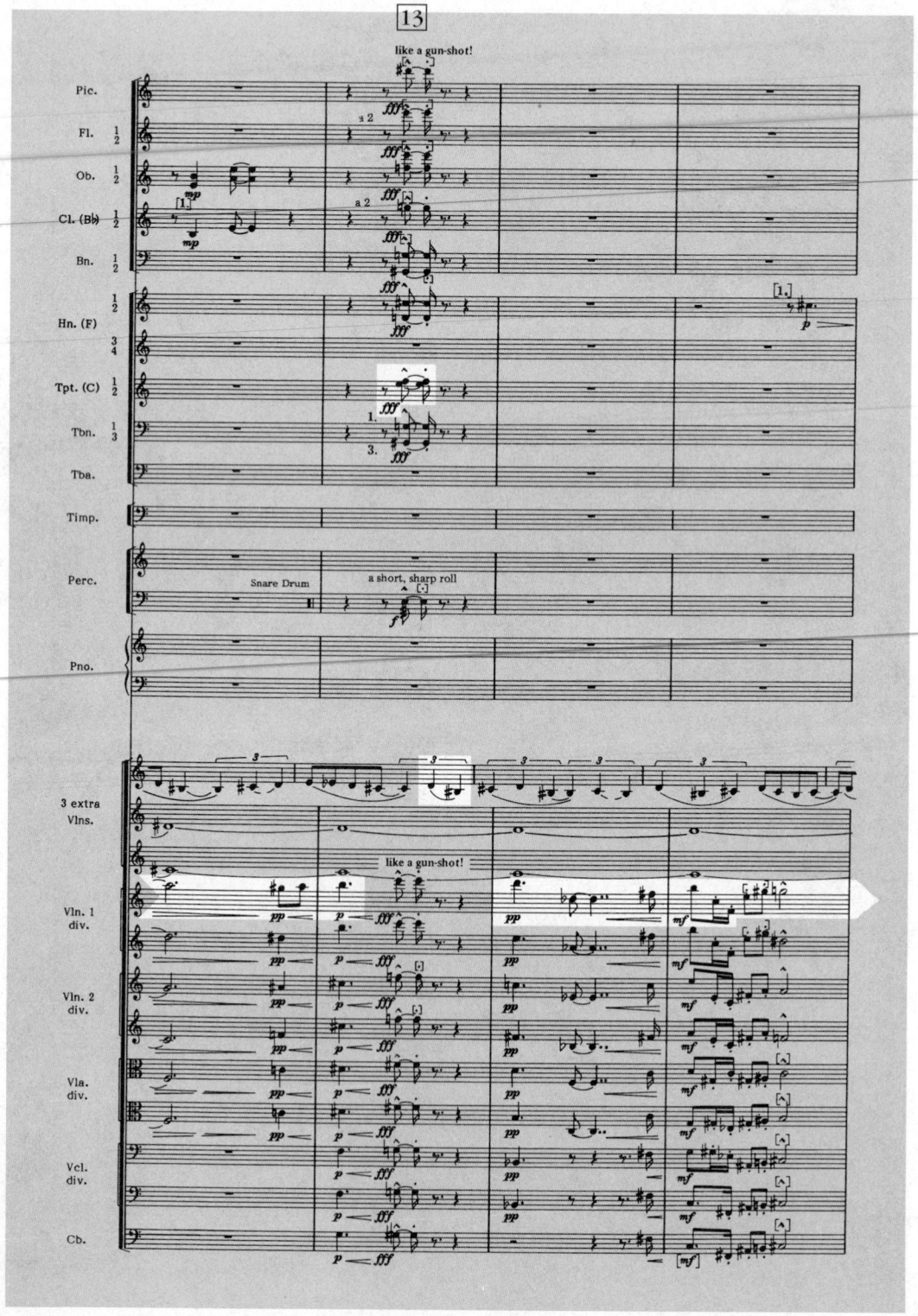
13
like a gun-shot!
Pic.
Fl.
Ob.
Cl. (B♭)
Bn.
Hn. (F)
Tpt. (C)
Tbn.
Tba.
Timp.
Perc.
Snare Drum
a short, sharp roll
Pno.
3 extra Vlns.
Vln. 1 div.
Vln. 2 div.
Vla. div.
Vcl. div.
Cb.
a 2
1.
3.

42
Più allegretto (♩ = about 92-96)
Pic.
Fl. 1
Ob. 1
Cl. (B♭) 1
Bn.
Hn. (F) 1 2 3 4
Tpt. (C) 1
Tbn. 1
Tba.
Timp.
Perc.
Pno.
Più allegretto (♩ = about 92-96)
3 extra Vlns.
Vln. 1 div.
Vln. 2 div.
Vla. div.
Vlc. div.
Cb.
one pizz., others arco

46
14
Più mosso
Pic.
Fl. 1
Ob. 1
Cl. (B♭) 1
Bn.
Hn. (F)
Tpt. (C)
Tbn.
Tba.
Timp.
Perc.
Bass Drum
Pno.
Più mosso
3 extra Vlns.
Vln. 1 div.
Vln. 2
Vla.
Vlc. div.
Cb.
Tutti, arco

* From this point on, Ives seems to think of the Timpani as high, medium, and low, rather than of definite pitches. This score reproduces the pitches Ives wrote. -Ed.

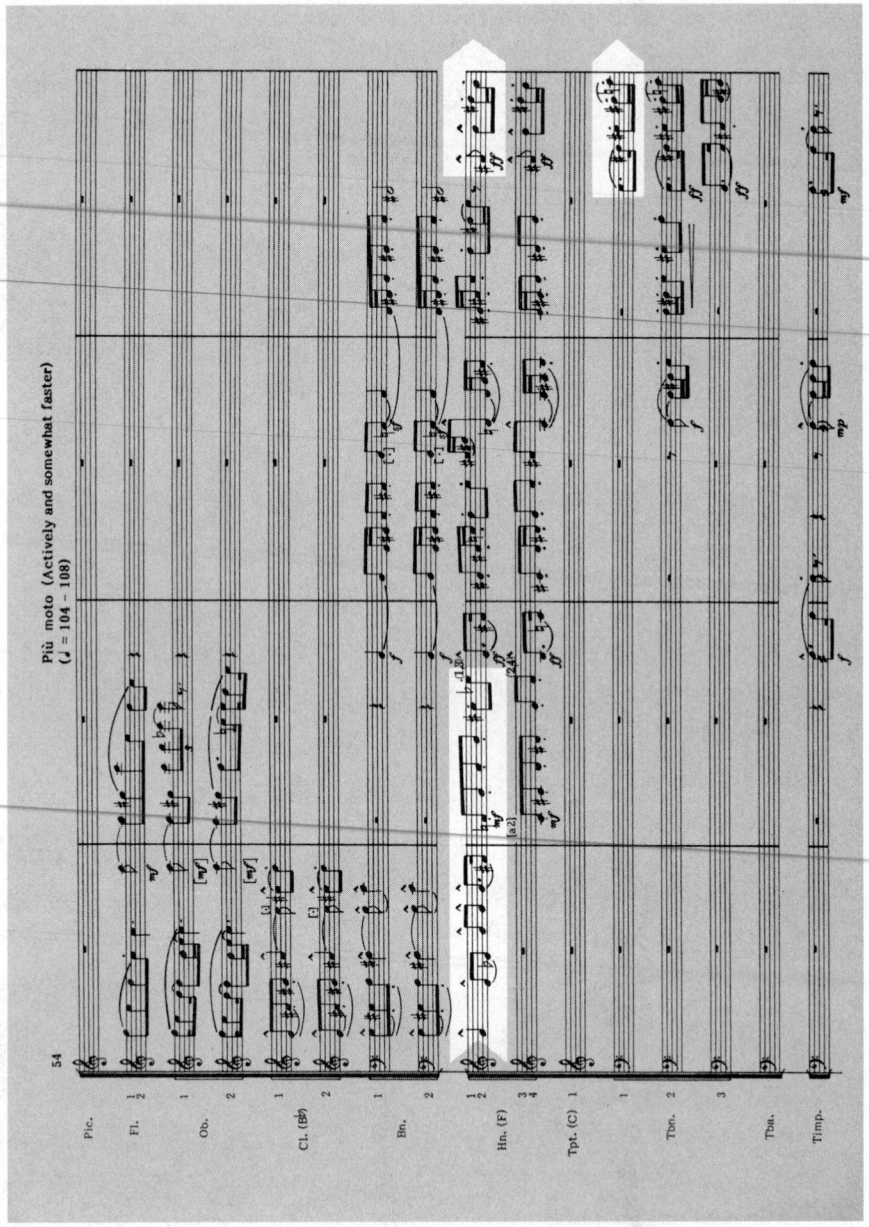
54
Più moto (Actively and somewhat faster)
(♩ = 104 – 108)
Pic.
Fl. 1 2
Ob. 1 2
Cl. (B♭) 1 2
Bn. 1 2
Hn. (F) 1 2 3 4
Tpt. (C) 1 1
Tbn. 2 3
Tba.
Timp.

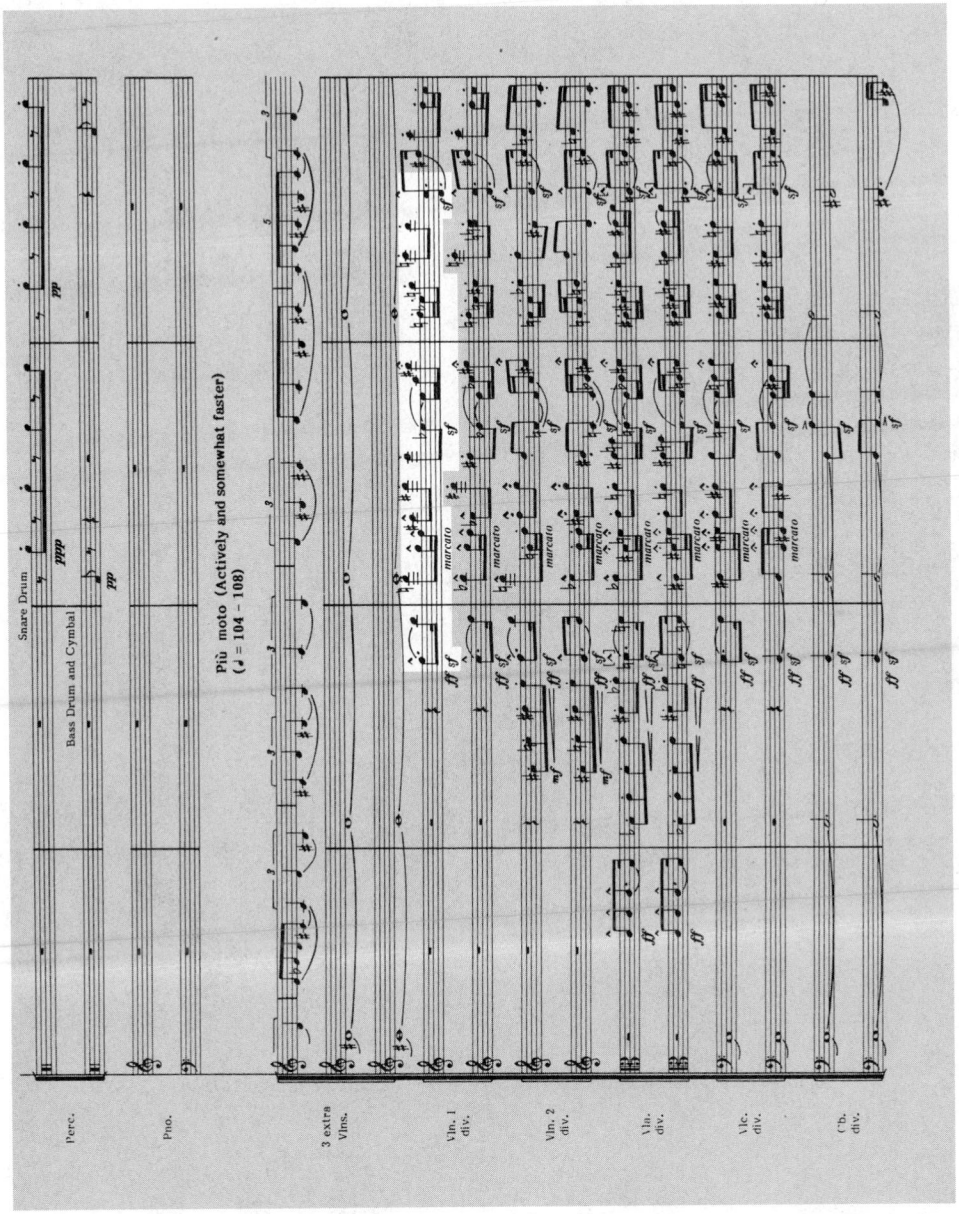
Perc.
Snare Drum
Bass Drum and Cymbal
Pno.
Più moto (Actively and somewhat faster)
(♩ = 104 – 108)
3 extra Vlns.
Vln. 1 div.
Vln. 2 div.
Vla. div.
Vle. div.
Cb. div.
marcato

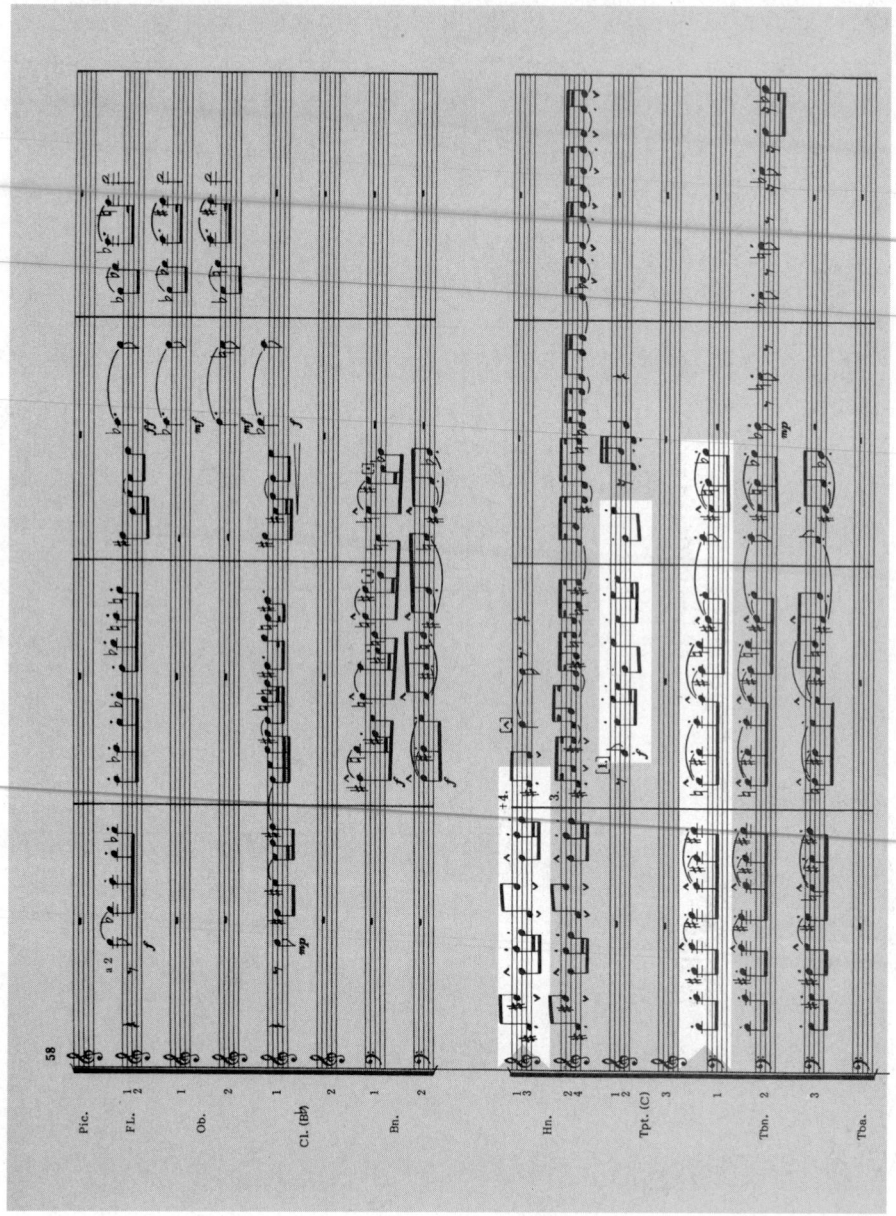
58
Pic.
Fl.
Ob.
Cl. (B♭)
Bn.
Hn.
Tpt. (C)
Tbn.
Tba.
a 2
mp
f
mf
+4.
3.
[2]
[1]

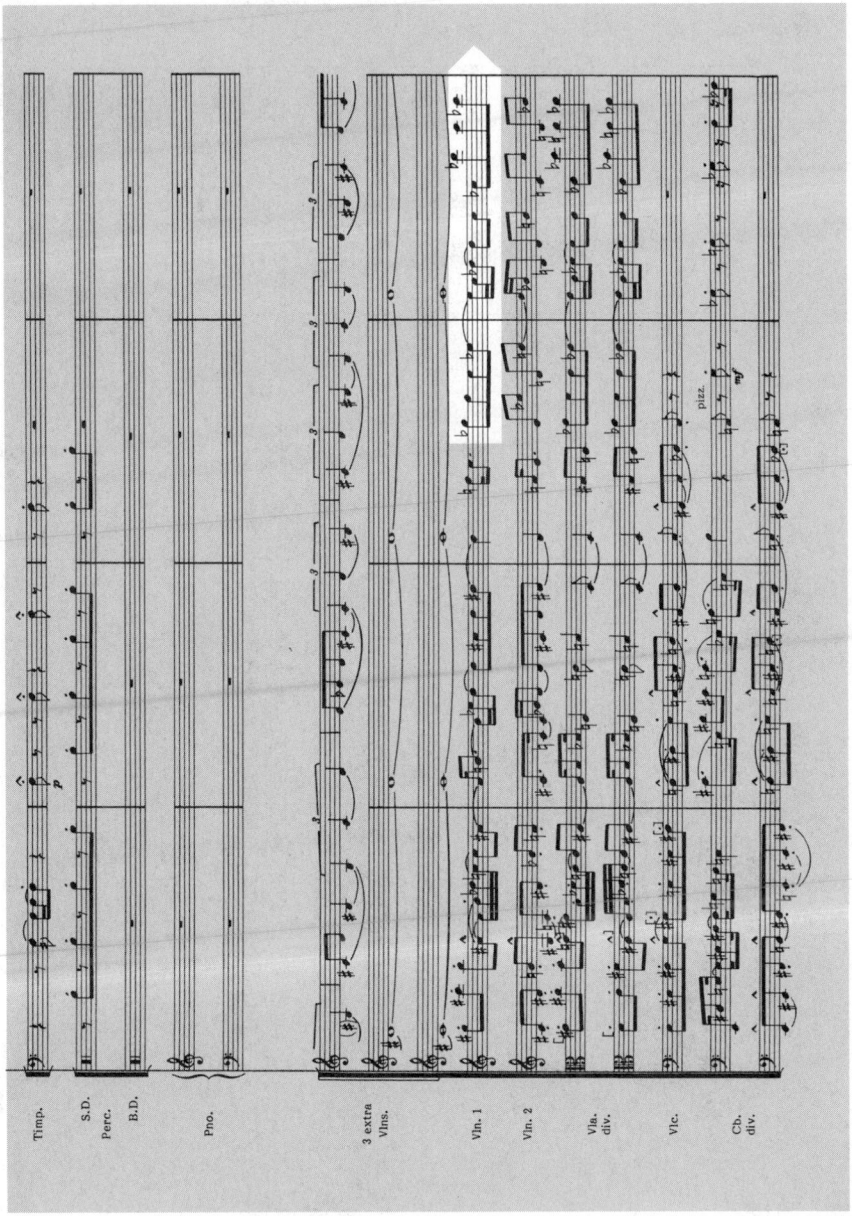
Timp.
S.D.
Perc.
B.D.
Pno.
3 extra Vlns.
Vln. 1
Vln. 2
Vla. div.
Vlc.
Cb. div.
p
pizz.
mf

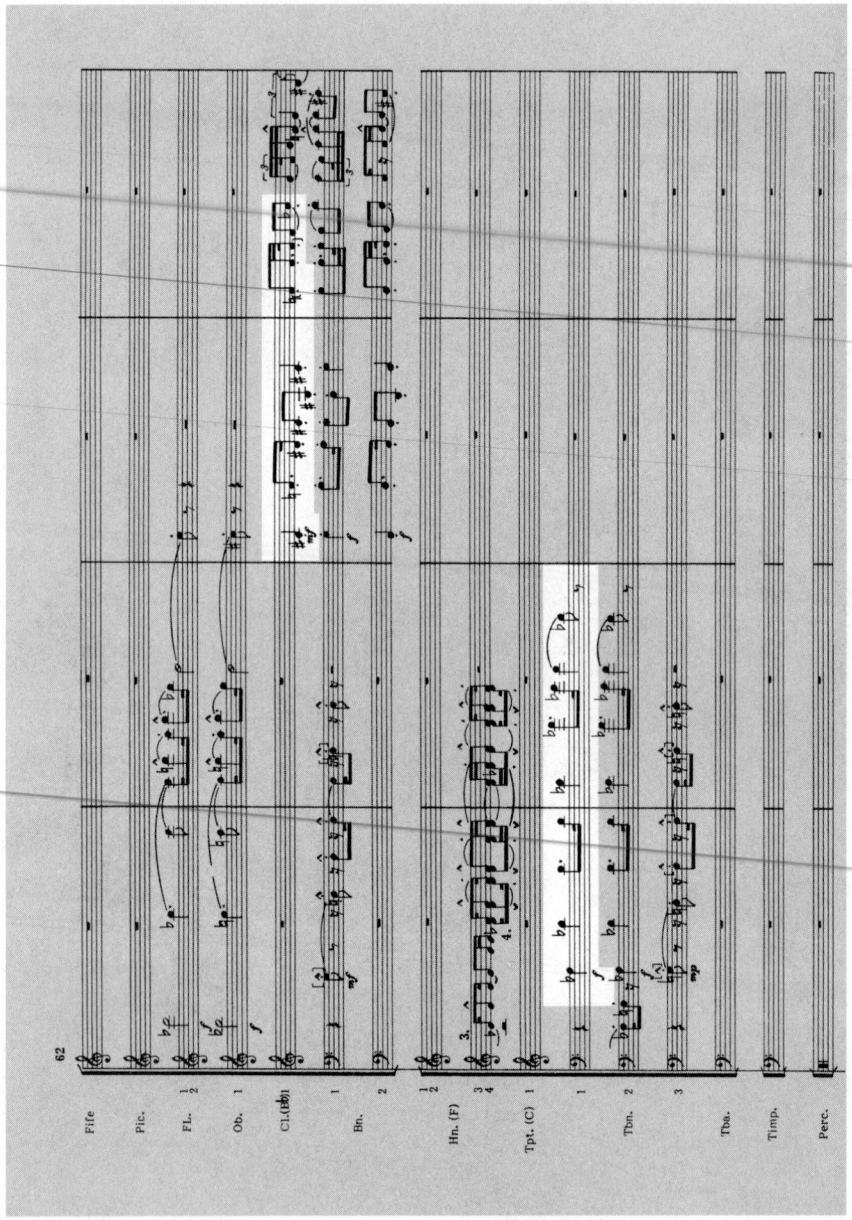
62
Fife
Pic.
Fl.
Ob.
Cl.
Bn.
Hn. (F)
Tpt. (C)
Tbn.
Tba.
Timp.
Perc.

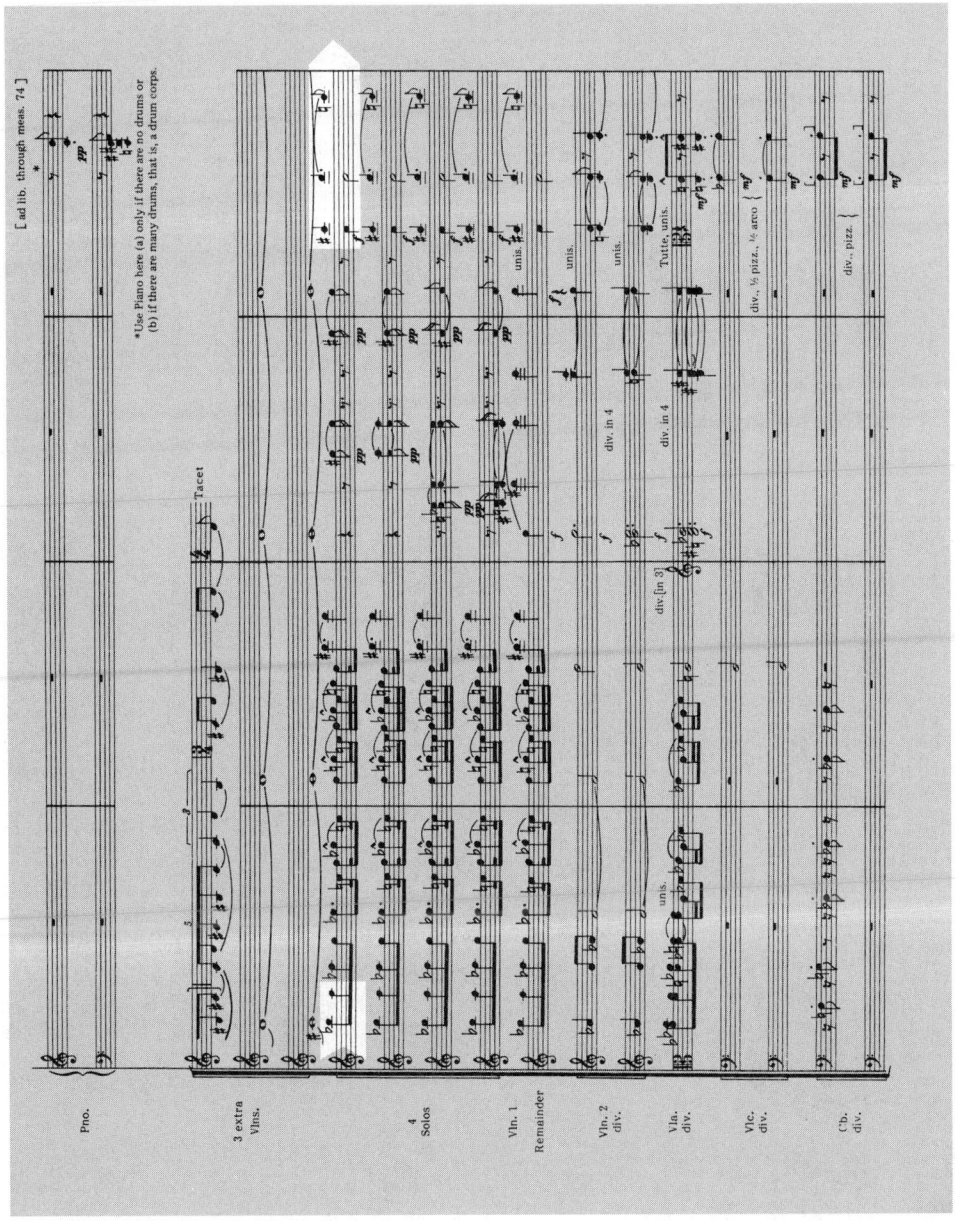
[ad lib. through meas. 74]
*Use Piano here (a) only if there are no drums or
(b) if there are many drums, that is, a drum corps.
Tacet
Pno.
3 extra Vlns.
4 Solos
Vln. 1 Remainder
Vln. 2 div.
Vln. div.
Vlc. div.
Cb. div.
unis.
div. in 4
div. [in 3]
Tutte, unis.
div., ½ pizz., ½ arco
div., pizz.

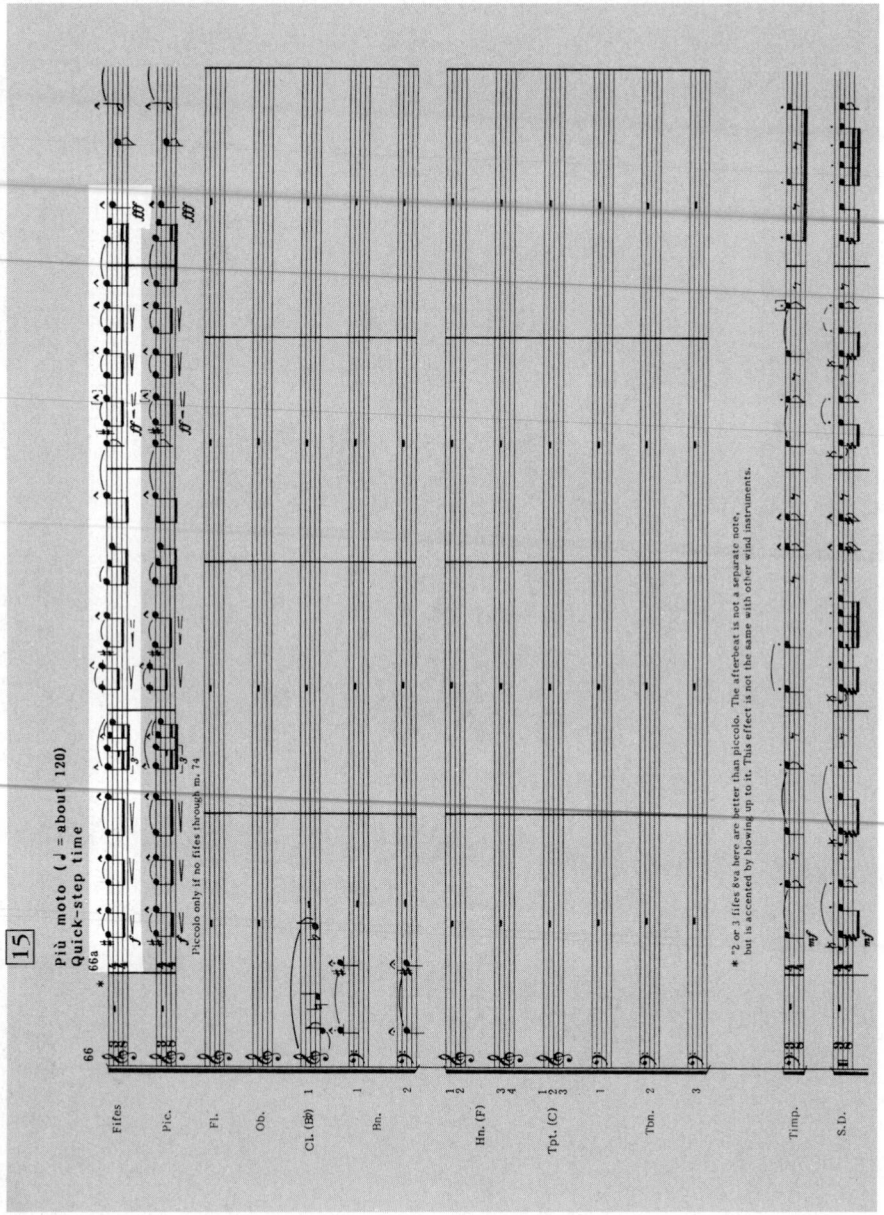
15
Più moto (♩ = about 120)
Quick-step time
66
* 66a
Piccolo only if no fifes through m. 74
Fifes
Pic.
Fl.
Ob.
Cl. (B♭) 1
1
Bn.
2
1
2
Hn. (F)
3
4
Tpt. (C)
1
2
3
1
Tbn.
2
3
Timp.
S.D.
* 2 or 3 fifes 8vb here are better than piccolo. The afterbeat is not a separate note,
but is accented by blowing up to it. This effect is not the same with other wind instruments.

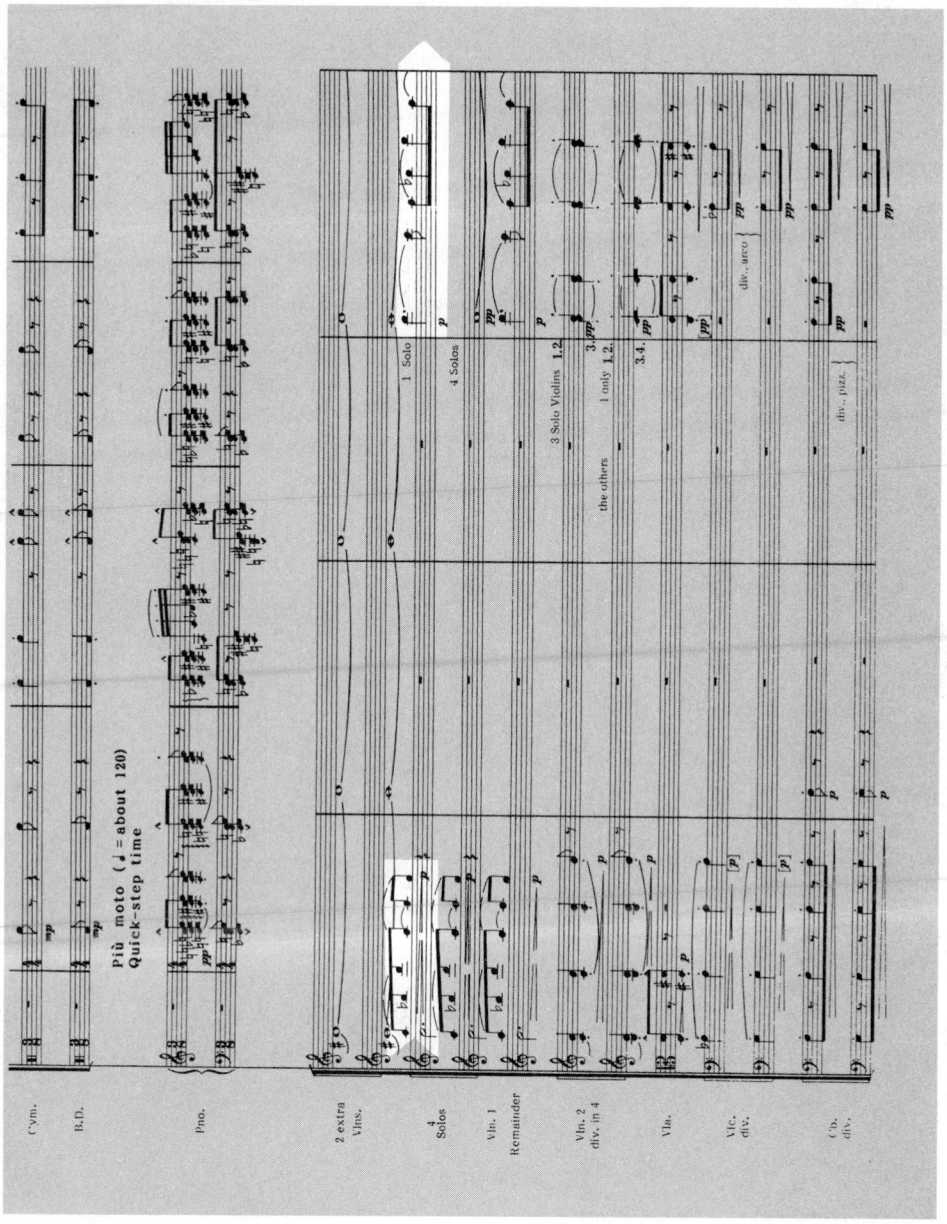
Cym.
B.D.
Pno.
Più moto (♩ = about 120)
Quick-step time
2 extra Vlns.
4 Solos
Vln. 1 Remainder
Vln. 2 div. in 4
Vla.
Vlc. div.
Cb. div.
1 Solo
4 Solos
3 Solo Violins 1.2
the others 1 only 1.2.
3.4.
div., arco
div., pizz.

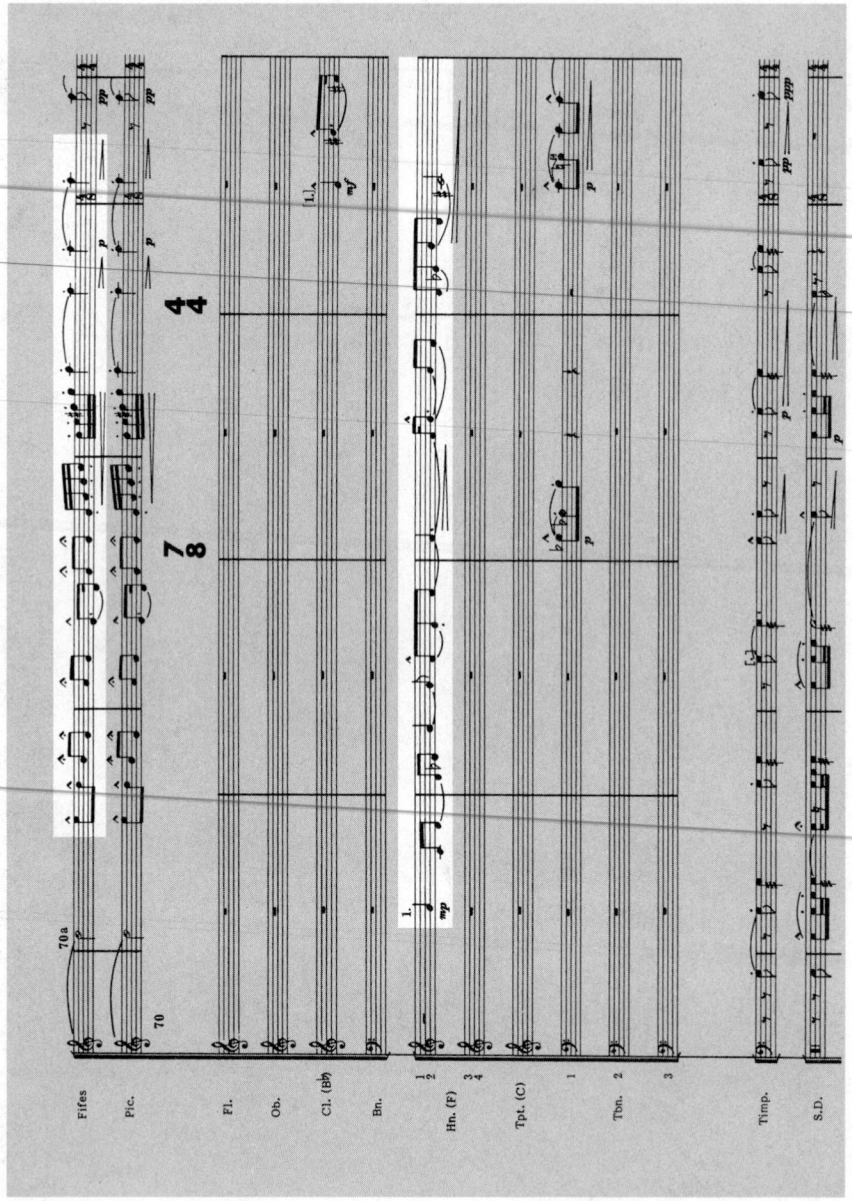
Fifes
Pic.
Fl.
Ob.
Cl. (B♭)
Bn.
Hn. (F)
Tpt. (C)
Ton.
Timp.
S.D.
70a
70
7/8
4/4
[L.]
mf
mp
p
pp
ppp

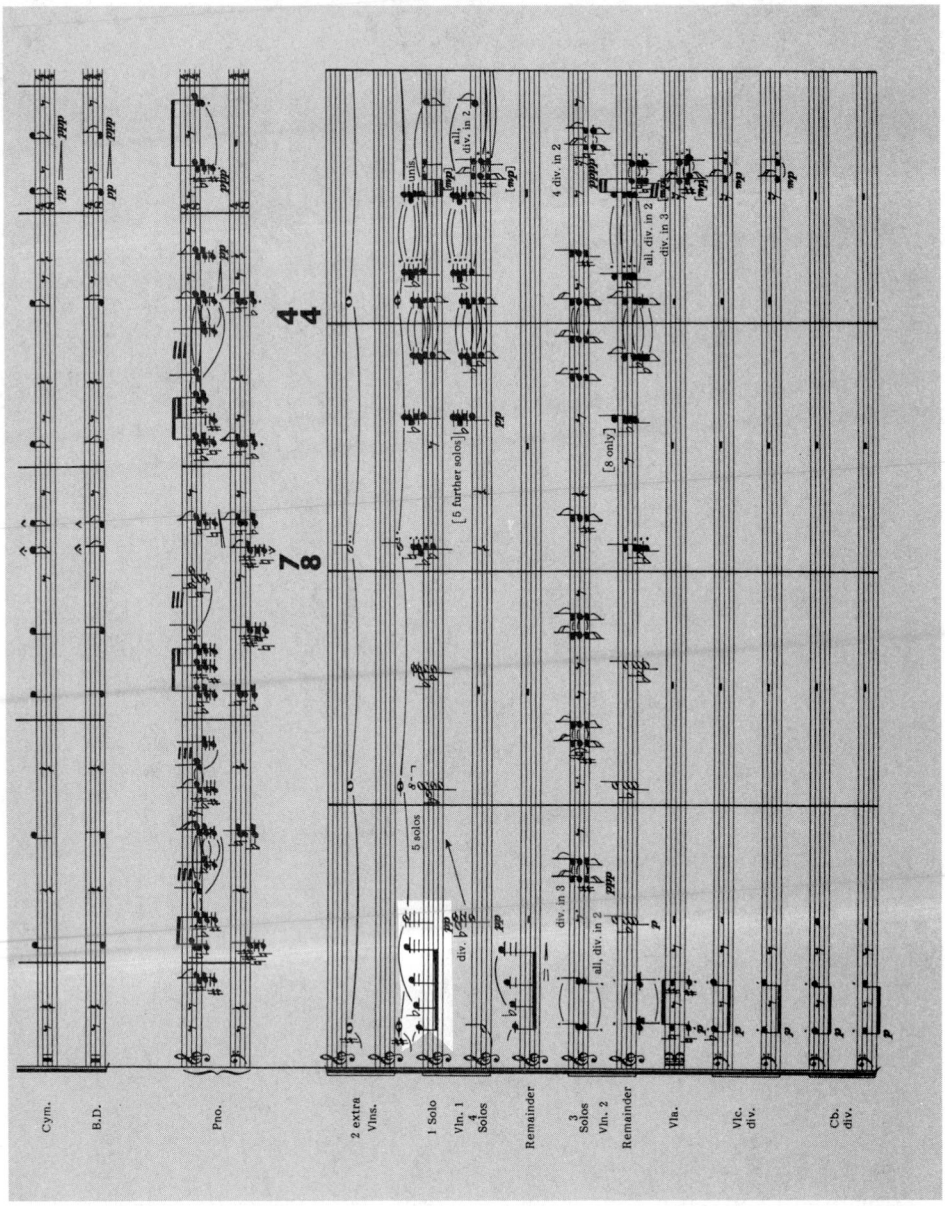
Cym.
B.D.
Pno.
2 extra Vlns.
1 Solo Vln. 1
4 Solos
Remainder
3 Solos Vln. 2
Remainder
Vla.
Vlc. div.
Cb. div.
5 solos
div.
div. in 3
all, div. in 2
[5 further solos]
unis.
all, div. in 2
[mp]
[dim.]
4 div. in 2
[8 only]
all, div. in 2
div. in 3
[mp]
[dim.]

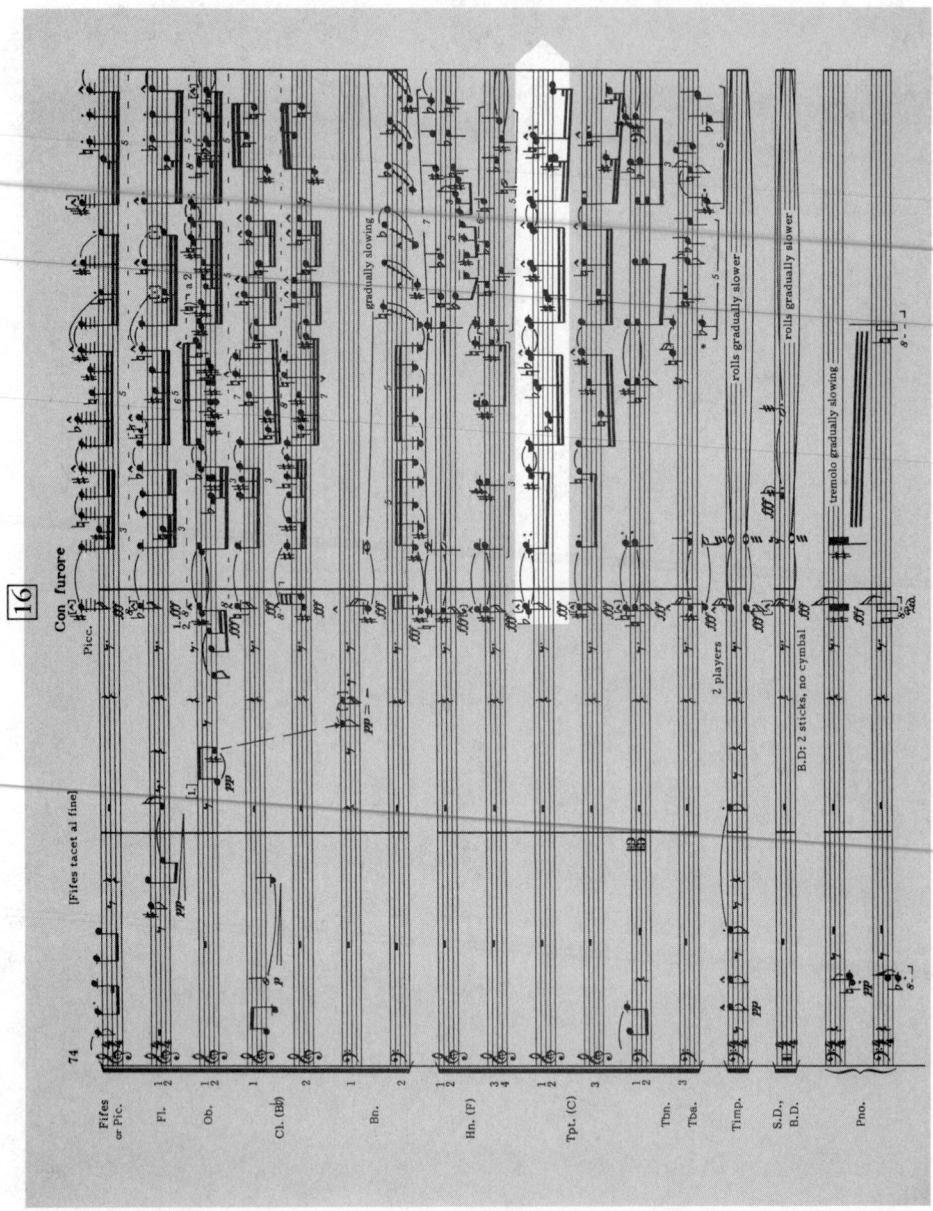
74
16
Con furore
[Fifes tacet al fine]
Fifes or Pic.
Picc.
Fl.
Ob.
Cl. (B♭)
a 2
Bn.
gradually slowing
Hn. (F)
Tpt. (C)
Tbn.
Tbs.
Timp.
2 players
rolls gradually slower
S.D., B.D.
B.D: 2 sticks, no cymbal
rolls gradually slower
Pno.
tremolo gradually slowing

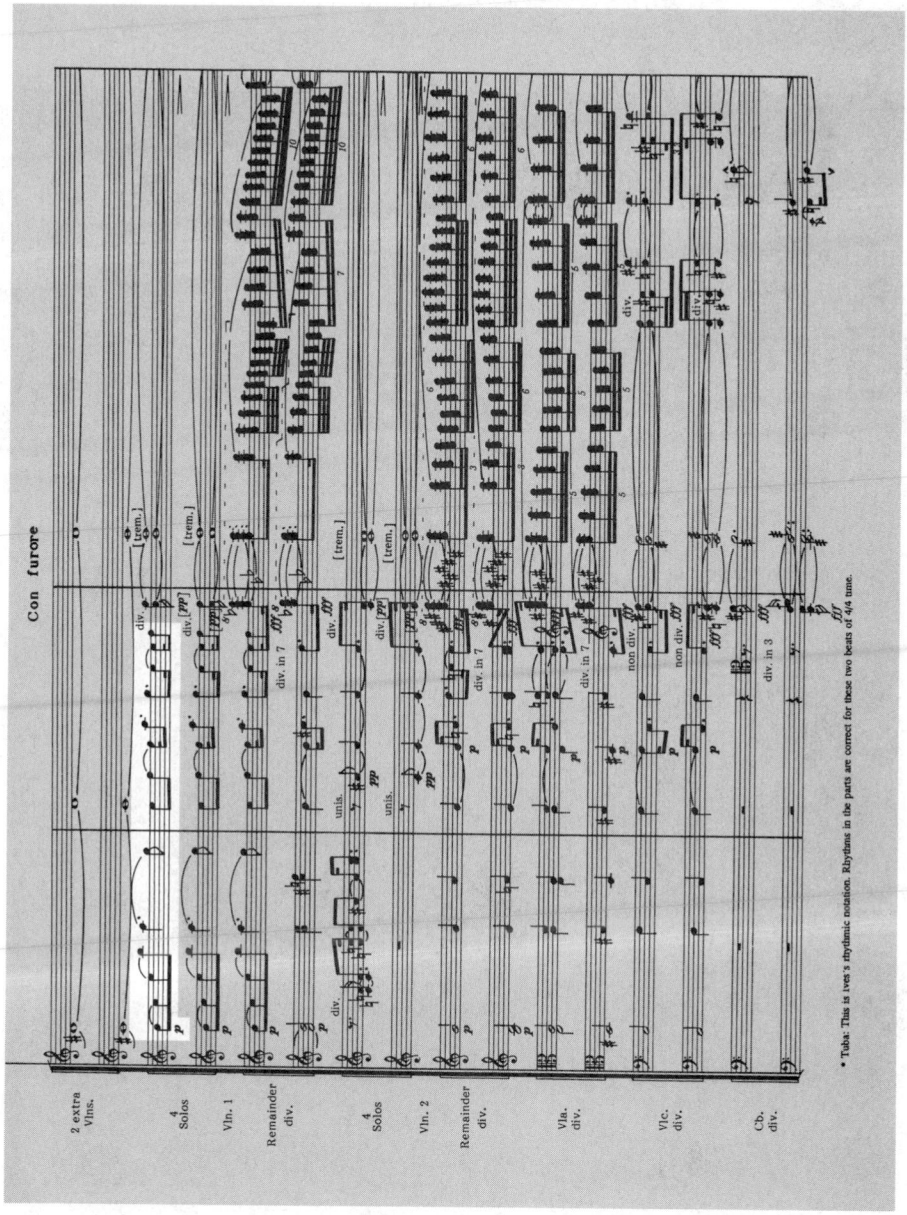
Con furore
2 extra Vlns.
4 Solos
Vln. 1
Remainder div.
4 Solos
Vln. 2
Remainder div.
Vla. div.
Vlc. div.
Cb. div.
[trem.]
div.
div. in 7
unis.
div. in 3
non div.
div. in 3
* Tuba: This is Ives's rhythmic notation. Rhythms in the parts are correct for these two beats of 4/4 time.

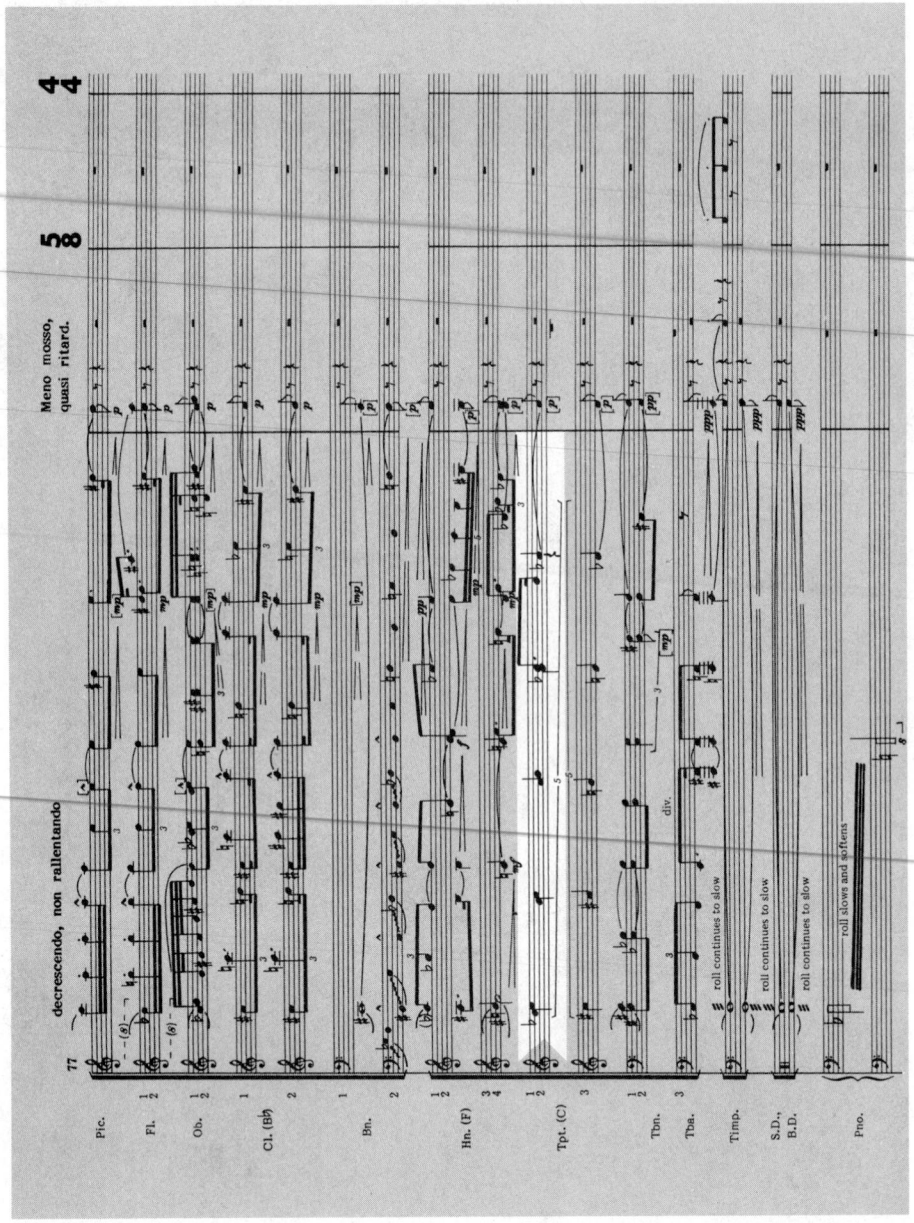
77
decrescendo, non rallentando
Meno mosso, quasi ritard.
Pic.
Fl.
Ob.
Cl. (B♭)
Bn.
Hn. (F)
Tpt. (C)
Tbn.
Tba.
Timp.
S.D., B.D.
Pno.
div.
roll continues to slow
roll continues to slow
roll continues to slow
roll slows and softens

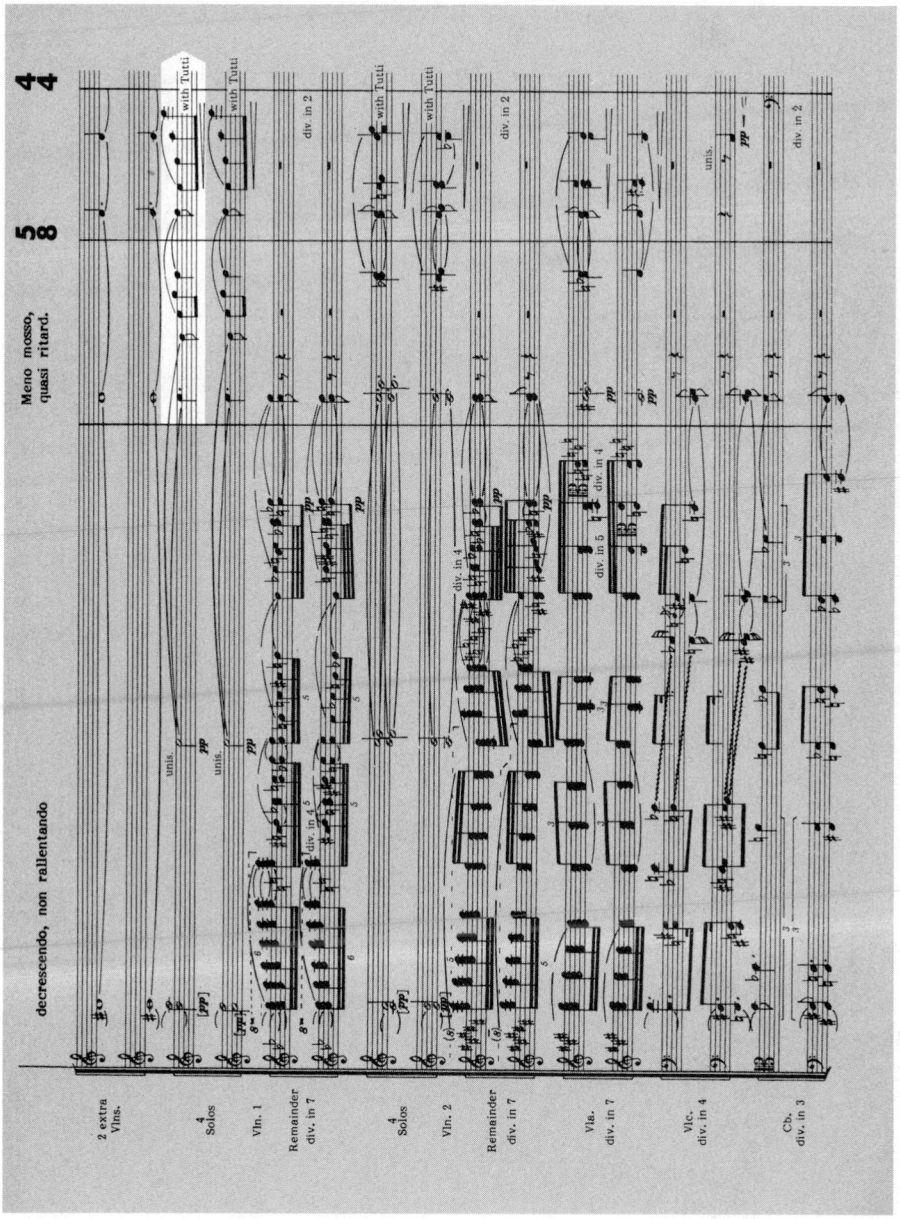
decrescendo, non rallentando
Meno mosso, quasi ritard.
5/8
4/4
2 extra Vlns.
4 Solos
Vln. 1
Remainder div. in 7
4 Solos
Vln. 2
Remainder div. in 7
Vlas. div. in 7
Vlc. div. in 4
Cb. div. in 3
unis.
with Tutti
div. in 2
div. in 4
div. in 5

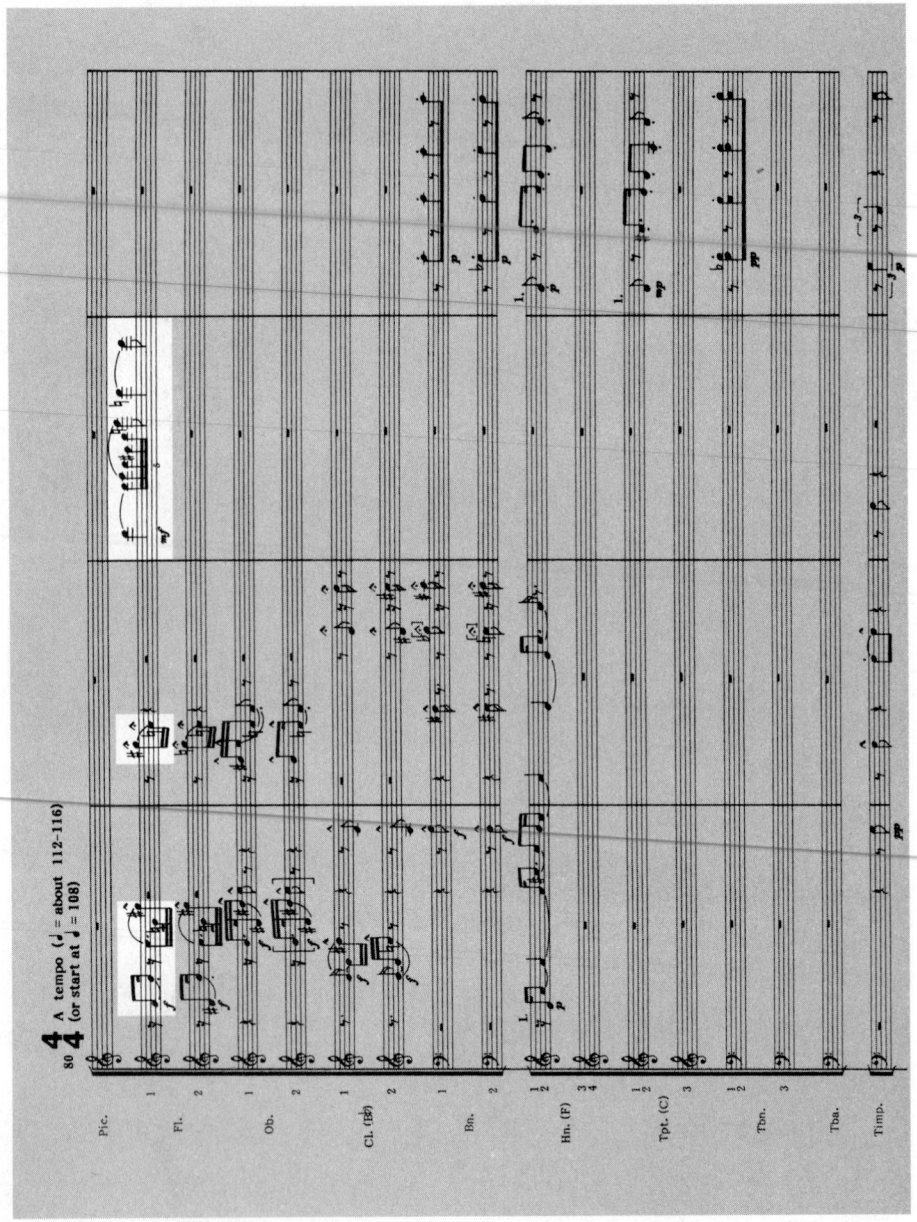
80
A tempo (♩ = about 112–116)
(or start at ♩ = 108)
Pic.
Fl.
Ob.
Cl. (B♭)
Bn.
Hn. (F)
Tpt. (C)
Tbn.
Tba.
Timp.

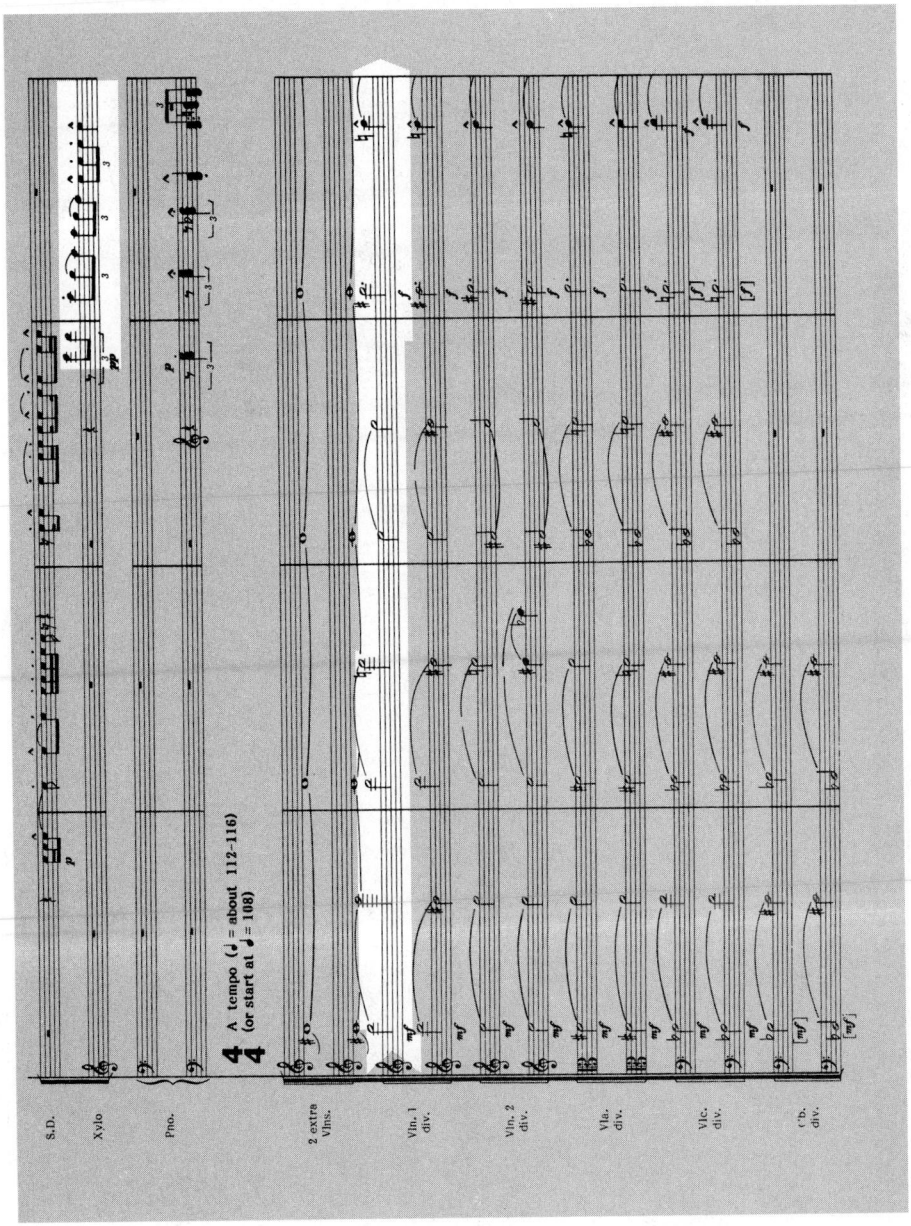
S.D.
Xylo
Pno.
A tempo (♩ = about 112–116)
(or start at ♩ = 108)
2 extra Vlns.
Vln. 1 div.
Vln. 2 div.
Vla. div.
Vlc. div.
C'b. div.

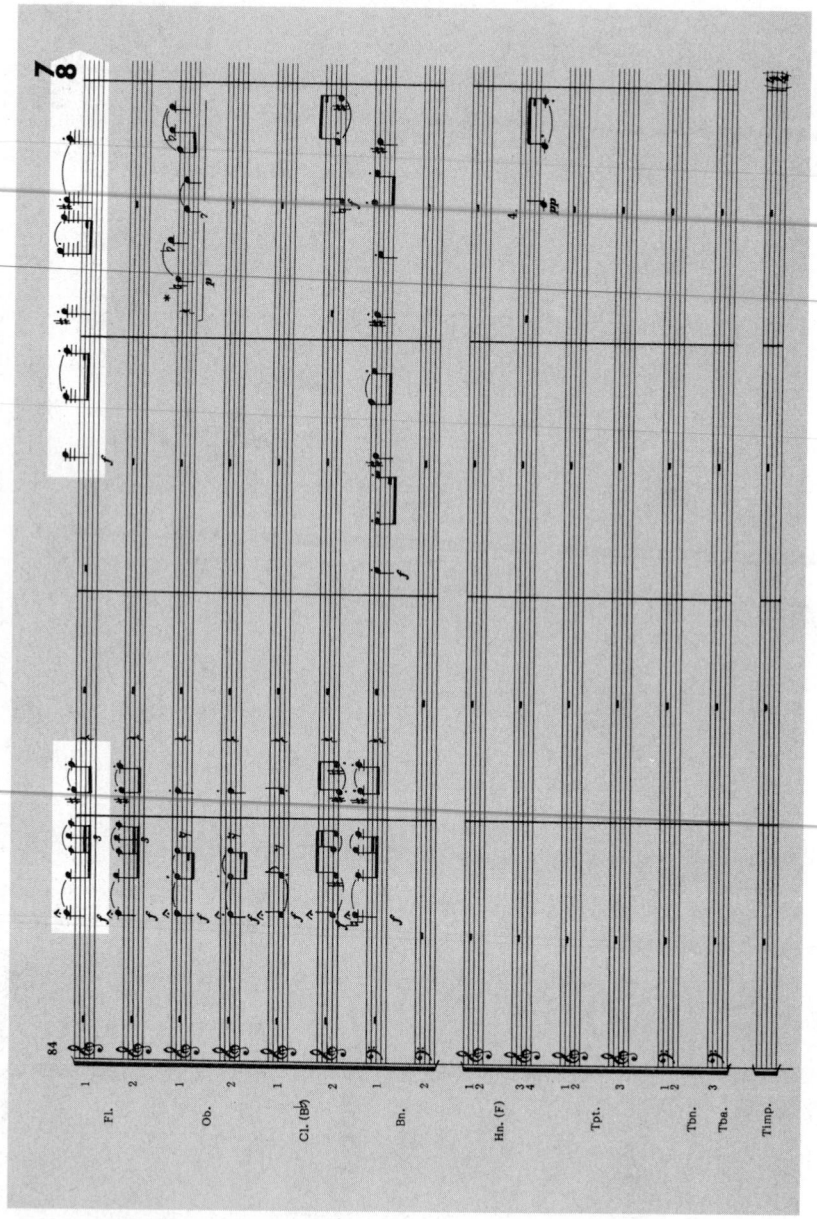
84
7
8
Fl.
Ob.
Cl. (B♭)
Bn.
Hn. (F)
Tpt.
Tbn.
Tba.
Timp.

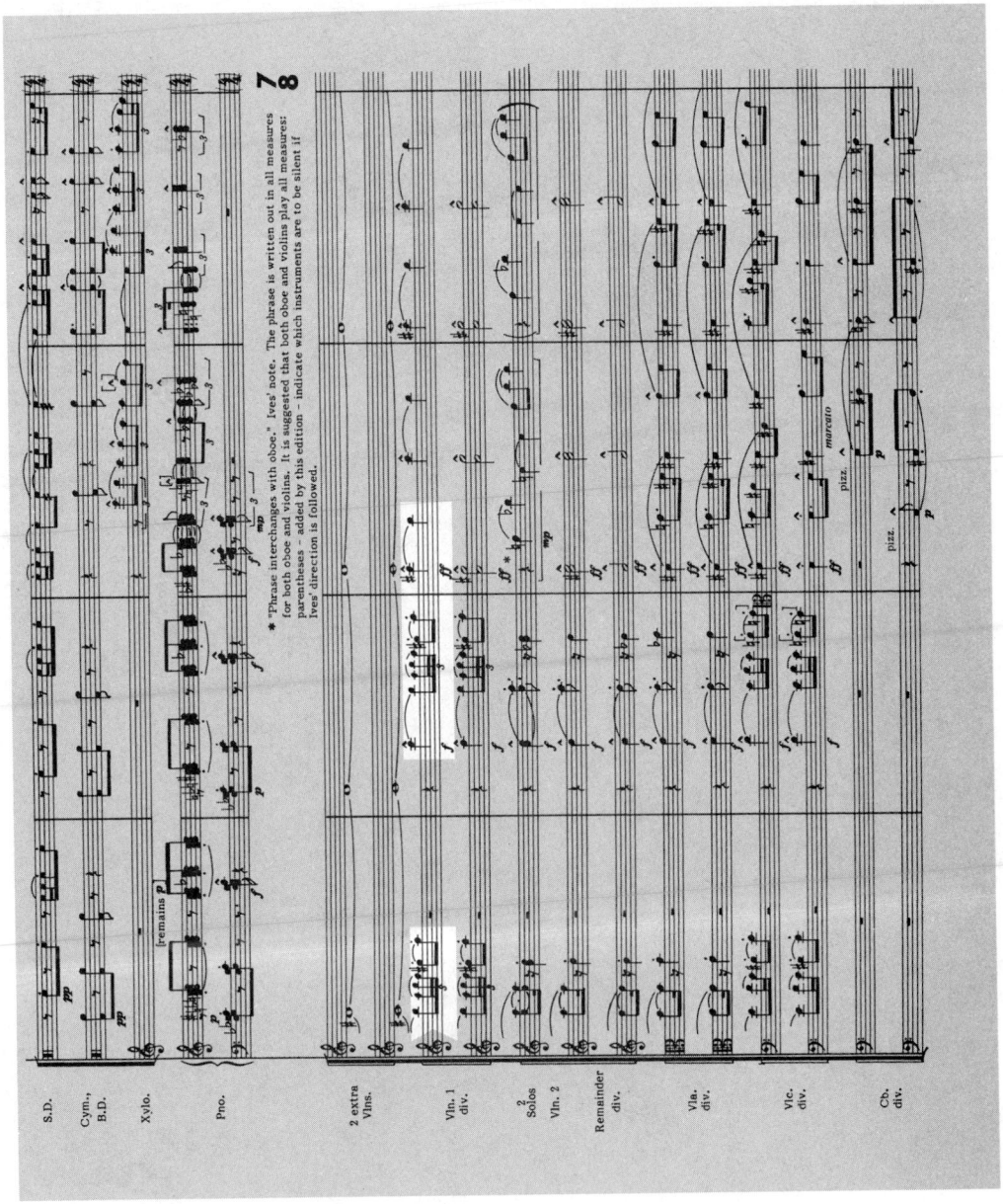
S.D.
Cym., B.D.
Xylo.
Pno.
[remains p]
7
8
* "Phrase interchanges with oboe." Ives' note. The phrase is written out in all measures for both oboe and violins. It is suggested that both oboe and violins play all measures; parentheses added by this edition– indicate which instruments are to be silent if Ives' direction is followed.
2 extra Vlns.
Vln. 1 div.
2 Solos
Vln. 2
Remainder div.
Vla. div.
Vlc. div.
Cb. div.
pizz.
marcato
pizz.

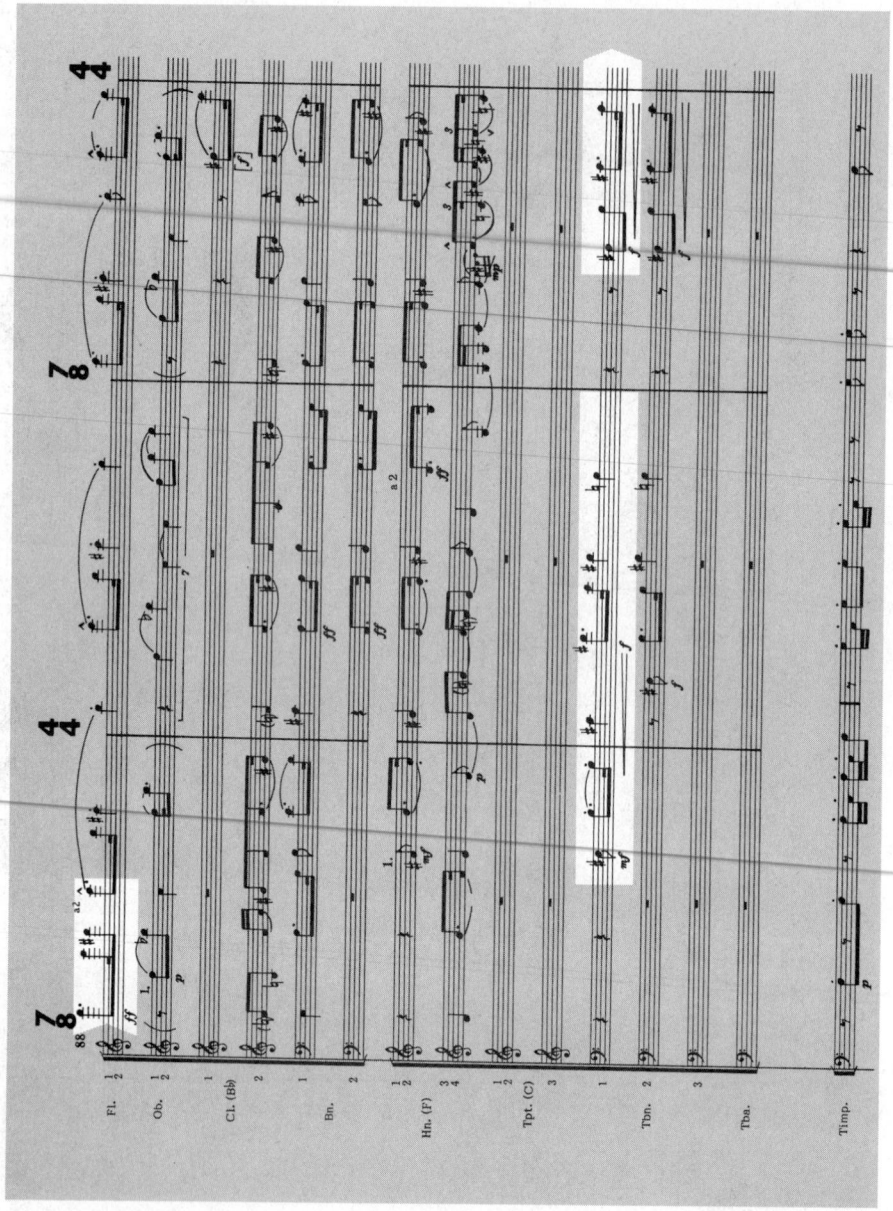
Fl.
Ob.
Cl. (B♭)
Bn.
Hn. (F)
Tpt. (C)
Tbn.
Tba.
Timp.
88
a2

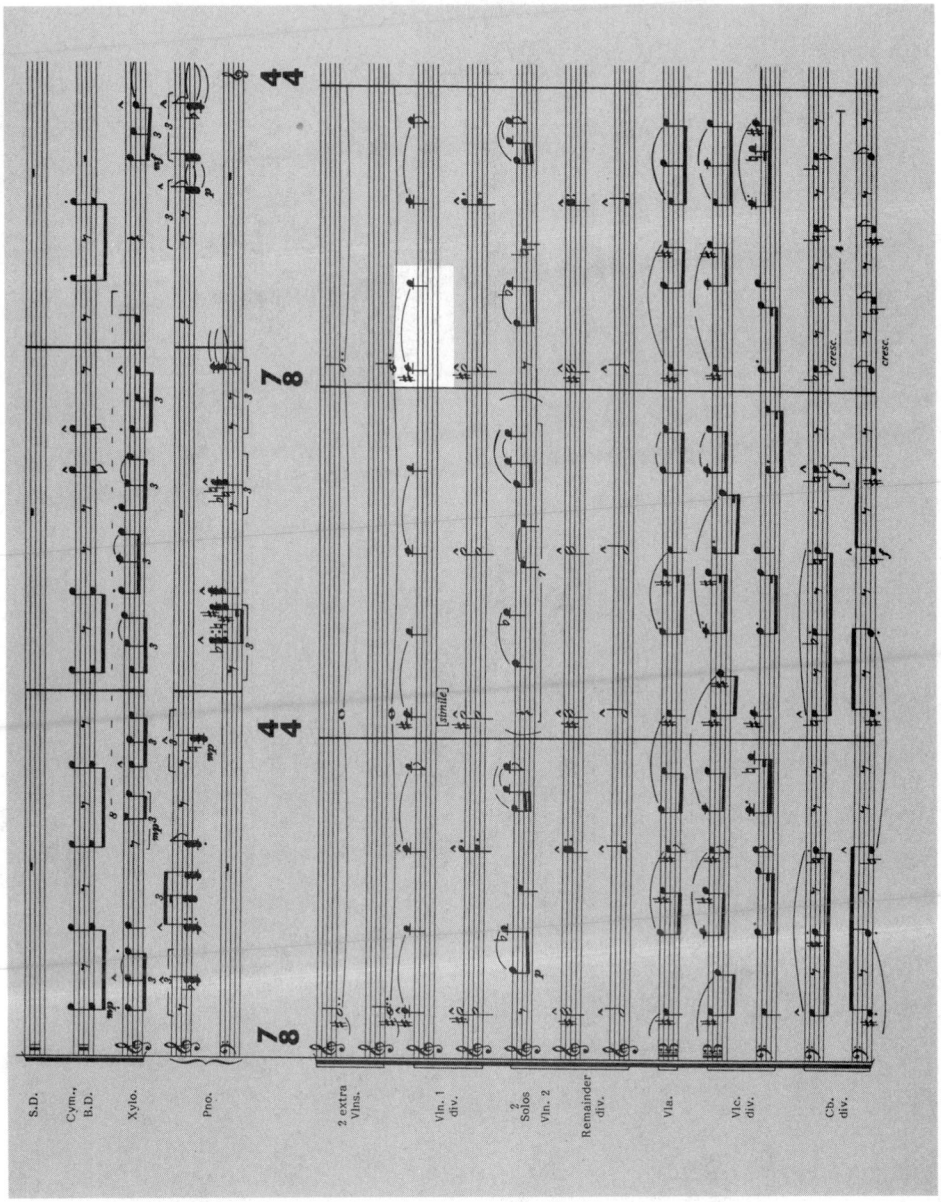
S.D.
Cym., B.D.
Xylo.
Pno.
2 extra Vlns.
Vln. 1 div.
2 Solos Vln. 2
Remainder div.
Vla.
Vlc. div.
Cb. div.
[similc]
cresc.
cresc.

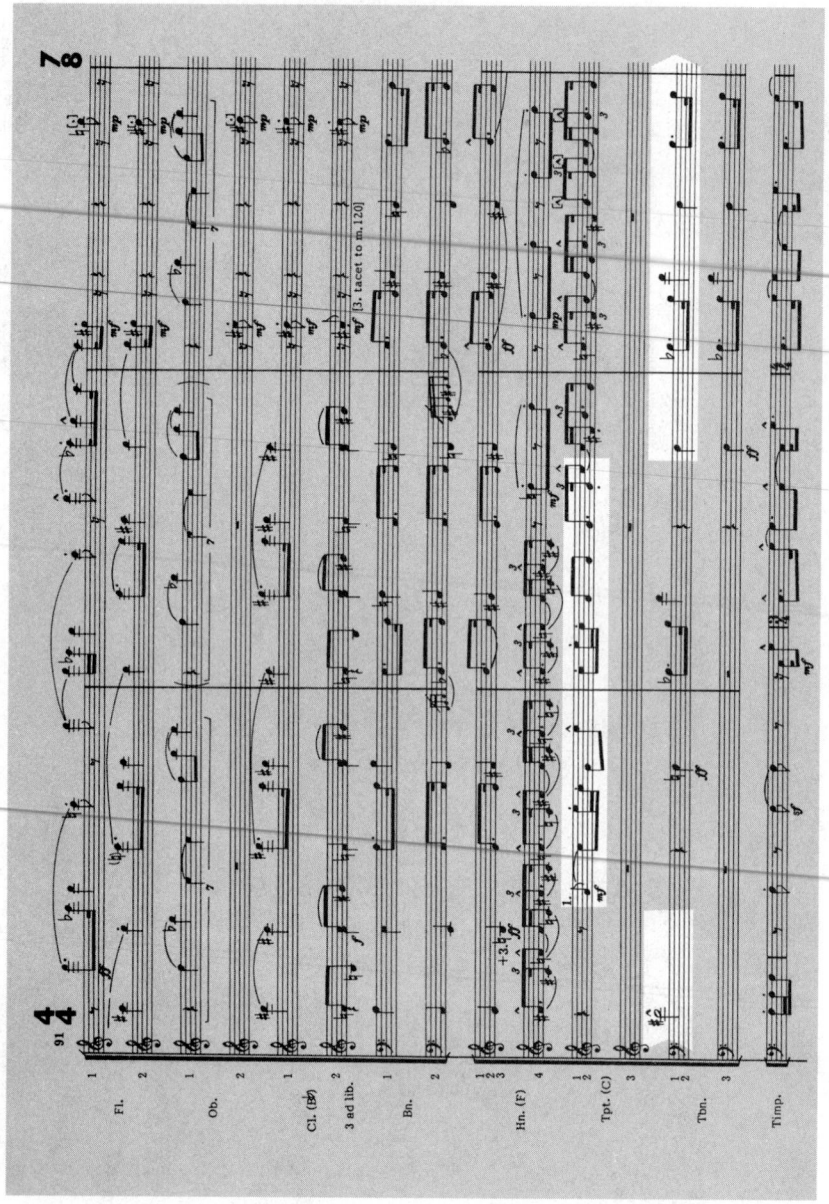
91
Fl.
Ob.
Cl. (B♭)
3 ad lib.
Bn.
Hn. (F)
Tpt. (C)
Tbn.
Timp.
[3. tacet to m.120]

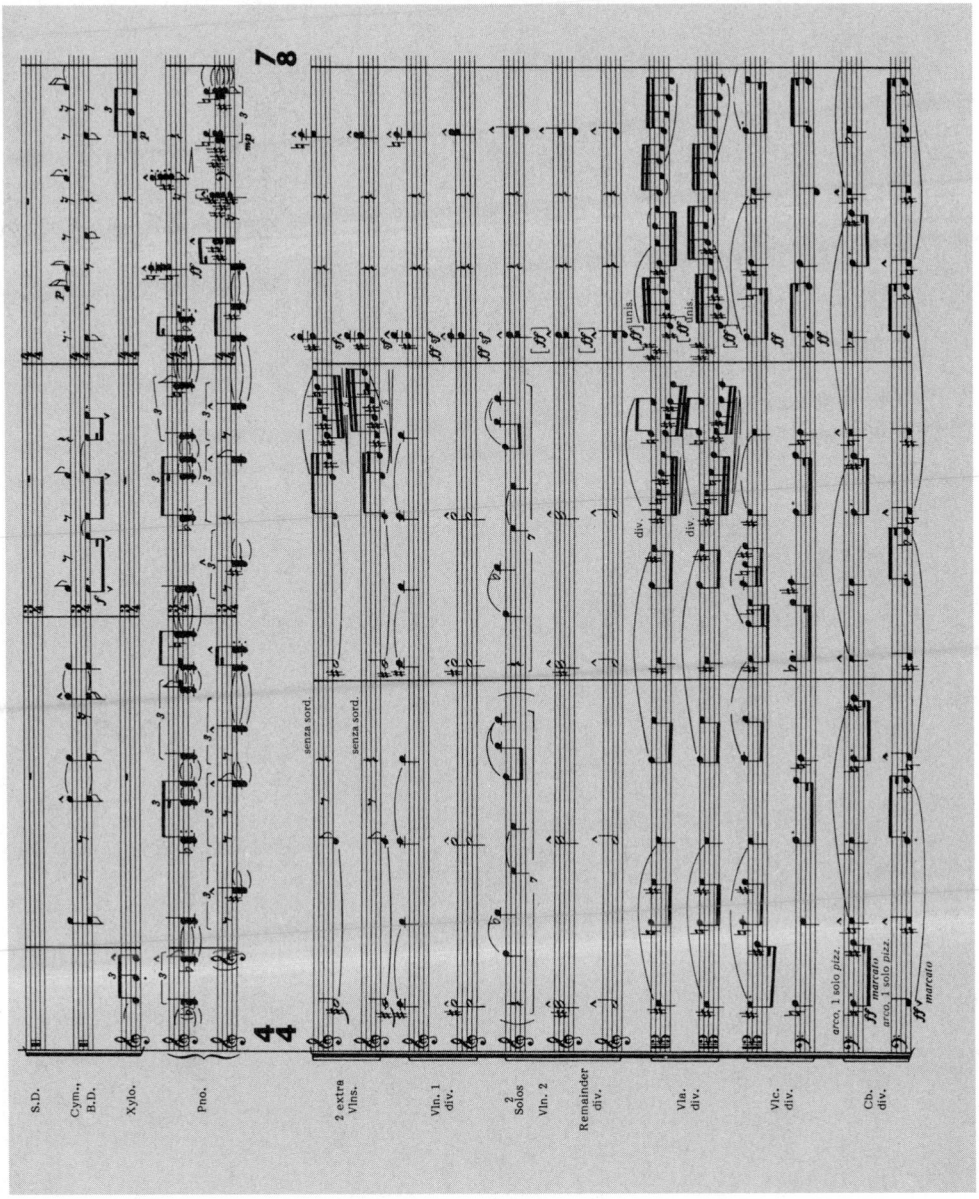
S.D.
Cym., B.D.
Xylo.
Pno.
2 extra Vlns.
senza sord.
senza sord.
Vln. 1 div.
2 Solos Vln. 2
Remainder div.
div.
unis.
Vla. div.
div.
unis.
Vlc. div.
arco, 1 solo pizz.
Cb. div.
arco, 1 solo pizz.
marcato
marcato

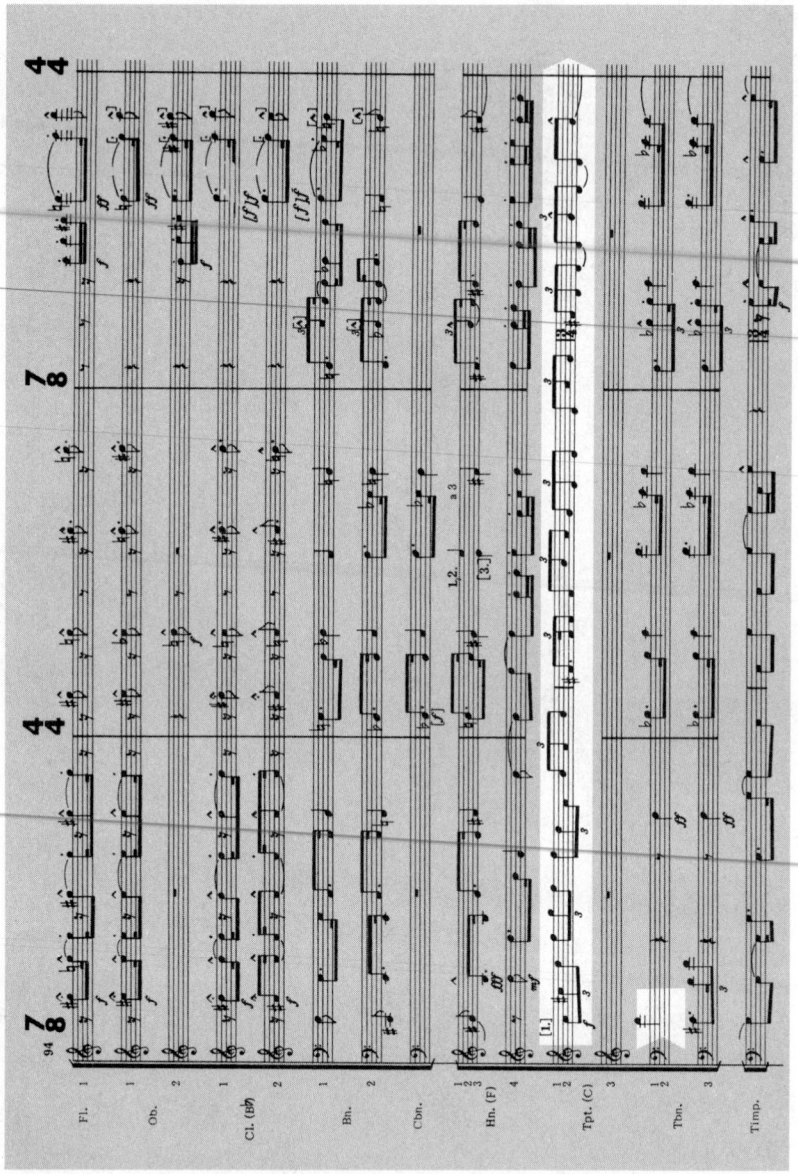
94
Fl. 1
Ob. 1
Ob. 2
Cl. (B♭) 1
Cl. (B♭) 2
Bn. 1
Bn. 2
Cbn.
Hn. (F) 1 2 3 4
Tpt. (C) 1 2 3
Tbn. 1 2 3
Timp.
[1.]
1.2.
a 3
[3.]

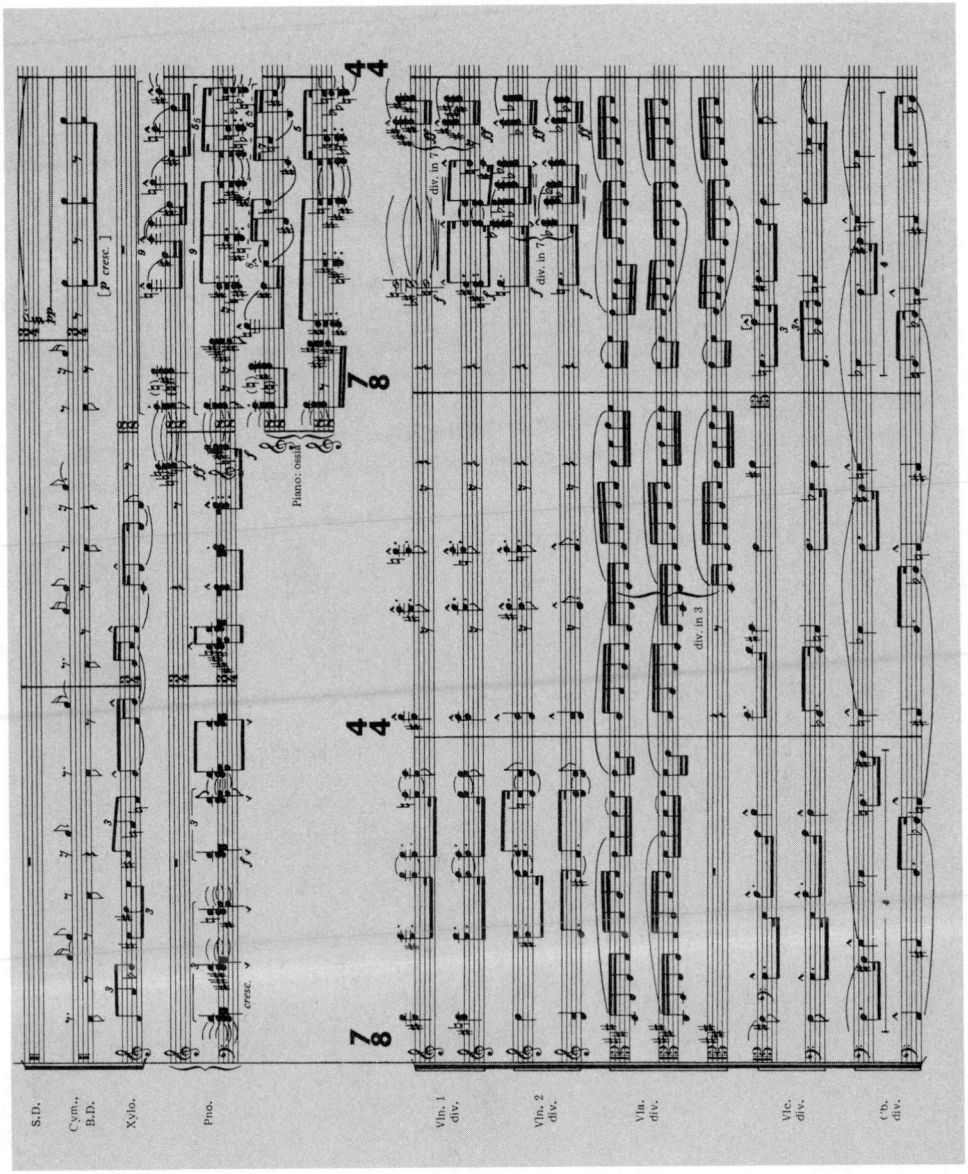
S.D.
Cym., B.D.
Xylo.
Pno.
[p cresc.]
cresc.
Piano: ossia
div. in 7
div. in 3
Vln. 1 div.
Vln. 2 div.
Vla. div.
Vlc. div.
Cb. div.

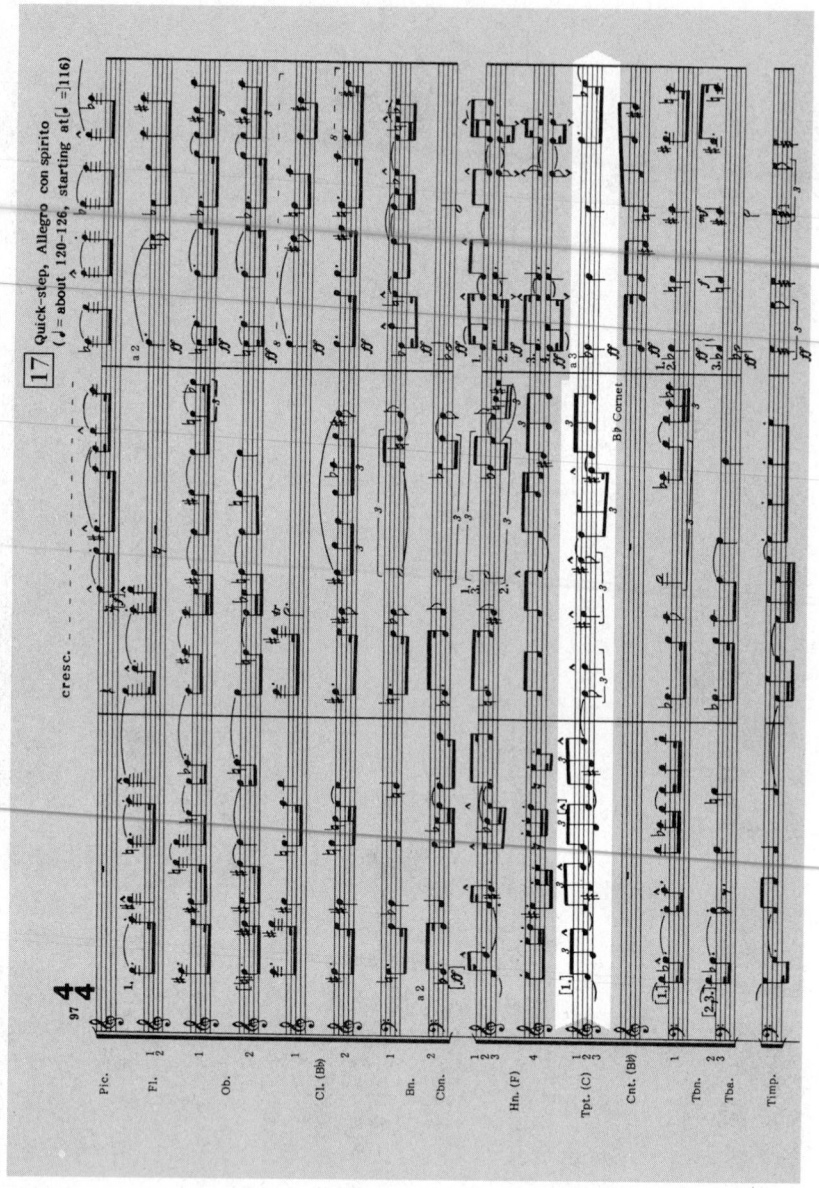
17 Quick-step, Allegro con spirito
(♩ = about 120–126, starting at [♩ =]116)
97
cresc.
Pic.
Fl.
Ob.
Cl. (B♭)
Bn.
Cbn.
Hn. (F)
Tpt. (C)
Cnt. (B♭)
Tbn.
Tba.
Timp.
a 2
a 3
B♭ Cornet

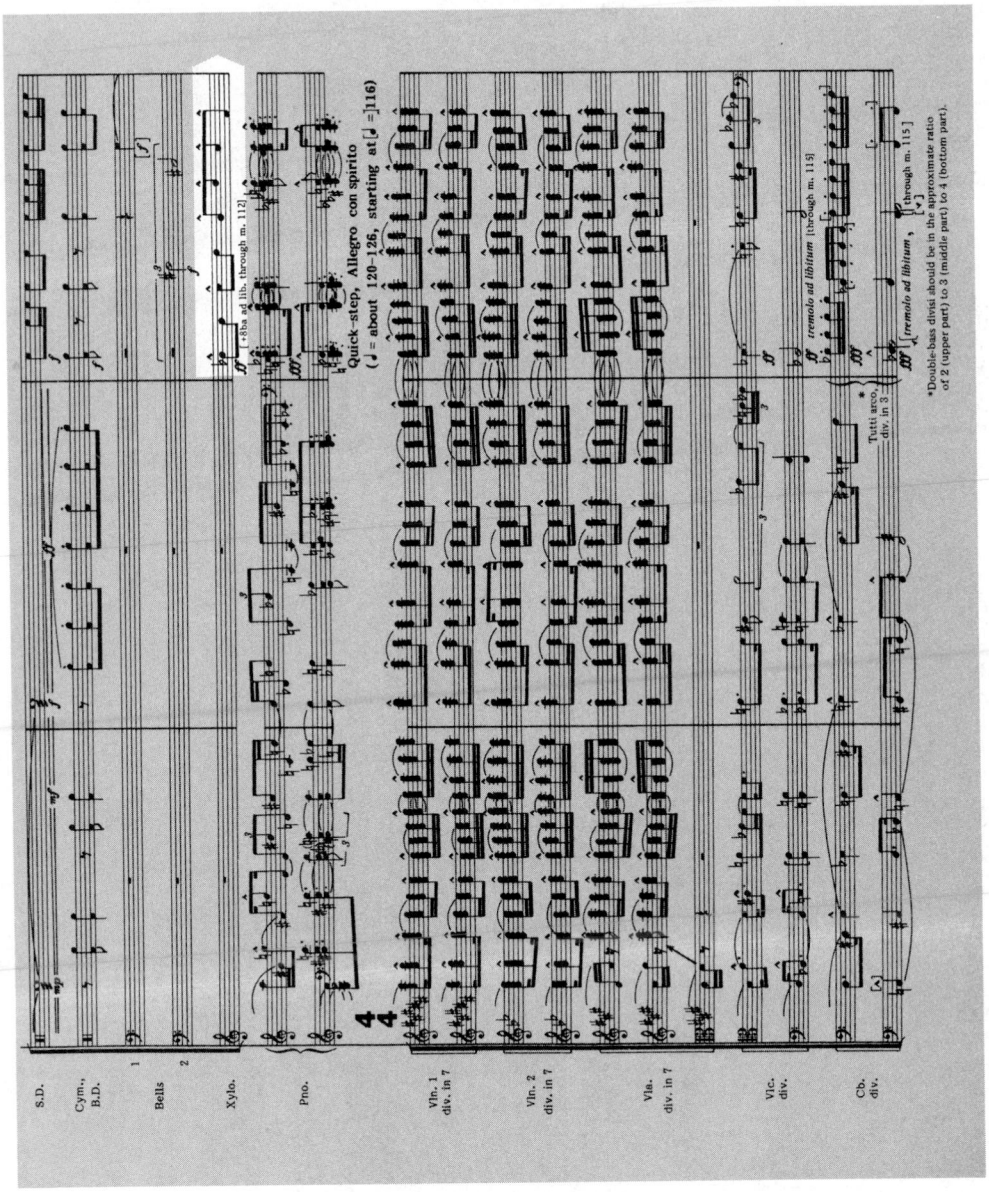
S.D.
Cym., B.D.
Bells
Xylo.
Pno.
Vln. 1 div. in 7
Vln. 2 div. in 7
Vla. div. in 7
Vlc. div.
Cb. div.
+tba ad lib. through m. 112]
Quick-step, Allegro con spirito
(♩ = about 120–126, starting at [♩ =♩116)
tremolo ad libitum [through m. 115]
tremolo ad libitum, [through m. 115]
Tutti arco, div. in 3
*Double-bass divisi should be in the approximate ratio of 2 (upper part) to 3 (middle part) to 4 (bottom part).

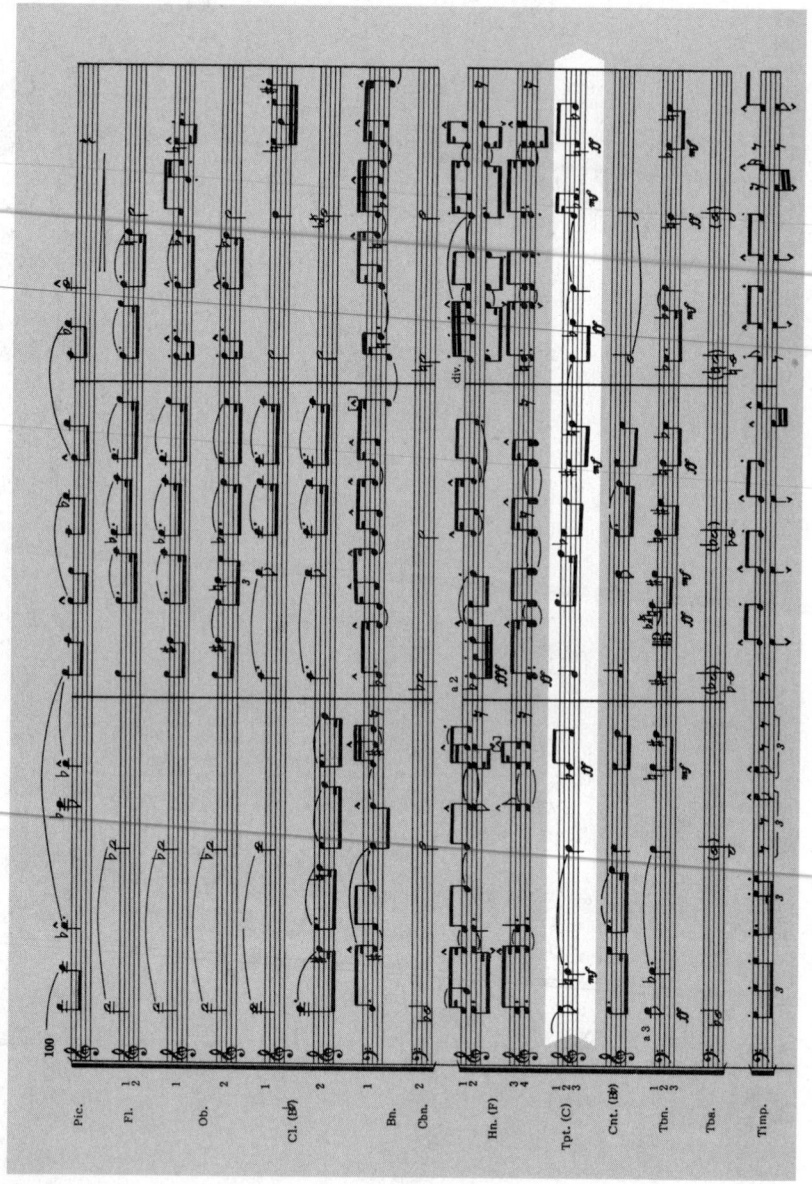
100
Pic.
Fl.
Ob.
Cl. (B♭)
Bn.
Cbn.
Hn. (F)
Tpt. (C)
Cnt. (B♭)
Tbn.
Tba.
Timp.
a 2
div.
a 3

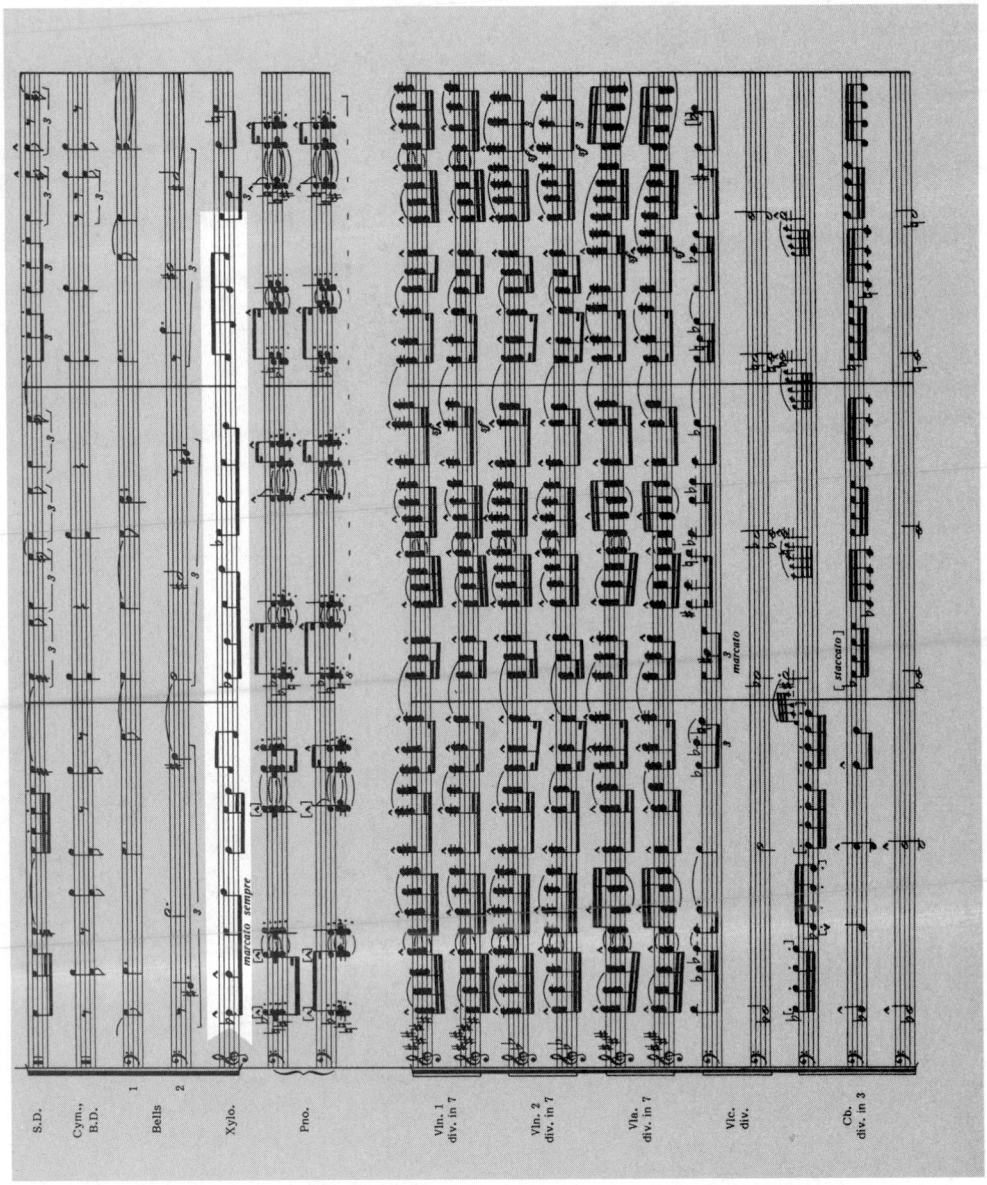
S.D.
Cym., B.D.
Bells
1
2
Xylo.
marcato sempre
Pno.
Vln. 1 div. in 7
Vln. 2 div. in 7
Vla. div. in 7
Vlc. div.
marcato
Cb. div. in 3
[staccato]

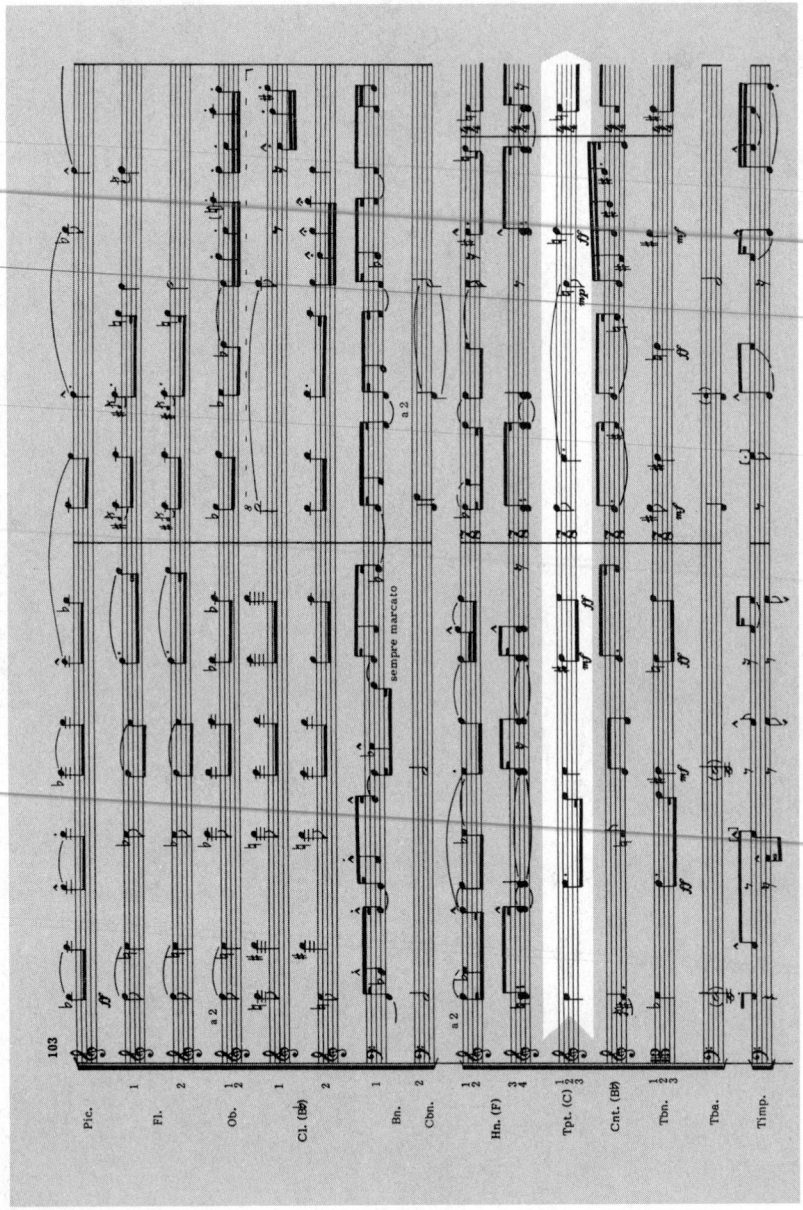
103
Pic.
Fl.
Ob.
Cl. (B♭)
Bn.
Cbn.
Hn. (F)
Tpt. (C)
Cnt. (B♭)
Tbn.
Tbe.
Timp.
a 2
sempre marcato

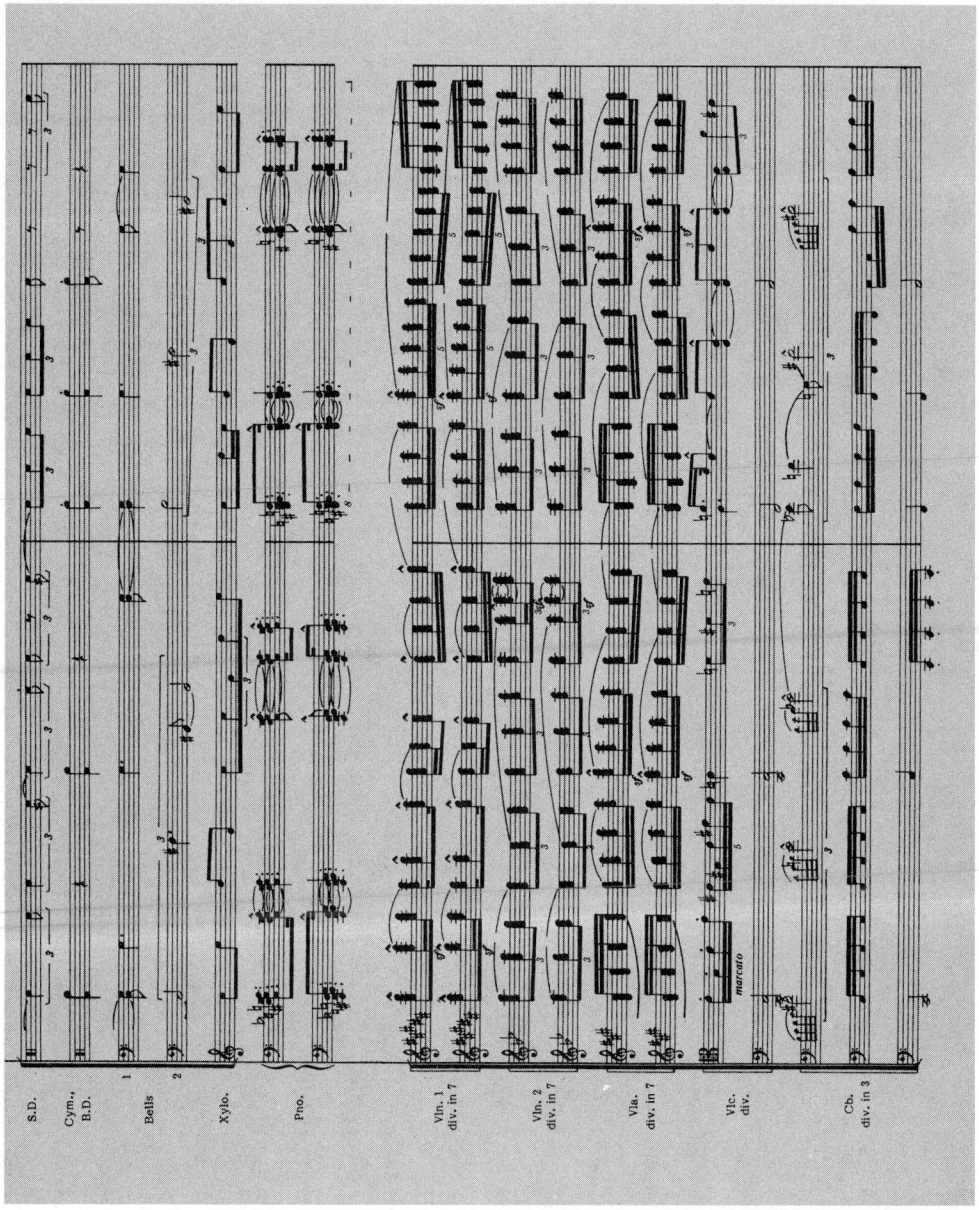
S.D.
Cym., B.D.
Bells
1
2
Xylo.
Pno.
Vln. 1 div. in 7
Vln. 2 div. in 7
Vla. div. in 7
Vlc. div.
Cb. div. in 3
marcato

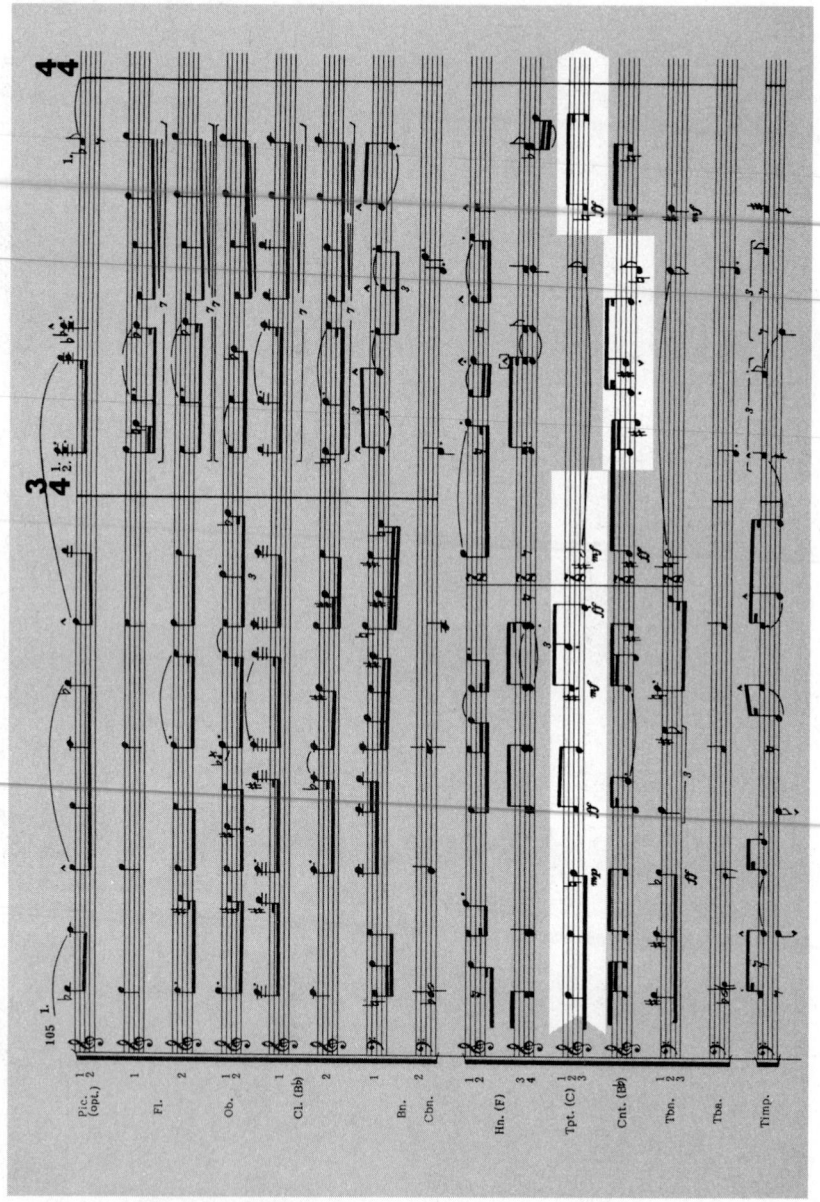
105
Pic. (opt.)
Fl.
Ob.
Cl. (B♭)
Bn.
Cbn.
Hn. (F)
Tpt. (C)
Cnt. (B♭)
Tbn.
Tba.
Timp.

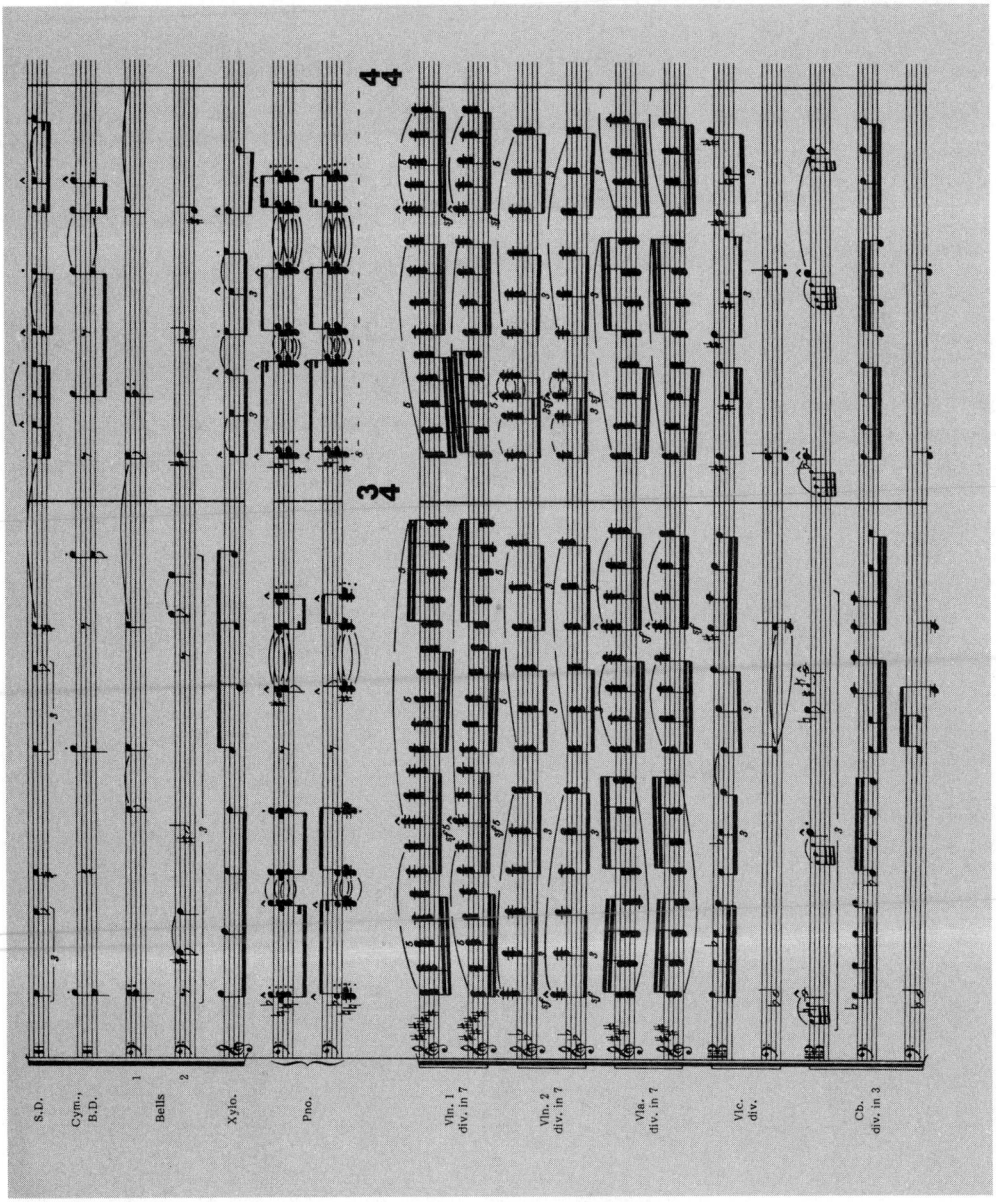
S.D.
Cym., B.D.
Bells
1
2
Xylo.
Pno.
Vln. 1 div. in 7
Vln. 2 div. in 7
Vla. div. in 7
Vlc. div.
Cb. div. in 3
3/4
4/4

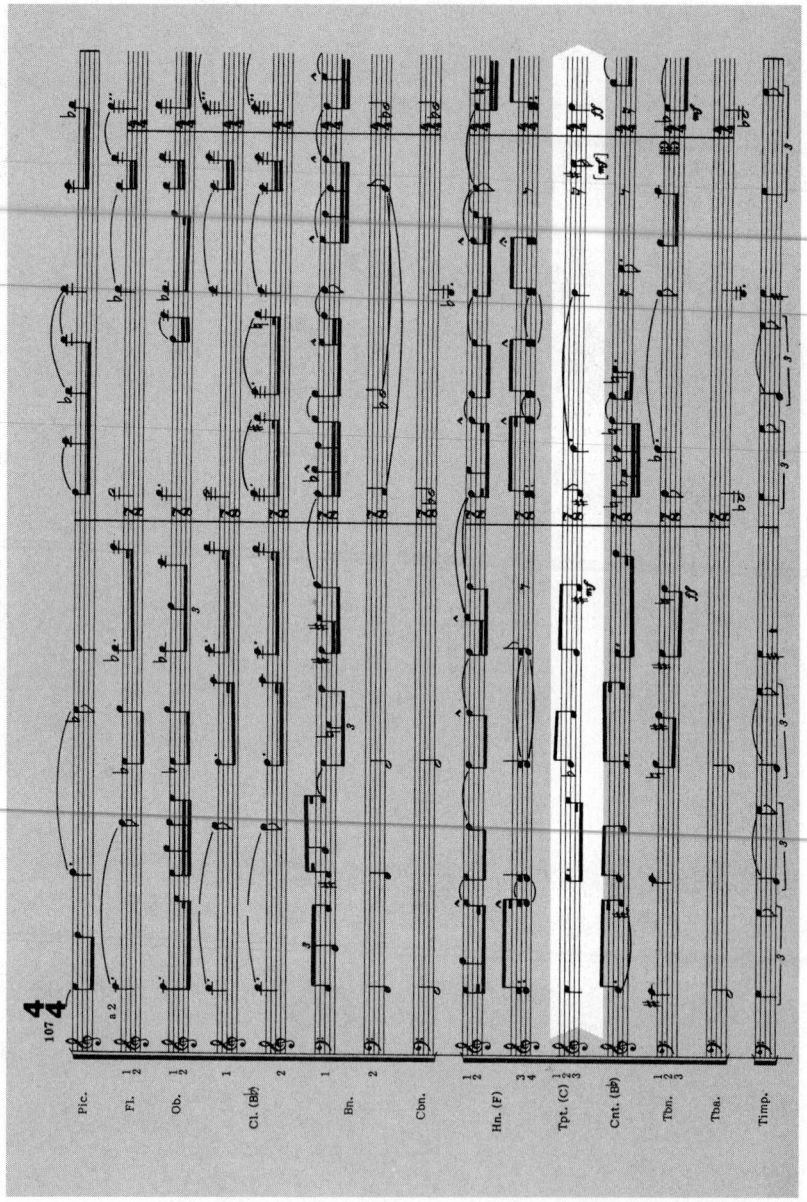
107
Pic.
Fl.
Ob.
Cl. (B♭)
Bn.
Cbn.
Hn. (F)
Tpt. (C)
Crt. (B♭)
Tbn.
Tba.
Timp.
a 2

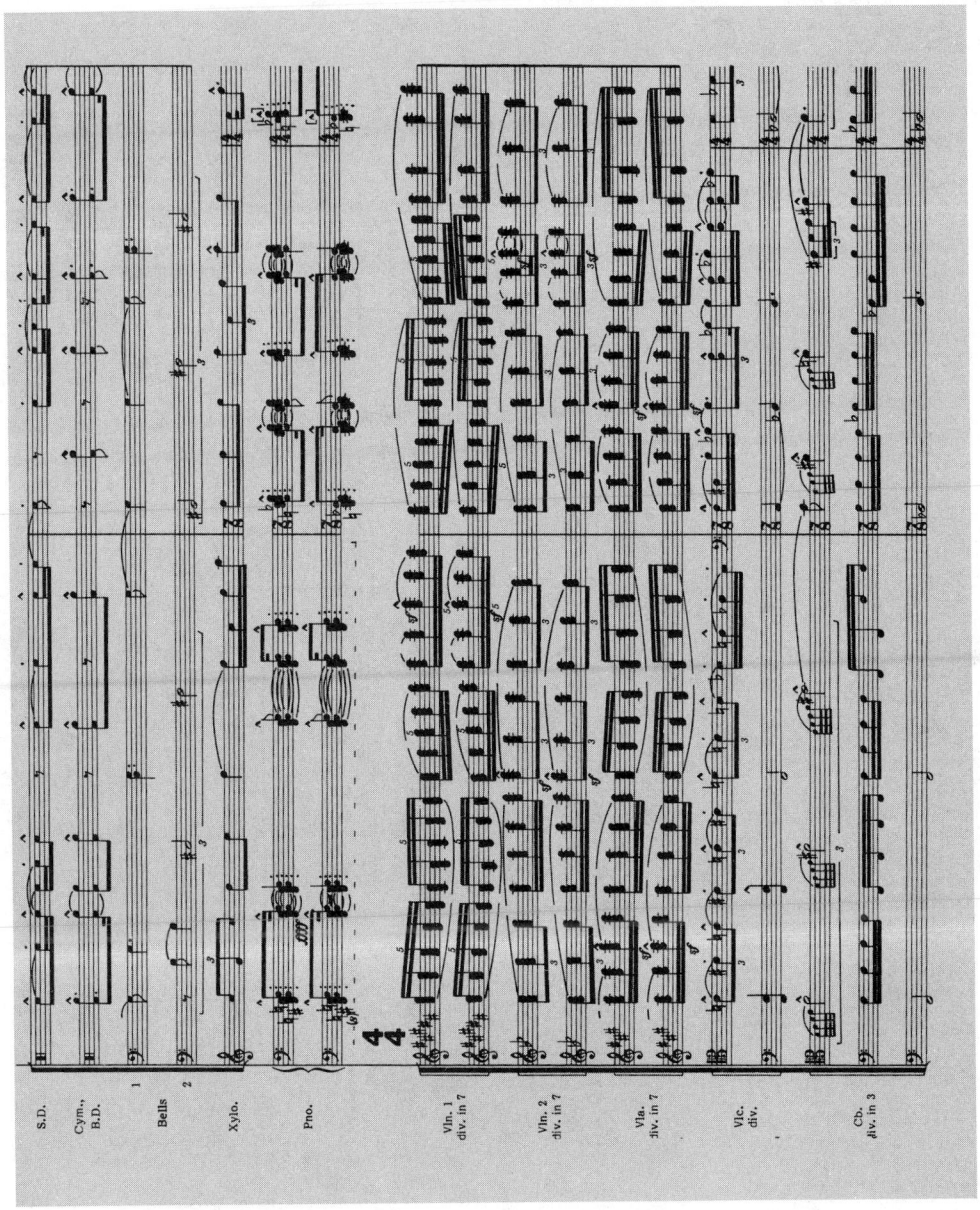
S.D.
Cym., B.D.
Bells
Xylo.
Pno.
Vln. 1 div. in 7
Vln. 2 div. in 7
Vla. div. in 7
Vlc. div.
Cb. div. in 3

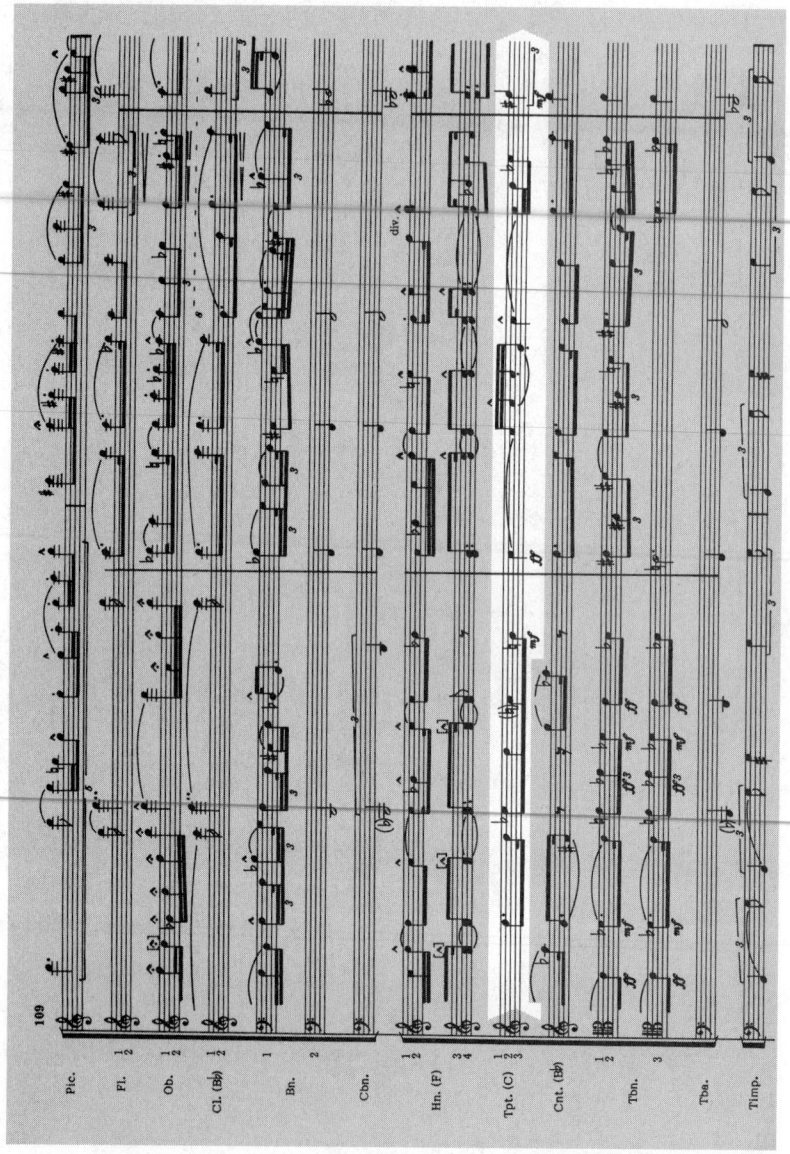
109
Pic.
Fl.
Ob.
Cl. (B♭)
Bn.
Cbn.
Hn. (F)
Tpt. (C)
Cnt. (B♭)
Tbn.
Tba.
Timp.
div.

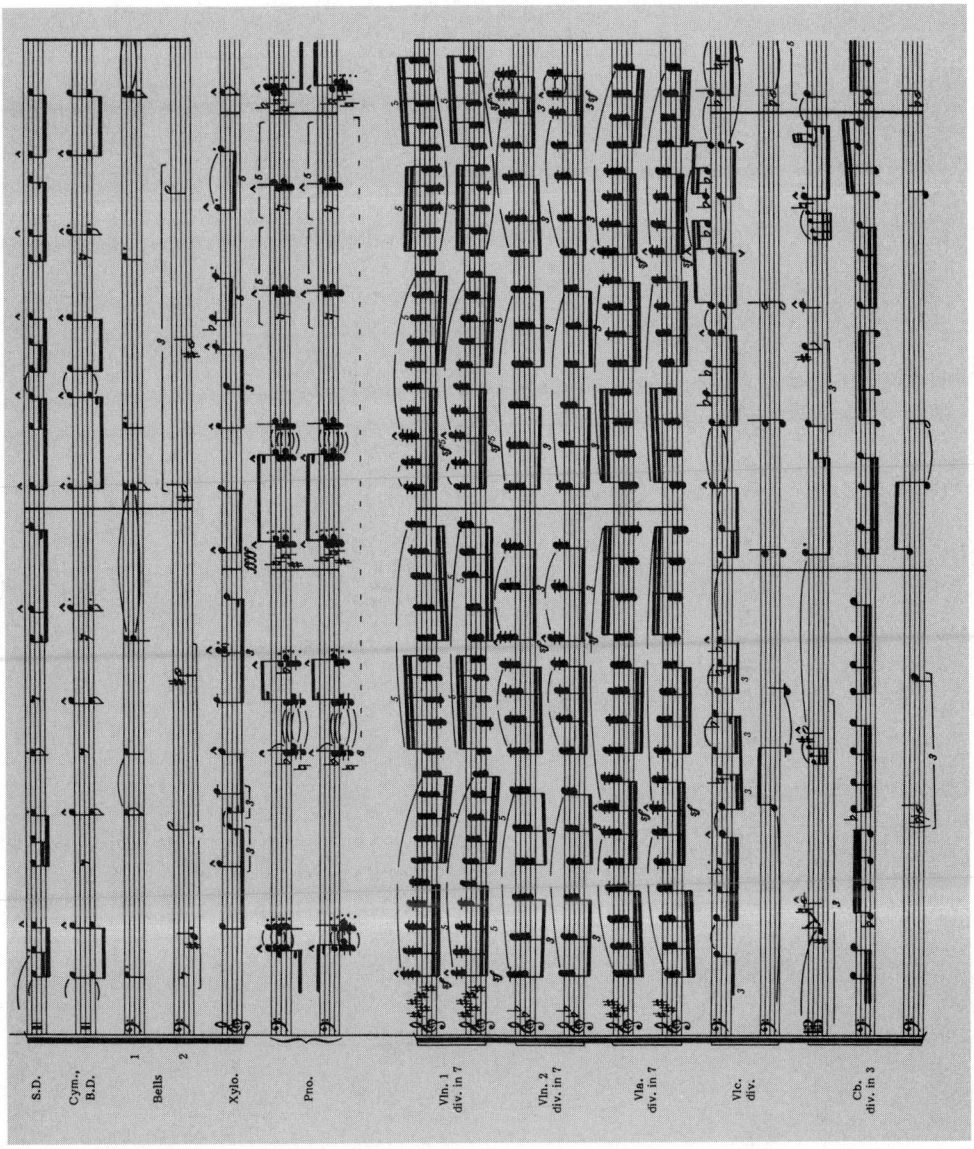
S.D.
Cym., B.D.
Bells
1
2
Xylo.
Pno.
Vln. 1 div. in 7
Vln. 2 div. in 7
Vla. div. in 7
Vlc. div.
Cb. div. in 3

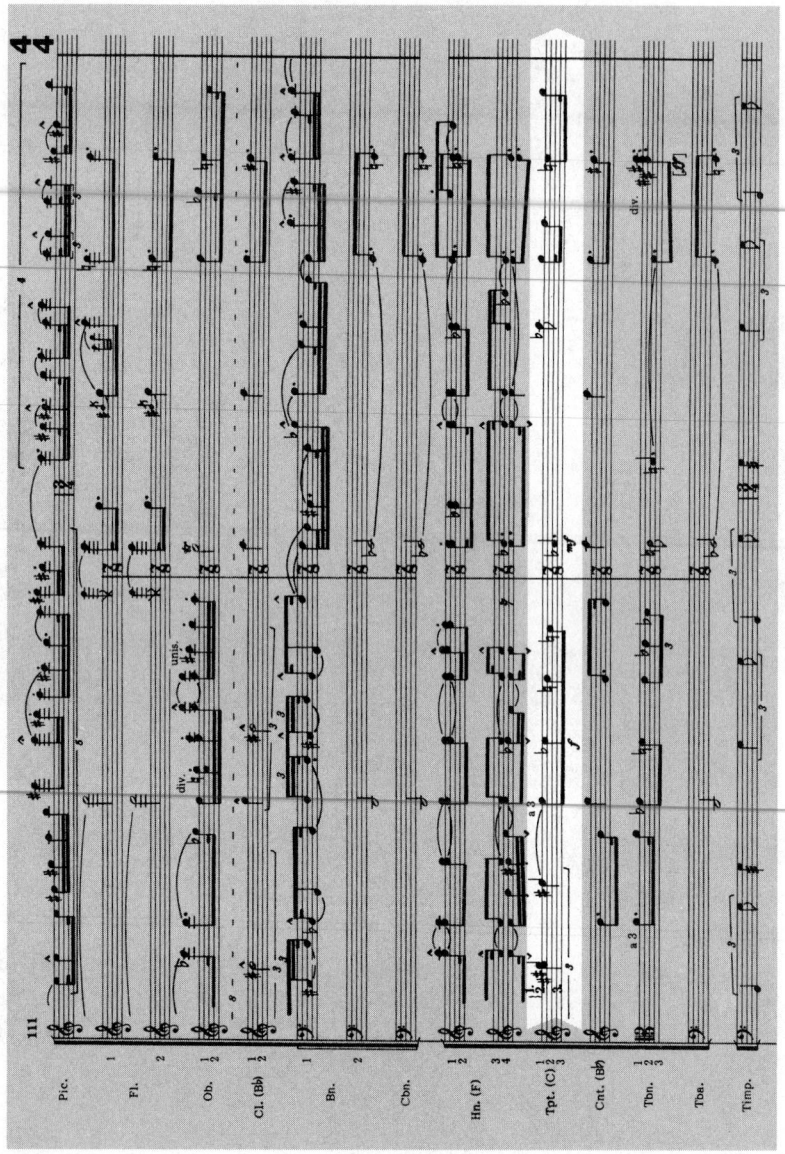
111
Pic.
Fl.
Ob.
Cl. (B♭)
Bn.
Cbn.
Hn. (F)
Tpt. (C)
Cnt. (B♭)
Tbn.
Tba.
Timp.
div.
unis.
a 3
div.

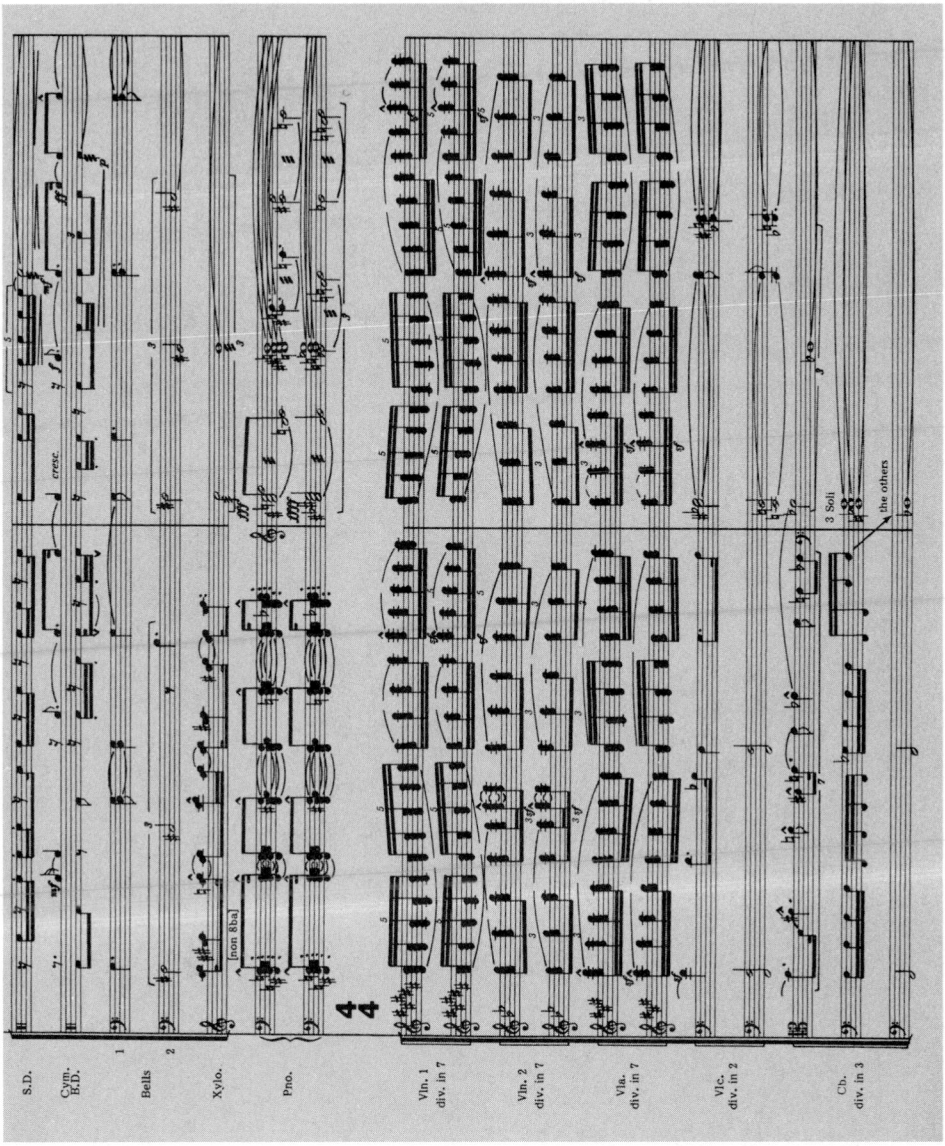
S.D.
Cym.
B.D.
Bells
1
2
Xylo.
Pno.
Vln. 1
div. in 7
Vln. 2
div. in 7
Vla.
div. in 7
Vlc.
div. in 2
Cb.
div. in 3
cresc.
[non 8va]
3 Soli
the others

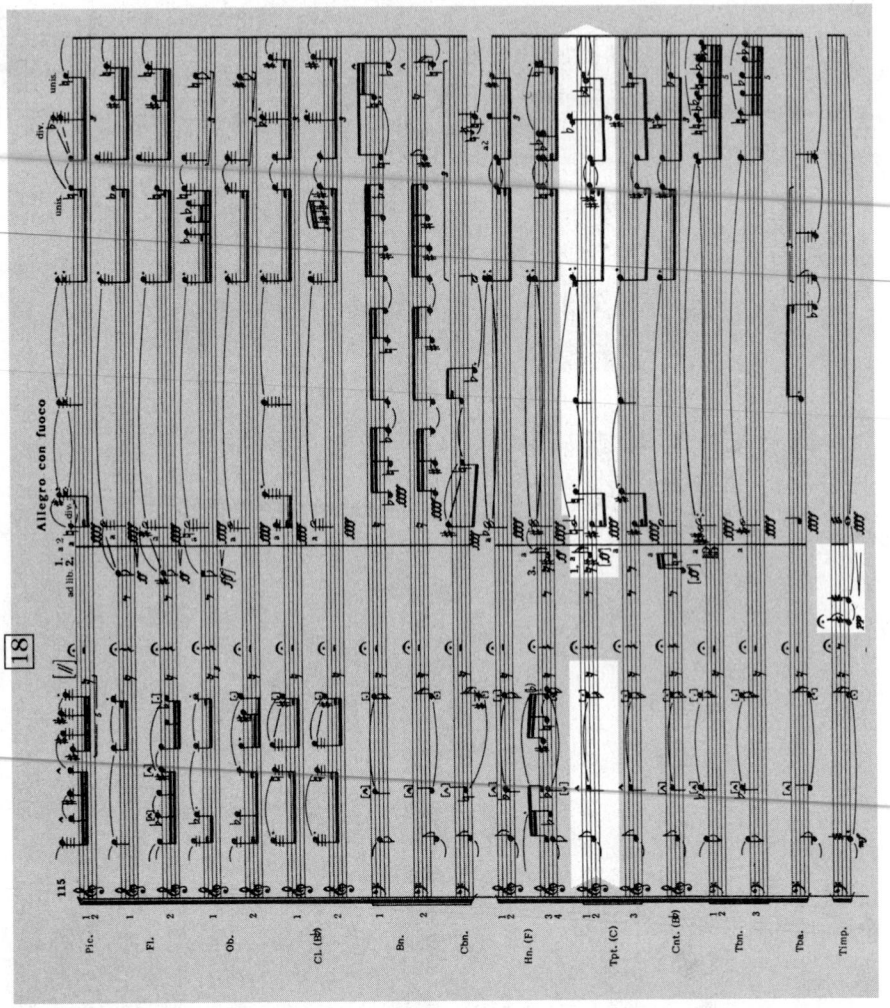
115
18
Allegro con fuoco
Pic.
Fl.
Ob.
Cl. (B♭)
Bn.
Cbn.
Hn. (F)
Tpt. (C)
Cnt. (B♭)
Tbn.
Tba.
Timp.

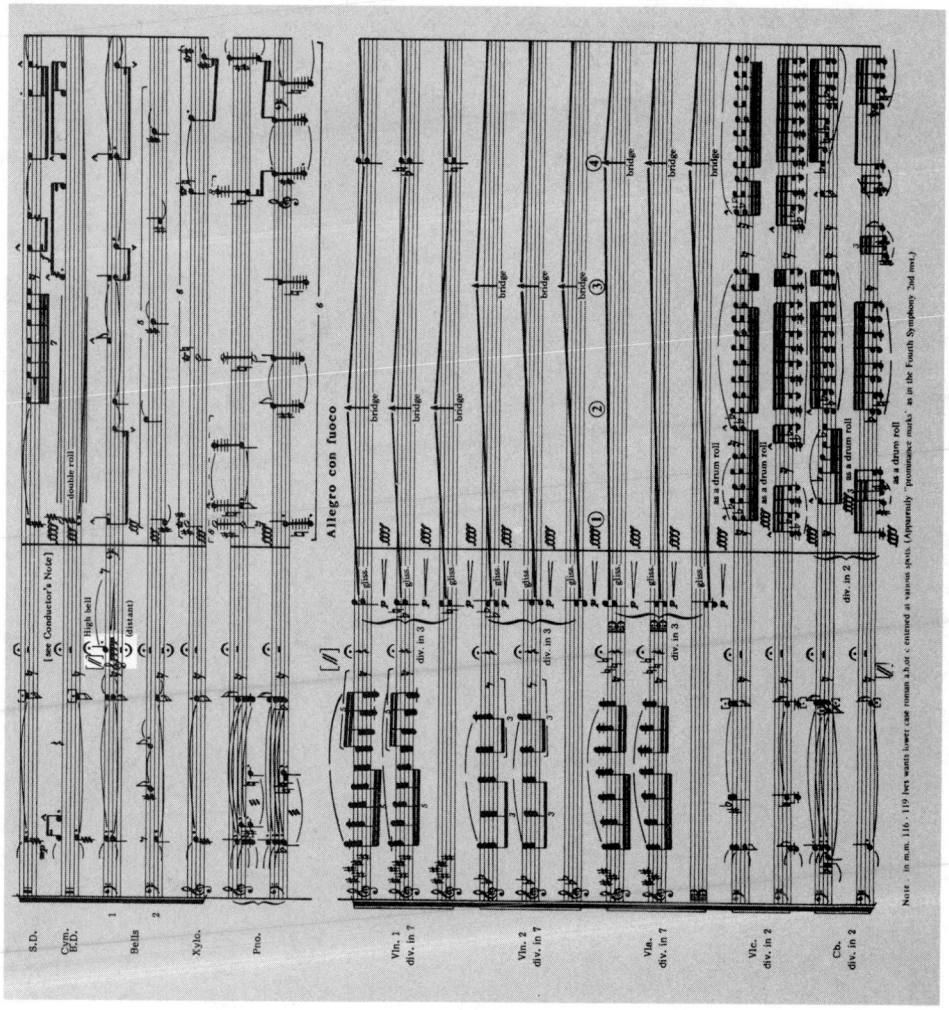
S.D.
Cym.
B.D.
[see Conductor's Note]
high bell
(distant)
Bells
Xylo.
Pno.
Allegro con fuoco
Vln. 1
div. in 7
Vln. 2
div. in 7
Vla.
div. in 7
Vlc.
div. in 2
Cb.
div. in 2
glss.
div. in 3
bridge
as a drum roll
Note: in m.m. 116-119 Ives wants lower case roman a,b,or c centered at various spots. (Apparently "pentatonic" marks, as in the Fourth Symphony 2nd mvt.)

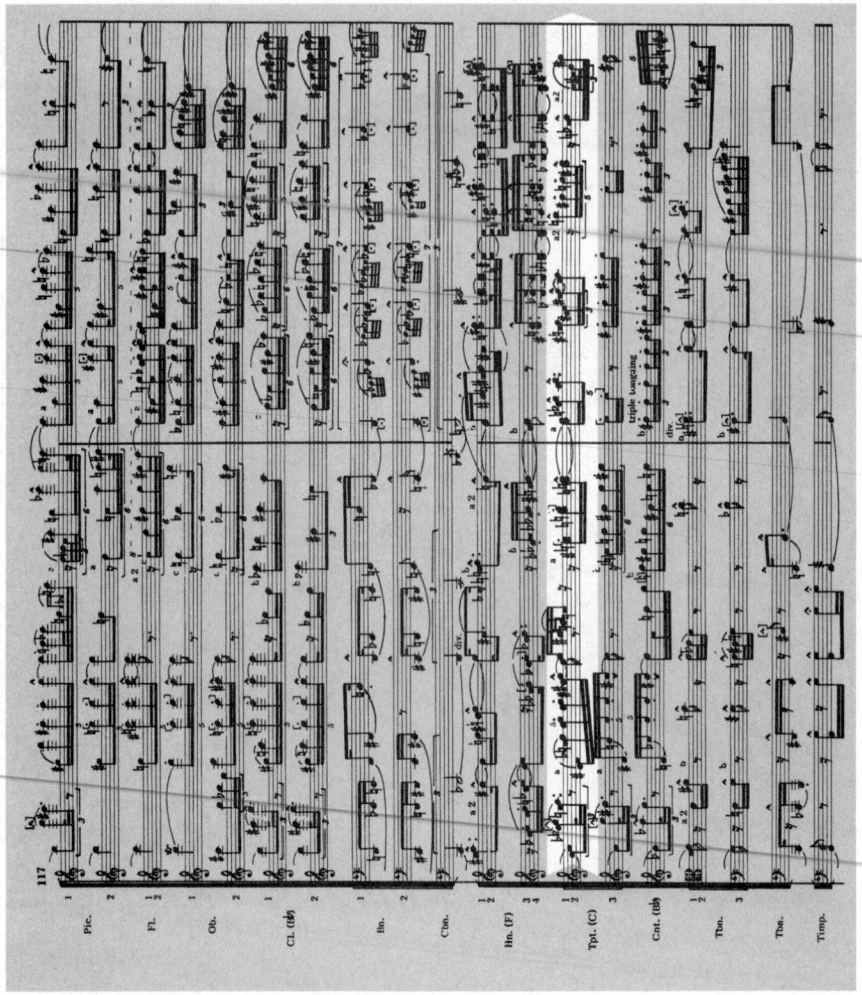
117
Pic.
Fl.
Ob.
Cl. (B♭)
Bn.
Cbn.
Hn. (F)
Tpt. (C)
triple tonguing
Cnt. (B♭)
Tbn.
Tba.
Timp.

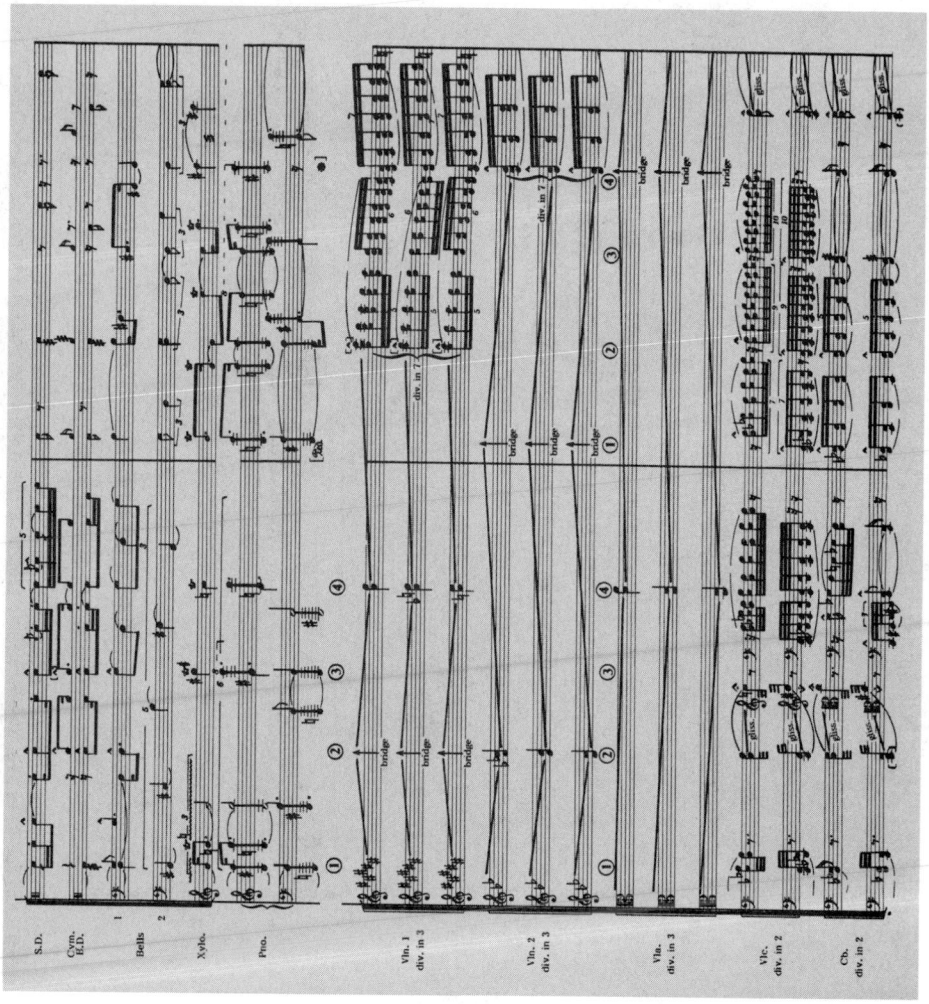
S.D.
Cym.
E.D.
Bells
Xylo.
Pno.
Vln. 1
div. in 3
Vln. 2
div. in 3
Vla.
div. in 3
Vlc.
div. in 2
Cb.
div. in 2
bridge
div. in 2
glss.

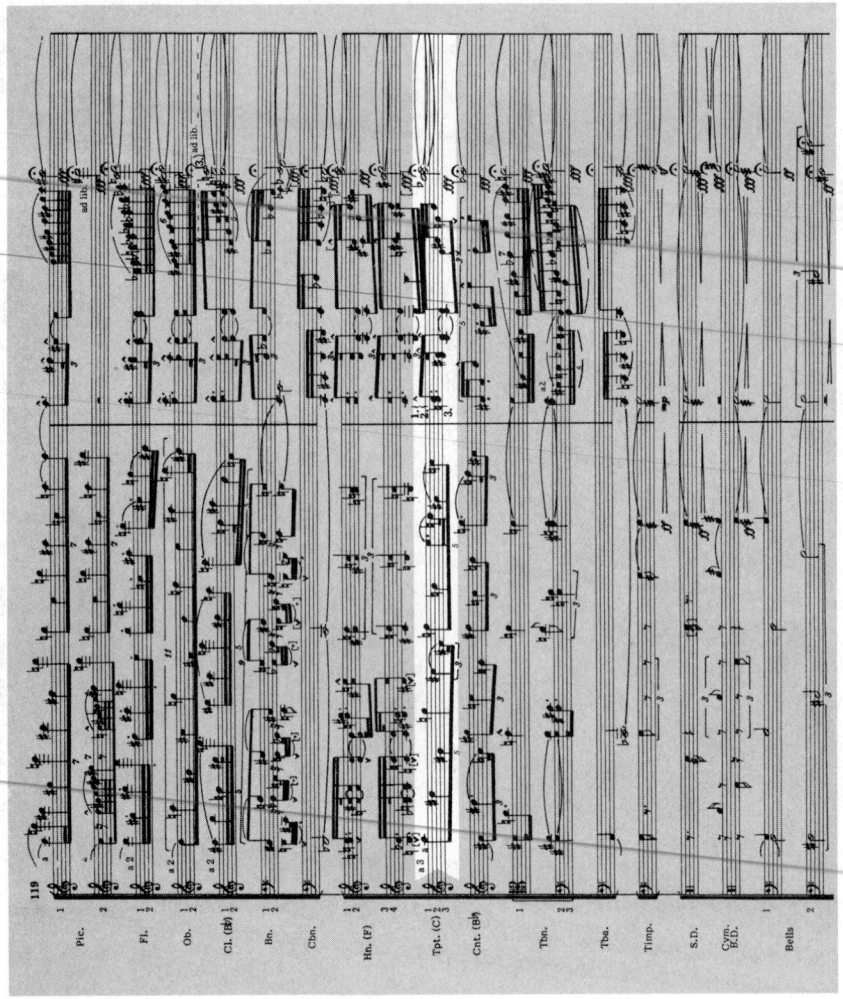
119
Pic.
Fl.
Ob.
Cl. (B♭)
Bn.
Cbn.
Hn. (F)
Tpt. (C)
Cnt. (B♭)
Tbn.
Tba.
Timp.
S.D.
Cym.
B.D.
Bells
ad lib.
a 2
a 3
1.
2.
3.

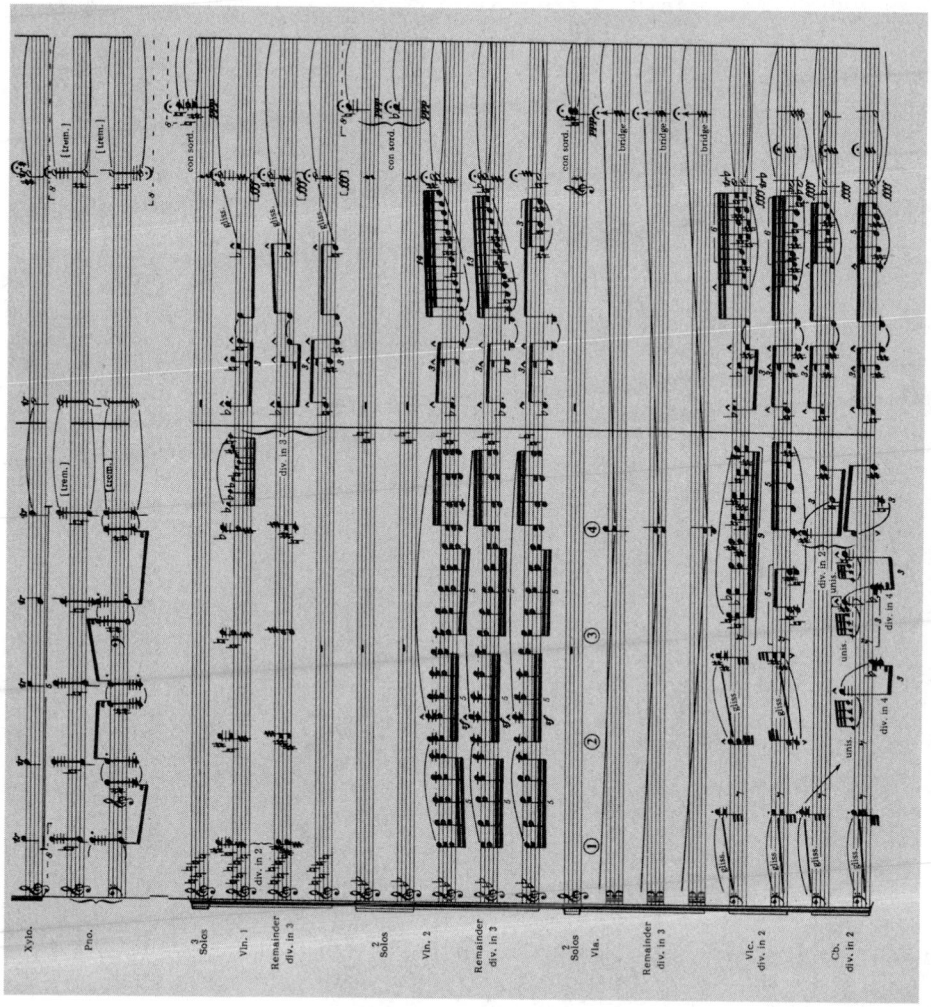
Xylo.
Pno.
[trem.]
[trem.]
[trem.]
[trem.]
con sord.
gliss.
gliss.
gliss.
div. in 2
div. in 3
con sord.
con sord.
2 Solos
Vln. 1
Remainder div. in 3
2 Solos
Vln. 2
Remainder div. in 3
2 Solos
Vla.
Remainder div. in 3
Vlc. div. in 2
Cb. div. in 2
con sord.
bridge
bridge
bridge
gliss.
gliss.
gliss.
gliss.
gliss.
gliss.
unis.
unis.
unis.
div. in 2
div. in 4
div. in 4

121
Meno mosso
"Not evenly, but as a falling rocket"
Pic.
Fl.
Ob.
Cl. (B♭)
Bn.
Cbn.
Hn. (F)
Tpt. (C)
Cnt. (B♭)
Tbn.
Tba.
Timp.
S.D.
Cym.
B.D.
Bells

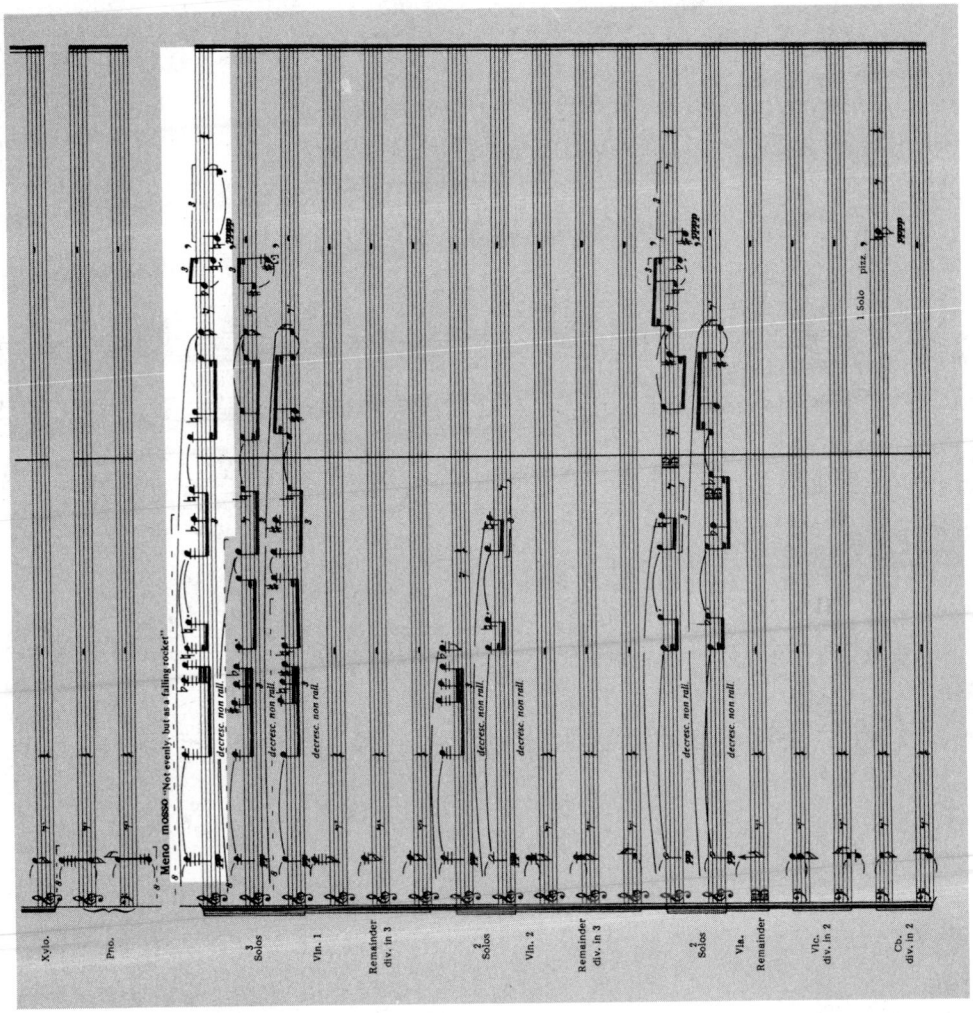
Xylo.
Pno.
Meno mosso "Not evenly, but as a falling rocket"
decresc. non rall.
3 Solos
Vln. 1
Remainder div. in 3
2 Solos
Vln. 2
Remainder div. in 3
2 Solos
Vla.
Remainder
Vlc. div. in 2
Cb. div. in 2
1 Solo
pizz.

24. *Maurice Ravel (1875–1937)*

8:7A/6 8:7/19 - 20

Chansons madécasses (Songs of Madagascar), Second Movement (1925–26)

© 1926 Durand S. A. Editions Musicales. Editions A.R.I.M.A. & Durand S. A. Editions Musicales. Joint publication. Used by permission of the publisher. Sole representative USA, Theodore Presser Company.

Sordina arco
pp
tans du ri va - - - ge.
8
pp
p
Du tems de nos pè-res, des blancs descen - di-rent dans cette î - le; on leur dit: Voi-là des
ter - res; que vos fem - mes les cul-ti - vent. Soy-ez jus-tes, soy-ez bons, et de-ve-nez nos frè -

-res.
Les blancs pro - mirent, et ce - pendant ils fai -
senza Sordina
poco crescendo
-saient des retranchemens. Un fort me-na-çant s'é - le-va; le tonner - re fut renfermé
dans des bouches d'airain;
crescendo e accelerando poco a poco
leurs prê - tres vou - lu - rent nous don-ner un Dieu

que nous ne connaissons pas; ils par-lè-rent en-fin d'o-bé-is-san-ce et d'escla-
FLAUTO
mf
cresc.
sempre cresc.
va-ge: plu-tôt la mort! Le car-na-ge fut long et ter-
♩=76
sempre cresc.
ri-ble; mais, mal-gré la fou-dre qu'ils vo-mis-saient, et qui é-cra-sait des armées en

pizz.
.tières, ils furent tous extermi - nés. Aoua! Aoua!
20
Allegro feroce
Quasi tromba
Allegro feroce
Mé.fi.ez-vous des blancs!
Allegro feroce ♩=168
Nous a - vons vu de nouveaux ty - rans, plus forts et plus nom - breux, plan -

-ter leur pa-vil - lon sur le ri - va - ge: le
ciel a com-bat - tu pour nous; il a fait tom - ber sur eux
les pluies, les tem - pê-tes et les vents em - poi-sonnés.

Molto ritenuto
Ils ne sont plus, et nous vi - vons, et nous vi-vons li - bres.
Molto ritenuto
Adagio
pp
Aoua! Aoua! Méfi-ez-vous des blancs, habitans du ri -
Adagio
pp
Sord.
p espressivo
Sordina
arco
p
I
II
va - - - ge.
ppp

TEXT AND TRANSLATION

Aoua! Aoua! Méfiez-vous des blancs,
habitans du rivage.
Du temps de nos pères, des blancs
descendirent dans cette île;
on leur dit: Voilà des terres; que
vos femmes les cultivent.
Soyez justes, soyez bons, et devenez nos
frères.
Les blancs promirent, et cependant
ils faisaient des retranchements.
Un fort mençant s'éleva; le tonnerre
fut renfermé dans des bouches d'airain;
leurs prêtres voulurent nous donner
un Dieu que nous ne connaissons pas;
ils parlèrent enfin d'obéissance et
d'esclavage; plûtot la mort!
Le carnage fut long et terrible; mais,
malgré la foudre qu'ils vomissaient,
et qui écrasait des armées entières,
ils furent tous exterminés.
Aoua! Aoua! Méfiez-vous des blancs!
Nous avons vu de nouveaux tyrans,
plus forts et plus nombreux,
planter leur pavillon sur le rivage;
le ciel a combattu pour nous;
il a fait tomber sur eux les pluies,
les tempêtes, et les vents empoisonnés.
Ils ne sont plus, et nous vivons, et
nous vivons libres.
Aoua! Aoua! Méfiez-vous des blancs,
habitans du rivage.

Aoua! Aoua! Do not trust the white men,
those who live on these shores.
From our father's time, white men
have descended upon this island;
they said: "Here is the soil; have
your women cultivate it.
Be fair, be kind, and become our
brothers."
The white men promised, and yet
they built entrenchments.
A menacing fort was erected;
thunder was enclosed in brass mouths;
their priests wished to give us a
God we did not know;
they finally spoke of obedience and
slavery; what's more, of death!
The carnage was long and terrible; but,
in spite of the lightning they belched forth,
annihilating whole armies, they
were all destroyed.
Aoua! Aoua! Do not trust the white men!
We have seen new tyrants,
stronger and more numerous,
raise their tents on the shore; the
heavens waged war for us,
unleashing rains, storms, and
poisonous winds.
They are gone, and we live, and
we live freely.
Aoua! Aoua! Do not trust the white men,
those who live on these shores.

25. Béla Bartók (1881–1945)

Music for Strings, Percussion, and Celesta, Fourth Movement (1936)

8:7A/7 — 7/21 - 24

3:3A/6 — 3/20 - 23

21 20

Allegro molto, ♩ ca. 130

Timp.
1. Vl.
2. Vl.
1. Vle.
1. Vlc.
1. Cb.
2. Cb.

f pizz. *p* pizz. cresc. *ff* pizz.

Timp.
1. Vl.
2. Vl.
1. Vle.
1. Vlc.
1. Cb.
3. Vl.
4. Vl.
2. Vle.

sim. *f*

© Copyright 1937 by Universal Edition, renewed 1964. © Copyright and renewal assigned to Boosey & Hawkes, Inc. for the USA. All rights reserved. Reprinted in the U.S. by permission of Boosey & Hawkes, Inc. Used in the world excluding the U.S. by permission of European American Music Distributors Corporation, agent for Universal Edition.

10
Timp.
1. Vl.
2. Vl.
1. Vle.
1. Vlc.
1. Cb.
3. Vl.
4. Vl.
2. Vle.
2. Vlc.
2. Cb.
arco
pizz.
f
mf

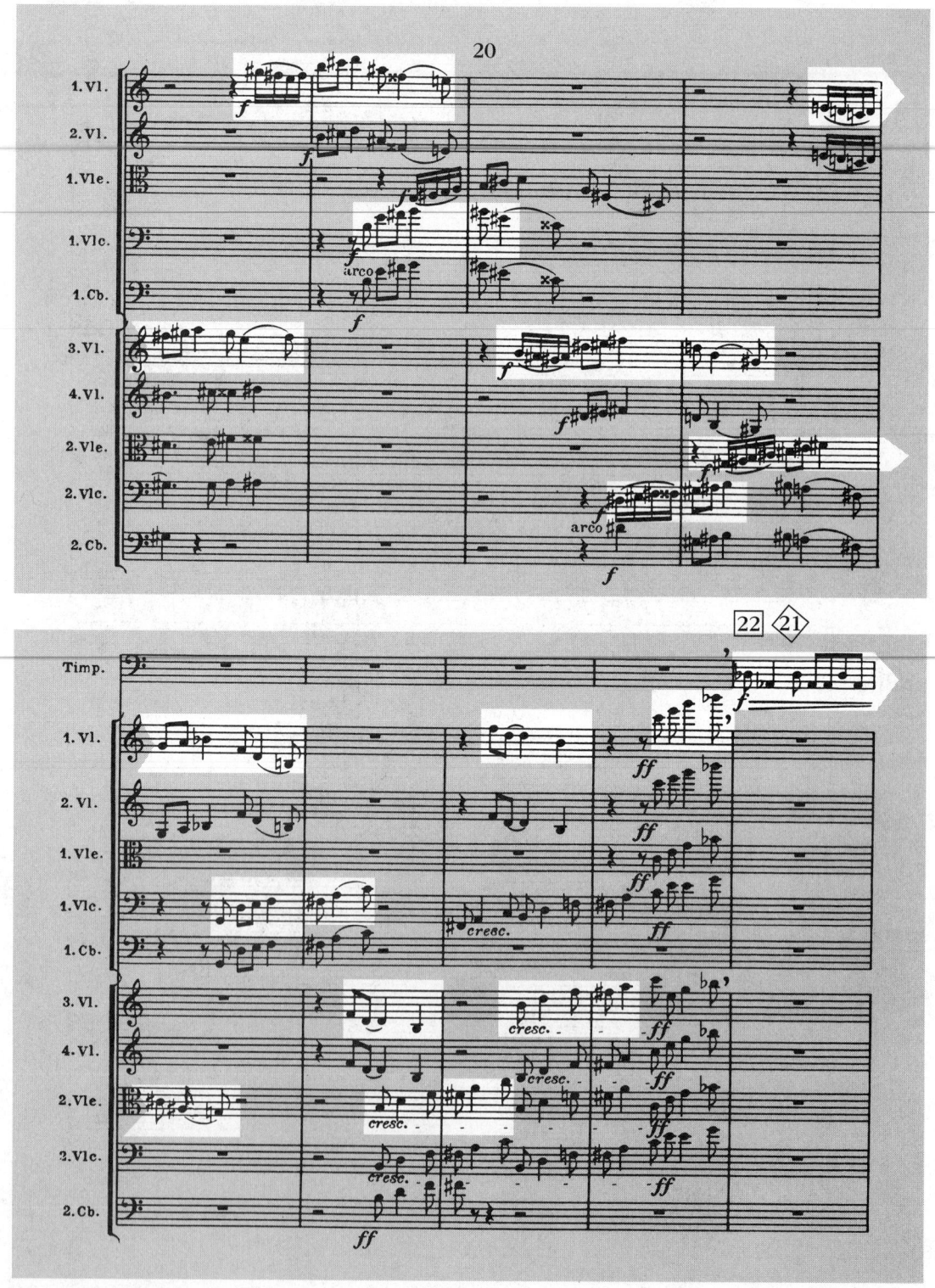
20
1. Vl.
2. Vl.
1. Vle.
1. Vlc.
1. Cb.
3. Vl.
4. Vl.
2. Vle.
2. Vlc.
2. Cb.
arco
arco
22
21
Timp.
cresc.
cresc.
cresc.
cresc.
cresc.
cresc.

30
Timp.
p
Pfte.
p, marcato
1. Vl.
pizz.
p
2. Vl.
pizz.
p
1. Vle.
pizz.
p
1. Vlc.
pizz.
p
1. Cb.
pizz.
p
3. Vl.
pizz.
p
4. Vl.
pizz.
p
2. Vle.
pizz.
p
2. Vlc.
pizz.
p
2. Cb.
pizz.
p

Timp.
cresc.
Pfte.
mf
cresc.
1. Vl.
cresc.
2. Vl.
cresc.
1. Vle.
cresc.
1. Vlc.
cresc.
1. Cb.
cresc.
3. Vl.
cresc.
4. Vl.
cresc.
2. Vle.
cresc.
2. Vlc.
cresc.
2. Cb.
cresc.

40
Timp.
Pfte.
1. Vl.
2. Vl.
1. Vle.
1. Vlc.
1. Cb.
3. Vl.
4. Vl.
2. Vle.
2. Vlc.
2. Cb.

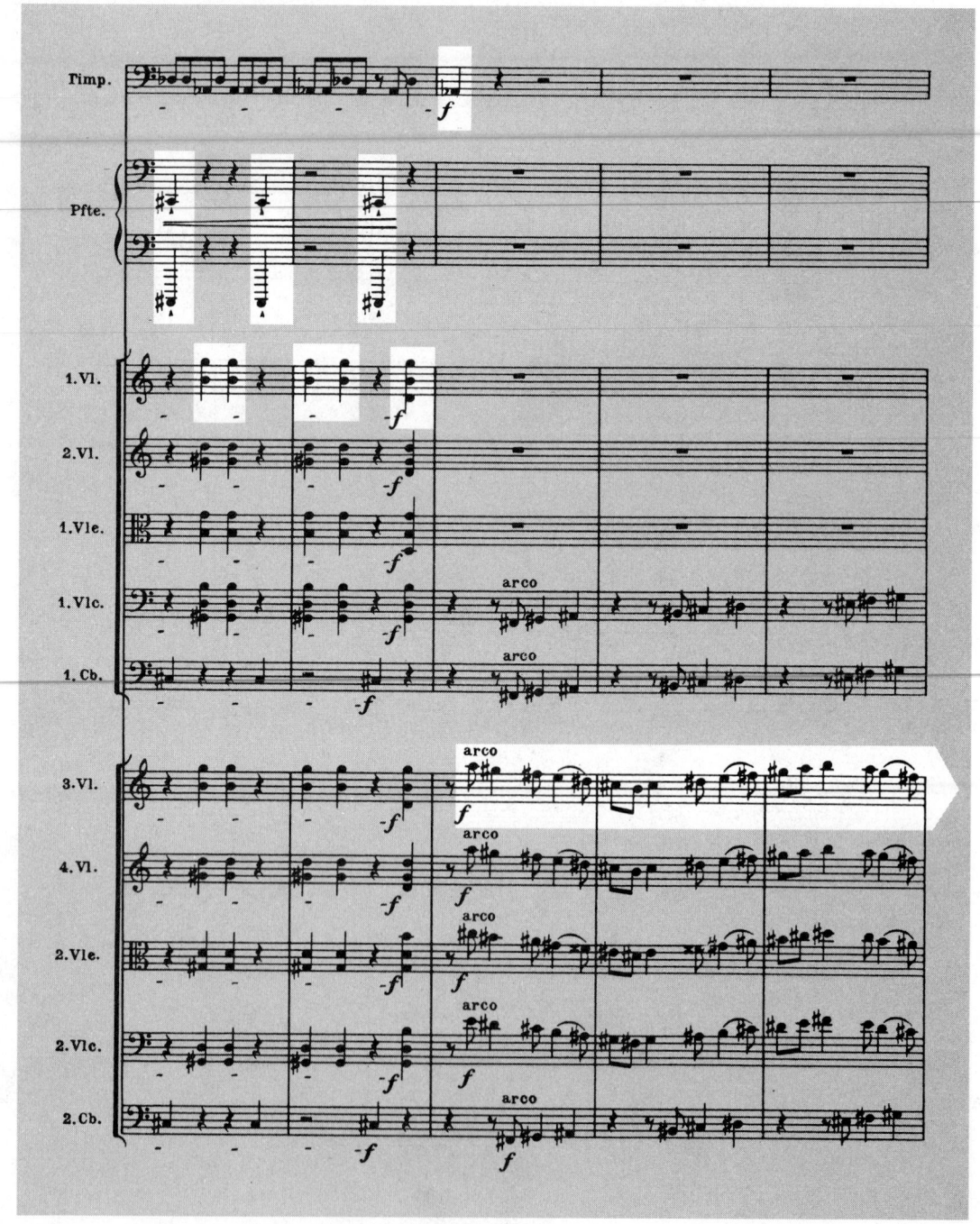
Timp.
Pfte.
1.Vl.
2.Vl.
1.Vle.
1.Vlc.
1.Cb.
3.Vl.
4.Vl.
2.Vle.
2.Vlc.
2.Cb.
arco

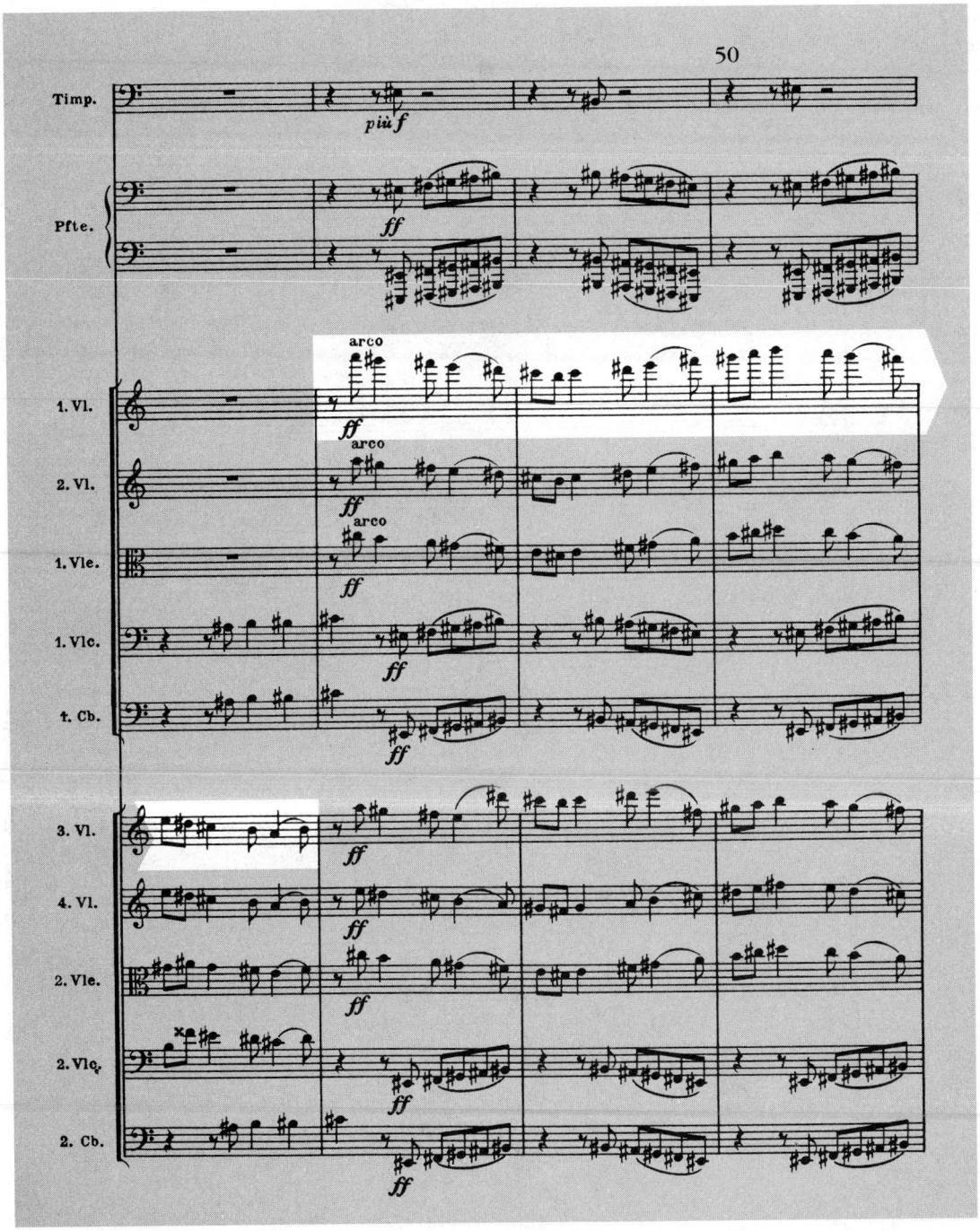
50
Timp.
più f
Pfte.
ff
arco
1. Vl.
2. Vl.
1. Vle.
1. Vlc.
1. Cb.
3. Vl.
4. Vl.
2. Vle.
2. Vlc.
2. Cb.

A Un poco meno mosso,
ca. 120
Timp.
Pfte.
1. Vl.
2. Vl.
1. Vle.
1. Vlc.
1. Cb.
3. Vl.
4. Vl.
2. Vle.
2. Vlc.
2. Cb.
ff

Timp.
ff
p
Pfte.
f
1. Vl.
p
2. Vl.
p
1. Vle.
p
1. Vlc.
p
1. Cb.
ff
mf
3. Vl.
ff
p
4. Vl.
ff
mf
2. Vle.
ff
mf
2. Vlc.
ff
mf
2. Cb.
ff
mf

60
Timp.
f
ff
Pfte.
ff
1. Vl.
cresc.
ff
2. Vl.
cresc.
ff
1. Vle.
cresc.
ff
1. Vlc.
cresc.
ff
1. Cb.
ff
3. Vl.
cresc.
ff
4. Vl.
ff
2. Vle.
f
ff
2. Vlc.
f
ff
2. Cb.
ff

Pfte.
1. Vl.
2. Vl.
1. Vle.
1. Vlc.
1. Cb.
3. Vl.
4. Vl.
2. Vle.
2. Vlc.
2. Cb.

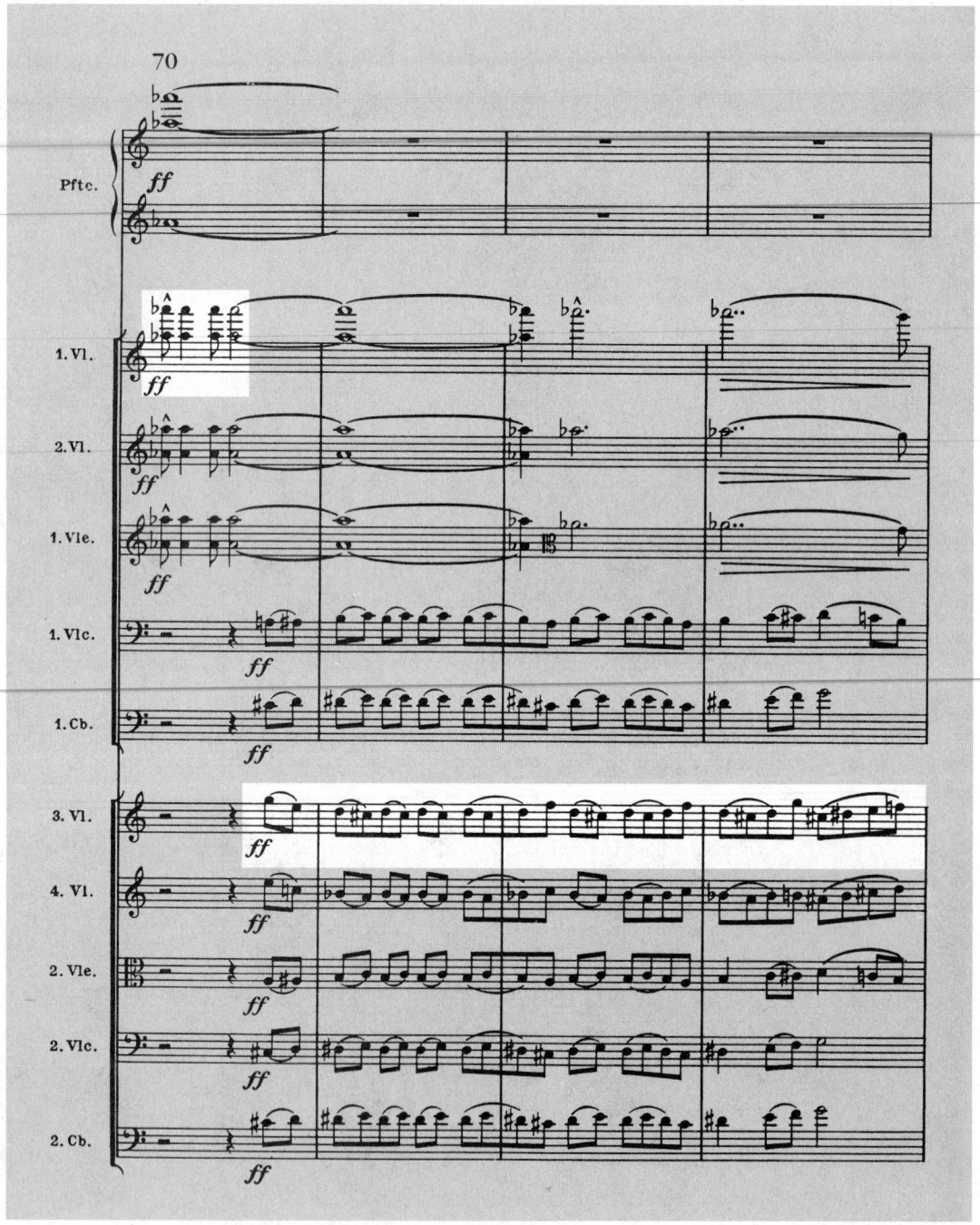
70
Pftc.
ff
1. Vl.
2. Vl.
1. Vle.
1. Vlc.
1. Cb.
3. Vl.
4. Vl.
2. Vle.
2. Vlc.
2. Cb.

B Ancora meno mosso, ♩ ca 112
Timp.
Arpa.
I.
Pfte. (a 4 m.)
II.
1. Vl.
2. Vl.
1. Vle.
1. Vlc.
1. Cb.
3. Vl.
4. Vl.
2. Vle.
2. Vlc.
2. Cb.

23
22
80
rallentando - - - - a tempo
Più
Timp.
Arpa.
I.
Pfte.
II.
1. Vl.
2. Vl.
1. Vle.
1. Vlc.
1. Cb.
3. Vl.
4. Vl.
2. Vle.
2. Vlc.
2. Cb.
ff
p
col legno
pizz.

mosso ♩ = ca 126
Arpa
I.
Pfte.
II.
sempre sim.
1. Vle.
mp
1. Vlc.
1. Cb.
2. Vle.
2. Vlc.
2. Cb.

90
Tamb.picc.
senza
corda
Arpa
I.
Pfte.
II.
sempre sim.
sempre sim.
1.Vl.
2.Vl.
1.Vle.
1.Vlc.
1.Cb.
ord.
col legno
3.Vl.
4.Vl.
2.Vle.
2.Vlc.
2.Cb.
col legno
col legno
ord.
col legno

Tamb.picc.
senza
corda
Arpa
I.
Pfte.
II.
1.Vl.
2.Vl.
1.Vle.
1.Vlc.
1.Cb.
3.Vl.
4.Vl.
2.Vle.
2.Vlc.
2.Cb.
ord.

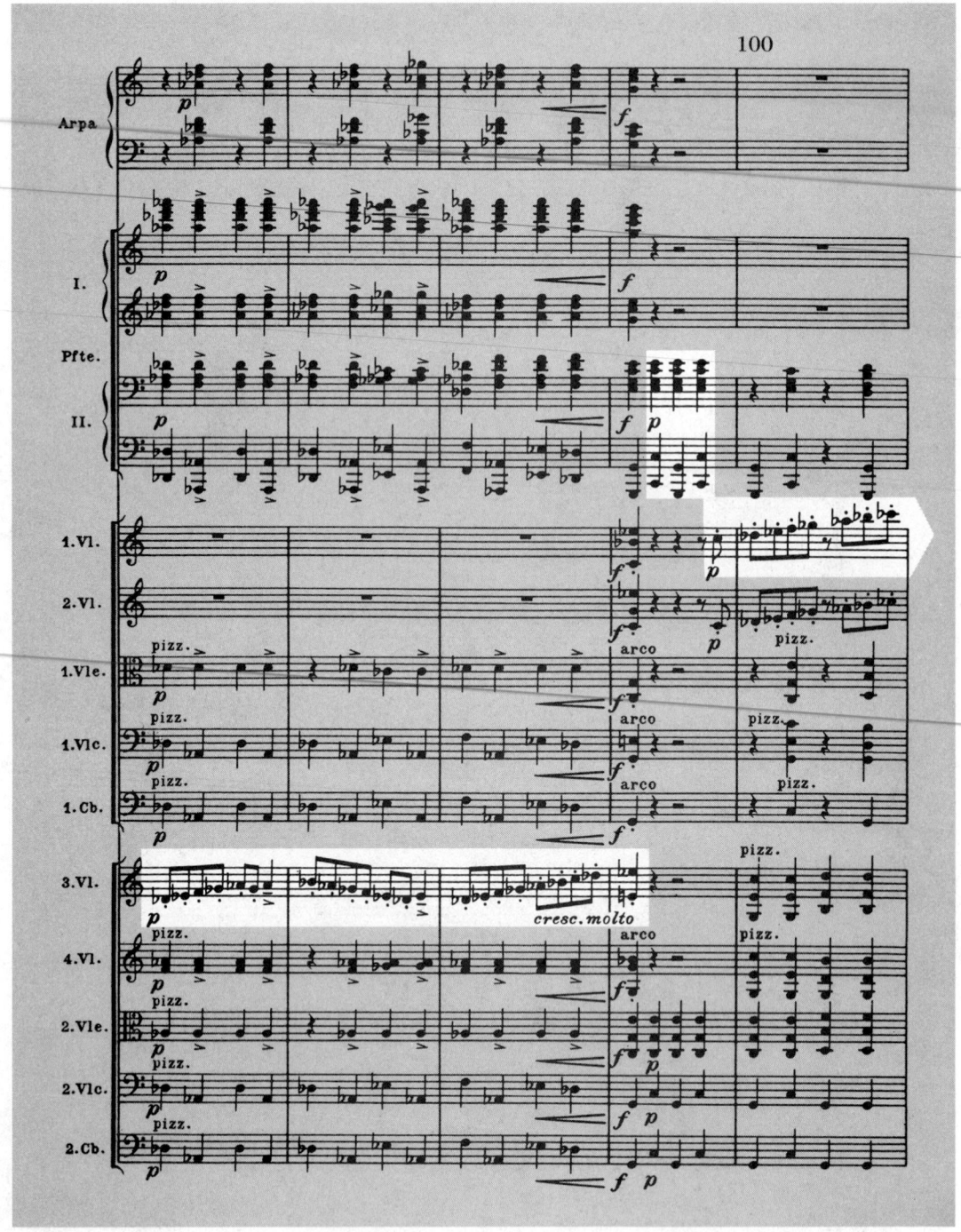
100
Arpa
I.
Pfte.
II.
1.Vl.
2.Vl.
1.Vle.
1.Vlc.
1.Cb.
3.Vl.
4.Vl.
2.Vle.
2.Vlc.
2.Cb.
pizz.
arco
cresc. molto

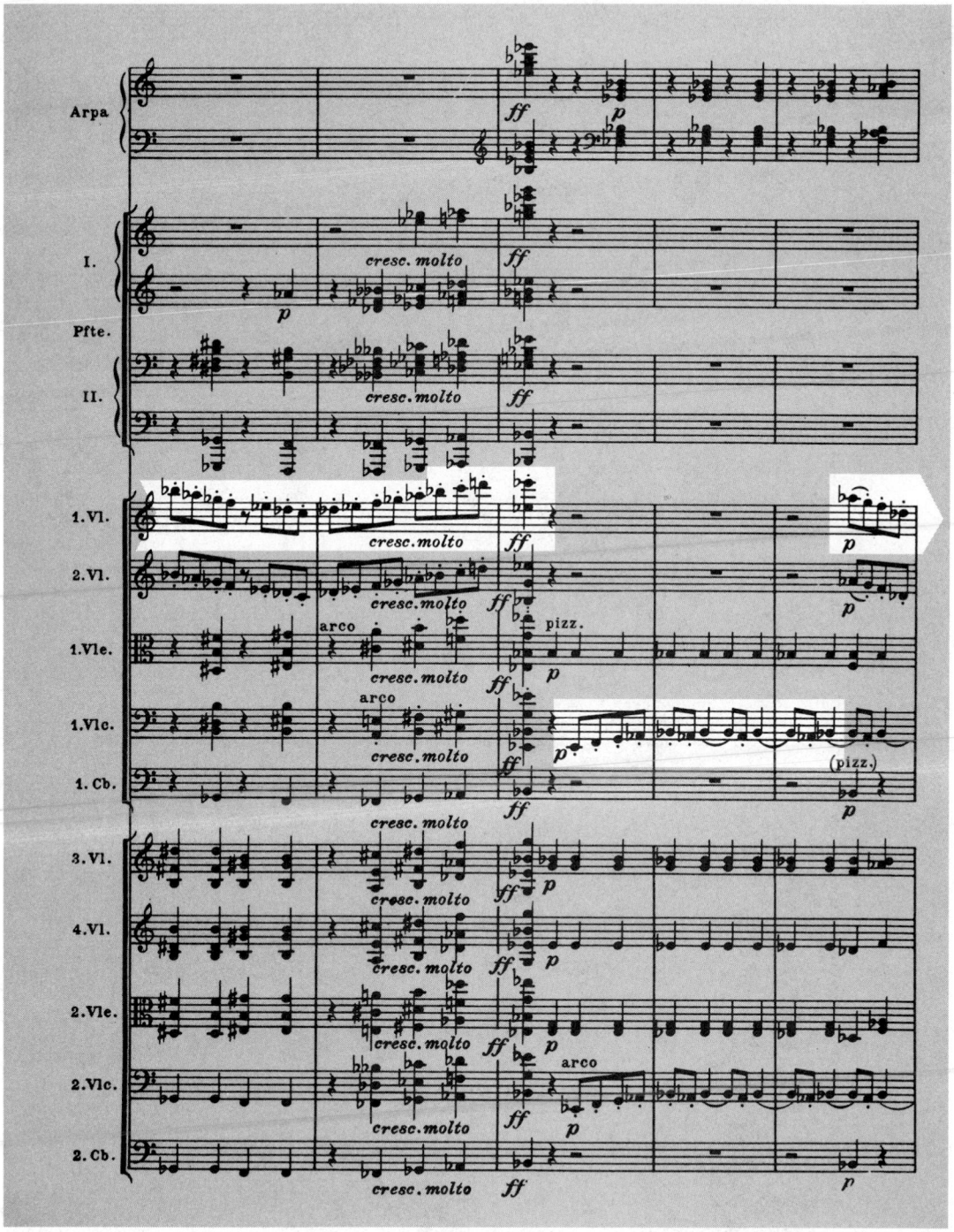
Arpa
I.
Pfte.
II.
1.Vl.
2.Vl.
1.Vle.
1.Vlc.
1. Cb.
3.Vl.
4.Vl.
2.Vle.
2.Vlc.
2. Cb.
cresc. molto
arco
pizz.
(pizz.)

110
Timp.
p
Arpa
Pfte.
p
1. Vl.
2. Vl.
1. Vle.
pp
1. Vlc.
pizz.
1. Cb.
3. Vl.
arco
p
4. Vl.
arco
pp
2. Vle.
pp
2. Vlc.
2. Cb.

D Un poco meno mosso, ♩ ca 120
Arpa
Pfte.
mf
f
p
1. Vl.
2. Vl.
1. Vle.
1. Vlc.
1. Cb.
3. Vl.
4. Vl.
2. Vle.
2. Vlc.
2. Cb.
cresc.
mf cresc.
arco
ff

120
Arpa
Pfte.
1. Vl.
2. Vl.
1. Vle.
1. Vlc.
1. Cb.
3. Vl.
4. Vl.
2. Vle.
2. Vlc.
2. Cb.
f

Tempo I
1. Vl.
2. Vl.
1. Vle.
1. Vlc.
1. Cb.
3. Vl.
4. Vl.
2. Vle.
2. Vlc.
2. Cb.
cresc.
cresc.

130
1. Vl.
2. Vl.
1. Vle.
1. Vlc.
1. Cb.
3. Vl.
4. Vl.
2. Vle.
2. Vlc.
2. Cb.

Arpa
Pfte.
1. Vl.
2. Vl.
1. Vle.
1. Vlc.
1. Cb.
3. Vl.
4. Vl.
2. Vle.
2. Vlc.
2. Cb.
f

E Un poco meno mosso, ca 120
140
Piatti
a 2
ppp
Arpa
p
sf
p
Pfte.
p
sf
p
1. Vl.
pp
sf
pp
2. Vl.
pp
sf
pp
1. Vle.
pp
sf
pp
1. Vlc.
pp
sf
pp
1. Cb.
pp
sf
pp
pizz.
3. Vl.
pp pizz.
sf
pp
4. Vl.
pp pizz.
sf
pp
2. Vle.
pp pizz.
sf
pp
2. Vlc.
pp pizz.
sf
pp
2. Cb.
pp
sf
pp

Piatti
Arpa
Pfte.
1. Vl.
2. Vl.
1. Vle.
1. Vlc.
1. Cb.
3. Vl.
4. Vl.
2. Vle.
2. Vlc.
2. Cb.
div.
div.
arco
arco
arco

Tempo I
150
Pfte.
mf
Ped.
1. Vl.
2. Vl.
1. Vlc.
3. Vl.
p
div.
4. Vl.
p
2. Vle.
p
arco
2. Vlc.
p
poco - - - - - a poco - -
Pfte.
* Ped. * Ped. * simile
Ped.
3. Vl.
cresc poco a poco (sin al ff)
div.
4. Vl.
cresc poco a poco (sin al ff)
2. Vle.
cresc poco a poco (sin al ff)
2. Vlc.
cresc poco a poco (sin al ff)

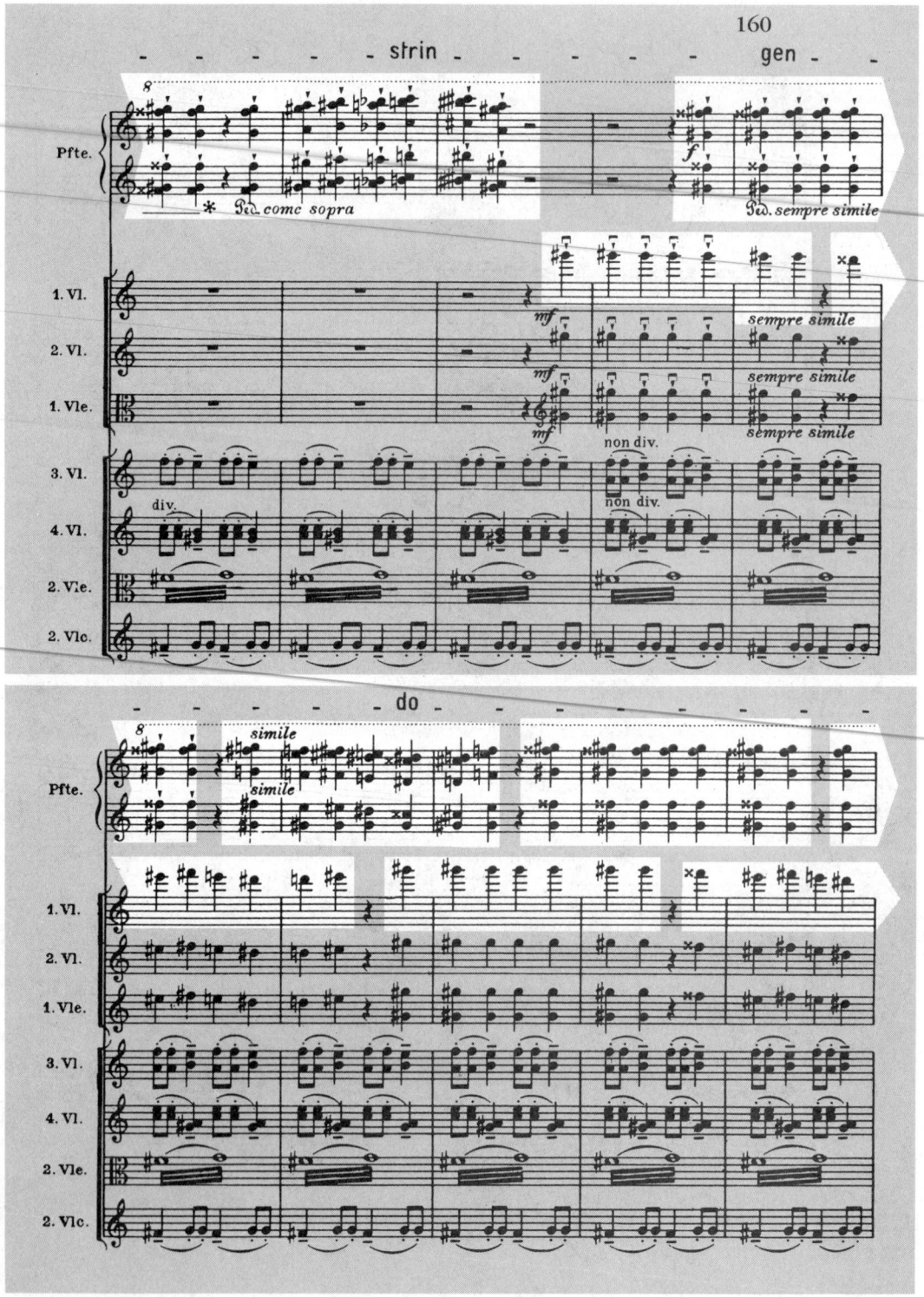
160
strin gen
Pfte.
comc sopra
sempre simile
1. Vl.
2. Vl.
1. Vle.
3. Vl.
4. Vl.
2. Vle.
2. Vlc.
mf
f
sempre simile
non div.
div.
do
simile
Pfte.
1. Vl.
2. Vl.
1. Vle.
3. Vl.
4. Vl.
2. Vle.
2. Vlc.

170
Arpa
Pfte.
ff
1. Vl.
f
simile
cresc.
2. Vl.
1. Vle.
1. Vlc.
sempre simile
3. Vl.
4. Vl.
2. Vle.
non div.
2. Vlc.

Xyl.
f
cresc.
Arpa
p gliss.
cresc.
Pfte.
8
1. Vl.
2. Vl.
1. Vle.
1. Vlc.
cresc.
pizz.
1. Cb.
f
3. Vl.
ff
4. Vl.
ff
2. Vle.
ff
2. Vlc.
ff
pizz.
2. Cb.
f

180
al
Xyl.
ff
Arpa.
ff
Pfte.
1. Vl.
ff
2. Vl.
ff
1. Vle.
ff
1. Vlc.
ff
1. Cb.
cresc.
ff
3. Vl.
4. Vl.
2. Vle.
2. Vlc.
2. Cb.
cresc.
ff

Vivacissimo, ♩ ca 176
Xyl.
Pfte.
1. Vl.
2. Vl.
1. Vle.
3. Vl.
4. Vl.
2. Vle.
2. Vlc.
2. Cb.
ff
arco
Presto strepitoso, ♩ 210
1. Vl.
2. Vl.
1. Vle.
1. Vlc.
1. Cb.
3. Vl.
4. Vl.
2. Vle.
2. Vlc.
2. Cb.

190
1. Vl.
2. Vl.
1. Vle.
1. Vlc.
1. Cb.
3. Vl.
4. Vl.
2. Vle.
2. Vlc.
2. Cb.
1. Vl.
2. Vl.
1. Vle.
1. Vlc.
1. Cb.
3. Vl.
4. Vl.
2. Vle.
2. Vlc.
2. Cb.

200
Timp.
f
ff
Pfte.
ff
1. Vl.
2. Vl.
1. Vle.
1. Vlc.
1. Cb.
3. Vl.
4. Vl.
2. Vle.
2. Vlc.
2. Cb.

24 23
F Molto moderato, ♪ ca 144
Timp.
mf
Cel.
p
Pfte.
1. Vl.
2. Vl.
1. Vle.
1. Vlc.
1. Cb.
f
3. Vl.
4. Vl.
p
IV
f, molto espr.
2. Vle.
f, molto espr.
2. Vlc.
f, molto espr.
2. Cb.
f

Timp.
Cel.
Pfte.
1. Vl.
2. Vl.
1. Vle.
1. Vlc.
1. Cb.
3. Vl.
4. Vl.
2. Vle.
2. Vlc.
2. Cb.

210
tr
Timp.
Cel.
Pfte.
mf, molto espr.
1. Vl.
2. Vl.
1. Vle.
1. Vlc.
1. Cb.
f, molto espr.
3. Vl.
4. Vl.
2. Vle.
2. Vlc.
2. Cb.
f

Timp.
Pfte.
1. Vl.
2. Vl.
1. Vle.
1. Vlc.
1. Cb.
3. Vl.
4. Vl.
2. Vle.
2. Vlc.
2. Cb.

Timp.
Pfte.
1. Vl.
2. Vl.
1. Vle.
1. Vlc.
1. Cb.
3. Vl.
4. Vl.
2. Vle.
2. Vlc.
2. Cb.

220
1. Vl.
2. Vl.
1. Vle.
1. Vlc.
3. Vl.
4. Vl.
2. Vle.
2. Vlc.
f
mf
p dolce
dim.
1. Cb.
2. Cb.

230
rallent. al Adagio, ♪ 84
1. Vl.
2. Vl.
1. Vle.
1. Vlc.
1. Cb.
3. Vl.
4. Vl.
2. Vle.
2. Vlc.
2. Cb.
sempre pp
Solo
f
dim.
pp

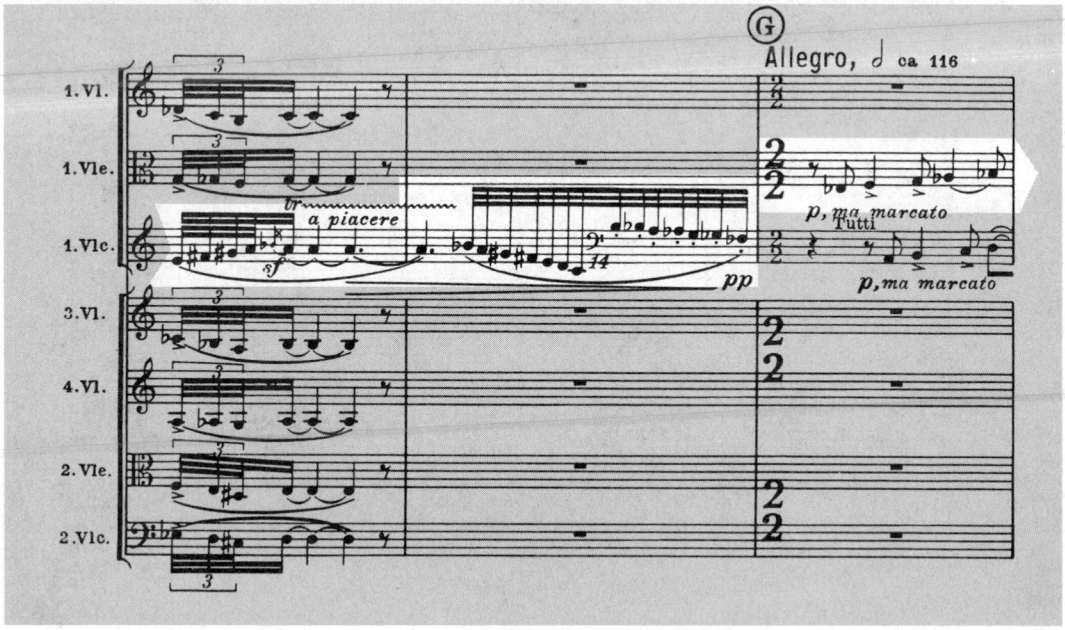
G
Allegro, 𝅗𝅥 ca. 116
1. Vl.
1. Vle.
1. Vlc.
3. Vl.
4. Vl.
2. Vle.
2. Vlc.
a piacere
p, ma marcato
Tutti
p, ma marcato
pp

1. Vl.
2. Vl.
1. Vle.
1. Vlc.
2. Vle.
2. Vlc.
mf, marcato
mp, marcato
mf
mf
mf
mp, marcato
mf
mp, marcato
240
accelerando
1. Vl.
2. Vl.
1. Vle.
1. Vlc.
3. Vl.
4. Vl.
2. Vle.
2. Vlc.
f, cresc.
ff

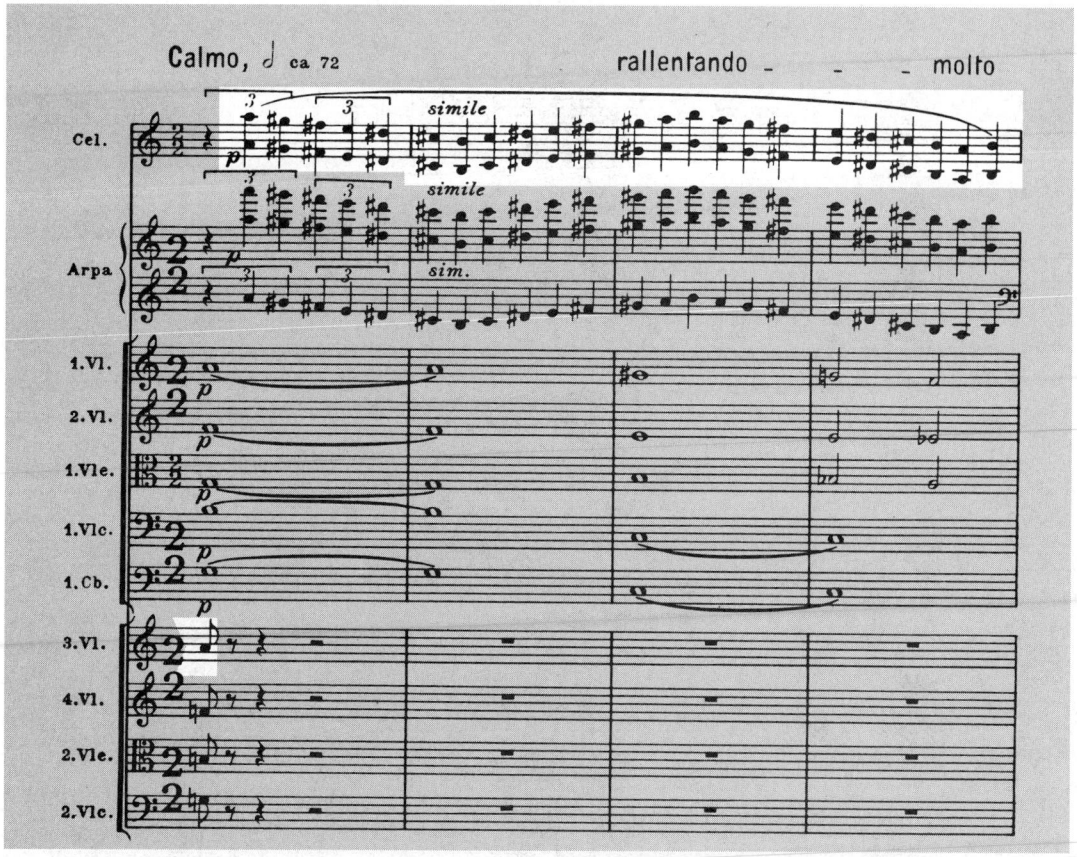
Calmo, ca 72
rallentando - - - molto
Cel.
simile
Arpa
simile
sim.
1.Vl.
2.Vl.
1.Vle.
1.Vlc.
1.Cb.
3.Vl.
4.Vl.
2.Vle.
2.Vlc.

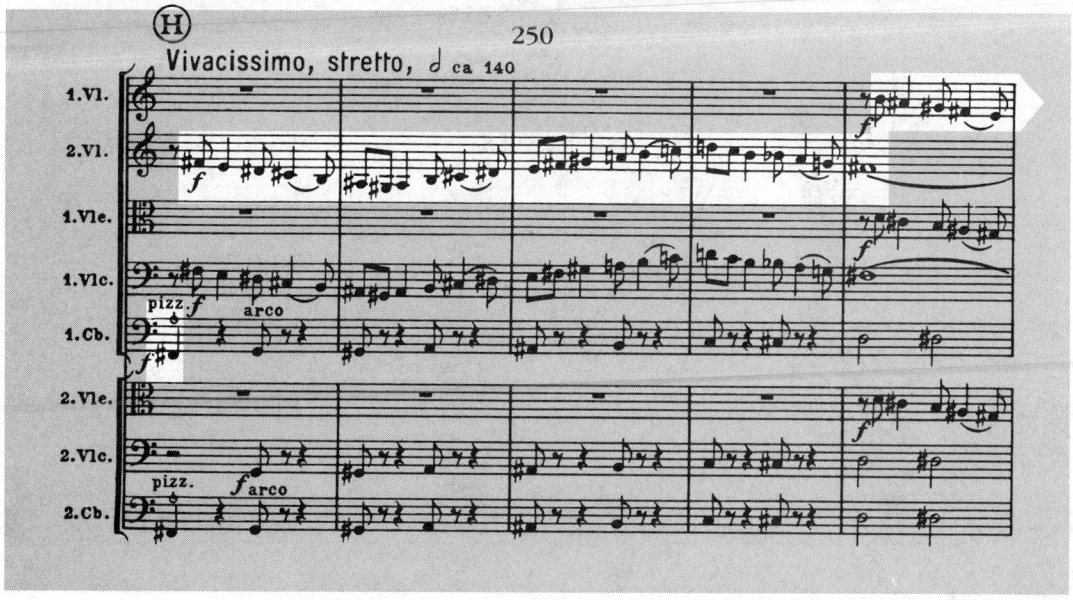
H
250
Vivacissimo, stretto, ca 140
1.Vl.
2.Vl.
1.Vle.
1.Vlc.
pizz.
arco
1.Cb.
2.Vle.
2.Vlc.
pizz.
arco
2.Cb.

1. Vl.
2. Vl.
1. Vle.
1. Vlc.
1. Cb.
3. Vl.
2. Vle.
2. Vlc.
2. Cb.
f

260
Tempo I
ca 130
Pfte.
f
ff
1. Vl.
2. Vl.
1. Vle.
1. Vlc.
1. Cb.
3. Vl.
4. Vl.
2. Vle.
2. Vlc.
2. Cb.
cresc.

Timp.
f
Pfte.
ff
1. Vl.
ff
2. Vl.
ff
1. Vle.
ff
1. Vlc.
ff
1. Cb.
ff
3. Vl.
4. Vl.
2. Vle.
2. Vlc.
2. Cb.

270
Timp.
Pfte.
1. Vl.
2. Vl.
1. Vle.
1. Vlc.
1. Cb.
3. Vl.
4. Vl.
2. Vle.
2. Vlc.
2. Cb.

Pfte.
f
1. Vl.
cresc.
2. Vl.
cresc.
1. Vle.
cresc.
1. Vlc.
cresc.
1. Cb.
cresc.
3. Vl.
cresc.
4. Vl.
cresc.
2. Vle.
cresc.
2. Vlc.
cresc.
2. Cb.
cresc.

I Meno mosso, ♩ ca 100
sempre rallentando
280
Arpa
ff
I.
ff
Pfte.
(a 4 m.)
II.
ff
Ped.
*
1. Vl.
più f, espr.
ff
IV
2. Vl.
più f, espr.
ff
1. Vle.
più f, espr.
2. Vlc.
più f, espr.
1. Cb.
più f
3. Vl.
più f
4. Vl.
più f
2. Vle.
più f
2. Vlc.
più f
2. Cb.
più f

al Largo
a tempo allarg.
a tempo
ca 100
(♩ 100)
(♩ 100)
Timp.
Xyl.
Arpa
gliss.
Re♯, Fa♯
I.
Pfte.
II.
1. Vl.
2. Vl.
1 Vle
1. Vlc.
1. Cb.
3. Vl.
4. Vl.
2. Vle.
2. Vlc.
2. Cb.
Budapest, 1936. szept. 7.
Durée d'exécution:
A = ca 50″
A-B = " 21″
B-C = " 9″
C-D = " 29″
D-E = " 19″
E-F = ca 55″
F-G = " 1′ 37″
G-H = " 18″
H-I = " 25″
I - = " 17″
ca 5′ 40″
I. = ca 6′ 30″
II. = " 6′ 55″
III. = " 6′ 35″
IV. = " 5′ 40″
ca 25′ 40″

26. *Igor Stravinsky (1882–1971)* 8:7B/1 8:7/25 - 40 MW

Petrushka, First Tableau (1911) 3:3A/3 3:3/7 - 15

"The Shrovetide Fair"

© Copyright by Edition Russe de Musique. © Copyright assigned to Boosey & Hawkes, Inc. Revised edition © copyright 1947, 1948 by Boosey & Hawkes, Inc.; copyright renewed.

Fl. I. II.
Cl. I.
Cl. II. III.
Fag. I. II.
Cont. F.
Cor. I. II.
Cor. III. IV.
Arpa I.
Arpa II.
Piano.
V. I.
V. II.
Viole.
tutti Celli.
C. B.
II.
I.
poco
mf
f
p
(détaché)
divisi
div.

Fl. I. II.
Ob. I.
I. Solo. espress. e cant.
Cl. I.
Cl. II. III.
Fag. I. II.
a 2
Cor. I. II.
Cor. III. IV.
Arpa I.
Arpa II.
Piano.
V. I.
V. II.
Viole.
Cello solo.
cant.

Fl. Picc. I. II.
Fl. I. II.
Ob. I. II.
Cl. I.
Cl. II. III.
Fag. I. II.
Cont. F.
Cor. I. II.
Cor. III. IV.
Arpa I.
Arpa II.
Celesta.
Piano.
V. I.
V. II.
Viole.
tutti Celli.
C. B.
a 2.
a 2. Soli
poco > etc. simile
poco > etc. simile
gliss.
sempre simile
(détaché)
(détaché)

Poco a poco accelerando e crescendo.
Fl. Picc. I. II.
Fl. I. II.
Ob. I. II.
Cl. I.
Cl. II. III.
Fag. I. II.
Cont. F.
Cor I. II.
Cor III. IV.
Tr. II. in Si♭.
mf marcato
Arpa I.
Arpa II.
Celesta.
Piano.
Poco a poco accelerando e crescendo.
V. I.
V. II.
Viole.
Celli.
C. B.

CURTAIN
Fl. Picc. I.II.
Fl. I. II.
Ob. I. II.
Ob. III.
Cl. I.
Cl. II. III.
Cor. I. II.
Cor. III. IV.
Pist. I in Si♭
Tr. II.
mf marcato
mf
Arpa I.
Arpa II.
Celesta.
Piano.
V. I.
V. II.
Viole.

26
8
SPECIAL CURTAIN
Fl. Picc. I.II.
Fl. I. II.
Ob. I. II.
Ob. III.
Cl. I.
Cl. II. III.
Fag. I. II.
Cor. I. II.
Cor. III. IV.
Pist. I. II.
Tr. I. II.
3 Trb.
Tamb. de Basque.
Arpa I.
Arpa II.
Celesta.
Piano.
V. I.
V. II.
Viole.
Celli.
f marcato
ore - scen - do sino al -
con mare.
div. a 3.

A SMALL GROUP OF TIPSY MERRYMAKERS, PRANCING, PASSES BY.
Fl. Picc. I. II.
Fl. I. II.
Ob. I. II.
Ob. III.
Cl. I.
Cl. II. III.
Cor. I. II.
fff sempre
Cor. III. IV.
Pist. I. II.
Tr. I. II.
3 Trb.
Bacch. di Tamb. milit.
Piatti
f
Bacch. di Tamb. milit.
Tam-T.
mf
V. I.
unis.
V. II.
Viole.
div. a 2
Celli:
C. B.
fff

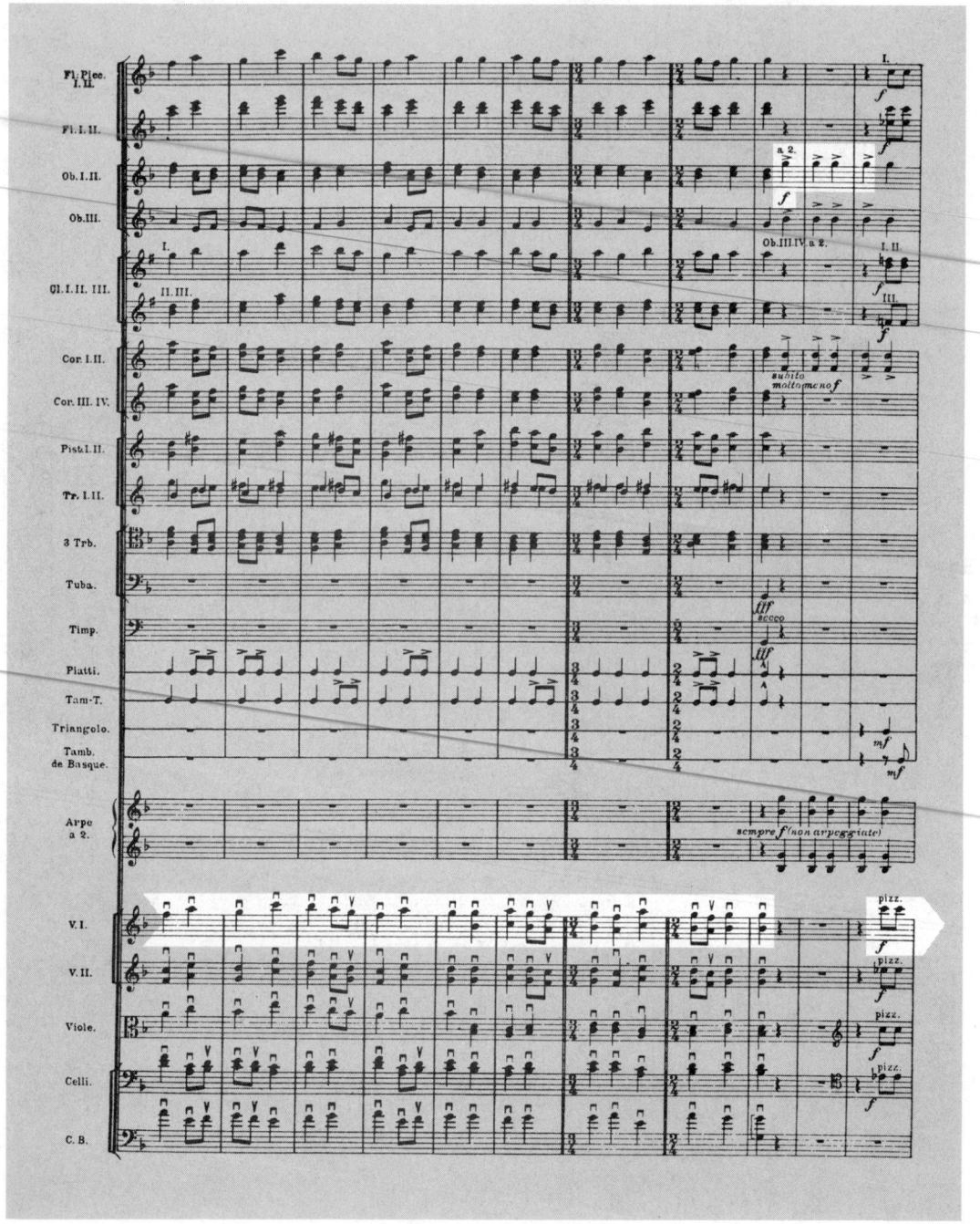
Fl. Picc. I. II.
Fl. I. II.
Ob. I. II.
Ob. III.
Cl. I. II. III.
Cor. I. II.
Cor. III. IV.
Pist. I. II.
Tr. I. II.
3 Trb.
Tuba.
Timp.
Piatti.
Tam-T.
Triangolo.
Tamb. de Basque.
Arpe a 2.
V. I.
V. II.
Viole.
Celli.
C. B.
a 2.
Ob. III. IV. a 2.
subito molto meno f
secco
sempre f (non arpeggiate)
pizz.

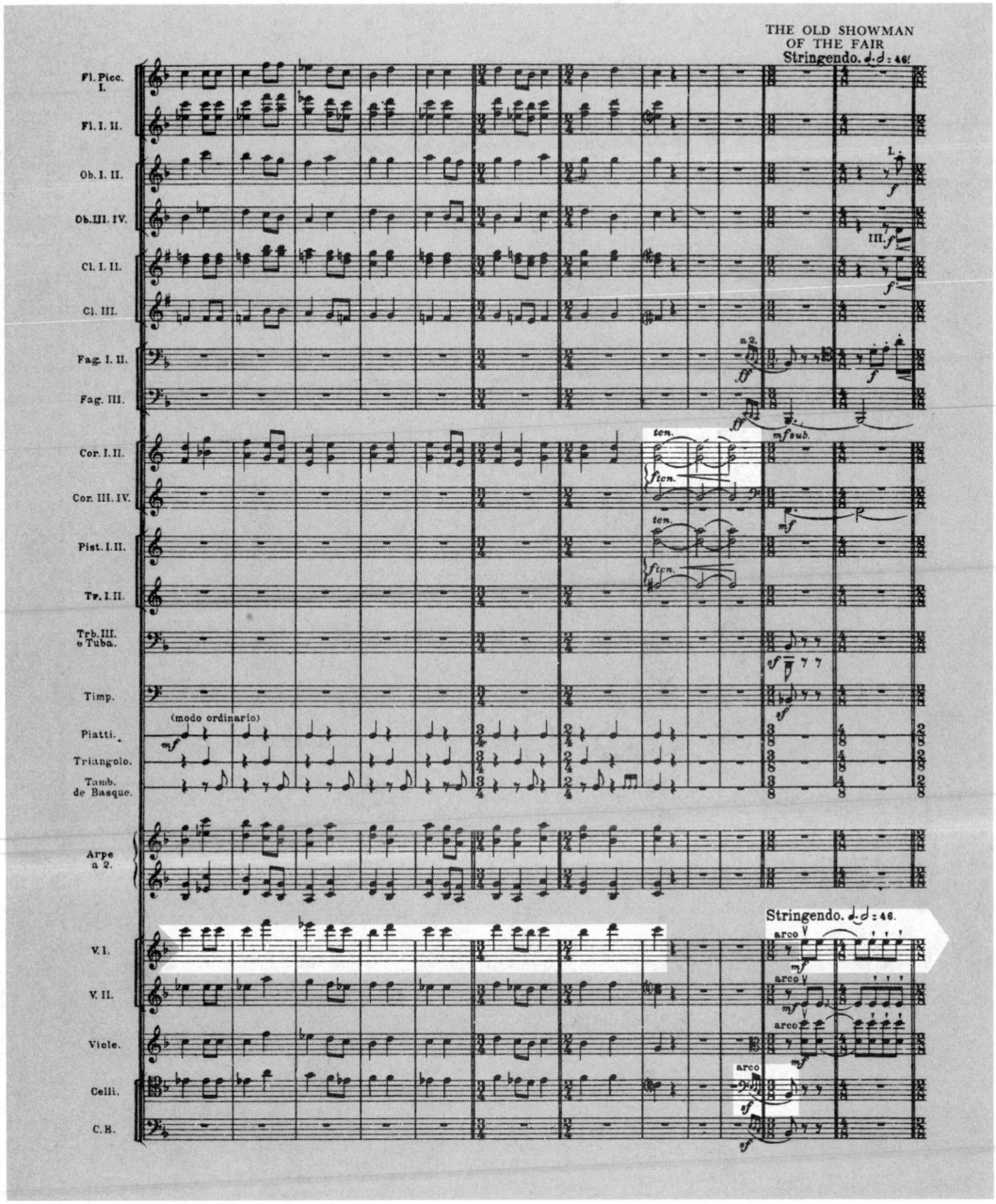
THE OLD SHOWMAN
OF THE FAIR
Stringendo.
Fl. Picc. I.
Fl. I. II.
Ob. I. II.
Ob. III. IV.
Cl. I. II.
Cl. III.
Fag. I. II.
Fag. III.
Cor. I. II.
Cor. III. IV.
Pist. I. II.
Tr. I. II.
Trb. III. e Tuba.
Timp.
Piatti.
(modo ordinario)
Triangolo.
Tamb. de Basque.
Arpe a 2.
V. I.
V. II.
Viole.
Celli.
C. B.
Stringendo.
arco

ENTERTAINS THE CROWD FROM THE HEIGHT OF HIS BOOTH.
Fl. Picc. I.II.
Fl. I. II.
Ob. I.
Ob. II.III.
Cl. I.II.
Cl. III.
Fag. I.II.
Fag. III.
Cor. III. IV.
Pist. I.II.
Tr. I.II.
Timp.
V. I.
V. II.
Viole.
Celli.
C. B.

27
9
Come prima. ♩: 138.
Fl. Picc. I. II.
Fl. I. II.
Ob. I. II.
Ob. III. IV.
Cl. I. II.
Cl. III.
Fag. I.
Fag. II. III.
Cor. I. II.
Cor. III. IV.
Pist. I. II.
Tr. I. II.
Trb. III. e Tuba.
Timp.
♩: 138. (Come prima)
(détaché)
V. I. div.
V. II. div.
Viole. div.
pizz
Celli.
C. B.
arco
subito meno f

28
10
IN THE CROWD APPEARS AN ORGAN-GRINDER WITH A STREET DANCER.
Meno mosso.
Stringendo.
Fl. Picc. I.
Fl. I.
Ob. I. II.
Cl. I. II.
Cl. III.
Cl. basso in Sib.
Fag. I. II.
Cor. I. II.
Cor. III. IV.
Trb. III. e Tuba.
Timp.
V. I. div.
V. II. div.
Viole. div.
Celli.
C. B.

Fl. Picc. I. II.
Fl. I. II.
Ob. I.
Ob. II. III.
Cl. I. II.
Cl. III.
Fag. I. II.
Fag. III.
Cor. II.
Cor. IV.
Pist. I. II.
Tr. I. II.
V. I.
V. II.
Viole
Celli
C. B.
a 2.
unis.

THE ORGAN-GRINDER BEGINS TO PLAY.
Come prima. ♩= 138.
Meno mosso. ♩= 100.
Fl. Picc. I. II.
Fl. I. II.
Ob. I.
Ob. II. III.
Cl. I. II. III.
Cl. basso
Fag. I.
Fag. II.
Fag. III.
Pist. I. II.
Tr. I.
V. I.
V. II.
Viole
Celli
C. B.
sempre p
meno f
div.
pizz.

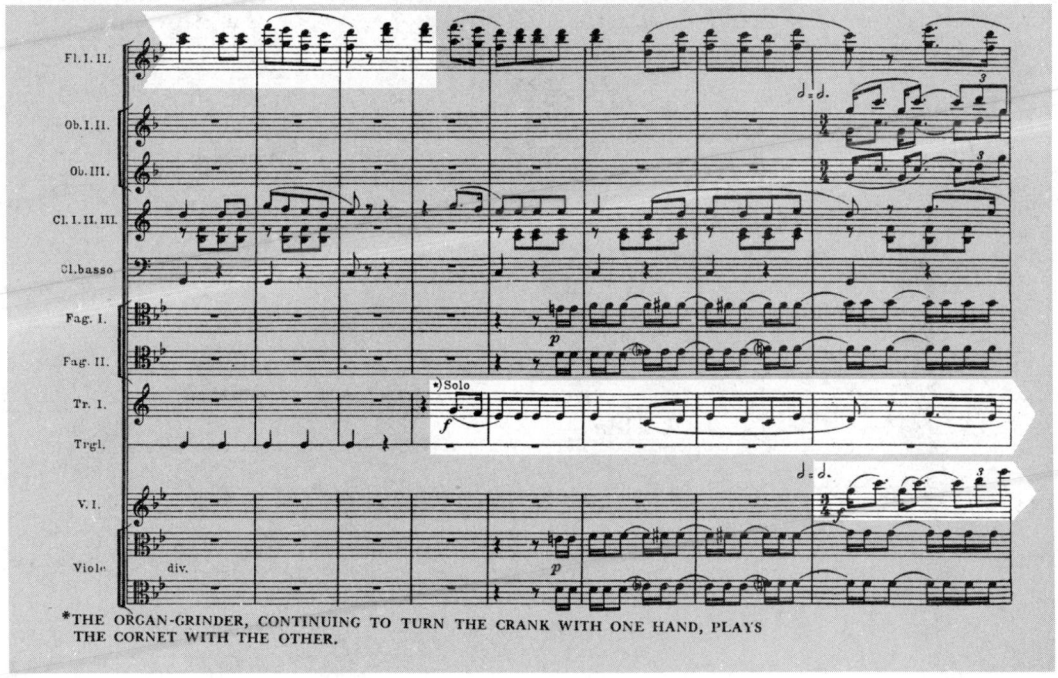

*THE ORGAN-GRINDER, CONTINUING TO TURN THE CRANK WITH ONE HAND, PLAYS THE CORNET WITH THE OTHER.

30
12
AT THE OTHER END OF THE STAGE, A MUSIC BOX PLAYS,
Fl. Picc. I.
Fl. I. II.
Ob. I. II.
Ob. III.
Cl. I. II.
Cl. III.
Cl. basso
Fag. I.
Fag. II.
Tr. I.
Campanelli
Celesta à 4 maains
V. I.
V. II.
Viole
Celli
stacc.
unis. pizz.
div.
pizz.

AROUND WHICH ANOTHER STREET DANCER DANCES.
Fl. Picc. I.
Fl. I.
Cl. I. II.
Cl. III.
Cl. basso
Camp.
Celesta à 4 mains
Piano
pp
THE FIRST DANCER
Fl. Picc. I.
Fl. I. II.
Cl. I. II.
Cl. III.
Cl. basso
Trgl.
Camp.
Celesta à 4 mains
Piano
mf

AGAIN BEATS THE TRIANGLE.
Fl. I. II.
Cl. I. II. III.
Trgl.
Camp.
Celesta à 4 mains
Piano
V. II.
div.
arco
arco

THE BARREL ORGAN AND
Stringendo.
Fl. Picc. I.
Fl. I. II.
Ob. I.
Ob. II. III.
Cl. I. II. III.
Cl. basso
Fag. I. II.
Cont. F.
Tr. I.
Solo
Trb. III Tuba
Timp.
Trgl.
Camp.
Celesta à 4 mains
Piano
V. I.
V. II.
Viole
Celli
C. B.
poco a poco cresc.
arco
Stringendo.
*THE ORGAN-GRINDER RESUMES PLAYING THE CORNET.

THE MUSIC BOX STOP PLAYING; THE SHOWMAN AGAIN ATTRACTS THE ATTENTION OF THE CROWD.
31
13
♩= 138 (Come prima)
Fl. I.
Fl. II.
Ob. I. II. III.
Cl. I.
Cl. II. III.
Fag. I. II.
Cont. F.
Cor. I. II.
Cor. III. IV.
Camp.
Arpa I
Arpa II
Piano
V. I.
V. II.
Viole
Celli
C. B.
div.
pizz.

Fl. picc. I.II.
Fl. I.II.
Ob. I. II.
Ob. III.
Cl. I.
Cl. II. III.
Fag. I.II.
Cor. I.II.
Cor. III.IV.
Tr. I.II.
Arpa I.
Arpa II.
Celesta.
Piano.
V. I. div.
V. II.
Viole.
a 2.
sempre à 2.
poco a poco
cresc.
cresc. poco a poco
mf marc.
f marc.
a 2
f gliss.
div.
più f

32
14
THE MERRYMAKERS RETURN.
Fl.picc. I.II.
Fl.I.II.
Ob.I.II.
Ob.III.
Cl.I.
Cl.II.III.
Fag.I.II.
Cor.I.II.
Cor.III.IV.
Pist.I.II.
Tr.I.II.
3 Trb.
Piatti.
Tam-T.
Tamb. de Basque.
Arpa I.
Arpa II.
Celesta.
Piano.
V.I. div.
V.II.
Viole.
Celli.
à 2.
sempre fff
ben marcato
sino al
Bacch.di Tamb.milit.
Bacch.di Tamb.milit.
unis.
arco div. a 3
a 2

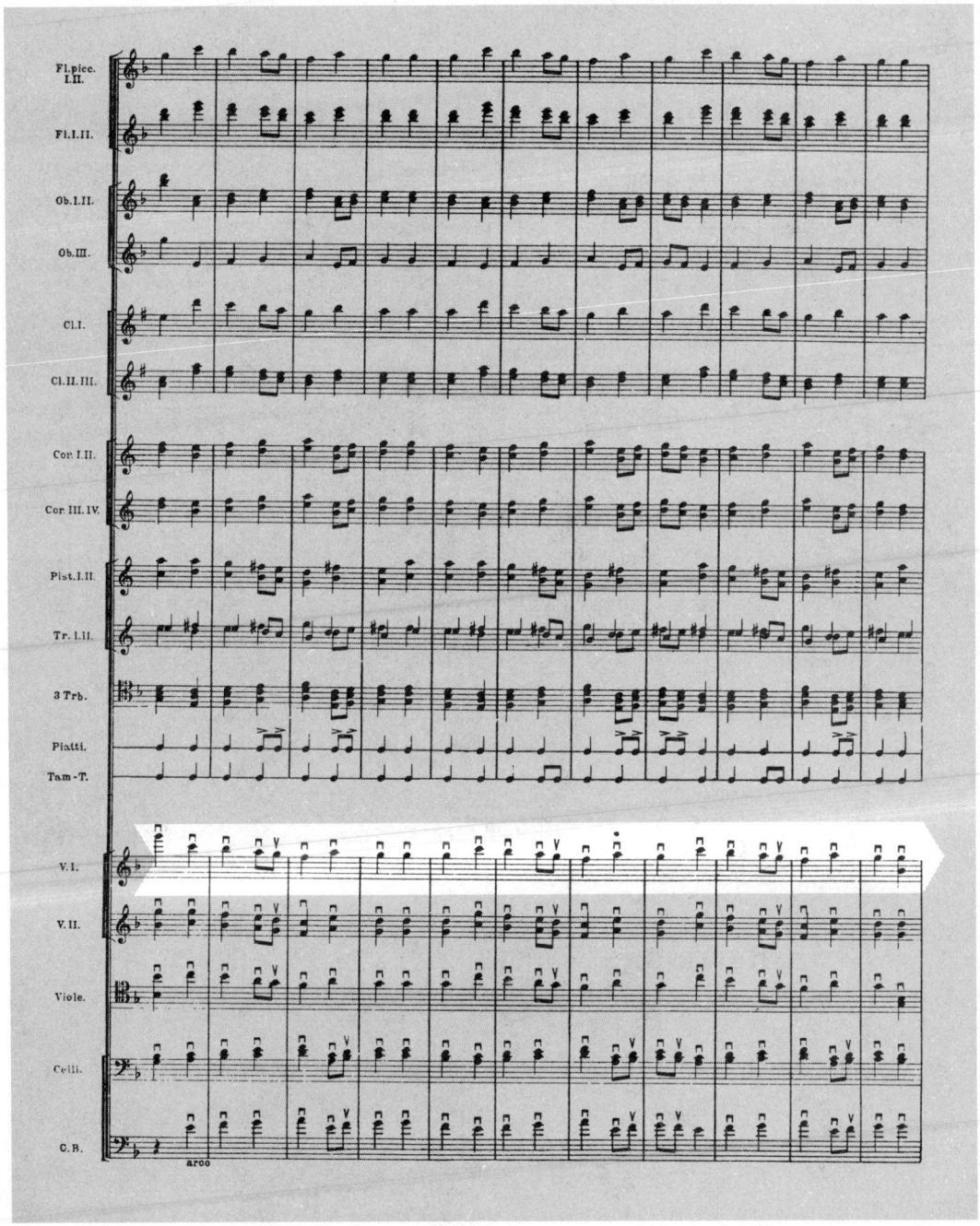
Fl.picc. I.II.
Fl.I.II.
Ob.I.II.
Ob.III.
Cl.I.
Cl.II.III.
Cor.I.II.
Cor.III.IV.
Pist.I.II.
Tr.I.II.
3 Trb.
Piatti.
Tam-T.
V.I.
V.II.
Viole.
Celli.
C.B.
arco

Fl.picc. I.II.
Fl. I. II
Ob. I. II.
Ob. III.
Cl. I. II. III.
Cor. I. II.
Cor. III. IV.
Pist. I. II.
Tr. I. II.
3 Trb.
Tuba.
Timp.
Piatti.
Tam-T.
Triangolo.
Tamb. de Basque.
Arpe a 2.
V. I.
V. II.
Viole.
Celli.
C. B.
a 2
III. IV. a 2.
subito meno f
fff
ecceo
(modo ordin.)
mf
sempre f (non arpeg.)
pizz.
f

stringendo
Fl. picc. I.
Fl. I. II
Ob. I. II. III. IV.
Cl. I. II.
Cl. III.
Fag. I. II.
Fag. III.
Cor. I. II.
Cor. III. IV.
Pi-t. I. II.
Tr. I.
Trb. III e Tuba
Timp.
Piatti.
Triangolo.
Tamb. de Basque.
Arpe a 2.
stringendo
V. I.
V. II.
Viole.
Celli.
C.B.

33
15
♩= 138. (Come prima).
Fl. picc. I.
Fl. I. II.
Ob. I.
Ob. II. III.
Cl. I. II.
Cl. III.
Fag. I.
Fag. II. III.
Cor. I. II.
Cor. III. IV.
Pist. I. II.
Trp. I. II.
Timp.
V. I. div.
V. II. div.
Viole.
Celli.
C.B.
(détaché)
pizz.

Fl. picc. I.
Fl. I. II.
Ob. I.
Ob. II. III.
Cl. I. II.
Cl. III.
Fag. I.
Fag. II. III.
Cor. I. II.
Cor III. IV.
Pist I. II.
Tr. I. II.
Tr. III e Tuba
Timp.
V. I. div.
V. II. div.
Viole
Celli
C. B.
a 2.
non div.
arco
simile

Fl. picc. I.
Fl. I. II.
Ob. I. II. III. IV.
Cl. I. II.
Cl. III.
Fag. II. III.
Cor. I. II.
Cor. III. IV.
Pist.-I.
Tr. I. II.
Tr. III. e Tuba.
Timp.
V. I.
V. II.
Viole
Celli
C. B.

Fl. picc. I.
Fl. I. II.
Ob. I. II. III. IV.
Cl. I. II. III.
Fag. I. II. III.
Cor. I. II.
Cor. III. IV.
Pist. I. II.
Tr. I. II.
Tr. III. e Tuba
Timp.
V. I.
V. II.
Viole
Celli
C. B.
sempre
unis
non div.
più

♩= 138 (Come prima)
Fl. picc. I.
Fl. I.
Fl. II.
Ob. I. II. III. IV.
Cl. I.
Cl. II.
Cl. III.
Fag. I. II.
Fag. III.
Cor. I. II.
Cor. III. IV.
Pist. I. II.
Trp. I. II.
3 Trb.
Timp.
Piatti
Trgl.
Tamb. de Basque
Camp.
Arpa I. II. a 2.
Piano.
Celesta.
V. I.
V. II.
Viole
Celli
sempre
simile
pizz.
arco

Fl. picc. I.
Fl. I.
Fl. II.
Ob. I. II.
Ob. III.
Ob. IV.
Cl. I.
Cl. II.
Cl. III.
Fag. I. II.
Cont. F.
Cor. I. II.
Cor. III. IV.
Pist. I. II. e Tr. I. II.
Piatti
Trgl.
Tamb. de Basque
Camp.
Arpa I. II. a 2.
Piano.
Celesta.
V. I.
V. II.
Viole.
Celli.
C. B.
Pist. a 2.
marcato
Tr. a 2.
marcato
arpa II.
glice.
arco
arco
arco
sul f

TWO DRUMMERS, STANDING IN FRONT OF
Molto crescendo sino al
Fl. picc. I.II.
Fl. I. II.
Ob. I.
Ob. III.IV.
Cl. I.
Cl. II.III.
Fag. I.II.III.
Cont. F.
Cor. I.II.
Cor. III.IV.
Pist. I.II.
Tr. I.II.
3 Trb. e Tuba
Timp.
bacchette di Tamb. milit.
cre - scen - do
Trgl.
Tamb. de Basque
Tamburin
Tamb. milit.
Dans la coulisse
a 2.
Arpa I.
Arpa II.
V. I.
enharm.
V. II.
Viole.
arco
Celli.
C.B.

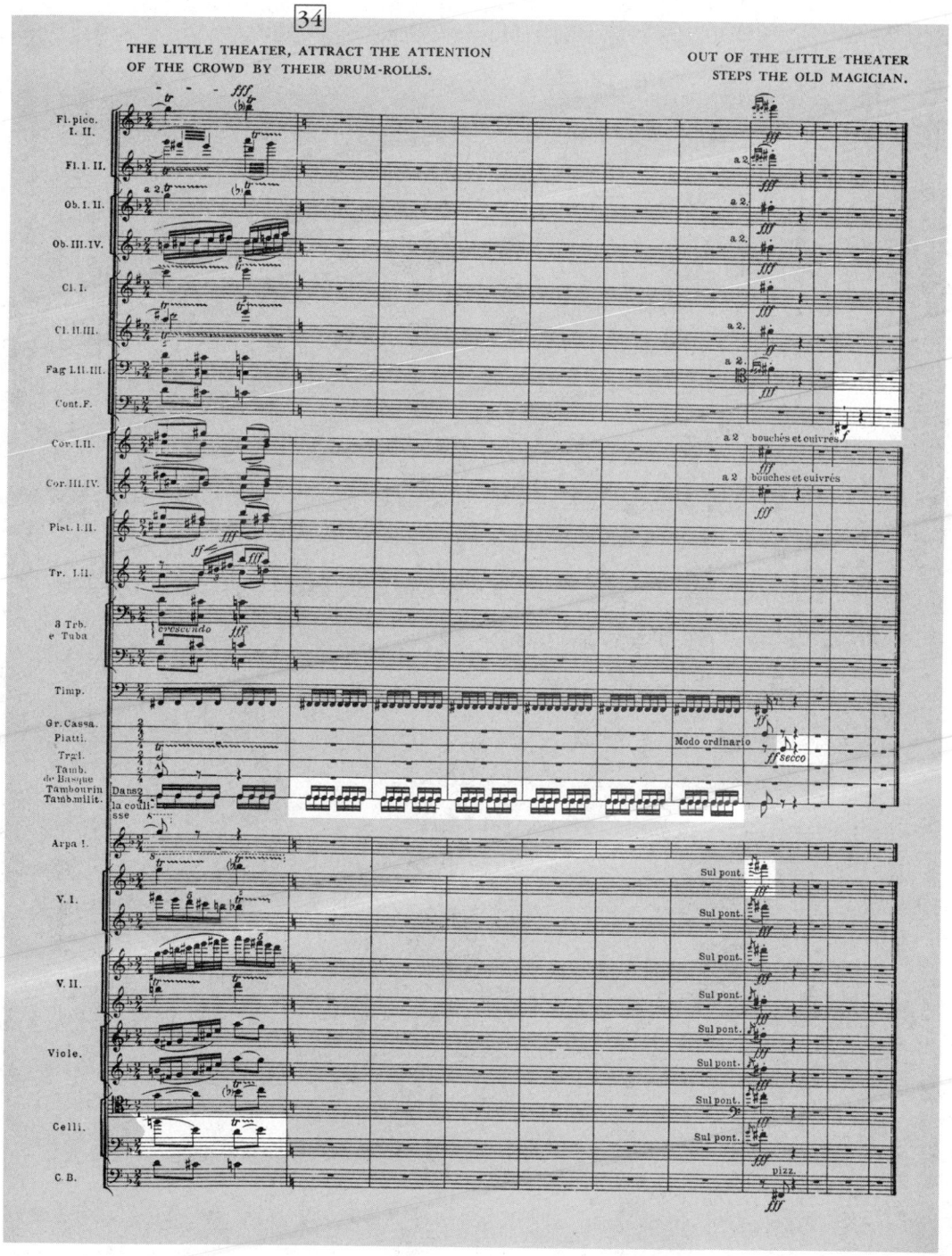
34
THE LITTLE THEATER, ATTRACT THE ATTENTION OF THE CROWD BY THEIR DRUM-ROLLS.
OUT OF THE LITTLE THEATER STEPS THE OLD MAGICIAN.
Fl. picc. I. II.
Fl. I. II.
Ob. I. II.
Ob. III. IV.
Cl. I.
Cl. II. III.
Fag. I. II. III.
Cont. F.
Cor. I. II.
Cor. III. IV.
Pist. I. II.
Tr. I. II.
3 Trb. e Tuba
Timp.
Gr. Cassa.
Piatti.
Trgl.
Tamb. de Basque
Tambourin
Tamburlit.
Arpa I.
V. I.
V. II.
Viole.
Celli.
C. B.
a 2.
a 2 bouchés et cuivrés
crescendo
Modo ordinario
ff secco
Dans la coulisse
Sul pont.
pizz.

"The Magic Trick"

THE CURTAIN OF THE LITTLE THEATER OPENS, AND THE CROWD SEES THREE PUPPETS: PETRUSHKA, A MOOR, AND A BALLERINA.
L'istesso tempo
Fl. Picc. I.
Fl. I.
Fl. II.
Ob. I.
Cor. Ingl.
Ob. IV = C. Ingl.
Solo
simile
mp cantabile
Cl. I.
Cl. II.
Fag. I.
Fag. II.
Cor. I. II.
Cor. III. IV.
Tr. I.
ouvert
Cel.
Arpa I.
Arpa II.
V. I.
V. II.
Viole
Colli
C. B.
div.
pizz.
arco
unis.
flautando
flaut.

THE MAGICIAN ANIMATES THEM BY TOUCHING THEM WITH HIS FLUTE.
Fl. Picc. I.
Fl. I.
Fl. II.
Ob. I.
Cor. Ingl.
Cl. I.
Cl. II.
Cor. I. II.
Cor. III. IV.
Pist. I.
Tr. I. II.
Camp.
Cel.
Arpa I.
Arpa II.
V. I.
V. II.
Viole
Celli
C. B.
Solo
mp cantabile
trem.
do ♯, mi ♮, sol ♯, la ♯, si ♯.
do ♮
gliss.
re ♯
re ♮, fa ♯, sol ♯, la ♭, si ♭.
uniss. pizz.
senza sord.
flaut.
div.

"Russian Dance"

37
Fl. Picc. I. II.
Fl. I. II.
Ob. I. II. III.
Cor. Ingl.
Cl. I. II.
Cl. III.
Fag. I. II.
Fag. III.
Cor. I. II.
Cor. III. IV.
Pist. I. II.
Trgl.
Tamb. de Basque
Xyloph.
Arpa I.
Arpa II.
Piano.
2 V. Soli.
V. I.
V. II.
3 sole
Viole
le altre
Celli
I.
a 2.
I. II.
III.
I. Solo
mf sempre grottesco
I. Solo.
mf sempre grottesco
con sord.
I. Solo marcato
gliss.
m. d.
m. g.
arco pp sempre
arco
pizz.
div. pizz.
f sub. meno f
poco
sempre - - simile
pizz.
sf sub. meno f
sf sub. meno f

Fl. Picc. I.
a 2.
Fl. I. II.
Ob. I.
Solo
stacc.
Cl. I.
Solo
Pist. I.
simile
senza sord.
Trgl.
Tamb. de Basque
Xyloph.
Arpa I.
Arpa II.
Piano
2 V. Soli
V. I.
gli altri
arco
pizz.
V. II.
sf sub. meno f
3 sole
Viole
le altre
sf sub. meno f
Celli
sf sub. meno f

Fl. Picc. I. II.
Fl. I. II.
Ob. I. II.
Cor. Ingl
Cl. I. II.
Cl. III.
Fag. I.
Fag. II. III.
Cor. I.
Pist. I. II.
Tr. I. II.
Xyloph.
Arpa I.
Arpa II.
Piano
2 V. Soli
Vni I.
gli altri
V. II.
3 sole
Viole
le altre
Celli div.
C. B.
p stacc.
p sub. stacc.
poco più f
p sub.
p poco marc.
sempre stacc.
pp stacc. leggiero
mf leggiero
arco
tutti stacc.
arco tutte
sim.
pizz.

crescendo sempre
Fl. Picc. I. II.
Fl. I. II
Ob. I. II.
Cor. Ingl.
Cl. I. II.
Cl. III.
Fag. I.
Fag. II. III.
Pist. I. II.
Tr. I. II.
Xyloph.
Arpa I.
Arpa II.
Piano.
V. I.
V. II
Viole.
Celli.
cresc.
sempre stacc.
crescendo sempre
crescendo sempre

38
Fl. Picc. I. II.
Fl. I. II.
Ob. I. II. III.
Cor. Ingl.
Cl. I II.
Cl. III.
Fag. I.
Fag. II. III.
Cor. I. II.
Cor. III. IV.
Pist. I. II.
Tr. I. II.
Xyloph.
Camp.
Arpa I.
Arpa II.
Piano.
V. I.
V. II.
Viole.
Celli.
C. B
a 2.
I. II.
I. II. III.
poco
mf poco
mp poco
f poco
glins.
Solo
gliss. poco a poco accel.
div.
stacc.
arco

Fl. Picc. I. II.
Fl. I. II.
Ob. I. II. III.
Cor. Ingl.
Cl. I. II. III.
Fag. I. II. III.
Cor. I. II.
Cor. III. IV.
Pist. I. II.
Tr. I. II.
Xyloph.
Camp.
Arpa I.
Solo
sol
Arpa II.
Piano.
V. I.
V. II.
Viole.
Celli.
C. B.

39
Fl. Picc. I. II.
Fl. I. II.
Ob. I. II. III.
Cor. ingl.
Cl. I. II. III.
Fag. I. II. III.
Cor. I. II.
Cor. III. IV.
Pist. I. II.
Tr. I. II.
Xyloph.
Camp.
G. Cassa.
Piatti.
Arpa I.
Arpa II.
Piano.
V. I.
V. II.
Viole.
Celli.
C. B.
(a 2.)
a 2.
I. Solo
II. Solo
III. Solo
poco marc. ma p
come sopra
[modo ordinario]
pizz.
gliss.
meno f
p sub.

Fl. Picc. I.II.
Fl. I. II.
Ob. I. II.
Cor. Ingl.
Cl. I. II.
Cl. III.
Fag I.
Fag II.
Fag III.
Cor. I. II.
Cor. III. IV.
Pist. I. II.
Tr. I.II.
G. Cassa.
Piatti.
Piano.
V. I.
V. II.
Viole.
Celli.
C. B.
I. Solo.
Solo
Solo
meno f
simile
simile
unis.
meno f
pizz.
pizz.
2 V-ni Soli
arco
scherzando
leggiero
cresc.

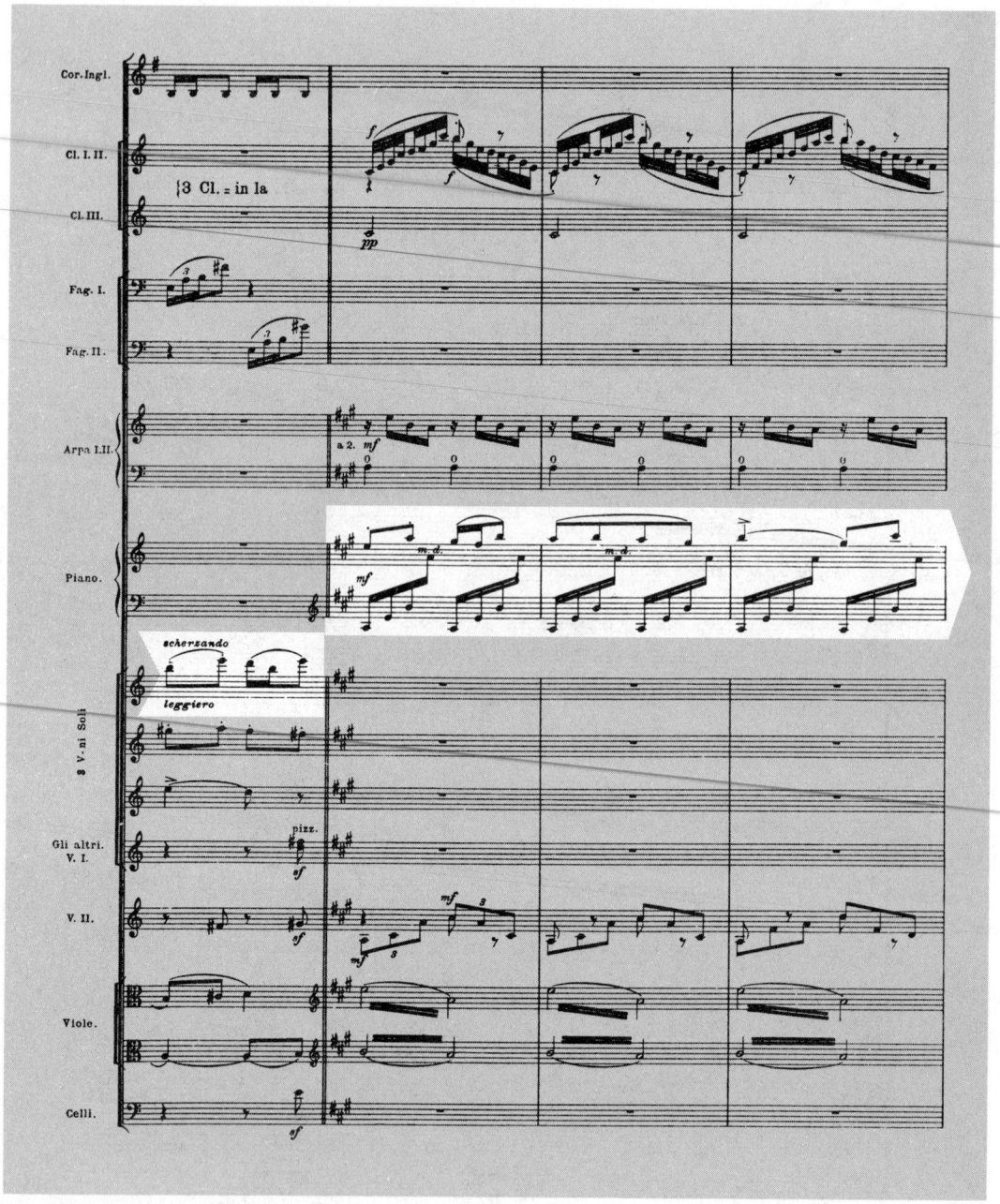
Cor. Ingl.
Cl. I. II.
Cl. III.
3 Cl. = in la
Fag. I.
Fag. II.
Arpa I.II.
a 2.
Piano.
schersando
leggiero
3 V.ni Soli
Gli altri V. I.
pizz.
V. II.
Viole.
Celli.

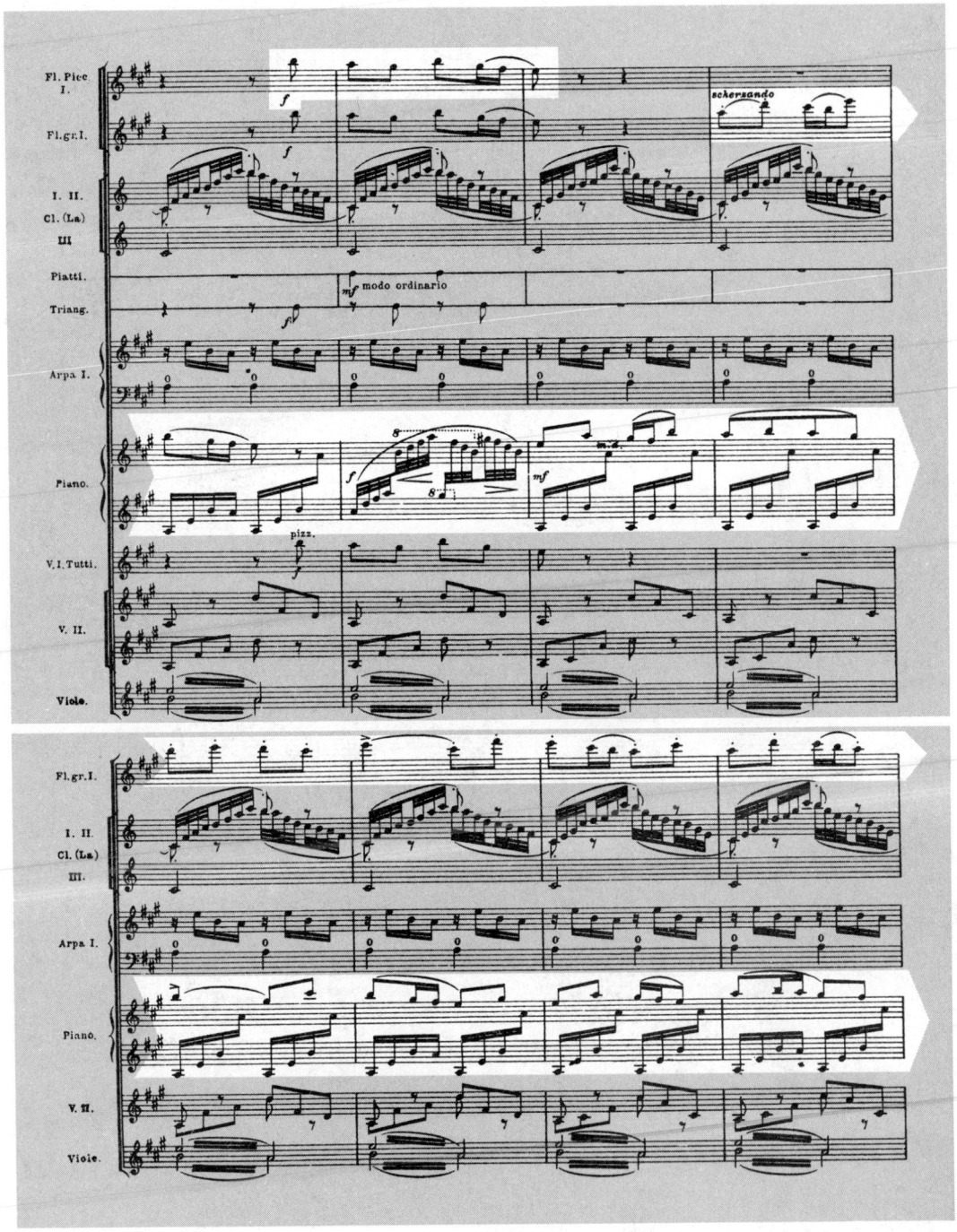
Fl. Picc I.
Fl. gr. I.
I. II.
Cl. (La)
III
Piatti.
Triang.
Arpa I.
Piano.
V. I. Tutti.
V. II.
Viole.
scherzando
modo ordinario
pizz.
Fl. gr. I.
I. II.
Cl. (La)
III.
Arpa I.
Piano.
V. II.
Viole.

I.
Fl.gr.I.II.
I. II.
Cl.(La)
III.
3 Cl. in si♭.
I. II.
Corni.
III. IV.
poco sf sub. p
sempre simile
sempre simile
Arpa I.
Piano.
pp sub.
V. solo.
mf scherzando
V. II.
Viole.
Solo.
Ob. I.
I. II.
Cl. (si♭)
III.
Cl. basso. (si♭)
simile
simile
Corni.
Piano.
V. solo.

poco a poco cresc.
Fl. Picc. I.
Fl. gr. I. II.
Ob. I. II.
Cl. I. II.
Cl. III.
Cl. bassò
Fag. I.
Fag. II.
Xyloph.
Piano.
V. solo.
simile
Poco meno (tranquillo)
pochiss. accel.
a tempo
rall.
Solo.
I. Solo.
Cor. Ingl.
Cl. I. II. III.
Cl. basso
Fag. I. II.
I. II. Corni.
III. IV.
pizz.
V. I.
V. II.
Viole.
Celli.
C.B.

40
Tempo I. (Allegro giusto.)
Cor. Ingl.
Tr. I.
con sord.
Piano.
f subito
V. I.
Fl. Picc. I. II.
Fl. gr. I. II.
Ob. I. II.
Cor. Ingl.
Cl. I. II.
Fag. I. II.
Tr. I.
Piano.
legato
V. I.
V. II.
Viole.
Celli.
ten.
arco
pizz.

Fl. Picc. I.II.
Fl.gr. I. II.
I. II.
Ob.
III.
Cl. I.II.
Fag. I. II.
Tr. I.
Arpa. I.
Piano.
V. I.
V. II.
Viole.
Celli.
I.
a 2.
mf
f
p
sf
(pizz.)
(arco)
pizz.
arco

Fl. Picc.
I. II.
Fl.gr. I. II.
I. II.
Ob.
III.
Cl.I.
Cl.II.III.
Fag.I.
Fag.II.III.
Cor.I.II.III.
Cor.IV.
Tr I.II.
Xyloph.
Arpa I.
Arpa II.
Piano.
V.I.
V.II.
Viole.
Celli.
C.B.
a 2.
arco
unis.
div.
pizz.

Fl. Picc. I. II.
Fl. gr. I. II.
I. II.
Ob.
III.
Cl. I.
Cl. II. III.
Fag. I.
Fag. II. III.
Cor. I. II. III.
Cor. IV.
Tr. I. II
Xyloph.
Arpa I.
Arpa II.
Piano.
V. I.
V. II.
Viole.
Celli.
C. B.
a 2.
cresc. ed accel.
unis.
arco
div.
pizz.

Editor's note: The last measure on this page is not played when continuing to the Second Tableau.

Editor's note: The Norton recording stops in the second measure of this page at the fermata.

27. Anton Webern (1883–1945)

8:7A/8 8:7/41 - 43

Symphony, Op. 21, Second Movement (1928)

Copyright 1929 by Universal Edition. Copyright renewed. All rights reserved. Used by permission of European American Music Distributors Corporation, sole U.S. and Canadian agent for Universal Edition.

II. Var.
sehr lebhaft (♩ = ca 84)
Kl.
Bkl.
1.
Hrn.
2.
ohne Dämpfer
Hrf.
1.Gg.
2.Gg.
Br.
Vlc.
pizz.
arco
rit.

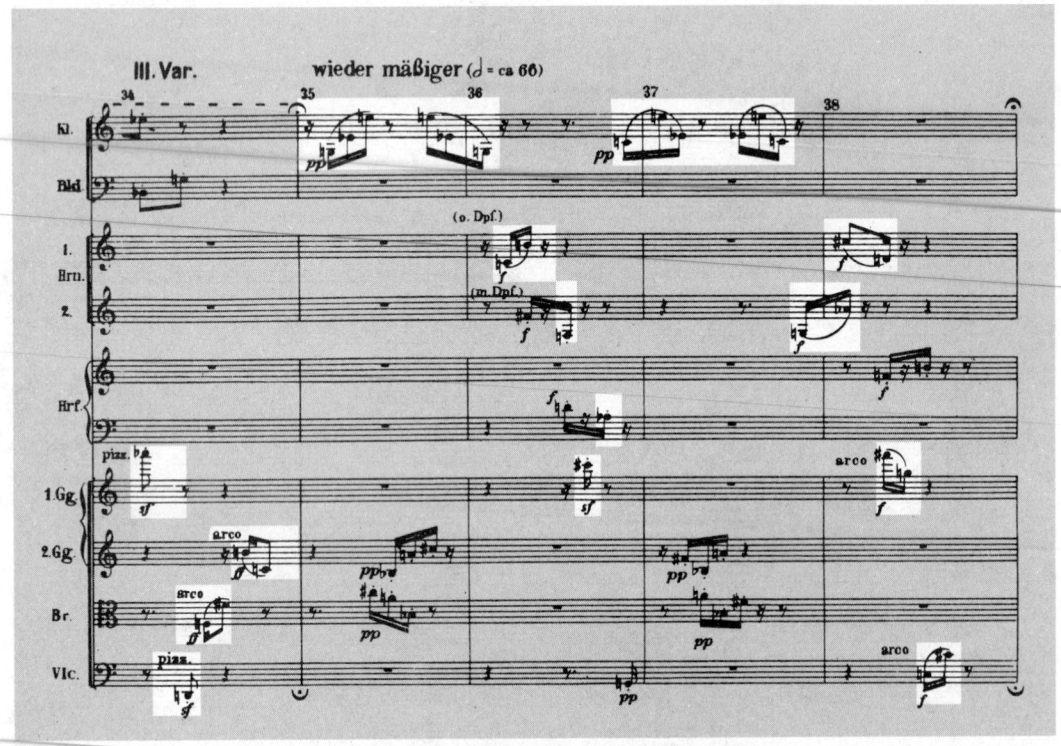
III. Var.
wieder mäßiger (𝅗𝅥 = ca 66)
34
35
36
37
38
Kl.
Bkl.
(o. Dpf.)
(m. Dpf.)
1.
Hrn.
2.
Hrf.
pizz.
arco
1.Gg.
2.Gg.
Br.
Vlc.

rit.
tempo
39
40
41
42
43
Kl.
Bkl.
gedämpft
offen
Dämpfer auf
1.
Hrn.
2.
Hrf.
pizz.
1.Gg.
2.Gg.
Br.
Vlc.

42
IV. Var.
molto rit. äußerst ruhig (♩ = ca 40)
molto rit.
Kl.
Bkl.
1. Hrn.
2.
m. Dpf.
(m. Dpf.)
Hrf.
1. Gg.
2. Gg.
Br.
Vlc.
Solo arco
(Solo)
Solo
V. Var.
rit. sehr lebhaft (♩ = ca 84)
Dämpfer ab
arco Alle (geteilt)
Alle (geteilt)

57
58
59
60
Kl.
Bkl.
1.
Hrn.
2.
Hrf.
1.Gg.
2.Gg.
Br.
Vlc.
pp
p
pp
cresc.
pp
cresc.
cresc.
pp
cresc.
pp

61
62
63
64
Kl.
Bkl.
1.
Hrn.
2.
Hrf.
1.Gg.
2.Gg.
Br.
Vlc.
mf
p cresc.
p cresc.
mp cresc.
mp cresc.
p
cresc.
p
cresc.
mp cresc.
mp cresc.

VI. Var.
rit. marschmäßig (♩ = ca 66), nicht eilen
Kl.
Bkl.
1. Hrn.
2.
o. Dpf.
Hrf.
1. Gg.
2. Gg.
Br.
Vlc.
mf cresc.
dim.
cresc.
gedämpft
offen

74
75
76
77
Kl.
Bkl.
1.
Hrn.
2.
Hrf.
1.Gg.
2.Gg.
Br.
Vlc.
43
VII. Var.
etwas breiter
rit.
tempo
rit.
tempo rit.
78 (♩ = ca 54)
79
80
81
82
83
(o. Dpf.)
(m. Dpf.)
pizz.
arco

tempo
rit.
tempo
Coda
rit.
84
85
86
87
88
89
Kl.
Bkl.
1.
Hrn.
2.
(o Dpf)
(m Dpf)
Hrf.
1. Gg.
2. Gg.
(pizz.)
arco
pizz.
Br.
Vlc.
tempo
rit.
tempo
rit.
tempo
90
91
92
93
94
95
96
97
98
99
Solo
f dim.
(Solo)
Solo pizz.
Solo
(pizz.)
1928
10 Min.

28. Alban Berg (1885–1935)

8:7B/2 8:7/44 - 47

Wozzeck, Act III, Scenes 4 and 5 (1922)

Full score copyright 1926 by Universal Edition A.G., Vienna. Full score copyright renewed. English translation copyright 1952 by Alfred A. Kalmus, London. English translation copyright renewed. Pocket score copyright 1955 by Universal Edition A.G., Vienna. Pocket score copyright renewed. All rights reserved. Used by permission of European American Music Distributors Corporation, sole U.S. and Canadian agent for Universal Edition and Alfred A. Kalmus.

Wozz
p
da regt sich was.
whispered loudly
Still!
Cel
As
pp
(frog croaks)
(mp)
accel
Etwas
230
(spoken)
(shouting)
Al-les still und tot.
Mör-der!
Str m D
pppp
Trp m D
ff
Holz
Hfe
gliss
(quasi Des-Dur)
rascher
235
again whispered
poco rit.
Mör - - - - der!!
Ha! da ruft's.
mf
gest Hr
Str
gliss (C-Dur)
Ces
(quasi Ces-Dur glissando)
Pos m D

(poco rit) - - - a tempo poco string - - - - - poco rit - - molto
staggers a few more steps, searching, and comes upon the corpse
(spoken)
Wozz
Nein_ ich selbst.
Ma-rie! Ma-
le-
p non legato e poco cresc - - - mf Str
molto pp
fehlende Akkordtöne
Wieder langsamer, aber nicht schleppend
(quasi Hauptzeitmaß)
gato
240
[quasi
rie! Was hast du für ei-ne ro - te Schnur um den Hals?
sempre pp
p espr
2 Solo Gg
Solo Vcl

Walzertempo
poco string
(breaking into song)
Wozz
Hast Dir das ro - te Hals - band ver-dient, wie die Ohr - ring - lein,
(2 Gg)
(Hrn)
hoch
Kl
Fl
poco cresc
richtige Lage
2 Solo Gg
Kl
poco cresc.
245
sempre string
mit Dei-ner Sün - - de!
(spoken)
Rasch (♩= 100-120)
mit Dei-ner Sün - - de!
Was hän - gen Dir die
Str
Holz
Fl
K Bs allein
250
schwar - zen Haa - re so wild_?!_ Mör - der!_ Mör -
(mit oberer 8va)
Holz
Pik
Holz
Xyl
Trp
(Holz)
Pauken

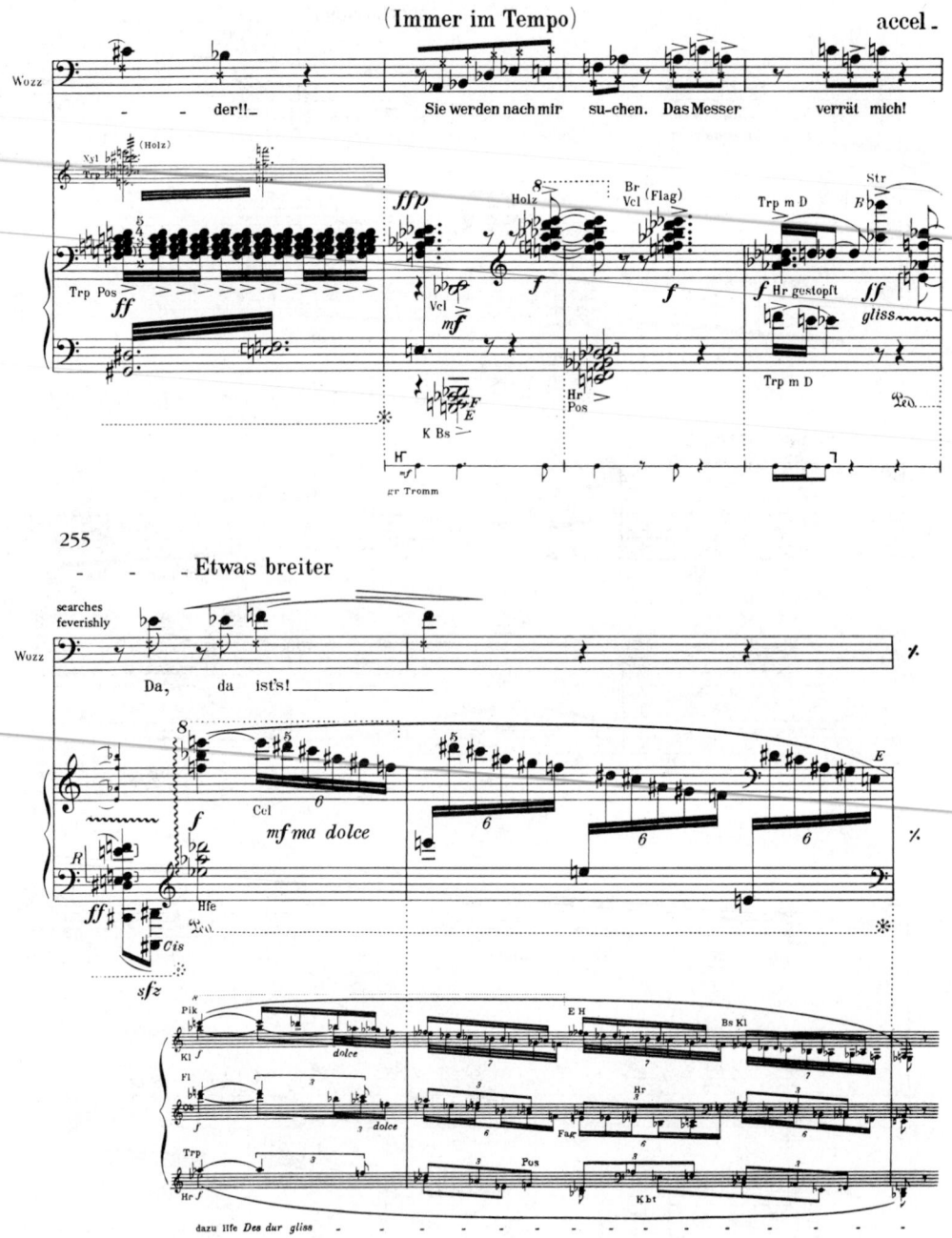
(Immer im Tempo)
accel.
Wozz
der!!
Sie werden nach mir su-chen. Das Messer verrät mich!
Xyl
Trp
(Holz)
Trp Pos
ff
ffp
Holz
Vcl
mf
f
Br
Vcl (Flag)
Trp m D
Str
f Hr gestopft
ff
gliss.
Hr
Pos
K Bs
gr Tromm
255
Etwas breiter
searches feverishly
Wozz
Da, da ist's!
Cel
mf ma dolce
Hfe
Cis
sfz
Pik
Kl
dolce
Fl
Trp
Hr
E H
Bs Kl
Fag
Pos
Kbt
dazu Hfe Des dur gliss

Wie zu Anfang dieser Szene
(♩= ca 100)
ritard
quasi Hauptzeitmaß
(♩= 80)
am Teich
throws the knife in
Wozz
So! da hin-un-ter!
Es taucht ins
ff Str
dimin
p
sfz
mf
poco a poco
Holz Blech Holz
260
The moon rises blood-red from the clouds
dunk-le Was-ser wie ein Stein.
Blech Holz Blech etc.
diminuendo
ppp
senza cresc
kleines Tamtam
freihängendes Becken
looks up
265
pp
A-ber der Mond ver-rät mich
Der Mond ist blu-
alle 1. Gg ohne D
ppp
verlöschen
(kl Tamtam Becken)
Hfe
verklingen lassen
gr Tamtam

270
Wozz
- tig. Will denn die gan-ze Welt es aus - plau-dern?! Das Messer,
(G Solo Gg m D)
G Br m D
alle Br o D
Wozz
es liegt zu weit vorn, sie findens beim Ba-den o-der wenn sie nach Muscheln tauchen.
wades into

Ganz frei ' a tempo
the pond
275
(with a somewhat singing voice)
(spoken)
Wozz
Ich find's nicht.
A-ber ich muß mich wa-schen.
Ich bin blu-tig.
Gg m D
ppp ged Blech allein.
pp
Pkn
mf
f Holz
pp
tief
Xyl
1.Gg m D richtig
2.Gg col leg gestr
(1.Gg)
moaning :
Da ein Fleck_ und noch ei-ner.
Weh!
molto espr.
Gg
2 Hfe
Hr
ff
poco f
sfz
hoch
tief
Vcl
K Bs,Pos u Tub
Br
Kl
Holz
Vcl

280
Wozz
Weh!
ich wa-sche mich mit
Blut
das
hoch
Vcl
(Hr Hfe)
K Bs
(Fag Hfe)
K Bs, Tub
K Bs, Pos
Kl
Bs Kl
Fag
K Fag
(he drowns . . .)
Was-ser ist Blut...
Blut...
pp (Beide Hände immer chromatisch)
Str
2. K Bs
sempre Ped
Holz u Hfe
Vcl dazu
Br dazu
(Str allein am Steg o D)
1. K Bs
3. K Bs

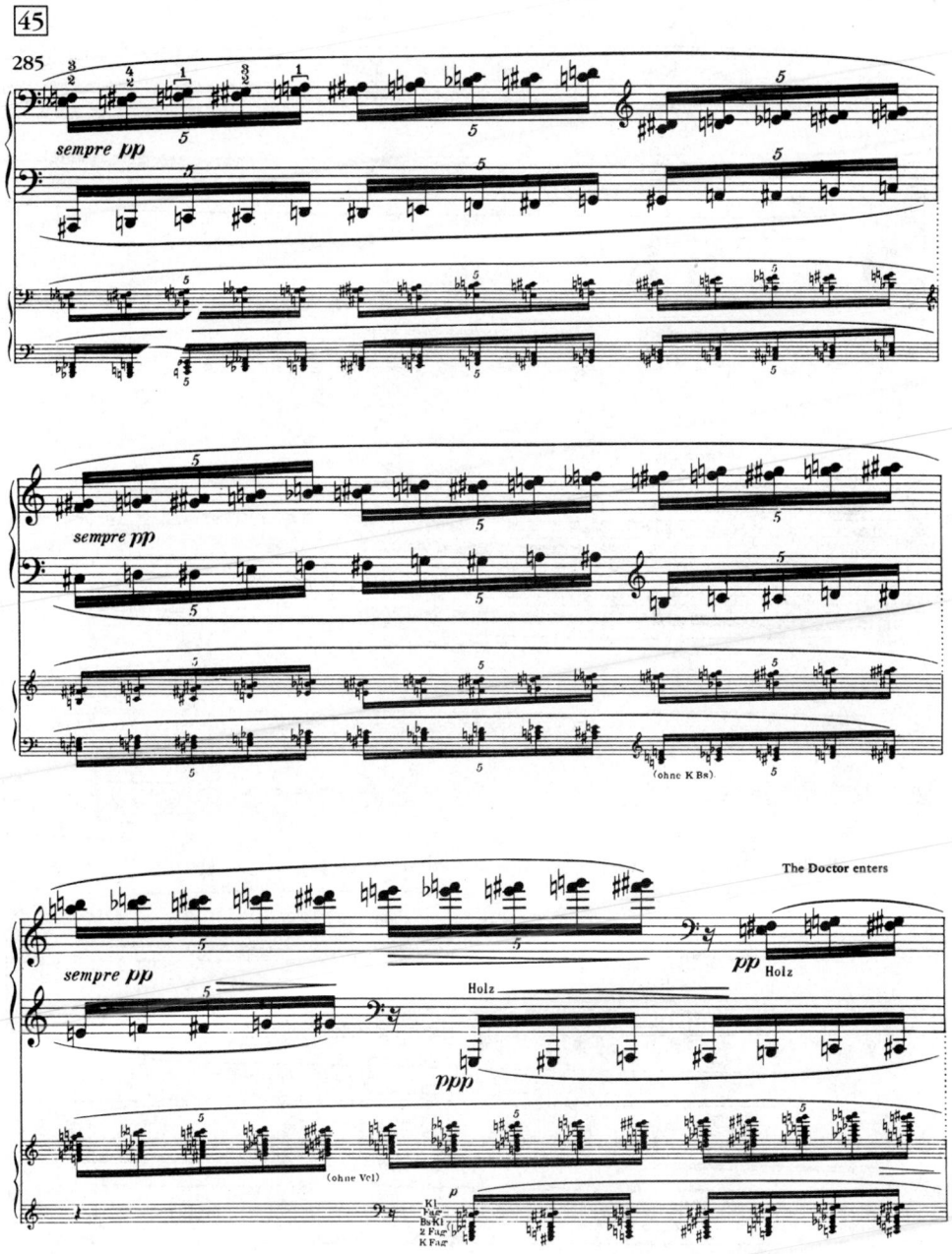
45
285
sempre pp
sempre pp
(ohne K Bs)
The Doctor enters
sempre pp
pp
Holz
Holz
ppp
(ohne Vcl)
p
Kl
Fag
Bs Kl
2 Fag
K Fag

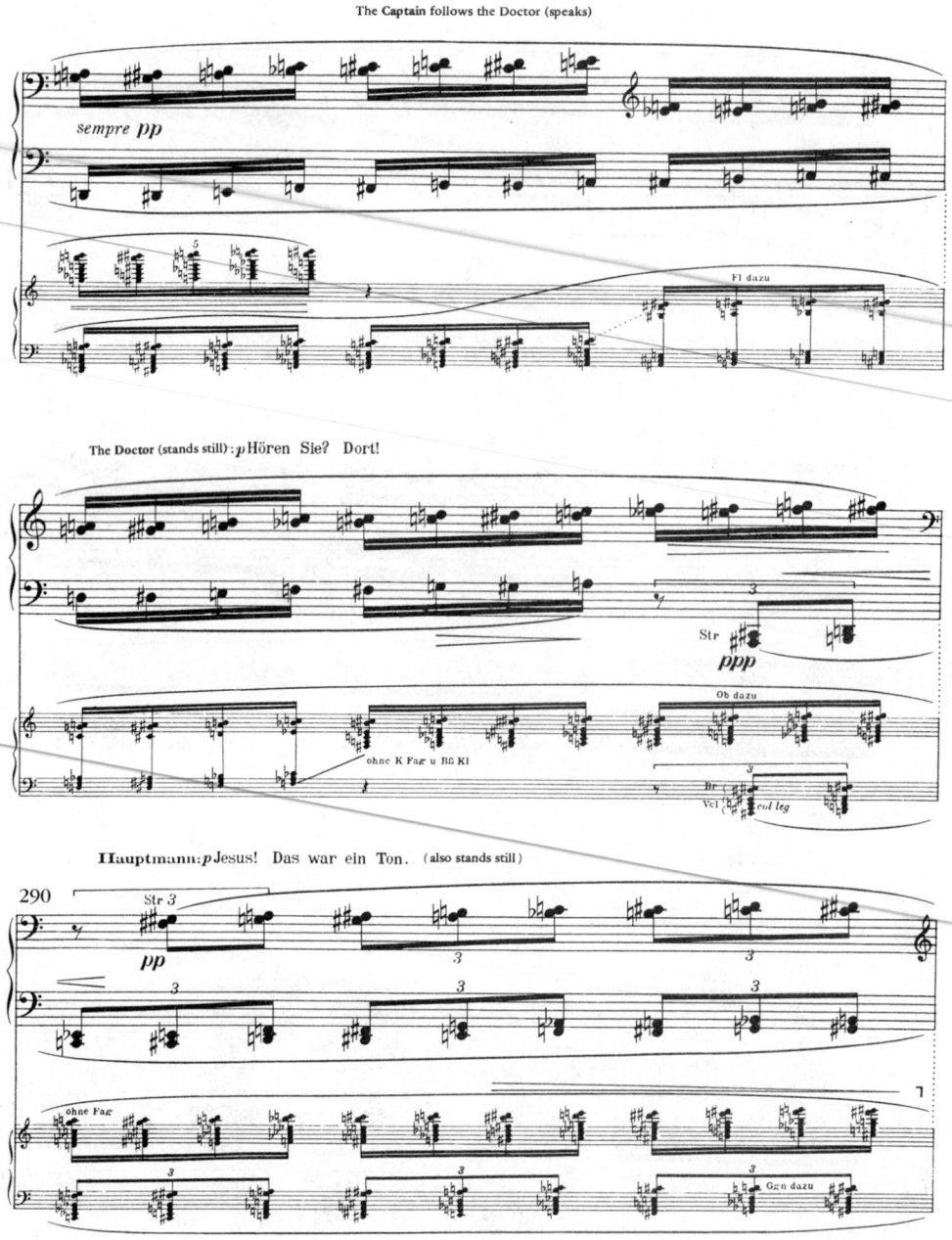
The Captain follows the Doctor (speaks)
sempre pp
Fl dazu
The Doctor (stands still): p Hören Sie? Dort!
Str
ppp
Ob dazu
ohne K Fag u Bß Kl
Br
Vcl
col leg
Hauptmann: p Jesus! Das war ein Ton. (also stands still)
290
Str
pp
ohne Fag
Ggn dazu

Doktor (pointing to the lake): Ja, dort!
Hauptmann: Es ist das Wasser
Fag
Hr
pp
ohne K Bß
Hr, Fag
im Teich. Das Wasser ruft. Es ist schon lange niemand ertrunken.
Gg
Br
Vcl
ppp
pp (Str m D)
Str (ohne K Bß)
Hauptmann: Kommen Sie, Doktor! Es ist
295
Trp Pos (m D)
Trp m D
Pos m D

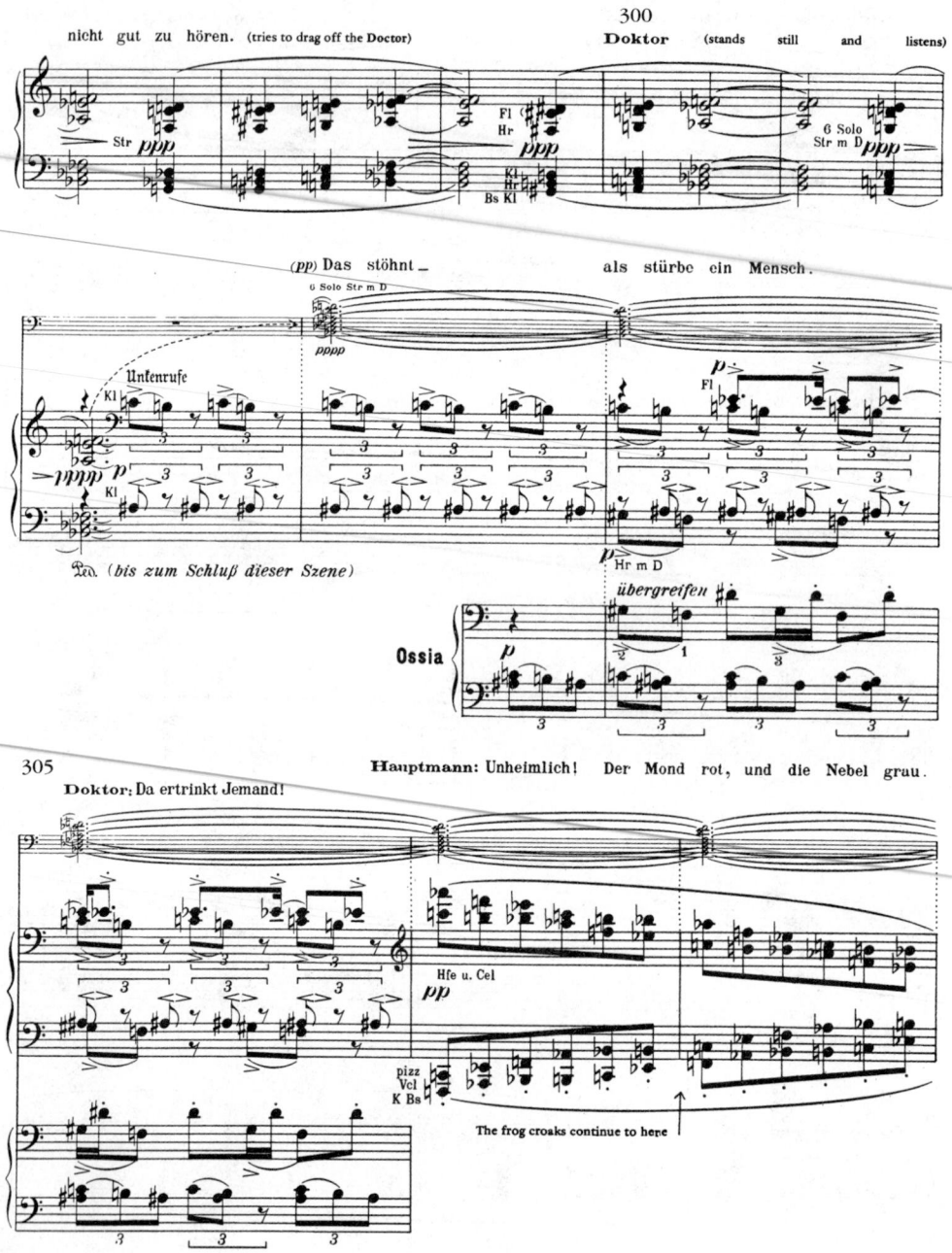
300
nicht gut zu hören. (tries to drag off the Doctor)
Doktor (stands still and listens)
Str
Fl
Hr
Kl
Hr
Bs Kl
6 Solo
Str m D
(pp) Das stöhnt
als stürbe ein Mensch.
6 Solo Str m D
Unkenrufe
Kl
Kl
Fl
Hr m D
(bis zum Schluß dieser Szene)
übergreifen
Ossia
305
Doktor: Da ertrinkt Jemand!
Hauptmann: Unheimlich! Der Mond rot, und die Nebel grau.
Hfe u. Cel
pizz
Vcl
K Bs
The frog croaks continue to here

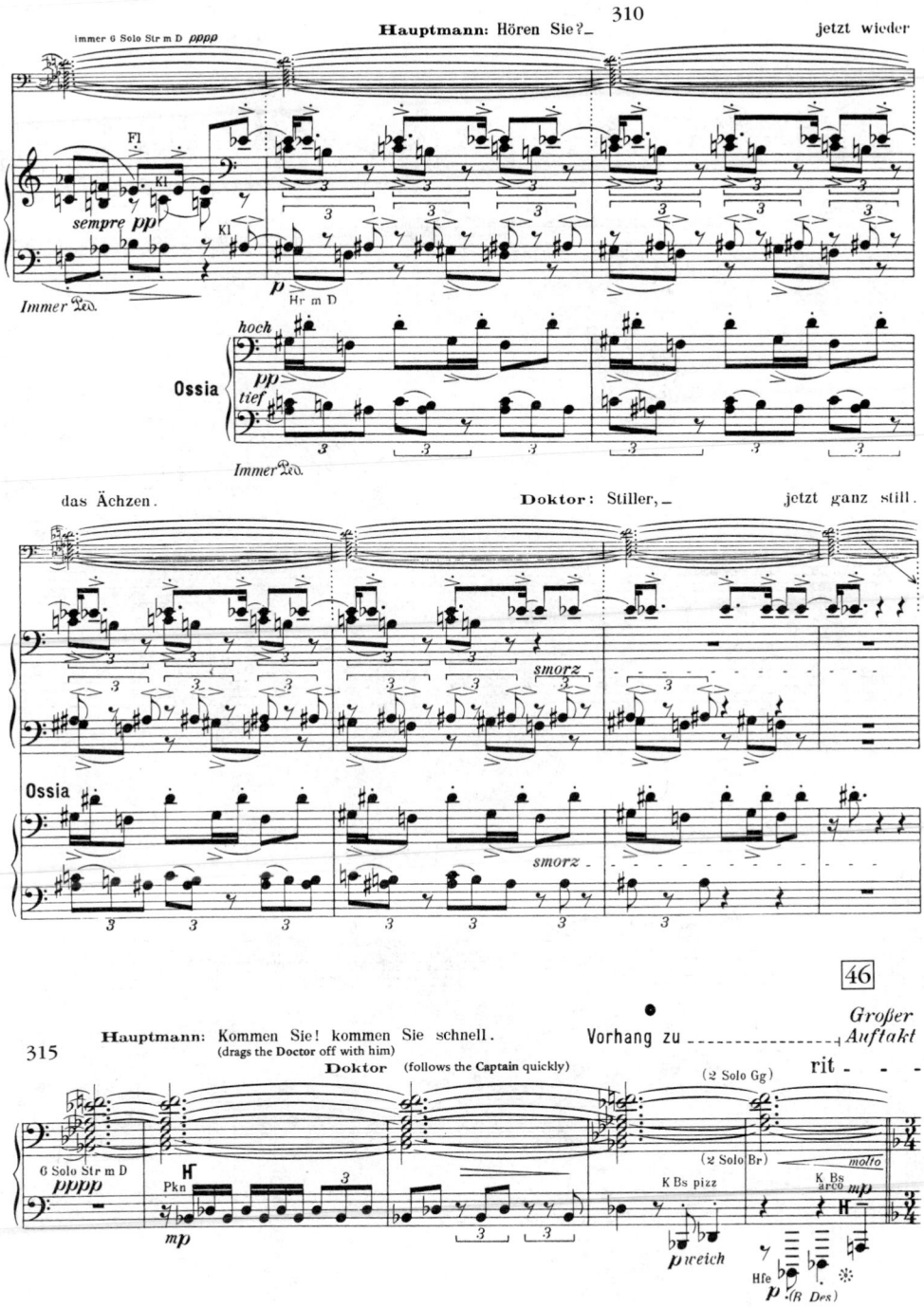
310
Hauptmann: Hören Sie?– jetzt wieder
immer 6 Solo Str m D pppp
Fl
Kl
sempre pp
Kl
p
Hr m D
Immer Ped.
hoch
pp
Ossia
tief
Immer Ped.
das Ächzen.
Doktor: Stiller,– jetzt ganz still.
smorz.
Ossia
smorz.
46
Großer Auftakt
Vorhang zu
rit - - -
315
Hauptmann: Kommen Sie! kommen Sie schnell.
(drags the Doctor off with him)
Doktor (follows the Captain quickly)
(2 Solo Gg)
(2 Solo Br)
molto
6 Solo Str m D
pppp
Pkn
mp
K Bs pizz
K Bs arco
mp
p weich
Hfe
p
(R Des)

320
Scene change
Adagio (♩= ♩= mindestens 46)
2.Gge
Br
p
(mp)
(K Bs)
Vcl dazu
2 Fag dazu
3. Fag u K Fag dazu
1.Ggn
p
Solo Gg
pp
II. Spieler
I. Spieler
325
Kl 2.Gg
Str
allein
p
Fag dazu
1. Hälfte Ggn
p
alle Ggn
mf
330
Ob dazu
Fl dazu
(Ob)
p
I
zurücktreten
Orig gra.
Hr
p
mp Hr
mf
3 Fag
p
Pos
mp
K Bs
II

I
II
1. Gg
Hfe
(1)
5
(4)
1. Pos u 2. Gg
etc
Pos
Str
Trp
Hfe (Ganzton Glissando)
335
nicht eilen
Holz u Trp
tief
1. Gg u. Pos
molto
sehr hoch
1. Gg dazu
2. Gg Trp
Br
Pos
Blech
Kbt Tamtam
Vcl div
340
klagend
Ggn
allein
(weg) espress
Vcl
Fag
Hr
(gest)
wie aus der Ferne, aber deutlich
meno p

string
molto
menop
1.Gg u 4 Ob
cresc
mp
Fag
mp
mf
cresc
Vcl
Holz
pp
Vcl u. K-B
345
Bedeutend bewegter
(♩= 80-84)
ff furioso
Trp
Ob
(pizz)
(tief)
f
Str trem
Pk trem
Pos
f
(gr Trommschlag)
350
je 4
Kl. Fl
(pizz)
pizz
fp
cresc
Hr
f
Trp
f
mf
Str
f
3 Pos
m D
f
cresc

rall
Wieder etwas breiter (Andante)
(Fl Kl)
(Trp)
Str u Ob
espr
Kl
weg!
(Pos) Hfe
rauschend
(cresc)
(Pke)
Hfe
355
Wieder drängend
Kl (Hfe)
(hoch) Ob
molto
col leg
Pos
Hrn u Fag (kl Tromm)
(tief)
(Br Vcl K Bs)
Wieder breiter
360
Ob
Trp Gg Xyl
cresc
Br
alles übertönend
Hr Vcl
Pos
Br Vcl
weg
3 Pos
(3 Pos)
Hr Vcl
(ff)
Hr
Holz Str Tub gr Tromm
1 Pos
2 Pos
3 Pos
etc
Fag BB Kl
cresc

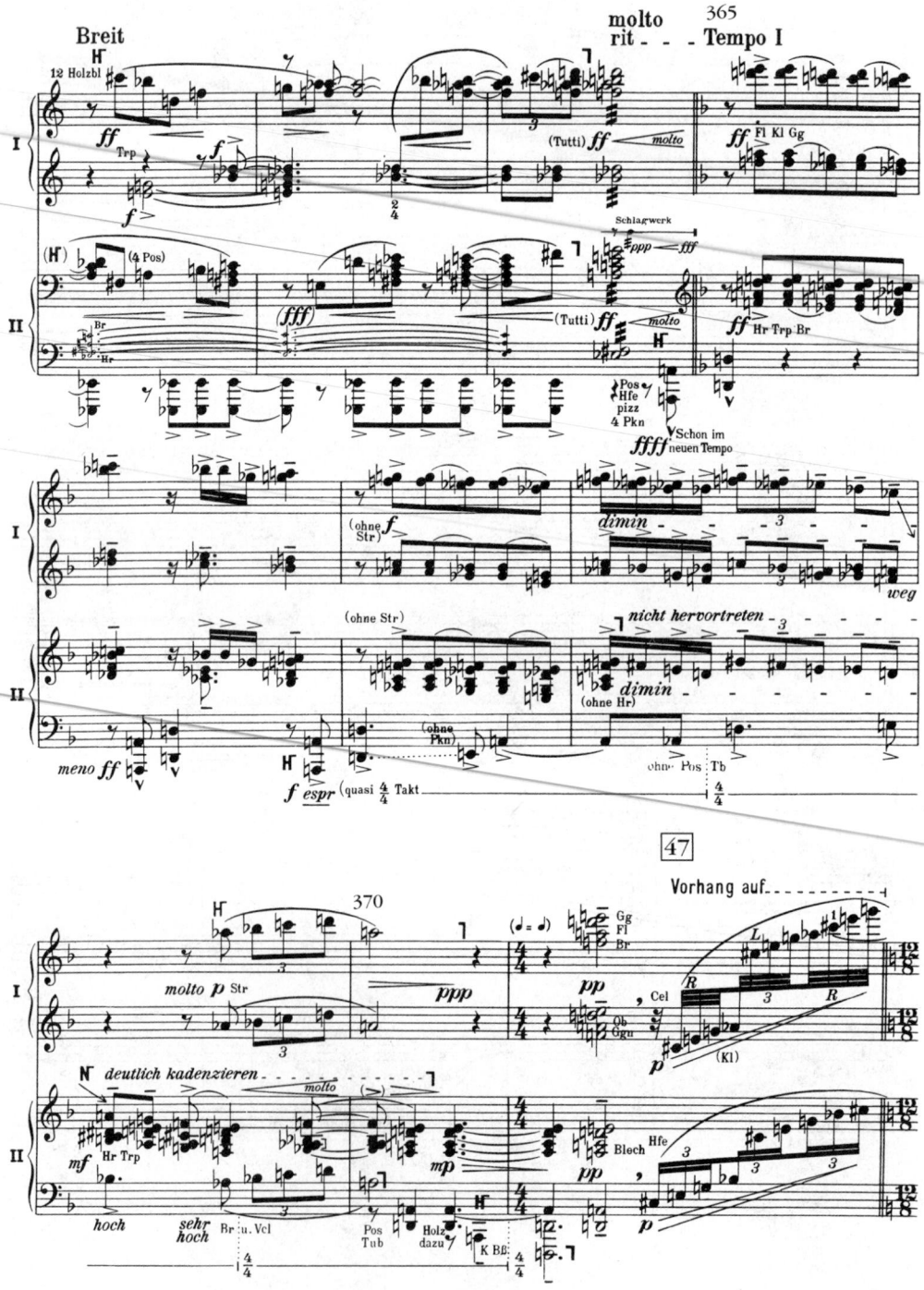
Breit
12 Holzbl
molto
rit - - -
365
Tempo I
Fl Kl Gg
(Tutti)
molto
Schlagwerk
(4 Pos)
Hr Trp Br
Pos
Hfe
pizz
4 Pkn
Schon im neuen Tempo
(ohne Str)
dimin
weg
nicht hervortreten
(ohne Hr)
(ohne Pkn)
ohne Pos Tb
meno ff
espr
(quasi 4/4 Takt
47
Vorhang auf
370
molto p Str
Gg
Fl
Br
Ob
Ogu
Cel
(Kl)
deutlich kadenzieren
Hr Trp
Blech
Hfe
hoch
sehr hoch
Br u. Vcl
Pos
Tub
Holz dazu
K Bb

5th (last) Scene In front of Marie's house (bright morning, sunshine)

Zweites Kind: Was is?
Erstes Kind: Weißt' es nit? Sie sind schon Alle 'naus.
(rall)
(♩. = 58)
Hfe
Es Kl
Trp m D
Tamtam
(Es Kl Trp)
Solo Gg m D
espr
Kl
Noch etwas langsamer
Wieder voriges Tempo
(♩. = 58)
380
Mariens Knabe (still riding)
Hopp,hopp!
Drittes Kind
(to Marie's child): Du! Dein Mutter ist tot!
1.Gg (Flag)
Br (Flag)
Br
Vcl (Flag)
Vcl
Rute
Ob
Fl
(Br)
Hrn Hfe
Pkn gedämpft
'poco rit - - - - - a tempo, ma sempre rubato
Mariens Knabe
Hopp,hopp! Hopp,hopp!
Zweites Kind: Wo is sie denn?
Erstes Kind: Draus liegt sie, am Weg, neben dem Teich.
1Gg
1 Trp m D
Es Kl
Str m D
Br
Vcl
(poco espr.)
poco
4 Hr m D
etc
kl Tromm gedämpft

385
Mariens Knabe
riding
Hopp,hopp! Hopp,hopp! Hopp,hopp!
Drittes Kind: Kommt – anschaun!
Alle Kinder run off
(poco rit.)
(Es Kl)
Xyl
Solo Kl
ganz ohne Ausdruck
Bs Kl
Solo Vcl
Str allein
Pke gedämpft
gr Tromm
dimin.
poco espress
Vorhang fällt
Mariens Knabe (alone) hesitates for a moment, then rides off after the other children
(ab) Leere Bühne
Etwas zögernd und molto rubato.
Allmählich wieder gleichmäßig fließend werden: Quasi Tempo I
[rit. acc. rit. acc. rit. acc. rit. acc. rit]
poco espress
Solo Hr
Trp m D
Solo Gg m D
Hr m D
sempre pp, ma molto espr
pp sempre senza cresc e dim.
Fl Cel
senza rit
390
(beide Hände hoch)
I
vierhändig
(tief)
II
Str m D ohne K BB
(Hfe)
molto p
ppp
End of the opera

TEXT AND TRANSLATION

SCENE FOUR

INVENTION ON A CHORD OF SIX NOTES

PATH IN THE WOOD BY THE POND. MOONLIGHT, AS BEFORE.

(WOZZECK STUMBLES HURRIEDLY IN, THEN STOPS, LOOKING AROUND FOR SOMETHING.)

WOZZECK

Das Messer? Wo ist das Messer? Ich hab's dagelassen. Näher, noch näher. Mir graut's . . . da regt sich was. Still! Alles still und tot.

The knife? Where is the knife? I left it there. Around here somewhere. I'm terrified . . . something's moving. Silence. Everything silent and dead.

(SHOUTING)

Mörder! Mörder!

Murderer! Murderer!

(WHISPERING AGAIN)

Ha! Da ruft's. Nein, ich selbst.

Ah! Someone called. No, it was only me.

(STILL LOOKING, HE STAGGERS A FEW STEPS FURTHER AND STUMBLES AGAINST THE CORPSE)

Marie! Marie! Was hast du für eine rote Schnur um den Hals? Hast dir das rote Halsband verdient, wie die Ohrringlein, mit deiner Sünde! Was hängen dir die schwarzen Haare so wild? Mörder! Mörder! Sie werden nach mir suchen. Das Messer verrät mich!

Marie! Marie! What's that red cord around your neck? Was the red necklace payment for your sins, like the earrings? Why's your dark hair so wild about you? Murderer! Murderer! They will come and look for me. The knife will betray me!

(LOOKS FOR IT IN A FRENZY)

Da, da ist's!

Here! Here it is!

(AT THE POND)

So! Da hinunter!

There! Sink to the bottom!

(THROWS THE KNIFE INTO THE POND)

Es taucht ins dunkle Wasser wie ein Stein.

It plunges into the dark water like a stone.

(THE MOON APPEARS, BLOOD-RED, FROM BEHIND THE CLOUDS. WOZZECK LOOKS UP.)

Aber der Mond verrät mich, der Mond ist blutig. Will denn die ganze Welt es ausplaudern? Das Messer, es liegt zu weit vorn, sie finden's beim Baden oder wenn sie nach Muscheln tauchen.

But the moon will betray me: the moon is blood stained. Is the whole world going to incriminate me? The knife is too near the edge: they'll find it when they're swimming or diving for snails.

(WADES INTO THE POND)

Ich find's nicht. Aber ich muss mich waschen. Ich bin blutig. Da ein Fleck—und noch einer. Weh! Weh! Ich wasche mich mit Blut—das Wasser ist Blut . . . Blut . . .

I can't find it. But I must wash myself. There's blood on me. There's a spot here—and another. Oh, God! I am washing myself in blood—the water is blood . . . blood . . .

(DROWNS)

(THE DOCTOR APPEARS, FOLLOWED BY THE CAPTAIN.)

CAPTAIN

Halt!

Wait!

DOCTOR *(STOPS)*

Hören Sie? Dort!

Can you hear? There!

CAPTAIN

Jesus! Das war ein Ton!

Jesus! What a ghastly sound!

(STOPS AS WELL)

DOCTOR *(POINTING TO THE POND)*

Ja, dort!

Yes, there!

CAPTAIN

Es ist das Wasser im Teich. Das Wasser ruft.
Es ist schon lange Niemand ertrunken.
Kommen Sie, Doktor!
Es ist nicht gut zu hören.

It's the water in the pond. The water is calling.
It's been a long time since anyone drowned.
Come away, Doctor.
It's not good for us to be hearing it.

(TRIES TO DRAG THE DOCTOR AWAY)

DOCTOR *(RESISTING, AND CONTINUING TO LISTEN)*

Das stöhnt, als stürbe ein Mensch.
Da ertrinkt Jemand!

There's a groan, as though someone were dying. Somebody's drowning!

CAPTAIN

Unheimlich! Der Mond rot, und die Nebel grau.
Hören Sie? . . . Jetzt wieder das Ächzen.

It's eerie! The moon is red, and the mist is grey.
Can you hear? . . . That moaning again.

DOCTOR

Stiller, . . . jetzt ganz still.

It's getting quieter . . . now it's stopped altogether.

CAPTAIN

Kommen Sie! Kommen Sie schnell!

Come! Come quickly!

(HE RUSHES OFF, PULLING THE DOCTOR ALONG WITH HIM.)

SCENE CHANGE

INVENTION ON A KEY (D MINOR)

SCENE FIVE

INVENTION ON A QUAVER RHYTHM

IN FRONT OF MARIE'S DOOR. MORNING. BRIGHT SUNSHINE.

(CHILDREN ARE NOISILY AT PLAY. MARIE'S CHILD IS RIDING A HOBBY-HORSE.)

CHILDREN

Ringel, Ringel, Rosenkranz, Ringelreih'n,
Ringel, Ringel, Rosenkranz, Ring . . .

Ring-a-ring-a-roses,
A pocket full of . . .

(THEIR SONG AND GAME ARE INTERRUPTED BY OTHER CHILDREN BURSTING IN.)

ONE OF THE NEWCOMERS

Du, Käthe! Die Marie!

Hey, Katie! Have you heard about Marie?

SECOND CHILD

Was ist?

What's happened?

FIRST CHILD

Weisst' es nit? Sie sind schon Alle 'naus.

Don't you know? They've all gone out there.

THIRD CHILD *(TO MARIE'S LITTLE BOY)*

Du! Dein' Mutter ist tot!

Hey! Your mother's dead!

MARIE'S SON *(STILL RIDING)*

Hopp, hopp! Hopp, hopp! Hopp, hopp!

Hop, hop! Hop, hop! Hop, hop!

SECOND CHILD

Wo ist sie denn?

Where is she, then?

FIRST CHILD

Draus' liegt sie, am Weg, neben dem Teich.

She's lying out there, on the path near the pond.

THIRD CHILD

Kommt, anschaun!

Come and have a look!

(ALL THE CHILDREN RUN OFF.)

MARIE'S SON *(CONTINUING TO RIDE)*

Hopp, hopp! Hopp, hopp! Hopp, hopp!

Hop, hop! Hop, hop! Hop, hop!

(HE HESITATES FOR A MOMENT AND THEN RIDES AFTER THE OTHER CHILDREN.)

END OF THE OPERA

LIBRETTO BY ALBAN BERG, AFTER GEORG BÜCHNER'S PLAY *WOYZECK* (1837)

Translated by Sarah E. Soulsby

29. *Sergei Prokofiev (1891–1953)* 8:7B/3 8:7/48 - 49

Alexander Nevsky, Seventh Movement (1939)

Words and music by Sergei Prokofiev. Copyright © 1945, 1949, 1966 by MCA Music Publishing, a division of MCA Inc. Copyright renewed. International copyright secured. All rights reserved.

f
на род - ной зем - ле не бы - вать вра - гу.
in our na - tive land foes shall ne - ver live.
f
ле не быть вра - гу,
land no foe shall live.
f
на род - ной зем - ле не бы - вать вра - гу.
in our na - tive land foes shall ne - ver live.
f
ле не быть вра - гу.
land no foe shall live.
maestoso
m.d.
ff

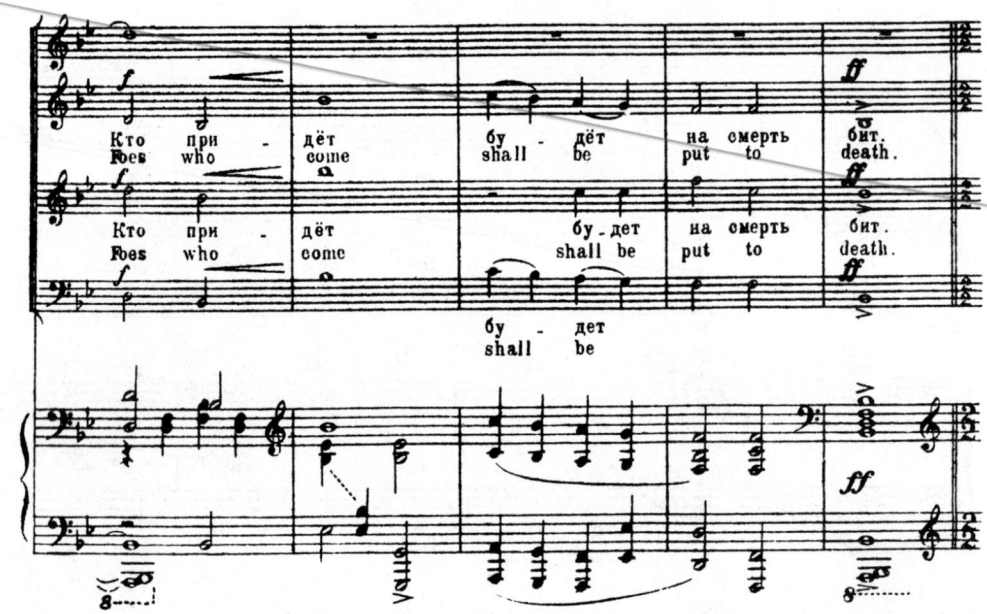
f
Кто при - дёт бу - дёт на смерть бит.
Foes who come shall be put to death.
ff
f
Кто при - дёт бу - дет на смерть бит.
Foes who come shall be put to death.
ff
f
бу - дет
shall be
ff

Allegro, ma non troppo ♩ = 84
Camp.
Xilof.
f Legni, Tr-be
Arpa, Archi
simile
ff
S.
Ве - се - ли - ся, пой,
Ce - le - brate and sing,
мать род - на - я Русь!
na - tive mo - ther Russ!
На - род - ной Ру - си
In our na - tive land
A.
Ве - се - ли - ся, пой,
Ce - le - brate and sing,
мать род - на - я Русь!
na - tive mo - ther Russ!
На - род - ной Ру - си
In our na - tive land

p subito
cresc.
не бы_вать вра_гу,
foes shall ne_ver live.
не ви_дать вра_гу
Foes shall ne_ver see
на_ших рус_ских сёл.
Rus_sian towns and fields.
p subito
cresc.
не бы_вать вра_гу,
foes shall ne_ver live.
не ви_дать вра_гу
Foesshall ne_ver see
на_ших рус_ских сёл.
Rus_sian towns and fields.
p
p subito
cresc.
S.
Кто при_дёт на Русь
They who march on Russ
f
бу_дет на смерть бит!
shall be put to death!
A.
Кто при_дёт на Русь
They who march on Russ
f
бу_дет на смерть бит!
shall be put to death!
T.
f
Не ви_дать вра_гу
Foes shall ne_ver see
B.
f
Не ви_дать вра_гу
Foes shall ne_ver see
f
V-ni
f espress.
m. d.
f

Т.
на - ших рус_ских сёл,
Rus - sian towns and fields,
кто при - дет на
They who march on
Русь,
Russ
В.
m. s.
А.
На Ру - си
In our Rus -
род - ной, на Ру-
sia great, in our
Т.
бу - дет на смерть бит.
shall be put to death.
На Ру - си
In our Rus
род - ной, на Ру-
sia great, in our
В.
m. d.
А.
- си боль - шой
na - tive Rus -
не бы_вать вра -
sia no foe shall -
Meno mosso ♩ = 138
- гу!
live!
Т.
- си боль - шой
na - tive Rus -
не бы_вать вра -
sia no foe shall -
- гу!
live!
В.
Meno mosso ♩ = 138
m. d.
f
p

Legni
Tr-be
f
Corni
f
Fl.
p
Archi pizz.
Fl.
Ob.
p

Fl.
Cl.
Cl.
p
Fl.
Archi
Fag.
mf
C. ing.
mp
Ob.
p
Sax.

49
Alti
Bassi
mf
На Ру -
In our
Fl
Cl.
Fg.
Sax.
p
-ся род - - ной, на Ру -
Rus - - sia great, in our
Fl.
Cl.
Fg.
Ob.
-ся боль - - шой не бы -
na - tive Rus - - sia no
Fl.
Ob.

-вать
foe
вра
shall
-гу.
live.
Cl.
Fl.
Cl.
Be
Ce
ce
le
Sax.
Ob.
-ли
-brate
ся,
and
пой,
sing,
mf
Fl.
Cl.
Fag.

мать
na - tive
род - на -
moth -
Cl.
S.
На Ру - сь род -
In our Rus - sia
A.
- я
er
Русь!
Russ!
T.
На Ру - сь род -
In our Rus - sia
B.
- я
er
Русь!
Russ!
Ob.
Fl.
Fl., Archi
f espress.
Corni, Cl. b

-ной, на Ру - си боль - шой не бы - вать вра - - гу.
great, in our na - tive Rus - sia no foe shall - live.
на Ру - си
in our
-ной, на Ру - си боль - шой не бы - вать вра - - гу.
great, in our na - tive Rus - sia no foe shall - live.
на Ру - си
in our на-
Ве - се - ли - ся, пой, мать род-на - я Русь!
Се - le - brate and sing, na-tive mo-ther Russ!
Ве - се - ли - ся, пой, мать род-на - я Русь!
Се - le - brate and sing, na-tive mo-ther Russ!

Più largamente
На ве - ли - кий празд - ник
To a fete in tri - umph
На ве - ли - кий празд - ник
To a fete in tri - umph
Camp.
Più largamente
Tr-be, Corni
Celli
Bassi
со - бра - ла - ся Русь. Ве - се - ли - ся,
all of Rus - sia came. Ce - le - brate, re -
со - бра - ла - ся Русь. Ве - се - ли - ся,
all of Rus - sia came. Ce - le - brate, re -
m.s.

Русь! Be ce - ли - ся, Русь, род -
joice, ce - le - brate and sing, our
Русь! Be ce - ли - ся, Русь, род -
joice, ce - le - brate and sing, our
Camp.
91
ff
Tr-ni
m.s. m.d.
m.s. m.d.
f pesante
poco allarg.
fff
на - я мать!
moth - er land!
на - я мать!
moth - er land!
poco allarg.
m.s.m.d.
m.s.
fff

30. Richard Rodgers (1902–1979)

My Funny Valentine (1937)

8:7B/4-5 8:7/50 - 53

3:3B/2 3:3/35 - 36

MW

Original Version, from *Babes in Arms* (1937)

Editor's note: Shorter Norton recording and *The Norton CD-ROM Masterworks,* volume 1, include Gerry Mulligan Quartet version only.

Words by Lorenz Hart. Music by Richard Rodgers. Copyright © 1937 by Chappell & Co. Copyright renewed. Rights on behalf of the estate of Lorenz Hart administered by W. B. Music Corp. The interest of Richard Rodgers for the extended term of copyright in the U.S. assigned to Williamson Music. International copyright secured. All rights reserved. Used by permission.

Cm
Fm
G
va - cant brow and thy tous - led hair con - ceal thy good in - tent. Thou
51
Cm
B♭7
E♭
G
G7+
no - ble, up - right, truth - ful, sin - cere and slight - ly dop - ey gent, you're
Refrain (slowly, with much expression)
Cm
Cm(B♮)
Cm7
My fun - ny Val - en - tine, Sweet com - ic
p
Cm6
A♭
Fm7
Val - en - tine, You make me smile with my

Fm6 G7 Fm G7 Cm G7
heart. Your looks are laugh - a - ble,
Cm7 Cm6 Ab Fm7
Un - pho - to - graph - a - ble, Yet, you're my fav - 'rite work of
Abm Bb7 Eb Bb7(Eb) Bb7 Eb Bb7(Eb) Bb7
art. Is your fig - ure less than Greek; Is your
mf
Eb Bb7(Eb) Bb7 Eb Bb7(Eb) Bb7 Ebmaj7 G7+ G7 Cm
mouth a lit - tle weak, when you o - pen it to speak, Are you

Abmaj7 Ab6 Ab7 G7 Cm Cm(B♮)
smart? But don't change a hair for me,
p
Cm7 Cm6 Ab D7♭5 G7
Not if you care for me, Stay lit - tle Val - en - tine,
poco a poco cresc.
Cm Eb7 Ab Abmaj7 Fm7 Bb7
stay! Each day is Val - en - tine's
f molto espr.
mf
1. Eb Ab7 G7 2. Eb
day. day.
mf
p 8va.

Gerry Mulligan Quartet Version (1953)

Transcribed by Evan Solot.

(+ drummer singing)
(saxophone only)
(drummer sings)
(saxophone)

53
36
3
3
3
arco

31. Louis Armstrong (c. 1898–1971) and the Savoy Ballroom Five

8:7B/6 8:7/54 - 59

West End Blues (1928), excerpt

Words and music by Joe Oliver and Clarence Williams. Copyright © 1928 by MCA Music Publishing, a division of MCA Inc. Copyright renewed. International copyright secured. All rights reserved.

56 Chorus 2—not transcribed

57 Chorus 3—not transcribed

58 Chorus 4—not transcribed

Chorus 5 (Solo trumpet)

32. Duke Ellington (1899–1974)

Ko-Ko (1940)

8:8A/1 8:8/1 - 8

3:3B/1 3:3/27 - 34

Copyright © 1940, 1943; (renewed) 1968, 1971, Robbins Music Corporation. All rights assigned to EMI Catalogue Partnership. All rights controlled and administered by EMI Robbins Catalog, Inc. International copyright secured. Made in USA. All rights reserved. Used by permission. Transcribed by David Berger.

2
28
A
Swing
A. Sax
A. Sax
T. Sax
T. Sax
B. Sax
Trb. 1
Trb. 2
Trb. 3
(to Plunger)
(to Plunger/mute)
Solo
Guitar
E♭m
Bass
Drums
HH (High hat)
A. Sax
A. Sax
T. Sax
T. Sax
B. Sax
Trb. 3
Guitar
A♭m
Bass
Drums

A. Sax
A. Sax
T. Sax
T. Sax
B. Sax
Trb. 3
Guitar
E♭m
B7
B♭7
E♭m
Piano
Bass
Drums

3
29
B
A. Sax
A. Sax
T. Sax
T. Sax
B. Sax
p
Tpt. 1
Tpt. 2
Tpt. 3
Plunger
Trb. 1
Trb. 2
Trb. 3
E♭m
Plunger/mute
YA YA
Guitar
Piano
Bass
Drums

A. Sax
A. Sax
T. Sax
B. Sax
Tpt. 1
Tpt. 2
Tpt. 3
Trb. 1
Trb. 2
Trb. 3
Guitar
Piano
Bass
Drums
A♭m
E♭m
B♭7
YA YA
YA YA
YA YA
YA YA
A♭m
E♭m
B♭7

4
30
C
A. Sax
A. Sax
T. Sax
B. Sax
Tpt. 1
Tpt. 2
Tpt. 3
Trb. 1
Trb. 2
Trb. 3
YA YA
YA YA
E♭m
E♭m
E♭m
Guitar
Piano
Bass
Drums

A. Sax
A. Sax
T. Sax
B. Sax
Tpt. 1
Tpt. 2
Tpt. 3
Trb. 1
Trb. 2
Trb. 3
Guitar
A♭m
E♭m
Piano
Bass
Drums

5
31
A. Sax
A. Sax
T. Sax
B. Sax
Tpt. 1
Tpt. 2
Tpt. 3
Trb. 1
Trb. 2
Trb. 3
(to open)
E♭m
(to open)
YA
YA YA
(to open)
Guitar
B♭7
E♭m
Piano
Bass
Drums

D
A. Sax
A. Sax
T. Sax
B. Sax
Tpt. 1
Tpt. 2
Tpt. 3
Guitar
E♭m
8va
Piano
Bass
Drums
A. Sax
A. Sax
T. Sax
B. Sax
Tpt. 1
Tpt. 2
Tpt. 3
Guitar
A♭m
E♭m
8va
Piano
Bass
Drums

A. Sax
A. Sax
T. Sax
B. Sax
Tpt. 1
Tpt. 2
Tpt. 3
Guitar
B♭7
E♭m
Piano
Bass
Drums

6
32
E
A. Sax
A. Sax
T. Sax
T. Sax
B. Sax
1/2 Open
Tpt. 1
Tpt. 2
Tpt. 3
Open
Trb. 1
Open
Trb. 2
Open
Trb. 3
E♭m
Guitar
Piano
Bass
Drums

A. Sax
A. Sax
T. Sax
T. Sax
B. Sax
Tpt. 1
Tpt. 2
Tpt. 3
Trb. 1
Trb. 2
Trb. 3
Guitar
A♭m
E♭m
A♭m
E7
Piano
Bass
Drums

7
33
F
A. Sax
A. Sax
T. Sax
T. Sax
B. Sax
Tpt. 1
Tpt. 2
Tpt. 3
(to open)
Open
(to open)
Open
(to open)
Open
Trb. 1
Trb. 2
Trb. 3
Guitar
A♭m
E7
E♭m
E♭m
Piano
Bass
Drums

A. Sax
A. Sax
T. Sax
T. Sax
B. Sax
Tpt. 1
Tpt. 2
Tpt. 3
Trb. 1
Trb. 2
Trb. 3
Guitar
A ♭m7
Piano
Bass
Solo
Solo
Drums
CR
HH
CR

8
34
G
A. Sax
A. Sax
T. Sax
T. Sax
B. Sax
Tpt. 1
Tpt. 2
Tpt. 3
Trb. 1
Trb. 2
Trb. 3
Guitar
B♭ 7-9
E♭ m7
Bass
Solo
Drums
HH
CR

A. Sax
A. Sax
T. Sax
T. Sax
B. Sax
Tpt. 1
Tpt. 2
Tpt. 3
Trb. 1
Trb. 2
Trb. 3
Guitar
A♭m7
Piano
Bass
Drums

B. Sax
Trb. 1
Trb. 2
Trb. 3
Bass
Drums
A. Sax
A. Sax
T. Sax
T. Sax
B. Sax
Tpt. 1
Tpt. 2
Tpt. 3
Trb. 1
Trb. 2
Trb. 3
Bass
Drums

33. Aaron Copland (1900–1990)

Billy the Kid, Scene 1, ***Street in a Frontier Town*** (1939, orchestral suite)

8:8A/2 8:8/9 - 11

3:3A/7 3:3/24 - 26

© Copyright 1941 by The Aaron Copland Fund for Music; copyright renewed. Reprinted by permission of Boosey & Hawkes, Inc., sole agent.

Picc.
Fl. 1
Bsn. 1
Tinwhistle
Vl. 1
Vl. 2
Vla.
solo
mp
solo
p

a tempo
rit.
Picc.
Fl. 1
Clar. 1
Bsn. 1
Bsn. 2
Trpt.
Harp.
Piano
solo
mp
solo
mp
p
solo
p
(Trpt.)
sfp
p
sfp
p
7
a tempo
rit.
Vl. 1
Vl. 2
Vla.
Vlc.
C.b.
pizz.
sf
pizz.
sf
pizz.
sf
(pizz.)
p
(pizz.)
p
arco
p

Picc.
Ob. 1
solo
p
(solo)
mp
Clar.
1
2
(solo)
mp
p
Trpt. 1
con sordino
mp
Vl.
1
2
(pizz.)
(pizz.)
Vla.
Vlc.

Picc.
Fl. 1
mp
Ob. 1
mp
Clar. 1
Bsn. 1
mf
Hr.
con sordino
mf
Trpt. 1
mp
♩ = 126
8
♩ = 126
Vl.
1
2
Vla.
arco
mf
Vlc.
mf

Picc.
Ob. 1
Bsn. 1
Hr. 1
Trpt. 1/2
con sordino
solo
mf
arco
Vl. 1
Vl. 2
Vla.
Vlc.

Picc.
Fl. 1/2
Ob. 1/2
Clar. 1/2
Bsn. 1/2
Hr.
Piano
a2
1st solo
solo
stacc.
p
9
Vl. 1
Vl. 2
Vla.
Vlc.

Picc.
Fl.
1
2
Ob.
Clar.
Bsn.
Hr.
Trpt.
Trb.
Tb.
Timp.
Piano
Vl.
Vla.
Vlc.
Cb.
(a2)
a2
(senza sord.)
pp
con sordino

Picc.
Fl.
Ob.
Clar.
Bsn.
Hr.
Trpt.
Trb.
Tb.
Timp.
Piano
Vl.
Vla.
Vlc.
Cb.
a2
senza sord.
stacc.
mp
10
piuz.

Bsn. 1 2
Hr.
Trb. 1
solo
mf poco marcato
Piano
mf stacc.
Vl. 1 2
Vla.
Vlc.
Cb.
mp

Picc.
Fl. 1 2
Ob. 1 2
Clar. 1 2
Bsn. 1 2
Hr.
Trpt. 1 2 3
(senza sord.)
solo
mf
con sordino
p
Trb. 1 2 3
Tb.
Timp.
Piano
stacc
mf
11
Vl. 1 2
Vla.
Vlc.
Cb.

Picc.
Fl. 1 2
1° solo
Ob. 1 2
Clar. 1 2
1° solo
Bsn 1 2
Hr.
Trpt. 1 2 3
Trb. 1 2 3
Tb.
Timp.
Perc.
Piano
Vl. 1 2
div.
pizz.
Vla.
pizz.
Vlc.
arco
Cb.
arco

Picc.
Fl. 1 2
Ob. 1 2
Clar. 1 2
Bsn. 1 2
Hr.
Trpt. 1 2 3
solo
mp
Trb. 1 2 3
Tb.
Timp.
Perc.
Piano
f
12
Vl. 1 2
unis. IV
arco IV
Vla.
Vlc.
Cb.

Picc.
Fl. 1 2
Ob. 1 2
Clar. 1 2
Bsn. 1 2
Hr.
Trpt. 1 2 3
Trb. 1 2 3
Tb.
Timp.
Perc.
Piano
Vl. 1 2
Vla.
Vlc
Cb.
solo
pizz.

Fl. 1/2
Clar. 1/2
Bsn 1/2
Hr.
Trpt. 1
Trb. 1
Piano
Vl. 1
Vl. 2
Vla.
Vlc.
Cb.
meno f
(senza sord.)
con sordino
solo
13
(pizz.)

Fl. 1/2
Clar. 1/2
Bsn. 1/2
Vl. 1
Vl. 2
Vla.
Vlc.
Cb.
p
pp
ppp
p dim. sempre

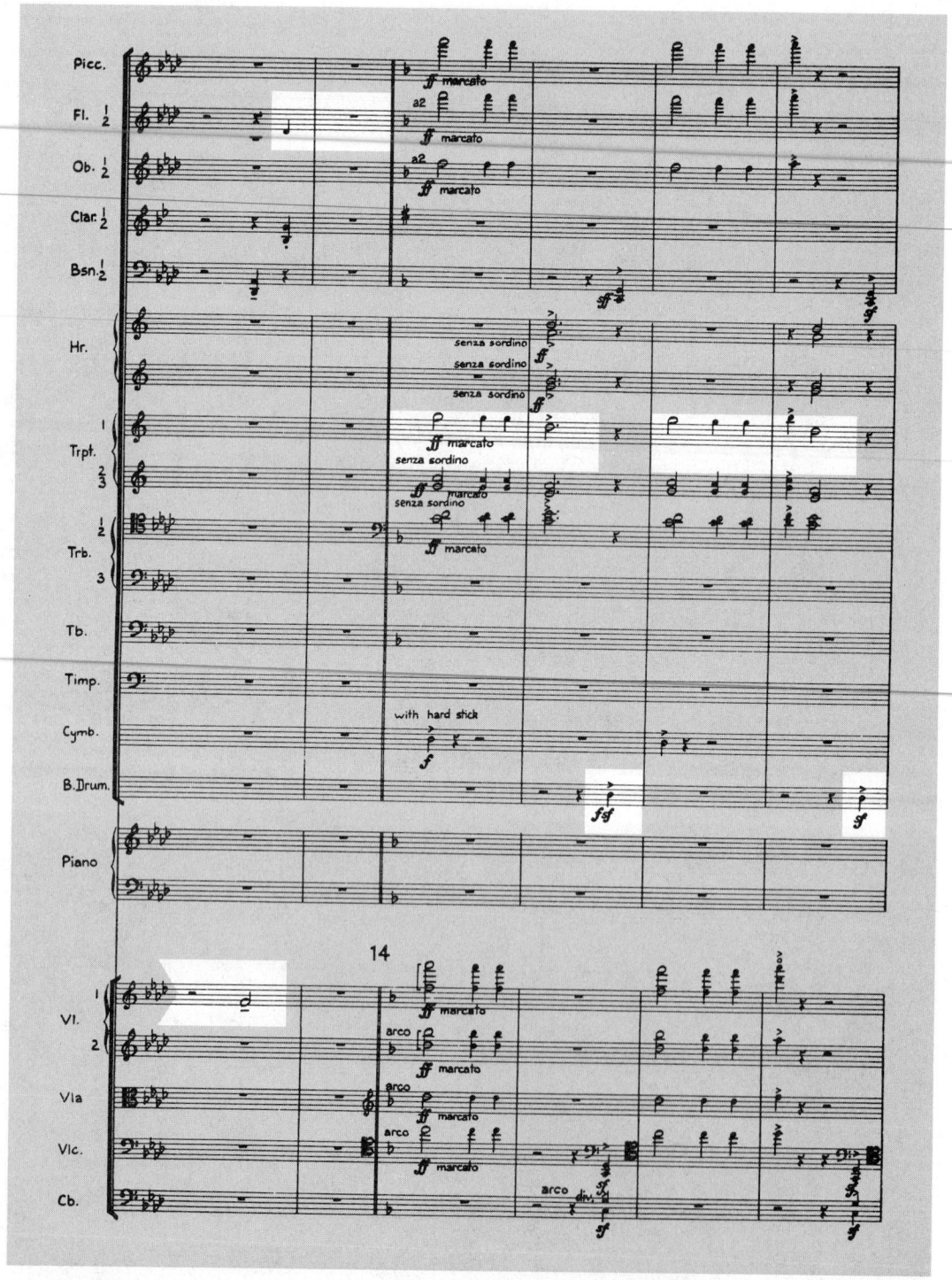
Picc.
Fl. 1 2
Ob. 1 2
Clar. 1 2
Bsn. 1 2
Hr.
Trpt. 1 2 3
Trb. 1 2 3
Tb.
Timp.
Cymb.
B.Drum.
Piano
Vl. 1 2
Vla
Vlc.
Cb.
ff marcato
a2
senza sordino
with hard stick
f
14
arco
div.

Picc.
Fl. 1 2
a2
Ob. 1 2
a2
Clar. 1 2
Bsn. 1 2
Hr.
Trpt. 1 2 3
Trb. 1 2 3
Tb.
Timp.
Cymb.
B. Drum
Piano
Vl. 1 2
Vla.
Vlc.
Cb.

10
25
♩ = ♩ precedente. (♩ = 138)
Picc.
Fl. 1 2
Ob. 1 2
a2
Clar. 1 2
Bsn. 1 2
f stacc.
Hr.
f stacc.
f stacc.
Trpt. 1 2 3
Trb. 1 2 3
f stacc.
senza sordino
f stacc.
Tb.
senza sordino
f stacc.
Timp.
Wood-bl.
f
mf
Sn. Drum.
f
Cymb.
B. Drum.
Piano
♩ = ♩ precedente. (♩ = 138)
15
Vl 1 2
f div.
f
Vla.
f
Vlc.
f pizz.
Cb.
f pizz.
f

Picc.
Fl. 1 2
Ob. 1 2
Clar. 1 2
Bsn. 1 2
a2 stacc.
f
Hr.
Trpt. 1 2 3
solo f
solo f
Trb. 1 2 3
Tb.
Timp.
Woodbl.
Cymb.
B.Drum.
Piano
Vl. 1 2
Vla.
arco
f
Vlc.
Cb.

Picc.
Fl. 1 2
Ob. 1 2
Clar. 1 2
Bsn. 1 2
mf
a2
mf
Hr.
Trpt. 1 2 3
stacc.
mf
stacc.
mf
Trb. 1 2 3
soli
mf legato, cantabile
Tb.
Timp.
Woodbl.
Cymb.
B.Drum.
Piano
16
Vla. 1 2
pizz.
mf
unis.
pizz.
mf
Vla
pizz.
mf
Vlc.
pizz.
arco
mf
Cb.
(pizz)
arco
mf

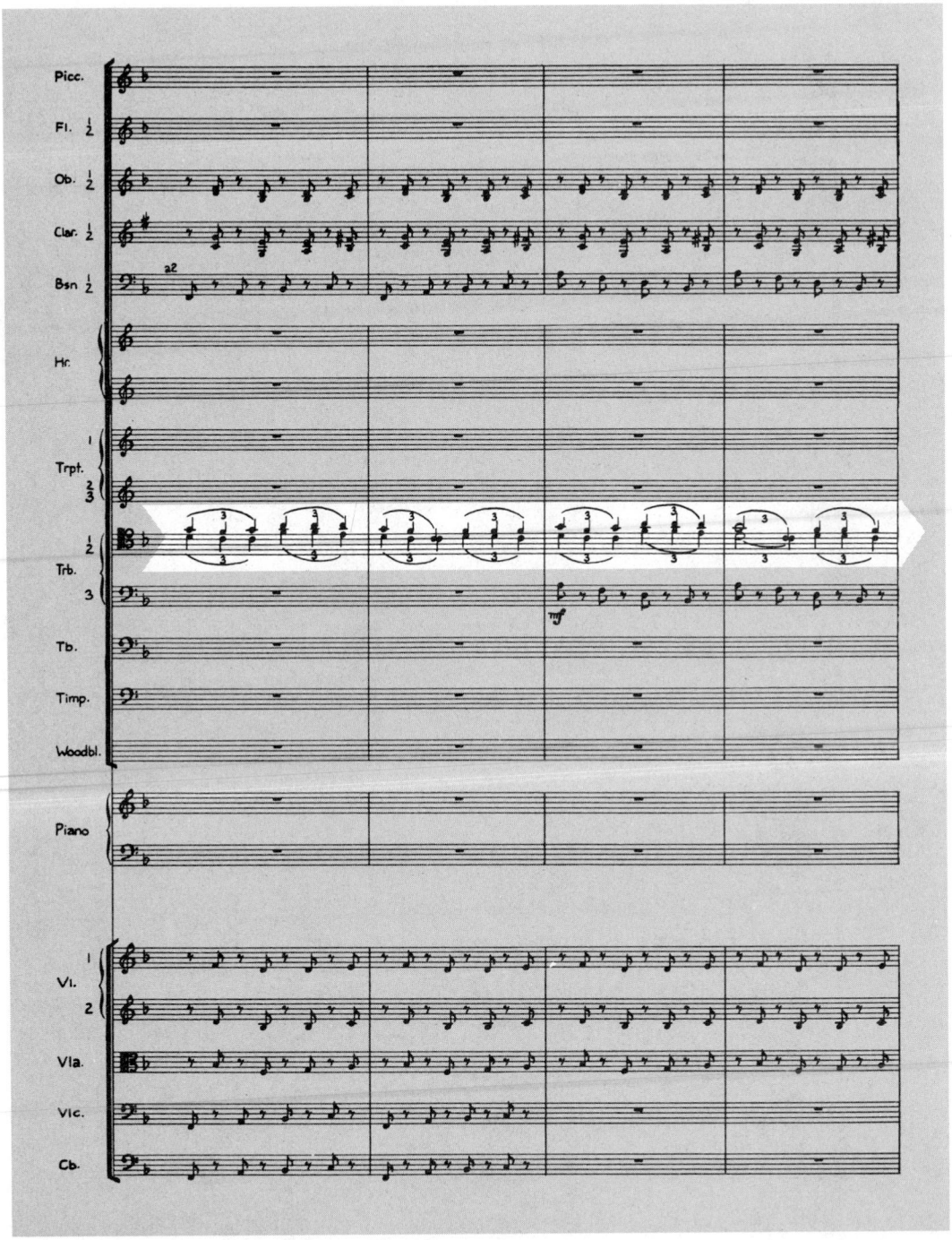
Picc.
Fl. 1 2
Ob. 1 2
Clar. 1 2
Bsn 1 2
a2
Hr.
Trpt. 1 2 3
Trb. 1 2 3
mf
Tb.
Timp.
Woodbl.
Piano
Vl. 1 2
Vla.
Vlc.
Cb.

Picc.
Fl. 1 2
Ob. 1 2
Clar. 1 2
Bsn. 1 2
a2
Hr.
Trpt. 1 2 3
Trb. 1 2 3
Tb.
Timp.
Woodbl.
Piano
Vl. 1 2
arco
div.
Vla.
Vlc.
C.b.
(arco)

Picc.
Fl. 1 2
Ob. 1 2
Clar. 1 2
Bsn. 1 2
Hr.
Trpt. 1 2 3
Trb. 1 2 3
Tb.
Timp.
Woodbl.
Piano
Vl. 1 2
Vla.
Vlc.
Cb.
a2
mf
con sordino
solo
17

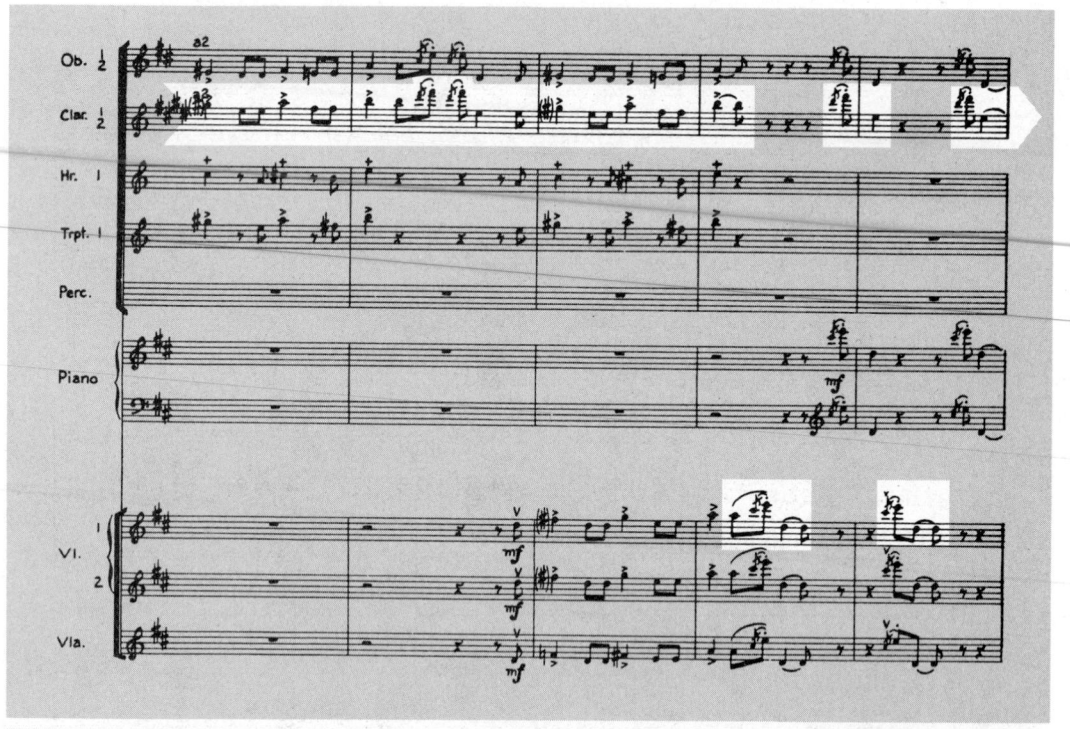
Ob. 1 2
Clar. 1 2
Hr. 1
Trpt. 1
Perc.
Piano
Vl. 1 2
Vla.
a2
mf

Picc.
Fl. 1 2
Ob. 1 2
Clar. 1 2
Perc.
Piano
Vl. 1 2
Vla.
Vlc.
solo
mf stacc.
a2
1° solo
Sleigh-bells
18
p
pizz.

Picc.
Fl. 1 2
a2
Ob. 1 2
Clar. 1 2
Bsn. 1 2
Hr.
Trpt. 1 2 3
Trb. 1 2 3
Tb.
Timp.
Sleigh.b.
Woodbl.
Piano
Vl. 1 2
Vla.
Vlc.
Cb.

Picc.
Fl. 1 2
a2
Ob. 1 2
Clar. 1 2
Bsn. 1 2
Hr. 1 2 3 4
solo
f cantabile
Trpt. 1 2 3
mf
Trb. 1 2 3
Tb.
Timp.
Perc.
Piano
19
Vl. 1 2
Vla.
legato, cantabile
arco
tenuto
Vlc.
Cb.
div.

Picc.
Fl. 1 2
Ob. 1 2
Clar. 1 2
Bsn. 1 2
Hr. 1 2 3 4
Trpt. 1 2 3
Trb. 1 2 3
Tb.
Timp.
Perc.
Vl. 1 2
Vla.
Vlc.
Cb.

Mexican Dance and Finale

Picc.
Fl. 1 2
Ob. 1 2
Clar. 1 2
Bsn. 1 2
1°
Hr.
Trpt. 1 2 3
Trb. 1 2 3
Tb.
Timp.
Woodbl.
Gourd.
Piano
Vl. 1 2
Vla.
Vlc.
Cb.

Picc.
Fl.
1
2
solo
Ob. 1/2
solo
Clar. 1/2
Bsn. 1/2
Hr.
Trpt.
1
2
3
Trb.
1/2
3
Tb.
Timp.
Woodbl.
Gourd.
Piano
22
Vl.
1
2
modo ordinario
modo ordinario
Vla.
modo ordinario
Vlc.
pizz.
Cb.

Picc.
Fl.
1
2
Ob. 1 2
Clar. 1 2
Bsn. 1 2
Hr.
Trpt.
1
2 3
Trb.
1 2
3
Tb.
Timp.
Woodbl.
Gourd.
Piano
23
Vl.
1
2
Vla
Vlc.
Cb.

Pict.
Fl. 1 2
Ob. 1 2
Clar. 1 2
Bsn. 1 2
1°
Hr.
1
Trpt.
2 3
1 2
Trb.
3
Tb.
Timp.
Woodbl.
Gourd.
Piano
1
Vl.
2
col legno
col legno
Vla
col legno
Vlc.
Cb.
(pizz.)

Picc.
Fl. 1 2
Ob. 1 2
Clar. 1 2
Bsn. 1 2
Hr.
1
Trpt.
2
3
1 2
Trb.
3
Tb.
Timp.
Woodbl.
Gourd.
Piano
1
Vl.
2
Vla.
Vlc
Cb.

Fl. 1 2
Ob. 1 2
Clar. 1 2
Hr.
Trpt. 1 2 3
24
Vl. 1 2
Vla.
Vlc.
mp
mf
arco
v legato
modo ordinario
arco modo ordinario

Ob. 1 2
Clar. 1 2
Bsn. 1 2
Hr.
Vl. 1 2
Vla.
Vlc.
solo mf
p
dim.

Ob. 1/2
Clar. 1/2
Bsn. 1/2
Hr.
solo mp
25
Vl. 1
Vl. 2
sul G....
mp
Vla.
(dim.)
Vlc.

Ob. 1/2
Clar. 1/2
Bsn. 1
Bsn. 2
Hr.
Vl. 1
Vl. 2
(sul G)
pizz.
Vla.
Vlc.

Fl. 1/2
Ob. 1/2
a2
Clar. 1/2
Bsn. 1/2
Glockenspiel
(sounds 8va higher)
25A
Vl. 1
Vl. 2
arco
Vla.
Vlc.

Fl. 1/2
Ob. 1/2
a2
Clar. 1/2
Hr.
senza sordino
(con sordino)
senza sordino
(con sordino)
Glockenspiel
Vl. 1
Vl. 2
Vla.
Vlc.

Fl. 1/2
Ob. 1/2
Clar. 1/2
Bsn. 1/2
Hr.
Glocksp.
a2
mf con intensita
26
Vl. 1
Vl. 2
Vla.
Vlc.
(a2)
Bsn 1/2
pizz
arco

Picc.
Fl. 1 2
Ob. 1 2
Clar. 1 2
Bsn. 1 2
Hr.
Trpt. 1 2 3
Trb. 1 2 3
Tb.
Timp.
Perc.
Piano
Vl. 1 2
Vla.
Vlc.
Cb.
(a2)
a2
senza sordino
solo
26A
(arco)

Picc.
Fl. 1/2
Ob. 1/2
Clar. 1/2
Bsn. 1/2
Hr.
Trpt. 1 2 3
Trb. 1/2 3
Tb.
Timp.
Perc.
Piano
Vl. 1 2
Vla.
Vlc.
Cb.
stacc.
(a2)
marc.
a2
senza sord.
senza sordino

Picc.
Fl. 1 2
Ob. 1 2
Clar. 1 2
Bsn. 1 2
(a2)
Hr.
Trpt. 1 2 3
Trb. 1 2 3
Tb.
Timp.
Glockspl.
Xyloph.
Cymb.
B. Drum
Piano
8va
27
Vl. 1 2
Vla.
Vlc.
Cb.

Picc.
Fl. 1 2
Ob. 1 2
Clar. 1 2
Bsn. 1 2
(a2)
Hr.
Trpt. 1 2 3
Trb. 1 2 3
Tb.
Timp.
Glockspl.
Xylph.
Cymb.
B.Drum
Piano
8va
Vl. 1 2
Vla.
Vlc.
Cb.

meno mosso
Picc.
Fl. 1 2
Ob. 1 2
Clar. 1 2
Bsn 1 2
Hr.
Trpt 1 2 3
Trb. 1 2 3
Tb.
Timp.
Glockspl
Xyloph.
Slapstick
Cymb.
B. Drum.
Piano
27A
meno mosso
Vl. 1 2
Vla.
Vlc.
Cb.
div.
pizz.
arco

34. *Ruth Crawford (1901–1953)* 8:8A/3 8:8/12 - 15

Rat Riddles, from Three Songs (1933)

Ruth Crawford, Rat Riddles *from* Three Songs for Voice. © *1933 New Music Edition. Theodore Presser Company.*

Editor's note: "N.B." (*nota bene*, "note well") and "(a)!" used to mark composer's cautionary accidentals.

Ostinati
Cl
Bn
Trp
Hrn
Trb
Concertanti
Alt
Ob
Ch bl
Tri
Tamb
Cym
Tr
Per
Pft
mf
(b)
tr
leggiero
cantando
8.
basso
Ostinati
Yl I
Yl II
Yla
Yc
B

Ostinati
Cl
Bn
Trp
Hrn
Trb
15
There was a gray
Concertanti
Alt
Ob
Pr
Ch.bl.
Tri.
Tamb.
Cym.
Tr.
Pft
tr
mp
(b)
(a) N.B!
(a)!
p
(a) N.B!
8
basso
Ostinati
Vl I
Vl II
Vla
Vc
B

Ostinati
Cl
Bn
Trp
Hrn
Trb
rat looked at me with green eyes out of a
20
Concertanti
Alt
Ob
mp
Ch.bl
Tri
Tamb
Cym
Dr
Per
Pft
(d)
leggiero
Ostinati
Vl I
Vl II
Vla
Vc
B

Ostinati
Cl
Bn
Trp
Hrn
Trb
rat- hole.
"Hel-lo, rat,"
I said,
"Is there
25
Concertanti
Alt
Ob
Per
Ch. bl.
Tri.
Tamb.
Cym.
Dr.
Pft
mf
fz
tr (b)
mf cresc. molto
ff
f
pp legato
Ostinati
Vl I
Vl II
Vla
Vc
B

13
Ostinati
Cl
Bn
Trp
Hrn
Trb
a-ny chance for me to get on- to the lan- guage of the rats ?"
30
Concertanti
Alt
Ob
mp
Ch bl
Tri
Tamb
Cym
Tr
Per
Pft
pp
Ostinati
Yl I
Yl II
Yla
Yc
B

Ostinati
Cl
Bn
Trp
Hrn
Trb
35
Concertanti
Alt
Ob
Ch.bl.
Tri.
Tamb.
Cym.
Pf
cantando
leggiero
Ostinati
Vl I
Vl II
Vla
Vc
B

Ostinati
Cl
Bn
Trp
Hrn
Trb
And the green eyes blinked at me,
40
Concertanti
Alt
Ob
tr
mp
p
Ch. bl.
Tri.
Tromb.
Cym.
Dr.
Per
cantando
Pft
basso
Ostinati
Yl I
Yl II
Yla
Yc
B

Ostinati
Cl
Bn
Trp
Hrn
Trb
blinked from a gray rat's rat-hole.
"Come a-gain, rat,"
45
Concertanti
Alt
Ob
Per
Ch.bl
Tri.
Tamb.
Cym.
Dr
Pft
mf
f
ff
mf cresc. molto
Ostinati
Vl I
Vl II
Vla
Vc
B

Ostinati
Cl
Bn
Trp
Hrn
Trb
I said,
"Slip me a couple of riddles; there must be
50
Concertanti
Alt
Ob
Ch bl.
Tri
Tamb
Gong
Tr
Pr
Pft
pp legato
16va
pp
Ostinati
Vl I
Vl II
Vla
Vc
B

14
Ostinati
Cl
Bn
Trp
Hrn
Trb
rid-dles
a-mong the rats."
55
Concertanti
Alt
Ob
Per
Ch.bl.
Tri.
Tamb.
Cym.
Pft
mp
tr
cantando
Ostinati
Yl I
Yl II
Yla
Yc
B

Ostinati
Cl
Bn
Trp
Hrn
Trb
Concertanti
Alt
And the green eyes
Ob
mf
tr
mp
p
Ch.bl.
Tri
Tamb
Cym
Br
Per
Pft
leggiero
8
basso
Ostinati
Yl I
Yl II
Yla
Yc
B

Ostinati
Cl
Bn
Trp
Hrn
Trb
rallentando e diminuendo
blinked at me and a whis- per came from the gray rat- hole :
60
Concertanti
Alt
Ob
Ch.bl.
Tri
Tamb
Cym
Tr
Per
Pft
mp
cantando
rallentando e diminuendo
Ostinati
Vl I
Vl II
Vla
Vc
B

Quasi recitativo
"Who do you think you are and why is a rat?
65
Alt
Dr
ppp
colla parte
mp
pp
mf
accel. e cresc.
Where did you sleep last night and why do you sneeze on Tuesdays?
(almost spoken)
ff
Grave
And why is the grave of a rat no
70
sostenuto
Ob
sostenuto cantando
p
sempre ppp
Pft
8 basso
deep- er than the grave of a man?"
75
f
un poco
(h)
pppp
mf

15
Ostinati
Cl
Bn
Trp
Hrn
Trb
ppp
tenuto sempre
molto sotto voce
Tempo primo
accel.
And the tail of a green-eyed rat
80
Concertanti
Alt
Ob
Per
Ch.bl.
Tri.
Tamb
Cym
Tir
mp
tr
mf
cantando
Pft
Tempo primo
accel.
Ostinati
Vl I
Vl II
Vla
Vc
B

Ostinati
Cl
Bn
Trp
Hrn
Trb
a tempo
ritenuto molto
whipped
and was
gone
at a
gray
rat-hole.
Concertanti
Alt
Ob
tr
Ch bl
Tri
Tamb
Cym
Tr
Per
Pft
a tempo
ritenuto molto
Ostinati
Yl I
Yl II
Yla
Yc
B

Ostinati
Cl
Bn
Trp
Hrn
Trb
a tempo
85
Concertanti
Alt
Ob
Per
Pft
p
8
basso
a tempo
Ostinati
Vl I
Vl II
Vla
Vc
B

35. *Witold Lutosławski (1913–1994)*

Jeux vénitiens (Venetian Games), First Movement (1961)

8:8A/5 8:8/18 - 19

STRUMENTI DELL'ORCHESTRA

2 flauti (II anche flauto piccolo)
1 oboe
3 clarinetti in si♭ (III anche clarinetto basso in si♭)
1 fagotto

1 tromba in do
1 corno in fa
1 trombone

percussione (4 esecutori)
I 3 timpani scordati (3 dimensioni)
II 3 tamburi (soprano, alto, tenore), tamburo rullante
III xilofono, 3 piatti sospesi (soprano, alto, tenore), tam-tam, 5 tom-tom
IV claves, vibrafono senza motore

arpa
pianoforte (2 esecutori; II anche celesta)

4 violini
3 viole
3 violoncelli
2 contrabbassi

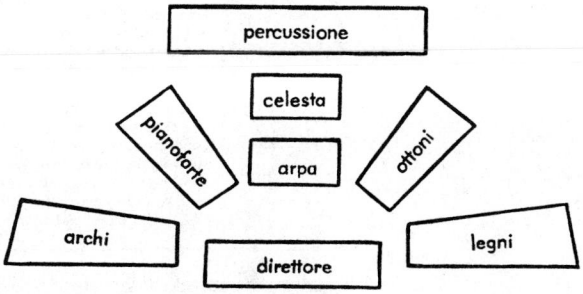

DURATA ca 13'

The piccolo, xylophone, and celesta are notated an octave lower, and the double-basses an octave higher, than they sound. All the other instruments are notated at their actual pitch. In this score the signs ♯ and ♭ apply only to the notes they precede. Notes without accidentals should always be read as naturals.

© 1962 by Moeck Verlag, Celle. © renewed. All rights reserved. Used by permission of European American Music Distributors Corporation, sole U.S. agent for Moeck Verlag, Celle.

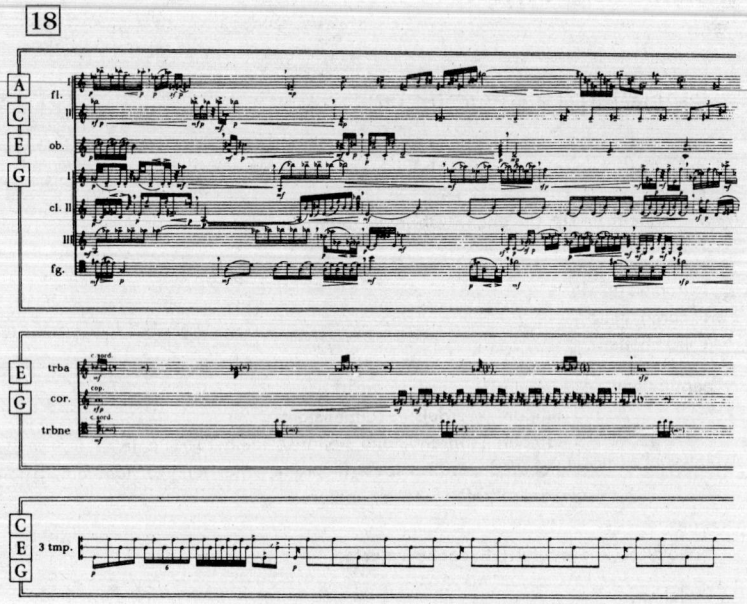

Order of performance: A B C D E F G H

Sections A C E G :

A is played by the woodwinds and percussion group; C by the woodwinds, kettledrums, and percussion; E by the woodwinds, brass, kettledrums, and percussion; G by the woodwinds, brass, kettledrums, percussion, and piano. The broken "bar lines" with a caesura above call for a caesura of optional length; on the length of the caesura will depend the density of the texture.

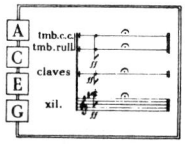

Duration of the particular sections: A = 12″, C = 18″, E = 6″, G = 24″. The conductor gives the sign for the beginning and end of each section (the beat showing the end of section A also indicates the beginning of section B, the beat showing the end of C, the beginning of D, etc.). When the sign for the end of each section is given, the performers must interrupt playing immediately. If by this time a player has already played his part to the end, he should repeat it

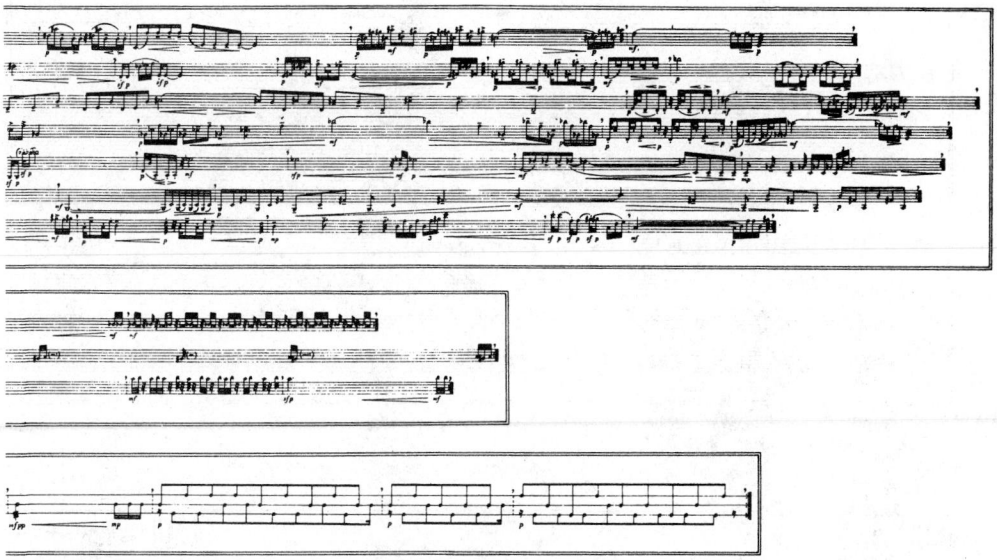

from the beginning of the section. In the following sections, which are indicated by the letters in the order C, E, G, the individual parts ought not to be played from the beginning but from any other phrase between two caesuras. Each musician should play his part with the same freedom as if he were playing it alone; the rhythmic values serve only as a guide, and the basic tempo is between ♪ = 140 and ♪ = 150.

Sections B D F H:

The bar lines, rhythmical values, and meter are intended merely for orientation: the music should be played with the greatest possible freedom. The number of notes at places like the third bar of section B in the first viola part depends on the strength of the player's bowing (*spiccato* or preferably *ricochet*). In section D the first violin part should be played independently of the conductor and the rest of the ensemble.

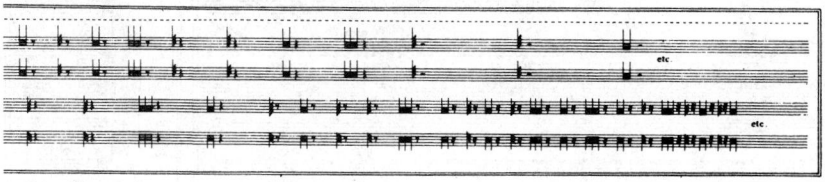

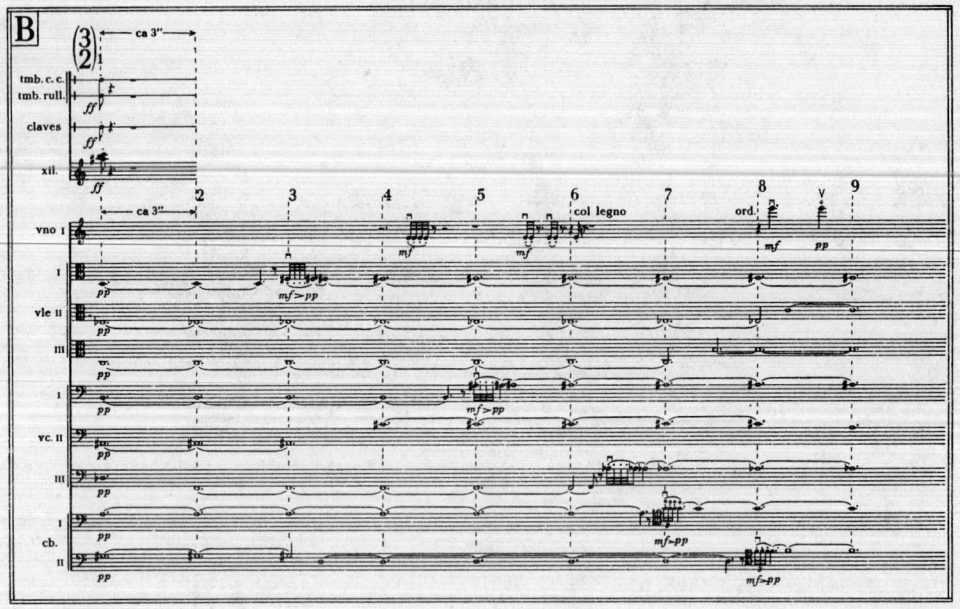

19

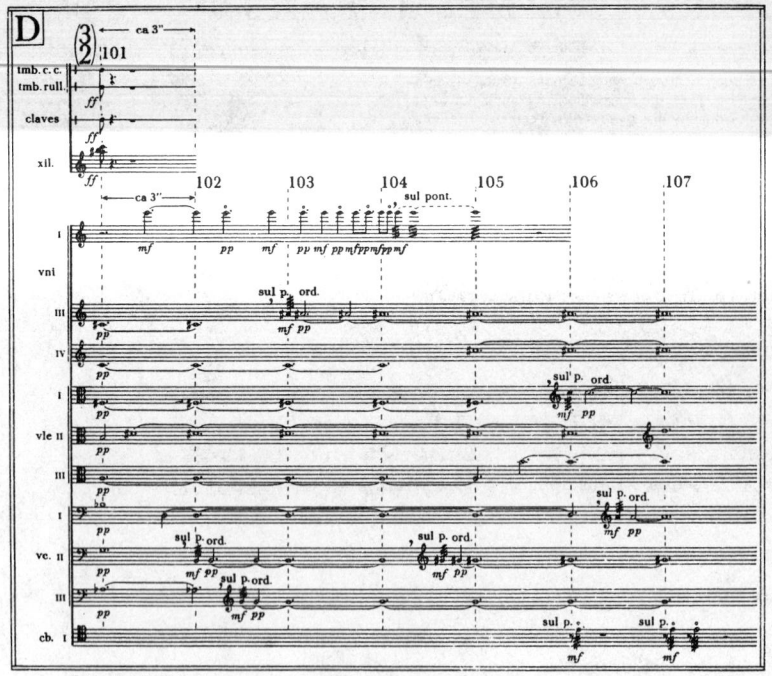

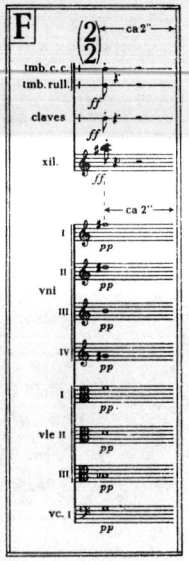

Edition Moeck - 5012

H
ca 3"
tmb. c. c.
tmb. rull.
claves
xil.
ca 3"
vni
vle II
vc.
sul p.
pizz.
pizz.
tmb. c. c.
tmb. rull.
claves
xil.
vni
vle
vc. I
pizz.

36. Elliott Carter (b. 1908)

8:8A/4 8:8/16 - 17

Sonata for Flute, Oboe, Cello, and Harpsichord, First Movement (1952)

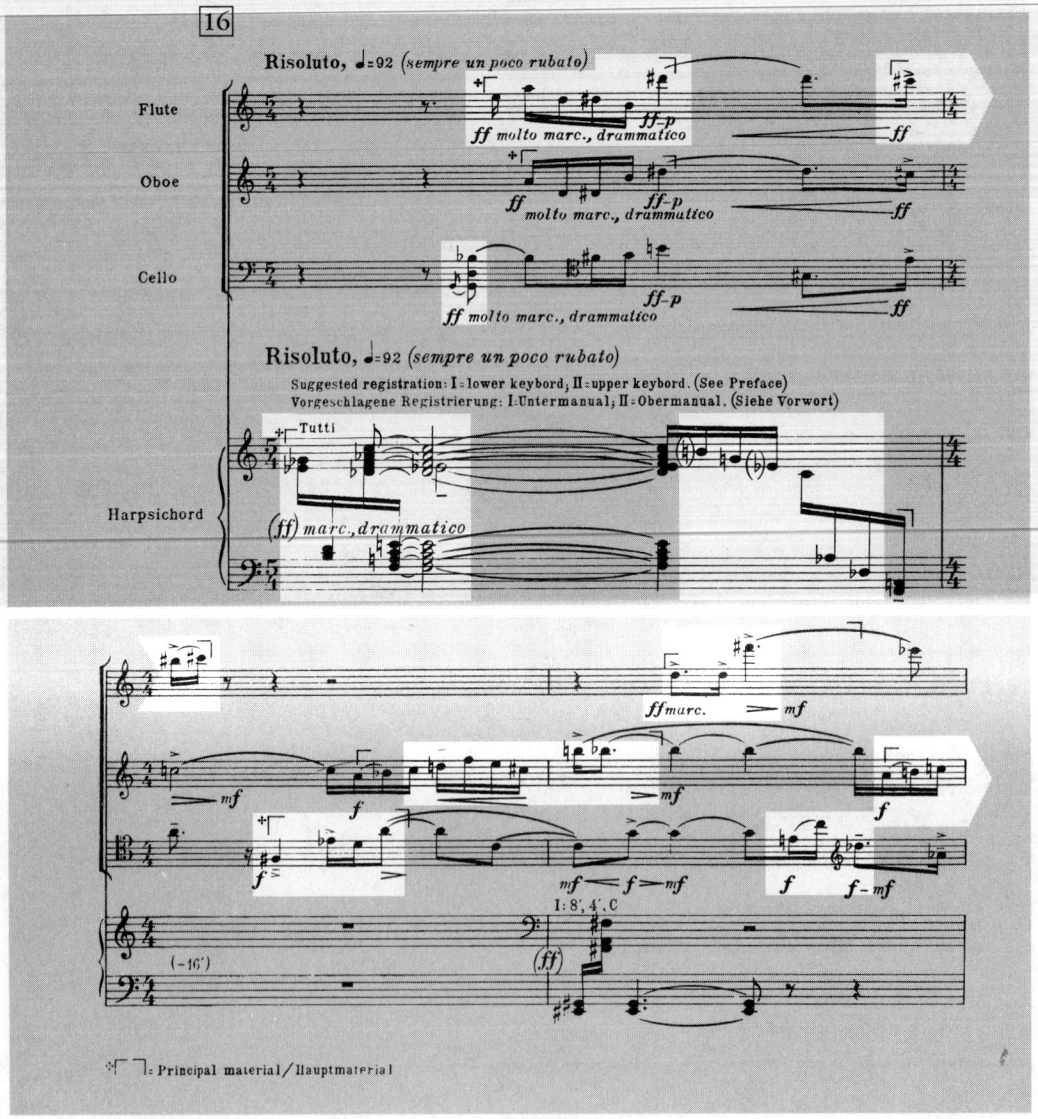

Copyright © 1960 (renewed) by Associated Music Publishers, Inc. (BMI). International copyright secured. All rights reserved. Reprinted by permission.

5
sf–mf
ff
mf
mf
f
mf
f
f–mf
f
mf
f
mf
5
f
mf
ff
f
mf
sff
f
mf
ff marcatiss.
ff
sff
f
fp
f sub.
ff marcatiss.
f
sff
(I:+16′,–8′,–C)
(II:+8′)

10
p–pp
pp
p
pp
p
I: 4′, 16′
II: 8′
(p)
L.II.
15
p
f
marc.
mf
pizz.
arco
+8′

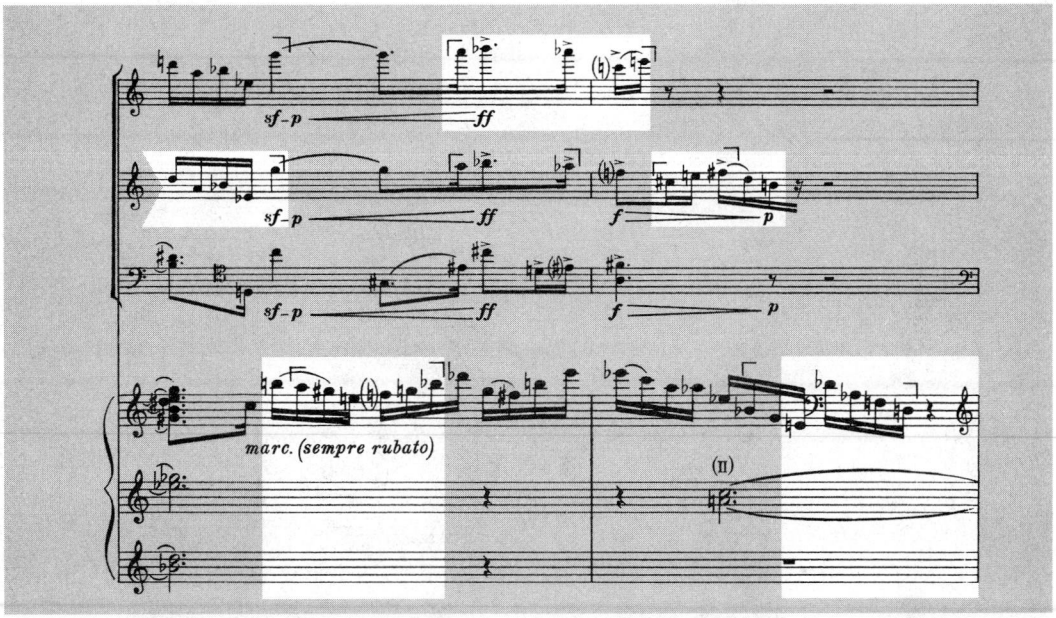
sf-p
ff
sf-p
ff
f
p
sf-p
ff
f
p
marc. (sempre rubato)
(II)

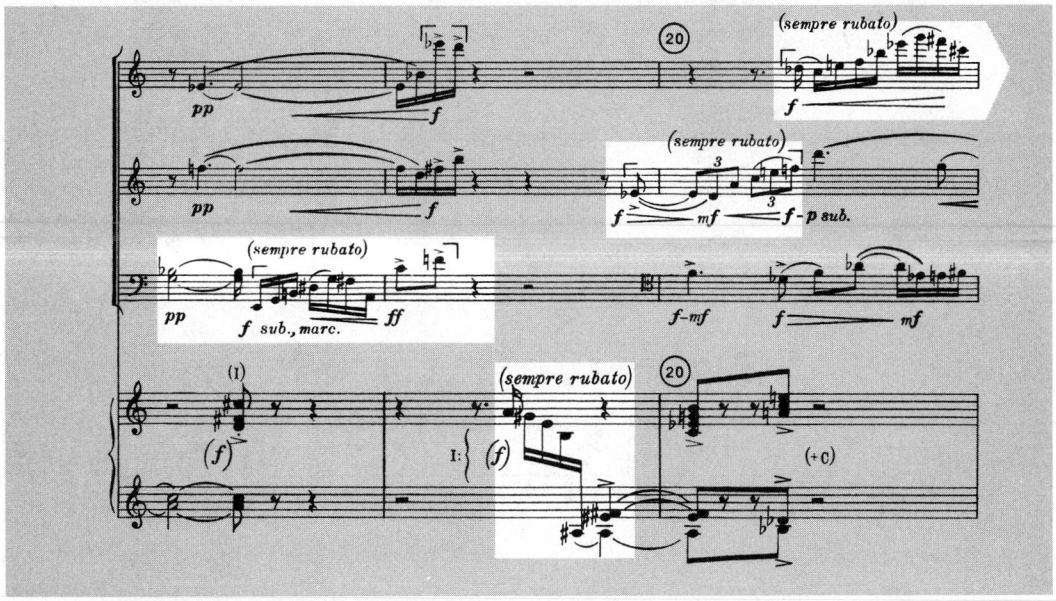
pp
f
20
(sempre rubato)
f
pp
f
(sempre rubato)
f
mf
f-p sub.
pp
(sempre rubato)
f sub., marc.
ff
f-mf
f
mf
(I)
(f)
(sempre rubato)
I:
(f)
20
(+C)

mf
f
ff
mf
p sub.
mf
ff
ff
f marc.
mf
f
Tutti
(ff)
ff
mf
f
f
f
f
marc.

25
ff
f
ff
mf
ff
f
ff marc.
ff
f
ff
mf
25
(ff)
molto marc.
(I:–4′,–16′,–8′)
f
meno f
f
mf
f
f–mf
f
f
meno f
f
marc. f–mf
f
f marc.
mf

30
17
Tempo giusto
(un poco più mosso)
f
mf
p
accompagnando
pp
3
mf
f
mf
30
Tempo giusto
(un poco più mosso)
Melodic outline/Melodiegang:
Solo al fine
I:$\frac{1}{2}$8', C
(mf) resonante
4
3
2
35
rubato
mf espr.
rubato
3
mf
f
rubato
mp espr.
f
35
(colle parti)

40
p pp mf
pp
pp p
pizz.
mf
40
giusto
(+4')
p pp
f p sub. f ff
p
(più f)

45
f
p
pp
pp
pp
(sempre ptzz.)
f
pp
pp
45
mp
dim.
mp
pp
mp
pp

50
pp
p
mf–pp
mf
arco
p
50
etc.
II:8′
(-4′)
(meno f)
55
pp
p
pizz.
pp
55
Melodic outline/Melodiegang:
I:½8′, C
(mf)
(II)

60
fp
p
3
più p
arco
pp
f
ff
60
65
mf
p
pp
poco rit.
poco rit.
pizz.
poco rit.
pp
65
etc.
poco rit.

37. *Milton Babbitt (b. 1916)*

8:8A/6 8:8/20

Phonemena, excerpt (1969–70)

Editor's note: This work was originally conceived with synthesized accompaniment. The composer prepared this piano/vocal score for study purposes.

Copyright © 1979 by C. F. Peters Corporation, 373 Park Avenue South, New York, NY 10016. International copyright secured. All rights reserved. Alle Rechte vorbehalten.

9
LE - - Ō HĀ MA LAW - - GŌ
11
LE MAH DĀ THAH SHĒ
13
LŌ ZHU SU JAW TŌ HAH
15
DĒ SHE WĀ - E TŌ SHĒ MI ZA

17
BŌ RU
YŪ SHU RU I
20
SHA MĀ YU ZAW THA GAW
22
FE GĀ - VA THA FĒ THĒ AH VŪ
24
BU WI DAW THŪ JU - - THU LŪ CHU HU THŪJ

27
PE MAH Ē VI
30
CHĒ WĒ E GĀ HI LE Ā RŌ VAW - - L YAH
33
Ō ZŌ AW YŌ BAH SHŌ PŌ LUH SAW PA SAH RA
35
ZE RA ZHA SHA YU KU SHU TU SHU

38
GU ZU PŌ THI
MAW- BĒ
40
VŪ JU - Ū HU JU TĀ SŪ U
42
VŪ WŪ MU RŪ ZHUH KUH
WU NGU RU
44
BĀ SHUH LE THE RĀ LE SHĀ LAW LE

47
GA THI HE SĒ DI RAH ZHA TI DĒ AH
50
FI DĒ WĒ GA KAH MAW PŌ WU RŪ
52
MĀ NAH RA LU CHU LU - NU ZŪ LŪ
54
GAW - MA - LE VŌ NU ZHE JŌ HU CHA DĒ THAH JAH

56
YĒ FU SŌ SHU DAW RI BŌ - A
59
PI VĒ PE SHE VĀ KŪR Ē - -
62
Z
THŌ-
65
- A WO - A THA JAW THA WA CHŌ THAW GAH NA ZHŌ

38. Leonard Bernstein (1918–1990)

Symphonic Dances from *West Side Story* (1957/1961), excerpts

8:8A/7 8:8/21 - 24

3:3B/3 3:3/37 - 40

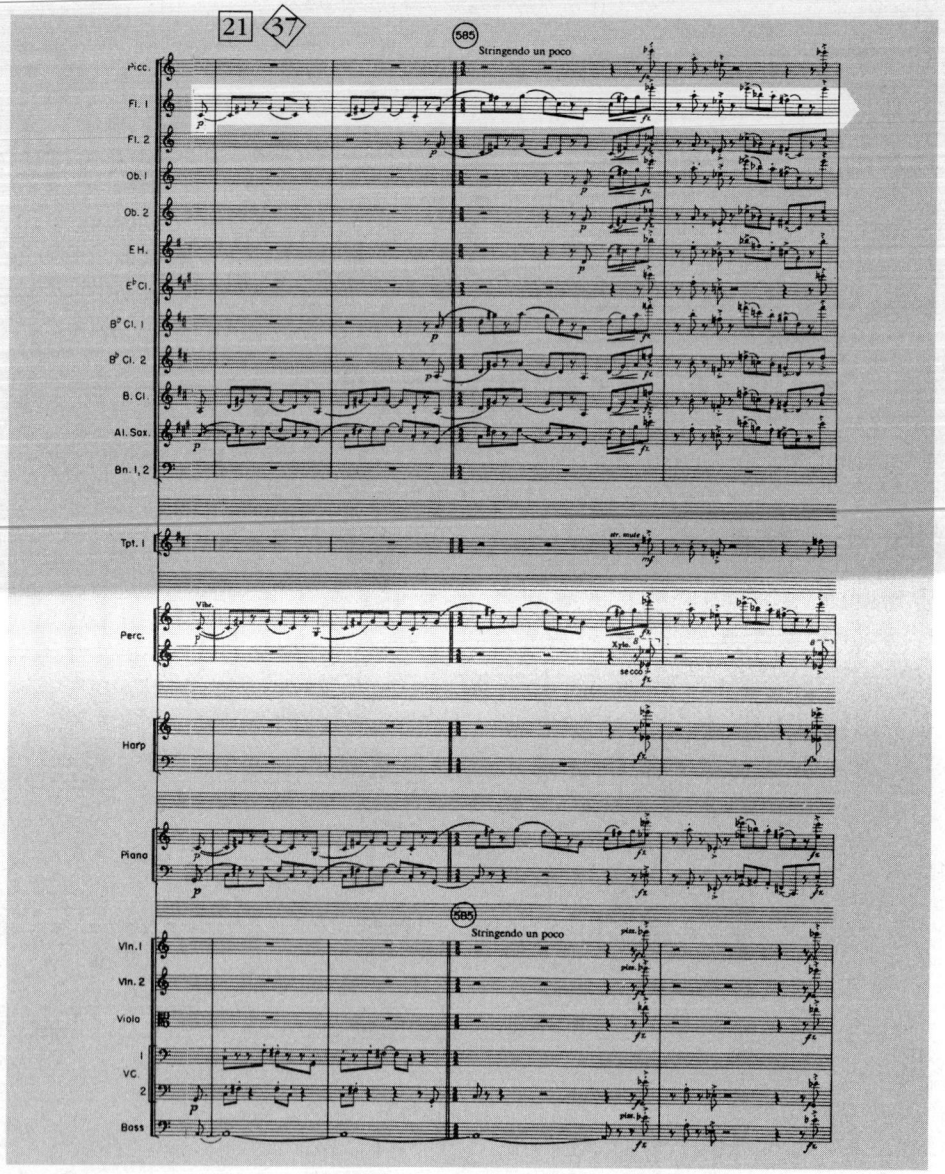

© Copyright 1951 by The Estate of Leonard Bernstein; copyright renewed. Reprinted by permission of Boosey & Hawkes, Inc., sole agent.

589
♩= 88
Picc.
Fl. 1
Fl. 2
Ob. 1
Ob. 2
E.H.
E♭ Cl.
B♭ Cl. 1
B♭ Cl. 2
B. Cl.
Al. Sax.
Bn. 1, 2
Tpt. 1
Perc.
Vibr.
Xylo.
Cymb.
Harp
Piano
To Celesta
Celesta
Vln. 1
Vln. 2
Viola
Vc. 1
Vc. 2
Bass
Solo
Soli
3 Soli Celli
sans sord.
I. Solo
pizz.
arco

595
Fl. I
B. Cl.
Bn. I
Vbr.
Harp
Celesta
Vln. I
Vln. 2
Viola
I
VC.
2
Bass
con sord.
3 Soli
Tutti: div.
4 Basses pizz.
vc. Solo

601
Fl. I
B. Cl.
Al. Sax.
Perc.
Harp
Piano
Vln. I
Vln. 2
Viola
I
VC.
2
Bass
dim. molto
non cresc.
Vibr.
Bongos
via sord.
div. a 3

Fugue
607
Fl. 1
B Cl.
Al. Sax
Tpt. 1
Tight cup mute
pp
cresc.
molto
Perc.
(Vibr.)
Brush on Cymb.
pp
Harp
Piano
607
Vc.
Bass
612
1
Tpt. 2
3
molto
sfz
Perc.
Brush on Cymb.
Vibr.
pp
Bongo
sfz
612
Harp
pp
Piano
Bass
pizz.
pp

22
38
620
Fl. 1
Fl. 2
Hn. 1
Tpt. 1
Solo
Tight mute
cresc.
Perc.
Brush on Cymb.
Vibr.
Harp
Pedal gliss.
VC.
arco
unis.
con sord.
625
Flutter
Hn. 1,3
Hn. 2
Tpt. 2
Tpt. 3
mollo
III. open
Sm. Dr.
Bongo

Fl. 1
Fl. 2
Ob. 1, 2
E H.
B♭ Cl. 1
B♭ Cl. 2
Al. Sax.
Hn. 1, 3
Hn. 2, 4
Tpt. 1
Trb. 1
Perc.
Harp
Piano
Vln. 1
Vln. 2
Viola
VC.
Bass
Flutter
632
With a Jazz feel
con sord.
cup mute
Vibr.
Sn. Dr.
Bongo
Brush on Cymb.
Pedal glss.
Tutti
cresc.

Fl. 1
Fl. 2
Ob. 1, 2
E.H.
B♭ Cl. 1
B♭ Cl. 2
Al. Sax.
Flutter
Hn. 1, 3
Hn. 2, 4
Tpt. 2
Trb. 1, 2
Trb. 3
open
II open
con sord.
Perc.
Vibr.
Tenor Dr.
Brush on Cymb.
Harp
Piano
Vln. 1
Vln. 2
Viola
VC.
Bass
senza sord.
pizz.

637
Picc.
Fl. 1, 2
Flutter
Tight
Ob. 1, 2
E.H.
B♭ Cl. 1
B♭ Cl. 2
Al. Sax.
Hn. 1, 3
Hn. 2, 4
Tpt. 1
Tpt. 2
Tight cup mute
Flutter
Trb. 1, 2
cresc.
molto
Trb. 3
Vibr.
Perc.
Bongo
Brush on Cymb.
Tenor Dr.
Harp
Piano
637
Vln. 1
Vln. 2
Viola
VC.
Bass
cresc.
molto

644
Picc.
Fl. 1
Fl. 2
Ob. 1,2
B♭ Cl. 1
B♭ Cl. 2
B. Cl.
Al. Sax.
Bn. 1
Hn. 1,3
Hn. 2,4
Tpt. 1
Trb. 1
Perc.
Vibr.
Bongo
Brush on Cymb.
Harp
Piano
644
Vln. 1
Vln. 2
Viola
VC.
Bass
arco
senza sord.
cresc.

Picc.
Fl. 1
Fl. 2
Ob. 1, 2
B♭ Cl. 1
B♭ Cl. 2
Al. Sax.
Bn. 1
Bn. 2
Hn. 1, 3
Hn. 2, 4
Tpt. 2
Tpt. 3
Trb. 1, 2
Trb. 3
Perc.
Vibr.
Xylo.
Bongo
Brush on Cymb.
Harp
Piano
Vln. 1
Vln. 2
Vla.
Vc.
Bass
Flutter
molto
div. pizz.

649
Picc.
Fl. 1
Ob. 1,2
E.H.
E♭Cl.
B♭Cl. 1,2
B. Cl.
Al. Sax.
Bn. 1
Bn. 2
Hn. 1,3
Hn. 2,4
Tpt. 1
Tpt. 2
Trb. 1,2
Trb. 3
Perc.
Vibr.
Bongo
Brush on Cymb.
Tenor Dr.
Piano
649
Vln. 1
Vln. 2
Vla.
Vc.
Bass
cresc.
molto
Flutter

Picc.
Fl. 1, 2
Ob. 1, 2
E.H.
E♭Cl.
B♭Cl. 1, 2
B. Cl.
Al. Sax.
Bn. 1, 2
Hn. 1, 3
Hn. 2, 4
Tpt. 1
Tpt. 2
Tpt. 3
Trb. 1, 2
Trb. 3
Perc.
Harp
Piano
Vln. 1
Vln. 2
Vla.
Vc.
Bass
656
cresc. sempre
con sord.
con sord. (str. mute)
Vibr.
Xylo.
Rim on Sn. Dr.
Brush on Cymb.
Sn. Dr.
Tmpe:
B.D.

Picc.
Fl. 1, 2
Ob. 1, 2
E. H.
E♭ Cl.
B♭ Cl. 1, 2
B. Cl.
Al. Sax.
Bn. 1, 2
Hn. 1, 3
Hn. 2, 4
Tpt. 1
Tpt. 2
Tpt. 3
Trb. 1, 2
Trb. 3
Perc.
Xylo.
Rim on Sn. Dr.
Trups: Sn. Dr.
B. Dr.
Sn. Drum
Harp
Piano
Vln. 1
Vln. 2
Vla.
Vc.
Bass
Flutter
div.

661
Picc.
Fl. 1, 2
Ob. 1, 2
E. H.
E♭Cl.
B♭Cl. 1, 2
B. Cl.
Al. Sax.
Bn. 1, 2
Hn. 1, 3
Hn. 2, 4
Tpt. 1
Tpt. 2
Tpt. 3
Trb. 1
Trb. 2, 3
Perc.
Rim
Trips.
Sn. Drum
Piano
661
Vln. 1
Vln. 2
Vla.
Vc.
Bass

666
Picc.
Fl. 1, 2
Ob. 1, 2
E.H.
E♭ Cl.
B♭ Cl. 1, 2
B. Cl.
Al. Sax.
Bn. 1, 2
Hn. 1, 3
Hn. 2, 4
Tpt. 1
Tpt. 2, 3
Trb. 1
Trb. 2, 3
Tuba
open
Xyl.
Bs. Dr.
Perc.
(Trap.)
add Cymb.
Solo Jazz break (Traps.)
Piano
666
Vln. 1
Vln. 2
Vla.
Vc.
Bass

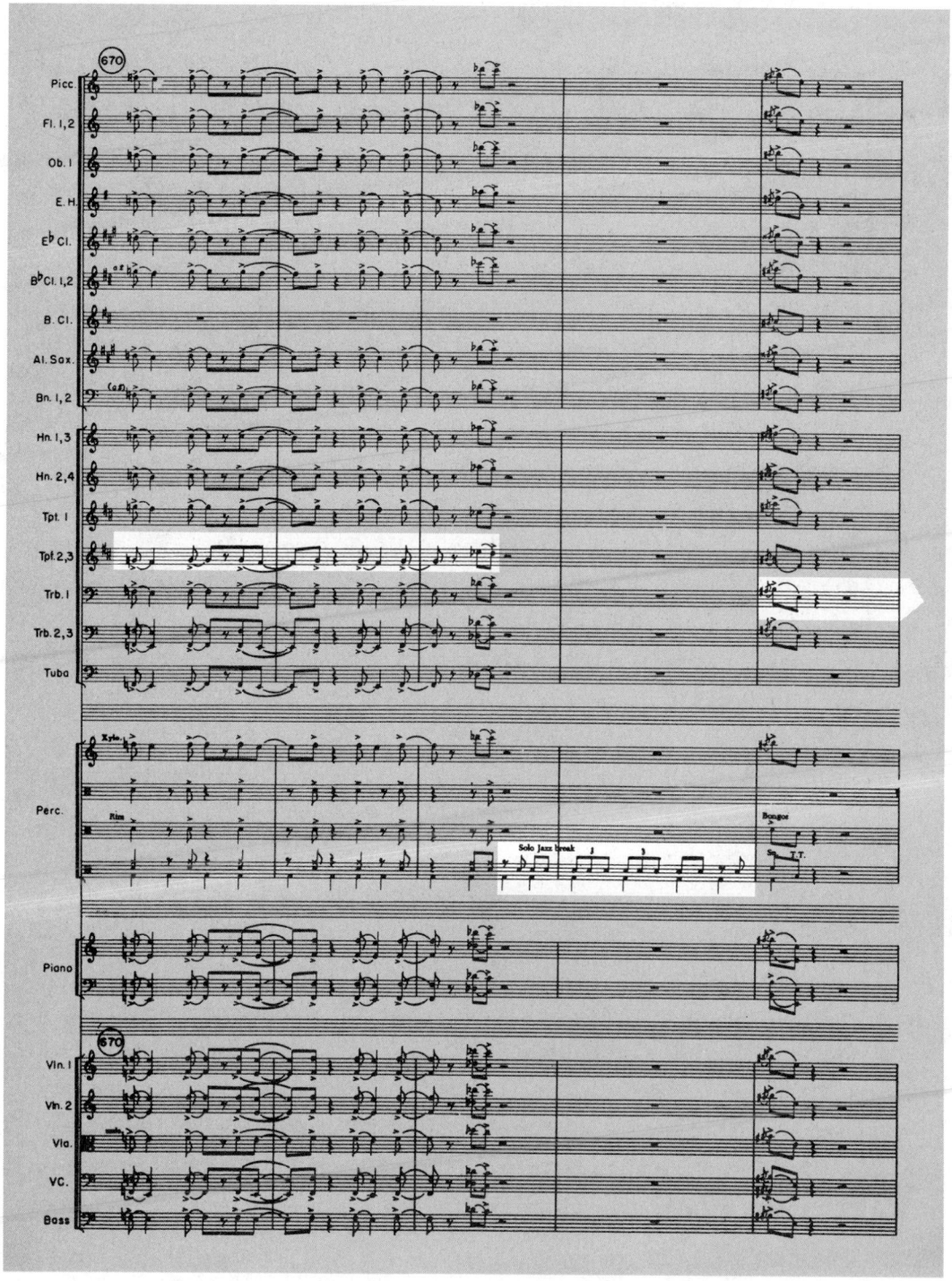
670
Picc
Fl. 1,2
Ob. 1
E. H.
E♭ Cl.
B♭ Cl. 1,2
B. Cl.
Al. Sax.
Bn. 1,2
Hn. 1,3
Hn. 2,4
Tpt. 1
Tpt. 2,3
Trb. 1
Trb. 2,3
Tuba
Xyl.
Perc.
Rim
Solo Jazz break
Bongos
Sm. T.T.
Piano
670
Vln. 1
Vln. 2
Vla.
Vc.
Bass

676
Picc.
Fl. 1, 2
Ob. 1, 2
E. H.
E♭ Cl.
B♭ Cl. 1, 2
B. Cl.
Al. Sax.
Bn. 1, 2
C-Bn.
Hn. 1, 3
Hn. 2, 4
Tpt. 1
Tpt. 2, 3
Trb. 1
Trb. 2, 3
Tuba
Xylo.
Sn. Dr.
Perc.
Bongos
2 Pitches
3 Pitches
Toms-Toms
Piano
676
Vln. 1
Vln. 2
Vla.
Vc.
Bass

681
Picc.
Fl. 1, 2
Ob. 1, 2
E.H.
E♭ Cl.
B♭ Cl. 1, 2
B. Cl.
Al. Sax.
Bn. 1, 2
Hn. 1, 3
Hn. 2, 4
Tpt. 1
Tpt. 2, 3
Trb. 1
Trb. 2, 3
Tuba
Perc.
Xylo.
Sn. Dr.
(ord.)
R.S.
Bongos
Cym.
Tom-Toms
Tim.
Sn. Drum
Piano
681
Vln. 1
Vln. 2
Vla.
Vc.
Bass
div.

23
39
685
690
Picc.
Fl. 1, 2
Ob. 1, 2
E. H.
E♭ Cl.
B♭ Cl. 1, 2
B. Cl.
Al. Sax.
Bn. 1, 2
C-Bn.
Hn. 1, 3
Hn. 2, 4
Tpt. 1
Tpt. 2, 3
Trb. 1
Trb. 2, 3
Tuba
Perc.
Timp.
Bongos
Sn. Dr. Jazz
Bass Dr.
Tom-Toms
Sn.
Vibr.
Hi-Hat
Sn. Drum
Harp
Piano
Vln. 1
Vln. 2
Vla.
Vc.
Bass

694
Picc.
Fl. 1, 2
Ob. 1, 2
E. H.
E♭ Cl.
B♭ Cl. 1, 2
B. Cl.
Al. Sax.
Bn. 1, 2
C-Bn.
Hn. 1, 3
Hn. 2, 4
Tpt. 1
Tpt. 2, 3
Trb. 1
Trb. 2, 3
Tuba
Timp.
Perc.
Vibr.
Hi-Hat
Sm. Dr.
Tenor Dr.
B. Drum
Harp
Piano
Vln. 1
Vln. 2
Vla.
Vc.
Bass
694

Picc.
Fl. 1, 2
Ob. 1, 2
E.H.
E♭ Cl.
B♭ Cl. 1, 2
B. Cl.
Al. Sax.
Bn. 1, 2
C-Bn.
Hn. 1, 3
Hn. 2, 4
Tpt. 1
Tpt. 2, 3
Trb. 1
Trb. 2, 3
Tuba
Perc.
Vibr.
Timp.
Bongos
Hi-Hat
Bass Dr.
Sn. Dr.
Piano
To Harp
Harp
Vln. 1
Vln. 2
Vla.
VC.
Bass
702
unis.
pizz.
arco
Soli
dim. molto

706
Picc.
Fl. 1
Fl. 2
Ob. 1, 2
E. H.
E♭ Cl.
B♭ Cl. 1, 2
B. Cl.
Al. Sax.
Bn. 1, 2
C-Bn.
Hn. 1, 3
Hn. 2, 4
Tpt. 1
Tpt. 2, 3
Trb. 1, 2
Trb. 3
Tuba
Perc.
Vibr.
Harp
Celesta
706
3 Solo Vla.
3 Soli
1
VC.
2
Bass
arco
pizz.
arco Tutti

710
Picc.
Fl. 1
Fl. 2
Ob. 1, 2
E.H.
E♭ Cl.
B♭ Cl. 1, 2
B. Cl.
Al. Sax
Bn. 1, 2
C-Bn.
Hn. 1, 3
Hn. 2, 4
Tpt. 1
Tpt. 2, 3
Trb. 1, 2
Trb. 3
Tuba
Vibr.
Perc
Sn. Dr.
Bass Dr.
Bongo
Hi-Hat
Celesta
710
Vln. 1
Vln. 2
Vla.
VC.
Bass
Tutti arco
Tutti
arco
pizz.
1. pizz.
ff sempre

716
Picc.
Fl. I
B.Cl.
Al. Sax.
Bn. I
Perc.
Vibr.
Xylo.
Harp
Piano
Vln. I
Vln. 2
VC.
Bass
2 players
721
Snap fingers
2 Pitched Drs.
marcato

24
40
Molto allegro
727
733
Picc
Fl. 1, 2
Ob. 1, 2
E.H.
E♭Cl.
B♭Cl. 1, 2
B. Cl.
Al. Sax.
Bn. 1, 2
C-Bn.
Hn. 1, 3
Hn. 2, 4
Tpt. 1, 2
Tpt. 3
Trb. 1, 2
Trb. 3
Tuba
Perc.
Vibr.
Timp.
Cymb.
B. Drum
Xylo.
SUSP. CYM.
3 Pitches
Sn. Dr.
Harp
Piano
Molto allegro
Vln. 1
Vln. 2
Vla.
VC.
Bass
ff subito
marcato
arco
div.

Picc.
Fl. 1, 2
Ob. 1, 2
E.H.
E♭ Cl.
B♭ Cl. 1, 2
B. Cl.
Al. Sax.
Bn. 1, 2
C-Bn.
Hn. 1, 3
Hn. 2, 4
Tpt. 1, 2
Tpt. 3
Trb. 1, 2
Trb. 3
Tuba
Perc.
Xylo.
Cymb.
3 Pitches
Timp.
Bass Dr.
Harp.
Piano
Vln. 1
Vln. 2
Vla.
VC. 1
VC. 2
Bass
737
737
II. senza sord.

743
Picc.
Fl. 1, 2
Ob. 1, 2
E.H.
E♭ Cl.
B♭ Cl. 1, 2
Al. Sax.
Bn. 1, 2
C-Bn.
Hn. 1, 3
Hn. 2, 4
Tpt. 1, 2
Tpt. 3
Trb. 1
Trb. 2
con sord.
cuivré
glissando
Xylo.
Timp.
Perc.
Cymb.
3 Pitches
Sn. Dr.
Harp
Piano
marcato
743
Vln. 1
Vln. 2
Vla.
Vc.
Bass
div.

750
756
Picc.
Fl. 1, 2
Ob. 1, 2
E♭ Cl.
B♭ Cl. 1, 2
Bn. 1, 2
Hn. 1, 3
Hn. 2, 4
Tpt. 1
Tpt. 2
Tpt. 3
Trb. 1
Trb. 2
Trb. 3
Tuba
Perc.
Timp.
Sn. Drum
Piano
Vln. 1
Vln. 2
Vla.
Vc.
Bass
con sord.
1. Solo
glissando
senza sord.
cresc.

760
Picc.
Fl. 1, 2
Ob. 1, 2
E. H.
E♭ Cl.
B♭ Cl. 1, 2
B. Cl.
Al. Sax.
Bn. 1, 2
C-Bn.
Hn. 1, 3
Hn. 2, 4
Tpt. 1
Tpt. 2
Tpt. 3
Trb. 1
Trb. 2
Trb. 3
Perc.
Timp.
Sn. Drum
Xylo.
Rim
Harp
Piano
Vln. 1
Vln. 2
Vla.
Vc.
Bass
pizz.
senza sord.
con sord.

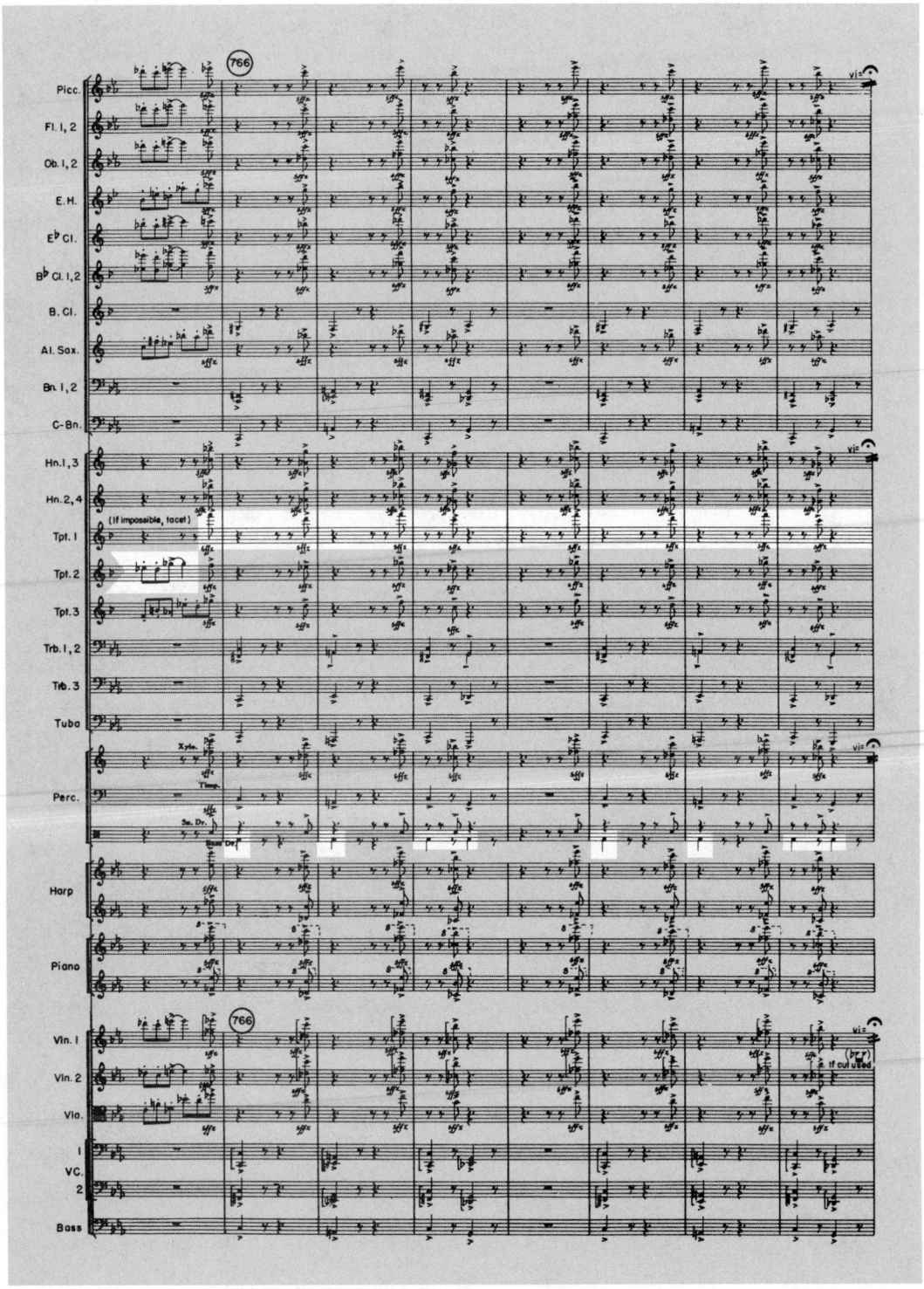
766
Picc.
Fl. 1, 2
Ob. 1, 2
E.H.
E♭ Cl.
B♭ Cl. 1, 2
B. Cl.
Al. Sax.
Bn. 1, 2
C-Bn.
Hn. 1, 3
Hn. 2, 4
(If impossible, tacet)
Tpt. 1
Tpt. 2
Tpt. 3
Trb. 1, 2
Trb. 3
Tuba
Xylo.
Timp.
Perc.
Sm. Dr.
Bass Dr.
Harp
Piano
766
Vln. 1
Vln. 2
Vla.
1
Vc.
2
Bass
vis
(harp)
If cut sized

773
780
B♭ Cl. 1
Bn. 1
Solo
pp
tempre staccato
Perc.
Wood Block
Cymb.
Tamb.
Vln. 1
Vln. 2
Vla.
Vc.
pizz.
785
Picc.
B♭ Cl. 2
B. Cl.
Bn. 2
cresc. poco a poco
mf
cresc.
Hn.
1
2
Xylo.
Perc.
Vln. 1
Vln. 2
Vla.
Vc.

793
Picc.
Fl. 1
Fl. 2
Ob. 1
Ob. 2
E.H.
E♭ Cl.
B♭ Cl. 1
B♭ Cl. 2
B. Cl.
Al. Sax.
Bn. 1, 2
Hn. 1, 3
Hn. 2, 4
Tpt. 1
Tpt. 2, 3
Trb. 1
Trb. 2
Perc.
Xylo.
Sn. Drum
Harp
Piano
Vln. 1
Vln. 2
Vla.
Vc.

798
803
Picc.
Fl. 1
Fl. 2
Ob. 1
Ob. 2
E. H.
E♭ Cl.
B♭ Cl. 1
B♭ Cl. 2
B. Cl.
Al. Sax.
Bn. 1
Bn. 2
Hn. 1,3
Hn. 2,4
Tpt. 1
Tpt. 2,3
Trb. 1,2
Trb. 3
Perc.
Xylo.
Sn. Dr.
Rim shot
Cymb.
Piano
Solo
Vln. 1
Vln. 2
Vla.
Vc.
Bass

808
Picc.
Fl. 1, 2
Ob. 1, 2
E. H.
E♭ Cl.
B♭ Cl. 1, 2
B. Cl.
Al. Sax.
Bn. 1, 2
cresc. molto
glissando
molto
Hn. 1, 3
Hn. 2, 4
Tpt. 1
Tpt. 2
Tpt. 3
Trb. 1, 2
(approximately 3 bars long)
Perc.
Xylo.
Bongos
Piano
cresc.
L.H. loco
Vln. 1
Vln. 2
Vla.
Vc.
Bass
808

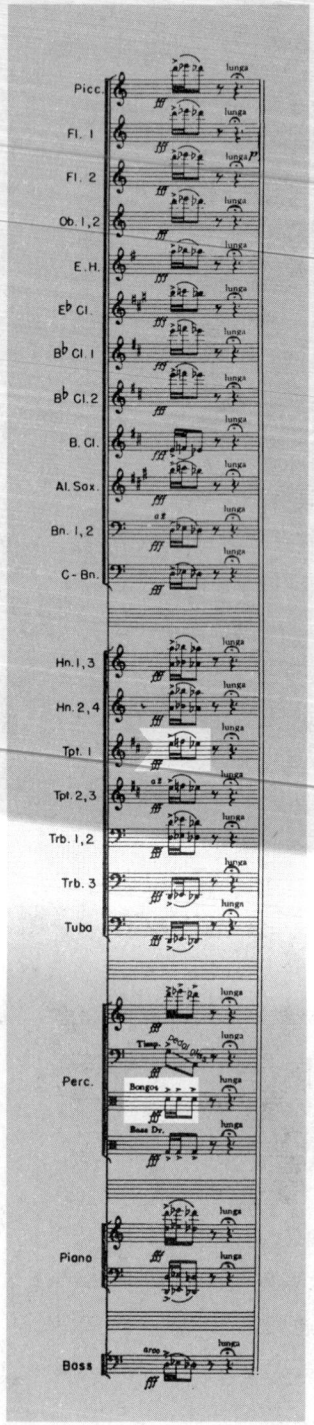
Picc.
Fl. 1
Fl. 2
Ob. 1, 2
E.H.
E♭ Cl.
B♭ Cl. 1
B♭ Cl. 2
B. Cl.
Al. Sax.
Bn. 1, 2
C-Bn.
Hn. 1, 3
Hn. 2, 4
Tpt. 1
Tpt. 2, 3
Trb. 1, 2
Trb. 3
Tuba
Perc.
Timp.
Bongos
Bass Dr.
Piano
Bass
arco
lunga

39. György Ligeti (b. 1923)

Désordre (Disorder) from Etudes for Piano, Book I (1985)

8:8A/8 — 8:8/25 - 27

3:3B/7 — 3:3/49 - 51

Composer's directions: Use the pedal very discreetly throughout the entire piece.

© *B. Schott's Soehne, Mainz, 1986. All rights reserved. Used by permission of European American Music Distributors Corporation, sole U.S. and Canadian agent for the publishers B. Schott's Soehne, Mainz.*

26
50

8bassa
crescendo poco a poco
8bassa
8va
fff più crescendo
8bassa
27
51
8va
fff crescendo molto
8bassa
Ped.
poco
simile
simile
simile
simile
mf
fff sub.
fff

Composer's directions:

*Dynamic balance: the right hand should play somewhat louder than the left, so that the accented chords in both hands sound equally loud (until the end of the piece).

Gradually add more pedal (but always sparingly).

*Gradual crescendo (until the end): the accents gradually become *ff*, then *fff* (with the right hand constantly louder), the eighth notes gradually *mp*, then *mf*.

8va
8va
8va
8va
8va
8va

40. Pierre Boulez (b. 1925)

8:8A/9 8:8/28 - 30

Le marteau sans maître (The Hammer Without a Master), Nos. 1, 3, 7 (1953–54; revised 1957)

1. *Avant "L'artisanat furieux" (Before "Furious Artisans")*

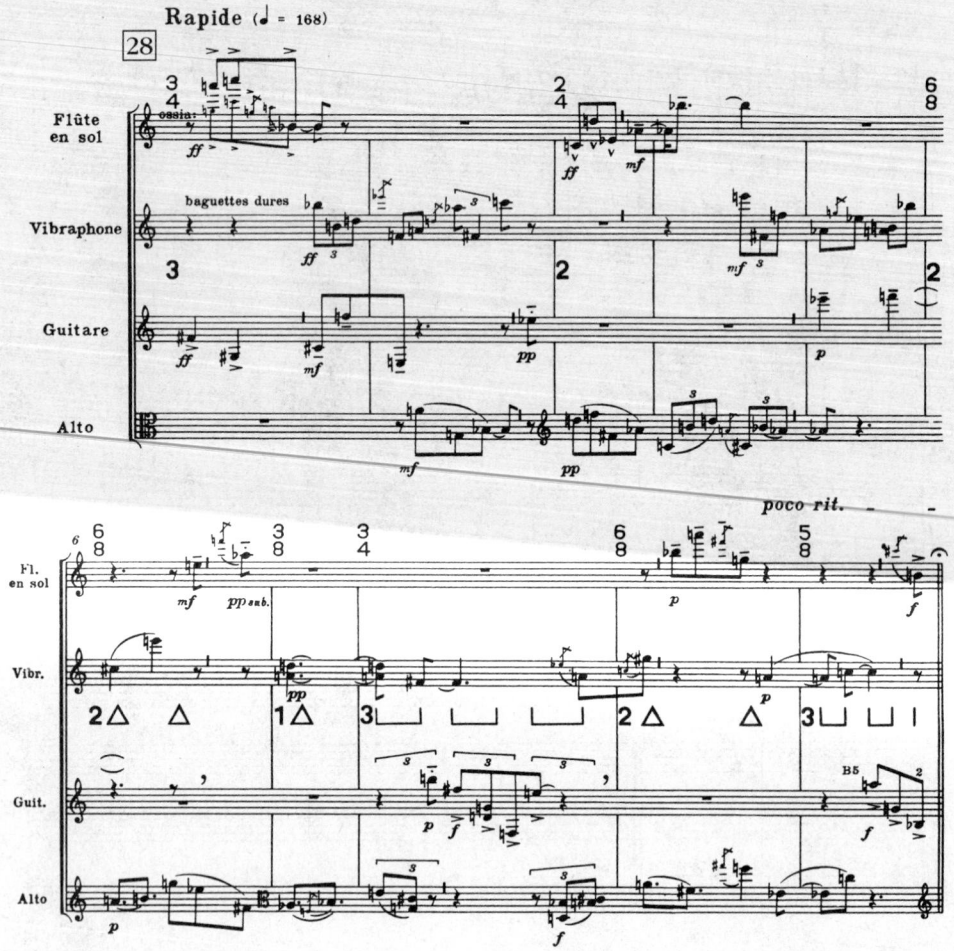

© Copyright 1954 by Universal Edition (London) Ltd., London. Final version: © copyright 1957 by Universal Edition (London) Ltd., London. © Copyrights renewed. Poèmes de René Char. © Copyright 1964 by Jose Corti Editeur, Paris. © Copyright renewed. All rights reserved. Used by permission of European American Music Distributors Corporation, sole U.S. and Canadian agent for Universal Edition (London) Ltd., London.

a tempo
11
Fl. en sol
Vibr.
Guit.
Alto
pizz.
arco
B 10
poco rit.
a tempo
17
p sub.
24
pour 4

presser - - - a tempo
Fl. en sol
Vibr.
Guit.
Alto
arco
pizz.
pour 4
pour 6
poco rit.
a tempo
cresc.

46
Fl. en sol
Vibr.
Guit.
Alto
presser
pour 4
pp sub.
arco
a tempo
53
pour 6
pizz.
f sub.
59
(pizz.)
p sub.
pp sub.

poco rit.
a tempo
Fl. en sol
Vibr.
Guit.
Alto
pour 6
pizz.
arco
poco rit.

a tempo
presser - - - - a tempo
Fl. en sol
Vibr.
Guit.
Alto
pizz.
arco
poco rit. a tempo
pour 4
presser - - - - a tempo - poco rit.
a tempo
presser
ff sub.
p sub.
arrêt assez court

3. *L'artisanat furieux (Furious Artisans)*

Fl. en sol
Voix
ca - da - vre dans le pa - nier
(♩ = 84)(♩. = 56)
(♩ = 126)
(♩. = 56) (♩ = 84)
senza dim.
cresc. al
tenuto senza dim.
Flzg.
Et che-vaux de
la - bours dans le fer à

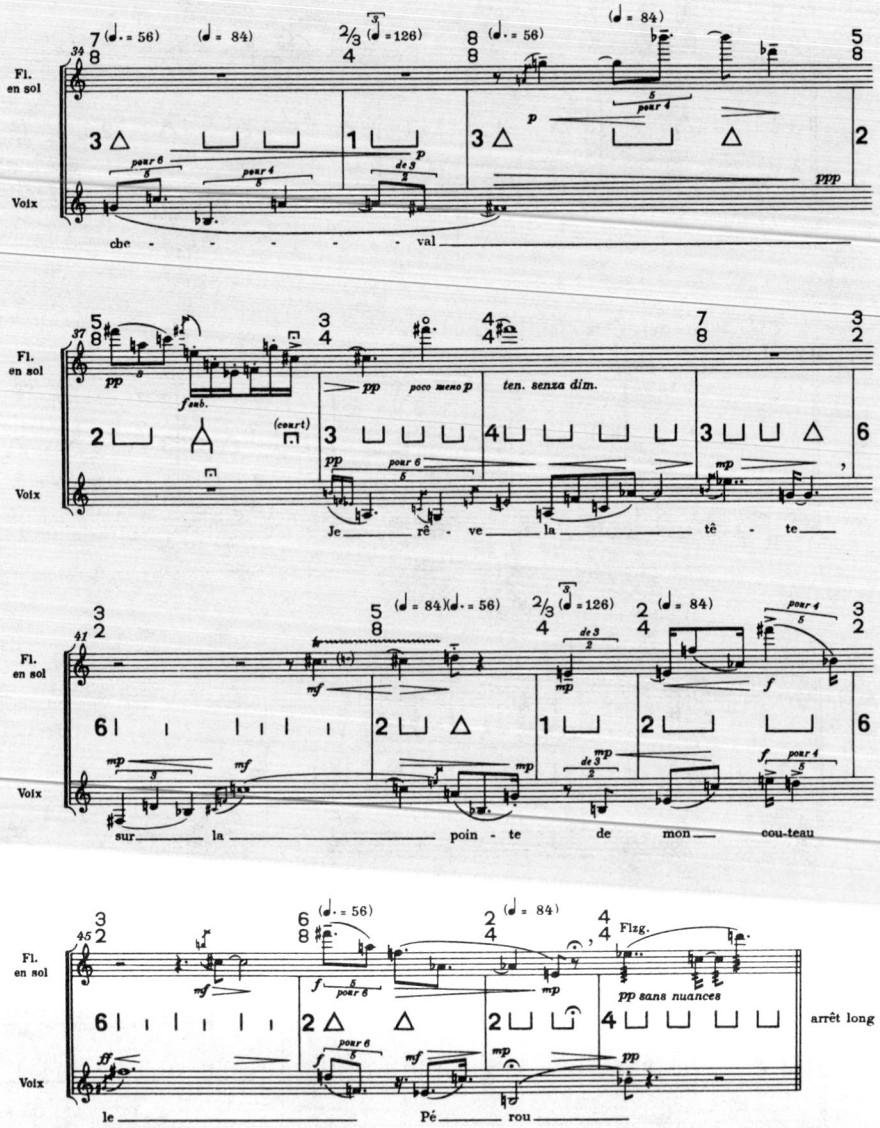

TEXT AND TRANSLATION

La roulotte rouge au bord du clou
Et cadavre dans le panier
Et chevaux de labours dans le fer à cheval
Je rêve la tête sur la pointe de mon couteau le Pérou

The red caravan at the prison's edge
And a corpse in the basket
And the work horses in the horseshoe
I dream of Peru with my head on the point of my knife

7. *Après "L'artisanat furieux"* (*After "Furious Artisans"*)

sempre accelerando
cédez
Fl. en sol
Vibr.
Guit.
(♩ = 208)
accelerando
molto
A tempo subito (♩ = 168)
très court
sempre ff
pour 4
sec
accelerando
pour 6
sempre f

(♩ = 208)
(♩. = 138)
beaucoup plus vif
poco rit.
accelerando
revenir au Tempo
Fl. en sol
Vibr.
Guit.
rit.
Tempo
più ritard.
accele
court
rando
poco a poco
accele
ff sempre
pp sub.
f sempre
(non accentué)

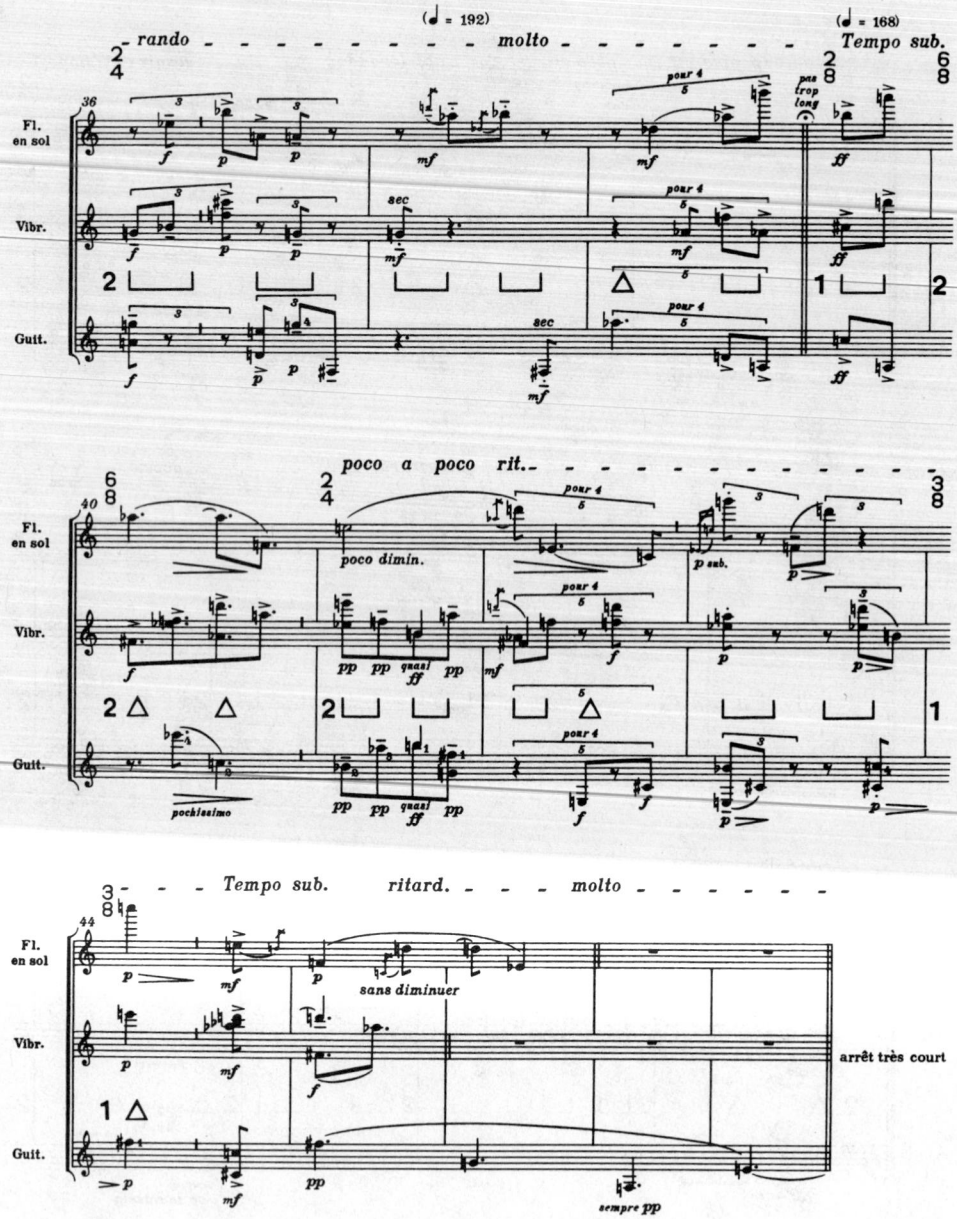
(♩ = 192)
(♩ = 168)
rando
molto
Tempo sub.
Fl. en sol
Vibr.
Guit.
pas trop long
sec
pour 4
poco a poco rit.
poco dimin.
p sub.
pp
quasi ff
pochissimo
Tempo sub.
ritard.
molto
sans diminuer
arrêt très court
sempre pp

41. *George Crumb (b. 1929)*

Ancient Voices of Children, First Movement: *El niño busca su voz* (1970)

8:8B/1 — 8:8/31 - 33

3:3B/6 — 3:3/46 - 48

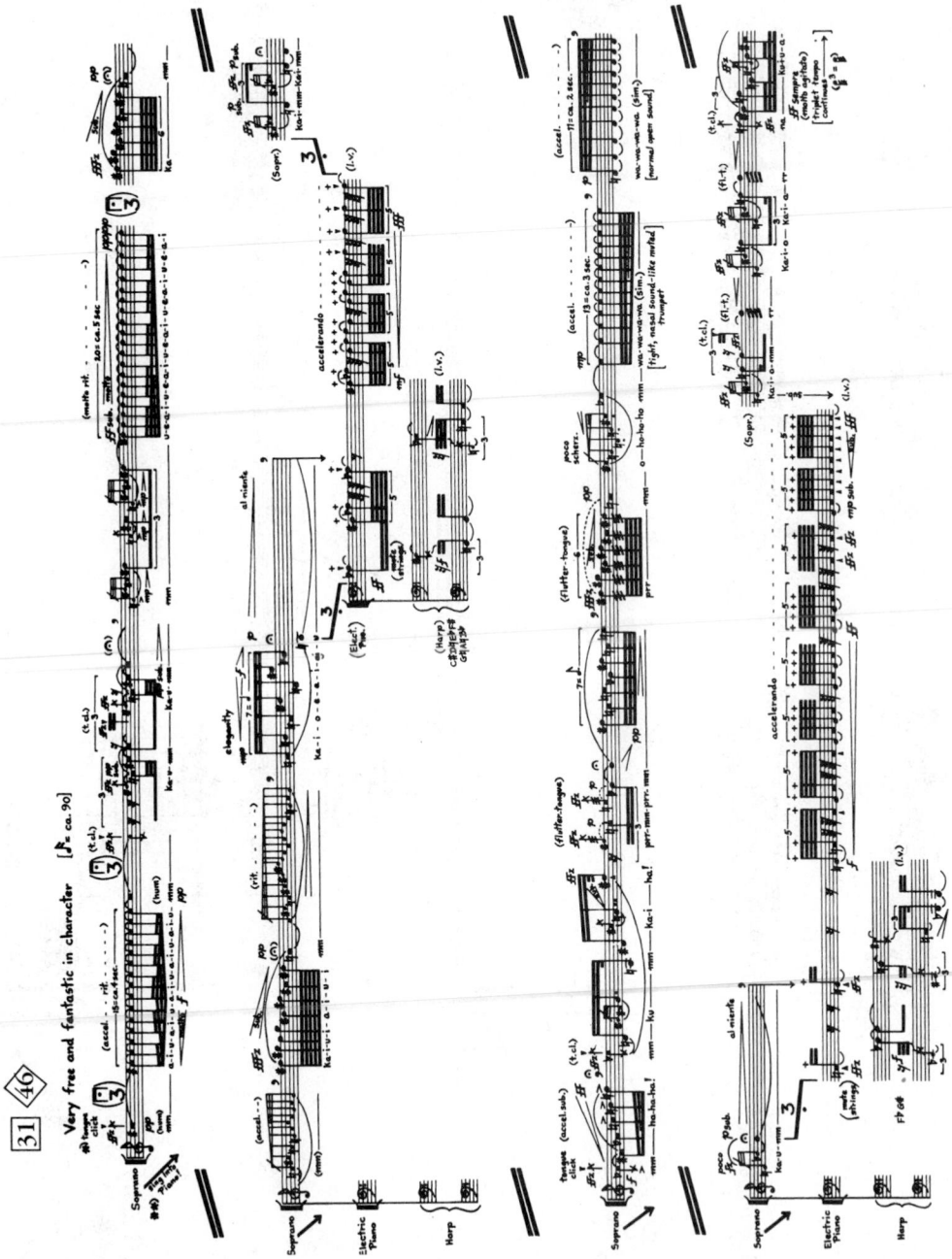

Copyright © 1970 by C. F. Peters Corporation, 373 Park Avenue South, New York, NY 10016. Reprinted with permission of the publishers who published the score of the complete work under Peters Edition No. 66303.

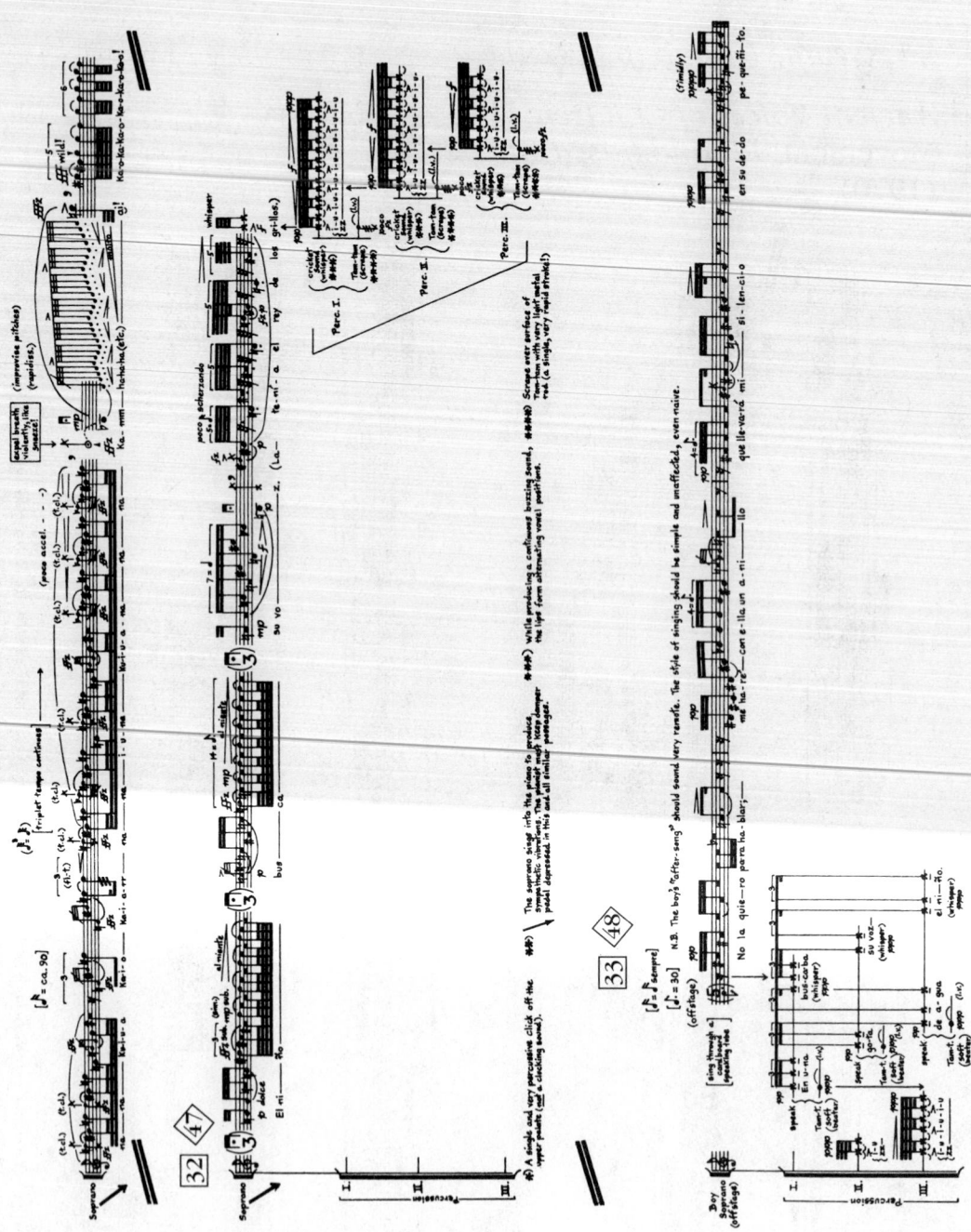
32
47
33
48
Soprano
Boy Soprano (offstage)
Percussion
Perc. I.
Perc. II.
Perc. III.
(improvise pitches)
(repeatless)
equal breath violently, like sneeze!
triplet tempo continues
(poco accel. - - - -)
(r.d.)
(f.d.)
[♩. = ca. 90]
Ka-i-a-ra
Ka-i-a-ra
Ka-o-ka-ka-o-ka-o-ka-o-ka!
wild!
Ka-ra-ra
Ka-ra-ra
Ka-i-a-ra
Ka-i-a-ra
Ka-i-a

TEXT AND TRANSLATION

El niño busca su voz.
(La tenía el rey de los grillos.)
En una gota de agua
buscaba su voz el niño.

No la quiero para hablar;
me haré con ella un anillo
que llevará mi silencio
en su dedo pequeñito.

The little boy is looking for his voice.
(The king of the crickets had it.)
In a drop of water
the little boy looked for his voice.

I don't want it to speak with;
I will make a ring of it
so that he may wear my silence
on his little finger.

FEDERICO GARCÍA LORCA

Translated by W. S. Merwin

42. Joan Tower (b. 1938)

Petroushskates (1980)

8:8B/2 8:8/34 - 37

3:3B/9 3:3/55 - 58

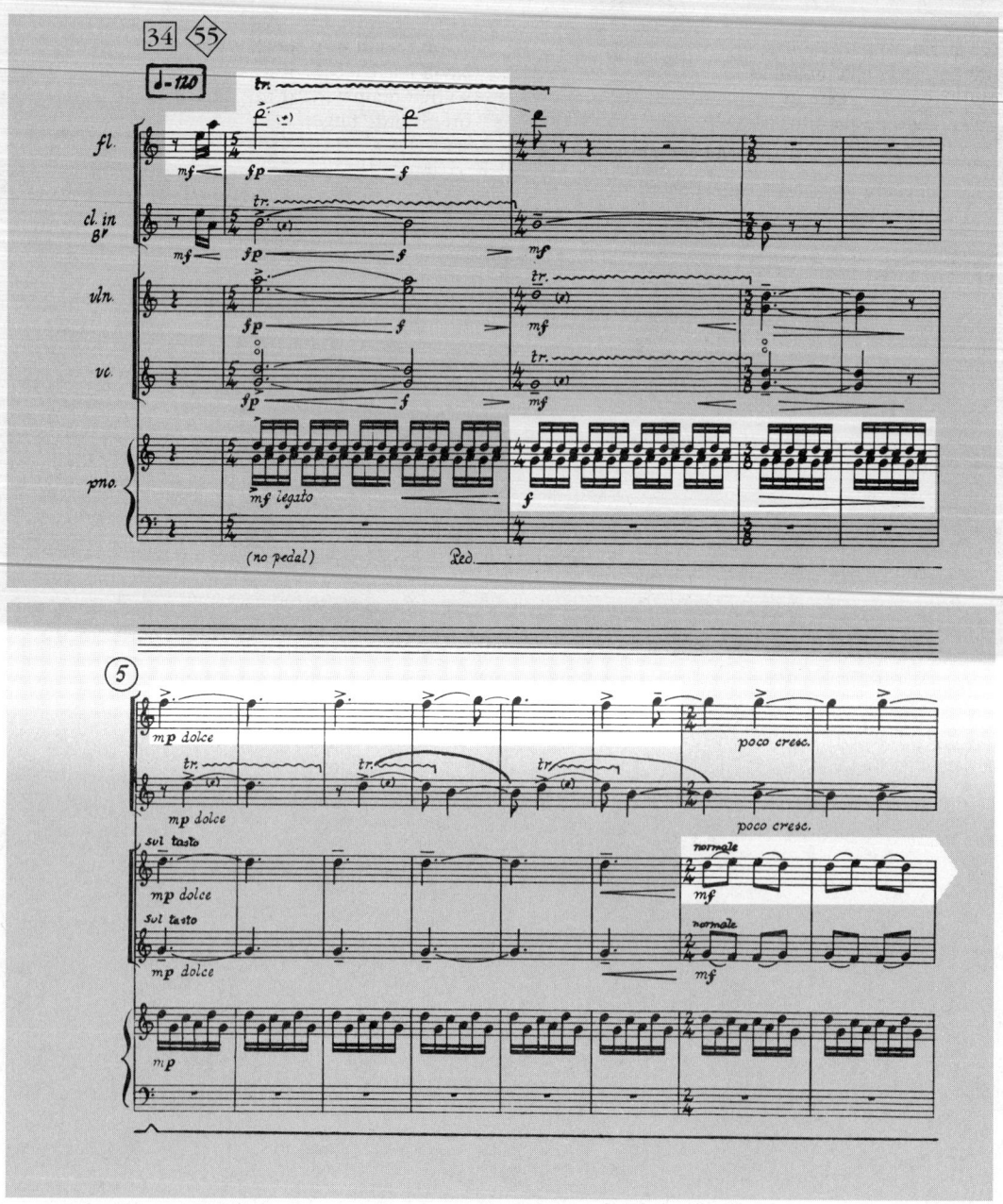

Copyright © 1983 (renewed) by Associated Music Publishers, Inc. (BMI). International copyright secured. All rights reserved. Reprinted by permission.

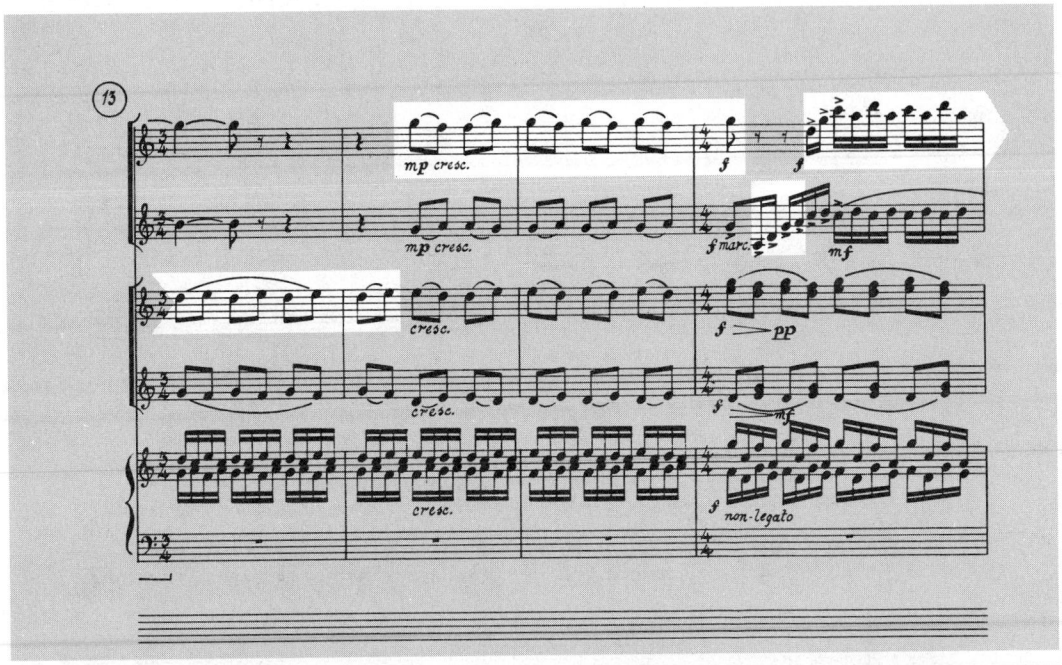
13
mp cresc.
mp cresc.
f
f
f marc.
mf
cresc.
cresc.
f
pp
f
mf
cresc.
f
non-legato

17
cresc.
cresc.

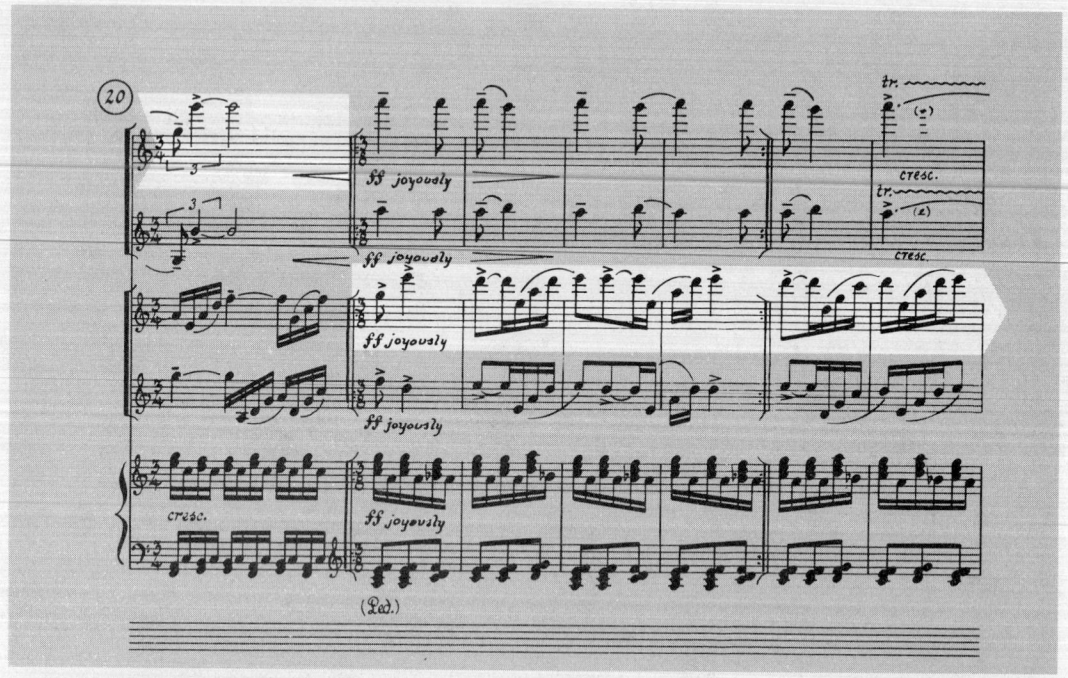
20
tr.
cresc.
ff joyously
ff joyously
ff joyously
ff joyously
ff joyously
cresc.
(Ped.)

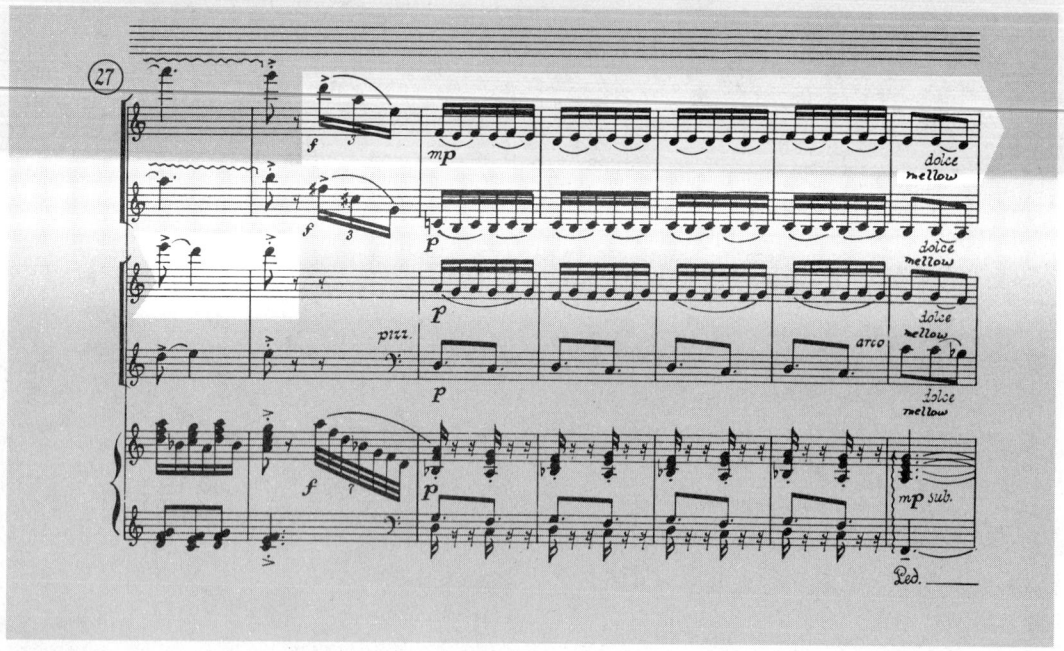
27
f
mp
dolce
mellow
p
pizz.
arco
mp sub.
Ped.

34
Rit.
Rit.
tr.
mp
Rit
p
pizz.
arco
Rit.
mp
dim.
Rit.
dim.
p
(Ped.)
mf
35
56
40
ca. ♩ = 40 (♩ = 80)
5:4
pp dolce
pp
mf
pp dolce singing
pp dolce
pizz.
pp dolce
ppp dolce
pp dolce

43
cresc. poco

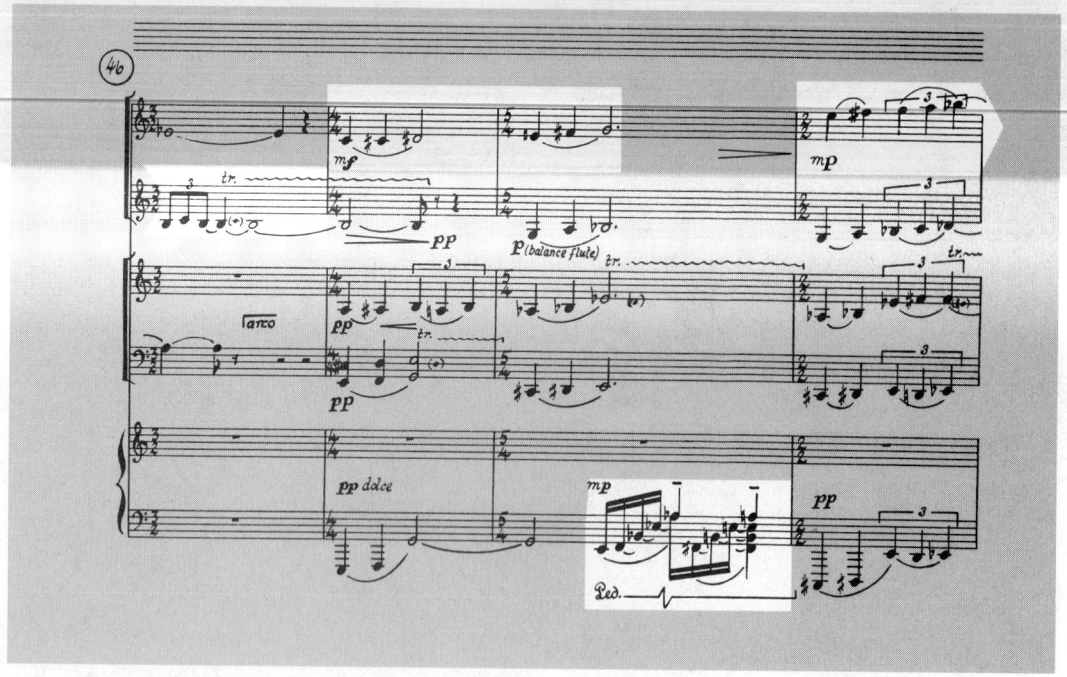
46
tr.
mf
pp
p (balance flute)
mp
arco
pp dolce
Ped.

50
Rit. poco
tr.
cresc.
Ped.

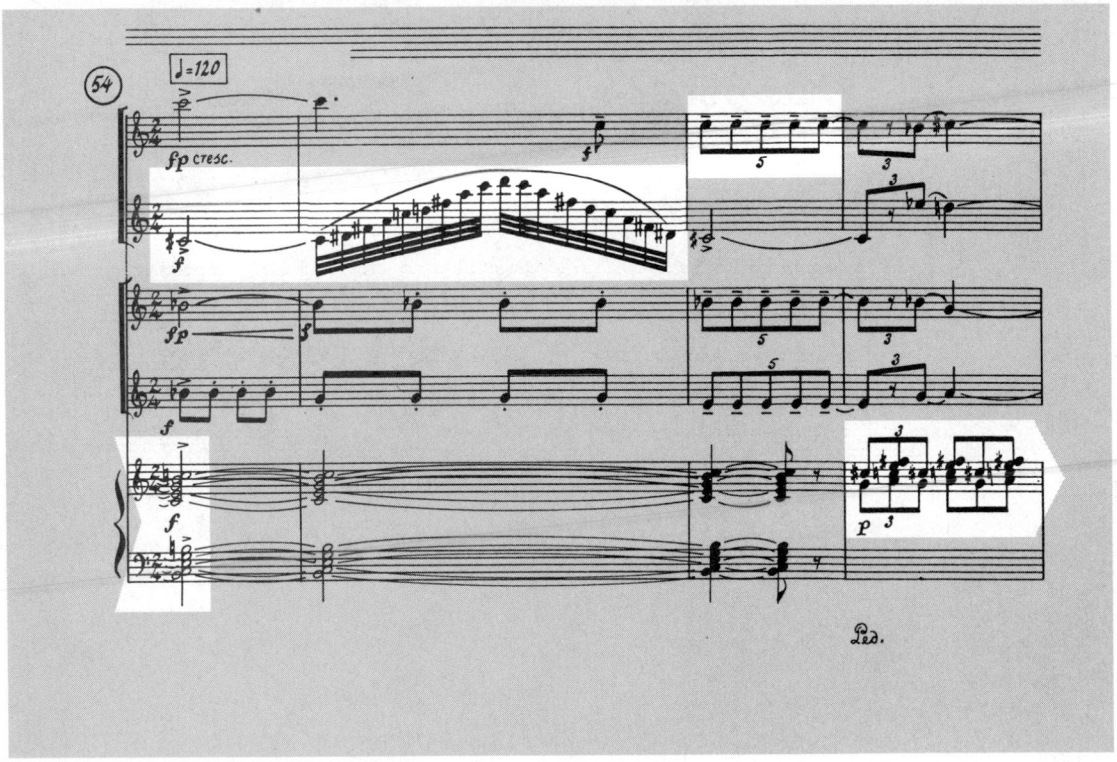
54
♩=120
fp cresc.
f
p
Ped.

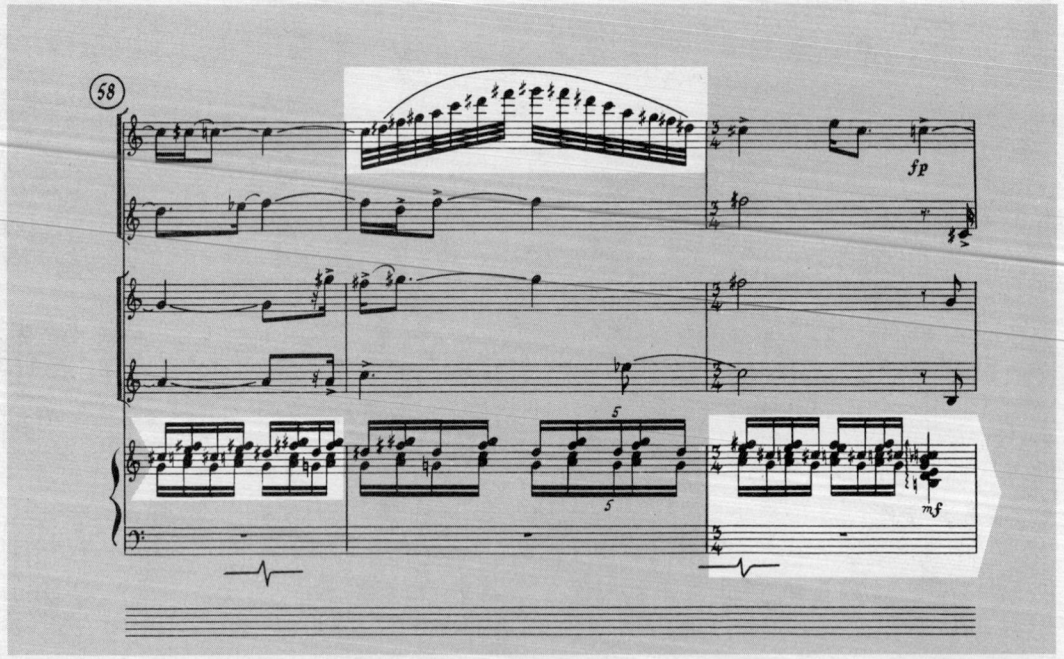
58
fp
mf

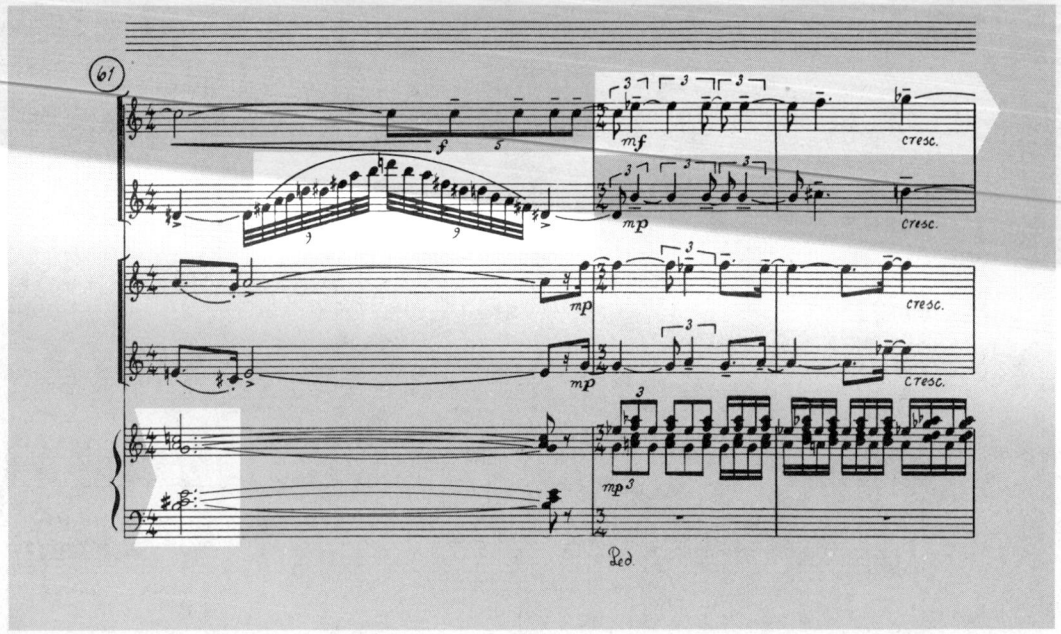
61
mf
cresc.
mp
cresc.
mp
cresc.
mp
cresc.
mp
Ped.

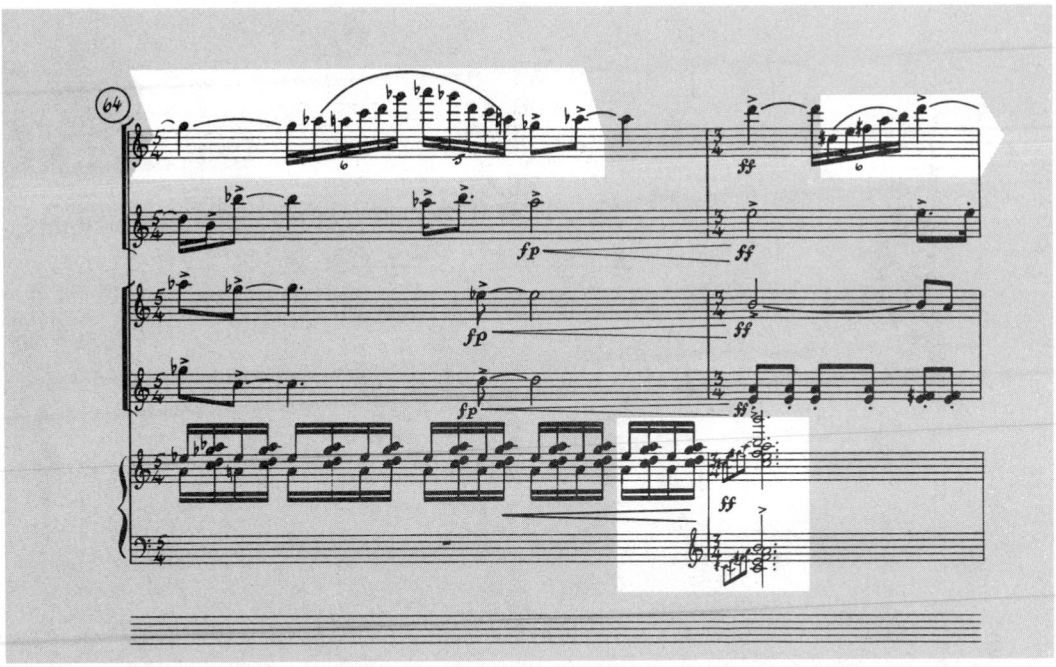
64
fp
ff
fp
ff
fp
ff
ff

66
p sub
p sub
p sub.
p sub.
mp
dim. molto
pp
Ped.

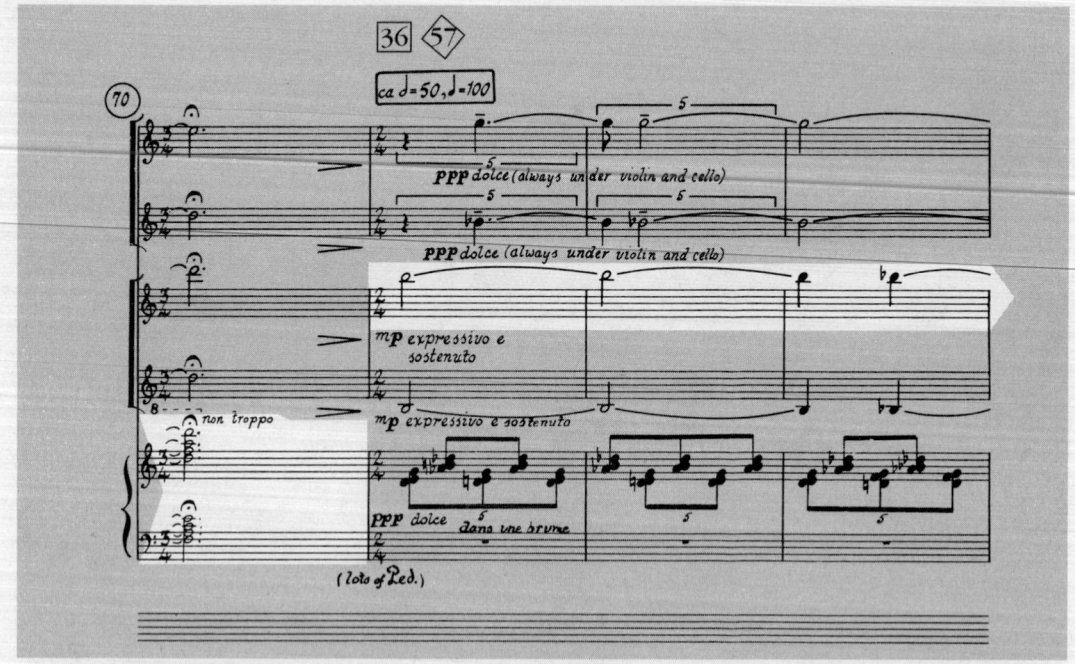
36
57
ca ♩=50, ♩=100
70
ppp dolce (always under violin and cello)
ppp dolce (always under violin and cello)
mp expressivo e sostenuto
mp expressivo e sostenuto
non troppo
ppp dolce dans une brume
(lots of Ped.)

74

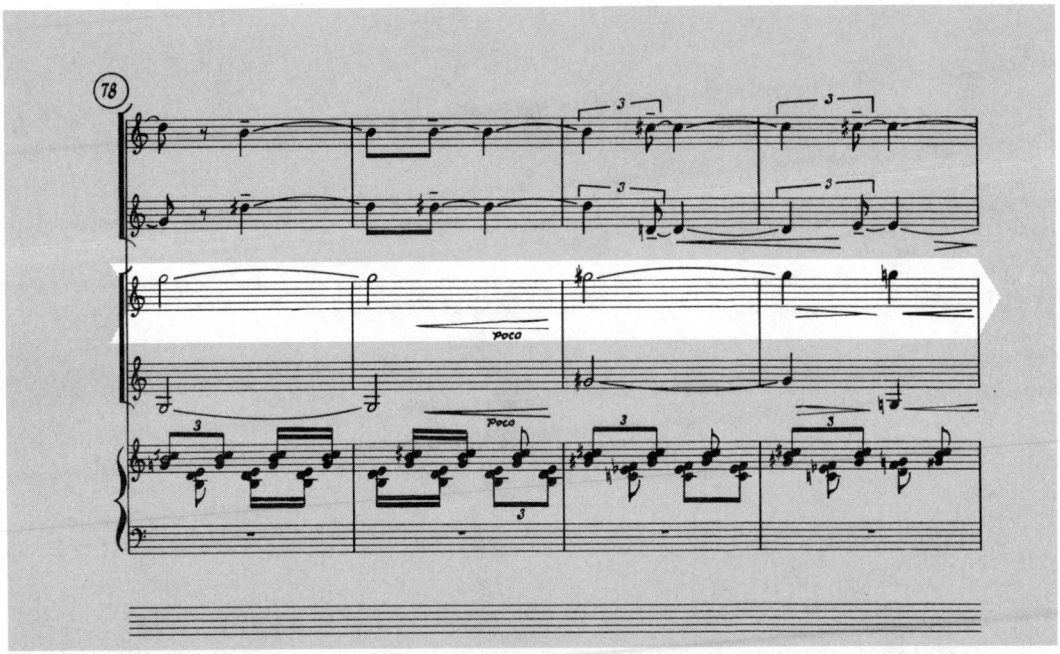
78
poco
poco

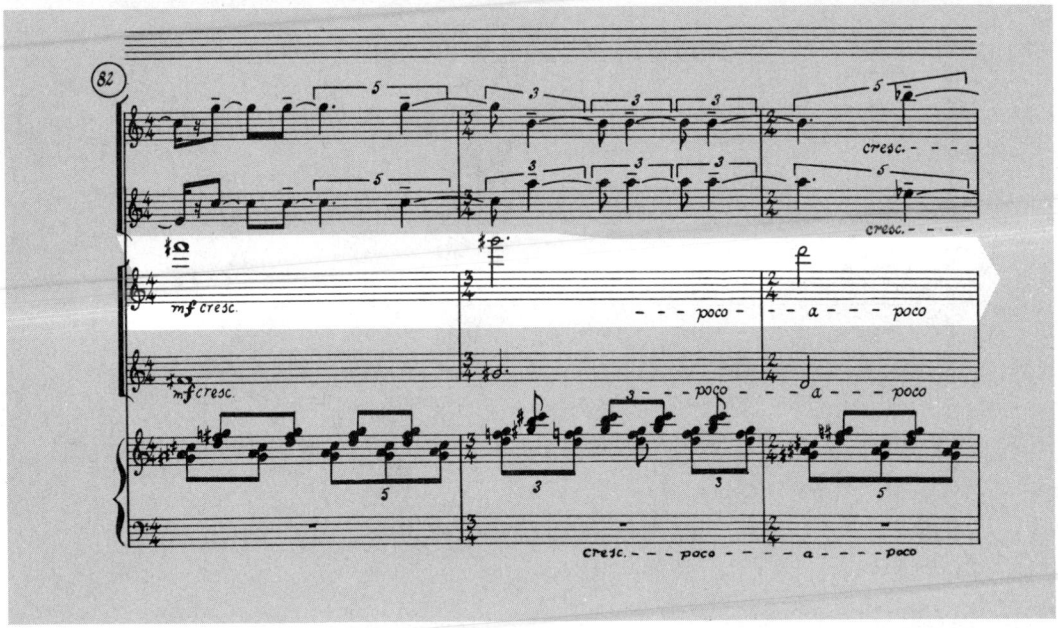
82
cresc.
cresc.
mf cresc.
poco a poco
mf cresc.
poco a poco
cresc. poco a poco

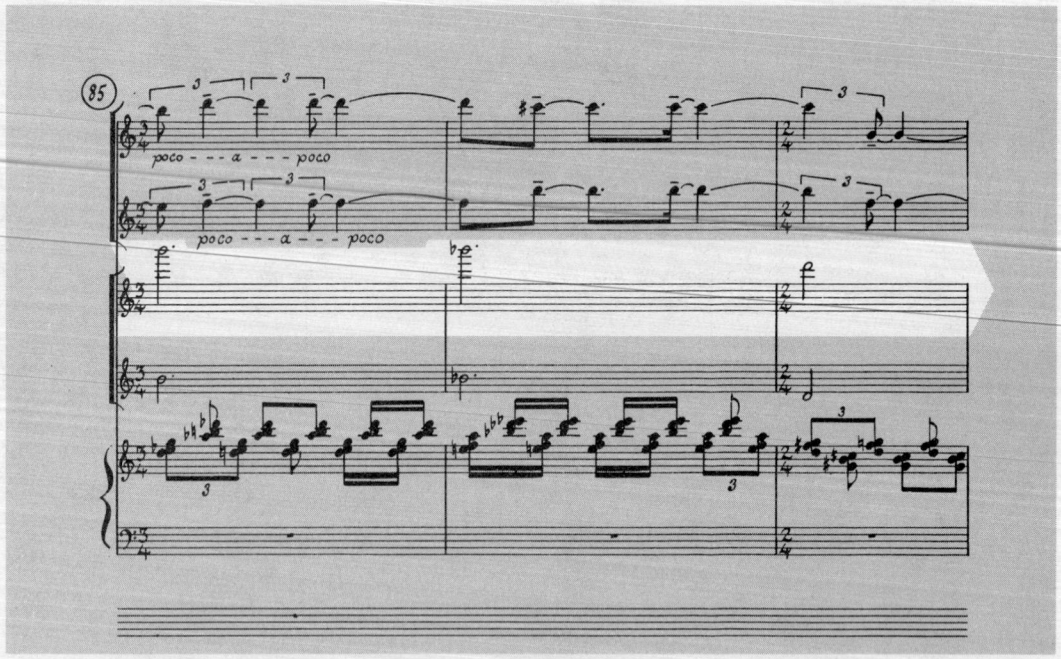
85
poco - - - a - - - poco
poco - - - a - - - poco

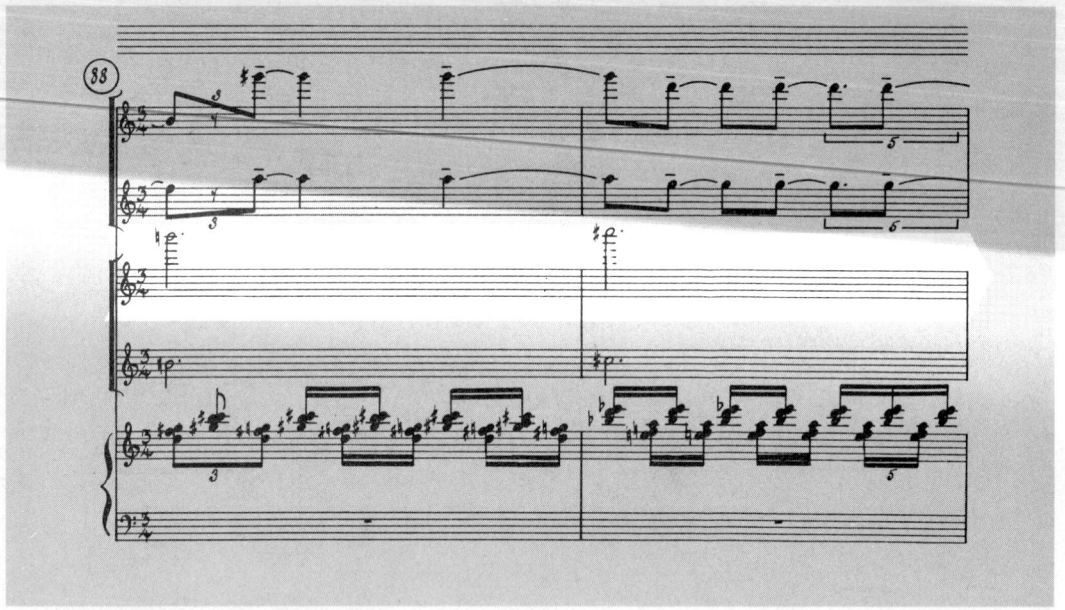
88

90
accel. poco to - - -
accel. poco to - - -
(slower tremolo)
accel. poco to - - -
increase tremolo speed
37
58
ossia
♩= 120
94
ff lively
ff lively
ff lively
ff lively
ff lively
(8va)
Ped.

98
loco
102
ff strong
legato
mf sub.

106
mf cresc.
f
cresc.
cresc.
mf cresc.

109
ff
ff
ffp
ff
ffp
ff
ff

112
ff
energico
f
ff
f
117
ff

122
6
6
ffp
ff energico
ffp
fp

127
f

133
p
138
energico
ffz

142
energico
mp
mf
mf
mf
sffz

146
ff energico
* press silently cluster of black and white notes
keep below C and catch notes with sost. pedal
sost. Ped.

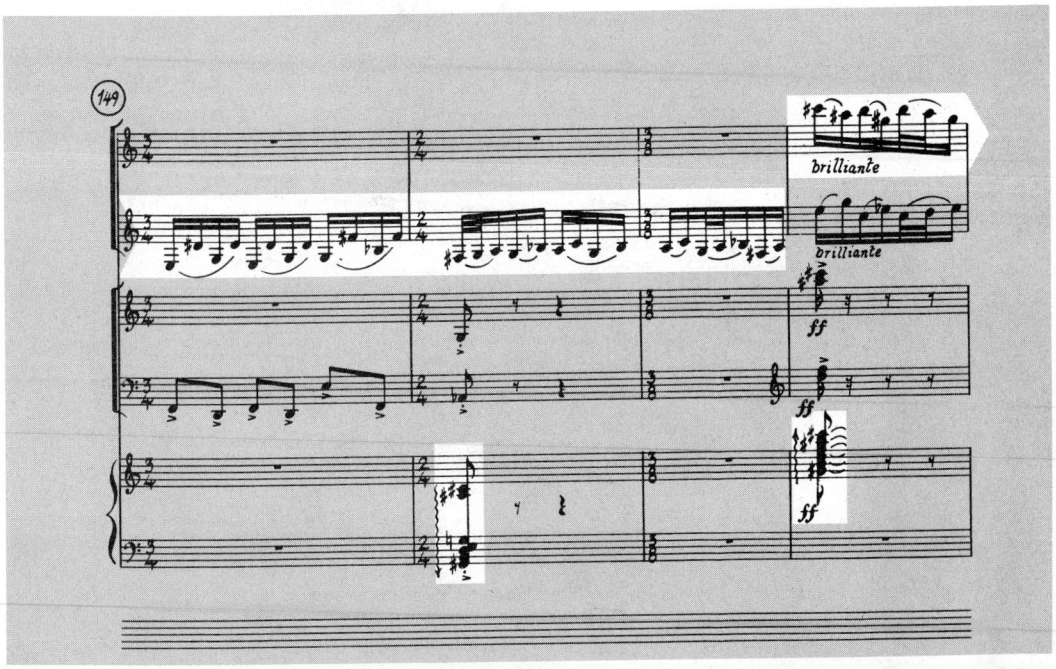
149
brillante
brillante
ff
ff
ff

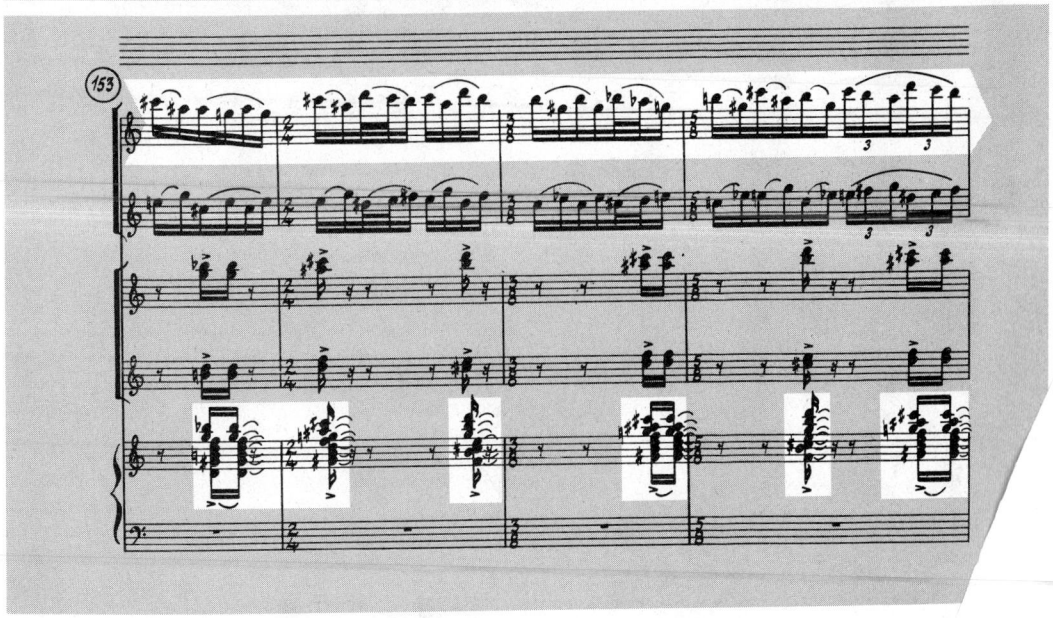
153

157
ff
160
ff
ff
ff
ff
mp
cresc.
ff

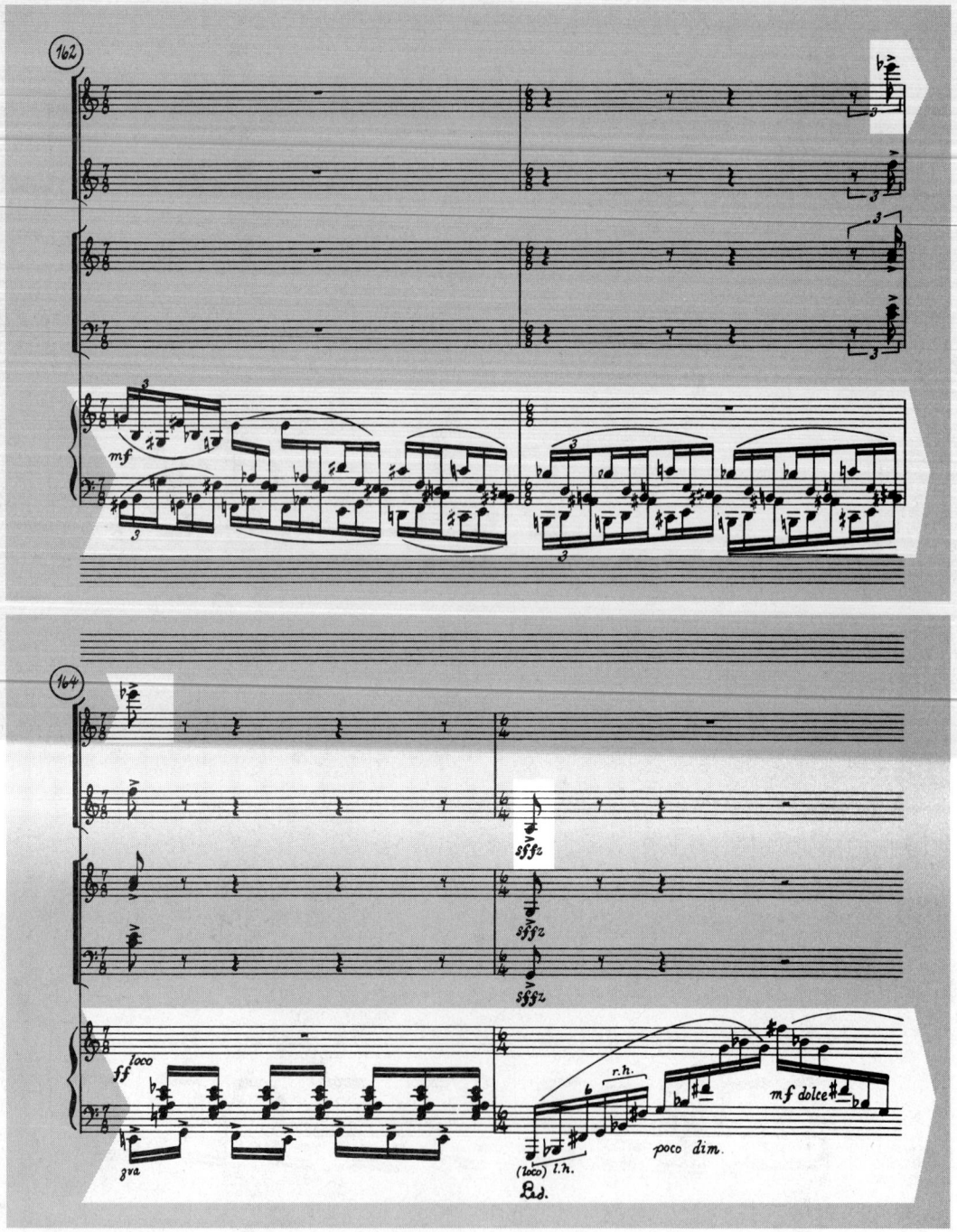
162
mf
164
sfz
sfz
sfz
ff loco
gra
r.h.
(loco) l.h.
poco dim.
mf dolce

166
r.h.
l.h.
cresc.
molto
167
mp
molto
sffz
mp
molto
ff agitato
mp
molto
ff agitato
ff
sffz

169
mf cresc. molto
ff agitato
mf
mf
cresc. molto
r.h.
l.h.
sffz
Ped.
* ossia
172
8va
ff agitato
mf cresc. molto
ff agitato
ff agitato
mf cresc. molto
ff agitato
r.h.
l.h.
sffz
sffz
Ped.

175
*ossia
8va
mf
ff agitato
178
r.h.
l.h.
Ped.

*ossia
179
f
Ped.
*ossia
(Ped.)

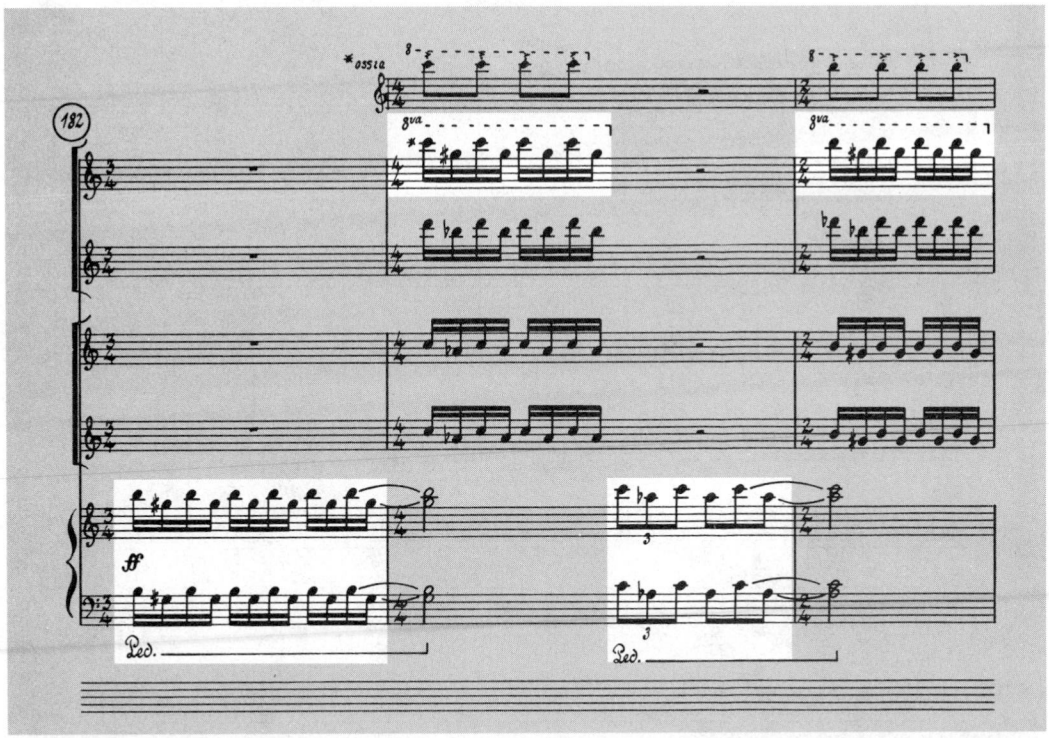
182
*ossia
8va
ff
Ped.

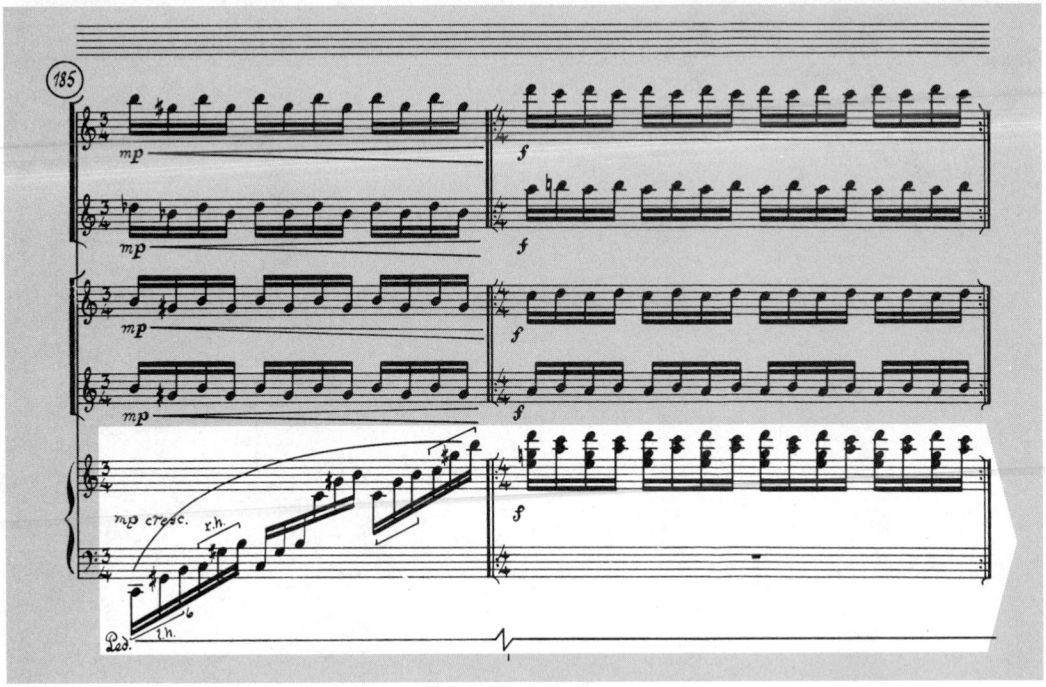
185
mp
f
mp cresc.
r.h.
l.h.
Ped.

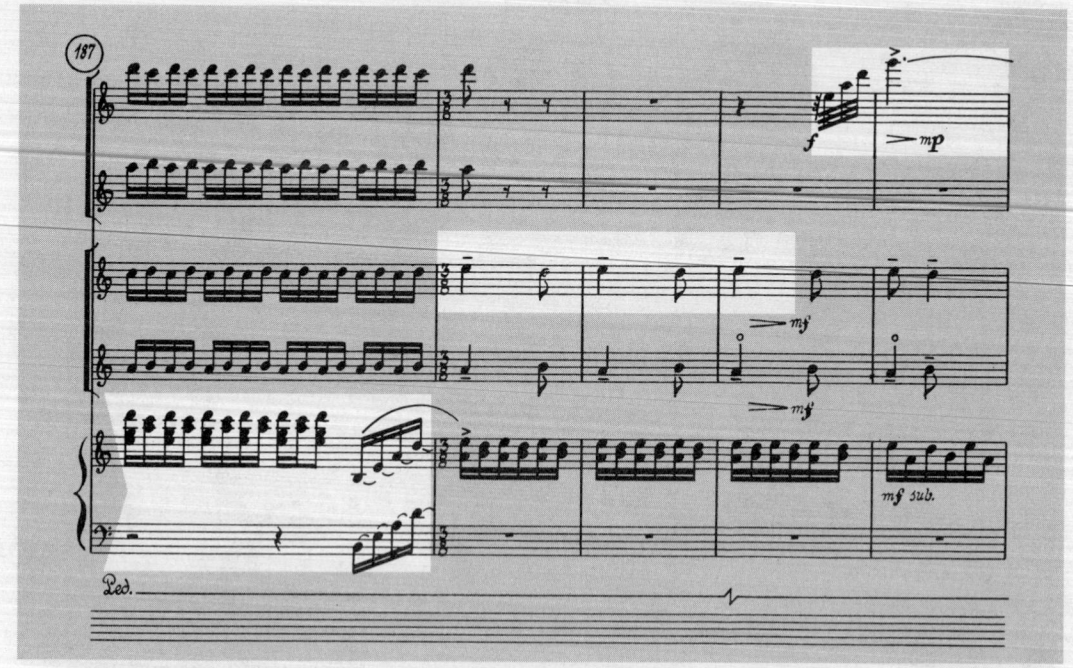
187
f
mp
mf
mf
mf sub.
Ped.

192
mf
f
f
fp
tr.
f
tr.
f
fp
(Ped.)

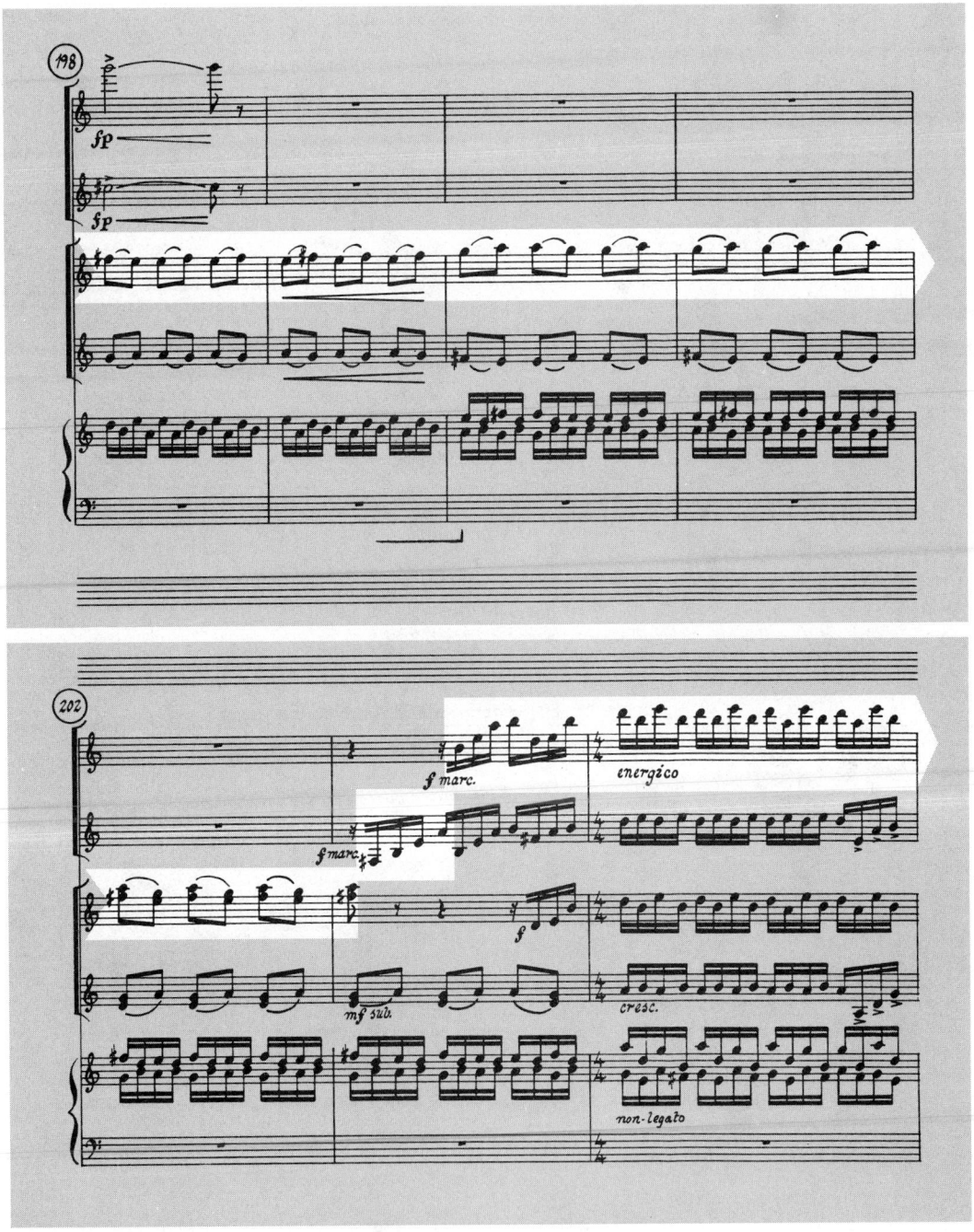
198
fp
fp
202
f marc.
energico
f marc.
f
mf sub.
cresc.
non-legato

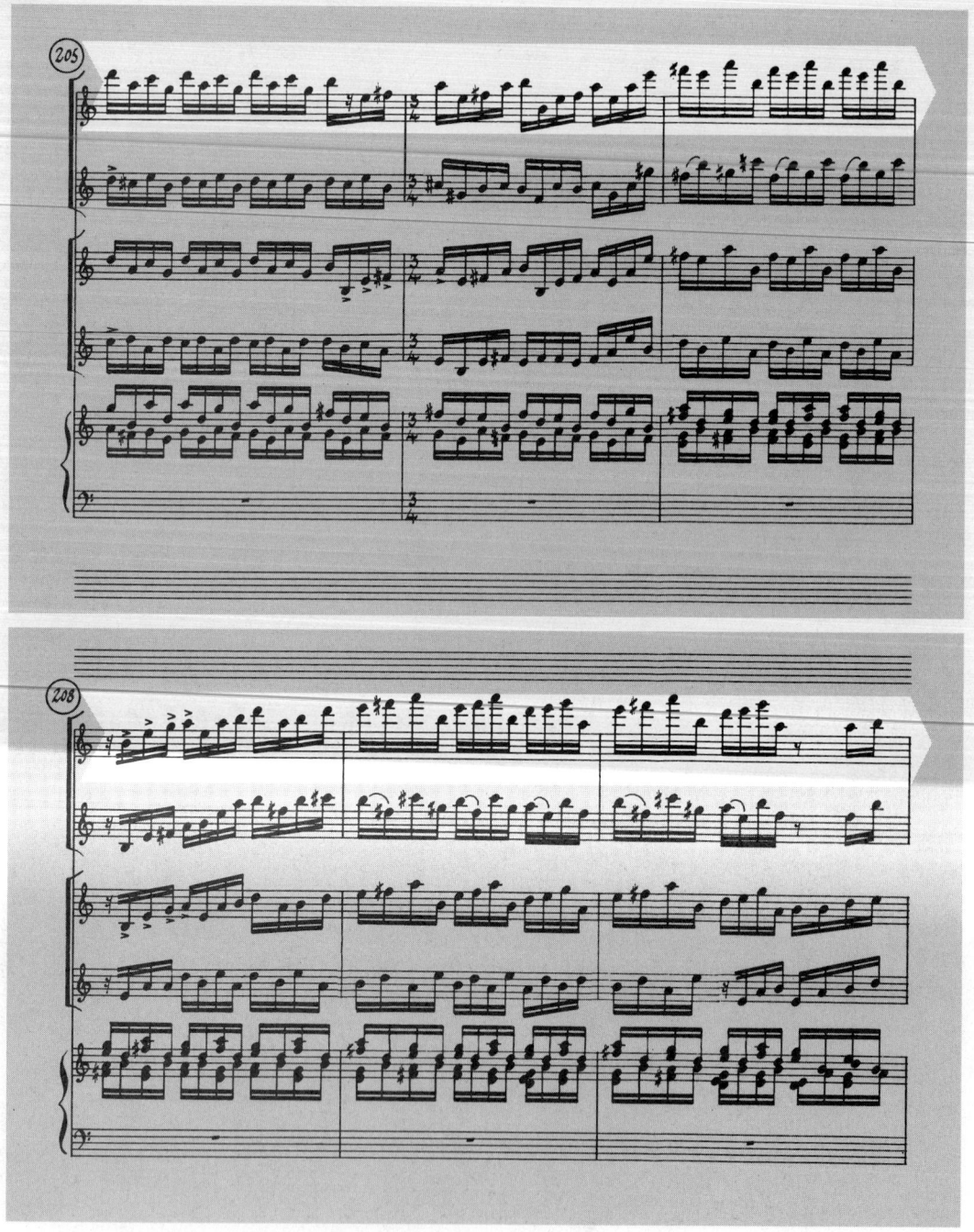
205
208

211
8
brilliante
brilliante
brilliante
brilliante
brilliante
(Ped.)

216
(8)
(Ped.)

221
(8)
8
8
22b
(8)
tr.
mp cresc.
mf
mp
mf
mp cresc.
mf
(8)
(8)
mf cresc.
Ped.

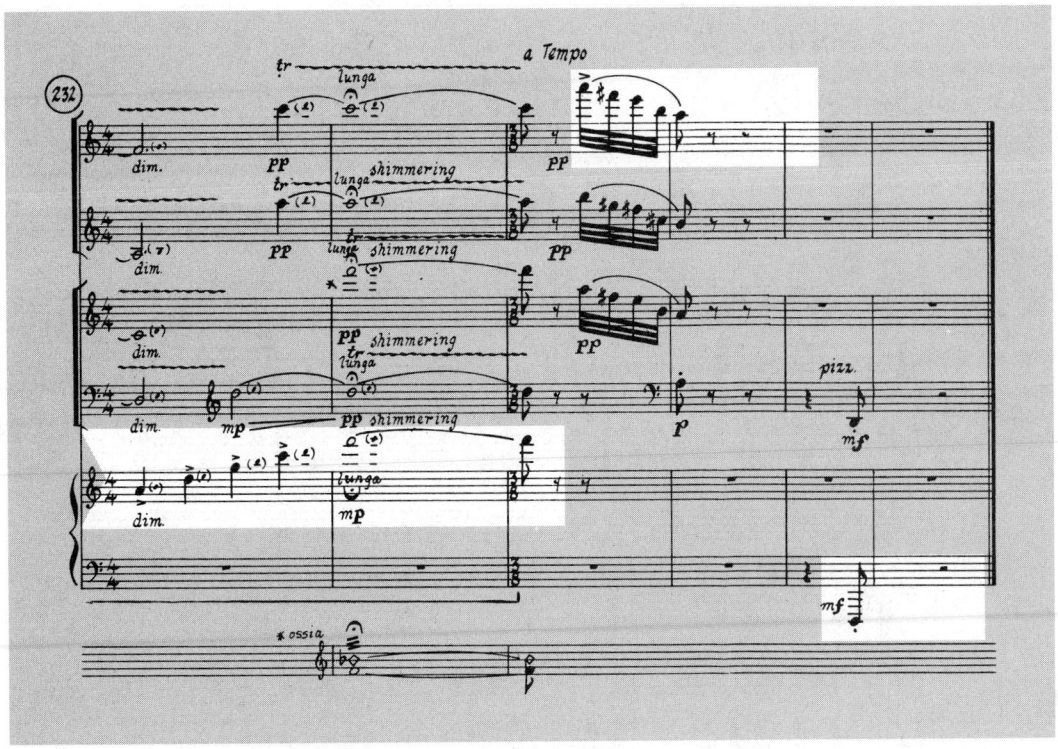
232
tr
lunga
a Tempo
dim.
pp
shimmering
mp
pizz.
p
mf
* ossia

43. *John Adams (b. 1947)*

8:8B/3 8:8/38 - 39

Nixon in China, Act I, Scene 3, Finale (1987)

© Copyright 1987 by Hendon Music, Inc. Reprinted by permission of Hendon Music, Inc.

NIXON
SO EN - JOYED A DIN - NER, NOR HAVE I HEARD
(342)
529
NIXON
PLAYED BET - TER THE MU - SIC THAT I LOVE OUT -
532
NIXON
SIDE A - MER - I - CA.
536
NIXON
I MOVE A VOTE OF THANKS TO ONE AND ALL WHOSE
540

NIXON
EF - FORTS MADE THIS POS - SI - BLE.
544
NIXON
NO ONE WHO HEARD COULD BUT AD - MIRE YOUR EL - O - QUENT RE - MARKS, PRE -
548
NIXON
MIERE, AND MIL - LIONS MORE HEAR WHAT WE SAY THROUGH
551
NIXON
SAT - TEL - LITE TECH - NO - LO - GY THAN EV - ER
554

NIXON
HEARD A PUB - LIC SPEECH BE - FORE.
559
NIXON
NO ONE IS OUT OF TOUCH.
563
NIXON
NO ONE NO ONE NO ONE IS OUT OF TOUCH.
566
NIXON
569
½ Ped
UNA CORDA

NIXON
(3+2)
TE - LE - COM - MU - NI - CA - TION HAS
574
NIXON
BROAD - CAST YOUR MES - SAGE IN - TO SPACE.
8VA
YET
579
Ped
NIXON
(3+2+2)
SOON OUR WORDS WON'T BE RE - CALLED WHILE WHAT WE DO CAN CHANGE THE
8VA
8VA
584
Ped
Ped
NIXON
WORLD.
8VA
LOCO
8VA
LOW
8VA
LOCO
(Ped.)
588
(Ped)

NIXON
592
597
WE HAVE AT TIMES BEEN EN - E - MIES
602
WE STILL HAVE DIF - FERENCES
(FALSETTO)
GOD KNOWS,
607
BUT LET US,

NIXON
IN THESE NEXT FIVE DAYS
611
NIXON
START A LONG MARCH
615
CRESC. POCO A POCO
NIXON
ON NEW HIGH-WAYS,
IN DIF-FERENT LANES,
620
f
Ped
(Ped)
NIXON
BUT PAR-AL-LEL
AND HEAD-ING FOR A
4:9
625

NIXON
SIN - GLE GOAL
630
AGITATO
NIXON
THE WORLD
634
NIXON
WATCH - ES AND LIS TENS.
4:4
WE MUST SEIZE THE
638
NIXON
HOUR
WE MUST SEIZE THE HOUR
642

NIXON
WE MUST SEIZE THE HOUR.
WE
647
NIXON
MUST SEIZE THE HOUR
AND SEIZE THE
651
39
NIXON
DAY.
FULL CHORUS
CHEERS!
CHEERS!
CHEERS!
CHEERS!
656

SOPRANOS
CHEERS! CHEERS! CHEERS! CHEERS! CHEERS! CHEERS! CHEERS! CHEERS! CHEERS!
ALTOS
CHEERS! CHEERS! CHEERS! CHEERS! CHEERS! CHEERS! CHEERS! CHEERS! CHEERS!
TENORS
CHEERS! CHEERS! CHEERS! CHEERS! CHEERS! CHEERS! CHEERS! CHEERS! CHEERS!
BASSES
CHEERS! CHEERS! CHEERS! CHEERS! CHEERS! CHEERS! CHEERS! CHEERS! CHEERS!
660
NIXON
THISSS IS THE HOUR!
SOPRANOS
CHEERS! CHEERS! CHEERS! CHEERS! CHEERS!
ALTOS
CHEERS! CHEERS! CHEERS! CHEERS! CHEERS!
TENORS
CHEERS! CHEERS! CHEERS! CHEERS! CHEERS!
BASSES
CHEERS! CHEERS! CHEERS! CHEERS! CHEERS!
665
ad

PAT
AND YOURS!
CHOU
YOUR HEALTH! TO DOC-TOR KISS-IN-GER!
SOPRANOS
ALTOS
TENORS
BASSES
CHEERS!
670
KISSINGER
NEW FRIENDS AND PRES-ENT COM-PAN-Y!
674
Led

NIXON
TO CHAIR-MAN MAO!
TO CHAIR-MAN MAO!
CHOU
THE U. S. A.!
THE U. S.
SOPRANOS
CHEERS!
ALTOS
CHEERS!
TENORS
CHEERS!
BASSES
CHEERS!
678
CHOU
A. !
SOPRANOS
CHEERS! CHEERS! CHEERS! CHEERS! CHEERS! CHEE RS!
ALTOS
CHEERS! CHEERS! CHEERS! CHEERS! CHEERS! CHEE RS!
TENORS
CHEERS! CHEERS! CHEERS! CHEERS! CHEERS! CHEE RS!
BASSES
CHEERS! CHEERS! CHEERS! CHEERS! CHEERS! CHEE RS!
682

SOPRANOS
CHEERS! CHEERS! CHEERS! CHEERS! CHE CHE CHE CHE CHE CHE CHEE - - - - - - - - - - - RS!
ALTOS
CHEERS! CHEERS! CHEERS! CHEERS! CHE CHE CHE CHE CHE CHE CHEE - - - - - - - - - - - RS!
TENORS
CHEERS! CHEERS! CHEERS! CHEERS! CHE CHE CHE CHE CHE CHE CHEE - - - - - - - - - - - RS!
BASSES
CHEERS! CHEERS! CHEERS! CHEERS! CHE CHE CHE CHE CHE CHE CHEE - - - - - - - - - - - RS!
686
PAT
HAVE YOU FOR-GOT-TEN WASH-ING-TON?
CHOU
WASH-ING-TON'S BIRTH_-DAY!
SOPRANOS
CHEERS!
ALTOS
CHEERS!
TENORS
CHEERS!
BASSES
CHEERS!
690

PAT
NIXON
WASH-ING-TON'S BIRTH-- DAY!
WASH-ING-TON'S BIRTH-- DAY!
WASH-ING-TON'S BIRTH--- DAY!
CHOU
WASH-ING-TON'S BIRTH-- DAY!
WASH-ING-TON'S BIRTH--- DAY!
KISSINGER
WASH-ING-TON'S BIRTH-- DAY!
WASH-ING-TON'S BIRTH-- DAY!
WASH-ING-TON'S BIRTH--- DAY!
SOPRANOS
WASH-ING-TON'S BIRTH-- DAY!
WASH-ING-TON'S BIRTH-- DAY!
ALTOS
WASH-ING-TON'S BIRTH-- DAY!
WASH-ING-TON'S BIRTH-- DAY!
TENORS
WASH-ING-TON'S BIRTH-- DAY!
WASH-ING-TON'S BIRTH-- DAY!
BASSES
WASH-ING-TON'S BIRTH-- DAY!
WASH-ING-TON'S BIRTH-- DAY!
694

PAT
WASH-ING-TON'S BIRTH-- DAY! WASH-ING-TON'S BIRTH-- DAY! WASH-ING-TON'S CHEERS! CHEERS!
NIXON
WASH-ING-TON'S BIRTH-- DAY! WASH-ING-TON'S BIRTH-- DAY! WASH-ING-TON'S BIRTH - DAY!
CHOU
WASH-ING-TON'S BIRTH-- DAY! WASH-ING-TON'S BIRTH-- DAY! WASH-ING-TON'S BIRTH - DAY!
KISSINGER
WASH-ING-TON'S BIRTH-- DAY! WASH-ING-TON'S BIRTH-- DAY! WASH-ING-TON'S BIRTH - DAY!
SOPRANOS
WASH-ING-TON'S BIRTH-- DAY! WASH-ING-TON'S BIRTH-- DAY! WASH-ING-TON'S CHEERS! CHEERS!
ALTOS
WASH-ING-TON'S BIRTH-- DAY! WASH-ING-TON'S BIRTH-- DAY! WASH-ING-TON'S CHEERS! CHEERS!
TENORS
WASH-ING-TON'S BIRTH-- DAY! WASH-ING-TON'S BIRTH-- DAY! WASH-ING-TON'S CHEERS! CHEERS!
BASSES
WASH-ING-TON'S BIRTH-- DAY! WASH-ING-TON'S BIRTH-- DAY! WASH-ING-TON'S CHEERS! CHEERS!
697

PAT
SOPRANOS
ALTOS
TENORS
BASSES
CHEERS!
701
705

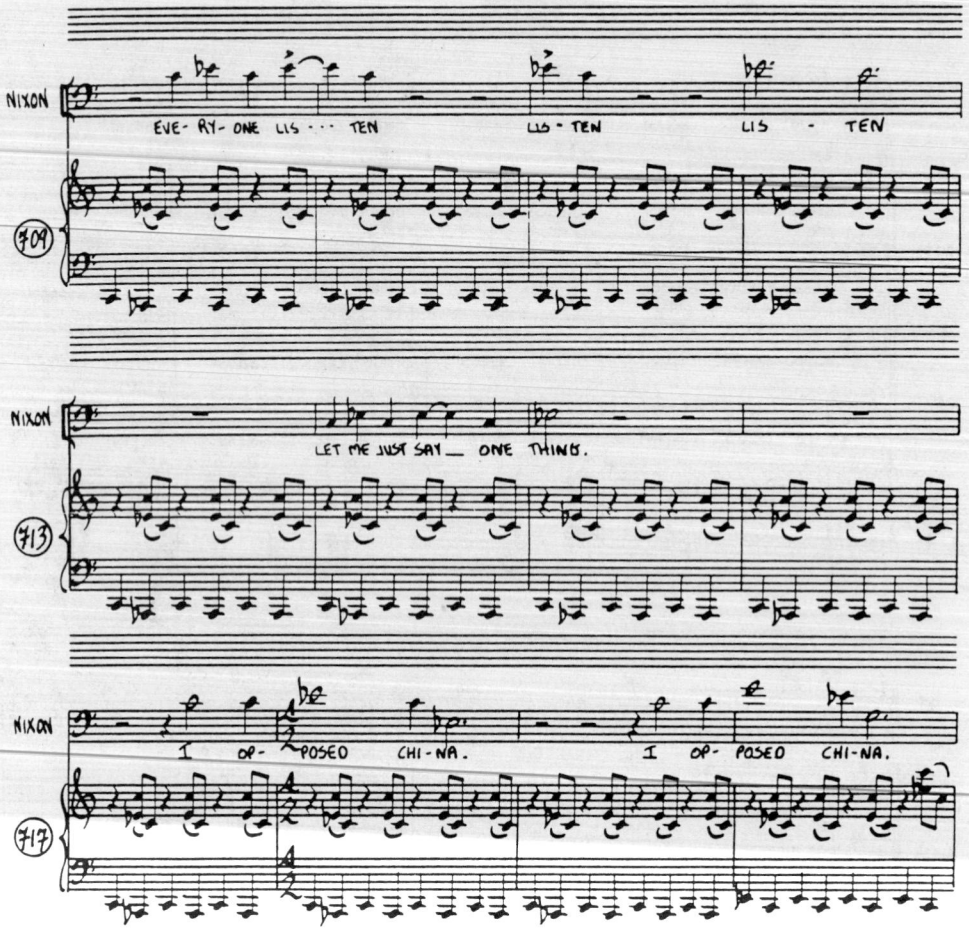
NIXON
EVE- RY- ONE LIS ··· TEN
LIS - TEN
LIS - TEN
709
NIXON
LET ME JUST SAY ONE THING.
713
NIXON
I OP- POSED CHI-NA.
I OP- POSED CHI-NA.
717

(SOFTLY)
NIXON
I OP- POSED CHI-NA. I WAS WRONG.
SOPRANOS
ALTOS
TENORS
BASSES
CHEERS! CHEERS! CHEERS!
(721)
f
CHEE - - - - - - - - - - - - RS!
(725)

SOPRANOS
CHEERS! CHEERS! CHEERS!
CHEE - - - - - - - - - - - - - - - RS!
CHEERS! CHEERS! CHEERS! CHEERS!
ALTOS
CHEERS! CHEERS! CHEERS!
CHEE - - - - - - - - - - - - - - - RS!
CHEERS! CHEERS! CHEERS! CHEERS!
TENORS
CHEERS! CHEERS! CHEERS!
CHEE - - - - - - - - - - - - - - - RS!
CHEERS! CHEERS! CHEERS! CHEERS!
BASSES
CHEERS! CHEERS! CHEERS!
CHEE - - - - - - - - - - - - - - - RS!
CHEERS! CHEERS! CHEERS! CHEERS
729
PAT
WHAT DID YOU SAY,
NIXON
I WAS WRONG.
I WAS
KISSINGER
BOT - TOMS UP, MIS - TER PRES - I - DENT.
SUBITO
SOPRANOS
CHEERS!
CHEERS! CHEERS! CHEERS! CHEERS! CHEERS! CHEERS!
SUBITO
ALTOS
CHEERS!
CHEERS! CHEERS! CHEERS! CHEERS! CHEERS! CHEERS!
SUBITO
TENORS
CHEERS!
CHEERS! CHEERS! CHEERS! CHEERS! CHEERS! CHEERS!
SUBITO
BASSES
CHEERS!
CHEERS! CHEERS! CHEERS! CHEERS! CHEERS! CHEERS!
732

PAT
SWEET - HEART? WHAT DID YOU SAY, SWEET - HEART?
NIXON
WRONG WAS WRONG I WAS WRONG. I WAS
CHOU
THE U. S. A. MIS - TER
KISSINGER
MIS - TER PRES - I - DENT. BOT - TOMS UP, MIS - TER
SOPRANOS
CHEERS! CHEERS! CHEERS! CHEERS! CHEERS! CHEERS! CHEERS! CHEERS!
ALTOS
CHEERS! CHEERS! CHEERS! CHEERS! CHEERS! CHEERS! CHEERS! CHEERS!
TENORS
CHEERS! CHEERS! CHEERS! CHEERS! CHEERS! CHEERS! CHEERS! CHEERS!
BASSES
CHEERS! CHEERS! CHEERS! CHEERS! CHEERS! CHEERS! CHEERS! CHEERS!
736

PAT
I CAN'T CATCH EVE - RY WORD IN ALL THIS NOISE.
NIXON
WRONG I OP - POSED CHI- NA. I WAS WRONG. I -
CHOU
PRES - I - DENT PRES ··· I - DENT PRES - I - DENT PRES - I - DENT
KISSINGER
PRES - I - DENT PRES ··· I - DENT PRES - I - DENT PRES - I - DENT
SOPRANOS
CHEERS! CHEERS! CHEERS! CHEERS! CHEERS! CHEERS! WE
ALTOS
CHEERS! CHEERS! CHEERS! CHEERS! CHEERS! CHEERS! WE
TENORS
CHEERS! CHEERS! CHEERS! CHEERS! CHEERS! CHEERS! WE
BASSES
CHEERS! CHEERS! CHEERS! CHEERS! CHEERS! CHEERS! WE
740

PAT
A - MER - - - - - - - I - CA THE BEAU - - - - - - - TI -
NIXON
DEAS THAT WE HAVE EN-TER- TAINED IN FORM-ER YEARS GROW IN A
CHOU
LOOK DOWN AND SEE WHAT THE
KISSINGER
YOU WON'T BE - LIEVE HOW MOVED I AM
SOPRANOS
HAVE AT TIMES BEEN EN - E - MIES THE
ALTOS
HAVE AT TIMES BEEN EN - E - MIES THE
TENORS
HAVE AT TIMES BEEN EN - E - MIES THE
BASSES
HAVE AT TIMES BEEN EN - E - MIES THE
744

PAT
FUL A ----- MER - I - CA A ----- MER - I -----
NIXON
MIGHT TO TOUCH THE STARS. I-DEAS THAT WE HAVE EN-TER- TAINED GROW IN A
CHOU
CHI - NESE PEO - PLE HAVE DONE TO
KISSINGER
YOU WON'T BE - LIEVE HOW MOVED I AM. YOU
SOPRANOS
CHI - NESE PEO - PLE ARE RE - NOWNED. WE
ALTOS
CHI - NESE PEO - PLE ARE RE - NOWNED. WE
TENORS
CHI - NESE PEO - PLE ARE RE - NOWNED. WE
BASSES
CHI - NESE PEO - PLE ARE RE - NOWNED. WE
748

PAT
... CA THE BEAU - TI - FUL A - - - - MER - I -
NIXON
NIGHT TO TOUCH THE STARS. I - DEAS THAT WE HAVE EN - TER - TAINED GROW IN A
CHOU
EARN THIS PRAISE LOOK DOWN AND
KISSINGER
WON'T BE - LIEVE HOW MOVED I AM.
SOPRANOS
HAVE AT TIMES BEEN EN - E - MIES. THE
ALTOS
HAVE AT TIMES BEEN EN - E - MIES. THE
TENORS
HAVE AT TIMES BEEN EN - E - MIES. THE
BASSES
HAVE AT TIMES BEEN EN - E - MIES. THE
752

PAT
CA THE BEAU - - - - - - TI - FUL A - - - - - - - - - - - - - - - - -
NIXON
NIGHT TO TOUCH THE STARS. I-DEAS THAT WE HAVE EN-TER - TAINED GROW IN A
CHOU
THINK WHAT THE CHI - NESE PEO - PLE HAVE
KISSINGER
THIS IS THE HOUR! THIS IS THE HOUR!
SOPRANOS
CHI - NESE PEO - PLE ARE RE - NOWNED. WE
ALTOS
CHI - NESE PEO - PLE ARE RE - NOWNED. WE
TENORS
CHI - NESE PEO - PLE ARE RE - NOWNED. WE
BASSES
CHI - NESE PEO - PLE ARE RE - NOWNED. WE
356

PAT
(A)
NIXON
NIGHT TO TOUCH THE STARS. I-DEAS THAT WE HAVE EN-TER- TAINED GROW IN A
CHOU
DONE HAVE DONE HAVE DONE HAVE DONE
KISSINGER
YOU WON'T BE - LIEVE HOW... THE CHI-NESE PEO-PLE THE CHI-NESE PEO-PLE
SOPRANOS
HAVE AT TIMES BEEN EN - E - MIES. WE MUST
ALTOS
HAVE AT TIMES BEEN EN - E - MIES. WE MUST
TENORS
HAVE AT TIMES BEEN EN - E - MIES. WE MUST
BASSES
HAVE AT TIMES BEEN EN - E - MIES. WE MUST
760

PAT
(A) MER - I CA!
NIXON
NIGHT TO TOUCH THE STARS. TO TOUCH THE STARS.
CHOU
TO EARN THIS PRAISE.
KISSINGER
THE CHI-NESE PEO-PLE THE CHI-NESE PEO-PLE
SOPRANOS
BROAD - CAST SEEDS OF GOOD - WILL.
ALTOS
BROAD - CAST SEEDS OF GOOD - WILL.
TENORS
BROAD - CAST SEEDS OF GOOD - WILL.
BASSES
BROAD - CAST SEEDS OF GOOD - WILL.
764

(34242)
769
PAT
SPRING IS HERE. I LOVE YOU DEAR. SPRING IS HERE. I LOVE YOU DEAR.
NIXON
IT'S LIKE A DREAM. IT'S LIKE A DREAM. IT'S LIKE A DREAM. IT'S LIKE A
CHOU
COM-RADES AND FRIENDS BROTH-ERS A-GAIN! COM-RADES AND FRIENDS BROTH-ERS A-GAIN!
KISSINGER
YOU CAN'T BE-LIEVE HOW MOVED I
773
f
* Ped
PAT
SPRING IS HERE. I LOVE YOU DEAR. SPRING IS HERE. I LOVE YOU
NIXON
DREAM. IT'S LIKE A DREAM. IT'S LIKE A DREAM. IT'S LIKE A DREAM. IT'S LIKE A
CHOU
COM-RADES AND FRIENDS BROTH-ERS A-GAIN! COM-RADES AND FRIENDS BROTH-ERS A-GAIN
KISSINGER
AM. YOU WON'T BE-LIEVE HOW MOVED I
777

PAT
DEAR.
NIXON
DREAM.
CHOU
KISSINGER
AM.
781
785

PAT
I LOVE YOU, DEAR THE SPRING IS HERE I LOVE YOU, DEAR THE SPRING IS HERE
NIXON
IT'S LIKE A DREAM. IT'S LIKE A DREAM. IT'S LIKE A DREAM. IT'S LIKE A
CHOU
TO CHAIR-MAN MAO THE U. S. A. TO CHAIR-MAN MAO THE U. S. A.
KISSINGER
YOU WON'T BE - LIEVE HOW MOVED I
789
PAT
I LOVE YOU, DEAR THE SPRING IS HERE I LOVE YOU, DEAR THE SPRING IS
NIXON
DREAM. IT'S LIKE A DREAM. IT'S LIKE A DREAM. IT'S LIKE A
CHOU
TO CHAIR-MAN MAO THE U. S. A. TO CHAIR-MAN MAO THE U. S.
KISSINGER
AM. YOU WON'T BE - LIEVE HOW MOVED I
793

PAT
HERE!
NIXON
OPERA!
CHOU
A.!
KISSINGER
AM.
SOPRANOS
CHEERS! CHEERS! CHEERS! CHEERS! CHEERS! CHEERS! CHEERS! CHEERS! CHEERS! CHEERS!
ALTOS
CHEERS! CHEERS! CHEERS! CHEERS! CHEERS! CHEERS! CHEERS! CHEERS! CHEERS! CHEERS!
TENORS
CHEERS! CHEERS! CHEERS! CHEERS! CHEERS! CHEERS! CHEERS! CHEERS! CHEERS! CHEERS!
BASSES
CHEERS! CHEERS! CHEERS! CHEERS! CHEERS! CHEERS! CHEERS! CHEERS! CHEERS! CHEERS!
797

SOPRANOS
CHEE
CHEERS! CHEERS! CHEERS!
CHEE
ALTOS
CHEERS! CHEERS! CHEERS!
TENORS
CHEE
CHEERS! CHEERS! CHEERS!
CHEE
BASSES
CHEE
CHEERS! CHEERS! CHEERS!
CHEE
301
SOPRANOS
CHEERS! CHEERS!
CHEERS!
ALTOS
CHEERS! CHEERS!
CHEERS!
TENORS
CHEERS! CHEERS!
CHEERS!
BASSES
CHEERS! CHEERS!
CHEERS!
304
ff

809
814
818
822
2+3+2
826
(829)

44. *Tod Machover (b. 1952)*

Bug-Mudra, excerpt (1989–90)

8:8B/4 8:8/40 - 42

3:3B/8 3:3/52 - 54

Composer's Note on *Bug-Mudra*

Bug-Mudra is scored for two guitarists (one electric and one acoustic) and one percussionist (who plays an electronic mallet controller and acoustic cymbals), each of whose playing is converted to MIDI data and interpreted in specially developed hyper-instrument software. (A hyper-instrument is one that is electronically enhanced based on computer monitoring of the performer's musical interpretation.) The musical result is computed according to the functions assigned to each instrument in each section and produced as sound by an array of synthesis gear. Additionally, the conductor wears a hand-and-finger-sensing device known as the Exos Dexterous Hand Master, which is used to control a second hyper-instrument system. This system interprets the hand gestures of the conductor (measuring the bend of each joint of each finger) and maps them to real-time control of a pair of automated mixers that shape the levels, panning, frequencies, etc., of the sounds from the other hyper-instruments. The major components of the entire setup are shown in the diagram on the following page.

There is also a tape part, which plays the entire length of the piece, providing time code information that controls the performance. The time base information (i.e., bars, time signatures, and tempi) is precisely maintained through the use of SMPTE time code. Thus, the hyper-instruments know exactly (within 1/100 of a second) what the current place in the performance is, as well as the beat and metric structure. This information enables the system to change behavior rapidly and in synchronization with the music. For example, in one section, the electric guitar's timbre is switched repeatedly between an electric bass sound transposed two octaves down to a synthesized guitar sound transposed two octaves up. In another case, notes are fed into the guitar synchronized with rapid notes on the tape so that the tape part sounds the correct note regardless of what the guitarist plays. Also, the fret board has been remapped so that each position produces a slightly different timbre; thus, the guitarist controls articulation, timbre, and phrase shape, while the tape controls the pitch.

The relationship between the hand gesture (controlled by the conductor wearing the Hand Master glove) and the sonic result changes in the different sections of the piece. The hand is used at times to shape complex, inharmonic spectra, the thumb is tied into the panning of one group of channels, and finger movement is mapped to levels of the different performers with an automatic smoothing function. This hyper-instrument system represents the most powerful and complex performance environment created to date.

Bug-Mudra Hyper-Instrument Performance System

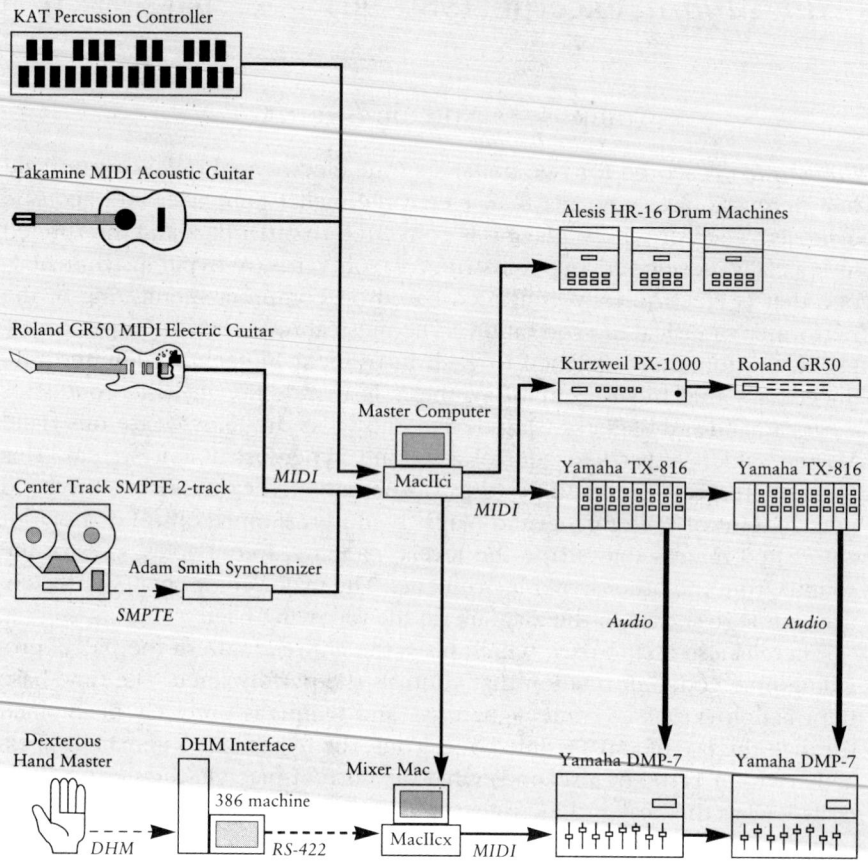

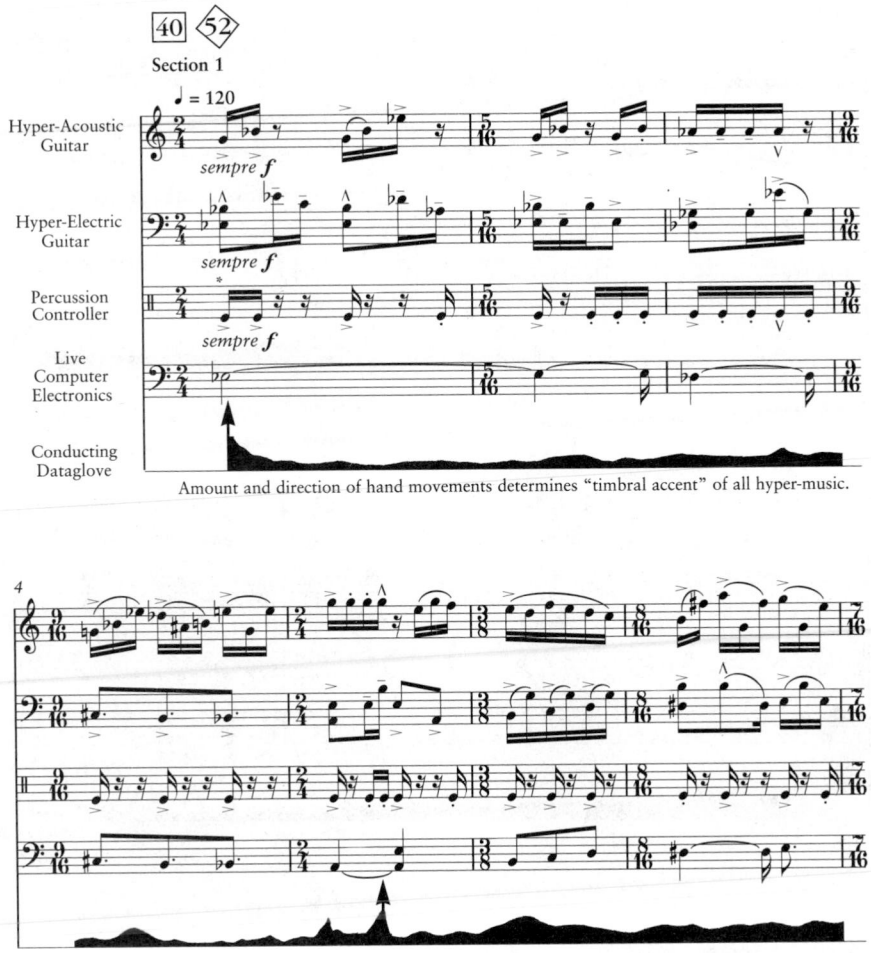

*In non-pitched sections (no 𝄞) *any* percussion sound may be chosen and played in specified rhythm. Play on 4-octave *KAT controller* or equivalent. All these are noted on bottom line of staff. Notes above this bottom line are to be played on *acoustic cymbals*, lo-to-hi: 𝄞

© Copyright by Editions Ricordi, Paris. Reprinted by permission of Hendon Music, Inc., agent, and Tod Machover.

sf
sf
sempre f

18
22
26

29

32

35

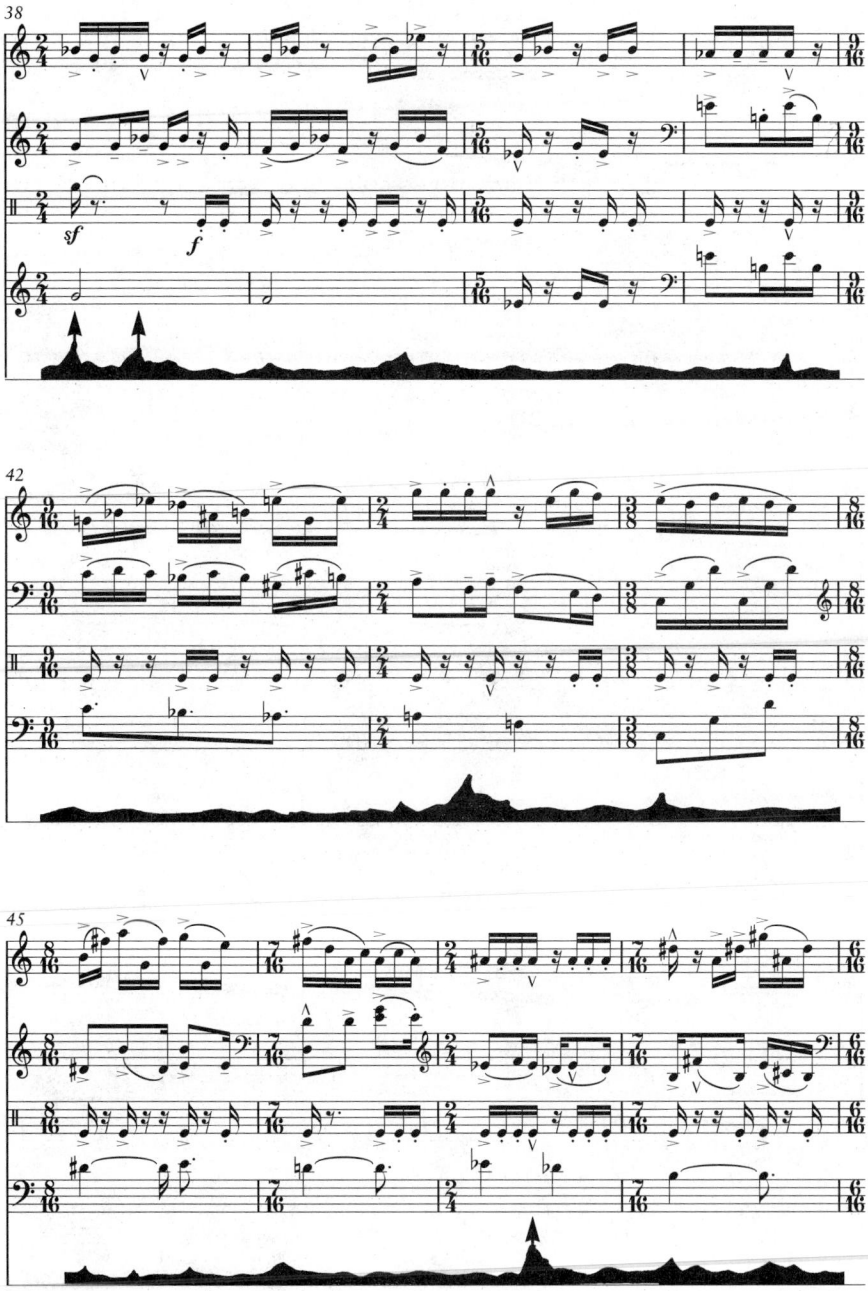
38
sf
f
42
45

49
52
56

59
sf

62

66
sf
f

70
74
77

80
"woodblocks"
mf
poco f
83
87

91
"normal" (any timbre)
sf
95
99

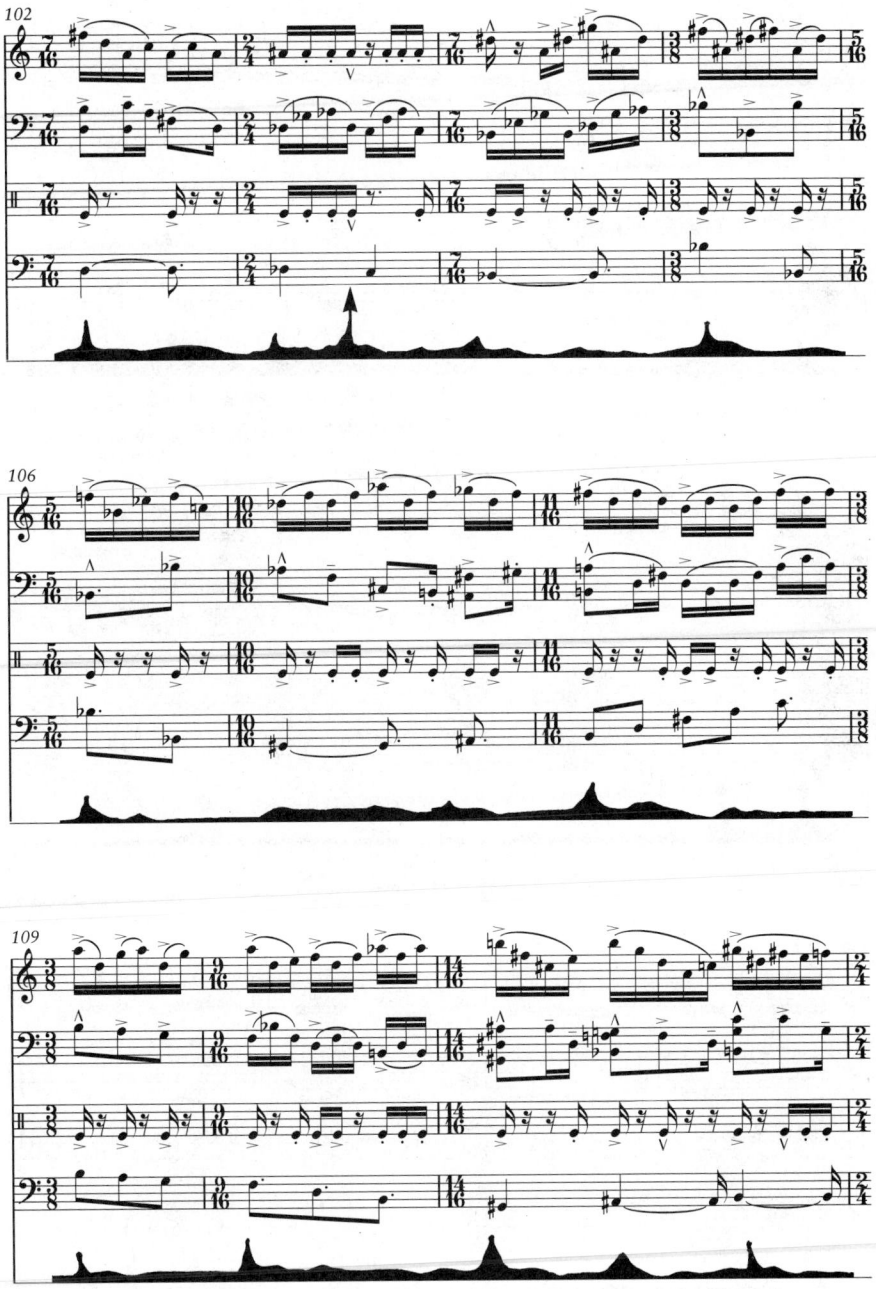
102
106
109

112
sf
sf
sf
sfp

115
sf

118

122
sf

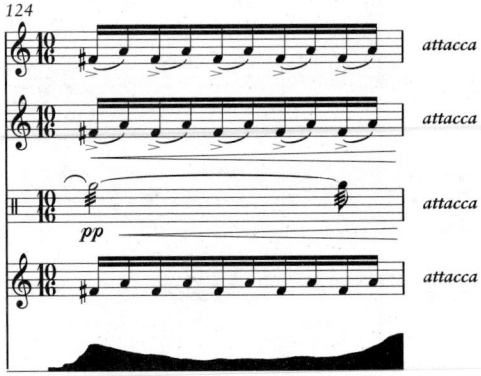
124
attacca
attacca
attacca
attacca
pp

Conduct beats with dataglove (synchronizes computer part). Amount of movement (small→large) determines degree of rhythmic quantizing (none→lots) for hyper-instruments.

*Improvise rhythm on running sixteenth notes. Constantly leave rests and pauses in texture. Place accents irregularly. Live playing will be "quantized" into exact sixteenth notes by the computer. Choose wood, claves and other dry sounds, not traditional "drum-set" material. These are generally found in octaves 2 and 3 of the KAT.

1 E: hyper-event triggered on these notes.

130
mf
sf
mf
sf
sf
mf
sf
mf
sf
mp
f
sf (hyper-trigger)
mp
- - - (beats; movement = sync) - - -

132
mp f mf sf mp sf mf sff mp poco f sf
sf mf sf mp mp sf (hyper-trigger)
- - - (beats; movement = sync) - - -

134
mf
mp
mf
mp
sf
mp
mp
sf (hyper-trigger)
E
sff
sf (hyper-trigger)
- - - (beats; movement = sync) - - -

136
sff
poco f
sf
mf
sff
sf
mf
sf
mf
sf (hyper-trigger)
- - - (beats; movement = sync) - - -

138
mf
sff
mf
sf
sff
sf
mp
lyrical
mp
mf
sf (hyper-trigger)
- - - (beats; movement = sync) - - -

**Hyper-electric guitar*: Until ms. 157, notes are fed automatically to 6 guitar strings. Fret = timbre. Play fast, furiously, and with great rhythmic complexity/irregularity.

150
sf
sf
ff
sf
p
sf
sff
mf
ff
sf
mf
(continue auto-notes)
- - - (beats; movement = sync) - - -

156
(continue auto-notes)
same timbres, precise rhythms
acoustic cymbals
- - - (beats; movement = sync) - - -

Continue with beats. Arrow indicates very large downbeat; enhances accent and synchronization.

161
mf
sf
mp
sf
mp
sf
mf
mf
f
- - - (beat; arrows) - - -

164
f
mf
sf
f
- - - (beat; arrows) - - -

**Hyper-electric guitar*: Play notes on low E string. Complex patterns transferred automatically to other strings.

**Back to improvised sixteenths, quantized by computer, again using wood sounds. Continue until measure 176.

169
poco f
sf
p
f
- - - (beat; arrows) - - -

171
3
3
p
- - - (beat; arrows) - - -

173
ff
sf sf sf
sff
p
3
3
- - - (beat; arrows) - - -

175
ff
5
f
3
sempre f
ff
- - - (beat; arrows) - - -

177
3
mp
sffp
ff

179
sffp
sff
f
mf
ff
attacca
"normal"
attacca
attacca
attacca
attacca
attacca
attacca
attacca
attacca
attacca
- - - (beat; arrows) - - -

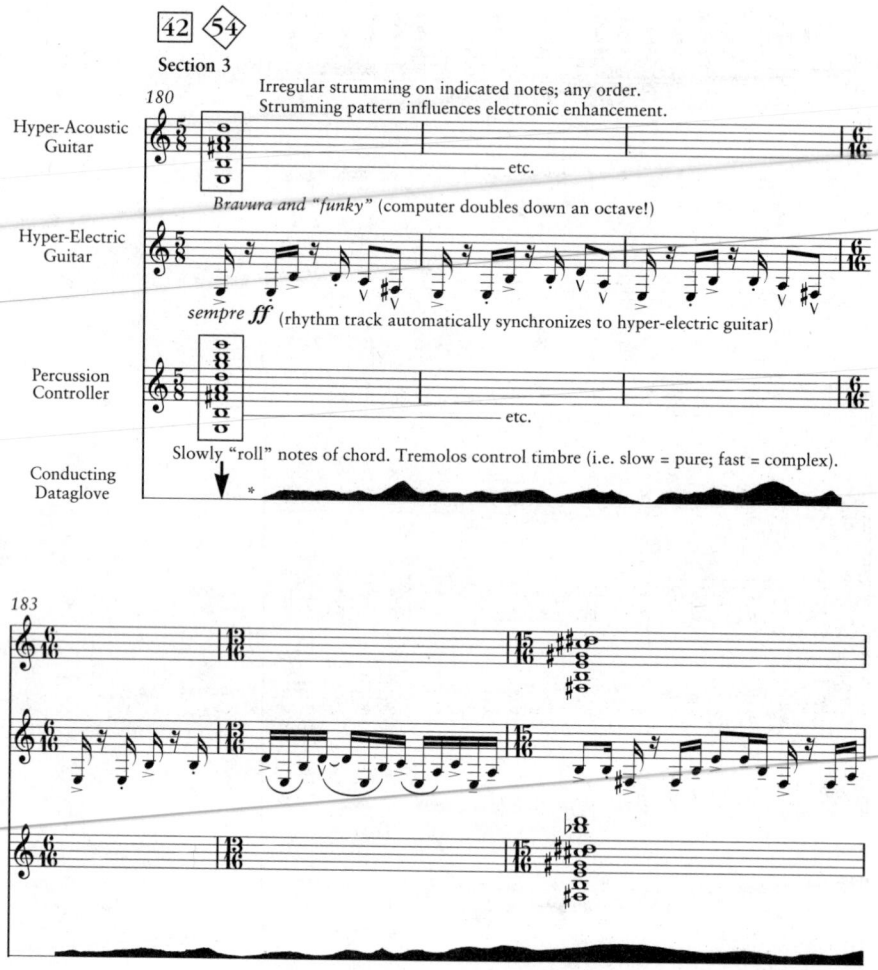

*Right-hand conducting stops. Timbre shaping of all hyper-music from dataglove. Position of hand, speed/continuity of movement, and position of fingers sculpts timbre density and determines spectral content.

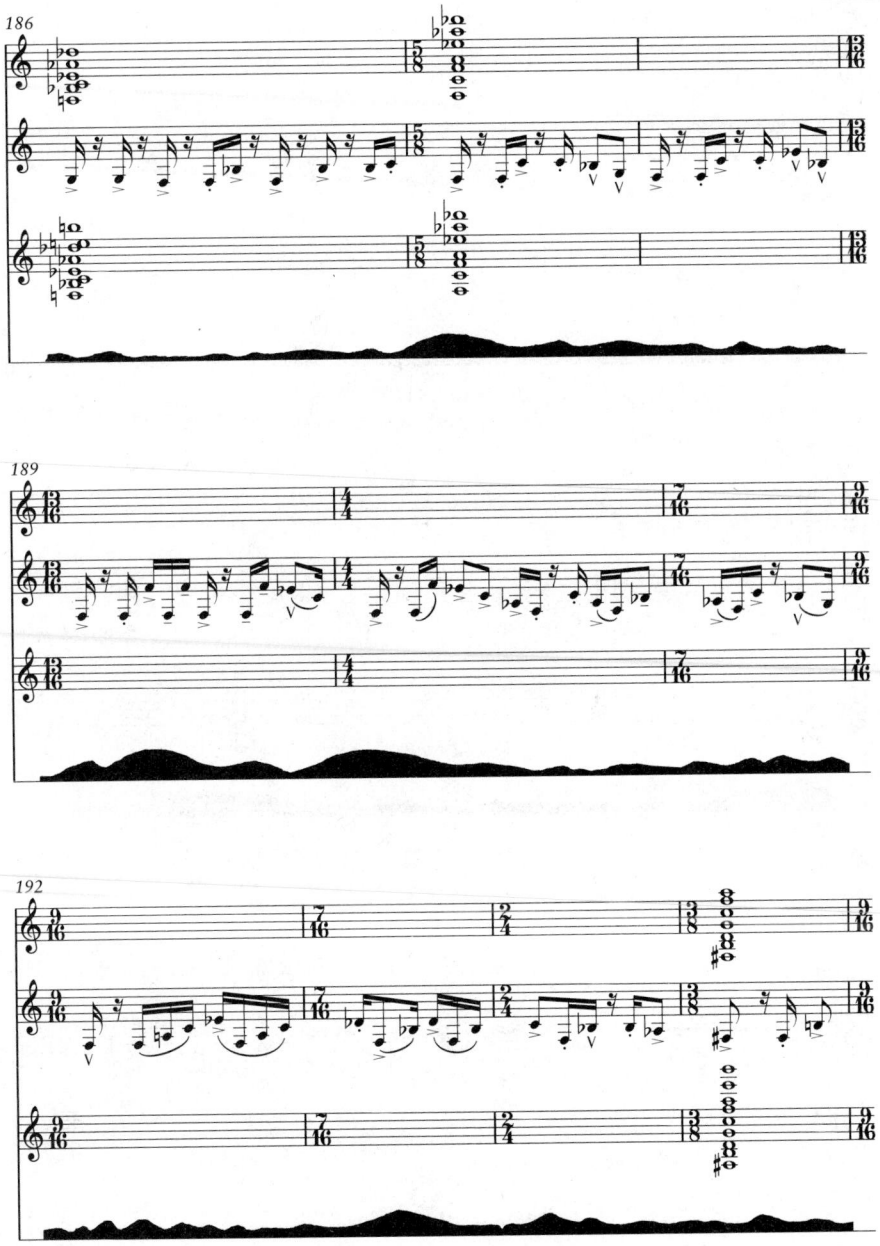
186
189
192

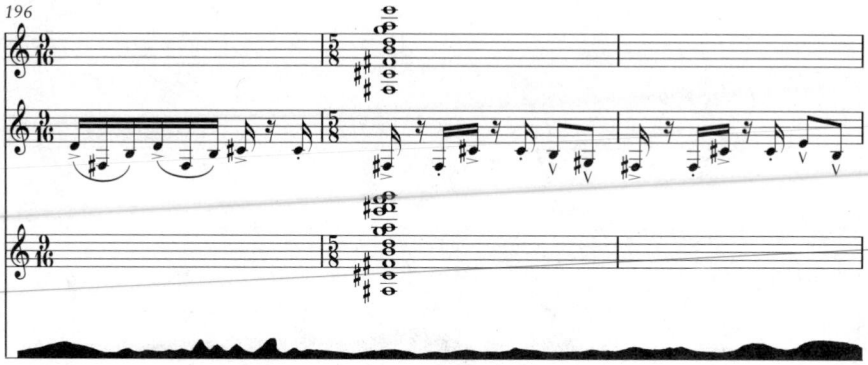
196

199

202

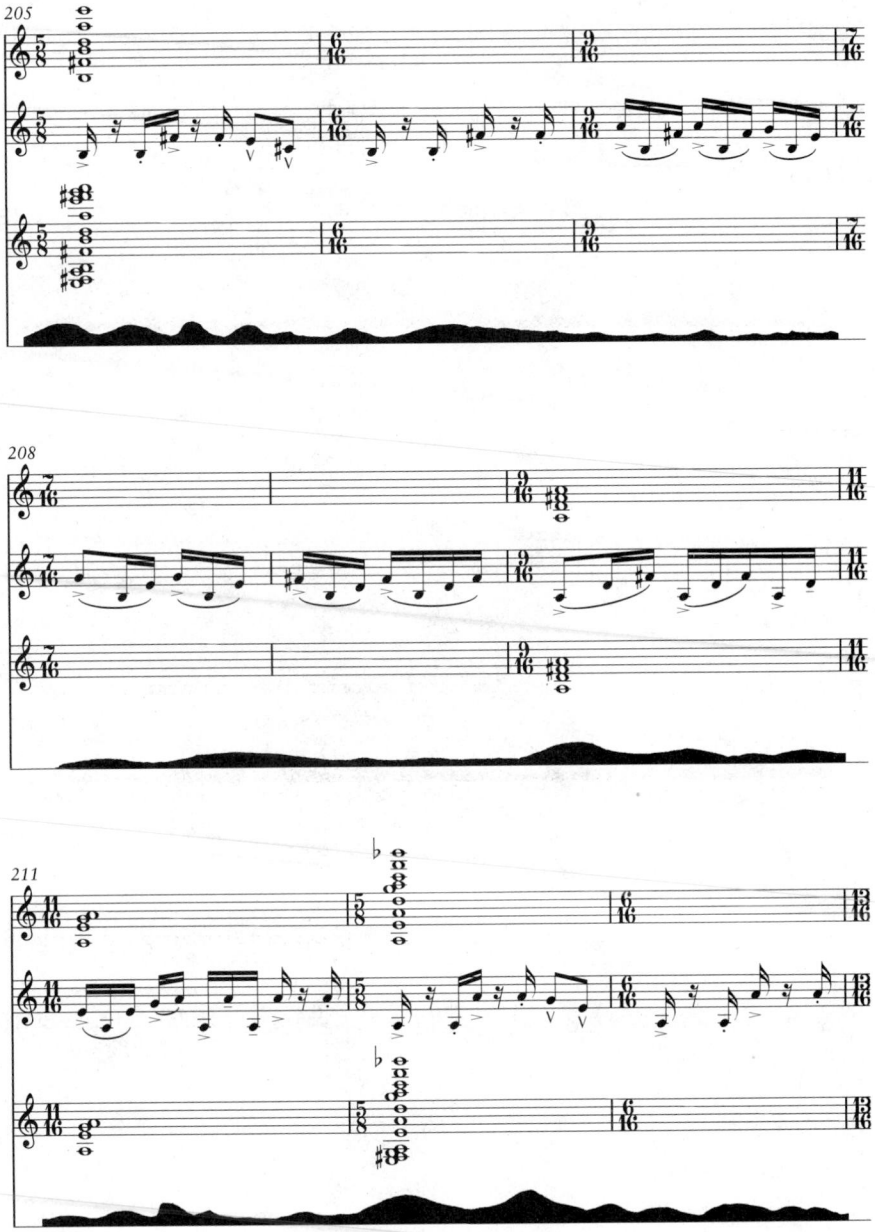
205
208
211

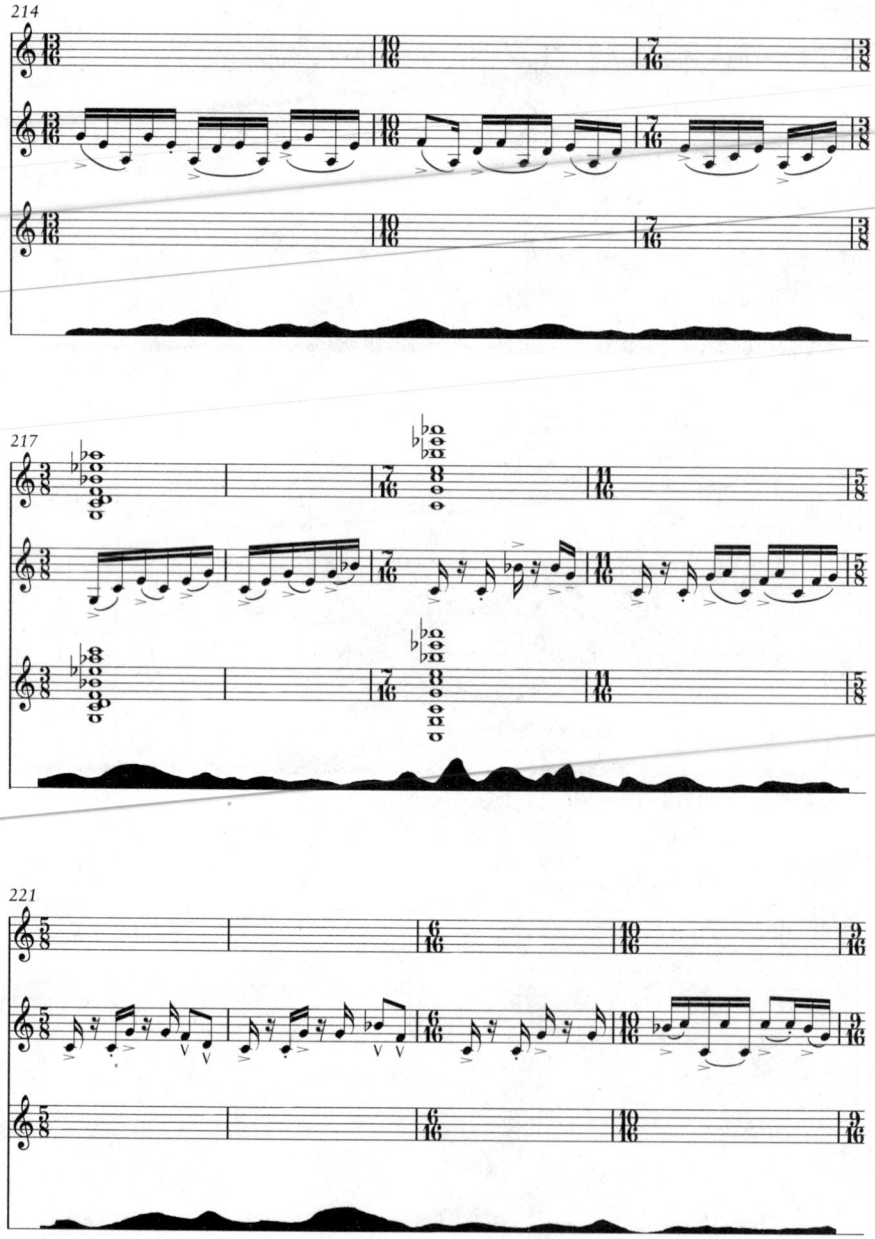
214
217
221

225

228

231

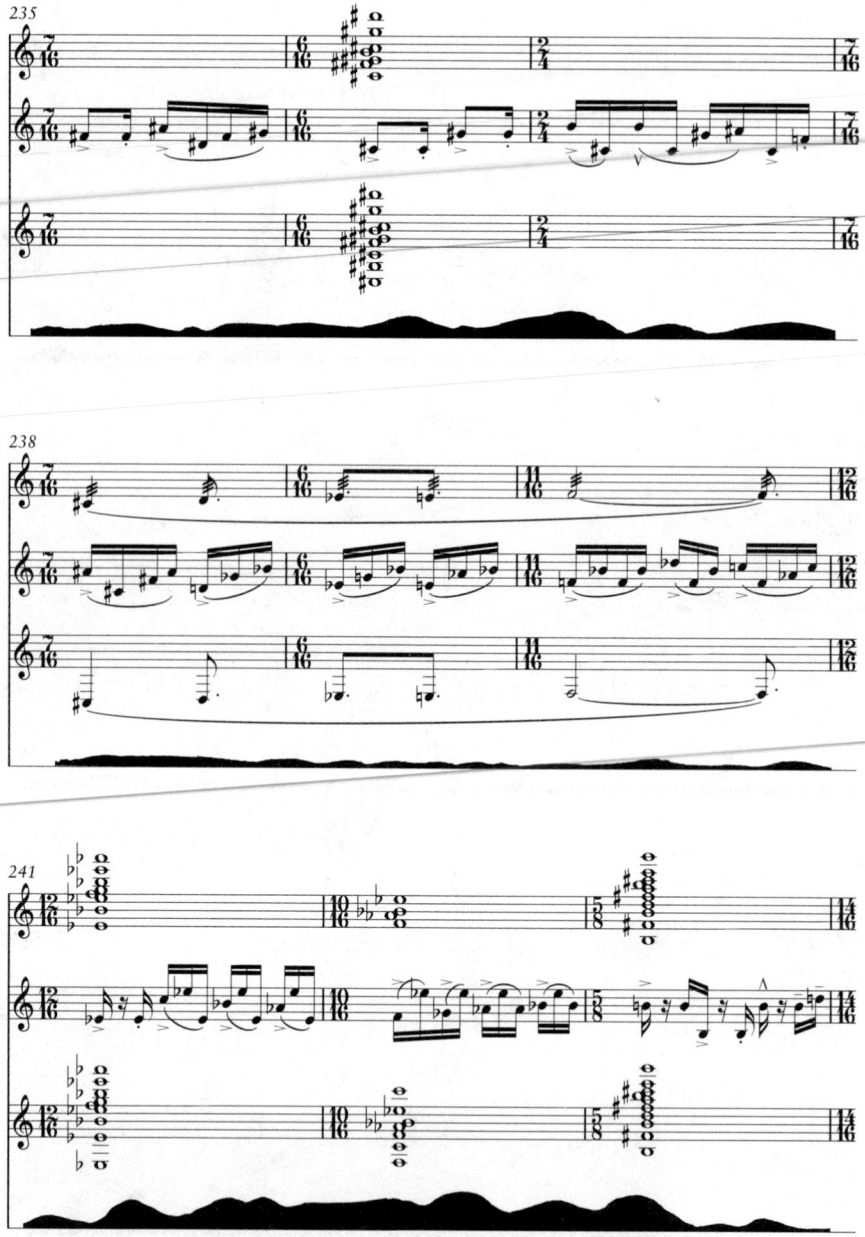
235
238
241

244
247

Appendix A

Reading a Musical Score

CLEFS

The music for some instruments is written in clefs other than the familiar treble and bass. In the following example, middle C is shown in the four clefs used in orchestral scores:

The *alto clef* is primarily used in viola parts. The *tenor clef* is employed for cello, bassoon, and trombone parts when these instruments play in a high register.

TRANSPOSING INSTRUMENTS

The music for some instruments is customarily written at a pitch different from its actual sound. The following list, with examples, shows the main transposing instruments and the degree of transposition. (In some modern works—such as the Stravinsky example included in this anthology—all instruments are written at their sounding pitch.)

Instrument	*Transposition*	*Written note*	*Actual sound*
Piccolo Celesta	sounds an octave higher than written		
Trumpet in F	sounds a fourth higher than written		
Trumpet in E	sounds a major third higher than written		
Clarinet in E♭ Trumpet in E♭	sounds a minor third higher than written		

Instrument	*Transposition*	*Written note*	*Actual sound*
Trumpet in D Clarinet in D	sounds a major second higher than written		
Clarinet in B♭ Trumpet in B♭ Cornet in B♭ French horn in B♭, alto	sounds a major second lower than written		
Clarinet in A Trumpet in A Cornet in A	sounds a minor third lower than written		
French horn in G Alto flute	sounds a fourth lower than written		
English horn French horn in F	sounds a fifth lower than written		
French horn in E	sounds a minor sixth lower than written		
French horn in E♭ Alto saxophone	sounds a major sixth lower than written		
French horn in D	sounds a minor seventh lower than written		
Contrabassoon French horn in C Double bass	sounds an octave lower than written		
Bass clarinet in B♭ Tenor saxophone (written in treble clef)	sounds a major ninth lower than written		
(written in bass clef)	sounds a major second lower than written		
Bass clarinet in A (written in treble clef)	sounds a minor tenth lower than written		
(written in bass clef)	sounds a minor third lower than written		
Baritone saxophone in E♭ (written in treble clef)	sounds an octave and a major sixth lower than written		

Appendix B

Instrumental Names and Abbreviations

The following tables set forth the English, Italian, German, and French names used for the various musical instruments in these scores, and their respective abbreviations (when used). Latin voice designations and a table of the foreign-language names for scale degrees and modes are also provided.

WOODWINDS

English	*Italian*	*German*	*French*
Piccolo (Picc.)	Flauto piccolo (Fl. Picc.)	Kleine Flöte (Kl. Fl.)	Petite flûte
Flute (Fl.)	Flauto (Fl.); Flauto grande (Fl. gr.)	Grosse Flöte (Gr. Fl.)	Flûte (Fl.)
Alto flute	Flauto contralto (fl. c-alto)	Altflöte	Flûte en sol
Oboe (Ob.)	Oboe (Ob.)	Hoboe (Hb.); Oboe (Ob.)	Hautbois (Hb.)
English horn (E. H.)	Corno inglese (C. or Cor. ingl., C.i.)	Englisches Horn (E. H.)	Cor anglais (C. A.)
E♭ clarinet	Clarinetto piccolo (clar. picc.)		
Clarinet (C., Cl., Clt., Clar.)	Clarinetto (Cl., Clar.)	Klarinette (Kl.)	Clarinette (Cl.)
Bass clarinet (B. Cl.)	Clarinetto basso (Cl. b., Cl. basso, Clar. basso)	Bass Klarinette (Bkl.)	Clarinette basse (Cl. bs.)
Bassoon (Bsn., Bssn.)	Fagotto (Fag., Fg.)	Fagott (Fag., Fg.)	Basson (Bssn.)

English	*Italian*	*German*	*French*
Contrabassoon (C. Bsn.)	Contrafagotto (Cfg., C. Fag., Cont. F.)	Kontrafagott (Kfg.)	Contrebasson (C. bssn.)
Alto saxophone	Sassofone	Saxophon	Saxophone
Tenor saxophone			
Baritone saxophone			
	BRASS		
French horn (Hr., Hn.)	Corno (Cor., C.)	Horn (Hr.) [*pl.* Hörner (Hrn.)]	Cor; Cor à pistons
Trumpet (Tpt., Trpt., Trp., Tr.)	Tromba (Tr.)	Trompete (Tr., Trp.)	Trompette (Tr.)
Trumpet in D	Tromba piccola (Tr. picc.)		
Cornet	Cornetta	Kornett	Cornet à pistons (C. à p., Pist.)
Trombone (Tr., Tbe., Trb., Trm., Trbe.)	Trombone [*pl.* Tromboni (Tbni., Trni.)]	Posaune (Ps., Pos.)	Trombone (Tr.)
Bass trombone			
Tuba (Tb.)	Tuba (Tb., Tba.)	Tuba (Tb.) [*also* Basstuba (Btb.)]	Tuba (Tb.)
Ophicleide	Oficleide	Ophikleide	Ophicléide
	PERCUSSION		
Percussion (Perc.)	Percussione	Schlagzeug (Schlag.)	Batterie (Batt.)
Kettledrums (K. D.)	Timpani (Timp., Tp.)	Pauken (Pk.)	Timbales (Timb.)
Snare drum (S. D.)	Tamburo piccolo (Tamb. picc.)	Kleine Trommel (Kl. Tr.)	Caisse claire (C. cl.); Caisse roulante
	Tamburo militare (Tamb. milit.)		Tambour militaire (Tamb. milit.)

English	*Italian*	*German*	*French*
Bass drum (B. drum)	Gran cassa (Gr. Cassa, Gr. C., G. C.)	Grosse Trommel (Gr. Tr.)	Grosse caisse (Gr. c.)
Cymbals (Cym., Cymb.)	Piatti (P., Ptti., Piat.)	Becken (Beck.)	Cymbales (Cym.)
Tam-Tam (Tam.-T.)			
Tambourine (Tamb.)	Tamburino (Tamb.)	Schellentrommel; Tamburin	Tambour de Basque (T. de B., Tamb. de Basque)
Triangle (Trgl., Tri.)	Triangolo (Trgl.)	Triangel	Triangle (Triang.)
Glockenspiel (Glocken.)	Campanelli (Cmp.)	Glockenspiel	Carillon
Bells; Chimes	Campane (Cmp.)	Glocken	Cloches
Antique cymbals	Crotali; Piatti antichi	Antike Zimbeln	Crotales; Cymbales antiques
Sleigh bells	Sonagli (Son.)	Schellen	Grelots
Xylophone (Xyl.)	Xilofono	Xylophon	Xylophone
Cowbells		Herdenglocken	
Crash cymbal			Grande cymbale chinoise
Siren			Sirène
Lion's roar			Tambour à corde
Slapstick			Fouet
Wood blocks			Blocs chinois

STRINGS

Violin (V., Vl., Vln., Vi.)	Violino (V., Vl., Vln.)	Violine (V., Vl., Vln.); Geige (Gg.)	Violon (V., Vl., Vln.)
Viola (Va., Vl., *pl.* Vas.)	Viola (Va., Vla.) [*pl.* Viole (Vle.)]	Bratsche (Br.)	Alto (A.)
Violoncello; Cello (Vcl., Vc.)	Violoncello (Vc., Vlc., Vcllo.)	Violoncell (Vc., Vlc.)	Violoncelle (Vc.)

English	*Italian*	*German*	*French*
Double bass (D. Bs.)	Contrabasso (Cb., C. B.) [*pl.* Contrabassi or Bassi (C. Bassi, Bi.)]	Kontrabass (Kb.)	Contrebasse (C. B.)
	OTHER INSTRUMENTS		
Harp (Hp., Hrp.)	Arpa (A., Arp.)	Harfe (Hrf.)	Harpe (Hp.)
Piano	Pianoforte (P.-f., Pft.)	Klavier	Piano
Celesta (Cel.)			
Harpsichord	Cembalo	Cembalo	Clavecin
Harmonium (Harmon.)			
Organ (Org.)	Organo	Orgel	Orgue
Guitar		Gitarre (Git.)	
Mandoline (Mand.)			

Voice Designations

Soprano (S)
Alto (A)
Tenor (T)
Bass (B)

Singstimme	Voice
Rezitation	Voice in Sprechstimme
Chor	Chorus

Names of Scale Degrees and Modes

SCALE DEGREES

English	*Italian*	*German*	*French*
C	do	C	ut
C-sharp	do diesis	Cis	ut dièse
D-flat	re bemolle	Des	ré bémol
D	re	D	ré
D-sharp	re diesis	Dis	ré dièse
E-flat	mi bemolle	Es	mi bémol
E	mi	E	mi
E-sharp	mi diesis	Eis	mi dièse
F-flat	fa bemolle	Fes	fa bémol
F	fa	F	fa
F-sharp	fa diesis	Fis	fa dièse
G-flat	sol bemolle	Ges	sol bémol
G	sol	G	sol
G-sharp	sol diesis	Gis	sol dièse
A-flat	la bemolle	As	la bémol
A	la	A	la
A-sharp	la diesis	Ais	la dièse
B-flat	si bemolle	B	si bémol
B	si	H	si
B-sharp	si diesis	His	si dièse
C-flat	do bemolle	Ces	ut bémol

MODES

major	maggiore	dur	majeur
minor	minore	moll	mineur

Appendix C

Glossary of Musical Terms Used in the Scores

The following glossary is not intended to be a complete dictionary of musical terms, nor is knowledge of all these terms necessary to follow the scores in this book. However, as listeners gain experience in following scores, they will find it useful and interesting to understand the composer's directions with regard to tempo, dynamics, and methods of performance.

In most cases, compound terms have been broken down in the glossary and defined separately, as they often recur in varying combinations. A few common foreign-language particles are included in addition to the musical terms. Note that names and abbreviations for instruments and for scale degrees will be found in Appendix B.

a The phrases *a 2*, *a 3* (etc.) indicate the number of parts to be played by 2, 3 (etc.) players; when a simple number (1, 2, etc.) is placed over a part, it indicates that only the first (second, etc.) player in that group should play.

ab Off.

aber But.

accelerando (accel.) Growing faster.

accentato, accentué Accented.

accompagnando Accompanying.

accompagnemento Accompaniment.

accordato, accordez Tune the instrument as specified.

adagio Slow, leisurely.

affettuoso With emotion.

affrettare (affrett.) Hastening a little.

agitando, agitato Agitated, excited.

al fine "The end"; an indication to return to the start of a piece and to repeat it only to the point marked "fine."

alla breve Indicates two beats to a measure, at a rather quick tempo.

allargando (allarg.) Growing broader.

alle, alles All, every, each.

allegretto A moderately fast tempo (between allegro and andante).

allegrezza Gaiety.

allegro A rapid tempo (between allegretto and presto).

allein Alone, solo.

allmählich Gradually (*allmählich wieder gleich mässig fliessend werden*, gradually becoming even-flowing again).

alta, alto, altus (A.) The deeper of the two main divisions of women's (or boys') voices.

am Steg On the bridge (of a string instrument).

ancora Again.

andante A moderately slow tempo (between adagio and allegretto).

andantino A moderately slow tempo.

Anfang Beginning, initial.

anima Spirit, animation.

animando With increasing animation.

animant, animato, animé, animez Animated.

aperto Indicates open notes on the horn, open strings, and undamped piano notes.

a piacere The execution of the passage is left to the performer's discretion.

appassionato Impassioned.
appena Scarcely, hardly.
apprensivo Apprehensive.
archet Bow.
archi, arco Played with the bow.
arditamente Boldly.
arpeggiando, arpeggiato (*arpegg.*) Played in harp style, i.e., the notes of the chord played in quick succession rather than simultaneously.
arrêt Break (as in *arrêt long*, long break).
articulato Articulated, separated.
assai Very.
assez Fairly, rather.
attacca Begin what follows without pausing.
a tempo At the original tempo.
auf dem On the (as in *auf dem G*, on the G string).
Ausdruck Expression.
ausdrucksvoll With expression.
äusserst Extreme, utmost.
avec With.

bachetta, bachetti Drumsticks (*bachetti di spugna*, sponge-headed drumsticks).
baguettes Drumsticks (*baguettes de bois*, wooden drumsticks; *baguettes d'éponge*, sponge-headed drumsticks; *baguettes dures*, hard mallets; *baguettes midures*, medium-hard mallets or drumsticks.
bass, bassi, basso, bassus (*B.*) The lowest male voice.
battere, battuta, battuto (*batt.*) To beat.
beaucoup A lot.
Becken Cymbals.
bedeutend bewegter With significantly more movement.
behaglich heiter Pleasingly serene or cheerful.
beider Hände With both hands.
ben Very.
bewegt Agitated.
bewegter More agitated.
bisbigliando, bispiglando (*bis.*) Whispering.
bis zum Schluss dieser Szene To the end of this scene.
blasen Blow.
Blech Brass instruments.
bogen (*bog.*) Played with the bow.
bois Woodwind.
bouché Muted.
breit Broadly.
breiter More broadly.
brilliante Brilliant.
brio Spirit, vivacity.
burden Refrain.

cadenza (*cad.*, *cadenz.*) An extended passage for solo instrument in free, improvisatory style.
calando (*cal.*) Diminishing in volume and speed.
calma, calmo Calm, calmly.
cantabile (*cant.*) In a singing style.
cantando In a singing manner.
canto Voice (as in *col canto*, a direction for the accompaniment to follow the solo part in tempo and expression).
cantus An older designation for the highest part in a vocal work.
capriccio Capriciously, whimsically.
cedendo Yielding.
cédez Slow down.
changez Change (usually an instruction to retune a string or an instrument).
chiuso See *gestopft*.
chromatisch Chromatic.
circa (ca.) About, approximately.
coda The last part of a piece.
col, colla, colle, coll' With the.
colore Colored.
come prima, come sopra As at first, as previously.
commodo Comfortable, easy.
con With.
corda String; for example, *seconda (2a) corda* is the second string (the A string on the violin).
corto Short, brief.
court Short.
crescendo (cres.) An increase in volume.
cuivré Played with a harsh, blaring tone.

da capo (D.C.) Repeat from the beginning.
dal segno (D.S.) Repeat from the sign.
Dämpfer (dpf.) Mutes.
dazu In addition to that, for that purpose.

de, des, die Of, from.
début Beginning.
deciso Determined, resolute.
declamando In a declamatory style.
decrescendo (decresc., decr.) A decreasing of volume.
dehors Outside.
delicato Delicate, delicately.
dem To the.
détaché With a broad, vigorous bow stroke, each note bowed singly.
deutlich Distinctly.
d'exécution Performance.
diminuendo, diminuer (dim., dimin.) A decreasing of volume.
distinto Distinct, clear.
divisés, divisi (div.) Divided; indicates that the instrumental group should be divided into two parts to play the passage in question.
dolce Sweetly and softly.
dolcemente Sweetly.
dolcissimo (dolciss.) Very sweetly.
dolore, doloroso With sorrow.
Doppelgriff Double stop.
doux Sweetly.
drammatico Dramatic.
drängend Pressing on.
dreifach Triple.
dreitaktig Three beats to a measure.
dur Major, as in *G dur* (G major).
durée Duration.

e, et And.
eilen To hurry.
ein One, a.
elegante Elegant, graceful.
Empfindung Feeling.
energico Energetically.
espansione Expansion, broadening.
espressione With expression.
espressivo (espr., espress.) Expressively.
etwas Somewhat, rather.
expressif Expressively.

facile Simple.
falsetto Male voice singing above normal range, with light sound.
feroce Fierce, ferocious.
fin, fine End, close.
Flatterzunge (Flzg.), flutter-tongue A special tonguing technique for wind instruments, producing a rapid, trill-like sound.
flebile Feeble, plaintive, mournful.
fliessend Flowing.
forte (f) Loud.
fortepiano (fp) Loud, then soft immediately.
fortissimo (ff) Very loud (*fff* indicates a still louder dynamic).
forza Force.
forzando (fz) Forcing, strongly accented.
forzandissimo (ffz) Very strongly accented.
fou Frantic.
frappez To strike.
frei Freely.
freihäng., freihängendes Hanging freely. An indication to the percussionist to let the cymbals vibrate freely.
frisch Fresh, lively.
fuoco Fire.
furioso Furiously.
furore Fury, rage.

ganz Entirely, altogether.
Ganzton Whole tone.
gedämpft (ged.) Muted.
geheimnisvoll Mysteriously.
geschlagen Pulsating.
gestopft (gest.) Stopping the notes of a horn; that is, the hand is placed in the bell of the horn to produce a muffled sound. Also *chiuso*.
geteilt (get.) Divided; indicates that the instrumental group should be divided into two parts to play the passage in question.
getragen Sustained.
gewöhnlich As usual.
giocoso Humorous.
giusto Moderately.
glissando (gliss.) Rapid scales produced by running the fingers over all the strings.
gradamente Gradually.
grande Large, great.
grandezza Grandeur.
grandioso Grandiose.
grave Slow, solemn; deep, low.
grazioso Gracefully.
Griffbrett Fingerboard.
grosser Auftakt Big upbeat.
gut Good, well.

Hälfte Half.
Hauptzeitmass Original tempo.

hauteur réelle In the octave notated, designation for transposing French horns.
hervortreten Prominent.
hoch High, nobly.
Holz Woodwinds.
Holzschlägel Wooden drumstick.

im gleichen Rhythmus In the same rhythm.
immer Always.
in Oktaven In octaves.
insensibilmente Slightly, imperceptibly.
intensa Intensely.
istesso tempo Duration of beat remains unaltered despite meter change.

jeu Playful.
jusqu'à Until.

kadenzieren To cadence.
klagend Lamenting.
kleine Little.
klingen To sound.
komisch bedeutsam Very humorously.
kurz Short.

langsam Slow.
langsamer Slower.
languendo, langueur Languor.
l'archet See *archet*.
largamente Broadly.
larghetto Slightly faster than largo.
largo A very slow tempo.
lasci, lassen To abandon.
lebhaft Lively.
lebhafter Livelier.
legatissimo A more forceful indication of *legato*.
legato Performed without any perceptible interruption between notes.
légèrement, leggieramente Lightly.
leggierissimo Very light.
leggiero (legg.) Light and graceful.
legno The wood of the bow (*col legno gestrich*, played with the wood).
lent Slow.
lentamente Slowly.
lento A slow tempo (between andante and largo).
l.h. Abbreviation for "left hand."
liricamente Lyrically.
loco Indicates a return to the written pitch, following a passage played an octave higher or lower than written.
Luftpause Pause for breath.
lunga Long, sustained.
lusingando Caressing.

ma, mais But.
maestoso Majestic.
marcatissimo (marcatiss.) With very marked emphasis.
marcato (marc.) Marked, with emphasis.
marcia March.
marschmässig, nicht eilen Moderate-paced march, not rushed.
marziale Military, martial, march-like.
mässig Moderately.
mässiger More moderately.
melodia Melody.
même Same.
meno Less.
mezzo forte (mf) Moderately loud.
mezzo piano (mp) Moderately soft.
mindestens At least.
misterioso Mysterious.
misura Measured.
mit With.
moderatissimo A more forceful indication of *moderato*.
moderato, modéré At a moderate tempo.
moins Less.
molto Very, much.
mordenti Biting, pungent.
morendo Dying away.
mormorato Murmured.
mosso Rapid.
moto Motion.
mouvement (mouv., mouvt.) Tempo.
muta, mutano Change the tuning of the instrument as specified.

nach After.
naturalezza A natural, unaffected manner.
nel modo russico In the Russian style.
neuen New.
nicht Not.
niente Nothing.
nimmt To take; to seize.
noch Still.
non Not.
nuovo New.

obere, oberer (ob.) Upper, leading.
oder langsamer Or slower.
offen Open.

ohne Without.
ondeggiante Undulating movement of the bow, which produces a tremolo effect.
ordinario (ord., ordin.) In the usual way (generally canceling an instruction to play using some special technique).
ossia An alternative (usually easier) version of a passage.
ôtez vite les sourdines Remove the mutes quickly.
ottava Octave (as in *8va*, octave higher than written; *8 basso*, *8 bassa*, octave lower than written; *16 va*, two octaves higher than written).
ottoni Brass.
ouvert Open.

parte Part (*colla parte*, *colle parti*, the accompaniment is to follow the soloist[s] in tempo).
passionato Passionately.
passione Passion, emotion.
Paukenschlägel Timpani stick.
pavillons en l'air An indication to the player of a wind instrument to raise the bell of the instrument upward.
pedal, *pedale (ped., P.)* (1) In piano music, indicates that the damper pedal should be depressed; an asterisk indicates the point of release (brackets below the music are also used to indicate pedaling); (2) on an organ, the pedals are a keyboard played with the feet.
per During.
perdendosi Gradually dying away.
pesante Heavily.
peu Little, a little.
piacevole Agreeable, pleasant.
pianissimo (pp) Very soft (*ppp* indicates a still softer dynamic).
piano (p) Soft.
piena Full.
più More.
pizzicato (pizz.) The string plucked with the finger.
plötzlich Suddenly, immediately.
plus More.
pochissimo (pochiss.) Very little, a very little.
poco Little, a little.
poco a poco Little by little.
ponticello (pont.) The bridge (of a string instrument).
portamento Continuous smooth and rapid sliding between two pitches.
portando Carrying.
position naturel (pos. nat.) In the normal position (usually canceling an instruction to play using some special technique).
possibile Possible.
precedente Previous, preceding.
precipitato Rushed, hurried.
premier mouvement (1er mouvt.) At the original tempo.
prenez Take up.
préparez Prepare.
presque Almost, nearly.
presser To speed up.
prestissimo A more forceful indication of *presto*.
presto A very quick tempo (faster than allegro).
prima, *primo* First, principal.
punto Point.

quarta Fourth.
quasi Almost, as if.
quinto Fifth.

rallentando (rall., rallent.) Growing slower.
rapidamente Quickly.
rapide Rapid, fast.
rapidissimo (rapidiss.) Very quickly.
rasch Quickly.
rascher More quickly.
rauschend Rustling, roaring.
recitative, *recitativo (recit.)* A vocal style designed to imitate and emphasize the natural inflections of speech.
rein Perfect interval.
resonante Resonating.
respiro Pause for breath.
retenu Held back.
revenir au tempo Return to the original tempo.
r.h. Abbreviation for "right hand."
rianimando Reanimating.
richtig Correct (*richtige Lage*, correct pitch).
rien Nothing.
rigore di tempo Strictness of tempo.
rigueur Rigor, strictness.
rinforzando (rf, rfz, rinf.) A sudden accent on a single note or chord.
risoluto In a resolute or determined manner.

ritardando (rit., ritard.) Gradually slackening in speed.
ritenuto (riten.) Immediate reduction of speed.
ritmato, ritmico Rhythmic.
ritornando, ritornello (ritor.) Refrain.
rubato A certain elasticity and flexibility of tempo, consisting of slight accelerandos and ritardandos according to the requirements of the musical expression.
ruhig Quietly.

saltando Leaping.
sans Without.
Schalltrichter Horn.
scherzando (scherz.) Playful.
schlagen To strike in a usual manner.
Schlagwerk Striking mechanism.
schleppen, schleppend Dragging.
Schluss Cadence, conclusion.
schnell Fast.
schneller Faster.
schon Already.
Schwammschägeln Sponge-headed drumstick.
scorrevole Flowing, gliding.
sec, secco Dry, simple.
secunda Second.
sehr Very.
semplice Simple.
semplicità Simplicity.
sempre Always, continually.
senza Without.
sforzando (sf., sfz.) With sudden emphasis.
sforzandissimo (sff, sffz) With very loud, sudden attack.
simile (sim.) In a similar manner.
sin Without.
Singstimme Singing voice.
sino al Up to the . . . (usually followed by a new tempo marking, or by a dotted line indicating a terminal point).
si piace Especially pleasing.
smorzando (smorz.) Dying away.
sofort Immediately.
soli, solo (s.) Executed by one performer.
sonoro Sonorous, resonant.
sopra Above; in piano music, used to indicate that one hand must pass above the other.
soprano (S.) The voice classification with the highest range.
sordini, sordino (sord.) Mute.
sostenendo, sostenuto (sost.) Sustained.
sotto voce In an undertone, subdued, under the breath.
sourdine (sourd.) Mute.
soutenu Sustained.
spiel, spielen Play (an instrument).
Spieler Player, performer.
spirito Spirit, soul.
spiritoso In a spirited manner.
spugna Sponge.
staccato (stacc.) Detached, separated, abruptly, disconnected.
stentando, stentare, stentato (stent.) Delaying, retarding.
stesso The same.
Stimme Voice.
stimmen To tune.
strascinare To drag.
straziante Agonizing, heart-rending.
Streichinstrumente (Streichinstr.) Bowed string instruments.
strepitoso Noisy, loud.
stretto In a non-fugal composition, indicates a concluding section at an increased speed.
stringendo (string.) Quickening.
subito (sub.) Suddenly, immediately.
sul On the (as in *sul G*, on the G string).
superius In older music, the uppermost part.
sur On.

tacet The instrument or vocal part so marked is silent.
tasto Fingerboard (as in *sul tasto*, bow over the fingerboard).
tasto solo In a continuo part, this indicates that only the string instrument plays; the chord-playing instrument is silent.
tempo primo (tempo I) At the original tempo.
teneramente, tenero Tenderly, gently.
tenor, tenore (T.) The highest male voice.
tenuto (ten., tenu.) Held, sustained.
tertia Third.
tief Deep, low.
timbre Tone color.
touche Key; note.
toujours Always, continually.

tranquillo Quietly, calmly.
tre corde (t.c.) Release the soft (or *una corda*) pedal of the piano.
tremolo (trem.) On string instruments, a quick reiteration of the same tone, produced by a rapid up-and-down movement of the bow; also a rapid alternation between two different notes.
très Very.
trill (tr.) The rapid alternation of a given note with the diatonic second above it. In a drum part, it indicates rapid alternating strokes with two drumsticks.
tromba Trumpet (as in *quasi tromba*, trumpet-like).
Trommschlag (Tromm.) Drumbeat.
troppo Too much.
tutta la forza Very emphatically.
tutti Literally, "all"; usually means all the instruments in a given category as distinct from a solo part.

übergreifen To overlap.
übertonend Drowning out.
umstimmen To change the tuning.
un One, a.
una corda (u.c.) With the "soft" pedal of the piano depressed.
und And.
unison (unis.) The same notes or melody played by several instruments at the same pitch. Often used to emphasize that a phrase is not to be divided among several players.
unmerklich Imperceptible.

velocissimo Very swiftly.
verklingen lassen To let die away.
vibrare To sound.
vibrato (vibr.) To fluctuate the pitch on a single note.
vierfach Quadruple.
vierhändig Four-hand piano music.
vif Lively.
vigoroso Vigorous, strong.
violento Violent.
viva, vivente, vivo Lively.
vivace Quick, lively.
vivacissimo A more forceful indication of *vivace*.
voce Voice (as in *colla voce*, a direction for the accompaniment to follow the solo part in tempo and expression).
volles Orch. Entire orchestra.
vorbereiten Prepare, get ready.
Vorhang auf Curtain up.
Vorhang zu Curtain down.
vorher Beforehand, previously.
voriges Preceding.

Waltzertempo In the tempo of a waltz.
weg Away, beyond.
weich Mellow, smooth, soft.
wie aus der Fern As if from afar.
wieder Again.
wie zu Anfang dieser Szene As at the beginning of this scene.

zart Tenderly, delicately.
Zeit Time; duration.
zögernd Slower.
zu The phrases *zu 2*, *zu 3* (etc.) indicate the number of parts to be played by 2, 3 (etc.) players.
zum In addition.
zurückhaltend Slackening in speed.
zurücktreten To withdraw.
zweihändig With two hands.

Appendix D

Concordance Table for Recordings and The Enjoyment of Music *Listening Guides*

The following table provides cross-references to the Listening Guides (LG) in the various versions of *The Enjoyment of Music*, seventh edition, by Joseph Machlis and Kristine Forney (New York: W.W. Norton, 1995). The following abbreviations are used throughout: C for the Chronological version; S for the Standard version, and Sh for the Shorter version. The table also summarizes the location of each work and its individual movements within the various recordings sets (see "Note on Recordings," p. xiv). Because of copyright restrictions, several contemporary works included on the recordings and in the Listening Guides do not appear in *The Norton Scores*.

Listening Guides				*Norton Scores*	*8-CD*	*8-Cas*	*3-CD*	*3-Cas*
C	Sh	S	*Composer, Title*	*Page*	*Set*	*Set*	*Set*	*Set*
36	—	29	MENDELSSOHN, *A Midsummer Night's Dream*, Overture	62	5/13	5A/3	—	—
37	20	2	SCHUBERT, *Erlkönig (Erlking)*,*	1	5/1	5A/1	2/20	2A/4
38	—	3	BRAHMS, *Vergebliches Ständchen (Futile Serenade)*	247	5/47	5B/4	—	—
39	21	4	CHOPIN, Polonaise in A-flat major, Op. 53*	117	5/24	5A/5	2/27	2A/5
40	—	5	CHOPIN, Prelude in E minor, Op. 28, No. 4	116	5/22	5A/4	—	—
41	—	6	LISZT, *Wilde Jagd (Wild Hunt)*, Transcendental Etude No. 8	168	5/35	5A/6	—	—
42	22	7	C. SCHUMANN, Scherzo in D minor, Op. 10	226	6/6	6A/2	2/31	2B/1

*Included in *The Norton CD-ROM Masterworks*, Volume I.

Listening Guides C	Sh	S	Composer, Title	Norton Scores Page	8-CD Set	8-Cas Set	3-CD Set	3-Cas Set
43	23	8	BERLIOZ, *Symphonie fantastique*, Fifth Movement	8	5/8	5A/2	2/37	2B/2
44	24	9	MUSORGSKY, *Pictures at an Exhibition*					
			Promenade	317	6/23	6B/1	—	—
			The Hut on Fowl's Legs	322	6/24	6B/2	—	—
			The Great Gate of Kiev	352	6/27	6B/2	2/42	2B/3
45	—	10	BRAHMS, Symphony No. 4, Fourth Movement	252	6/12	6A/3	—	—
46	—	11	DVOŘÁK, Symphony No. 9 in E minor, *From the New World*, Second Movement	424	6/43	6B/6	—	—
47	—	12	R. SCHUMANN, Piano Concerto in A minor, First Movement	127	5/28	5B/1	—	—
48	25	13	BRAHMS, *A German Requiem*, Fourth Movement	236	5/42	5B/3	2/49	2B/4
49	26	14	VERDI, *La traviata*					
			Act II, Finale (complete)	189	6/1	6A/1	—	—
			Act II, Finale (second part only)	200	—	—	3/1	3A/1
50	27	15	WAGNER, *Die Walküre*					
			Act III, "Farewell" and "Magic fire" music	179	5/38	5B/2	—	—
			Act III, "Magic fire" music (only)	183	—	—	2/54	2B/5
51	—	16	BIZET, *Carmen*, Act I (excerpt)	283	6/15	6A/4	—	—
52	28	17	LEONCAVALLO, *Pagliacci*, Act I, Canio's Aria*	442	6/46	6B/7	2/56	2B/6
53	—	18	TCHAIKOVSKY, *The Nutcracker*					
			March	377	6/34	6B/3	—	—
			Dance of the Sugar Plum Fairy	401	6/37	6B/4	—	—
			Trepak	410	6/40	6B/5	—	—
54	—	54	MAHLER, *Das Lied von der Erde (The Song of the Earth)*, Third Movement	447	6/48	6B/8	—	—
55	—	55	STRAUSS, *Der Rosenkavalier* (The Cavalier of the Rose), Act III, Trio	489	7/5	7A/2	—	—
56	29	56	DEBUSSY, *Prélude à "L'après-midi d'un faune" (Prelude to "The Afternoon of a Faun")*	458	7/1	7A/1	3/3	3A/2

*Included in *The Norton CD-ROM Masterworks*, Volume I.

Listening Guides C	Sh	S	Composer, Title	Norton Scores Page	8-CD Set	8-Cas Set	3-CD Set	3-Cas Set
57	—	57	RAVEL, *Chansons madécasses (Songs of Madagascar)*, Second Movement	570	7/19	7A/6	—	—
58	30	58	STRAVINSKY, *Petrushka*					
			First Tableau (complete)	628	7/25	7B/1	—	—
			First Tableau (first part only)*	628	—	—	3/7	3A/3
59	31	59	SCHOENBERG, *Pierrot lunaire*					
			No. 18, "Der Mondfleck"*	499	7/7	7A/3	3/16	3A/4
			No. 21, "O alter Duft aus Märchenzeit"	505	7/9	7A/4	3/18	3A/5
60	—	60	BERG, *Wozzeck*, Act III, Scenes 4 and 5	692	7/44	7B/2	—	—
61	—	61	WEBERN, Symphony, Op. 21, Second Movement	684	7/41	7A/8	—	—
62	—	62	PROKOFIEV, *Alexander Nevsky*, Seventh Movement	717	7/48	7B/3	—	—
63	32	63	BARTÓK, *Music for Strings, Percussion, and Celesta*, Fourth Movement	578	7/21	7A/7	3/20	3A/6
64	—	64	IVES, *The Fourth of July*, from *A Symphony: New England Holidays*	509	7/11	7A/5	—	—
65	—	65	CRAWFORD, *Rat Riddles*, from Three Songs (1933)	799	8/12	8A/3	—	—
66	33	66	COPLAND, *Billy the Kid*, Scene 1, *Street in a Frontier Town*	758	8/9	8A/2	3/24	3A/7
67	—	67	LOUIS ARMSTRONG AND THE SAVOY BALLROOM FIVE, *West End Blues*	737	7/54	7B/6	—	—
68	34	68	ELLINGTON, *Ko-Ko*	739	8/1	8A/1	3/27	3B/1
69	35	69	RODGERS, *My Funny Valentine*					
			Original Version	730	7/50	7B/4	—	—
			Gerry Mulligan Quartet Version*	734	7/52	7B/5	3/35	3B/2
70	36	70	BERNSTEIN, Symphonic Dances from *West Side Story*, excerpts: *Cool* (Fugue) & "Rumble"	840	8/21	8A/7	3/37	3B/3
71	—	71	DYLAN, *Mister Tambourine Man* by the Byrds	—	8/43	8B/5	—	—
72	37	72	*Black Magic Woman/Gypsy Queen* by Santana	—	8/44	8B/6	3/41	3B/4
73	38	73	*That's Why I Choose You* by Ladysmith Black Mambazo	—	8/46	8B/7	3/43	3B/5

*Included in *The Norton CD-ROM Masterworks*, Volume I.

Listening Guides C	Sh	S	*Composer, Title*	*Norton Scores Page*	*8-CD Set*	*8-Cas Set*	*3-CD Set*	*3-Cas Set*
74	—	74	CARTER, Sonata for Flute, Oboe, Cello, and Harpsichord, First Movement	822	8/16	8A/4	—	—
75	—	75	BOULEZ, *Le marteau sans maître (The Hammer Without a Master)*					
			No. 1	880	8/28	8A/9	—	—
			No. 3	886	8/29	8A/10	—	—
			No. 7	889	8/30	8A/11	—	—
76	—	76	LUTOSŁAWSKI, *Jeux vénitiens (Venetian Games)*, First Movement	817	8/18	8A/5	—	—
77	39	77	CRUMB, *Ancient Voices of Children*, First Movement	893	8/31	8B/1	3/46	3B/6
78	40	78	LIGETI, *Désordre (Disorder)*, from Etudes for Piano, Book I	875	8/25	8A/8	3/49	3B/7
79	—	79	BABBITT, *Phonemena* (excerpt)	833	8/20	8A/6	—	—
80	41	80	MACHOVER, *Bug-Mudra* (excerpt)	961	8/40	8B/4	3/52	3B/8
81	42	81	TOWER, *Petroushskates*	896	8/34	8B/2	3/55	3B/9
82	—	82	ADAMS, *Nixon in China*, Act I, Scene 3, Finale	928	8/38	8B/3	—	—

Index of Forms and Genres

ABA form: *see* ternary form
aleatoric music:
LUTOSŁAWSKI, *Jeux vénitiens*, I (p. 817)
aria:
BIZET, *Carmen*, Act I, Habanera (p. 306)
LEONCAVALLO, *Pagliacci*, Act I, Canio's Aria (p. 443)
VERDI, *La traviata*, Act II, Finale (p. 189)
art song: *see* song

ballet music:
COPLAND, *Billy the Kid* (p. 758)
DEBUSSY, *Prélude à "L'après-midi d'un Faune"* (p. 458)
STRAVINSKY, *Petrushka* (p. 628)
TCHAIKOVSKY, *The Nutcracker* (p. 377)
blues:
ARMSTRONG, *West End Blues* (p. 737)
ELLINGTON, *Ko-Ko* (p. 739)

cadenza:
ROBERT SCHUMANN, Piano Concerto in A minor, Op. 54 (p. 161)
cantata:
PROKOFIEV, *Alexander Nevsky* (p. 717)
chamber music:
BOULEZ, *Le marteau sans maître* (p. 880)
CARTER, Sonata for Flute, Oboe, Cello, and Harpsichord (p. 822)
CRAWFORD, *Rat Riddles* (p. 799)
CRUMB, *Ancient Voices of Children* (p. 893)
RAVEL, *Chansons madécasses* (p. 570)
SCHOENBERG, *Pierrot lunaire* (p. 499)
TOWER, *Petroushskates* (p. 896)
choral music:
BRAHMS, *A German Requiem* (p. 236)
PROKOFIEV, *Alexander Nevsky* (p. 717)
chorus, operatic:
ADAMS, *Nixon in China*, Act I, Scene 3 (p. 928)
BIZET, *Carmen*, Scene from Act I (p. 283)
VERDI, *La traviata*, Act II, Finale (p. 196)
concert overture: *see* overture
concerto:
ROBERT SCHUMANN, Piano Concerto in A minor, Op. 54 (p. 127)

dance music:
BERNSTEIN, Symphonic Dances from *West Side Story* (p. 840)
TCHAIKOVSKY, *The Nutcracker*, Act II (p. 377)
double-exposition form: *see* first-movement concerto form
durchkomponiert song: *see* through-composed song

electronic music:
BABBITT, *Phonemena* (p. 833)
MACHOVER, *Bug-Mudra* (p. 961)
ensemble, operatic:
ADAMS, *Nixon in China*, Act I (p. 928)
STRAUSS, *Der Rosenkavalier*, Act III, Trio (p. 489)
VERDI, *La traviata*, Act II, Finale (p. 196)
etude:
LIGETI, *Désordre*, from Etudes for Piano (p. 875)
LISZT, *Wilde Jagd* (p. 168)

film music:
PROKOFIEV, *Alexander Nevsky* (p. 717)
first-movement concerto form:
ROBERT SCHUMANN, Piano Concerto in A minor, Op. 54 (p. 127)
fugue:
BERNSTEIN, Symphonic Dances from *West Side Story*, *Cool* (p. 840)

incidental music:
MENDELSSOHN, *A Midsummer Night's Dream* (p. 62)
interlude, orchestral:
BERG, *Wozzeck*, Act III (p. 706)

jazz:
ARMSTRONG, *West End Blues* (p. 737)

ELLINGTON, *Ko-Ko* (p. 739)
RODGERS, *My Funny Valentine*, Gerry Mulligan Quartet (p. 734)

Lied: *see* song

march:
TCHAIKOVSKY, *The Nutcracker*, Act II, *March* (p. 377)
Mass, Requiem:
BRAHMS, *A German Requiem* (p. 236)
musical theater:
BERNSTEIN, Symphonic Dances from *West Side Story* (p. 840)
RODGERS, *My Funny Valentine* (p. 730)

operatic scene:
ADAMS, *Nixon in China*, Act I, Finale (p. 928)
BERG, *Wozzeck*, Act III, Scenes 4 and 5 (p. 692)
BIZET, *Carmen*, Scene from Act I (p. 283)
LEONCAVALLO, *Pagliacci*, Act I, Canio's Aria (p. 442)
STRAUSS, *Der Rosenkavalier*, Act III, Trio (p. 489)
VERDI, *La traviata*, Act II, Finale (p. 189)
WAGNER, *Die Walküre*, Act III, Scene 3 (p. 179)
orchestral music:
BARTÓK, *Music for Strings, Percussion, and Celesta* (p. 578)
BERLIOZ, *Symphonie fantastique* (p. 8)
BERNSTEIN, Symphonic Dances from *West Side Story* (p. 840)
BRAHMS, Symphony No. 4 in E minor (p. 252)
COPLAND, *Billy the Kid* (p. 758)
DEBUSSY, *Prélude à "L'après-midi d'un faune"* (p. 458)
DVOŘÁK, Symphony No. 9 in E minor *(New World)* (p. 424)
IVES, *The Fourth of July* (p. 509)
LUTOSŁAWSKI, *Jeux vénitiens* (p. 817)
MENDELSSOHN, *A Midsummer Night's Dream* (p. 62)
MUSORGSKY, *Pictures at an Exhibition* (p. 317)
ROBERT SCHUMANN, Piano Concerto in A minor (p. 127)
STRAVINSKY, *Petrushka* (p. 628)
TCHAIKOVSKY, *The Nutcracker*, Act II (p. 377)
WEBERN, Symphony, Op. 21 (p. 684)
overture:
MENDELSSOHN, *A Midsummer Night's Dream*, Overture (p. 62)

passacaglia:
BRAHMS, Symphony No. 4 in E minor (p. 252)
piano music:
CHOPIN, Polonaise in A-flat major, Op. 53 (p. 117); Prelude in E minor, Op. 28, No. 4 (p. 116)
LIGETI, *Désordre*, from Etudes for piano (p. 875)
LISZT, *Wilde Jagd* (p. 168)
CLARA SCHUMANN, *Scherzo*, Op. 10 (p. 226)
polonaise:
CHOPIN, Polonaise in A-flat major, Op. 53 (p. 117)
prelude:
CHOPIN, Prelude in E minor, Op. 28, No. 4 (p. 116)
DEBUSSY, *Prélude à "L'après-midi d'un faune"* (p. 458)
program music:
BERLIOZ, *Symphonie fantastique* (p. 8)
COPLAND, *Billy the Kid* (p. 758)
DEBUSSY, *Prélude à "L'après-midi d'un faune"* (p. 458)
IVES, *The Fourth of July* (p. 509)
MENDELSSOHN, *A Midsummer Night's Dream*, Overture (p. 62)
MUSORGSKY, *Pictures at an Exhibition* (p. 317)
STRAVINSKY, *Petrushka* (p. 628)
program symphony:
BERLIOZ, *Symphonie fantastique* (p. 8)

recitative:
LEONCAVALLO, *Pagliacci*, Act I, Canio's Aria (p. 442)
VERDI, *La traviata*, Act II, Finale (p. 189)
ritornello:
CRAWFORD, *Rat Riddles* (p. 799)
rondo:
BARTÓK, *Music for Strings, Percussion, and Celesta*, IV (p. 578)
BRAHMS, *A German Requiem*, IV (p. 236)

scherzo and trio:
CLARA SCHUMANN, *Scherzo*, Op. 10 (p. 226)
solo voice (in chamber ensemble):
BABBITT, *Phonemena* (p. 833)
BOULEZ, *Le marteau sans maître*, III (p. 886)
CRAWFORD, *Rat Riddles* (p. 799)
CRUMB, *Ancient Voices of Children*, I (p. 893)
RAVEL, *Chansons madécasses*, I (p. 570)
SCHOENBERG, *Pierrot lunaire* (p. 499)
solo voice (in orchestral music):
MAHLER, *Das Lied von der Erde*, III (p. 886)

RODGERS, *My Funny Valentine* (p. 730)
sonata-allegro form:
MENDELSSOHN, *A Midsummer Night's Dream*, Overture (p. 62)
song:
BRAHMS, *Vergebliches Ständchen*, Op. 84, No. 4 (p. 247)
CRAWFORD, *Rat Riddles* (p. 799)
CRUMB, *Ancient Voices of Children,* I (p. 893)
MAHLER, *Das Lied von der Erde* (p. 447)
RAVEL, *Chansons madécasses* (p. 570)
RODGERS, *My Funny Valentine* (p. 730)
SCHOENBERG, *Pierrot lunaire* (p. 499)
SCHUBERT, *Erlkönig* (p. 1)
song-cycle (excerpt):
BOULEZ, *Le marteau sans maître* (p. 880)
CRUMB, *Ancient Voices of Children* (p. 893)
MAHLER, *Das Lied von der Erde* (p. 447)
RAVEL, *Chansons madécasses* (p. 570)
SCHOENBERG, *Pierrot lunaire* (p. 499)
strophic song form (modified):
BRAHMS, *Vergebliches Ständchen*, Op. 84, No. 4 (p. 247)
suite:
MUSORGSKY, *Pictures at an Exhibition* (p. 317)
TCHAIKOVSKY, *The Nutcracker* (p. 377)
symphony:
BERLIOZ, *Symphonie fantastique* (p. 8)
BRAHMS, Symphony No. 4 in E minor (p. 252)
DVOŘÁK, Symphony No. 9 in E minor *(New World)* (p. 424)
WEBERN, Symphony, Op. 21 (p. 684)

ternary form:
DEBUSSY, *Prélude à "L'après-midi d'un faune"* (p. 458)
DVOŘÁK, Symphony No. 9 in E minor *(New World)*, II (p. 424)
LISZT, *Wilde Jagd* (p. 168)
MAHLER, *Das Lied von der Erde*, III (p. 447)
TCHAIKOVSKY, *The Nutcracker*, Act II, *March* (p. 377), *Dance of the Sugar Plum Fairy* (p. 401), *Trepak* (p. 410)
ternary form (modified):
CHOPIN, Polonaise in A-flat major, Op. 53 (p. 117)
theme and variations:
WEBERN, Symphony, Op. 21, II (p. 684)
three-part form: *see* ternary form
through-composed song:
CRUMB, *Ancient Voices of Children*, I (p. 893)
SCHUBERT, *Erlkönig* (p. 1)
twelve-bar blues: *see* blues
twelve-tone music:
BOULEZ, *Le marteau sans maître* (p. 880)
WEBERN, Symphony, Op. 21, II (p. 684)

variations: *see* theme and variations

Donated
To
St. Francis College